MAYA® Character Animation

Second Edition

Production Editor Patrick Cunningham

Book Designer EO Communication

Graphic Illustrator Jae-jin Choi

Compositors Ann Lee, Woon-young Hong

Proofreader Jae-jin Choi

Indexer Ann Lee

Cover Designer EO Communication

Cover Illustrator Jae-jin Choi

This English edition published by Sybex, Inc.

Originally published in Korea 2004 by YoungJin.com, Seoul, Korea.

All rights reserved.

Library of Congress Control Number: 2004100470

ISBN: 0-7821-4328-8

Manufactured in Korea

10 9 8 7 6 5 4 3 2 1

MAYA® Character Animation

Second Edition

http://www.arcstudios.com

INTRODUCTION

It has been over 10 years since I first came into contact with computer graphics.
Every year new technologies that change the graphics industry are developed. With the introduction of Maya, the once vague and unfamiliar territory of character animation became easier and faster work in.

Maya was still a newcomer to the world of computer graphics when my first book, more of a how-to manual for Maya, was published. It received favorable attention from students and professionals of computer graphics. Many people came to know me through my first book, and it provided me with the opportunity to release this, my second book.

As someone who sincerely likes animation, I have chosen Maya as my preferred tool. It has proven to be a good tool, allowing me to quickly and easily convey my thoughts and ideas. However, tools are just tools. As time goes by, good tools will develop into even better tools, or they will fade from the limelight to make way for better tools. That is why tools should be regarded as simply tools. Placing an absolute value on them is not desirable.

I have come into contact with many software programs in my career. I started out studying and working with Max, and I have also used Animation Master, a simple yet powerful tool, to make characters. Working in a television studio, I learned how to use Softimage and Alias Power Animator. Although Alias was the tool I used most often, I learned to use Softimage on my own because I was impressed with its animation features.

Maya is the only tool that I have used faithfully for any length of time, and I have become quite familiar with it. Through this book, I will explain how to effectively convey whatever it is you want to convey using Maya. However, the methods described here are merely those that I prefer and are not the only ways to do things. Read this book and use my methods as a roadmap to find your own unique method.

Beginners have a tendency to concentrate on learning how to easily control characters. They refer to many tutorials and study books. Character Setup can be very complex and difficult because how the characters are controlled is greatly dependent on how they move. As you work, you will realize that this is not a big problem. Of course, many factors go into Character Setup, and these factors can come together to reduce the time you spend on it and enhance the precision of the final result.

However, neither simple nor complex setups are always best. Many animators prefer having many components that they can control themselves. A simpler setup can give greater control to animators. The important thing is to effectively breathe life into your characters. This should be the main focus of your study, not Character Setup.

Although the computer is a good tool for expressing your imaginative thoughts, imagination is something you are going to have to work on yourself. I believe that simply spending a lot of time thinking is more important than learning how to use the tools. How will something be made and how will it be expressed? How far does your imagination run when you see a nice picture? These thoughts, I believe, are far more important than any tool.

My dream is to create a work of art that contains all the sensibilities, beauty, and culture of Korea and then share it with people from around the world so that they can come to better understand us. Each Korean will add his or her own unique drawings and unique styles to this masterpiece. I pray that this dream will come true soon.

In closing, I would like to thank all those who have worked so hard to make this book a reality.

First of all, I would like to thank my wife and my best friend for always standing by me in all that I do, for believing in me, and for giving me strength. Although she jokingly calls me her "roommate" because I come home late every night, she always gives me strength and courage. I also want to thank my two lovely daughters, whom I love the most in this world.

I would like to thank everyone at ARC studio for giving all of themselves to the publication of this book. I would like to thank all those who work at SBS (Seoul Broadcasting System). Thanks to Vice-director Lee Sung-ho, Lee Jong-jeong, and Professor Nelson Shin for guiding me through my dissertation. In such a short time, you have awakened me to the basics of animation. I would also like to thank Professor Oh Geun-je, who has always guided me from afar. I would like to thank Byeong-hak Ahn, for editing this book, and Jeon Hee-kyeong, who suffered much because my manuscript was late.

Jae-jin Choi

HOW TO READ THIS BOOK...

This book is an advanced study in Character Animation. As follows, those new to Maya will find this book to be quite difficult. For those who have had some experience with Maya, I explain the basic menus for each example in this book, so you should have no trouble following along.

This book deals mostly with Subdivision Surface and Polygon Modeling methods. It covers basic Character Setup and several adaptations thereof to aid your understanding.

An example of the language used to describe menu commands follows: [Modeling > Create > NURBS Primitives > Sphere]. When something like this appears in the text, simply follow each menu item in sequence to arrive at the final menu choice.

Maya is made to support a 3-button mouse, which will be depicted in this book as LMB, MMB, and RMB. LMB means Left Mouse Button, MMB means Middle Mouse Button, and RMB means Right Mouse Button.

The supplementary CD-ROM, which comes with this book, includes all the data necessary for following along with the examples in the book. It contains the Model Data and Mapping Source, which are used in the CHARACTER Project. The Movies folder contains video clips and the Still Images folder contains still cuts.

Tom While visitng New Orleans in the year 2000, I came across an amusing doll.

It was the figure of a small doll playing the saxophone.

I thought that it would be a great to use as the subject of an animation, and I used it as the main character of this book.

14

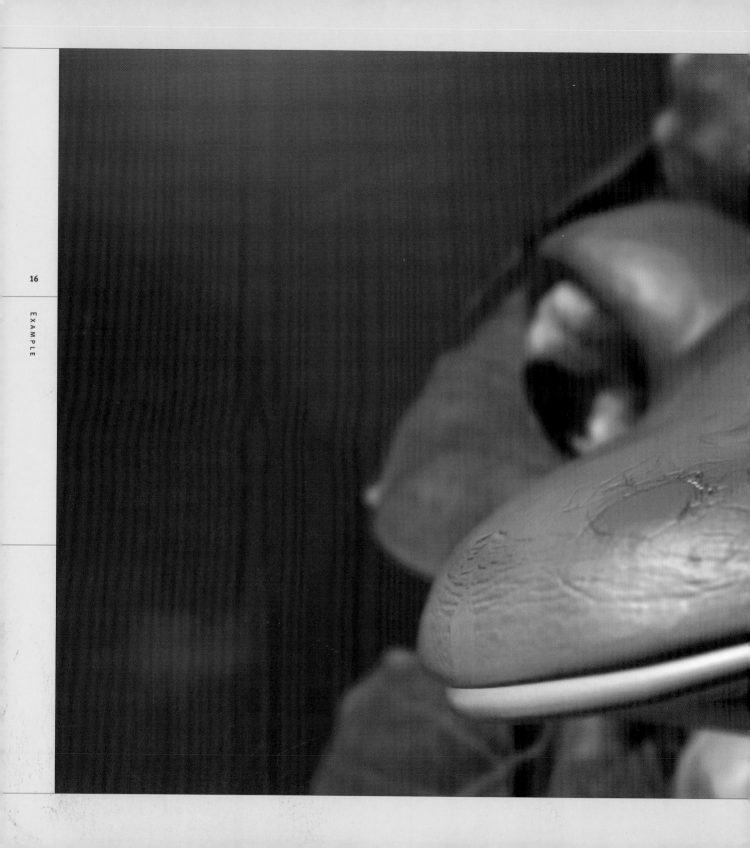

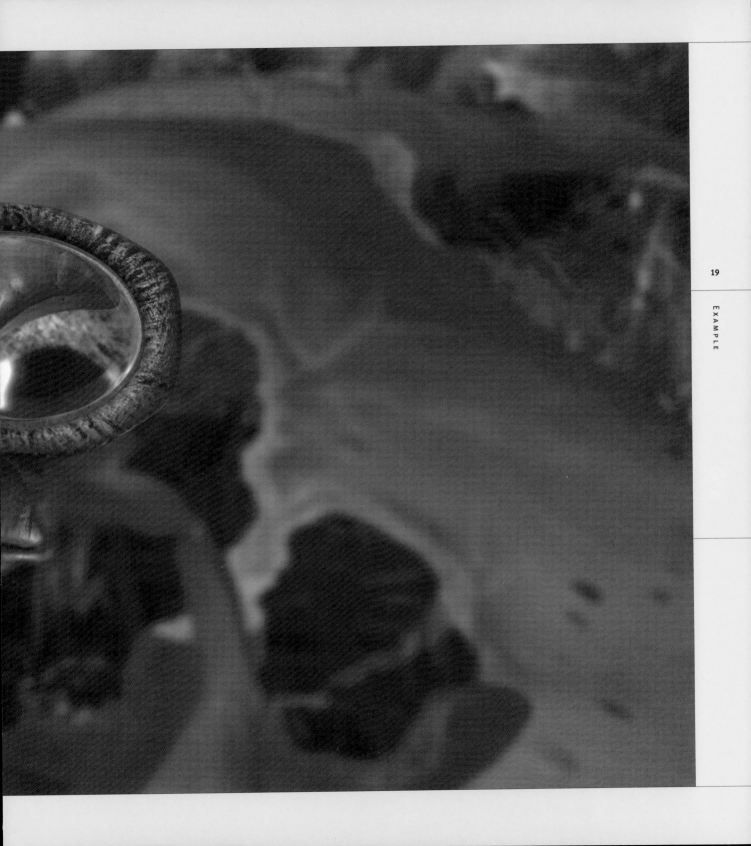

GP32 CF   Despite having a limited amount of time, with the help of friends, I was able to complete this.
The video clip is included in the supplementary CD-ROM.
I would like to thank all those who worked day
and night to make this project a success.

Image by Won-sub Lim

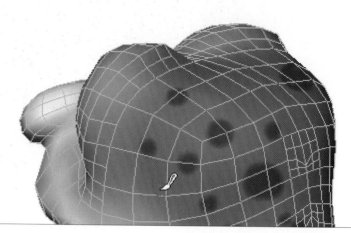

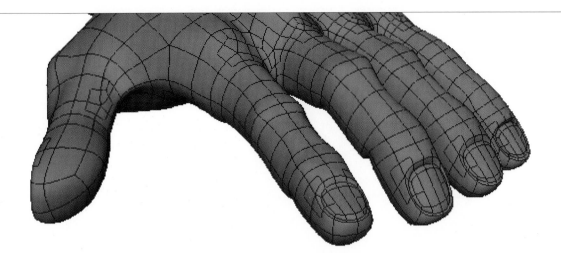

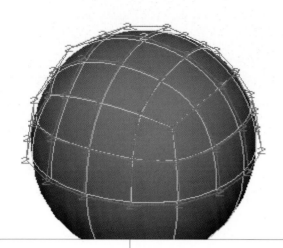

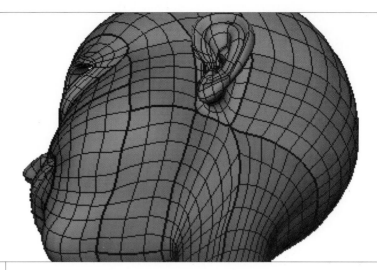

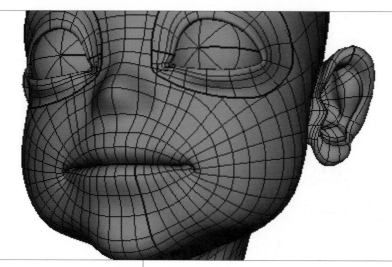

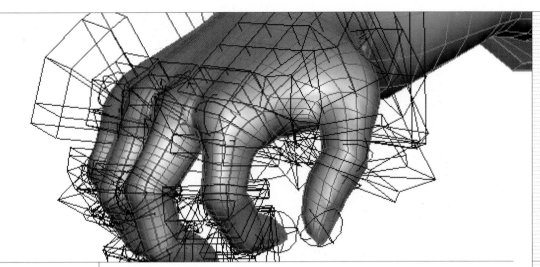

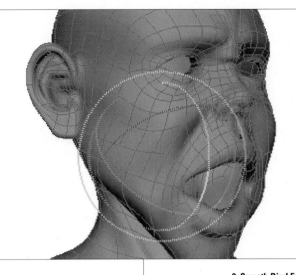

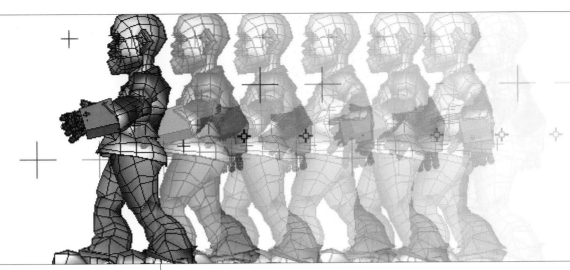

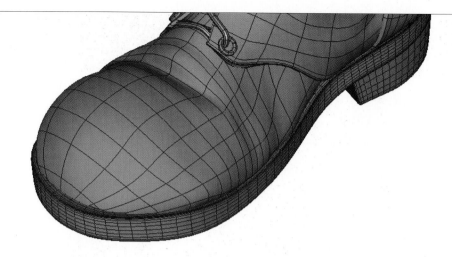

Chapter 9 _ Render Utility & Mapping Techniques   532

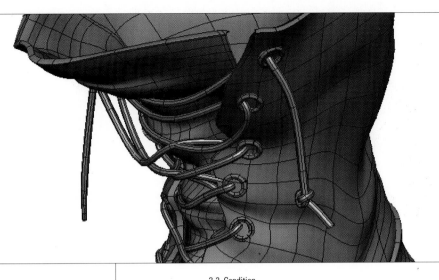

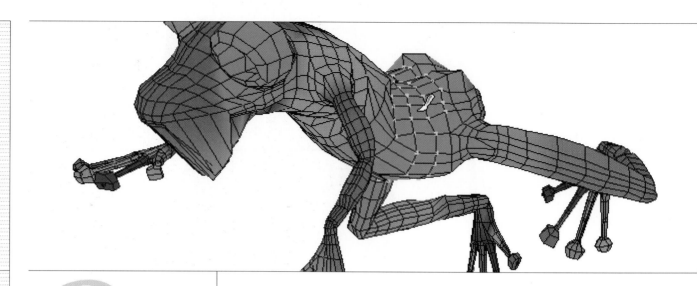

CONTENTS

p a r t

2

Maya and Beyond

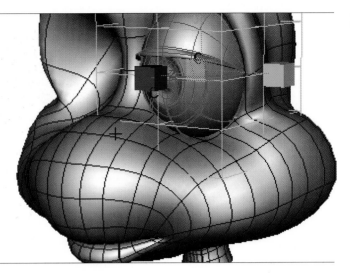

part 3

Making an Animation with Maya

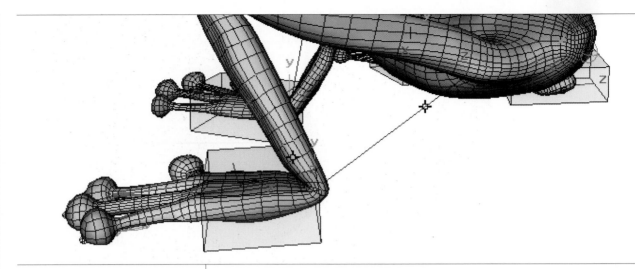

Chapter 13 _ Character Setting   752

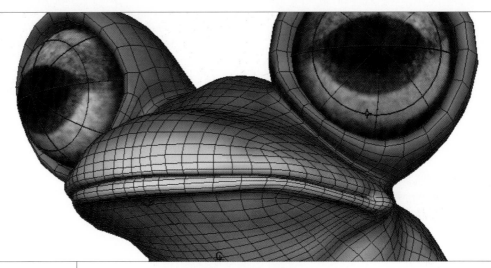

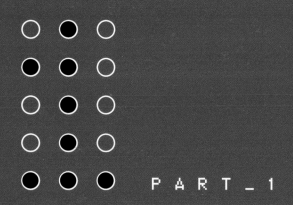

PART_1

CHARACTER MODELING

1 Subdivision & Polygon Modeling

Many of Maya's features have seen great improvements in recent updates to the software. In modeling, the most noteworthy point is the improvement in Subdivision Modeling. The Polygon menu has also been partially improved to make modeling using Subdivision Surfaces easier.

Subdivision Surface Modeling is a technique that uses continuous surface slicing to make the initial line segment or mesh resemble a smooth curve. The biggest advantage to this method is that it allows us to make random surface slices like Polygon, while maintaining the smooth curvature of NURBS. Currently, almost all types of software offer this kind of feature, which is enough to portray almost all kinds of characters or items.

In this chapter, we will learn how to use these menus through a tutorial, which will show us just how easy it is to approach modeling.

1. POLYGON MENU

Before we can begin Subdivision Modeling, we must fully understand the related Polygon menu. This is because Subdivision Modeling is based on the Polygon Modeling method. Although there are many facets to the Maya Polygon menu, we will look at only those necessary for Subdivision Modeling.

1-1. CREATE POLYGON TOOL

(Modeling > Polygons > Create Polygon Tool)

This menu is used to make polygons. Although other polygon-based modelers use splines to make polygons, Maya does not offer this type of feature. Therefore, in order to make polygons, we need to use this tool.

Select [Modeling > Polygons > Create Polygon Tool] and then click on the desired point while clicking the LMB as shown in Figure 1-1 to make the polygon.

When the polygon is complete, as shown in Figure 1-2, press the Enter key to finish making the polygon.

Figure 1-1 Polygon Modeling   Figure 1-2 Completing the Polygon Model by Pressing the Enter Key

Users can also create polygons with holes. First, make the polygon as shown in Figure 1-3 using the Create Polygon Tool and then, instead of pressing the Enter key, click on the inside of the polygon model with the LMB while holding down the Ctrl key and then, releasing the Ctrl key, create the desired shape as shown in Figure 1-4.

To continue making holes, press the Ctrl key, instead of the Enter key, to make the desired shapes. Press the Enter key when you are finished.

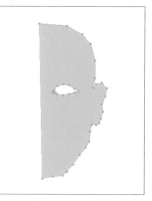

Figure 1-3 Polygon Modeling

Figure 1-4 Making a Polygon with Holes

1-2. APPEND TO POLYGON TOOL

(Modeling > Polygons > Append to Polygon Tool)

This tool is used to make a new face (surface plane). Users can use this tool on a polygon that has already been made to create the desired shape or surface and create a new face.

First, select [Modeling > Polygons > Append to Polygon Tool] and then, as shown in Figure 1-5, click the LMB on the edge to which you wish to add the face. The selected edge now becomes the first edge of the new face, and the pink rectangle that appears shows the direction of the edge.

As shown in Figure 1-6, clicking any point in the window will create a line and a new point. Observing the picture, you can see that one side of the edge appears as dotted lines. This indicates that points can continue to be added in this direction to create a face.

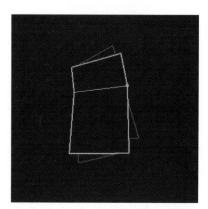

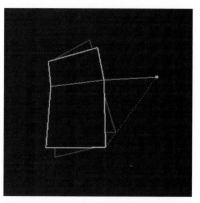

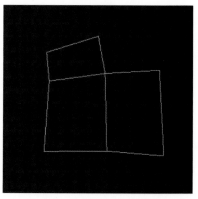

Figure 1-5 Selecting the Edge   Figure 1-6 Location of the Point   Figure 1-7 Completing the Image by Pressing the Enter Key

When the desired result is achieved (Figure 1-7), press the Enter key to exit from the Append to Polygon Tool.

Although we can continue to use the Append to Polygon Tool to make new faces to trim the shape of the polygon, it is also used quite frequently to fill in holes.

Let's look at the picture below. Figure 1-8 shows a polygon model with a face erased in the forehead to reveal a gaping hole. This tool is very effective for filling in such holes.

Select [Modeling > Polygons > Append to Polygon Tool], and then select the edge that is indicated in Figure 1-9.

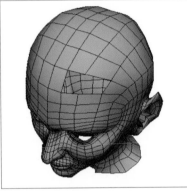
Figure 1-8 A Polygon Model with an Erased Face

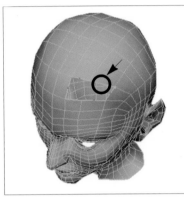
Figure 1-9 Selecting the Edge

Then, select the second edge as shown in Figure 1-10. This will create a new surface as shown. Exit from the Append to Polygon Tool by pressing the Enter key to create the new surface shown in Figure 1-11.

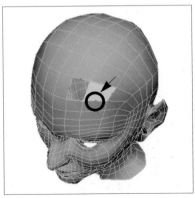
Figure 1-10 Selecting the Second Edge

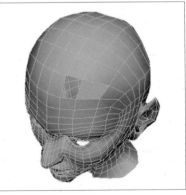
Figure 1-11 Completing the Image by Pressing the Enter Key

1-3. COMBINE

(Modeling > Polygons > Combine)

This tool combines together two separate polygons.

Let's see how to use this tool by looking at the following example. Figure 1-12 shows us the process of modeling a hand. This model shows the process of detailing the pointer finger. After working on most of the details, similar shapes can be made by copying and pasting. Although this model is basically a duplicate of the polygon model used to make the fingers, in the end, they must all be merged to blend the edges together. To merge together all the edges, all polygons must be recognized as one object.

Let's see how this is done.

First, as shown in Figure 1-13, select the faces of the polygon that will be copied.

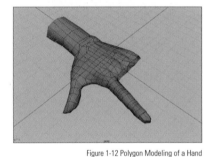

Figure 1-12 Polygon Modeling of a Hand   Figure 1-13 Selecting the Face to be copied

Select [Modeling > Edit Polygons > Duplicate Face]. The selected face will be copied as shown in Figure 1-14. Click the LMB on the area indicated in Figure 1-14 and then arrange it as shown in Figure 1-15. Finally, adjust the values for the size, location, and rotation.

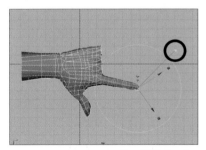
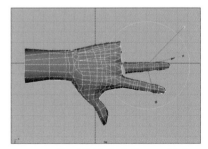

Figure 1-14 Duplicate Face   Figure 1-15 Adjusting the Placement of the Finger

We now need to use the Merge Edge Tool to blend together the edge of the hand and the duplicated finger. This is because the two polygons are two separate objects. The Merge Edge Tool is used to link together one polygon with its displaced edge.

Therefore, the Combine Tool must be used to combine the two polygons into one.

Select the two polygons and then select [Modeling > Polygons > Combine] to make one polygon as shown in Figure 1-16.

Figure 1-17 shows the use of the Merge Edge Tool to blend the edge of the finger with the hand. More instructions on how to use the Merge Edge Tool can be found in the back of this book.

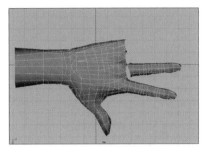

Figure 1-16 The Combined Polygon

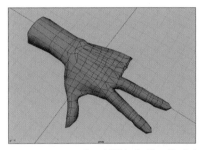

Figure 1-17 Using the Merge Edge Tool

1-4. SPLIT POLYGON TOOL

(Modeling > Edit Polygons > Split Polygon Tool)

This tool is used to slice a surface by adding an edge to a polygon face. Generally, when modeling polygons, it is more effective to split surfaces at random while modeling detailed areas to achieve optimal data and clean modeling data. This tool is used frequently for this purpose.

The following is a good example. Figure 1-18 shows a polygon cube that has been reduced in scale, to approximate the shape of a hand model.

Select [Modeling > Edit Polygons > Split Polygon Tool] and the edges marked "A" and "B," in this order, as shown in Figure 1-19. Before removing your hand from the mouse, drag it from side to side to position it. After making the selections, press the Enter key to exit from this step.

Figure 1-18 Adjusting the Scale of the Polygon Cube

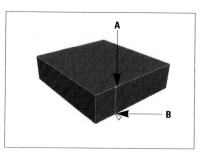

Figure 1-19 Using the Split Polygon Tool

Users can select edges to continue splitting the surface. Before pressing the Enter key to exit from this step, click on the desired edge to continue splitting the face.

1-5. EXTRUDE FACE

(Modeling > Edit Polygons > Extrude Face)

This tool allows us to create a new face by extruding a face.

Let's use it in conjunction with the Split Polygon Tool, which was explained above, to see how it works. Figure 1-20 shows how the surface was split by adding edges using the Split Polygon Tool.

Select the polygon object, press the RMB as shown in Figure 1-21, and select Face from the Marking Menu.

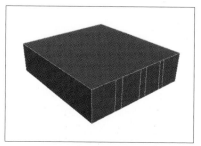

Figure 1-20 Using the Split Polygon Tool

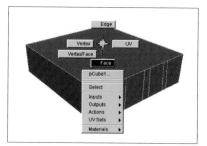

Figure 1-21 Selecting Face from the Marking Menu

As shown in Figure 1-22, select the face while holding down the Shift key on the keyboard.

Select [Modeling > Edit Polygons > Extrude Face].

As shown in Figure 1-23, select one axis of the Manipulator Move icon and then move the face to reveal the new, extruding face.

Figure 1-22 Selecting the Face

Figure 1-23 Executing Extrude Face

Continue to model by repeatedly applying Extrude Face.

1-6. EXTRUDE EDGE

(Modeling > Edit Polygons > Extrude Edge)

This feature was first added to version 3. Whereas Extrude Face, which we looked at above, is used to model by extruding the face, this tool extrudes edges to make a new face.

After making a new polygon cube and then selecting it, press the RMB as shown in Figure 1-24 and select the edge.

As shown in Figure 1-25, select one axis of the Manipulator Move icon and move the edge to create a new, extruding edge.

Figure 1-24 Selecting the Edge

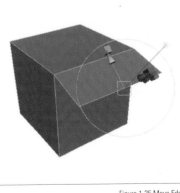

Figure 1-25 Move Edge

Keep one thing in mind when using Extrude Face and Extrude Edge: Use Keep Faces Together when extruding several faces or edges at a time. This option is used by setting [Modeling > Polygons > Tool Options > Keep Faces Together] to On. To see how this option is used, look at Figure 1-26. Select several faces and then apply Extrude Face and adjust the scale. Because Keep Faces Together is set to Off, we can see that each of the surfaces is separate from each other. In Figure 1-27, we set the Keep Faces Together option to On and then applied Extrude Face and adjusted the scale. We can see that the surfaces are connected now. The same holds true for extruding edges. Figure 1-28 shows the extruding of the edges with the Keep Faces Together option set to Off, and Figure 1-29 shows the edges extruded with this option set to On.

Figure 1-26 Keep Face Together; Off

Another thing to keep in mind when using these two tools is the use of the Manipulator. When these two tools are used to execute Extrude, the Manipulator appears as in Figure 1-30.

The Manipulator contains the tools for Move, Rotate, and Scale. A represents Move, B represents Scale, and C represents Rotate. When D is clicked, the extruded face or edge will be centered on the center of the extruded face or edge, which is the central axis of Transform. This is shown in Figure 1-31. When this is clicked again, the central axis will return to its original position. Test the Move and Scale Tools to see the difference between the two.

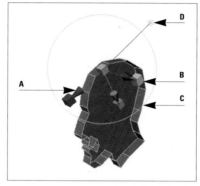

Figure 1-30 Manipulator Tool

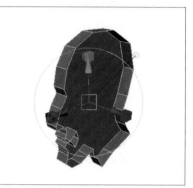

Figure 1-31 Changing the Central Axis of the Manipulator

1-7. MERGE EDGE TOOL

(Modeling > Edit Polygons > Merge Edge Tool)

This tool merges the edges of polygons. We saw earlier how this tool was used to combine two, separate polygon objects when using the Combine Tool. Figure 1-32 is the same example that was used earlier to explain the Combine Tool.

As shown, copy the face of the finger to model the fingers and then rearrange them and apply the Combine command to combine the two polygon objects into one. Now, because these two surfaces are separated from each other, as shown in Figure 1-32, we combine them into one using the Merge Edge Tool.

Select [Modeling > Edit Polygons > Merge Edge Tool] and select the *A* edge shown in Figure 1-33. Then, as shown in Figure 1-33, the color of the selected edge will change and all of the edges will turn pink.

Figure 1-27 Keep Face Together; On

Figure 1-28 Keep Face Together; Off

Figure 1-29 Keep Face Together; On

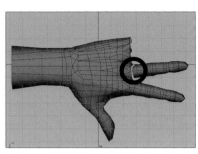

Figure 1-32 Polygons separated after applying the Combine Command.

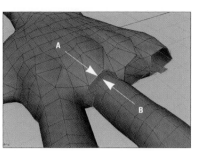

Figure 1-33 Applying the Merge Edge Tool

As shown in Figure 1-33 select the edge marked "B" and then, press the Enter key to combine the two edges. Instead of pressing the Enter key, users can also click the LMB on an empty space in the window to continue using the Merge Edge Tool to merge other edges together.

1-8. SPLIT VERTEX TOOL
(Modeling > Edit Polygons > Split Vertex)

This tool is used to divide a vertex into two to slice an edge. For example, let's suppose that we modeled the figure of a closed mouth as shown in Figure 1-34. This tool comes in handy should we want to split the upper and lower lips to model the inside of the mouth. Select the vertex you wish to divide. Select the areas marked in Figure 1-34. Select [Modeling > Edit Polygons > Split Vertex] and then move the vertex, as shown in Figure 1-35, to divide the selected vertex. If the Split Vertex Tool has been applied excessively, combine the vertices together using the Merge Edge Tool.

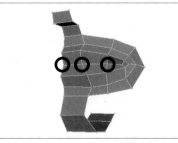

Figure 1-34 Selecting Vertex

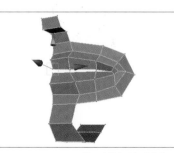

Figure 1-35 Applying Split Vertex

2. SUBDIVISION SURFACE MENU

Several Maya upgrades have brought many improvements to Subdivision Surface. This type of modeling technique is offered in almost all programs. Although the names are slightly different from program to program, the basic concept is the same.

The following is the main concept behind Subdivision Surface.

Although NURBS (Non-Uniform Raditional B-Spline) is normally used for smooth curves and complex models, it has one fatal flaw: NURBS surfaces require rectangular lattice structure to link each control vertex (CV), and that causes them to form surfaces.

In other words, triangular structures cannot exist, and we cannot freely divide Isoparms in patch units as we did for the edges in Polygon as we learned earlier. Those experienced with NURBS modeling are probably familiar with this disadvantage.

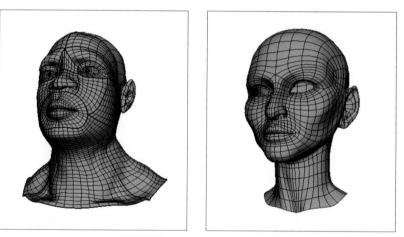

Figure 1-36 NURBS Modeling   Figure 1-37 Subdivision Surface Modeling

The solution to this is Subdivision Surface. This method is similar to Polygon Modeling, and the output is a B-Spline structure. In existing NURBS Patch (Multi-Surface) Modeling, it was impossible to create one attachment due to the disadvantage mentioned earlier. Therefore, Stitch or Global Stitch was used to fit together adjacent curves so that it appeared to be linked when rendered. However, Subdivision Surfaces allow all surfaces to be attached and transformed into any shape. In addition, necessary surfaces can also be added in parts to create more detailed modeling.

If you are not familiar with Subdivision Surfaces, you might find them easier to understand if you first just browse through the explanation of the menu here and then run through the tutorial in the back before coming back and reading this section over more carefully.

This modeling technique radically simplifies the previously complex and intricate field of character modeling. Control of this technique is also quite simple. Choosing to use this method, say, to make a character and model it using Blend Shape to create many different facial expressions will make your work much faster and easier.

Maya's Subdivision Surface is a revolutionary tool. Although this will be covered in more detail in the back of this book, this tool is revolutionary because meshes can be divided into various levels, depending on the accuracy of the model, for more effective modeling. However, there are also disadvantages. Using Subdivision Surface to bind joints conspicuously lowers the speed of the system and because it uses the Polygon Mapping method, it is extremely difficult to make the mapping axis. Also, the data is much larger than NURBS or Polygon.

In this chapter, we will look at the menus related to Subdivision Surfaces. You can put your knowledge to use by following along with the modeling tutorial in back.

2-1. POLYGONS TO SUBDIV

(Modify > Convert > Polygons to Subdiv)

Subdivision Surfaces, for the most part, use polygon objects. In other words, Polygons to Subdiv is the command used to convert polygon objects into Subdivision Surfaces. (NURBS can be changed to Subdivision Surfaces. To do so, use NURBS to Subdiv.)

After making one primitive polygon cube ([Create > Polygon Primitives > Cube]) as shown in Figure 1-36, adjust the size appropriately in the window. After selecting the polygon object, select [Modify > Convert > Polygons to Subdiv]. As shown in Figure 1-37, the selected polygon cube has been changed into a subdivision surface. To make the surface appear as smooth as it does in Figure 1-37, press **3** on the keyboard to set the Smoothness of the subdivision surface to Fine.

Figure 1-38 Polygon Primitive Cube

Figure 1-39 Polygons to Subdiv Surface

Let's look at the Convert to Subdiv option.

Selecting [Modify > Convert > Polygons to Subdiv ⬛] will create the option window shown in Figure 1-40.

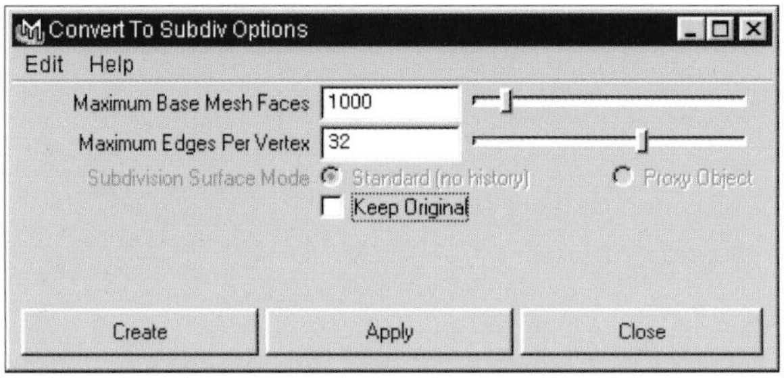

Figure 1-40 Convert to Subdivision Option Window

● Maximum Base Mesh Faces

We set the value of the face to the maximum value in order to successfully convert the original surface to a Subdivision Surface. For example, let's suppose we have a polygon object with a face value of 900. The Maximum Base Mesh Faces must be set to 1000, a value greater than 900, for the Subdivision Surface to be made. A Subdivision Surface will not be made if the value is set to less than 900, and an error message will appear.

● Maximum Edges Per Vertex

The concept is similar to the option above, but this option is used to set the maximum value for the edge of a vertex.

● Keep Original

This option is used to create a new Subdivision Surface while maintaining the original object. Setting this option to On will activate Standard and Proxy Object. This option will be explained in greater detail in the back of this book.

2-2. SUBDIV TO POLYGONS

(Modify > Convert > Subdiv to Polygons)

This is the tool used to convert subdivision surfaces to polygon objects.

To convert the subdivision surface shown in Figure 1-41 to a polygon, select it and then apply [Modify > Convert > Subdiv to Polygons] to convert it to the polygon shown in Figure 1-42.

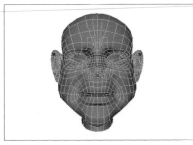

Figure 1-41 Subdivision Surface

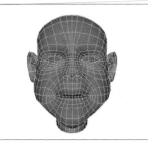

Figure 1-42 After Applying Subdiv to Polygons

Selecting [Modify > Convert > Subdiv to Polygons ☐] will create the Convert Subdiv To Polygons options window as shown in Figure 1-43.

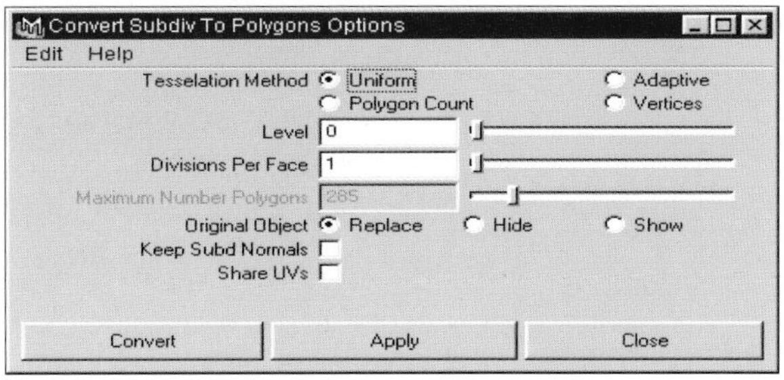

Figure 1-43 The Convert Subdiv To Polygons Options Window

● **Tesselation Method**

Users can use one of the following three methods to convert subdivision surfaces to polygons.

Uniform

Uniform Tessellation creates polygon objects using the same intermediary values of each of the subdivision surfaces.

Adaptive

Adaptive Tessellation creates many more polygons in detailed regions to express the precision of the subdivision surface models.

Polygon Count

This is basically the same as Uniform Tessellation. This value can be raised to increase the number of polygons, but the number entered is not the same as the number of polygons.

The Difference Between Uniform and Adaptive Let's look at the subdivision surface shown below in Figure 1-44. This figure is a portion of the finger to which a surface has been added to depict the fingernail. In the figure below, the subdivision surface is set to Standard Mode, displaying the Subdiv Mesh Point and Subdiv Mesh Edge from [Display > Subdiv Surface Component].

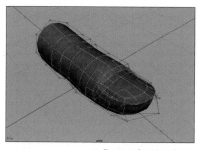

Figure 1-44 Subdivision Surface

Let's look at the difference between Uniform and Adaptive when converting to polygons when adding surfaces to particular areas for partial depiction, as we did here, or using Refine Selected Components (refer to "2-17. Portraying Detail in Another Level" for more information) to make a subdivision surface. The image in Figure 1-45 was made using the default values in the Options window and applying Uniform Tessellation. As shown here for Uniform Tessellation, it is made using the intermediary values of the subdivision face. However, the image in Figure 1-46, which was made by applying Adaptive Tessellation, adds surfaces at random for more precise delineation and adds many polygons to the created surface.

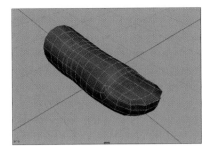

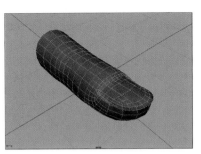

Figure 1-45 Tessellation Method; Uniform   Figure 1-46 Tessellation Method; Adaptive

Level This option can only be used for Uniform Tessellation. It decides how many surfaces will be tessellated in the display level of the subdivision surface. For example, if the level is set to 3, it will be converted to a polygon at that level. (More detailed information on levels can be found in "2-17. Portraying Detail in Another Level.")

Divisions Per Face This decides how many times each surface will be sliced. This is an option that can be used in both Uniform and Adaptive Tessellation. The greater the value, the greater the number of surfaces there will be for a smoother model.

Maximum Number of Polygons This option is used when the Tessellation Method is set to Polygon Count. The greater the value, the smoother the model will be.

Vertices

Vertices are used when calculating the level points of the selected subdivision surface as polygon vertices to make polygon objects.

Let's look at the following figures. Figure 1-47 shows a simple polygon cube made as a subdivision surface. The Display Level for this object is 0. Selecting the Vertices as 0 and then executing it gives us the polygon seen in Figure 1-48.

The Subdiv Mesh Points and Subdiv Mesh Edges are displayed in Figures 1-47 and 1-49 to help you better understand. Extract Vertices must be executed in Object Mode.

Users can convert back and forth from Object Mode to Component Mode in Maya by pressing the F8 key.

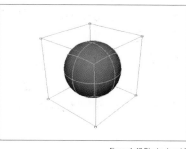

Figure 1-47 Display Level 0

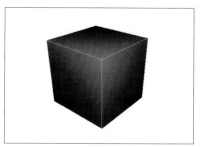

Figure 1-48 Executing Extract Vertices

The Display Level in Figure 1-49 was set to 1, and Figure 1-50 was achieved by executing Extract Vertices at Level 0.

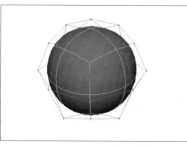

Figure 1-49 Display Level 1

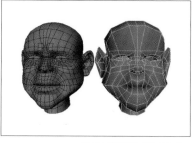

Figure 1-50 Executing Extract Vertices

Levels are defined in the Convert Subdiv To Polygons options window. Open the Convert Subdiv To Polygons Options window by selecting [Modify > Convert > Subdiv to Polygons ▢], and enter the desired value for the Level.

2-3. FULL CREASE AND PARTIAL CREASE EDGE/ VERTEX

(Modeling > Subdiv Surface)

This tool can be used to make or delete Crease in Edge or vertex.

Full Crease is the option used to make a sharp corner when transforming the subdivision surface of a selected edge. Sharp corners can also be made for selected vertices.

Partial Crease also alters the subdivision surface due to the selected Edge or Vertex, but, unlike the Full Crease, does not make a sharp corner. This option is very useful for making smooth ridgelines, like when making character lips.

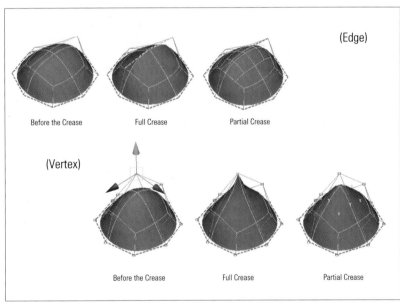

Figure 1-51 Full Crease and Partial Crease

To apply Full Crease, first, select the edge or point and then select [Modeling > Subdiv Surfaces > Full Crease Edge/Vertex].

To apply Partial Crease, first, select the edge or point and then select [Modeling > Subdiv Surfaces > Partial Crease].

This command only works in Standard Mode. It will not work in Polygon Proxy Mode.

Users can also adjust the sharpness of the Partial Crease by, first, applying the Crease, then raising the Detail Level of the Crease, and then removing the Crease.

The sharpness of the Crease is determined by how much the level is raised before the Crease is removed. However, users should know that there are many possible values. In order to adjust the sharpness of the Partial Crease, first, select Edge in the Subdivision Surface as shown in Figure 1-52, and then select [Modeling > Subdiv Surfaces > Full Crease Edge/Vertex].

An acute angle is made with respect to the selected Eedge as shown in Figure 1-53. This was done with the Display Level set to 0.

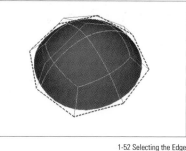
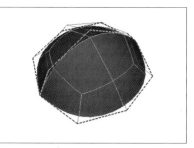

1-52 Selecting the Edge

Figure 1-53 Executing Full Crease Edge/Vertex with the Level Set to 0

In the current state (with the Edge selected), select [Modeling > Subdiv Surfaces > Refine Selected Components]. Press the RMB and set the Display Level to 2 from the Marking Menu as shown in Figure 1-54. To add more detail, repeat this step one more time. With the edge selected, select [Modeling > Subdiv Surfaces > Uncrease Edge/Vertex] to adjust the angle as shown in Figure 1-55.

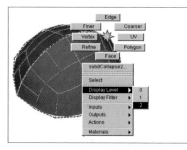

Figure 1-54 Adjusting the Display Level

Figure 1-55 Uncrease Edge/Vertex

2-4. UNCREASE EDGE/VERTEX

(Modeling > Subdiv Surfaces > Uncrease Edge/Vertex)

After using Crease to adjust the angle on the subdivision surface, the Crease is removed using this command. The image in Figure 1-56 shows the application of a Full Crease. In this state, select the Edge and then select [Modeling > Subdiv Surfaces > Uncrease Edge/Vertex] to return the model to its original, uncreased state as shown in Figure 1-57.

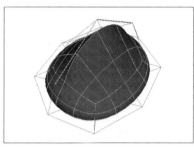

Figure 1-56 Execution of Full Crease

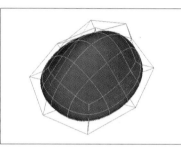

Figure 1-57 Executing Uncrease

2-5. MIRROR

(Modeling > Subdiv Surfaces > Mirror)

This option is used to Mirror Copy a subdivision surface. Figure 1-58 shows a completed model of just one half of a face. In order to make the other half, select this object and then select [Modeling > Subdiv Surfaces > Mirror] to make the mirror copy as shown in Figure 1-59.

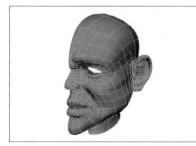

Figure 1-58 Subdivision Surface

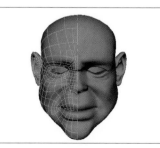

Figure 1-59 Mirror Copy of the Subdivision Surface

We can open the Mirror Options window to determine along which axis the Mirror Copy will be made.

Select [Subdiv Surfaces > Mirror ▢] to reveal the Options window shown in Figure 1-60. Select the axis along which you want the mirror copy to be made. If you normally work in front view, select the X-axis.

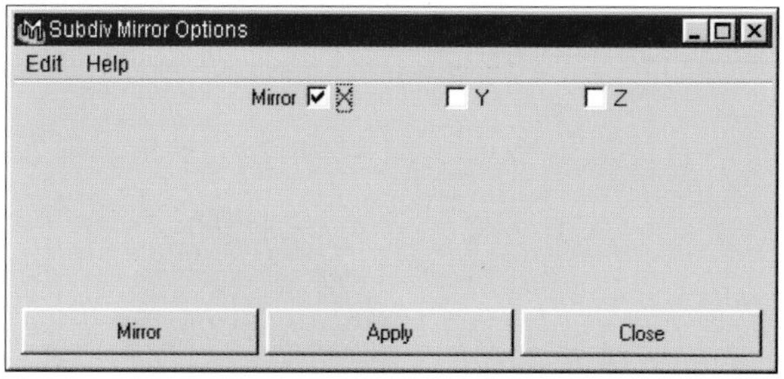

Figure 1-60 The Subdiv Mirror Options Window

2-6. ATTACH

(Modeling > Subdiv Surfaces > Attach)

This option is used to attach together two subdivision surfaces. As shown in Figure 1-61, select the object and its mirror copy, which we made in the previous step, and then select [Modeling > Subdiv Surfaces > Attach] to attach the two subdivision surfaces together as shown in Figure 1-62.

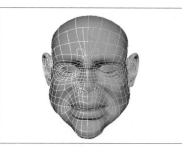

Figure 1-61 Selecting Both Subdivision Surfaces

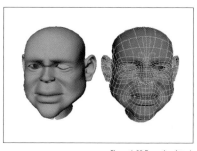

Figure 1-62 Executing Attach

Selecting [Subdiv Surfaces > Attach ▢] will open the Options window shown in Figure 1-63.

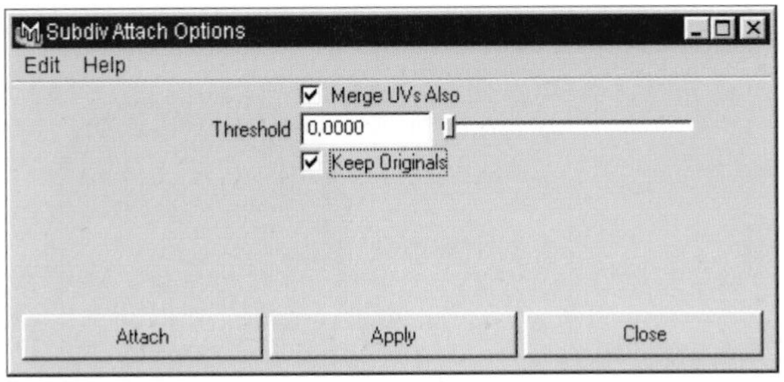

Figure 1-63 Subdiv Attach Options Window

Merge UVs Also

If the model to attach has a UV-axis, the axes on both sides of the model will also merge. Refer to Chapter 2, "Polygon, Subdivision Surface Mapping," for more detail on subdivision and polygon mapping.

Threshold

When two objects are attached on a variety of different levels, sometimes, the two surfaces do not form a clean attachment. In this instance, adjust this value for a clean fit between the two objects.

Keep Originals

When this option is turned on, a new attached object will be made separate from the original object. When turned off, the original object will be deleted.

2-7. MATCH TOPOLOGY

(Modeling > Subdiv Surfaces > Match Topology)

Match Topology is linked to [Animation > Deform > Create Blend Shape]. Generally, there is no need to execute this option as a separate step. This is because when [Animation > Deform > Create Blend Shape] is executed, Match Topology is executed automatically. When subdivision surfaces are made using Blend Shape, the same number of vertices are needed at every level, but when using Match Topology, the number of vertices is fixed automatically. Let's look at Figure 1-64. The number of vertices is different for each model at Level 1 (shown on the left and right). We can see that there are more vertices on the right for a more precise transformation of the shape.

Generally, Level 0 must have the same
number of vertices.
If Level 0 has a different number of
vertices, a Match Topology or Blend
Shape will not be made.

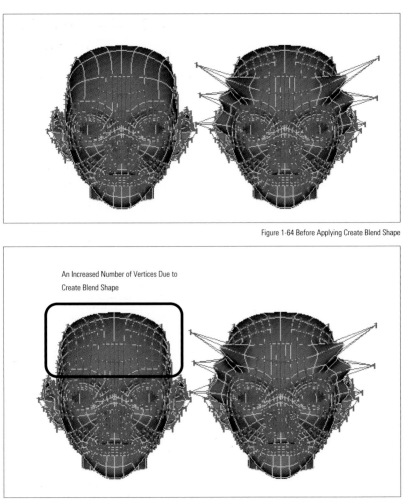

Figure 1-64 Before Applying Create Blend Shape

An Increased Number of Vertices Due to
Create Blend Shape

Figure 1-65 After Applying Create Blend Shape

The picture above, Figure 1-65, shows the results after applying Create Blend Shape.
Comparing the model on the left in Figure 1-65 to the model in Figure 1-64, we can see
that there is an increase in the number of vertices. In this way, when Blend Shape is used
in Maya, it automatically matches the number of vertices between the two models. This
is called Match Topology.
If the vertices have been adjusted for any level, excluding Level 0, for necessary
alterations, Maya automatically matches the vertices and applies Blend Shape.

2-8. CLEAN TOPOLOGY

(Modeling > Subdiv Surfaces > Clean Topology)

This option is needed for more effective subdivision surface modeling.

This option is used to delete vertices that have not been edited in the various levels of the subdivision surface. In other words, unedited vertices are deleted to improve work speed and the amount of data is also reduced.

For example, let's suppose that we selected a face or vertex and applied [Modeling > Subdiv Surface > Refine] to divide the levels. Then, if only a few vertices have been edited, unnecessary vertices, which have not been edited, will remain. In these instances, this option is used to automatically delete the unedited vertices.

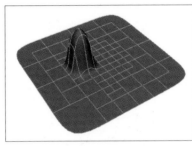

Figure 1-66 Before Applying Clean Topology

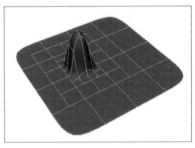

Figure 1-67 After Applying Clean Topology

2-9. COLLAPSE STANDARD

(Modeling > Subdiv Surfaces > Collapse STANDARD)

This option initializes the level in standard mode.

For example, let's suppose we have the situation shown here. The Display Level in Figure 1-68 is set to 0 and the Display Level for Figure 1-69 is set to 1. At times, you may need to randomly initialize the Display Level 1 in Figure 1-69 to Display Level 0. Display Levels are further explained in "2-17. Portraying Detail in Another Level."

The tool used at this time is Collapse Standard.

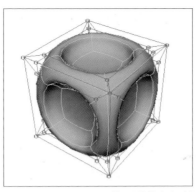

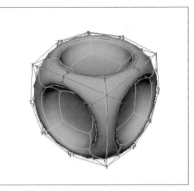

Figure 1-68 Display Level: 0   Figure 1-69 Display Level: 1

Select the Subdivision Surface and apply [Modeling > Subdiv Surfaces > Collapse Standard ▢] to open the Subdiv Collapse Options window. In this window, set the Number of Levels to Collapse to 1 and then press the Collapse button or the Apply button at the bottom. This will take the Subdivision Surface at Display Level 1, shown in Figure 1-69, and make the new Subdivision Surface at Display Level 0 shown in Figure 1-70.

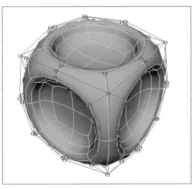

Figure 1-70 Number of Levels to Collapse: 1

2-10. STANDARD MODE AND POLYGON PROXY MODE

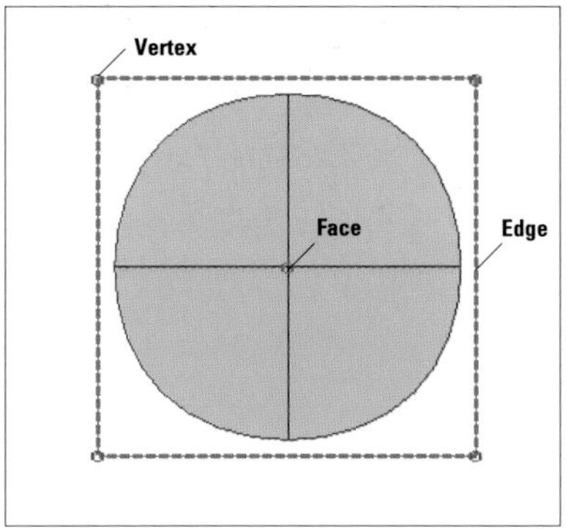

Figure 1-71 Standard Mode

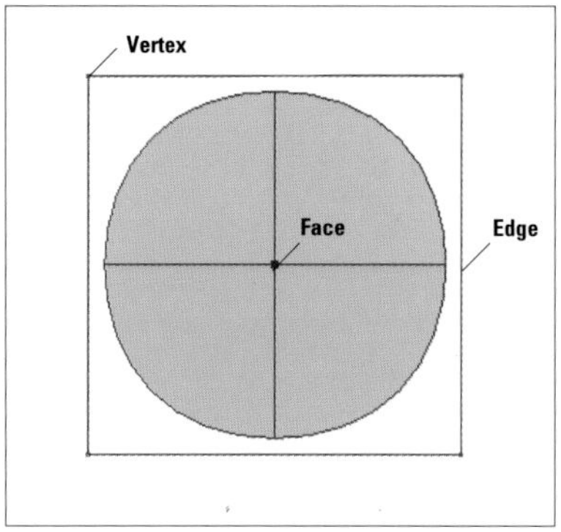

Figure 1-72 Polygon Proxy Mode

Subdivision Surface modeling usually occurs in Standard or Polygon Proxy Modes. Each of these modes has their own unique characteristics when used in modeling. Let's find out more about these two different modes.

1. Standard Mode

In Standard Mode, we can select the vertex, edge, or face in the Display Level and translate them or control them using Rotate or Scale as shown in Figure 1-73. Keyframing is also possible. However, this mode does not have a Construction History. In addition, in this mode, levels can be raised in parts to add more detail. It is also easier to subdivide points using Display Levels for more precise, partial modeling.

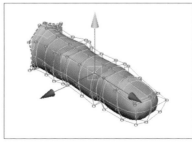

Figure 1-73 Working in Standard Mode

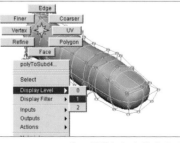

Figure 1-74 Selecting the Display Level

Figure 1-74 shows us how to view Display Levels. Place the mouse over the subdivision surface, click the RMB, and then select the desired level from the Marking Menu or enter the Display Level in the Channel Box.

This type of modeling becomes the strategic point for optimizing subdivision surface modeling. Conversion from Polygon Proxy Mode to Standard Mode is possible at any time during the modeling.

To convert from Polygon Proxy Mode to Standard Mode, select [Modeling > Subdiv Surfaces > Standard Mode] or select the Subdivision Surface and click the RMB and select Standard Mode from the Marking Menu.

2. Polygon Proxy Mode

Changing to Polygon Proxy Mode will create a coinciding polygon on the basic mesh (Level 0) of the Subdivision Surface.

Everything in the polygon proxy mode is linked through the Construction History. Therefore, basic Polygon Tools and features can be used to alter the basic mesh (Level 0) of the subdivision surface.

When using basic Polygon Tools, their use will be recorded in the Channel Box. However, when converting to Standard Mode, the Construction History will be deleted.

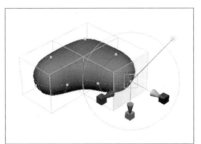

Figure 1-75 Working in Polygon Proxy Mode
(Executing the Face Extrude Command)

Figure 1-76 Working in Polygon Proxy Mode
(Deleting the Selected Face)

For example, let's suppose you are modeling in Standard Mode and want to extrude or delete the face. This can be done by converting to Polygon Proxy Mode, as shown in Figure 1-75, and selecting and extruding the face or by deleting the selected face as shown in Figure 1-76.

• It is a good idea to convert periodically to Standard Mode when working in Polygon Proxy Mode. This will delete the History and prevent unexpected results.

• Some features (Boolean, Bevel, Reduce, etc.) cannot be used in Polygon Proxy Mode.

Users can convert from Polygon Proxy Mode to Standard Mode at any time during the modeling. Switching from Polygon Proxy Mode to Standard Mode is done either by selecting [Modeling > Subdiv Surfaces > Polygon Proxy Mode] or by selecting the Subdivision Surface and clicking the RMB and selecting Standard Mode from the Marking Menu.

2-11. CONVERT SELECTION TO FACE

(Modeling > Subdiv Surfaces > Convert Selection To Face)

This option is used for selecting faces within a component.

In other words, let's suppose that we selected a vertex at random in the Subdivision surface of Figure 1-77. Applying this option with the vertex selected will automatically cause the faces linked to the selected vertex to be selected as shown in Figure 1-78. The remaining edges, vertices and UVs use the same command. Try using the command for each of these to gain a better understanding of how this command works.

Figure 1-77 Selecting the Vertex

Figure 1-78 Executing Convert Selection to Face

2-12. REFINE SELECTED COMPONENTS

(Modeling > Subdiv Surfaces > Refine Selected Components)

This option is used to raise the level of the selected components.

Selecting a vertex in Level 0 and applying this command will cause the area around the vertex to be divided into Level 1. Level 1 will be divided into Level 2, Level 2 will be divided into Level 3, and so on to create greater subdivision of the surface.

For example, let's suppose we are modeling the nose of a character as shown in Figure 1-79. Let's suppose that we want to create a more precise modeling of the nose. However, the levels around this area are not further subdivided making precise modeling impossible with this current structure. It is at times like this that we apply the command to raise the levels. As shown here, select the vertex in the desired area and apply [Modeling > Subdiv Surfaces > Refine Selected Components] to divide the area around the selected vertex to Level 2 as shown in Figure 1-80.

Figure 1-79 Selecting the Vertex

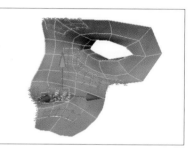

Figure 1-80 Executing Refine Selected Components

2-13. EXPAND SELECTED COMPONENTS
(Modeling > Subdiv Surfaces > Expand Selected Components)

When the levels are divided using the Refine command, only the levels around the selected vertex will be divided. This command is used to expand the divided level. Let's suppose we have a divided level as shown in Figure 1-81. Select the desired vertex and apply [Modeling > Subdiv Surfaces > Expand Selected Components] to expand the level as shown in Figure 1-82.

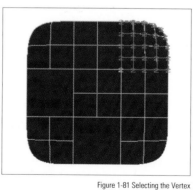

Figure 1-81 Selecting the Vertex

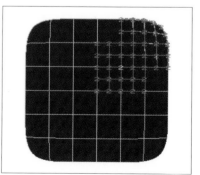

Figure 1-82 Executing Expand Selected Components

2-14. COMPONENT DISPLAY LEVEL

(Modeling > Subdiv Surfaces > Component Display Level)

Users can also use [Modeling > Subdiv Surfaces > Component Display Level] to select the Display Level as above.

If the Display Level is currently set to 1, apply [Modeling > Subdiv Surfaces > Component Display Level > Finer, Coarse, Base], and select Finer to change to Display Level 2. Coarser changes a current Level 1 to 0, and Base returns a level to Level 0.

In other words, Finer increases the current Display Level one at a time, while Coarser decreases it one step at a time.

2-15. COMPONENT DISPLAY FILTER

(Modeling > Subdiv Surfaces > Component Display Filter)

This menu is used to display only the edited vertices in the current level.

For example, let's suppose that we had modified a few points of Figure 1-83, which is at Level 1. Selecting the vertex, apply [Modeling > Subdiv Surfaces > Component Display Filter > Edits] to display only the modified vertices shown in Figure 1-84.

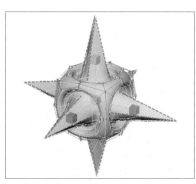
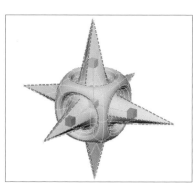

Figure 1-83 Modifying Vertices Using the Scale Tool

Figure 1-84 Display Filter = Edits

UV Borders can only be verified through the UV Texture Editor ([Window > UV Texture Editor...]).
By making the UV boundary thick, we can easily see which UVs have not been linked.
Adjust the size of the Normal by opening the Attribute Editor. After expanding the Subdiv Surface Display, set the Normals Display Scale to the desired size.

Selecting [Modeling > Subdiv Surfaces > Component Display Filter > All] will display all the points again.

2-16. DISPLAYING SUBDIVISION SURFACES COMPONENTS

We can model subdivision surfaces in standard mode by displaying the vertices, edges and faces of the subdivision surface.
To display these components, select the subdivision surface, apply [Display > Subdiv Surface Components] and choose between Vertices, Edges, Faces, and Normals (Shaded Mode).

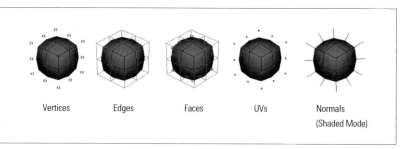

Figure 1-85 Subdivision surface components

We can also select the Subdivision Surface and press Ctrl+A key to open the Attribute Editor (shown below in Figure 1-86) to display the components of the Subdivision Surface.
Select the desired component in the Subdiv Component Display Section of the Attribute Editor.

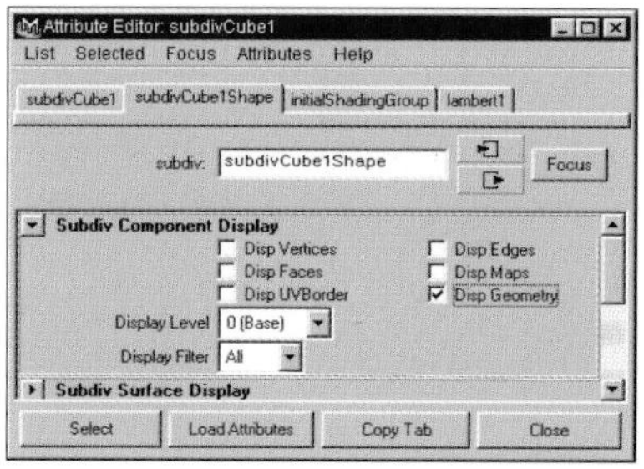

Figure 1-86 Attribute Editor

Users can also use the Marking Menu to quickly display the components of the Subdivision Surface and select them to make the shape of the surface. As shown in Figure 1-87, place the mouse over the subdivision surface and click the RMB. Then, select the desired component from the marking menu.

A more general method is to use the Components Mask.

Select the Subdivision Surface and then press F8 to convert to Component Mode. Then, as shown in Figure 1-88, select the desired component from the Components Mask.

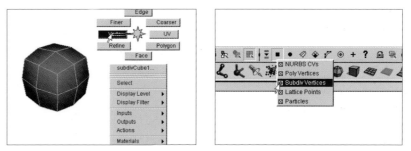

Figure 1-87 Selection Using the Marking Menu　　Figure 1-88 Making the Selection from the Components Mode

2-17. PORTRAYING DETAIL IN ANOTHER LEVEL

Subdivision surfaces offer levels for depicting detail. Users can use these levels to more accurately model an area of their choice. A maximum of 13 (0-12) levels can be made in the base mesh. A subdivision surface generally has two levels, 0 and 1. Selecting the vertex, edge, or face and then applying [Modeling > Subdiv Surfaces > Refine Selected Components] will create another layer. We can confirm this by selecting the Subdivision Surface in standard mode, clicking the RMB, and selecting Display Level from the Marking Menu.

Let's look at how to use this through a simple example.

Figure 1-89 on the next page shows the base mesh at Display Level 0. Level 0 is called a Base Mesh. Figure 1-90 illustrates the selection of Display Level 1 in the Marking Menu.

Figure 1-89 Display Level = 0

Figure 1-90 Display Level = 1

The figures above are models of a finger. Users will require more mesh points, edges, or faces to depict the fingernails.

The option Refine Selected Components is used to raise the Display Level of the selected area. First, select the edge of the area where the fingernail will be placed as shown in Figure 1-91. (You may also select the point or the face.) After selecting the edge, select [Modeling > Subdiv Surfaces > Refine Selected Components] to raise the Display Level to 2 as shown in Figure 1-92.

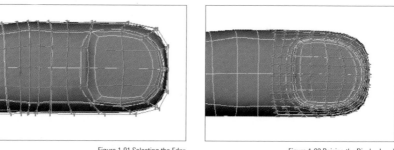

Figure 1-91 Selecting the Edge

Figure 1-92 Raising the Display Level

In this way, we can create more accurate modeling in a given section by raising the Display Level.

You may continue to select the point, edge, or face and apply Refine Selected Components to raise the Display Level up to 12.

1. Selecting the Display Level

Display Levels are selected in the following manner. First, they can be selected using the Marking Menu. This is done by placing the mouse over the subdivision surface, clicking the RMB, and setting the Display Level to the desired value in the Marking Menu as shown in Figure 1-93.

In selecting Display Levels using the Channel Box, we must first select the subdivision surface or its components (vertices, etc.) to display the Display Levels in the Channel Box (below the polyToSubdShape node) as shown in Figure 1-94. Clicking on the value using the LMB will display the level allowing us to select the desired level.

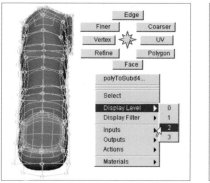

Figure 1-93 Selecting Levels Using the Marking Menu

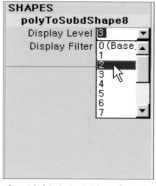

Figure 1-94 Selecting Levels Using the Channel Box

2-18. DEFINING THE SMOOTH VALUE FOR THE SUBDIVISION SURFACE

The Subdivision Surface, much like NURBS, can define how smooth the surface will be displayed.

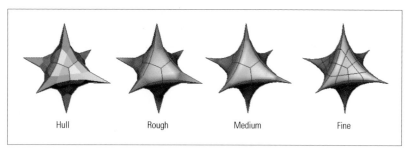

Figure 1-95 Smooth Values for the Subdivision Surface

Select one of the smooth values, depicted above, from [Display > Subdiv Smoothness].
Hull is the lowest setting and portrays the surface in angles. Being the lowest setting, the speed in which it is displayed is the fastest.
Rough, Medium, and Fine (using the respective shortcut keys of 1, 2, and 3) represent increasingly smoother and more accurate displays, which conversely, leads to lower view speeds.

3. QUICK START TUTORIAL

Up until now, we looked at the basic Polygon and Subdiv Surfaces menus for the purposes of learning how to model using subdivision surfaces. It is very difficult to understand subdivision surfaces through a simple explanation of the menus.
The following tutorial was designed to facilitate a general understanding of subdivision surface modeling.
A brief explanation will be offered on how to create comparatively simple characters and how to texturize them using Maya's 3D Paint feature.

step 1 Subdivision surfaces use polygons as their base. First, use [Modeling > Polygons > Create Polygon Tool] to make the polygon shown in Figure 1-96. In order to remain faithful to the example given here, try to make the same shape and vertices shown here.

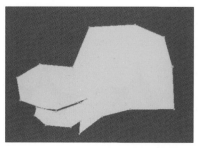

Figure 1-96 Using the Create Polygon Tool

It does not matter what direction the figure is drawn, just as long as it takes on the same shape. When you have finished drawing the shape, press the Enter key to exit from this tool. You can edit the vertices to modify portions of the shape.

Check the box to make sure that the [Modeling > Polygons > Tool Options > Keep Faces Together] option is turned on.

Select the model, click the RMB, and select Edge from the Marking Menu. Select all the edges of the polygon, and select [Modeling > Edit Polygons > Extrude Edge].
This will create the Extrude Manipulator shown in Figure 1-97.

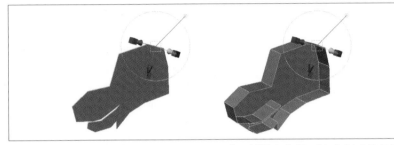

Figure 1-97 Moving the Edges Using the Extrude Manipulator

Use the Manipulator as shown to move the edges so that they extrude from the page.

 Select the polygon, and then click RMB to select the face. As shown in Figure 1-98, select the side and neck surfaces and then press the Delete key to remove.
After selecting the polygon again, select [Modify > Convert > Polygon to Subdiv] to convert the polygon to a subdivision surface.

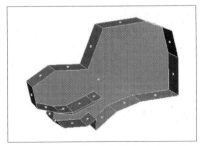

Figure 1-98 Selecting the Face to Delete

Figure 1-99 Converting to Subdivision Surface

Select the subdivision surface and select [Edit > Duplicate ◘] to open the Options window, as shown in Figure 1-100. In the window, set Scale X to -1, the Geometry Type to Instance, and then press the Duplicate button at the bottom.

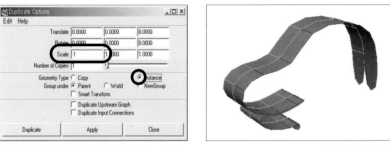

Figure 1-100 The Duplicate Options Window

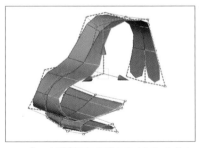

Figure 1-101 Mirror Copy

Because the subdivision surface was mirror copied and the Type was set to Instance, only one side of the subdivision surface is made with the remaining portion matched automatically to create the overall modeling.

To make partial modifications, select the subdivision surface, click the RMB, and select Vertex from the Marking Menu. After selecting several vertices to verify the attachment between the vertex and the vertex edge, select [Display > Subdiv Surface Components > Edge].
This will display both the vertex and the edge as shown in Figure 1-102.

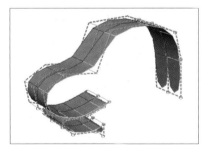

Figure 1-102 Subdiv Surface Component Display

Figure 1-103 Trimming the Shape by Adjusting the Vertex

To make the overall shape, adjust the vertex of the subdivision surface, as shown above in Figure 1-103, to form the shape. There is no need to make your picture look exactly like the one shown here. Just try to make it as similar as you can.

step 3 Now that we're done with the basics, it's time to start making the surfaces to complete the overall shape.

First, in order to make the surface, select the subdivision surface, and then either click the RMB and select Polygon from the Marking Menu or select [Modeling > Subdiv Surfaces > Polygon Proxy Mode] to convert the subdivision surface to Polygon Proxy Mode.

Figure 1-104 Polygon Proxy Mode

Most of the overall surfaces will be made using Extrude Edge or Face. First, in order to extrude the edge, select the edge inside the mouth as shown in Figure 1-105. Select the mode so that the borders of the edge are clearly visible and then open the Options window by selecting [Display > Custom Polygon Display] and select Border Edge from Highlight.

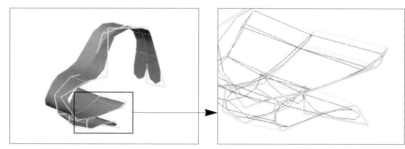

Figure 1-105 Selecting the Edge to Extrude

Select [Modeling > Edit Polygons > Extrude Edge]. This will create the Extrude Manipulator shown in Figure 1-106. In the beginning, the Manipulator will fit itself to the local axis of the edge. Moving the extruded edge at this time will cause to edge to move abnormally. To prevent this from happening, click on the area indicated in Figure 1-106 to fit the Manipulator to the World axis.

This will create an appropriate extrusion of the edge as shown in Figure 1-107.

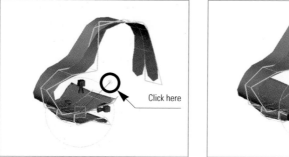

Figure 1-106 Extrude Edge

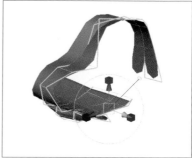

Figure 1-107 Moving the Edge

After moving back to standard mode, adjust the overall vertex as shown in Figure 1-108 to make the overall shape. Again, an accurate recreation is not necessary. Just make sure you represent how the inside of the mouth is organized.

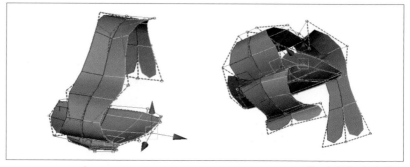

Figure 1-108 Trimming the Shape

After moving back to Polygon Proxy Mode, extrude the respective edges as shown in Figure 1-109 to make the surface.

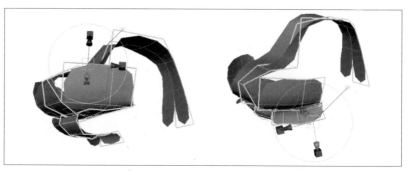

Figure 1-109 Extrude Edge

Attach the separated edges by selecting [Modeling > Edge Polygons > Merge Edge Tool]. As shown in Figure 1-110, selecting Edge A, the edge we wish to adhere, will cause all edges to turn pink. At this time, select Edge B to merge together Edges A and B. Continue to merge the edges to achieve the result shown in Figure 1-111.

Figure 1-110 Merge Edge Tool

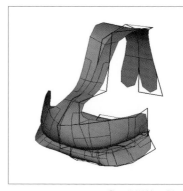

Figure 1-111 Merge Edge Tool

Extrude the edges as shown in Figure 1-112 to make the surface, and use the Merge Edge Tool to merge the edges in the back.

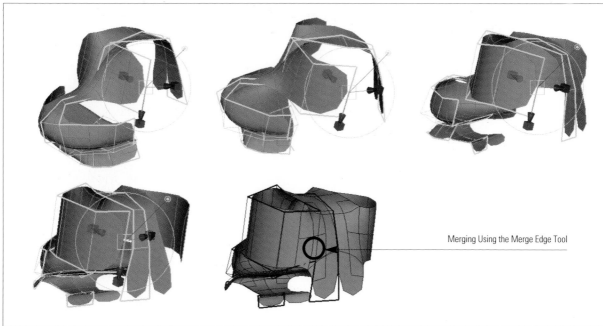

Merging Using the Merge Edge Tool

Figure 1-112 Extrude Edge and Merge Edge Tool

Select the model and then select [Modeling > Polygons > Append to Polygon Tool]. Selecting Edges 1 and 2, in succession, will create a preview of the filled surface as shown in Figure 1-113. To fill in the surface, press the Enter key. Select all the other edges in consecutive order and apply the Append to Polygon Tool to fill in the surfaces.

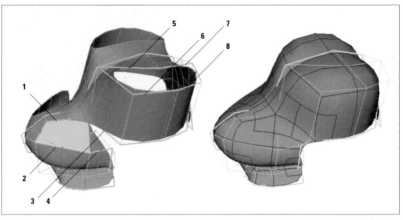

Figure 1-113 Using the Append to Polygon Tool

As shown in Figure 1-114, use Extrude Edge and Merge Edge Tool to make the lateral face and merge the edges together as shown.

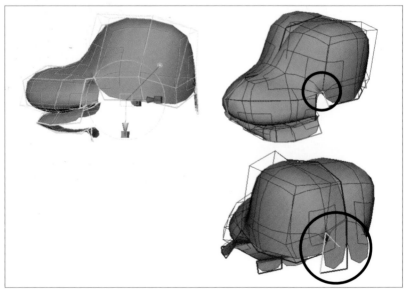

Figure 1-114 Extrude Edge & Merge Edge Tool

Fill in the holes on the chin by using the Append to Polygon Tool as shown in Figure 1-115.

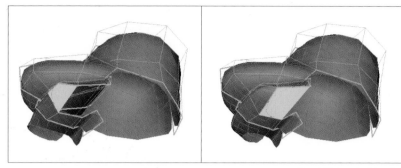

Figure 1-115 Append to Polygon Tool

Now it's time to model the slightly more complex region of the mouth. Figure 1-116 shows an extrusion of the edges around the mouth. If you have followed the tutorial faithfully up until this point, your edges should take on the configuration shown here. Extrude this edge.

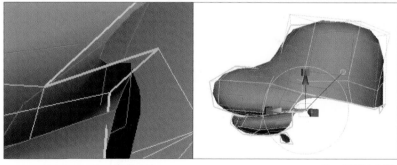

Figure 1-116 Extrude Edge

In standard mode, adjust the vertex so that the surface appears to spread as in Figure 1-117. Merge the edges together in Polygon Proxy Mode as shown in Figure 1-118.

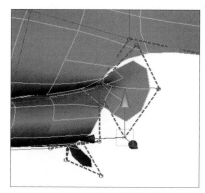

Figure 1-117 Modifying the Shape

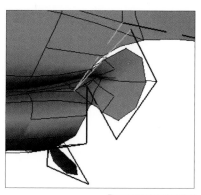

Figure 1-118 Merge Edge Tool

The next steps involve making the remaining surfaces. Each of the steps is illustrated using pictures, and you should have no problem following along to complete the next few steps.

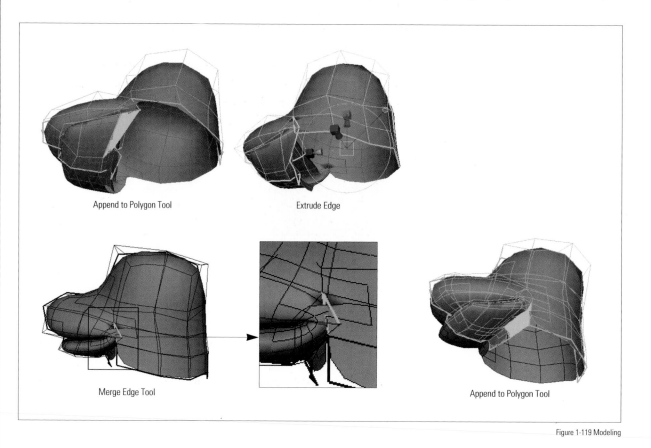

Append to Polygon Tool

Extrude Edge

Merge Edge Tool

Append to Polygon Tool

Figure 1-119 Modeling

After the surfaces have been made, revert back to standard mode and adjust the vertices to trim the overall shape of the character.

Figure 1-120 shows the process of trimming the character.

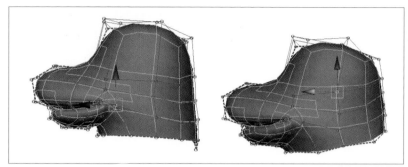

Figure 1-120 Modifying the Shape

step 4   Let's now find out how to use Extrude Face to model the other eye and the nose. First, we need to revert back to polygon proxy mode.

As shown in Figure 1-121, select the face where the nose will be made. Select [Modeling > Edit Polygons > Extrude Face] to slightly extrude the selected face. Repeat this step 2 more times until it looks like the character shown in Figure 1-122.

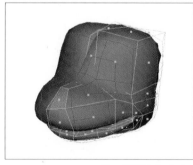

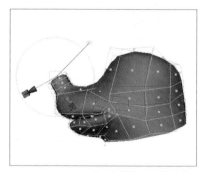

Figure 1-121 Selecting the Face   Figure 1-122 Executing Extrude Face

Select the inside of the nose as shown in Figure 1-123, and press the Delete key to erase. Select the face where the eye will be made and execute Extrude Face. Adjust the Manipulator until you get the result shown in Figure 1-124.

Figure 1-123 Selecting the Face to Delete

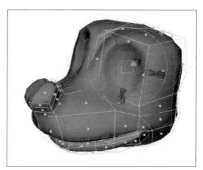

Figure 1-124 Executing Extrude Face

Convert back to standard mode to trim the shape.

We will now begin adding more detail to the model. First, in order to model the eyes, make a sphere and position it in the eye socket. Make the sphere by selecting [Create > NURBS Primitives > Sphere] and, after moving it to the position of the eye as shown in Figure 1-125, adjust the size as shown.

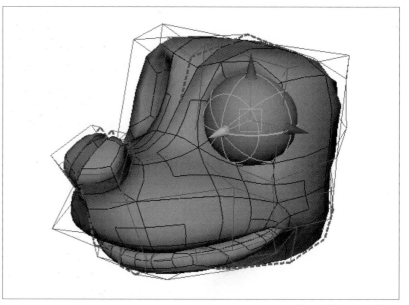

Figure 1-125 Arranging the Sphere

Now, adjust the vertices to trim the overall shape.

This process is illustrated in Figure 1-126.

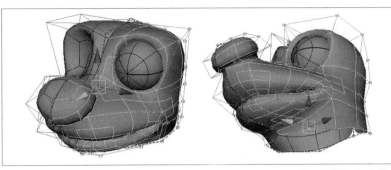

Figure 1-126 Trimming the Shape

To make modifications to portions of the surface, revert to polygon proxy mode, select the model, and then apply [Modeling > Edit Polygons > Split Polygon Tool] to slice the edge as shown in Figure 1-127.

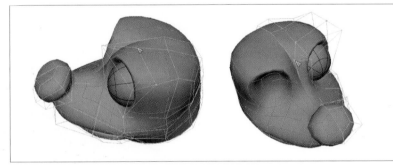

Figure 1-127 Split Polygon Tool

Go back to standard mode.

Let's attempt to divide the levels of the subdivision surface to depict greater detail. First, place the mouse over the subdivision surface, click the RMB, and then select Display Level 1 from the Marking Menu as shown in Figure 1-128. As the subdivision surface is raised to Level 1, greater detail is added to the surfaces and the vertices. Adjust the vertices in Level 1 to model the area around the eye as shown in Figure 1-129.

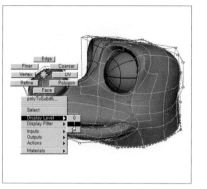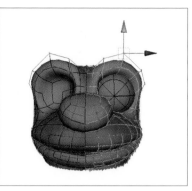

Figure 1-128 Selecting the Display Level   Figure 1-129 Trimming the Shape in Level 1

To add greater detail, select the vertex of the area you wish to modify, as shown in Figure 1-130, click the RMB, and select Refine from the Marking Menu. Selecting [Modeling > Subdiv Surfaces > Refine Selected Components] will divide the model into Level 2, as shown in Figure 1-131, to increase the number of vertices, which can be adjusted. As follows, detail can be added to a particular region in Polygon Proxy Mode without having to add additional surfaces.

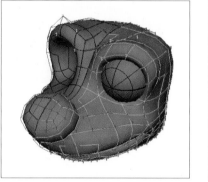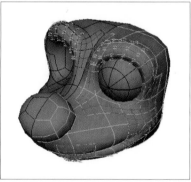

Figure 1-130 Selecting the Vertex   Figure 1-131 After Applying Refine

step 5 Set the Display Level of the subdivision surface to 1.
Click the RMB and, after selecting Edge from the Marking Menu, select the edge of Level 1 as shown in Figure 1-132. Select [Modeling > Subdiv Surfaces > Full Crease Edge/Vertex]. This will create an acute angle in the selected edge. Use the vertex to make the shape as shown in Figure 1-133.

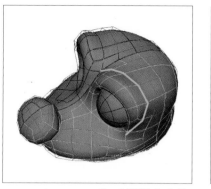

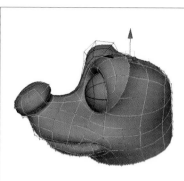

Figure 1-132 Selecting the Edge

Figure 1-133 Trimming the Shape

After modifying the shape, prepare for the next step by deleting the half of the model that was copied using Instance.

step 6 As the final step in modeling, we need to mirror the model that we made and attach it.

Before we can do this, however, we need to first examine the following situation. It is very difficult to obtain a precise attachment if the vertex, which is linked to the central edge of the model shown in Figure 1-134, is off the Grid Center Line of the window. Therefore, in such cases, we need to select all the vertices, as shown in Figure 1-135, press the X key on the keyboard to create the Grid Snap, and then match the X-axis of the grid to the center line as shown.

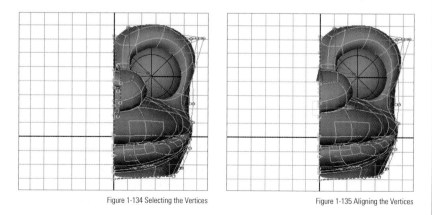

Figure 1-134 Selecting the Vertices

Figure 1-135 Aligning the Vertices

Select the subdivision surface, select [Modeling > Subdiv Surfaces > Mirror ◨] to open the Option window, select the X-axis and then press the Mirror button. If the polygon was modeled in side view from the beginning, the X-axis must be the base.

A mirror copy of the model will appear as in Figure 1-136. Select both subdivision surfaces, and then select [Modeling > Subdiv Surfaces > Attach]. The two models will attach to become one as shown in Figure 1-137.

Figure 1-136 Mirror

Figure 1-137 Attach

We have now completed a modeling of a character using subdivision surfaces.
Greater detail and more accurate modeling will be covered later in this book.

● **Texturing Subdivision Surface Model**

Now, we will look at how to create a simple subdivision surface texture. Again, greater detail will be covered later in this book.

Through this process, we will learn how easy and quickly we can create a simple texture.

step 1 Select the subdivision surface, click the RMB and then select Face from the Marking Menu. Select the entire face of the subdivision surface. Select [Modeling > Subdiv Surfaces > Textures > Automatic Mapping ◨] to open the Options window and make the configurations shown in Figure 1-138. (Refer to Chapter 2 "Polygon, Subdivision Surface Mapping," for more information.)

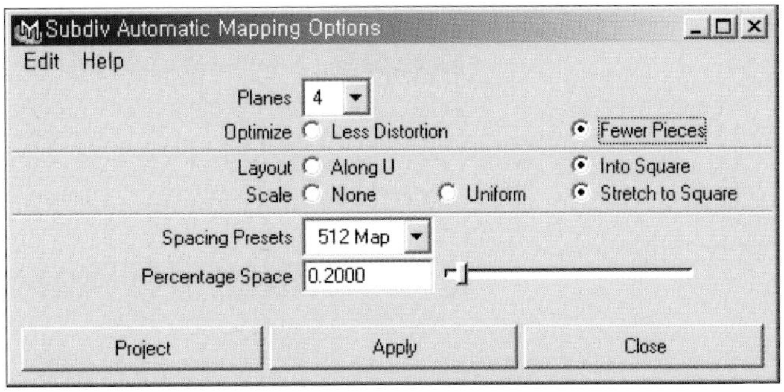

Figure 1-138 Options Window

Click the Project button at the bottom of the window.

Open the UV Texture Editor by selecting [Windows > UV Texture Editor] to automatically create the UV on the subdivision surface as shown in Figure 1-139.

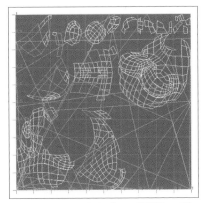

Figure 1-139 UV Texture Editor

step 2 Because we cannot paint directly on the subdivision surface, we must
convert it to a polygon first.

Select the model and then select [Modify > Convert > Subdiv to Polygon ▱] to open the
Options window. Make the configurations shown in Figure 1-140, and then press the
Convert button at the bottom.

Figure 1-140 Options Window

Select [Edit > Delete by Type > History] to delete the history of the polygon object. Hide
the subdivision surface by selecting the model and pressing the Ctrl+H key.

Figure 1-141 The Converted Polygon Model

step 3 Select the Polygon Model and then select [Rendering > Texturing > 3D Paint Tool] to open the Tool Settings window.

As shown in Figure 1-142, click the Assign Textures button in the File Texture Section to open the window that asks for the texture size (shown in Figure 1-143). Enter **512**, and then click the Assign Textures button.

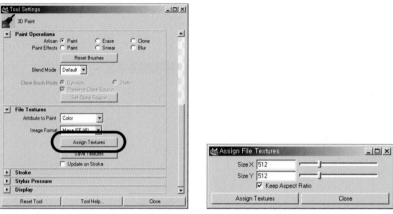

Figure 1-142 Tool Settings Window

Figure 1-143 Configuring the Texture Size

In the color section of the Tool Settings window, shown in Figure 1-144, click on the Color Box next to the Flood Color to open the Color Chooser window. From there, we can make a more specific color choice.

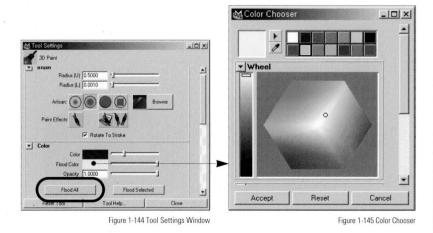

Figure 1-144 Tool Settings Window

Figure 1-145 Color Chooser

Click on the Flood All button in the Tool Settings window, shown in Figure 1-144.

We can see that the polygon model is filled in with the color we chose.
To paint the model, click on the Color Box next to Color, as shown in Figure 1-144, and select an appropriate color. As shown in Figure 1-146, check Reflection X under Stroke Selection in the Tool Setting window. This option allows us to paint symmetrically to the X-axis with respect to the absolute axis in the window as shown in Figure 1-147.

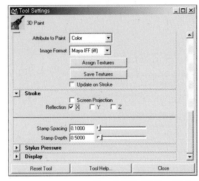

Figure 1-146 Tool Settings Window

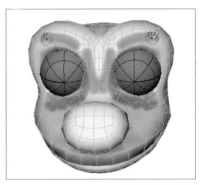

Figure 1-147 Reflect Paint

Now, use the desired colors to paint the model as shown in Figure 1-148. The brush size can be adjusted in the Brush Section. Opacity is used to adjust the opacity of the color in Color Sections. Flip back and forth between these options to create the desired texture.

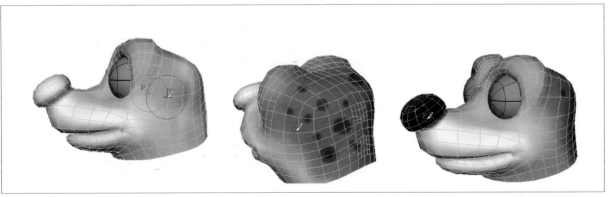

Figure 1-148 Painting Texture

step 4 When you have completed painting the model, click on the Save Texture button in the Tool Settings window as shown in Figure 1-149.

Select [Windows > Rendering Editors > Multilister]. You can see the texture file we just made in Figure 1-150.

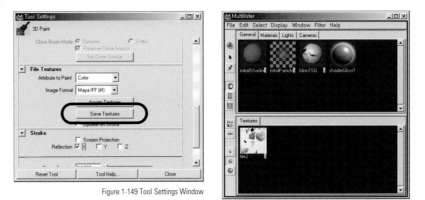

Figure 1-149 Tool Settings Window

Figure 1-150 Multilister

Make a new shader and place the texture in the color. Reveal again the subdivision surface, which was hidden earlier, by selecting [Display > Show > All] and assign this shader to the subdivision surface.

Hide or delete the polygon object.

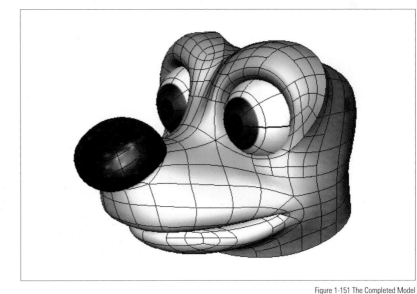

Figure 1-151 The Completed Model

2 Polygon, Subdivision Surface Mapping

The first step to successful and effective subdivision surface modeling is to understand the mapping environment.

Mapping and subdivision surface modeling are closely related. Using Maya 4 or higher, we can create a map axis directly on the subdivision surface. When deemed convenient, creating a map axis during the modeling process is very effective.

Although there are many ways to assign the axis, I will first explain the method that I use most often and then I will explain several other methods.

In order to map the subdivision surface, users must first have a firm understanding of polygon mapping.

1. POLYGON MAPPING

Textures are generally made in the shape of a rectangle and applied to individual objects. It is very easy to apply this rectangular texture to a NURBS object because the rectangle is the basic unit of the NURBS. For this reason, when a NURBS is made, a U or V texture axis is also made automatically. However, in the case of a polygon, an infinite number of angles can come from a rectangle. This presents us with the problem of how we can apply this rectangular texture to the many-sided polygon. In answer to this problem, Maya offers options that will allow us to apply many different mapping axes to a polygon. Texture Space, a 2D map axis system, allows us to assign a UV-axis to the polygon.

First, let's look at the basic menu for polygon mapping. The menu can be found under [Modeling > Edit Polygons > Texture].

1-1. ASSIGN SHADER TO EACH PROJECTION

This tool applies a random checker texture to individual mapping types, allowing us to see a preview of the applied texture without assigning a separate texture to the polygon object.

To use this tool, first set the [Modeling > Edit Polygons > Texture > Assign Shader to Each Projection] to 'On', make a polygon cube, select the face, and then select [Modeling > Edit Polygons > Texture > Planar Mapping]. This will display the checker texture, as shown in Figure 2-1, showing us the manner in which the current mapping axis has been applied.

Maya offers many different methods for making a UV-axis on the polygon object.

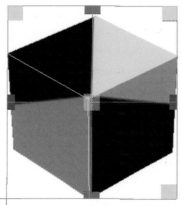

Figure 2-1 Assign Shader to Each Projection

1-2. CREATE UV

Maya offers many different methods for making a UV-axis on the polygon object.
The following figure (Figure 2-2) illustrates the different ways of making a UV-axis on a
polygon object using Maya.

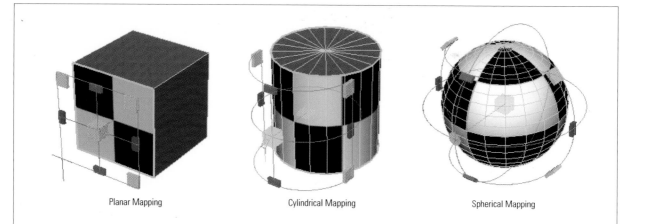

Planar Mapping   Cylindrical Mapping   Spherical Mapping

Figure 2-2 Basic Mapping Types

Each of the mapping types comes with a manipulator used for reediting the UV-axis.
Users can use the manipulator to adjust the size, repetition and rotation of the texture.
Figure 2-3 illustrates how to use the manipulator.

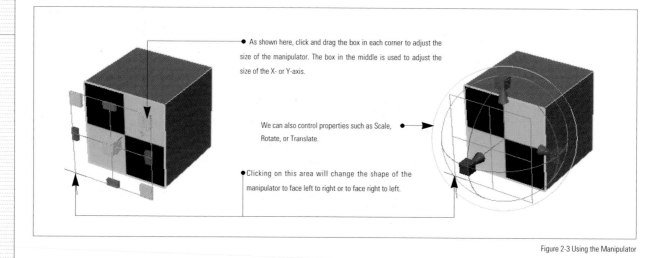

As shown here, click and drag the box in each corner to adjust the
size of the manipulator. The box in the middle is used to adjust the
size of the X- or Y-axis.

We can also control properties such as Scale,
Rotate, or Translate.

Clicking on this area will change the shape of the
manipulator to face left to right or to face right to left.

Figure 2-3 Using the Manipulator

```
INPUTS
   polyPlanarProj1
   polyCube1
Projection Center 0
Projection Center 0
Projection Center 0.5
  Image Center X 0.5
  Image Center Y 0.5
        Rotate X 0
        Rotate Y 0
        Rotate Z 0
Projection Width 1
Projection Height 1
  Image Scale U 1
  Image Scale V 1
  Rotation Angle 0
```

Figure 2-4 Channel Box

If the History is still alive, the manipulator can be displayed and modified at any time throughout the process.

Select the object and observe the Channel Box INPUTS. You should be able to see the name of the Planar Projections as shown in Figure 2-4. Click on the name, and select from the Minibar to display and work with the manipulator.

1. Planar Mapping

Planar mapping allows us to project the UV-axis of the object along the plane to make the texture map. The following example illustrates how to use planar mapping along with the options Smart Fit, Fit to Best Plane, and Fit to Bounding Box. It is also possible to use the manipulator to precisely situate a texture in the needed area.

step 1 Press F11 on the keyboard or place the mouse over the object, click the RMB, and then select Face from the Marking Menu to select the face of the polygon.

step 2 Open the Options window by selecting [Modeling > Edit Polygons > Texture > Planar Mapping ❑], and check the box next to Smart Fit to select this option. If this option is not selected, we will not be able to select Fit to Best Plane or Fit to Bounding Box options either. Check either Fit to Best Plane or Fit to Bounding Box.

step 3 Click on the Project button at the bottom of the Polygon Planar Projection Options window.

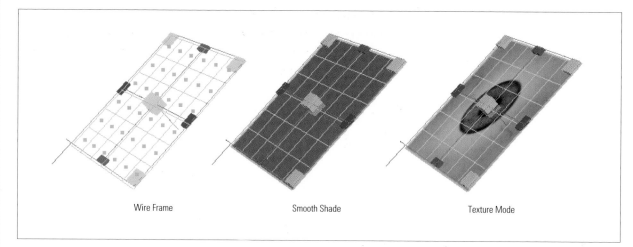

Wire Frame   Smooth Shade   Texture Mode

Figure 2-5 Planar Mapping

step 4 Use the Manipulator to position the texture of the polygon face. We can do this by moving the texture, as shown in Figure 2-6, or by adjusting the size and rotating it. Also, these properties can also be modified through the Channel Box.

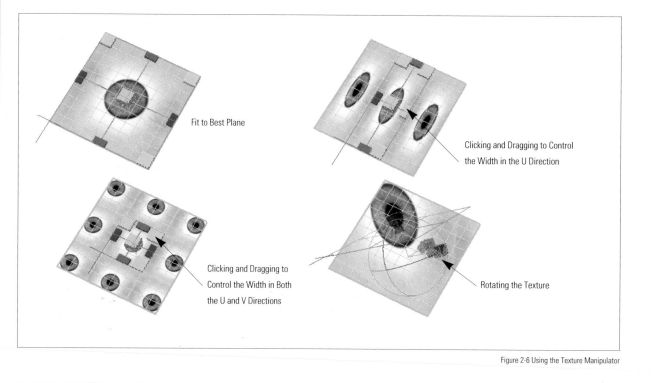

Fit to Best Plane

Clicking and Dragging to Control
the Width in the U Direction

Clicking and Dragging to
Control the Width in Both
the U and V Directions

Rotating the Texture

Figure 2-6 Using the Texture Manipulator

Polygon Planar Projection Options

Open the Options window by selecting [Edit Polygons > Texture > Planar Mapping ☐].
This will open the Polygon Planar Projection Options window as shown in Figure 2-7.
Let's take a look at how to use each of these options.

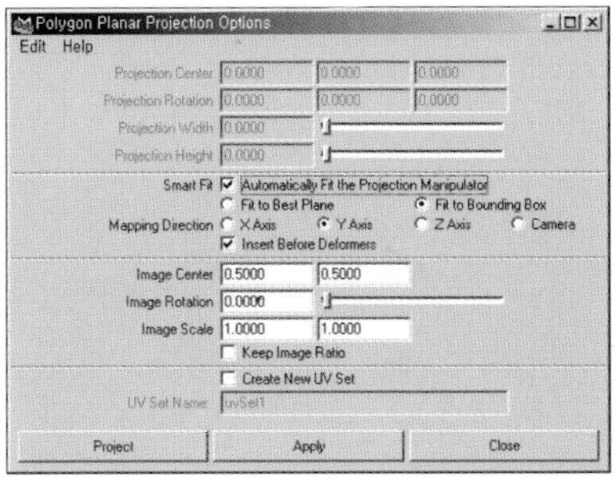

Figure 2-7 Polygon Planar Projection Options Window

Smart Fit

When this option is turned off, we can indicate the location of the manipulator by
entering in the values directly for Projection Center, Rotation, Projection Width, and
Height at the bottom of the Options window.

These values can also be adjusted using the Channel Box, the Attribute Editor, or the
Manipulator. When this option is turned on, we can also select the Fit to Best Plane or Fit
to Bounding Box options.

Fit to Best Plane

Selecting the Fit to Best Plane option will automatically snap into place the projection of
all the faces to create an optimal texture mapping for the face. In other words, the
projection will occur with respect to the border edge of the selected face. When this
option is turned on, we will not be able to use the Mapping Direction option.

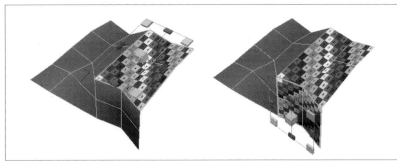

Figure 2-8 Projection with Respect to the Border Edge of the Selected Face

Fit to Bounding Box

When this option is selected, the texture will be projected vertically along the specified axis inside the bounding box of the polygon object and the manipulator will snap. With this option, we can use the mapping direction option to select along which axis we will make the projection.

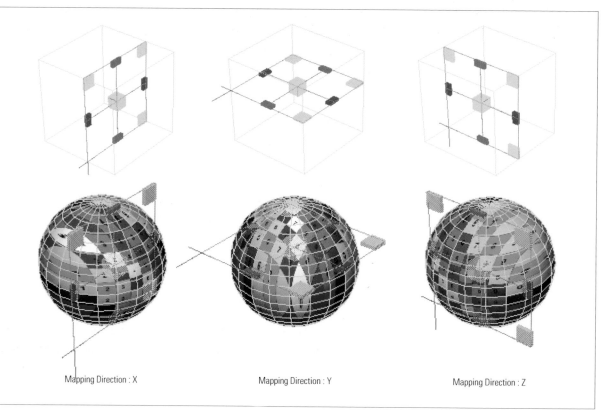

Mapping Direction : X   Mapping Direction : Y   Mapping Direction : Z

Figure 2-9 Mapping Direction

We can also select [Shade > Bounding Box] from the Panel menu in Windows to view the bounding box.

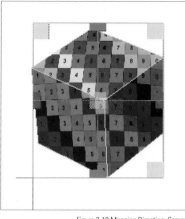

Figure 2-10 Mapping Direction: Camera

Camera

Selecting Camera from the mapping direction will make the projection along the viewpoint of the camera.

Insert Before Deformers

The default setting for this option is On. This option depends on whether the polygon object is influenced by the Deformer. For example, if the polygon is set to Joint and Binding and the texture mapping is done with this option turned off, the texture axis will not be able to follow the transformation of the object. To prevent this from happening, it is more convenient to work with this option always set to On.

Image Center

This option displays the UV center of the projection. Changing this value will cause the center to move.

Image Rotation

This option allows us to configure the UV rotation angle inside the 2D window. The image is rotated by dragging the slider bar or by typing the values.

Image Scale

This option sets the width (U) or height (V) of the 2D mapping along the center.

Keep Image Ratio

When this option is turned on, the width and height of the image is maintained and when this option is turned off, the image is aligned along the coordinates 0, 1 inside the UV Texture Editor.

Create New UV Set

When this option is turned on, a new UV set is made. The name of the UV set can be entered in the UV Set Name Field.

2. Cylindrical Mapping and Spherical Mapping

The Cylindrical Projection Mapping creates a texture mapping in the shape of a cylinder around the object.

Spherical Projection Mapping creates a texture mapping in the shape of a sphere around the object.

 step 1 Press the F11 key on the keyboard, or select the object and select Face from the Marking Menu to select the face of the polygon. We can also select the face of what we wish to map.

Open the Options window by selecting [Modeling > Edit Polygons > Texture > Cylindrical Mapping or Spherical Mapping 🗖].

Change the values in the Options window as needed.

Figure 2-11 Options Window

step 2 Click on the Project button at the bottom of the Options window. This will create a manipulator on the selected face as shown in Figure 2-12.

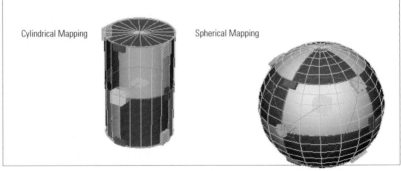

Figure 2-12 Cylindrical and Spherical Mapping

If the [Polygons > Tool Options > Convert Selection] option is turned on, there is no need to select all the faces in order to make a projection map for the entire object.

When this option is turned on, simply select the object on which you wish to make a projection map and make the projection using the desired projection type.

Note: This feature is improved in Maya virsions 4.5 and later.

As needed, users may use the manipulator to place the texture over the polygon face or arrange the texture over the object using the Channel Box or Attribute Editor.

The options in the Options window are, basically, the same as the options for planar mapping.

Cylindrical & Spherical Mapping Tip

When cylindrical or spherical mapping are used, problems arise at the joints or seams. This is because the UV values do not spread out and the opposite ends link together.

For example, let's suppose we applied a cylindrical mapping to the polygon object shown in Figure 2-13. Select all of the faces on the object and select [Modeling > Edit Polygons > Texture > Cylindrical Mapping] to create the manipulator shown in Figure 2-14.

Looking at the Channel Box, we can see that the Projection Horizontal Sweep value is set to 180. This is the default value. When this value is set to 180, the manipulator will only encircle half the object as shown in Figure 2-14. If this value is set to 360, the manipulator will completely encircle the object.

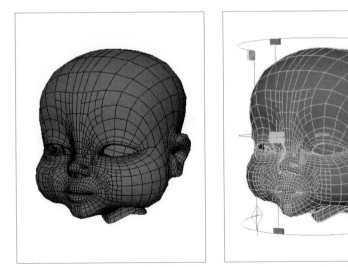

Figure 2-13 Polygon Object

Figure 2-14 Cylindrical Mapping

In the current state, select [Window > Texture Editor] to view the Texture Editor, as shown in Figure 2-15. Currently, the UV coordinates have not been made accurately. As we can tell by looking at Figure 2-15, we can see that a portion of the UV is twisted.

The following note applies only to users of Maya version 4. If you have version 4.5 or later, you may ignore this.

The value for the Projection Center does not need to be exactly 0.0001. Due to the problem in version 4, this Projection Center value may be adjusted to avoid the problem seen in Figure 2-15.

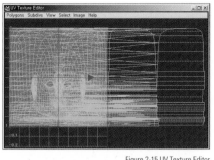

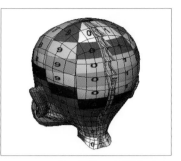

Figure 2-15 UV Texture Editor   Figure 2-16 Incorrected UV Coordinates

As we can see in the figure above, despite the fact that all the UVs of the polygon are within the texture axis, they still deviate. This will lead to a twisting of the textures in the back of the head as seen in Figure 2-16.

The answer to this problem lies in adjusting the Projection Center. Select polyCylProj1 from Channel Box INPUTS and fix the value of the Projection Center to 0.0001.

Looking at the UV Texture Editor, we can see that the polygon UV coordinates lie within the texture axis (see Figure 2-17) to prevent the texture in the back of the head from twisting (see Figure 2-18).

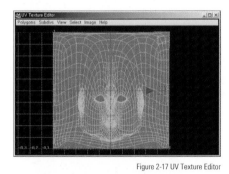

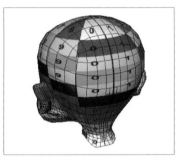

Figure 2-17 UV Texture Editor   Figure 2-18 Corrected UV Coordinates

The same principle holds true for spherical mapping.

3. Automatic Mapping

This option is very convenient for preventing partial UV distortion in planar, cylindrical, or spherical projection. When Automatic Mapping is executed, the polygon UV values in the texture space are cut out from repeating UV meshes and divided within the 0, 1 coordinates of the texture. In other words, this prevents repeating UV values and/or distorted images in planar, cylindrical, or spherical projection.

However, as convenient as this option is, it is not without its disadvantages. The allotment of the textures for each face is relatively small. Therefore, there is a tremendous amount of texture loss.

Figure 2-19 shows a comparison of each mapping type with automatic mapping.

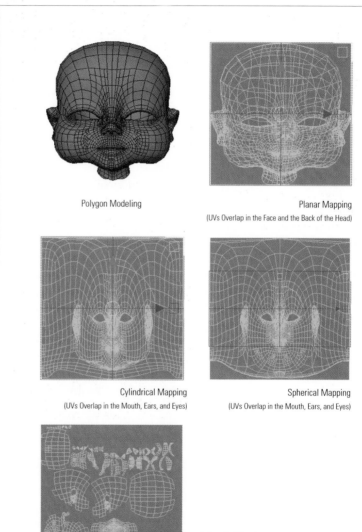

Polygon Modeling

Planar Mapping
(UVs Overlap in the Face and the Back of the Head)

Cylindrical Mapping
(UVs Overlap in the Mouth, Ears, and Eyes)

Spherical Mapping
(UVs Overlap in the Mouth, Ears, and Eyes)

Automatic Mapping
(There are no overlapping UV regions and all overlapping regions are spread out.)

Figure 2-19 Comparing Mapping for Each Type

Let's look at the options for Automatic Mapping. Select [Modeling > Edit Polygons > Texture > Automatic Mapping ▣] to open the Automatic Mapping Options window as shown in Figure 2-20.

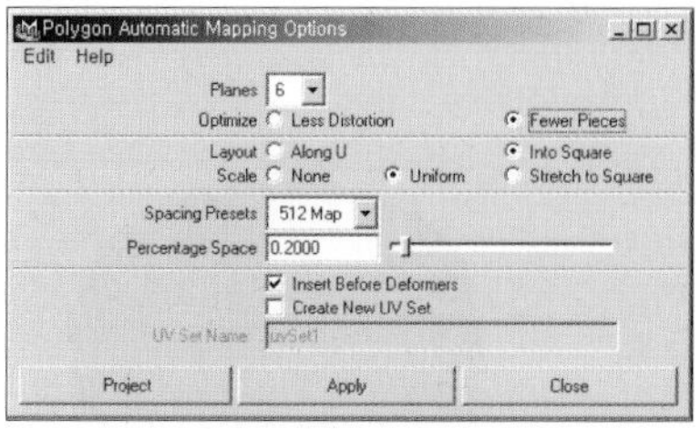

Figure 2-20 Automatic Mapping Options Window

Planes

Specify the number of planes. The higher this number, the more the UV distortion is prevented. The default value is 6.

Optimize

This option determines how the projection will be optimized.

Less Distortion This creates equal projection of all the planes. Although this can be used to optimize the projection of any face, it can also create many divided fragments. This option is very convenient for creating symmetrical surfaces in the projection of symmetrical models.

Fewer Pieces This option is used to project each plane until the ideal projection is achieved. It also increases the number of face fragments and lowers the number overall. This is the default setting.

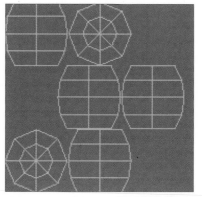

Figure 2-21 Less Distortion

Figure 2-22 Fewer Pieces

Layout

This option specifies the location within the texture space where the U and V mesh fragments will be arranged.

Along U Arranges the fragment along the U-axis.

Into Square Arranges the fragment in the 0, 1 texture space. This is the default setting.

Figure 2-23 Along U

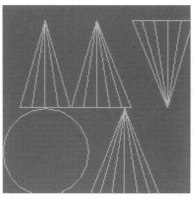

Figure 2-24 Into Square

Scale

This option decides how the U and V mesh fragments will be scaled within the texture space.

None No scaling.

Uniform Does not change the width and height proportion and scales the fragment fixedly in the 0-1 texture space. This is the default setting.

Stretch to Square Stretches the fragments fixedly in the 0, 1 texture space. This can also cause the fragments to become crooked.

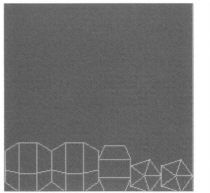

Figure 2-25 Along U, Uniform

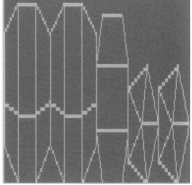

Figure 2-26 Along U, Stretch to Square

Spacing Presets

In Maya, we can establish a bounding box for each fragment at random and we can decide how close to the bounding box the layout will be. Problems can arise when we use Texture Paint because when the fragments are laid out, the UV of other fragments can share pixels.

To avoid this, select the predetermined Free Set in this menu and decide how far apart the pixels between the bounding boxes will be in the layout. The predetermined resolution will decide how far apart the fragments will be arranged.

The lower the resolution, the farther apart the UVs will be between bounding boxes.

Percentage Space

When Custom is selected in the Spacing Presets, we can decide on the Percentage, which will determine how far apart the spacing will be.

Create New UV Set

Turning on this option will create and arrange a new UV set. Enter the name of the new set in the UV Set Name Field.

4. Create UVs Based on Camera

The Create UVs Based on Camera option is determined by the current Camera View. The UV will be made with respect to the projection of the face or polygon as selected in View Plain. As follows, the Geometry seen in the Perspective Drawing View and the Face seen in the UV Texture Editor after this option is applied is the same.

step 1 Select the face in which the UV will be made. Press the F11 key on the keyboard or click the RMB to select Face from the Marking Menu. If the [Modeling > Polygons > Tool Options > Convert Selection] option is turned on, we can select the polygon object instead of the face.

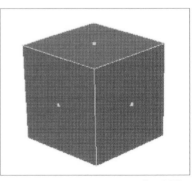

Figure 2-27 Face

step 2 Select [Edit Polygons > Texture > Create UVs Based on Camera]. A UV will be made in the selected face, and the texture will be mapped. As we can see in Figure 2-28, the geometrical shape seen in Perspective View and in the UV Texture Editor is the same.

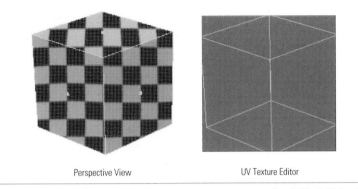

Perspective View   UV Texture Editor

Figure 2-28 Create UVs Based on Camera

To make a UV set with respect to the camera view, select [Edit Polygons > Texture > Create UVs Based on Camera ▢] to open the Options window. Set the Create New UV Set to On, enter the Set name, and then click the Apply button.

5. Best Plane Texturing Tool

step 1 Select the polygon object, and then either press the F11 key or click RMB to select Face from the Marking Menu to display the face of the polygon object.

step 2 Select [Edit Polygons > Texture > Best Plane Texturing Tool]. Select the face of the polygon object in which the UV coordinates will be made. We can select one or more.

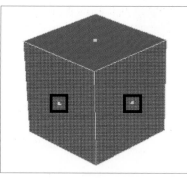
Figure 2-29 Selecting the Face

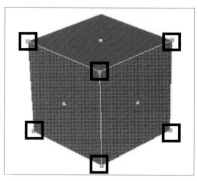
Figure 2-30 Selecting the Vertices

step 3 After selection of the faces is complete, as shown in Figure 2-29, press the Enter key on the keyboard. Now, select the vertices that surround the faces, as shown in Figure 2-30, press the Enter key. This will create the UV coordinates with respect to the selected vertices, as shown in Figure 2-31.

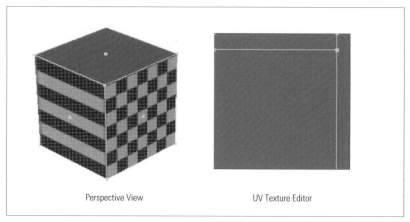

Perspective View   UV Texture Editor

Figure 2-31 Best Plane Texturing Tool

1-3. EDITING UVS

1. Normalize UVs

Normalizing the UVs will position them in the 0, 1 texture space. Select [Modeling > Edit Polygons > Texture > Normalize UVs ▢] to open the Options window shown in Figure 2-32.

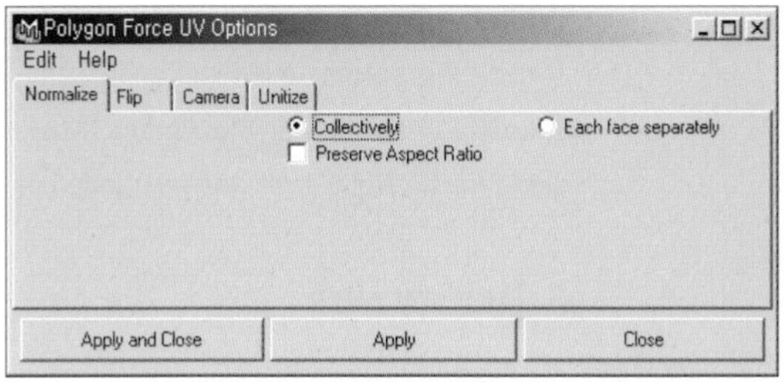

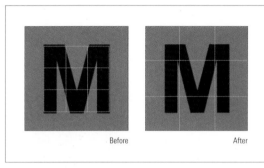

Figure 2-32 The Polygon Force UV Options Window

Collectively

This option will collectively normalize all the UVs in the selected face. In other words, all the texture coordinates in the selected face will be adapted to the 0, 1 texture space. This is the default setting.

Before　　　　　After

Figure 2-33 Collectively

Each Face Separately

Selecting this option will normalize the UVs in the selected face individually. In other words, each of the selected faces will be positioned within the borders of the 0, 1 texture space.

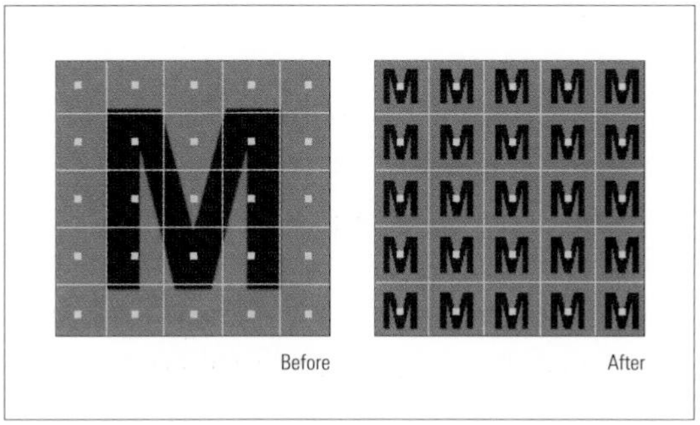

Before　　　　　After

Figure 2-34 Each Face Separately

Preserve Aspect Ratio

Turning this option on will uniformly scale the UV in the direction of U and V.

The default setting for this option is set to Off. In this case, the UV is unequally scaled along the U- and V-axes and positioned in the 0, 1 texture space.

2. Unitize UVs

Unitize UVs arranges the UVs of the selected face within the boundaries of the 0, 1 texture space.

To apply this option, first, select the desired face and select either [Edit Polygons > Textures > Unitize UVs] or [UV Texture Editor > Edit > Unitize UVs].

3. Flip UVs

This option will flip the UVs from left to right or from top to bottom.

For example, let's suppose the following situation.

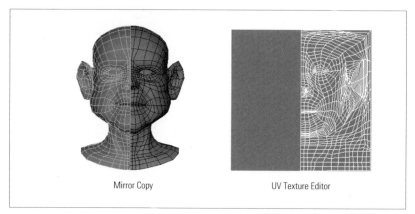

Mirror Copy   UV Texture Editor

Figure 2-35 Mirror Copying the Polygon and the UV Coordinates

Looking at Figure 2-35, we can see that when the polygon is mirror copied, the UV coordinates are not mirrored. In this case, the textures on the left and right side of the faces can be shared preventing us from using different textures. To spread out the UV, use Flip UVs.

To select this option, select the face of the model and then select [Edit Polygons > Textures > Flip UVs ▣] to open the Options window. In this window, set the Direction to Horizontal, and the Coordinate to Local. Click the Apply button to flip the left and right sides of the UV as shown in Figure 2-36.

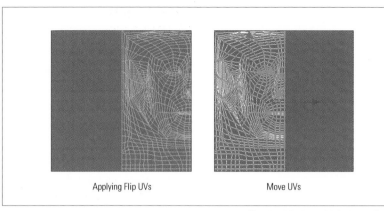

Applying Flip UVs   Move UVs

Figure 2-36 Adjusting the UV after Applying Flip UVs

To spread out the UV, select the UV, as shown in the figure above, and move it.

Taking a quick look at the options, Direction determines the direction, Horizontal flips the left and right sides, as shown in the figure, and Vertical flips the top and bottom.

Coordinate refers to the central axis. Selecting Local will flip the UVs across the center of the selected face, and selecting Global will flip the UVs with respect to the Texture Coordinate 0, as shown in Figure 2-37.

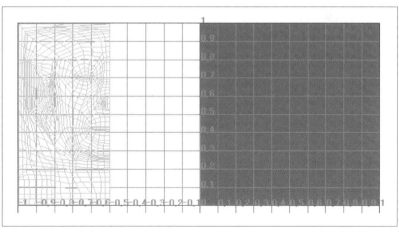

Figure 2-37 Coordinate: Global

4. Rotate UVs

This is the tool used for rotating UVs. However, because the same effect can be achieved by simply selecting the UV in the UV Texture Editor, pressing the E key on the keyboard, and using the Rotate Tool, this tool, in itself, is not very useful. Select the desired UV and then select [Edit Polygons > Textures > Rotate UVs ☐] to open the Options window. In the Options window, type the Rotate value and then click the Rotate button.

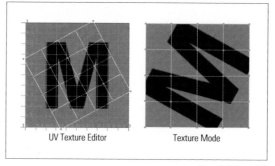

UV Texture Editor   Texture Mode

Figure 2-38 Rotate UVs

5. Map UV Border

This tool aligns the UV border to the texture border. For example, select the UV, as shown in Figure 2-39, and apply [Edit Polygons > Textures > Map UV Border] to align the UV border to the texture border as shown.

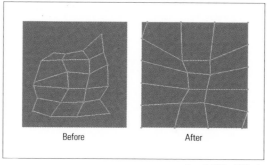

Before   After

Figure 2-39 Map UV Border

6. Straighten UV Border

This feature was added to Maya with the release of version 4. It is used to straighten out twisted UV borders. Previously, such twisted borders were straightened using the Map UV Border or by editing each of the UVs. However, this option allows us to quickly and easily straighten UV borders.

Before using this feature, set the Construction History to On and then select the polygon object. Select [Display > Custom Component Display ▢] to open the Custom Polygon Display Options window, as shown in Figure 2-40.

As shown here, check Texture Borders under Highlight to turn this option on.

This thickens the UV border to facilitate selection of the border.

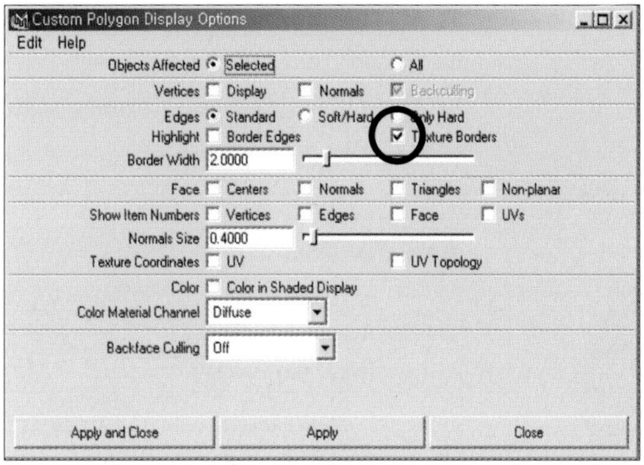

Figure 2-40 Custom Polygon Display Options Window

To apply Straighten UV Border, select the UVs in the border. Selecting [Edit Polygons > Textures > Straighten UV Border] will straighten out the selected UV borders as shown in Figure 2-41 on the next page.

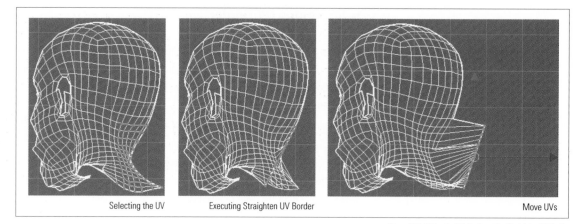

| Selecting the UV | Executing Straighten UV Border | Move UVs |

Figure 2-41 Editing the UVs by Executing Straighten UV Border

Selecting [Edit Polygons > Textures > Straighten UV Border ▢] will create the Options window shown in Figure 2-42.

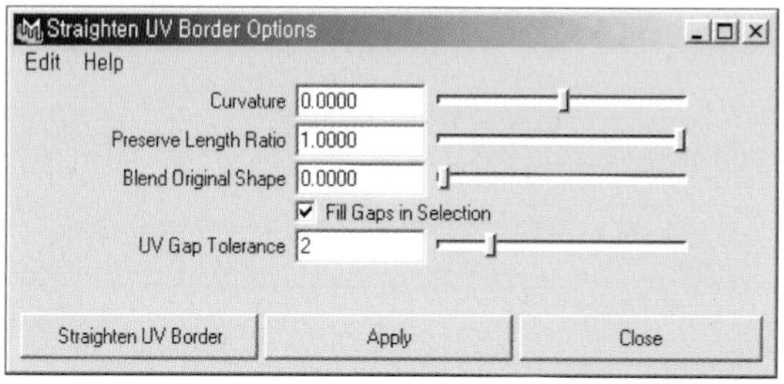

Figure 2-42 Options Window

Curvature

This option pushes in or pulls out the border of the selected UV according to the specified amount. The Default value is set to 0, which means that the border makes a straight line. Adding to or taking away from this value will scale the UV border within the axis to create a curve.

The concavity or convexity of the curve depends on whether this value is "+" or "−." Figure 2-43 on the next page shows a simple example.

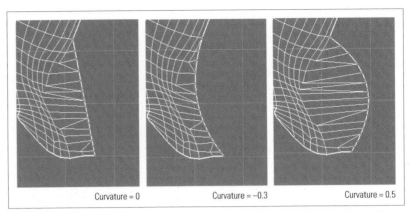

| Curvature = 0 | Curvature = −0.3 | Curvature = 0.5 |

Figure 2-43 Changes in the Border Depending on the Curvature

Preserve Length Ratio

This feature adjusts the size of the Texture Edge when the UV border is straightened out. When the value is set to 1, Maya preserves the original edge length and when the value is set to 0, it calculates the average length. Between 0 and 1, a proportional value of the length is calculated and applied.

Blend Original Shape

This option applies a blend according to the given value that fits with the shape of the original border. At 0, the border is straightened out and at 1, the shape of the original border is preserved.

Between 0 and 1, a proportional value of the length is calculated and applied.

Fill Gap in Selection, UV Gap Tolerance

This option is used when the UV border is severely twisted making selection of the UV very difficult. The following figure shows us how to use this option.

Let's take a look at Figure 2-44. If, as in Figure A, UV Straighten is not applied to the area marked by the circle, a small area is selected, as shown in Figure B, and it is possible that the UV, marked by a circle in Figure B, will not be selected. In this instance, if we use Fill Gap in Selection, even UVs that are not selected will be straightened, as shown in Figure C. UV Gap Tolerance is an option that specifies the permissible limits. If the UV border of an area that was not selected is not straightened, all we need to do is simply raise this value.

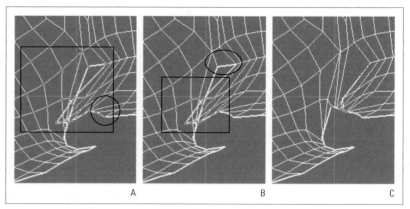

Figure 2-44 Using Fill Gap in Selector

7. Relax UVs

Relax UVs causes twisted UVs to straighten out automatically. This option is very useful when used together with Map UV Border.

Select [Modeling > Edit Polygons > Textures > Relax UVs] to open the Options window shown in Figure 2-45.

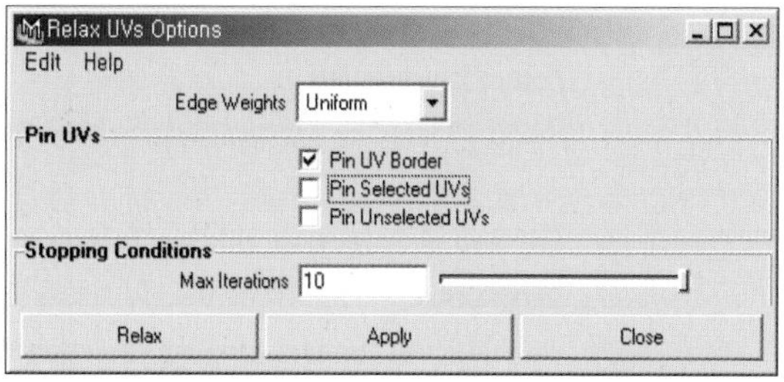

Figure 2-45 Relax UVs Options Window

Edge Weights

This determines how the UV Relax will be applied to the edge.

Uniform All edges are set to the same length and relaxed. This is the default setting.

World Space This applies the Relax while maintaining the angle of the original world space. It is also limited by the fixed UV border.

Pin UV Border

When this option is turned on, the UV border is maintained and the rest is relaxed.

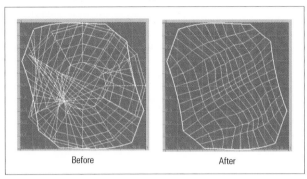

Before   After

Figure 2-46 Pin UV Border

Pin Selected UVs

When this option is turned on, the selected UV is not relaxed, but fixed and all the other UVs that have not been selected are relaxed.

Pin Unselected UVs

This relaxes only the UVs that have not been selected.

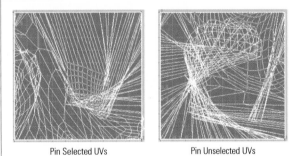

Pin Selected UVs   Pin Unselected UVs

Figure 2-47 Relax Options

Max Iteration

Here, we can enter the value to determine how many times we wish to repeat the Relax. Ideal Relaxes require several repetitions. For example, setting this value to 10 is the same thing as setting this value to 1 and repeating the Relax ten times.

The default for the Layout UVs is the loaded plug in.
The name of this plug-in is "polyUVsPlus.so." If you cannot see the menu, load this plug-in by selecting [Windows > Plug-in Manager].

8. Layout UVs

Layout UVs gives us a layout of the surfaces with overlapping meshes and arranges them so that they do not overlap in the texture axis.
For example, execute Planar Mapping, as shown in Figure 2-48 and then execute Layout UVs. As shown in the figure, we can see that all the overlapping surfaces are separated.

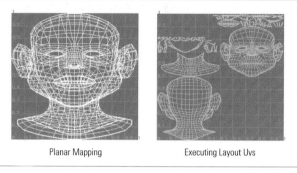

Planar Mapping | Executing Layout Uvs

Figure 2-48 Layout UVs

Although in most cases, we achieve optimal results by using the default value, if you wish to modify the option, select [Modeling > Edit Polygons > Textures > Layout UVs ❐] to open the Options window.

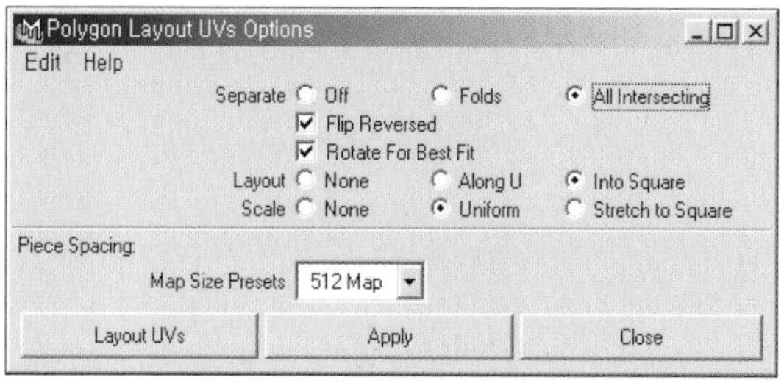

Figure 2-49 Polygon Layout UVs Options Window

Separate

This determines how the surface will be divided for the layout.

Off This does not separate the overlapping surfaces and only applies it in Scale Options.

Folds This divides only the surfaces that lie in the direction opposite the normal direction of the overlapping surfaces. This option will make your work faster and is very effective for large models, however, it may leave behind overlapping portions.

All Intersecting Divides all surfaces with overlapping UVs. This is the default setting.

Flip Reverse

This option will flip surfaces that are facing the direction opposite the normal.

Rotate For Best Fit

This automatically rotates surfaces and rearranges them inside the texture axis for the optimum effect.

Layout

This determines the location inside the texture space where the UV mesh fragments will be arranged.

None A layout is not made in the texture space after the surfaces are divided. Some surfaces will overlap with other surfaces.

Along U Arranges the surfaces along the U-axis. This is the default setting.

Into Square Arranges the surfaces within the 0, 1 texture space.

Scale

Establishes the scale method of the UV mesh fragments inside the texture space.

None No scaling.

Uniform Scales the surfaces fixedly within the 0, 1 texture space without changing the width/height ratio. This is the default setting.

Stretch to Square Stretches out the surfaces to fix them in the 0, 1 texture space. This may cause the surfaces to twist.

Map Size Presets

Maya creates random bounding boxes for each fragment and determines how close the layout will come to these bounding boxes. In the fragment layout, UVs can exchange pixels, which can lead to problems when using Texture Paint.

To avoid such problems, select the predetermined Free Set in this menu to spread out the pixels between bounding boxes in the layout. Each of the fragments will be arranged with some spacing between them as determined by the specified resolution.

The lower the resolution, the larger the UV spacing between bounding boxes.

Space

Selecting Custom from Spacing Presets allows us to specify the Percentage, which will determine how far apart the spacing will be.

9. Cut UVs

This command allows us to select the edge and divide the UV.

Selecting the edge to divide, select [Modeling > Edit Polygons > Textures > Cut UVs] to divide and move the UVs as shown below.

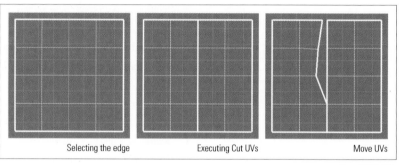

Selecting the edge   Executing Cut UVs   Move UVs

Figure 2-50 Cut UVs

10. Sew UVs

This links together edges that have been cut.

Select the edge you wish to link as shown, and then select [Modeling > Edit Polygons > Textures > Sew UVs] to link together the selected edges.

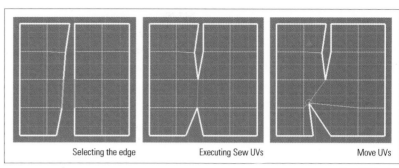

| Selecting the edge | Executing Sew UVs | Move UVs |

Figure 2-51 Sew UVs

11. Move and Sew UVs

This command allows us to move and link together UVs. In other words, executing this command will move and link the UV of the smaller surface to the UV of the larger surface.

This command can be executed automatically, or it can be executed manually as needed.

Manual Execution

Select the desired edge as shown in Figure 2-52 and then select [Modeling > Edit Polygons > Textures > Move and Sew UVs ▢]. This will open the Options window. In the window, set the Limit Piece Size to Off and then click the Apply button.

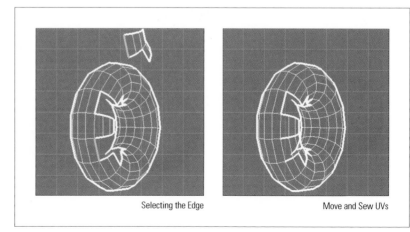

| Selecting the Edge | Move and Sew UVs |

Figure 2-52 Manual Execution

Automatic Execution

This method can be used to obtain fairly decent results by organizing the many surfaces that have been divided through the use of Layout UVs or Automatic Mapping.

As shown in Figure 2-53, select all the edges of the layout and then select [Modeling > Edit Polygons > Textures > Move and Sew UVs] to open the Options window. In the window, set the Limit Piece Size to On, enter the maximum number of faces to link, and then click the Apply button.

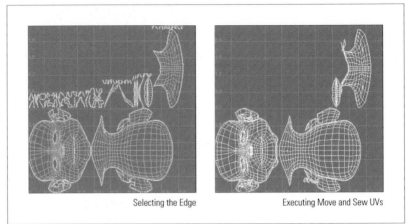

Selecting the Edge   Executing Move and Sew UVs

Figure 2-53 Automatic Execution

12. Merge UVs

Although this menu is basically similar to Sew UVs, this following illustrates a unique use of it.

For example, let's suppose we have the polygon model shown in Figure 2-54. This model shows a surface, which was made by sharing a portion of the edge and extruding a new edge. Looking at the Texture View, we can see the division of each of the UVs.

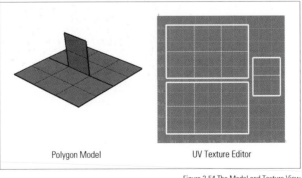

Polygon Model   UV Texture Editor

Figure 2-54 The Model and Texture View

Let's suppose that we want to link together the divided UVs to evenly distribute the textures of the horizontal face in this model. Select the edge in the UV Texture Editor and then execute Sew UVs. However, in this instance, the vertically extruded edge will link to the horizontal edge to give the result seen in Figure 2-55.

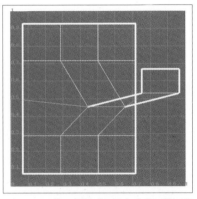

Figure 2-55 An Example Application of Sew UVs

This will make it difficult to select the UV-axis.

To organize the UVs in this model, we use the Merge UVs menu. Select the UVs to merge, as shown in Figure 2-56, and then select [Modeling > Edit Polygons > Merge UVs] to link the edges, which are not shared.

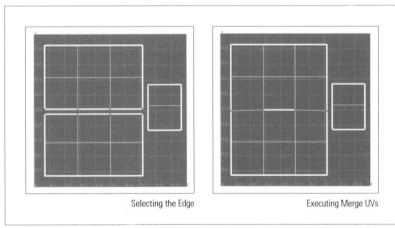

Selecting the Edge   Executing Merge UVs

Figure 2-56 Merge UVs

13. Delete UVs

This menu allows for partial deletion of UVs. After selecting the polygon face, as shown in Figure 2-57, select [Modeling > Edit Polygons > Textures > Delete UVs]. Opening the UV Texture Editor, we can see that the UVs have been deleted, as shown in Figure 2-58.

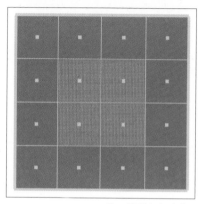

Figure 2-57 Selecting the Face

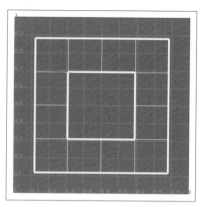

Figure 2-58 Deleted UVs

2. SUBDIVISION SURFACE MAPPING

Maya allows us to map directly on the subdivision surface. It offers 3 different types of mapping: Planar Mapping, Automatic Mapping, and Layout UVs.

2-1. PLANAR MAPPING

This is the most basic option, and it is similar in use to Polygon Mapping. However, one difference is that whereas Polygon Mapping allowed mapping in face units, Planar Mapping allows us to map in face units on the subdivision surface as well as in each display level.

Let's look at Figure 2-59. In this figure, a subdivision surface was made by selecting [Create > Subdiv Primitives > Sphere] and Planar Mapping was applied by selecting the face at Level 0. Although the rectangular hexahedron represents the axis at Level 0, in actuality, it represents a Level 1 UV-axis that will be made inside Level 0. If we were to convert to Polygon Mode in this state, the UV-axis will take on the form of a spread-out rectangular hexahedron.

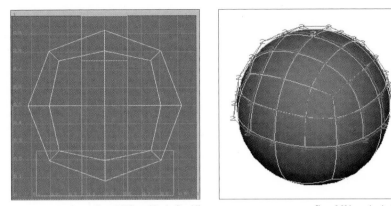

<table>
<tr><td>Figure 2-59 Planar Mapping (Level 0)</td><td>Figure 2-60 Increasing the Level</td></tr>
</table>

After increasing the level at random, as shown in Figure 2-60, select the face in Level 1, as shown in Figure 2-61. Apply Planar Mapping to make the axis in Level 2, as shown in Figure 2-62.

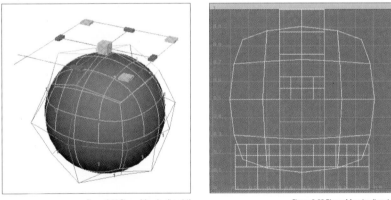

Figure 2-61 Planar Mapping (Level 1)

Figure 2-62 Planar Mapping (Level 1)

As we just saw, subdivision surface mapping allows us to map individually at each level. To map the entire axis, select Level 0 and then apply the mapping.

All basic options and the use of the manipulator are the same as for Polygon Mapping. Refer to the section on Polygon Mapping for more information.

2-2. AUTOMATIC MAPPING

Automatic Mapping is also similar to Polygon Mapping. Refer to the section on Polygon Mapping for more details.

To use Automatic Mapping, select the face to map in subdivision surface Level 0, as shown in Figure 2-63.

Select [Modeling > Edit Polygons > Textures > Automatic Mapping] and make the UV axis, shown in Figure 2-64, according to the given options.

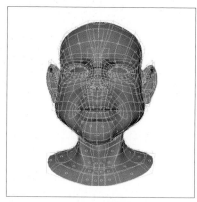

Figure 2-63 Selecting the Face

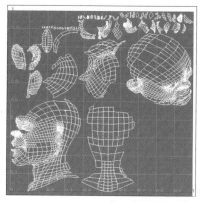

Figure 2-64 UV Texture Editor

2-3. LAYOUT UVS

Select the face of the subdivision surface, and then select [Modeling > Edit Polygons > Textures > Layout UVs] to make the UV-axis shown in Figure 2-65 according to the given options.

This option is also the same as Polygon Mapping. Refer to the section on Polygon Mapping for more details.

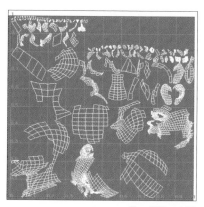

Figure 2-65 Layout UVs

3. UV TEXTURE EDITOR

The UV Texture Editor allows us to edit the UVs of the polygon or subdivision surface to make the optimal UV-axis.

Let's take a look at how to use the UV Texture Editor in this section.

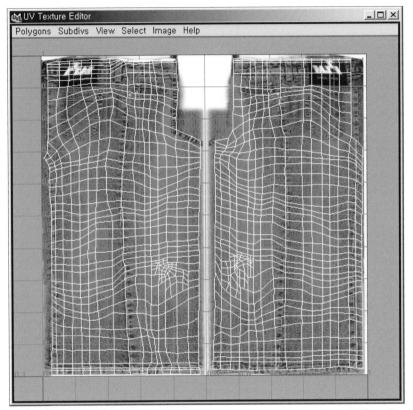

Figure 2-66 UV Texture Editor

Manipulation of the UV Texture Editor window is the same as that for View option. The UV Texture Editor is made up of five main menus: Polygons, Subdivs, View, Select, and Image. We have already covered most of the Polygons and Subdivs menu, so we will not cover them here. This section will be devoted to the other remaining menus.

3-1. UV SNAPSHOT

The Polygons and Subdivs menu has a UV Snapshot. This menu saves the UV-axis as an image file allowing us to refer to it when making a map source in an image processing program, such as Photoshop.

Loading the UV Snapshot will create the Options window, as shown in Figure 2-67.

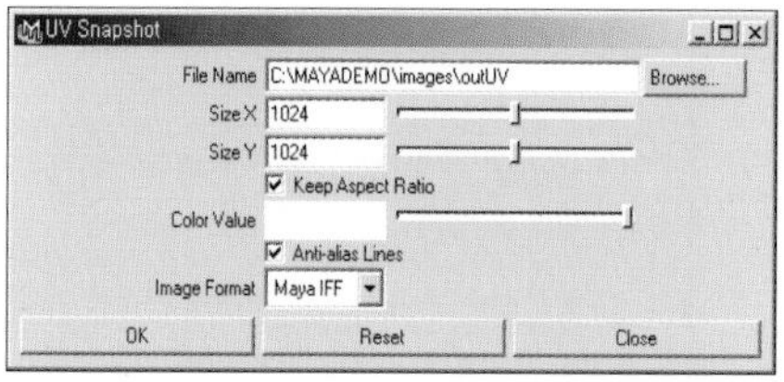

Figure 2-67 Options Window

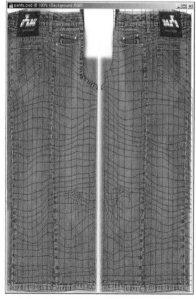

Figure 2-68 The Photoshop Work Window

Type the File Name and Size, and select the desired Format. If Photoshop has a plug-in that can read iff formats, then select iff. If not, select tga.

The iff, tga, and tiff formats all support 32-bits and can, therefore, include alpha channels when files are saved. Load this saved image in Photoshop. In most cases, the alpha channel will be included and the image will appear in a separate layer when loaded into Photoshop, as shown in Figure 2-68. This can be used as a reference in making the map source.

3-2. SUBDIVS MENU

The Subdivs menu is not included in the Maya main menu but exists as two menus in the UV Texture Editor. These two menus are Cut UVs and Move and Sew UVs.

Use of this menu is the same as for Polygon Mapping. Refer to the section on Polygon Mapping for more information.

3-3. VIEW

1. View Contained Face and View Connected Face

View Contained Face and View Connected Face allow us to verify which faces have been included or connected in the selected UV or Edge.

For instance, let's suppose that we have selected several UVs, as shown in the window in Figure 2-69.

Open the UV Texture Editor and select [View > View Contained Face] to display the faces included in the selected UV (see Figure 2-70). Selecting View Connected Face displays the connected faces in the selected UV (see Figure 2-71).

Figure 2-69 Select UVs

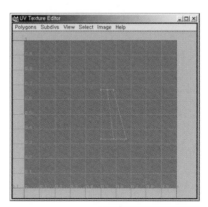

Figure 2-70 View Contained Face

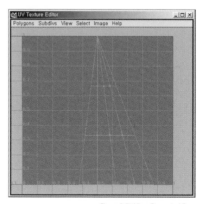

Figure 2-71 View Connected Face

2. Grid

When this option is turned off, the Grid will not be displayed in the UV Texture Editor. Selecting the Grid ⬚ will create the Options window, shown in Figure 2-72. This options window allows us to change the properties of the grid.

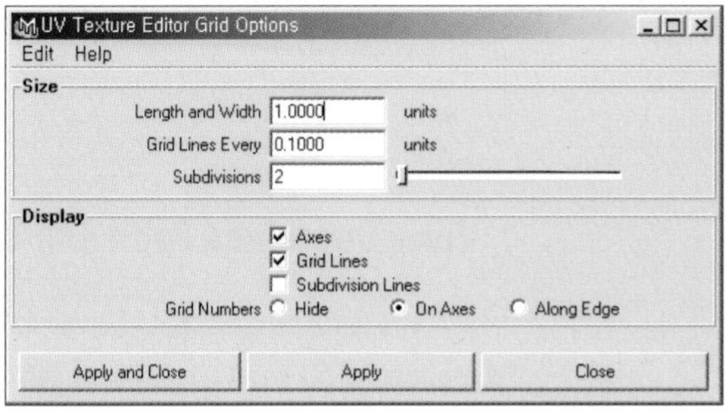

Figure 2-72 Options Window

Length and Width determines the proportions of the grid. Entering **2** will double the size of the current grid.

Grid Lines Every determines the spacing of the grid lines within the specified length and width. Subdivisions can be verified only if Subdivision Lines is checked in the Display Option. We can add more detailed lines to the current grid lines.

Axes displays the axes of the grid, and Grid Line displays the lines. Subdivision Lines subdivides the current grid line according to the indicated size.

Grid Number determines where the grid will be arranged according to the number of the grid units.

3. Frame All

Displays all of the indicated UVs in the window.

4. Frame Selected

Stretches out the selected UV to fill the screen.

3-4. SELECT

When selecting UVs, edges, or faces in the UV Texture Editor or Window, this option allows us to conveniently select elements that linked to our selections.

After selecting several UVs, select [Select > Select Contained Face or Convert Selection to Face] to select the face included in the selected UV or to select the faces linked to the selected UV. This option is used to select such linked elements.

3-5. IMAGE

1. Image Range

Selecting [Image > Image Range ⬛] will open the Image Range Options window as shown in Figure 2-73.

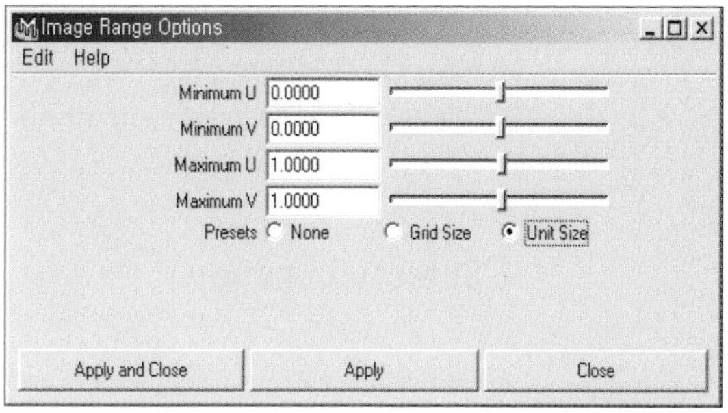

Figure 2-73 Options Window

Enter the values for Minimum U and V and Maximum U and V to use the grid coordinates to determine the scope of the displayed image.

The Presets at the bottom displays the image according to the predetermined coordinates.

Selecting Grid Size will display the texture inside the grid shown in the UV Texture Editor, and Unit Size will display it only within the actual texture axis.

2. Display Image

Turning this option off will not display the texture inside the UV Texture Editor.

3. Display Unfiltered

Turning this option on will prevent the image from being filtered so that it can be corrected.

4. Use Image Ratio

Turning this option on will display the image according to its length and width.

5. Pixel Snap

When this option is turned on and the Move Tool is used to edit the UV, a pixel snap will be applied to the image.
In order to use this option correctly, the Display Unfiltered option must be set to On.

6. Selected Image

If a different shader was used for each face unit to make the map, we can use this option to select the Shader Name to display the respective image.

7. UV Sets

If one object has several different UV sets, each with a different texture, we can use this option to select and display the texture used in each UV set.

Arc Studio

Arc Studio

3 Subdivision Surface Character Modeling

When you think of all the time and energy that is needed for NURBS Patch Modeling for character modeling, you will appreciate how much subdivision surface modeling will dramatically increase productivity. Maya offers a much more developed level of subdivision surfaces than other software programs. Maya allows detail modification through a unique hierarchy mode and, when binding, allows for the use of clusters in each level to create more fluid deformation in the surfaces.

We'll get to binding later, but first, we'll take a look at using subdivision surfaces for character modeling.

We will use a method whereby we first make the basic face shape and then transform it to create different types of faces.

Although different types of surface division will occur depending on the personality of the character we are making, we will use a fairly basic surface division here and modify it to create the shape of the character we want.

I cannot guarantee that the surface structure of the character used in this example is optimal, however, the basic surface division is such that it will allow the character to make a variety of different pronunciations and expressions. Even though you may have modeled one or two faces, much study is needed to understand how to apply them to different model shapes. This model needs its fair share of modifications here and there.

It is my wish that all of you will try this basic model and that it becomes an opportunity for you to think about how surface divisions occur as you try to create different expressions and shapes.

1. MAKING THE BASIC FACE

step 1 First, in order to make the face, use [Modeling > Polygon > Create Polygon Tool] to draw a lateral section of the face in side view. To remain faithful to the example outlined here, make sure you make as many vertices as there are in Figure 3-1. You do not have to worry about trying to make your face exactly the same as the one shown here. Just make sure you have the same number of vertices.

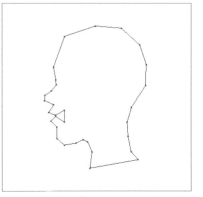

Figure 3-1 Create Polygon Tool

Click on this area to change the central axis of the Manipulator.

Figure 3-2 Extrude Edge

To extrude the edge of the polygon, select the polygon, click the RMB and then select Edge from the Marking Menu. After extruding the edge by selecting [Modeling > Edit Polygons > Extrude Edge], move the edge so as to maintain equal spacing in between, as shown in Figure 3-2.

Click on the area indicated in Figure 3-2 to change the central axis of the Manipulator.

Before converting the polygon into a subdivision surface, first verify the normal direction of the polygon. Check on [Shading > BackFace Culling] in the Panel menu to turn the option on. Then, observe the model and apply [Modeling > Edit Polygons > Normals > Reverse] to all surfaces that are facing the opposite direction so that they face the normal direction.

step 2 Before converting the polygon into a subdivision surface, delete unnecessary surfaces as shown in Figure 3-3.

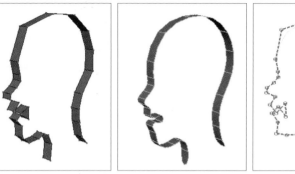

Figure 3-3 Deleting Unnecessary Faces   Figure 3-4 Polygon to Subdiv   Figure 3-5 Trimming the Face

Selecting the polygon model, apply [Modify > Convert > Polygon To Subdiv] to change the selected polygon into a subdivision surface as shown in Figure 3-4.

Selecting the subdivision surface to obtain an appropriate shape, click the RMB and select Vertex from the Marking Menu. Modify some of the vertices to trim the shape as shown in Figure 3-5.

Adjust the vertices in the front of the face to make the forehead, nose, lips, and chin.

Figure 3-7 Trimming the Face

step 3 Now we will extrude the edges to make the face shape. It is necessary that you pay attention here to see how the surfaces were divided for the modeling. One of the most important factors in subdivision surface modeling is how much the surface can be minimized in Level 0 to create a variety of different expressions and pronunciations. Optimizing the surfaces will allow us to model a character that can display a variety of different expressions with the least amount of effort on our part.

Therefore, it is advised that you should observe closely and understand the illustrations for each step in this process so that you may apply them to other character models.

First, in order to model the eye, we need to make an eyeball and arrange it in place. Because the eyeball determines the shape of the eye, make a NURBS Sphere and arrange it in place as shown in Figure 3-8.

In version 4, edges and vertices are not displayed simultaneously in the Component Mode of the subdivision surface. This makes it very difficult to determine how the vertices are linked in the Component Mode. To make this step easier, we can use the Hot Key. Select [Window > Setting/Preferences > Hot Key] to open the Hot Key Editor, select Display from Category and Toggle Mesh Edges from Commands and assign an appropriate shortcut key for the key field under Assign New Hot Key. In my case, I chose the letter "o."

Note: This functionality is improved in Maya versions 4.5 and later.

Figure 3-6 Hot Key Editor

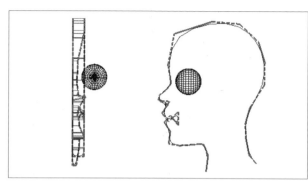

Figure 3-8 Making the NURBS Sphere and Positioning it in Place

We need to use the Polygon Menu for subdivision surface modeling. The most frequently used menus include Extrude Edge, Extrude Face, Merge Edge Tool, Split Polygon Tool, and Append to Polygon Tool. These menus are explained in detail in Chapter 1 and you can refer to it for more information.

To officially begin modeling, we select the subdivision surface, click the RMB, and select Polygon from the Marking Menu. We can also select [Modeling > Subdiv Surfaces > Polygon Proxy Mode] to convert to Polygon Mode.

Select the two edges between the eyes, as shown in Figure 3-9, and apply Extrude Edge twice to position it as shown. Trim the overall shape by modifying the vertices in Standard Mode.

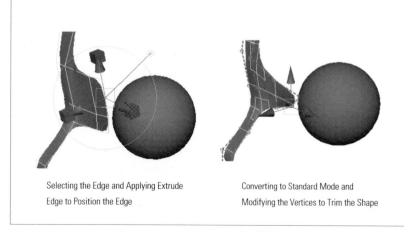

Selecting the Edge and Applying Extrude Edge to Position the Edge

Converting to Standard Mode and Modifying the Vertices to Trim the Shape

Figure 3-9 Applying Extrude Edge and Trimming the Shape

After converting to Polygon Proxy Mode, select the edges, as shown in Figure 3-10, and apply Extrude Edge to model the eye. It is a good idea to use the Manipulator to determine the Rotate and position values.

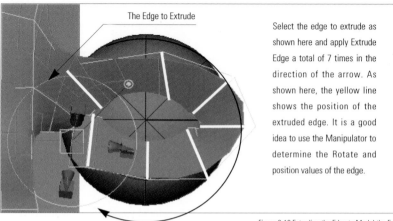

The Edge to Extrude

Select the edge to extrude as shown here and apply Extrude Edge a total of 7 times in the direction of the arrow. As shown here, the yellow line shows the position of the extruded edge. It is a good idea to use the Manipulator to determine the Rotate and position values of the edge.

Figure 3-10 Extruding the Edge to Model the Eye

Convert back to Standard Mode and move the vertices to trim the shape of the eye.
As shown in Figure 3-11, make the shape that surrounds the eyeball. Figure 3-12 shows us using [Modeling > Edit Polygons > Merge Edge Tool] to merge the edges of the surface surrounding the eye.

Merging the two edges
using the Merge Edge Tool.

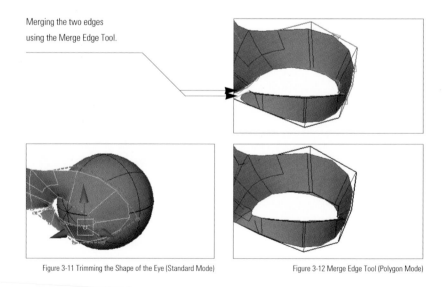

Figure 3-11 Trimming the Shape of the Eye (Standard Mode)

Figure 3-12 Merge Edge Tool (Polygon Mode)

At this point, you should be pretty comfortable working with these tools. I will refrain from written explanations for the next few steps and instead, rely on illustrated diagrams to depict the process of dividing surfaces.

For better understanding, I have shown these illustrations in Polygon Mode. Use Standard Mode to modify the shape by moving the vertices and use Polygon Proxy Mode when using Polygon Modeling. Assuming that each of the following steps were done in Polygon Proxy Mode, you should have no trouble working in this mode.

To model this area, select the face inside the mouth, as shown in Figure 3-13, and press the Delete key to delete this face.

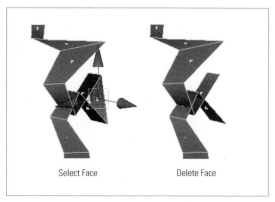

Select Face   Delete Face

Figure 3-13 Deleting the Face

The following illustration, Figure 3-14, shows the modeling for the mouth. Follow along with these illustrations to divide the surfaces.

Select the 2 edges making up the lips and the philtrum and apply Extrude Edge twice to position them.

Move the vertex to trim the shape of the lips. This is done in Standard Mode.

Extrude again the 2 edges that were extruded earlier to fix their shape and position.

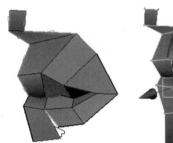

Use the Merge Edge Tool to merge the edges on either side.

Move the vertex to trim the shape of the lips. This is done in Standard Mode.

To make the nose, select the 3 edges of the nose and apply Extrude Edge once.

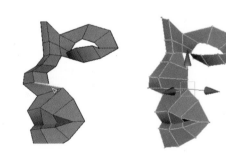

Use the Merge Edge Tool to merge both sides of the upper and lower edge.

Move the vertex to trim the shape of the lips. This is done in Standard Mode.

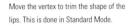

Figure 3-14 Modeling the Basic Shape of the Nose and Mouth

The following illustrations show how to connect the eyes and the forehead.

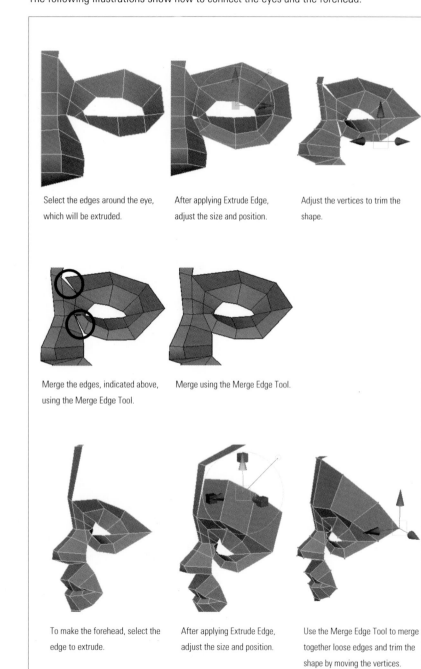

Select the edges around the eye, which will be extruded.

After applying Extrude Edge, adjust the size and position.

Adjust the vertices to trim the shape.

Merge the edges, indicated above, using the Merge Edge Tool.

Merge using the Merge Edge Tool.

To make the forehead, select the edge to extrude.

After applying Extrude Edge, adjust the size and position.

Use the Merge Edge Tool to merge together loose edges and trim the shape by moving the vertices.

Figure 3-15 Modeling the Eye and Forehead

The following illustrations show how to divide the surfaces of the cheek and chin.

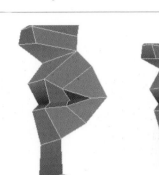

Select the edge to extrude.

After applying Extrude Edge, adjust the size and position.

Use the Merge Edge Tool to merge together loose edges.

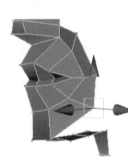

Adjust the vertices to trim the shape.

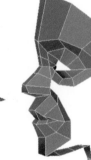

Select the edge to extrude.

After applying Extrude Edge, adjust the size and position.

Use the Merge Edge Tool to merge together loose edges.

Adjust the vertices to trim the shape.

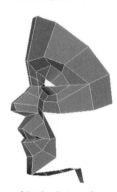

Select the edge to extrude.

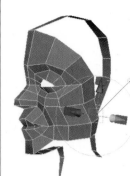

After applying Extrude Edge, adjust the size and position.

Use the Merge Edge Tool to merge together loose edges.

Adjust the vertices to trim the shape.

Select the edge to extrude.

After applying Extrude Edge, adjust the size and position.

After using the Merge Edge Tool to merge together loose edges, trim the shape by adjusting the vertices.

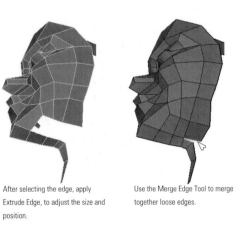
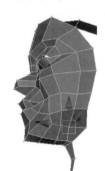

After selecting the edge, apply Extrude Edge, to adjust the size and position.

Use the Merge Edge Tool to merge together loose edges.

Adjust the vertices to trim the shape.

Figure 3-16 The Surface Structure of the Check and Chin

Now let's put the head together. It is a good idea to wrap up the head nicely because small changes will be made to this area. The following is the surface structure for the head.

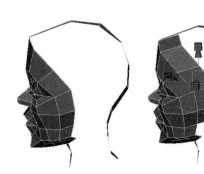

Select the edge to extrude.

After applying Extrude Edge, adjust the size and position.

After using the Merge Edge Tool to merge together loose edges, trim the shape by adjusting the vertices.

Select the edge to extrude.

After applying Extrude Edge, adjust the size and position.

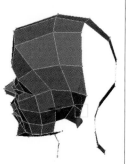

After using the Merge Edge Tool to merge together loose edges, trim the shape by adjusting the vertices.

Select the edge to extrude.

After applying Extrude Edge, adjust the size and position.

Trim the shape by adjusting the vertices.

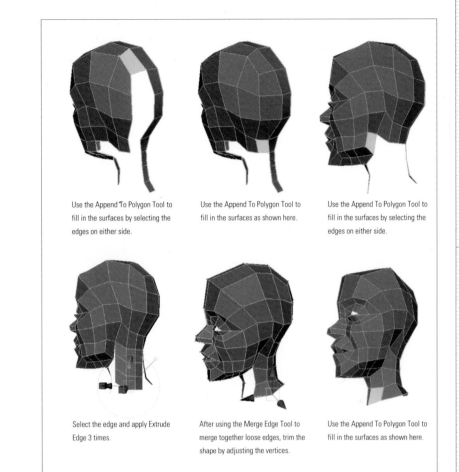

Use the Append To Polygon Tool to fill in the surfaces by selecting the edges on either side.

Use the Append To Polygon Tool to fill in the surfaces as shown here.

Use the Append To Polygon Tool to fill in the surfaces by selecting the edges on either side.

Select the edge and apply Extrude Edge 3 times.

After using the Merge Edge Tool to merge together loose edges, trim the shape by adjusting the vertices.

Use the Append To Polygon Tool to fill in the surfaces as shown here.

Figure 3-17 Completing the Head

step 4 We will now look at the process of making the ears. I believe that the ears have the most diverse surface structure of all the parts of our bodies. The entire surface structure, including the many folds of the ears, makes them very difficult to model.

We are going to need many surface divisions to create a precise model of the ear, which will lead to an increase in the amount of data needed. In most cases, however, the ear plays a relatively small role in the character model. Therefore, creating the general shape and adding a few details is more than enough.

Despite this, however, modeling the ear still calls for a rather large number of surface divisions.

I would need to devote a few dozen pages of this book to modeling the ear if I were to go over it step by step. Since I have already covered surface divisions for the face in detail, the step-by-step illustrations below (along with an analysis of the finished model) should be enough for you to understand how the ear is modeled.

In order to model the ear, first, extrude the portion of the face where the ear will be placed to create a lump.

Select the two faces shown in Figure 3-18, apply [Modeling > Edit Polygons > Extrude Face] to extrude the face, and then adjust the position, size, and rotation as shown in Figure 3-19.

Figure 3-18 Selecting the Face to Extrude

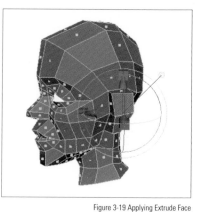

Figure 3-19 Applying Extrude Face

After applying Extrude, adjust the vertices to roughly shape the ear. Adjust the position and size of the ear by looking at it in both Front and Side views. Keep adjusting the shape until the desired shape is achieved.

We are basically modeling a big lump down to a small lump; therefore, it is a good idea to maintain a solid lump with the fewest number of vertices.

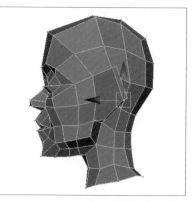

Figure 3-20 Modifying the Shape

To model the surface of the ear, divide the surfaces using the Split Polygon Tool as shown in Figure 3-21. For convenience, we have excluded the other portions of the face and restricted the illustration to the ear. Because this is a very complex modeling, it will be virtually impossible for you to achieve the same modeling result shown here. However, you should observe and understand the flow of the surfaces. If you find that you cannot understand the surface structure shown here, refer to FaceBASIC.mb.

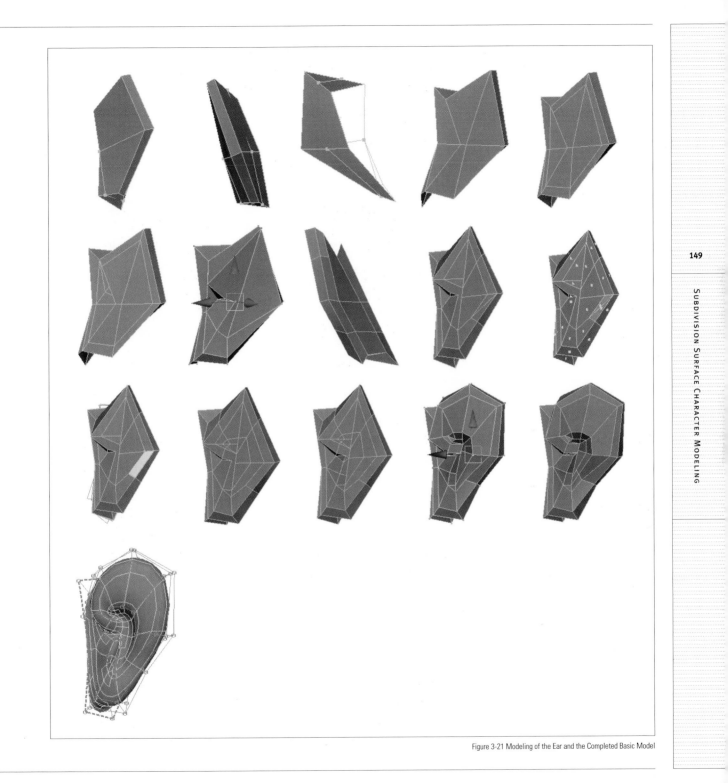

Figure 3-21 Modeling of the Ear and the Completed Basic Model

Figure 3-22 shows the shape of the completed basic model.

Although this model is not perfect, it is contains the essential factors for manipulating it into different shapes.

Since the opposite side was made using Mirror Copy, we do not need to apply Attach to these 2 models.

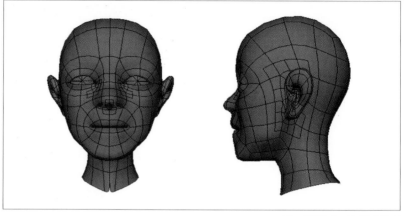

Figure 3-22 The Completed Basic Model

We can make changes to this model or use it as it is. However, it is more effective to make modifications before using it if we are going to clarify the character's personality and/or add dramatic expressions to certain parts of the face. Many of you will wonder why we need to make this basic model in the first place. We need this basic model in order to add the UV coordinates in the very next step. Although you may use the method that appeals to you, the most effective method to use right now to optimize the map environment of the subdivision surface is to perform part of the work manually to create the UV coordinate settings.

Using the Split Polygon Tool or some other polygon tool to modify the basic model will not greatly affect the UV coordinates of the setup model.

2. UV SETTING OF SUBDIVISION SURFACE

Let's take a look at how to add UV coordinates to the basic face. As I mentioned before, the manner and order in which you do the modeling is entirely up to you. The method that I will introduce here, in which the subdivision surface is bounded directly and the mapping is done through a 3D painting software, is one that I use most frequently.

If you make the modeling and the blend shape into a subdivision and convert it into a polygon for animation, this method will not be very effective.

There is a better and more convenient option. Refer to Chapter 2, "Polygon, Subdivision Surface Mapping," for more on polygon mapping environments.

2-1. CONVERT TO POLYGONS

step 1 To fix the UV map coordinates on the basic subdivision surface, convert it to Polygon Mode. We perform this conversion because the map environment of the subdivision surface is not yet as diversified as polygon.

The basic face was made at subdivision surface Level 0. Therefore, before converting to Polygon, we open the Convert Subdiv To Polygons Options window (see Figure 3-23) and set the Tessellation Method to Vertices and then make the settings in Level 0. We also need to convert the mirror copy to Polygon as well (see Figure 3-24).

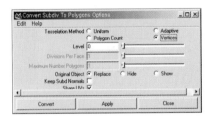

Figure 3-23 Convert Subdiv To Polygons Options Window

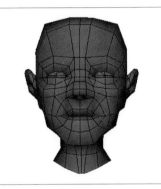

Figure 3-24 Convert To Polygon

step 2 Each of the converted polygons contains two segments, a left face and a right face. For a precise UV setting, we need to combine these two segments.

Select the two polygon faces, and apply [Modeling > Polygons > Combine]. Delete unnecessary data by selecting the model and applying [Edit > Delete by Type > History].

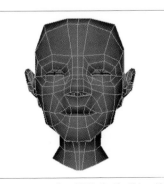

Figure 3-25 The Combined Polygon Model

2-2. USING CYLINDRICAL MAPPING

Now we will apply the UV coordinates by using Cylindrical Mapping, one of the polygon mapping types.

step 1 First verify that [Modeling > Polygons > Tool Options > Convert Selection] has been checked. If this option is turned off, check it to turn it on.

After selecting the polygon model, select [Modeling > Edit Polygons > Textures > Cylindrical Mapping] to open the Options window. Project the model using the default settings.

The Manipulator will appear, as shown in Figure 3-26.

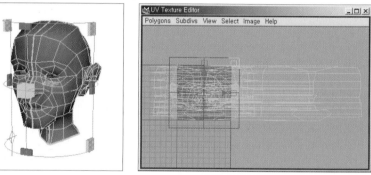

Figure 3-26 Cylindrical Mapping

Figure 3-27 UV Texture Editor

After opening the window by selecting [Window > UV Texture Editor], we can see that the UV deviates from the texture axis and that a portion of it is tangled, as shown in Figure 3-27. We perform the following step to correct this phenomenon.

step 2 As shown in Figure 3-28, enter **360** for the Projection Horizontal in the Channel Box. We can see that this causes the Projection Manipulator to wrap itself 360 degrees around the polygon object as shown here.

Looking at the UV Texture Editor, we can see that a portion of the UV still deviates from the texture axis and is tangled.

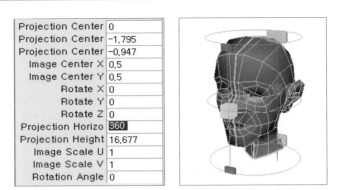

Projection Center	0
Projection Center	-1.795
Projection Center	-0.947
Image Center X	0.5
Image Center Y	0.5
Rotate X	0
Rotate Y	0
Rotate Z	0
Projection Horizo	360
Projection Height	16.677
Image Scale U	1
Image Scale V	1
Rotation Angle	0

Figure 3-28 Modifying the Projection Horizontal Value Using the Channel Box

step 3 Enter **0.00001** for the Projection Center in the Channel Box. Looking at the UV Texture Editor in Figure 3-29, we can see that most of the UVs fall in place inside the Texture Editor.

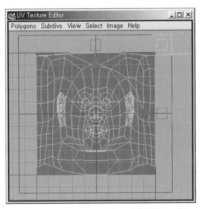

Figure 3-29 UV Texture Editor

2-3. UV EDITING

In modeling, we usually work on one half of the model and then use Mirror Copy to make the other copy in the end. Therefore, we delete one half of the basic model.

We apply Mirror Copy first and then combine the two halves for the mapping so we can accurately assign the texture to the other side. If we simply apply the Cylindrical Mapping to only one half of the face, the other side will take up all the texture and it becomes very difficult to make the settings that will allot the texture precisely to only one half of the face.

Because we have now completed the basic mapping, we can delete the other half of the face.

The following note applies only to users of Maya version 4. If you have version 4.5 or later, you may ignore this.

The value for the Projection Center does not have to be 0.00001 exactly.

A phenomenon occurs in version 4. When the center position changes slightly, the UV becomes properly aligned in the Texture Editor. Therefore, all we are doing is adjusting the center position slightly.

As we did not merge the two edges after combining them, we can simply separate the two objects back into their original states by using Separate.

step 1 After selecting the model, apply [Modeling > Edit Polygons > Separate]. This will divide the selected model back into its two original segments, as shown in Figure 3-30. Select the half that we no longer need and delete it. Looking at the UV Texture Editor (see Figure 3-31), we can see that only the UV coordinates for one half of the face remains.

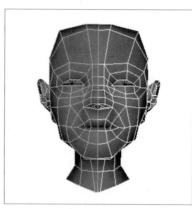

Figure 3-30 Applying Separate

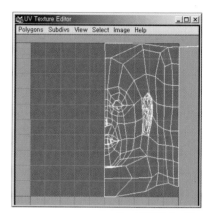

Figure 3-31 UV Texture Editor

step 2 As shown in Figure 3-32, click the RMB in the UV Texture Editor window and select UV from the Marking Menu.

As shown in Figure 3-33, select the portions of the UV, which deviate from the texture axis, and then move them inside the axis. Then, edit the edges so that they are aligned with the borders of the texture axis.

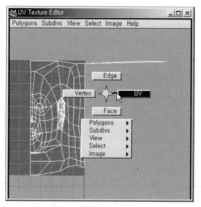

Figure 3-32 Selecting UV from the Marking Menu

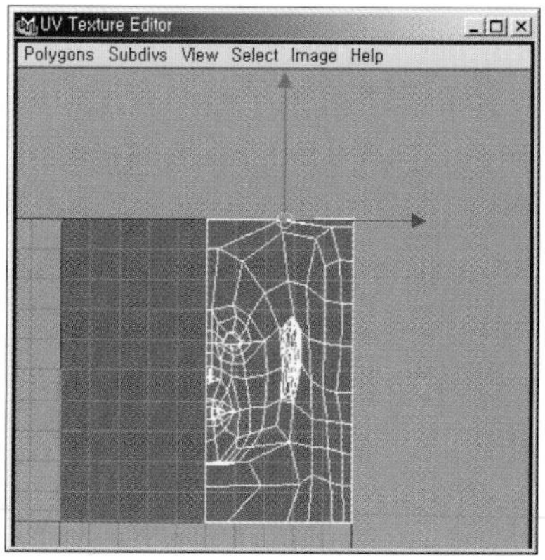

Figure 3-33 Editing the UVs

Let's take a look at Figure 3-34. Figure 3-34 shows the rearrangement of the UVs after editing. Although yours does not have to take on this form, the UVs must be rearranged with appropriate spacing in between. This is because we need to know what part of the character requires a lot of space before fixing the coordinates.

In general, it is a good idea to create ample spacing for the eyes, forehead, nose, cheeks, and mouth. Because these are areas of the face that have the most

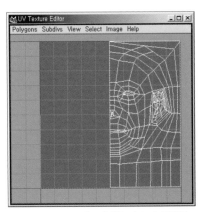

Figure 3-34 Completing the UV Editing.

exposure, we give them ample UV coordinates for high-resolution textures.

In contrast, the front and back of the head and the lower chin are areas that are not largely exposed and, therefore, do not require a lot of space.

The coordinates that we see in the figure are going to require some modifications to fit the personality of the character we are creating. We can see large spacing between the UVs in the lower neck. We leave this space for surface divisions in case we need to model portions of the lower part of the neck later. Because UVs are created automatically when the surface is divided, we do not need to modify them further.

For instance, let's suppose we have the situation in Figure 3-35. When the Split Polygon Tool is used to split the surface of the lower neck, as in Figure 3-35, the UV coordinates are also split automatically.

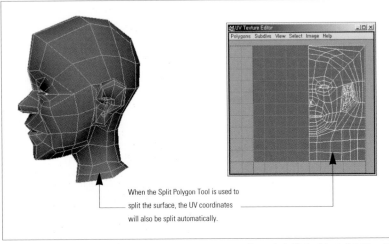

When the Split Polygon Tool is used to split the surface, the UV coordinates will also be split automatically.

Figure 3-35 Changes in the UV after Using the Split Polygon Tool

SUBDIVISION SURFACE CHARACTER MODELING

Once the settings for the UV are complete and we are finished using Extrude Edge, Extrude Face, and Append To Polygon Tool to make new surfaces, the UV coordinates will not crash. We have now finished looking at using subdivision surfaces to model the basic face shape and UV Mapping.

As I mentioned in the beginning, this is just one of the many methods that are available and you are encouraged to find the method that is most suited to your modeling environment.

Although the examples here have been explained in Polygon Mode, modeling is also possible in Polygon Proxy Mode, which should not be very difficult to understand.

3. TRANSFORMING THE BASIC FACE FOR FACE MODELING

We will now take our basic face and make our intended character. Here, we will learn how to depict detail using different levels. You will also learn how quick and easy it is to create a character using the basic face.

Figure 3-36 shows an edited version of the basic face. You can see that it is entirely different from the original basic face. In this section, we will look at how this face was created. No additional surfaces were added. We simply used the Split Polygon Tool to split the area of the lower neck to model a portion of the neck and the body. If you are familiar with this process already, I encourage you to let your imagination run free and create your own unique character.

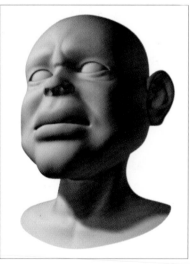

Figure 3-36 The Transformed Model

Before You Begin...

The model of the basic face and the transformed face model were created using Maya 3. Although I have tried to explain the process in terms of the latest version of Maya, there will be slight differences in some of the actual data. Also, just as everyone has their own working methods, some might find version 3 to be easier for subdivision surface modeling. Mapping setups are also easier in version 3.

3-1. IMPORT IMAGE PLAN

Open the image of the basic face, and then load the sketched image in View. So that you can more closely follow along with this example, I recommend that you use faceBASIC.mb, which is included in the supplementary CD-ROM. The supplementary CD-ROM contains an image file of this sketched image.

The image files are saved as CD-ROM/CHARACTER/sourceimages/facefront.jpg and faceside.jpg. Select [View > Image Plane > Import Image] from the window panel menu of both the front and side views to load facefront.jpg and faceside.jpg as shown in Figure 3-37.

When loading a sketched image into the image plan, it is a good idea to cut and load the image using Photoshop so that it fits the size in front and side views. Also, if you want to load the images in the same proportions, select [View > Default Home] from the View Panel Menu of each before loading the image.

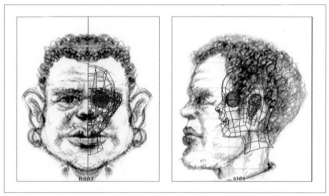

Figure 3-37 Loading the Images of the Front and Side Views

To adjust the color of the image plane, open the Attribute Editor (see Figure 3-38) and adjust the Color Gain to adjust the brightness. However, this can lead to a reduction in system speed on some graphic cards. If you don't like the white background, and want to change it, you should modify it in Photoshop before loading it into Maya.

Figure 3-38 Attribute Editor

Select the image plane, which was loaded in Front View, in Perspective View, and select imagePlane 1 from Channel Box INPUTS. As shown in Figure 3-39, enter **–13** for Center Z to move the image plane in the -Z direction.

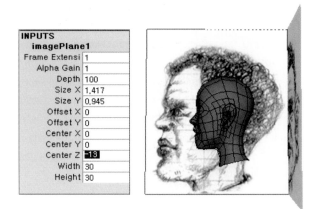

Figure 3-39 Moving the Image Plane

Select the model and adjust the scale so that it matches the size of the sketched image. Then, select [Edit > Duplicate ☐] to open the Options window (see Figure 3-40). In the Options window, set the Scale to –1, the Geometry Type to Instance, and then click the Duplicate button.

As shown in Figure 3-41, a mirror copy of the other side will be created.

Figure 3-41 The Mirror Copy of the Model

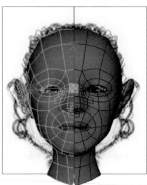

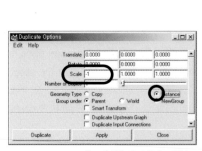

Figure 3-40 Duplicate Options Window

By setting the Geometry Type to Instance, modifying the vertices on one half automatically modifies the vertices on the other half to make observing the model shape easier.

We have now finished the basic steps. We now have to modify the vertices to plan the overall shape.

3-2. EDITING SUBDIVISION SURFACE MODEL

Let's begin editing the model. The first thing we need to do is to plan out a big lump. In other words, we need to first edit Level 0 of this subdivision surface. Modify the vertices in Level 0 to plan out a big lump and then work on the details later.

step 1 First, modify the vertices of the model in Side View so that it matches the edges of the sketched image. Modify the model, as shown in Figure 3-42, so as to keep the lump intact. Roughly map out the placement of the eye, ear, mouth, and chin.

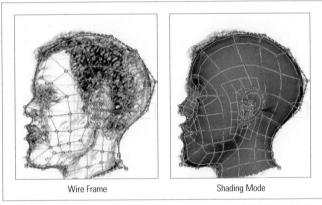

Wire Frame　　　　　　　　Shading Mode

Figure 3-42 Modifying the Outer Shape

step 2 Change the view to Front View, and modify the vertices to match the shape of the sketched image. Map out the overall shape of the face and the size and placement of the eyes, nose, mouth, and ears. Also, roughly map out the shape of the neck.

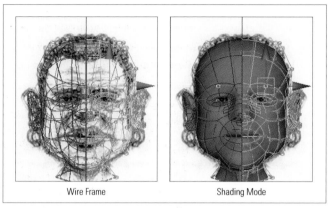

Wire Frame   Shading Mode

Figure 3-43 Modifying the Shape

step 3 After modifying the overall shape and the placement of the facial features, modify the vertices to add more detail. This modification is also done at Level 0. In trimming the shape, we must take care that the vertices and edges are arranged in keeping with the flow of the surface. This is done in order to obtain a more natural shape for the animation part later.

Figure 3-44 illustrates adding detail to the eye. Let's compare the sketch and model. In order to portray the personality of the character, we need to map out the surface to fit our intent (see Figure 3-44).

The importance of the arrows in Figure 3-44, which represent the flow of the surfaces, will become evident during the animation. It is important that we understand the flow of the surfaces before modeling so that we can more effectively portray the characteristic expressions of the character with the minimum of vertex movements.

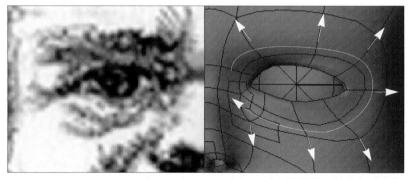

Figure 3-44 The Flow of the Surfaces in the Eye

Figure 3-45 shows the lips. Again, we must make sure that the surfaces are arranged to fit the flow of the muscles near the mouth.

As shown in the figure, make sure that the edge of the subdivision surface forms the lines of the mouth. Also, because the edges that make up the flow from the nose to the lower chin are crucial in determining the personality of the character, we must pay special attention to this point.

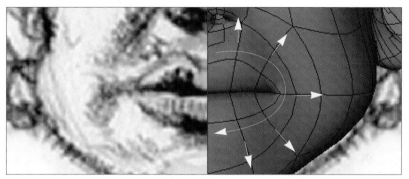

Figure 3-45 The Flow of the Surfaces in the Mouth

3-3. DIVIDING LEVELS FOR DETAILS

Once we have mapped out the big lump, we now need to divide the levels of the subdivision surface to depict the details. It is better keep the subdivision hierarchy levels to a minimum. The greater the number of levels we have, the better detail. However, this will also increase the amount of data.

Therefore, our goal is to complete the character with as few level divisions as possible. The extent of the levels will be determined by how the surfaces were split in the Polygon Mode in the beginning. If the surfaces were split appropriately, we can achieve effective detail with fewer level divisions. However, if this is not the case, more levels will be needed.

Which number is appropriate and how the surfaces are split is something that you will be able to determine through practicing and experimenting with different modeling methods. This character was divided into Levels 0-3. We will now learn how to use these levels to add detail. The important thing here is that we first create Level 1 and then add as much detail as possible to all areas of the face. If Level 1 is insufficient, then we move onto Level 2 and so forth.

step 1 Select the model and then, as shown in Figure 3-46, click the RMB and select [Display Level > 1] from the Marking Menu to display Level 1. Pressing the F8 key to switch to Component Mode will display Level 1 as shown in Figure 3-47.

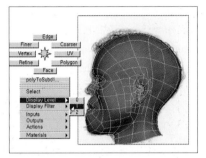

Figure 3-46 Selecting the Display Level

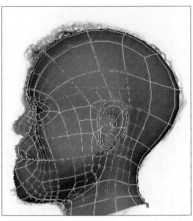

Figure 3-47 Display Level = 1

step 2 Adjust the vertices in each part of the face to add detail. Figure 3-48 illustrates adding detail to the eye. We used Level 0 to map out the general lump, and now, we modify the vertices within Level 1 to add more detail.

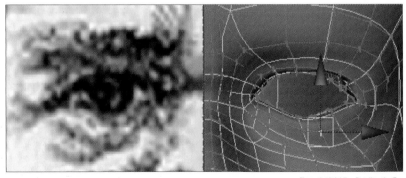

Figure 3-48 Adding Detail to the Eye

As we move to lower levels and modify the vertices to add detail, we must take care that we do not deviate too much from the placement of the vertices in the upper level. Deviating too much from the placement of the vertices in the upper level will create problems during the animation later. That is, surface changes can occur abnormally. This is because when we bind the model to the skeleton later on, this binding occurs at Level 0. Therefore, the lower levels should stay within the scope of Level 0. If the lower levels deviate too far from Level 0, the vertices of Level 0 will move. This will, in turn, affect the lower levels causing the shape to distort severely.

step 3 Modify the vertices to add detail to the nose. This process is illustrated in Figure 3-49. Detail the nose to the extent allowed in Level 1.

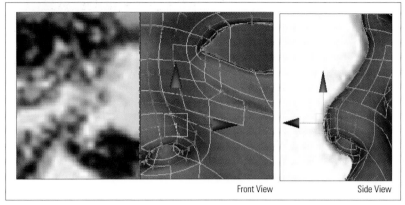

Front View   Side View

Figure 3-49 Detailing the Nose

In the same way, move the vertices of the mouth in Level 1 to create the shape. This is illustrated in Figure 3-50. As shown in the Front View of Figure 3-50, we also need to roughly create the character lines around the mouth.

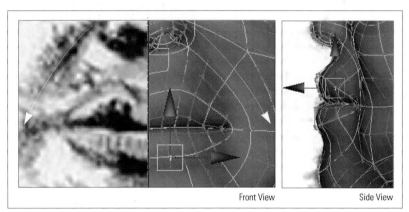

Front View   Side View

Figure 3-50 Detailing the Mouth

In the same way, create the overall shape. We must pay special attention to the ear. Because the structure of the ear is very complex, we must fully understand how the surfaces are arranged before modeling.

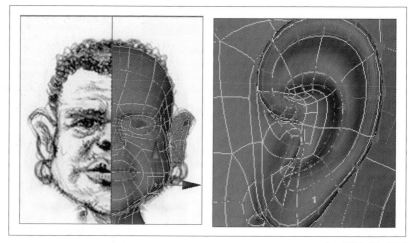

Figure 3-51 Depicting Detail

At times, we will need to go back to Level 0 to add detail to certain parts. This is necessary in order to create an effective, overall result. As I mentioned earlier, if you need to create drastic movement in Level 1, go back and modify Level 0 before doing so.

step 4 We will now divide the level 1 step further to add more detail. Select the vertices of the nose, as shown in Figure 3-52, click the RMB, and then select Refine from the Marking Menu. As shown in Figure 3-53, the vertices will convert to Level 2.

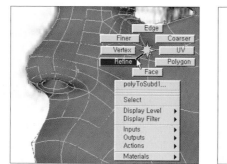

Figure 3-52 Refining the Selected Vertices.

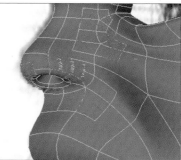

Figure 3-53 Level 2

Refine the necessary areas and divide them into Level 2 to add more detail. Figure 3-54 illustrates the division to Level 2 and the addition of more detail.

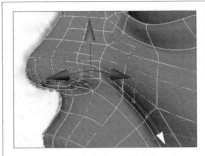

This shows the delineation of the nose. Modify the vertices to delineate the lateral muscles as shown, and organize the vertices in the direction of the arrows to model the character's personality.

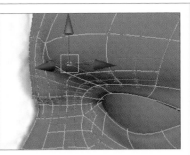

Match the area between the brows to fit the muscles of the forehead, and add wrinkles to portray the unique personality of the character.

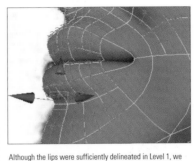

Although the lips were sufficiently delineated in Level 1, we modify the vertices to create the deep indentation below the lower lip.

The ears are very complex. Modify the vertices to create the detailed contours to fit the flow of the surface.

Figure 3-54 Detailing Each Part of the Face

Detail the other parts of the face as shown above. The wrinkles around the eyes and around the mouth can be sufficiently portrayed in Level 2.

step 5 A less than elaborate character can be completed at Level 2. However, adding more detail to the current surface structure is impossible. Figure 3-55 shows how to divide the subdivision surface to Level 3 for more elaborate detailing. We make the further division to Level 3 in order to tidy up the end of the nose and to emphasize the expression between the brows.

We can also do this, without having to divide the levels, by simply using the Split Polygon Tool to split the surface in the Polygon Proxy Mode. After testing various methods, you must select the method that will fully portray the character's expression.

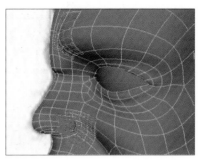
Figure 3-55 Level 3

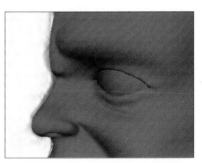
Figure 3-56 The Arranged Shading Mode

Figure 3-57 shows the arranged half of the model. Since we added mapping coordinates to the basic model in the beginning and did not add any other new surfaces, all that's left to do is to make a mirror copy of this character and attach the two sides to complete the modeling.

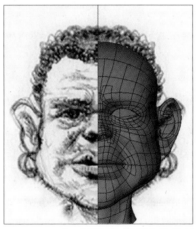
Figure 3-57 The Completed Half of the Model

3-4. MIRROR COPY AND ATTACH

As I mentioned in the beginning of this chapter, the modeling of this character was done using version 3. In newer versions, we are able to map directly in the subdivision surface. However, this mapping method lacks the variety of options found in Polygon Mode.
The mapping coordinates of a model that have been edited and converted to Subdivision Surface Mode will not perfectly convert when switching back to Polygon Mode. I was not able to find a method of carrying over the polygon coordinates to Standard Mode.

Mapping coordinates cannot be made on the subdivision surface in version 3; therefore, the coordinates of the polygon map are used. However, doing this in later versions creates many problems.

Therefore, I feel version 3 is better for modeling. However, this may not be the case for you. It is completely personal preference.

Although it will be quite difficult to model the style shown here in recent versions of Maya, it is not completely impossible. Perhaps there is a simpler way than the method I am about to describe to you, but I have not yet been able to find it. I will explain how to make the remaining half while maintaining the UV coordinates, which were set up in the beginning.

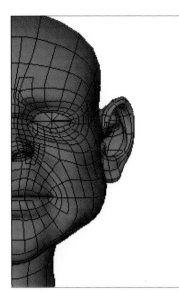

Figure 3-58 manHALF.mb Model

Use either your own completed file or load the example file from the supplementary CD-ROM (CD-ROM/CHARACTER/scenes/ manHALF.mb).

Because we have already created the mapping coordinates in the basic model, when we open this model in the UV Texture Editor, we can see that the UV coordinates for half of the face fill up half of the texture map as shown in Figure 3-59. The space on the other side is for the mirror copy that we will make of the face.

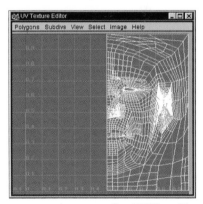

Figure 3-59 UV Texture Editor

step 1 First, select the model and select [Modeling > Subdiv Surface > Mirror] to open the Options window. In the window, check the X-axis and click the Mirror button. This will create a mirror copy of the model as shown in Figure 3-60.

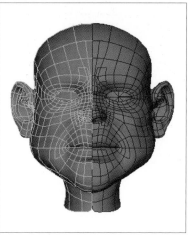

Figure 3-60 The Mirror Copy of the Subdivision Surface Model

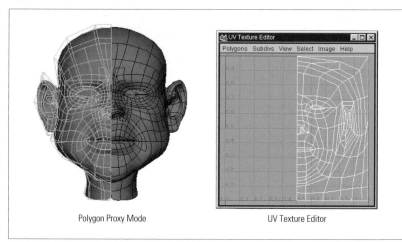

Polygon Proxy Mode   UV Texture Editor

Figure 3-61 Polygon Proxy Mode and the UV Texture Editor

step 2 Convert the mirror copy of the model to Polygon Proxy Mode. Open the UV Texture Editor in this mode. We can see that although the model has been mirrored, as shown in Figure 3-61, no change has been made to the texture map.

As of yet, no option is available that will also mirror the texture map of an object that has been mirror copied. As follows, you must manually mirror the texture map of an object that has been mirror copied.

step 3 To mirror the texture map, click the RMB in the current state and select UV from the Marking Menu.

Use the R key on the keyboard to adjust the scale. To create an accurate mirror copy, place the pivot point of the scale of the selected UV on the center of the texture map. The pivot point is gripped by pressing the Insert key on the keyboard in this state. Press the X key on the keyboard again to apply the Grid Snap, and place the X-axis on 0.5 of the texture grid as shown in Figure 3-62.

Converting to Scale Mode by pressing the 'R' key after selecting the UV

Pressing the Insert key to change the placement of the pivot and then displaying the pivot point.

Applying the Grid Snap by pressing the 'X' key and then centering the X-axis on the texture.

Figure 3-62 Moving the UV Pivot

To precisely mirror the UV, the UV must be scaled −1 along the X-axis from its current size. It is very difficult to scale −1 by hand. We need to enter the scaling value. Although a separate option does not exist, we can enter the scaling value using the Script Editor.

step 4 Press the Insert key again to change to Scale Mode and randomly adjust the X-axis, as shown in Figure 3-63. Press the Z key to delete the adjusted Scale value.

Select [Windows > General Editors > Script Editor] to open the Script Editor. Scroll down to the very bottom of the Script Editor, as shown in Figure 3-64. You should be able to see the Scale value for the UV.

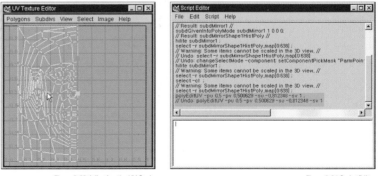

Figure 3-63 Adjusting the UV Scale

Figure 3-64 Script Editor

The structure for the scale in the Script Editor is "polyEditUV -pu 0.5 -pv 0.500629 -su -0.812348 -sv 1;". -pu and -pv refer to the current location of the UV and -su and -sv refer to the UV scale.

Because we need to change the scale in the U-direction, change the -su value to −1. Copy this script from the Script Editor, paste it at the bottom of the Script Editor as shown in Figure 3-65, and then change the -su value to −1. Use Ctrl+C and Ctrl+V to paste.

Press Ctrl+Enter to execute the script. As shown in Figure 3-66, this creates the scale −1 from the pivot point.

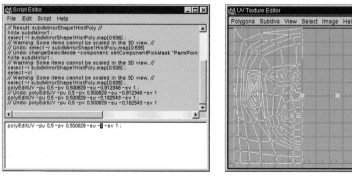

Figure 3-65 Script Editor   Figure 3-66 The Precisely Scaled UV

step 5 Convert the mirror copy of the face back to Standard Mode, and select the surface of both faces.

Select [Modeling > Subdiv Surface > Attach ▢] to open the Attach Options window.

Turn off Merge UVs Also and Keep Originals, and press the Attach button at the bottom.

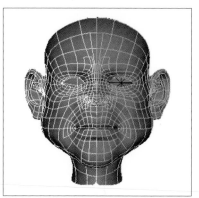
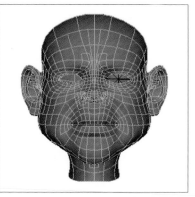

Figure 3-67 Selecting Both Surfaces in Standard Mode   Figure 3-68 Attach

Looking at Figure 3-69, we can see that by opening the UV Texture Editor, a mirror of the texture map is also created and that the UV coordinates are spread over the entire face.

In closing, click the RMB in the UV Texture Editor and select Edge from the Marking Menu. As shown in Figure 3-70, select all the edges, excluding the outer edges of the texture map. Select [Subdivs > Move and Sew UVs] from the menu at the top of the UV Texture Editor.

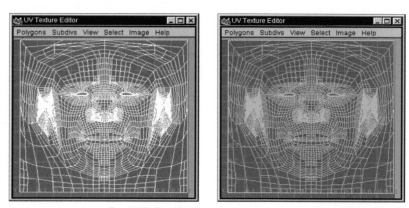

Figure 3-69 The Spread-Out UV   Figure 3-70 Move and Sew UVs

We have now completed making the shape of the face and have finished setting up the UV coordinates of its subdivision surface.

In applying Attach, some of the edges may not adhere together. In these instances, either raise the Threshold value in the Attach Options window or use [Modeling > Edit Polygons > Merge Edge Tool] after converting to Polygon Proxy Mode.

As a final step, make sure you select the model and select [Edit > Delete by Type > History] to delete the entire history.

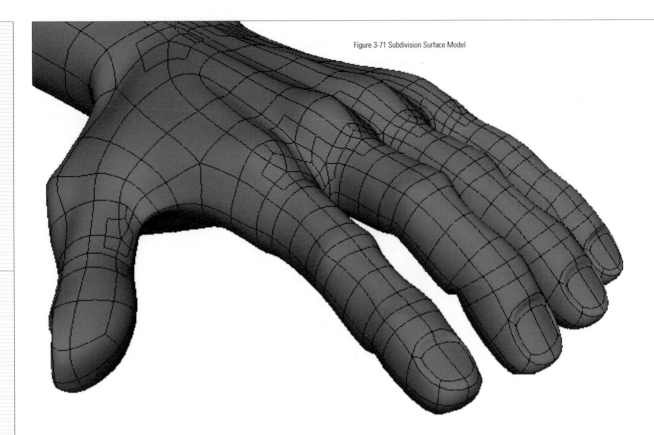

Figure 3-71 Subdivision Surface Model

4. HAND MODELING

In this section, we will look at how to model a hand using subdivision surfaces. This hand has a very complex surface structure. Therefore, it is very difficult to explain all the details that went into creating this hand. We will look, instead, at the overall modeling process. Referring to the finished hand model, which is offered in the supplementary CD-ROM, will help you understand better.

Before you begin...

I prefer to map in Polygon Mode rather than directly in the subdivision surface. Although this is completely a matter of preference, it also happens to be the most effective when using Deep Paint 3D, as we will see later in this section.

Mapping in Polygon Mode, as mentioned earlier, is somewhat difficult in recent versions of Maya. This hand and polygon mapping was done in version 3 and then loaded into the latest version.

If you have an environment that supports version 3, you can do the modeling in it.

If you will not be mapping directly in the subdivision surface and you will be using Polygon Mode, version 3 is not only faster, but is also more effective.

Although the steps here will be explained for the latest versions of Maya, version 3 uses the same options. Therefore, version 3 users should have no trouble following along.

Also, later in this section, we will link the UV setup process for mapping this hand with the modeling process. Although many other methods exist, I prefer this method because it is an effective method for explaining the mapping process using Deep Paint 3D.

When I begin subdivision surface modeling, I always think about the mapping process to come. In order to place the UV coordinates after perfectly completing the modeling, more planning time needs to be invested than if there were a small number of surfaces involved. I always make the general shape using the minimum amount of surfaces, set up the UV coordinates, and then split the surfaces to add detail.

This is something that you will have to get a feel for yourself after much practice.

4-1. MODELING A HAND

Basically, we will use the Polygon Primitive to make a cube and use this to model.
Make sure you understand the overall process before following along with the example.

step 1 After selecting [Modeling > Create > Polygon Primitives > Cube] to make a polygon cube, adjust the size as shown in Figure 3-72. This is the lump that will make up part of the back of the hand and the wrist.

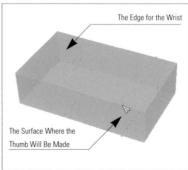

The Edge for the Wrist

The Surface Where the Thumb Will Be Made

Figure 3-72 Polygon Cube   Figure 3-73 Using the Split Polygon Tool

Split the surface, as shown in Figure 3-73, by selecting [Modeling > Edit Polygons > Split Polygon Tool]. We split the image first to ensure a place for the thumb and then to create the edge that will be used to make the wrist, as shown in the figure.

step 2 Use the Split Polygon Tool again to split the surfaces for the four fingers of the hand, as in Figure 3-74. Then, adjust the vertices to trim the shape. This will create the rough shape of a hand. Now, to convert back to the subdivision surface, select the polygon model and select [Modify > Convert > Polygon To Subdiv] to convert to the subdivision surface as shown in Figure 3-75.

Figure 3-74 Trimming the Shape

Figure 3-75 Convert to Subdivision Surface

step 3 The fingers will be modeled using Extrude Face. To extrude the face, select the face, as shown in Figure 3-76, and apply [Modeling > Edit Polygons > Extrude Face]. Position the extruded face as shown in Figure 3-77.

Figure 3-76 Selecting the Face

Figure 3-77 Extrude Face

Apply Extrude Face in the same way to make the diagram shown in Figure 3-78. Pay attention to how many joints were made in the finger. Three edges make up the joints, and these will become the edges for animating the joints later.

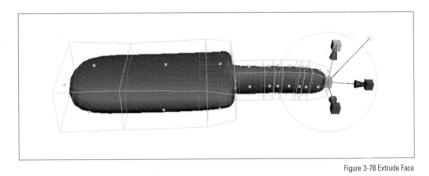

Figure 3-78 Extrude Face

Extrude the face of the thumb as shown in Figure 3-79.

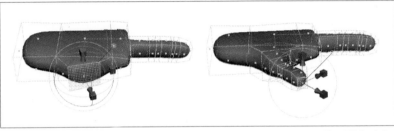

Figure 3-79 Extrude Face

step 4 The following sequence shows how to use the Split Polygon Tool to add more detail to the hand.

Let's take a look at how the surfaces are split.

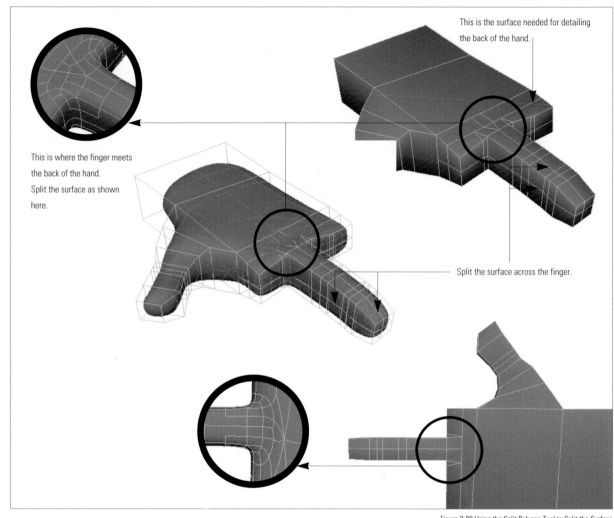

This is the surface needed for detailing the back of the hand.

This is where the finger meets the back of the hand.
Split the surface as shown here.

Split the surface across the finger.

Figure 3-80 Using the Split Polygon Tool to Split the Surface

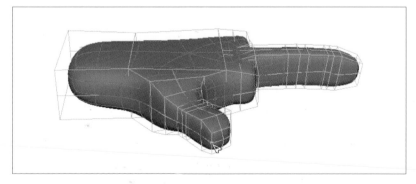

Figure 3-81 Split Polygon Tool

Split the surfaces of the thumb in the same way. As shown in Figure 3-81, make a lateral cut across the upper surface. We must split the surface so that it links with the lower surface.

step 5 After roughly splitting the surfaces using the Split Polygon Tool, we now need to add detail to portions of the hand. Select the model, click the RMB, and select Standard from the Marking Menu or select [Modeling > Subdiv Surface > Standard Mode] to convert from Polygon Mode to Standard Mode.

Add detail, as shown in Figure 3-82, by adjusting the vertices in Standard Mode.

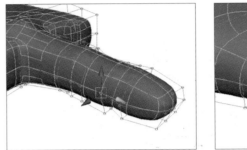
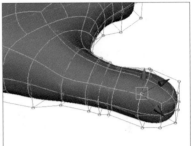

Figure 3-82-1 Adding Detail   Figure 3-82-2 Adding Detail

Follow the steps outlined in Figure 3-83 to add the fingernail. One thing to keep in mind is that when extruding two more faces at the same time, the [Polygons > Tool Options > Keep Faces Together] option must be turned on.

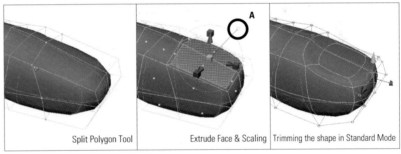

Split Polygon Tool   Extrude Face & Scaling | Trimming the shape in Standard Mode

Figure 3-83 Adding the Fingernail

Click on the area marked "A" in the figure, and adjust the scale to fit the Manipulator of the extruded face to the World axis.

We have now made the basic constituents of the hand. We have modeled the back of the hand, the thumb, and the middle finger. In the next step, we will link this process to mapping. The next step can be largely classified into two steps. First, in order to use polygon mapping, we can either place the mapping coordinates in the middle of the model or map directly in the final subdivision surface at the very end.

In addition, when working with version 3, we can also use polygon mapping after the modeling is complete. The modeling process, which will be explained here, can also be used in version 3.

1. Modeling and Mapping in Parallel

We will first look at how to use modeling and mapping in parallel. The modeling that we have completed so far is adequate for this method. In other words, although there are no specific details, the necessary components are in place. We have already made one of the four fingers, excluding the thumb; therefore, all that we have to do is copy and paste the finger we already made instead of making the remaining three fingers from scratch. The mapping coordinates will also use the polygon; therefore, once we make them for the one finger, we can copy and paste it for the other fingers. Adding the mapping coordinates to the modeling is a very effective method because it eliminates the need to add another surface using Extrude Face, Extrude Edge, or the Append Polygon Tool. The Split Polygon Tool splits the existing edge without affecting the UV coordinates.

To do this, we will need to convert the subdivision surface back to Polygon Mode. As follows, all work in the subdivision surface must be done in Display Level 0. Work in all other levels becomes useless upon conversion to the Polygon Mode.

Options Window   Selecting the face

Figure 3-84 Deleting Unnecessary Faces after Converting to Polygon Mode

step 1 Select the subdivision surface model, and select [Modify > Convert > Subdiv To Polygon ▢] to open the Options window. In the Options window, set the Tessellation Method to Vertices, the Level to 0, and the Original Object to Replace before clicking the Convert button. Select and delete the surface on the back of the wrist of the converted polygon, as shown in Figure 3-84.

After selecting the model, select [Windows > UV Texture Editor] to open the window. Select the UV of the model, and move it far away from the texture map as shown in Figure 3-85.

Figure 3-85 UV Texture Editor

step 2 To set up the mapping coordinates of the middle finger, select all the faces of the middle finger, as shown in Figure 3-86.

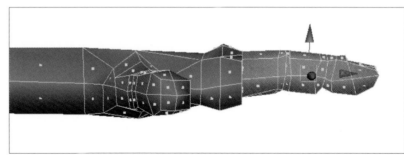

Figure 3-86 Selecting the Faces of the Finger

Select [Edit Polygons > Textures > Cylindrical Mapping]. If the options in the Channel Box are set to Default, the Rotate Z should be set to 90 and the Projection Horizontal to 360. (For more information, refer to the section on Polygon Mapping.) Adjust the Manipulator, as shown in Figure 3-87.

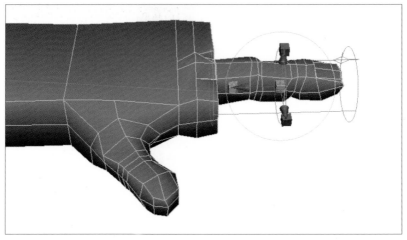

Figure 3-87 Cylindrical Mapping

Adjust the view in Perspective View, as shown in Figure 3-88, and select the face. Select [Edit Polygons > Texture > Planar Mapping ▣] to open the Options window. In the window, after setting the Mapping Direction to Camera, click the Project button. Open the UV Texture Editor, click the RMB, and select UV from the Marking Menu. Move the UV, to which the Planar Map has been applied, as shown in the figure.

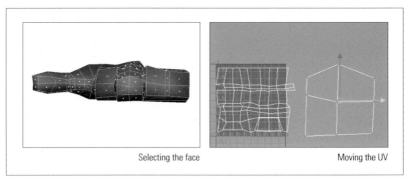

Selecting the face   Moving the UV

Figure 3-88 Planar Mapping

step 3 For smoother UV editing, select the polygon model and select [Display > Custom Polygon Display ▣] to open the Custom Polygon Display Options window, as shown in Figure 3-89. In the Options window, after turning on Texture Borders, click on the Apply and Close button at the bottom.

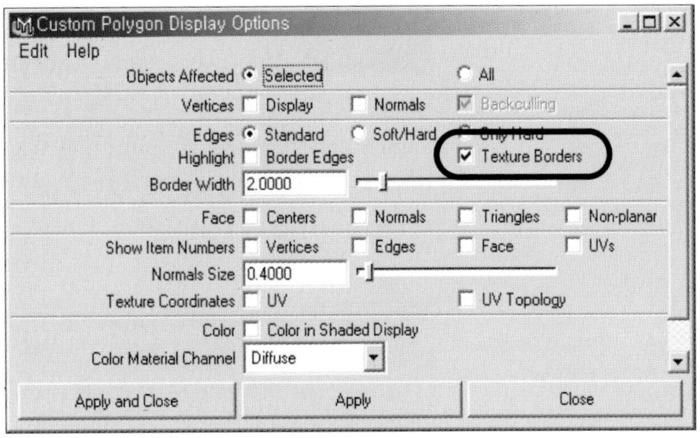

Figure 3-89 Options Window

Open the UV Texture Editor. It should closely resemble the configuration shown in Figure 3-90. In this case, fix the problem by following the steps illustrated below.

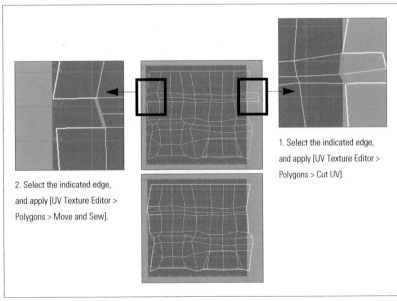

1. Select the indicated edge, and apply [UV Texture Editor > Polygons > Cut UV].

2. Select the indicated edge, and apply [UV Texture Editor > Polygons > Move and Sew].

Figure 3-90 Arranging the UVs

step 4 As shown in Figure 3-91, align the border UVs to the grid in the UV Texture Editor. This can be made easier by pressing the X key on the keyboard to apply the Grid Snap. We must make sure that all the bordering edges are attached. If a loose edge is discovered, select the edge and apply [UV Texture Editor > Polygon > Sew UVs]. After arranging the planar mapped faces of the finger, adjust the size and position as shown in Figure 3-92.

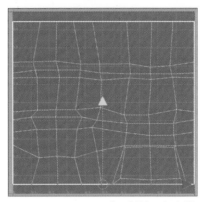

Figure 3-91 Arranging the UVs

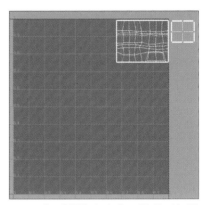

Figure 3-92 Adjusting the Size and Position of the UVs

After arranging the thumb in the same way, adjust its size and location as shown in Figure 3-93.

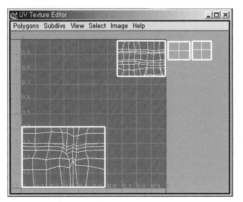

Figure 3-93 UV Texture Editor

step 5 Now, in order to set up the coordinates in back of the hand, select all of the faces, as shown in Figure 3-94, excluding the ones for the finger. As shown in the figure, either delete the faces for the positions of the other remaining fingers from the selection or delete them completely.

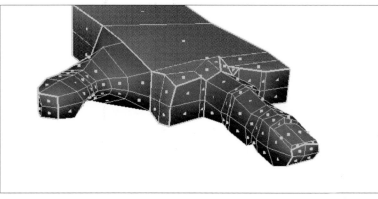

Figure 3-94 Selecting the Face

Select [Edit Polygons > Textures > Cylindrical Mapping] and adjust the Manipulator as shown in Figure 3-95. Open the UV Texture Editor, and adjust the location and size of the UV coordinates as shown in Figure 3-96.

Figure 3-95 Adjusting the Manipulator

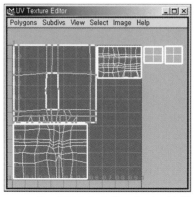

Figure 3-96 Adjusting the Size and Location of the UV

step 6 We have so far looked at the setup process for the UV coordinates. We will now look at how to make the remaining fingers and their respective UV coordinates. We will make the remaining fingers by copying and pasting the finger we have already made. First of all, duplicate the entire model as shown in Figure 3-97. After deleting all of the faces, excluding the ones for the finger, place it in the position for the index finger and adjust its size, as shown in Figure 3-98.

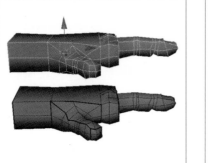

Figure 3-97 Duplicate Mode

Figure 3-98 Placing the Finger

Selecting the newly made finger and opening the UV Texture Editor, we can see the UV coordinates, as shown in Figure 3-99. We need to move the UV coordinates of the index finger because they currently overlap the ones for the middle finger. After moving the UVs, select the rest of the model by holding down the Shift key. This displays the coordinates for the rest of the model so that it is easier to pick out the UV coordinates we need.

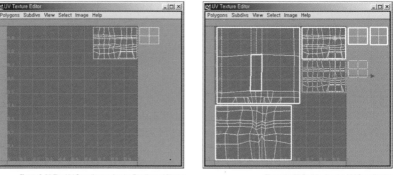

Figure 3-99 The UV Coordinates for the Duplicated Finger

Figure 3-100 Positioning the UV Coordinates

Make the remaining fingers in the same way and rearrange their respective UV coordinates. Refer to Figure 3-101 in making the remaining fingers.

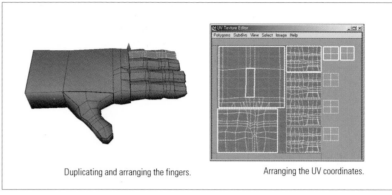

Duplicating and arranging the fingers.   Arranging the UV coordinates.

Figure 3-101 Making the Remaining Fingers

step 7 To attach the duplicated fingers to the hand, first, select and delete the faces where the fingers will be placed (Figure 3-102).

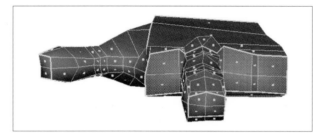

Figure 3-102 Selecting and Deleting the Faces

Add UV coordinates to the surfaces between the fingers by selecting [Edit Polygons > Textures > Planar Mapping] and arranging them at random in an empty space, as shown in Figure 3-104.

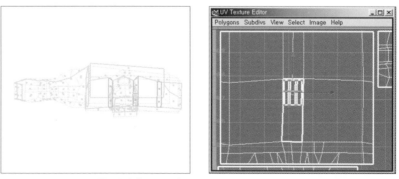

Figure 3-103 Selecting the Face   Figure 3-104 Arranging the UV

Finally, arrange all the UVs so that they look like the diagram in Figure 3-105.

By arranging the UVs in this way, a single page of textures will be made for all the surfaces of the hand. As follows, all the UVs of the hand must be inside the texture map.

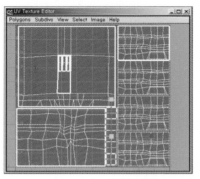

Figure 3-105 Final UV Arrangement

step 8 Convert all the polygons into subdivision surfaces.

Selecting the converted subdivision surface and opening the UV Texture Editor, we can see that the coordinates, which we added in the polygon, were maintained during the conversion (Figure 3-107).

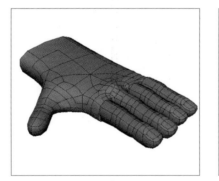 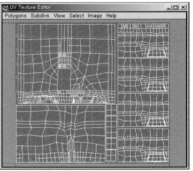

Figure 3-106 Convert To Subdivision Surface   Figure 3-107 The UV Coordinates of the Subdivision Surface

Attach each of the duplicated fingers. Selecting the hand and one of the fingers, select [Subdiv Surfaces > Attach ☐] to open the Attach Options window. In the window, turn both Merge UVs Also and Keep Originals off before clicking the Attach button at the bottom of the window.

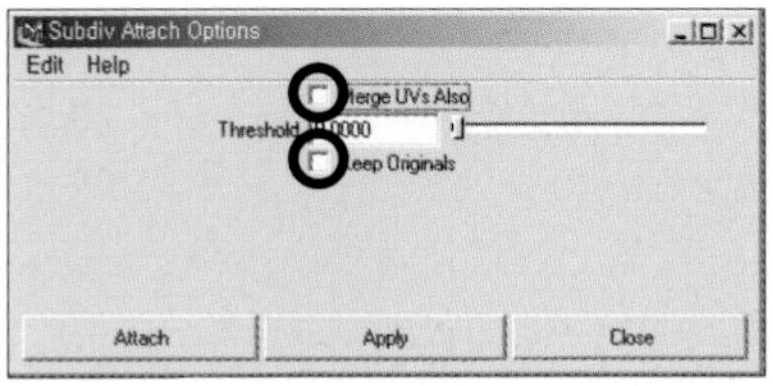

Figure 3-108 Options Window

Attach the remaining fingers in the same way.

To attach all the fingers, after converting the subdivision surface to Polygon Proxy Mode, use the Split Polygon Tool to split the surfaces so as to attach the remaining fingers, by referring to the structure of the middle finger. The surfaces are split because the edge of the finger and the edge of the hand must be the same in order to merge the edges together. This can be easily understood by looking at the way the middle finger is attached.

Figure 3-109 shows the hand in Polygon Mode so that we can more easily observe how the surfaces have been split. Conduct this surface splitting in Polygon Proxy Mode.

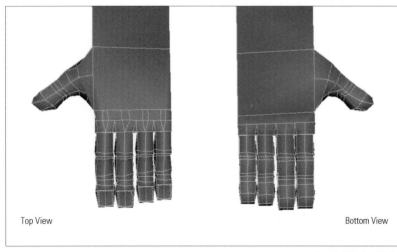

Top View   Bottom View

Figure 3-109 Surface Splitting

Now, use [Edit Polygons > Merge Edge Tool] to merge the edges of the fingers and the hand. Figure 3-110 shows the subdivision surface in Standard Mode after all the edges have been merged.

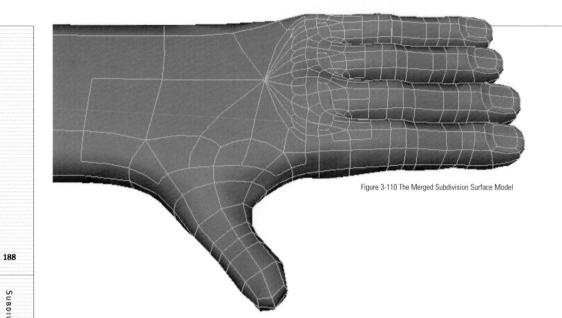

Figure 3-110 The Merged Subdivision Surface Model

In order to add detail, we use the Split Polygon Tool to split the surfaces. We must split the surfaces with respect to the structure of the finger. Figure 3-111 shows an example of splitting the surface of a polygon, which must be done at Level 0. Converting to Polygon Mode is the faster and more efficient method.

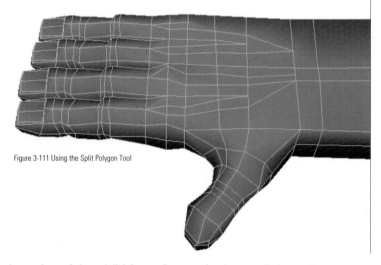

Figure 3-111 Using the Split Polygon Tool

Adjust the vertices of the subdivision surface to trim the overall shape. As necessary, convert back to Polygon Proxy Mode to use the Split Polygon Tool.

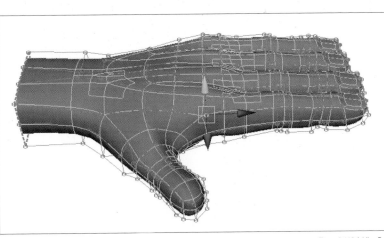

Figure 3-112 Adding Detail

note

Using the Split Polygon Tool or Merge Edge Tool in the Polygon Proxy Mode of the subdivision surface will dramatically lower the system speed. When working in Level 0, as we are here, the work will be much faster if we first work in Polygon Mode and then convert to Subdivision Surface Mode. We use Attach in the Subdivision Surface Mode instead of using Combine in the Polygon Mode because coordinates can be lost in the Polygon Mode when using Combine.

Split the surfaces and proceed with the modeling by referring to the CD-ROM/CHARACTER/scenes/subHAND.mb file.

Once the work in Level 0 is complete, we divide the level to add more detail. Because we split a sufficient number of surfaces in Level 0, completing our work in Level 1 will add a fair amount of detail to the hand. We do not want to create an unnecessary number of levels that could can increase the amount of data and lower our system speed.

Figure 3-113 illustrates how to add detail in Level 1. Follow the illustration to add sufficient detail to parts of the hand.

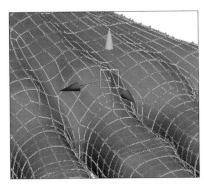

Figure 3-113-1 Adding Detail in Level 1

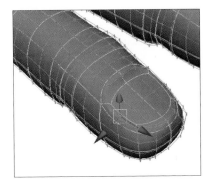

Figure 3-113-2 Adding Detail in Level 1

Use this method to complete the shape. Because we have already created the UV coordinates, we do not need to do so again.

Figure 3-114 shows the completed model of the hand.

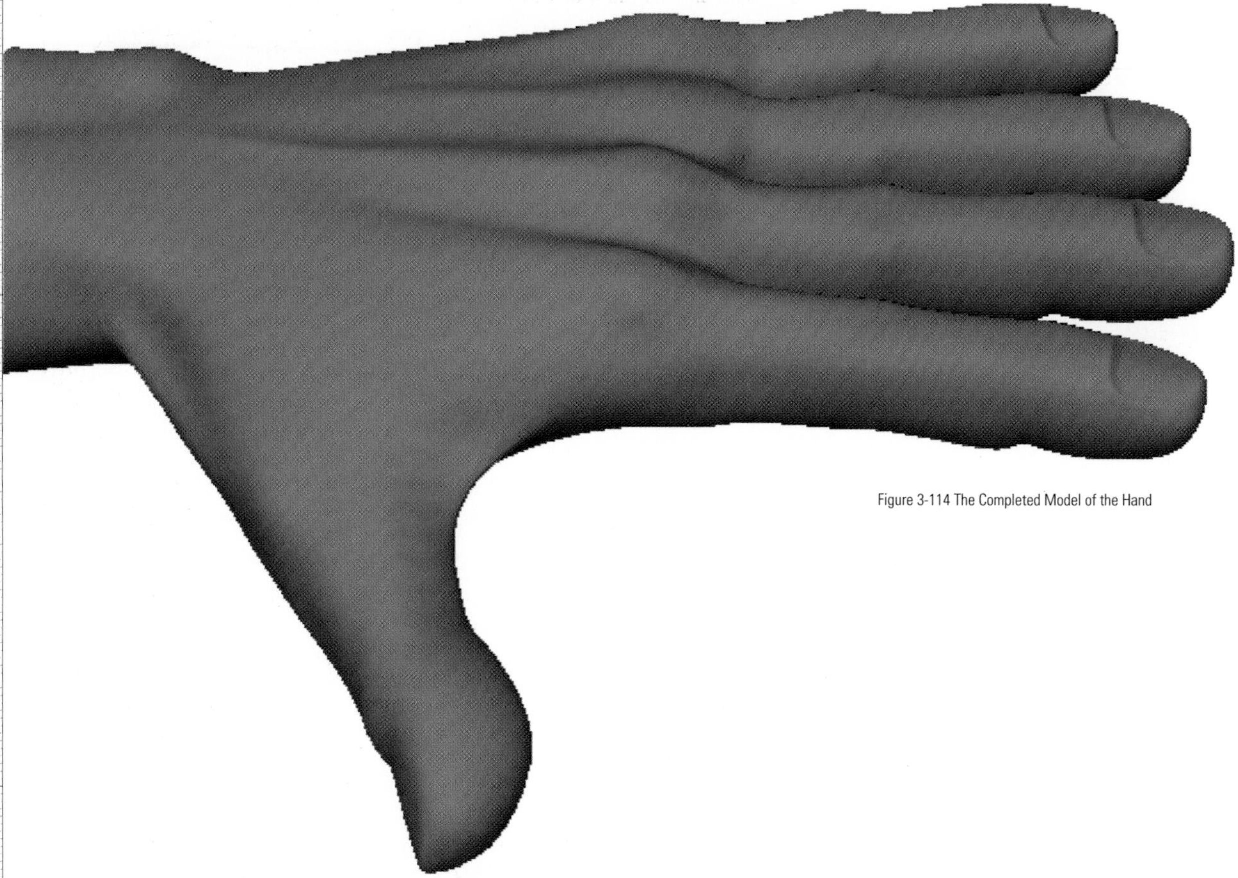

Figure 3-114 The Completed Model of the Hand

2. Using Subdivision Surface Mapping after Modeling

This is a comparatively faster method for modeling. However, in terms of mapping, it is rather difficult to set up optimized mapping coordinates for the use of 3D painting software.

The process of obtaining the model shown in Figure 3-115 is the same for both methods. We do not need to worry about the mapping coordinates here because they will be added directly to the subdivision surface later.

If you wish to add UV coordinates
as we did for the polygon map,
refer to page 694.

When modeling the hand, there is no need
to make another model of the same shape.
Once the middle finger has been modeled
to some extent, add the full details to the
middle finger and then copy and paste it to
make the other remaining fingers.

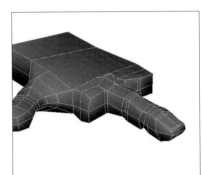

Figure 3-115 Polygon Model

step 1 Add detail to the middle
finger. After making the
overall shape in Level 0, add the details in
Level 1. Figure 3-116 shows the details
added to the middle finger.

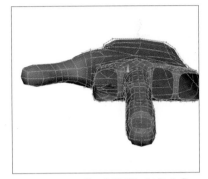

Figure 3-116 Adding Detail to the Finger

step 2 Let's look at how to create the fingernail. Follow the steps outlined in
Figure 3-117 to create the fingernail. Select portions of the edge and apply
[Subdiv Surfaces > Full Creases Edge/Vertex] to make an acute angle. Use the acute
angle and the vertices to quickly and easily make the fingernail.

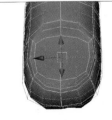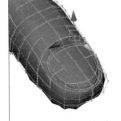

Select the edges to make the acute
angle.

Select [Subdiv Surfaces > Full
Creases Edge/Vertex] and move the
edges to make the shape.

Adjust the vertices to trim the
shape of the fingernail.

Figure 3-117 Adding Detail to the Fingernail

step 3 After making the fingernail, make a duplicate of the entire finger. Delete all the surfaces, excluding those of the finger, in Polygon Proxy Mode.

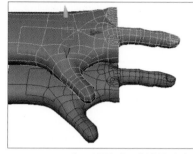

Figure 3-118 Duplicate Subdivision Surface

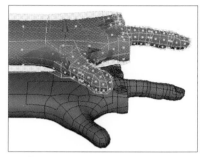

Figure 3-119 Selecting and Deleting Unnecessary Surfaces

After converting to Standard Mode, duplicate and arrange the finger by adjusting the scale for each.

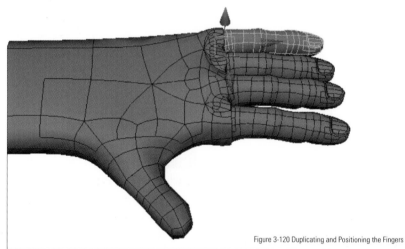

Figure 3-120 Duplicating and Positioning the Fingers

Attach all the fingers using [Subdiv Surfaces > Attach]. All of the attached fingers have loose edges. To easily attach the loose edges, press the **V** key on the keyboard to apply the Point Snap and align the vertices to the area where the finger meets the hand (see Figure 3-121).

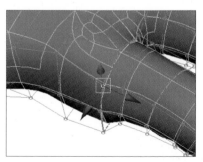

Figure 3-121 Aligning the Vertices using Point Snap

step 4 Converting to Polygon Proxy Mode, and select [Edit Polygons > Merge Multiple Edges ▢] to open the Options window. In the Options window, set the Threshold to 0.1 and then click the Sew button.

Figure 3-122 Options Window

All the edges, within a threshold of 0.1, will be merged. If some edges are still not merged, simply raise the Threshold value. Apply the Merge Multiple Edges Tool several times. Observing the hand in Standard Mode (see Figure 3-123), we can see that all the fingers have been neatly attached.

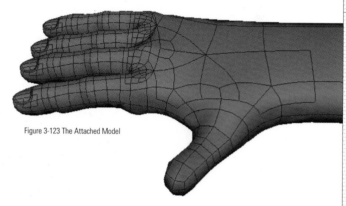

Figure 3-123 The Attached Model

Now, use the Split Polygon Tool in Polygon Proxy Mode to add detail. This process is the same as was described earlier. To make a more natural looking hand, make the fingers slightly different in shape as shown in Figure 3-124.

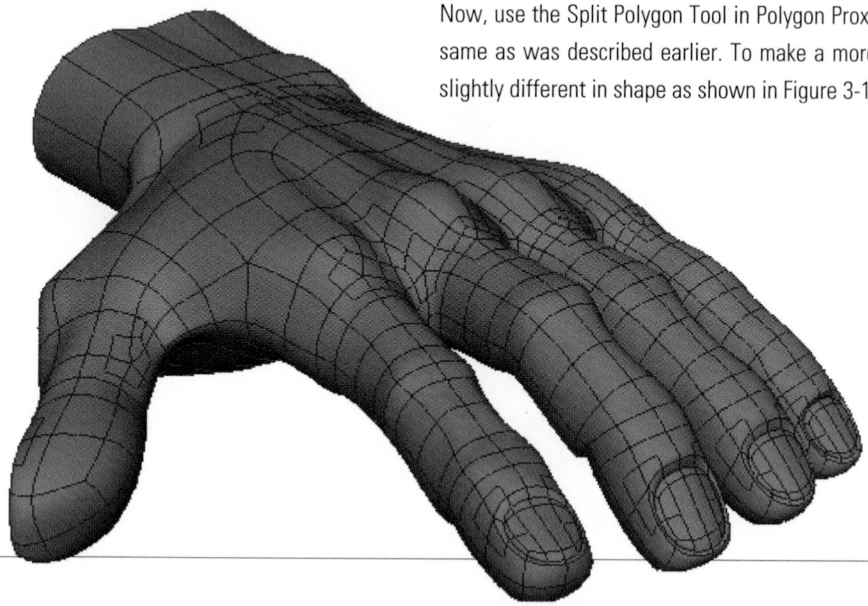

Figure 3-124 The Completed Model

step 5 Maya offers 3 different mapping types, which can be used to map directly on the subdivision surface.

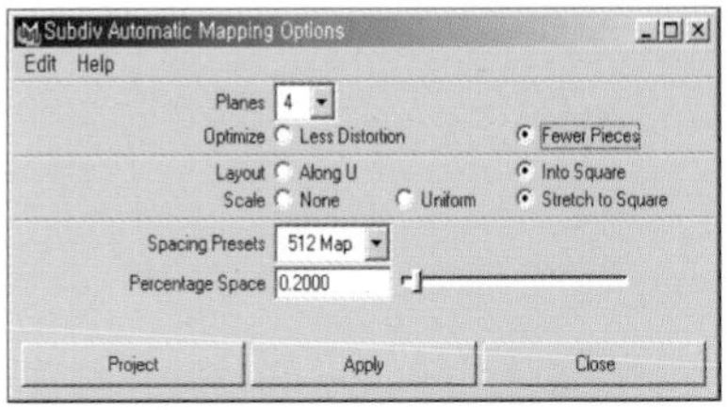

Figure 3-125 Options Window

These 3 mapping types are Planar Mapping, Automatic Mapping, and Layout UVs. Of these, Automatic Mapping and Layout UVs are the easiest and fastest ways to map. However, these two methods have some disadvantages pertaining to optimizing textures. Selecting all of the faces of the subdivision surface in Level 0, select [Subdiv Surfaces > Textures > Automatic Mapping ▣] to open the Options window. Configure the Option window, as shown in Figure 3-125, and press the Project button.

Opening the UV Texture Editor, we can see that all the UVs are spread out and do not overlap, as shown in Figure 3-126. However, the figure also shows that there are too many empty spaces within the texture map leading to a loss of texture.

We must rearrange the UVs, as shown in Figure 3-127, to optimize this situation to some degree.

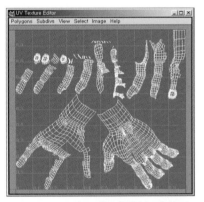

Figure 3-126 Automatic Mapping

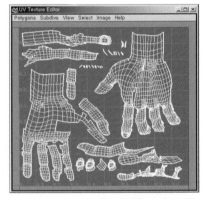

Figure 3-127 Rearranging the UVs.

Next, we look how to use Planar Mapping to obtain a more optimal map. In this case, we use Planar Mapping after selecting the surfaces of each section in each view so that they do not overlap or bend.

Before we begin, open the UV Texture Editor and move all the UVs out of the texture map to make selection of the UV easier.

Moving the UVs of the subdivision
surface, to which a mapping type
has been applied, in the Texture
Editor can dramatically lower the
system speed. In this instance,
delete the history of the subdivision
surface.

First of all, select the faces of the tops of each of the 4 fingers in Level 0.

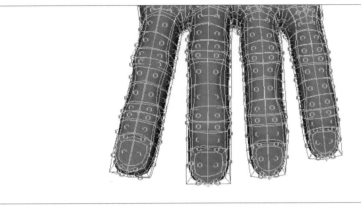

Figure 3-128 Selecting the Faces of the Subdivision Surface

Adjust the view in Perspective View so that all of the surfaces have enough room, as shown in Figure 3-128.

Select [Subdiv Surfaces > Textures > Planar Mapping] to open the Options window. In the Options window, set the Mapping Direction to Camera and then click the Project button.

A Planar Manipulator will be created, as shown in Figure 3-129. Opening the UV Texture Editor, we can see that the selected face is arranged inside the texture map as shown in Figure 3-130.

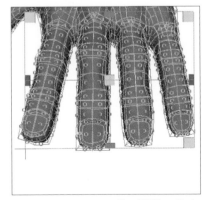

Figure 3-129 Planar Mapping

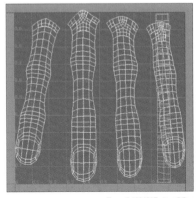

Figure 3-130 UV Texture Editor

After selecting the subdivision surface, select [Edit > Delete by Type > History] to delete the selected history and then move the UVs outside of the texture map in the UV Texture Editor.

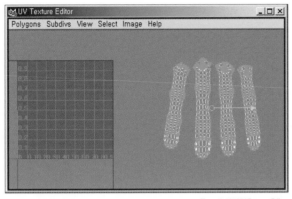

Figure 3-131 UV Texture Editor

In the same way, planar map all of the faces in their respective directions. Figure 3-132 shows the rearranged UV coordinates.

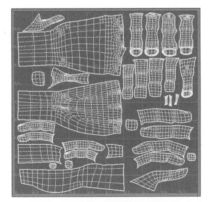

Figure 3-132 The Final UV Arrangement

We have, thus far, taken a look at modeling and mapping a hand. Many other methods exist and I recommend that you practice with each one of them and decide for yourselves which method you believe to be the most productive and effective.

5. OTHER MODELING

Up until now, we have looked at how to model character components. We also need to model the clothes and other parts of the character. We will now look at examples of these other models.

The subdivision surface modeling is the same as that for the character. Therefore, I will refrain from further explanation and rely on the figures to illustrate the modeling process. For this example, use the CD-ROM/CHARACTER/sourceimages/manFRONT.jpg and the manSIDE.jpg files as the image plane.

5-1. MODELING CLOTHES

Figure 3-133 shows the low polygon model of the jacket. I converted the subdivision surface to polygon mode so that you can easily understand the surface structure.

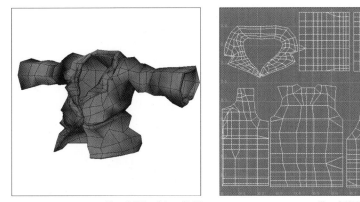

Figure 3-133 Low Polygon Model   Figure 3-134 UV Texture Editor

Make the model with large wrinkles to manifest the natural texture of the clothes.

Figure 3-134 shows the UV coordinates of the low polygon model.

First, we need to use the subdivision surface for the modeling. When modeling, we must make sure that the overall shape is modeled at Display Level 0. Then, we convert this to Polygon Mode.

In the Subdiv to Polygon Options window, set the Tessellation Method to Vertices and convert at Level 0.

Position the UV coordinates of the converted polygon, and convert them back to the Subdivision Surface Mode. Adjust the levels as needed to add detail.

Because we positioned all of the UV coordinates in Polygon Mode and then converted back to Subdivision Surface Mode, all of the UV coordinates are maintained, as shown in Figure 3-136.

Figure 3-135 Convert to Subdivision Surface

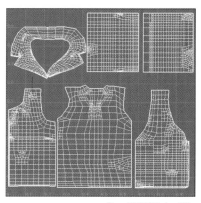

Figure 3-136 UV Texture Editor

The pants are modeled in the same fashion.

The following are illustrations of the subdivision surface model and UV coordinates, as seen in the UV Texture Editor, of the pants.

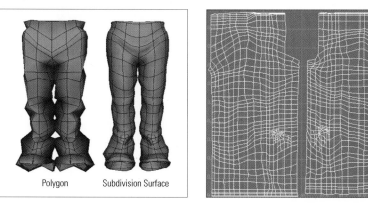

Polygon   Subdivision Surface

Figure 3-137 Modeling of the Pants

Figure 3-138 UV Texture Editor

5-2. OTHER MODELING

We will now look at how to model other accessory items. The shirt was made by using the NURBS Cylinder to adjust the CV, and the shoes were made in Subdivision Surface Mode. The buttons were also made in the Subdivision Surface Mode and then converted to Polygon Mode.

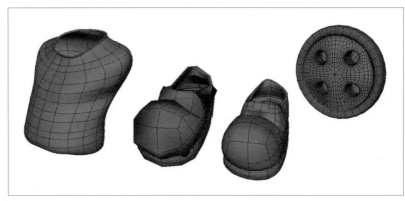

Figure 3-139 Other Modeling

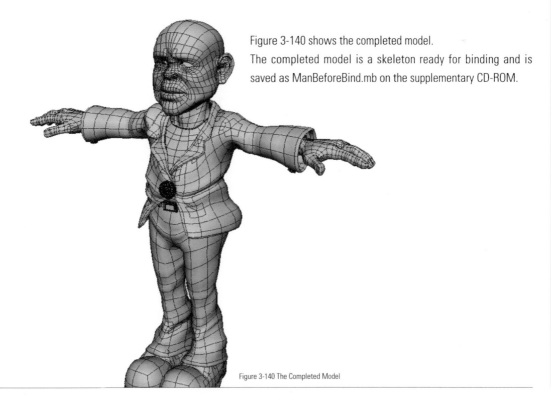

Figure 3-140 shows the completed model.
The completed model is a skeleton ready for binding and is saved as ManBeforeBind.mb on the supplementary CD-ROM.

Figure 3-140 The Completed Model

NURBS Modeling

Up until now, we have looked at Polygon and Subdivision Surface modeling in Maya. We will now look at NURBS modeling. There are 2 types of NURBS character modeling, the One Patch modeling method, commonly just called "modeling," and the Mult-Patch method, commonly called Multi Surface. Although the current trend in modeling is to work with subdivision surfaces, there are many advantages to using NURBS modeling and learning it will lead to many, diverse models.

In this chapter, we will look at the basic options for using NURBS modeling and at both simple One Patch modeling and Multi-Patch modeling.

If you are not yet familiar with the menus, I recommend that you understand them fully before starting the examples. Although there are many NURBS-related menus, I will only cover the ones necessary for character modeling.

1. UNDERSTANDING THE BASIC MENU

1-1. CURVE MENU (REBUILD) 🖾

This menu is accessed by selecting [Modeling > Edit Curves > Rebuild Curve] and is used to adjust a curve that has been drawn to assume the desired number of spans.
Selecting [Modeling > Edit Curves > Rebuild Curve ▢] will open the Rebuild Curve Options window shown in Figure 4-1.

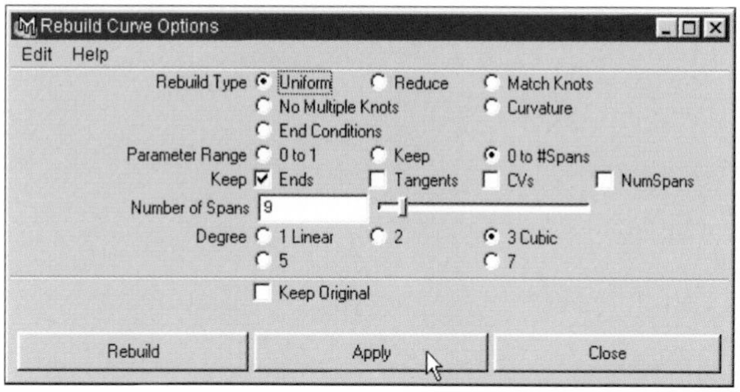

Figure 4-1 Rebuild Curve Options Window.

1. Rebuild Type

● Uniform

This option rebuilds the curve using a uniform Parameter value. When we use this option, however, we will not be able to adjust the values for Number of Spans and Degree.
This option is frequently used to rebuild curves in patch modeling.

● Reduce

This option rebuilds curves by deleting unnecessary knots based on the Tolerance Setting.

The higher the Tolerance Setting, the more knots are deleted.

If Global is checked for Use Tolerance, Maya uses the value in the Preference Setting ([Window > Setting/Preferences > Preferences]). If Local is checked, Maya uses the user's settings.

● Match Knots

This option rebuilds curves in accordance with the Degree, Knot, and Span values of another curve. To use this option, select the curve to rebuild and then select the other accordant curves while holding down the Shift key before executing this option. This option is effective in lofting several curves to make a surface.

For example, let's suppose that we have curves A-D, as in Figure 4-2 below. Let's also suppose that we will be rebuilding curves B-D based on curve A. To do so, select curves B-D, as in Figure 4-3, and then, holding down the Shift key, select curve A. Then, setting Rebuild Type to Match Knots will rebuild curves B-D based on curve A.

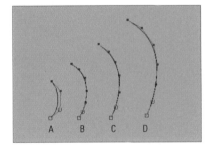

Figure 4-2 Curves to Rebuild

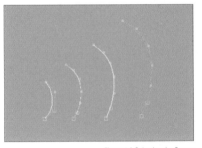

Figure 4-3 Selecting the Curves

● No Multiple Knots

This option deletes supporting curves that were created during the Rebuild process. The curves will assume the same degree value as the original curve.

● Curvature

This option will create a knot at the highest curvature. The curve will assume the degree value of the original curve, and the Use Tolerance value will be displayed. Use Tolerance is the same as the Reduce option, which was explained earlier. Using this option to rebuild the curve in Figure 4-4 will add many more knots to maintain the smooth curvature shown in Figure 4-5.

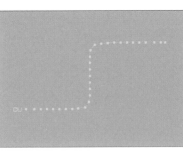

Figure 4-4 Before Rebuild
Figure 4-5 After Rebuild

We can draw the curve by selecting
No Multiple Knots.
Open the Tool Settings window,
shown in Figure 4-7, by selecting
[Create > CV Curve Tool] and turn
off Multiple End Knots.

Figure 4-7 Tool Setting Window

● End Conditions

This option will rebuild curves by specifying the location of the End CV and Knot of the curve. Selecting End Conditions will display 2 additional options for this condition, No Multiple Knots and Multiple Knots. Turn on the No Multiple Knots option, and the curve will be rebuilt in accordance with the End CV, as shown in Figure 4-6.

Figure 4-6 Rebuilding the Curve Using No Multiple Knots

Turning on the Multiple Knots option will align the curve to the End CV, and it will become easier to control the tangency related to the boundary of the curve.

Rebuilding the curve using End Conditions will apply the same degree value as the original curve.

2. Parameter Range

Although Parameter Range is not all that important in rebuilding curves, it becomes very important in rebuilding surfaces, which we will talk about later in this chapter.

Generally, in patch modeling, we use either Stitch or Global Stitch. This tool uses the Parameter Range value of the adjacent surface in attaching the two surfaces together and aligning their curvatures.

More information on this will be covered later in this chapter. Here, we will stick to looking at the Parameter Range for curve rebuilding.

● 0 to 1

This option sets the parameter from 0 to 1.

Draw a simple curve, set the parameter from 0 to 1 and then rebuild the curve. Opening the Attribute Editor, we can see that the Min Max Range has changed to 0 to 1.

● Keep

The parameter of the rebuilt curve maintains that of the original curve.

● 0 to # Span

This is the most frequently used option in patch modeling.

Selecting this option is the most fundamental step in rebuilding curves or surfaces.

Selecting this option will create a positive number of knots. This option is most commonly used in conjunction with Rebuild Type Uniform and creates a positive integer, which is easy to input.

Because this is such a basic and important option, we will use a very simple example to understand how it is used.

The curve in Figure 4-8 was made by first making one NURBS sphere, and then that sphere was made using Make Live. A Curve on Surface was made on top of this and then [Edit Curves > Duplicate Surface Curves] was applied to make a separate curve.

Figure 4-9 shows the Attribute Editor for this curve.

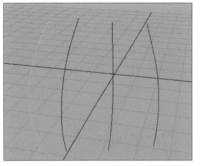

Figure 4-8 Duplicate Surface Curves   Figure 4-9 Curve made using the Attribute Editor.

As we can tell by looking at the Attribute Editor in Figure 4-9, curves generally made in this fashion do not have the same Span or Min Max value.

When such curves are lofted to make a surface, a surface with an irregular patch structure is made, as in Figure 4-10.

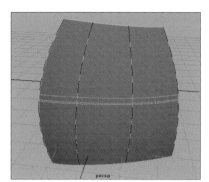

Figure 4-10 Surface made using Loft.

This makes our work very complicated. The whole point of NURBS modeling is that it must maintain a netted structure with isoparm adequate proportions. This becomes the most important factor for animation.

When using a curve to make a surface with either Loft or the Birail Tool, the surface is made with a uniformly distributed isoparm arrangement at the point where the first surface is made when the curves are rebuilt.

By rebuilding and lofting the curves in the following way, we get the surface with the evenly distributed isoparm arrangement shown in Figure 4-12.

First of all, after selecting the curve, select [Edit Curves > Rebuild Curve ⬛] to open the Options window (see Figure 4-11). In the Options window, set the Rebuild Type to Uniform, the Parameter Range to 0 to # Span, the Number of Spans to 3, and then rebuild all the curves. When using Loft to make these curves into a surface, we get the result seen in Figure 4-12.

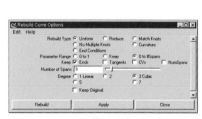

Figure 4-11 Rebuild Options Window

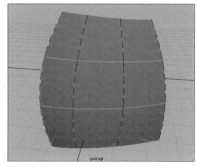

Figure 4-12 Surface Using Loft

Opening the Attribute Editor after rebuilding the curve, we can see that the Min Max value and the Span value are the same.

Knots are used, generally, to refer to edit points. A "span" is the curve unit that links edit points together in a NURBS curve or surface. In other words, selecting 0 to # Span, as we did above, means that the parameter of the curve we are to rebuild will coincide with the span number of the curve.

3. Keep

In order to specify the end point when we are rebuilding curves, Tangent, CV or Span number of the original curve, we must set Ends, Tangents, CV or NumSpans to On. NumSpans can only be used with the Uniform option.

4. Number of Spans

This option can be used only when the Rebuild Type is set to Uniform.
Typing in the desired value will rebuild the curve according to that number.

5. Degree

We use this option to specify the degree of the curve by entering the desired value.
We generally set this option to 3 Cubic. Setting this option to 1 Linear will rebuild the curve as a straight line.

6. Keep Original

When this option is selected, a new curve will be rebuilt while preserving the original curve. It is a good idea to turn this option off when rebuilding curves during patch modeling.

7. Use Tolerance

We can specify a given Tolerance value when the Rebuild Type is set to Reduce or No Multiple Knots. When this is option is set to Global, the values specified in Preferences are used, and when it is set to Local, the values entered by the user are used.

1-2. SURFACE MENU (BIRAIL, LOFT)

The tools that are most frequently used in Multi-Patch modeling are Birail and Loft. Both of these tools are very useful for making surfaces. Let's look at the basic menus and options of these tools.

1. Birail Tool

This tool follows a rail curve and uses one or more profile curves to make a surface. The [Modeling > Surface > Birail] menu includes the Birail 1 Tool, the Birail 2 Tool, and the Birail 3+ Tool. The numbers indicate how many profile curves will be used. In other words, the Birail 1 Tool will use one profile curve, the Birail 2 Tool will use 2 profile curves, and the Birail 3+ curve will use 3 or more curves.

Let's now look at how to use each of these tools.

● Birail 1 Tool 🛩

This tool uses one profile curve and 2 rail curves to make a surface.

Draw the curve shown in Figure 4-13. When drawing the curve, we must make sure that the starting and ending points of the curve (indicated with A and B in the drawing) coincide. If they do not, using the Birail Tool will produce an error and a surface will not be made.

Generally, to make sure that the starting and ending points meet, we use the Snap To Curve Mode. Draw the curve by pressing the C key on the keyboard or by clicking 🛩 in the Status Line. After drawing the curve, select [Modeling > Surfaces > Birail > Birail 1 Tool]. A "Select The Profile Curve" message will appear in the Help Line at the bottom of the window. Select the profile curve indicated in Figure 4-13.

A "Select Two Rail Curves" message will appear in the Help Line. In this case, select the rail curves, indicated in Figure 4-13, one at a time. A surface will be made as the profile curve follows the rail curve (see Figure 4-14).

If you cannot see the Help Line, select
[Display > UI Elements > Help Line] to
display the Help Line.

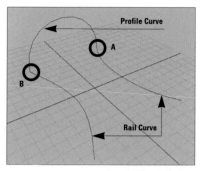

Figure 4-13 Drawing the Curve

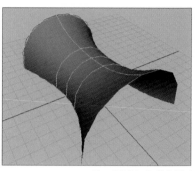

Figure 4-14 Using the Birail 1 Tool

Selecting [Modeling > Surfaces > Birail > Birail 1 Tool ▢] will open the Birail 1 Options
window (see Figure 4-15).

Figure 4-15 Birail 1 Tool Options Window

Transform Control

Transform Control can be Non Proportional or Proportional.

Let's see how these two options are different from each other.

As we can see in Figure 4-16, a Non Proportional rail curve maintains the height of the
surface even as it narrows. On the other hand, the surface height of a Proportional rail
curve, shown in Figure 4-17, gets proportionally smaller as it narrows.

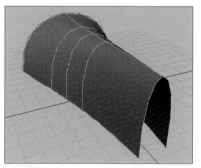

Figure 4-16 Non Proportional

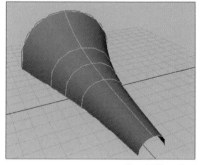

Figure 4-17 Proportional

This option can also be adjusted after making the surface.

After the surface is made, select it and then select the desired option from the INPUTS section of the Channel Box, as shown in Figure 4-18. Or, select the surface and modify the option in the Attribute Editor, as shown in Figure 4-19.

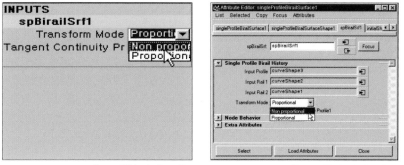

Figure 4-18 Using the Channel Box   Figure 4-19 Using the Attribute Editor

Continuity

The tangent of the surface succeeds the surface with the profile curve.

Because the Biral 2 and 3+ tools use a plural number of profile curves, the Continuity option contains both the profile option and rail option of each curve.

Rebuild

This option is basically the same as the Rebuild Curve, which we learned about earlier.

This option rebuilds the checked curve. For example, selecting Profile will rebuild the Profile Curve, and selecting First Rail and Second Rail will rebuild the first and second curves. Selecting one of these curves will display the Rebuild option, which is used in the same way as Rebuild Curve.

For example, checking Profile, First and Second Rail, setting the Rebuild Type to Uniform and Number of Span to 5, and then applying the tool will rebuild the curve and create the surface seen in Figure 4-20.

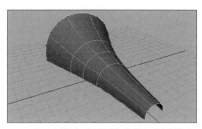

Figure 4-20 Using the Birail Tool with the Rebuild Option

Output Geometry

This allows us to select the geometry type. The default setting is NURBS. (Subdiv stands for subdivision surface.)

Tool Behavior

When Exit on Completion is set to On, we will be exited from the tool once it is used to make the birail surface. However, when this option is set to Off, we will be able to continue using the tool to make more birail surfaces. Setting Auto Completion to On will display a prompt at each step to automatically create the surface. However, when we set this option to Off we must select the curve and Birail Tool according to the specified sequence or press the Enter key to make the surface. The sequence of selection is first the Profile Curve, then the First Rail, and then the Second Rail.

● Birail 2 Tool

This tool is used in basically the same way as the Birail 1 Tool, with the only difference being that the Birail 2 Tool uses 2 profile curves. Using the curve we used in the example above, another profile curve is made at the end of the rail curve, as shown in Figure 4-21, so that 2 profile curves can be used.

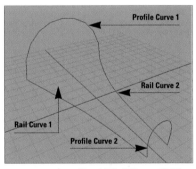
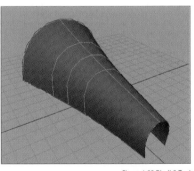

Figure 4-21 Profile Curve and Rail Curve   Figure 4-22 Birail 2 Tool

In the same way, the starting and ending points of the profile curve and rail curve must coincide. Select [Modeling > Surfaces > Birail > Birail 2 Tool], select profile curves 1 and 2 and then rail curves 1 and 2, in this order, to obtain the surface seen in Figure 4-22.

● Birail 3+Tool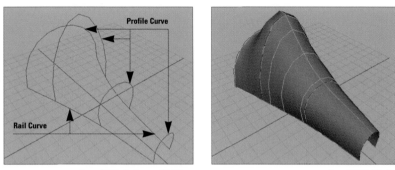

This tool is also used in basically the same way as the Birail Tools we saw earlier, with the only difference being that the Birail 3+ Tool uses 3 or more profile curves.

For instance, let s suppose that we added several more profile curves between the profile curves seen in Figure 4-21 (see Figure 4-23). After selecting [Modeling > Surfaces > Birail > Birail 3+ Tool], consecutively select each of the profile curves, press the Enter key, and consecutively select the 2 rail curves to obtain the surface seen in Figure 4-24.

Figure 4-23 Profile Curve and Rail Curve   Figure 4-24 Birail 3+ Tool

2. Loft Tool

This tool creates the surface that links curves together. Curve includes Curve on Surface, and Isoparm or Trim Edge can use the Loft Tool to make the surface. Let s suppose that we have 3 curves, as shown in Figure 4-25. In order to make the loft surface, first select the bottommost curve and then, holding down the Shift key, select the other 2 curves. The curve, which was selected last, will be shown in green. Selecting [Modeling > Surfaces > Loft] will create the loft surface that links together the curves in the order in which they were selected.

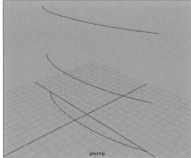

Figure 4-25 Curves to be Lofted   Figure 4-26 Loft Surface

We can also use Isoparm and a new curve to loft a surface, which has already been made, to make a new surface. As shown in Figure 4-27, select the isoparm of the surface, which has been made. Then, holding down the Shift key, select the new curve and then select [Modeling > Surfaces > Loft ☐] to make the new loft surface seen in Figure 4-28.

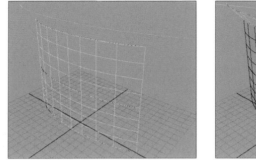

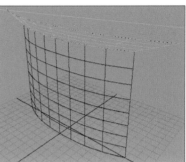

Figure 4-27 Selecting the Isoparm and the Curve

Figure 4-28 Loft Surface

Selecting [Modeling > Surfaces > Loft] will create the Loft Options window, shown in Figure 4-29.

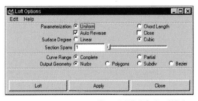

Figure 4-29 Loft Options Window

Parameterization

This option, which includes Uniform and Chord Length, is used to change the parameters of a loft surface. Selecting Uniform will give the surface uniform parameters in the V-direction. In other words, the surface isoparm of the profile curve, which was selected first, will be V(0), the second will be V(1) and so on. Selecting Chord Length will make the parameters, in the V-direction of the surface, based on the spacing of the profile curve. This option can come in very handy in certain situations.

Let's look at a simple example to illustrate the difference between these 2 options.

First, let's use this option to rearrange the curve used above.

As shown in Figure 4-30, select the profile curve in the middle and move it to the bottom to adjust the line spacing.

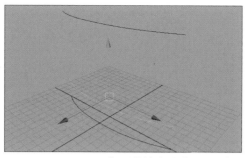

Figure 4-30 Adjusting the Spacing of the Curve

The two figures below (Figure 4-31 and Figure 4-32), show the Attribute Editor for the surface made by lofting the curve using Uniform and Chord Length, respectively.

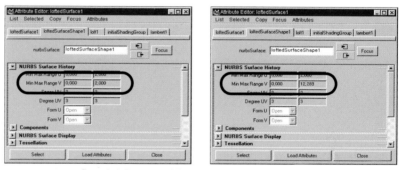

Figure 4-31 An Example Using Uniform

Figure 4-32 An Example Using Chord Length

Figure 4-31 above shows an example of using Uniform to loft the curve. We can see that both the Min Max Range V value and the Span value have been set to 2. In other words, this means that the bottommost curve in Figure 4-30 is 0, the middle curve is 1, and the topmost curve is 2.

Whereas Uniform imparts a uniform value to the curves, Chord Length, as we can see in Figure 4-31, creates parameters based on the spacing of the curve.

We will look at how these values affect Multi-Patch modeling when we talk about the Stitch option later. Here, we will look at the texture differences brought about by these 2 options. Observe the 2 figures below. Figure 4-33 is a rendering of a uniformly lofted surface to which Check Texture has been applied. We can see that this creates textural spacing based on the span. Figure 4-34 is a rendering of a surface, lofted using Chord Length, to which texture has been applied. We can see that, in this case, the texture is evenly applied without regards to the span.

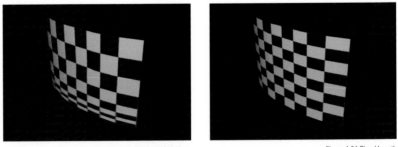

Figure 4-33 Uniform　　　　　　　　　　　　　　　Figure 4-34 Chord Length

Auto Reverse

This option automatically aligns differing curve directions, as we can see in Figure 4-35, to make the surface seen in Figure 4-36.

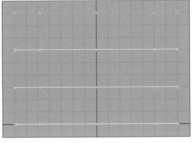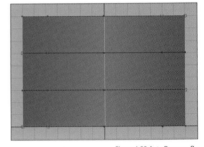

Figure 4-35 Differing Curve Directions　　　　　　　　　　Figure 4-36 Auto Reverse: On

When this option is turned off, the curves will be lofted in their various directions to produce a twisted surface (see Figure 4-37). In most cases, this option is usually left on.

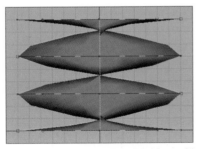

Figure 4-37 Auto Reverse : Off

Close

Turning this option on will close the loft surface in the V-direction (see Figure 4-38).

Figure 4-38 Close : On

Section Spans

This option will divide the span between each curve according to the designated value. The default value of 1 will create one span, which links the curves together as they are lofted. However, raising this value to 3 will create 3 spans between the curves, as shown in Figure 4-39.

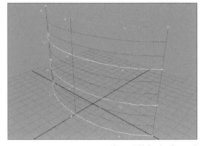

Figure 4-39 Section Spans : 3

Curve Range

Setting this option to Complete will create a surface by linking together the starting and ending points of the curve when lofted. However, sometimes, you will want only a certain portion of the curve to be lofted to make a surface. In this case, setting this option to Partial allows us to specify the scope of the curve that will be lofted to make the surface. Lofting the curve using the Partial option (Figure 4-40) will name the lofted curves "SubCurve 1, 2, 3, 4" and so forth, as we can see on the right side of the Channel Box in Figure 4-41.

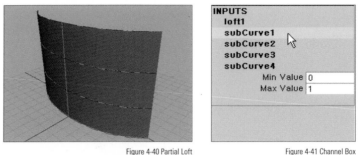

Figure 4-40 Partial Loft

Figure 4-41 Channel Box

Selecting SubCurve 1 from the Channel Box, as shown above, will display the Min Max Value. Adjusting this value allows us to adjust the range of the first curve used in the lofting process. We can also intuitively adjust the range by using the Manipulator.

Selecting SubCurve 4 from the Channel Box and selecting ▧ from the Minibar will create the Manipulator seen in Figure 4-43. Click the LMB on the Manipulator and drag to adjust the curve range.

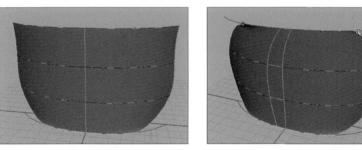

Figure 4-42 Min Value 0.2, Max Value 0.8

Figure 4-43 Using the Manipulator

Output Geometry

This allows us to specify the geometry of the created surface.

Selecting Polygon will display several options, which are used in basically the same way as the NURBS to Polygon option.

3. Attach Surface ▧

This command attaches 2 surfaces together.

Suppose we have 2 surfaces, as in Figure 4-44. Select the isoparm of each surface, and then apply the command to attach them together to create the surface seen in Figure 4-45.

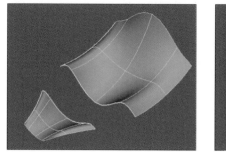

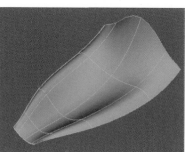

Figure 4-44 Selecting the Isoparm

Figure 4-45 Applying Attach Surface

Figure 4-46 illustrates the different uses of the Attach Surface command.

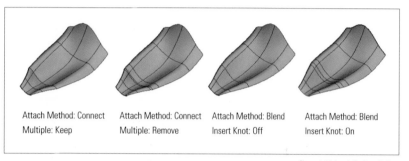

Attach Method: Connect
Multiple: Keep

Attach Method: Connect
Multiple: Remove

Attach Method: Blend
Insert Knot: Off

Attach Method: Blend
Insert Knot: On

Figure 4-46 Attach Surface Options

4. Attach Without Moving

This command attaches two surfaces together without moving them and creating a new patch (shown in yellow) to link them together, as shown in Figure 4-47 below.

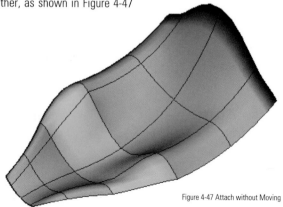

Figure 4-47 Attach without Moving

5. Open / Close Surface

This command is used to open a closed surface or to close an opened surface.
The Figure below shows the different uses of this command.

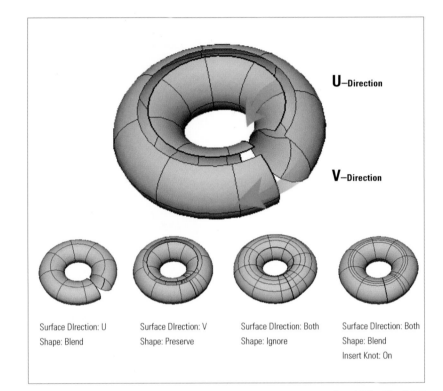

Surface DIrection: U
Shape: Blend

Surface DIrection: V
Shape: Preserve

Surface DIrection: Both
Shape: Ignore

Surface DIrection: Both
Shape: Blend
Insert Knot: On

Figure 4-48 Open/Close Options

6. Move Seam

In radial modeling, faces are usually made using one surface.
In this case, we commonly model one half of the face, use Mirror Copy to make the other side, apply Attach Surface to link the 2 sides together, and then use Open/Close Surface to close the surface.
However, this method presents a problem. That is, the starting and ending points of the closed surface are off to one side instead of remaining in the middle of the surface where they were before the surface was closed. Figure 4-49 shows the model before Open/Close Surface was applied, and Figure 4-50 shows the model after the application of Open/Close Surface.

The thick isoparm reflects the starting and ending points of the surface.

We can see in the figure that, indeed, the starting and ending points are pushed off to one side when the surface is closed.

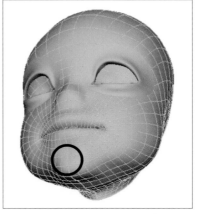

Figure 4-49 Before Applying Open/Close Surface

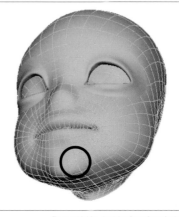

Figure 4-50 After Applying Open/Close Surface

This becomes a big problem when using Artisan. This makes it extremely difficult when using Artisan to model or when using the Reflect Paint option to modify the Skin Weight or Cluster Weight values.

Figure 4-51 shows the Artisan Sculpt Surface Tool Settings window. As we can see in the figure, turning on the Reflect option will make the starting and ending points the focal point (see Figure 4-52).

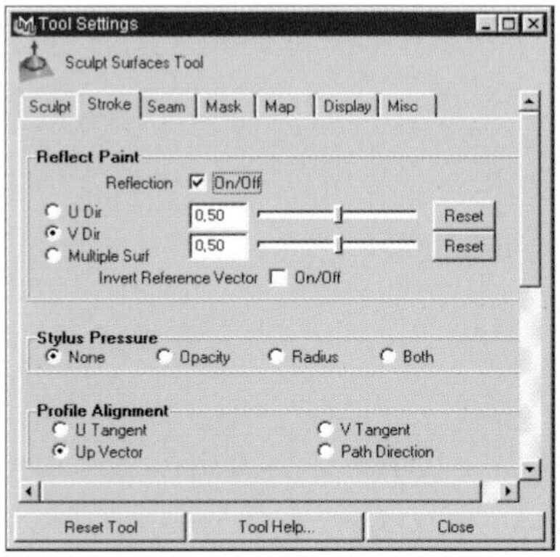

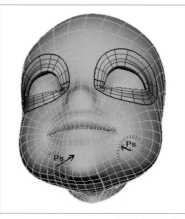

Figure 4-51 Tool Settings Window

Figure 4-52 Reflect Paint

Move Seam can only be used in uniform surfaces. An error will occur when Move Seam is applied in a chord length surface. If you decide to model by adding random isoparms, you must use Uniform Surface Rebuild.

This is very easy to confirm.

Open the Attribute Editor of the surface. If the Min Max Range value is an integer, it is Uniform. If it is a decimal number, it is Chord Length.

As we can see in Figure 4-52, this makes it very difficult to determine the symmetrical point. Although we can pinpoint it, somewhat, by slightly modifying the V Dir value in the Tool Settings window (see Figure 4-51), this is not exact. In this case, we must use Move Seam to change the position of the seam between the starting and ending points of the closed surface.

First of all, select the isoparm in the area that will be changed (here, it is included in the center) and then select [Edit NURBS > Move Seam] to position the selected isoparm on the seam.

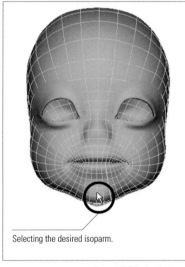

Selecting the desired isoparm.

Figure 4-53 Selecting the Isoparm

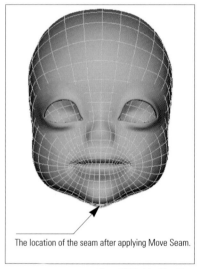

The location of the seam after applying Move Seam.

Figure 4-54 Applying Move Seam

Now, we have perfect vertical symmetry for using Artisan Reflect Paint.

This is also useful for preventing the source from accumulating on one side when making texture in mapping.

1-3. REBUILD SURFACE ▨

There are many different methods for making surfaces in patch modeling.
Depending on which method you use, each of the surfaces will have different parameters.
Patch modeling, in general, uses many surfaces and the curvatures of each are fit together often using Stitch or Global Stitch, which we will learn about later. However, undesirable results can occur if each of the surfaces has different parameters.
In such instances, we need to use Rebuild Surface to redefine the surface parameters.
In addition, if there are more than enough patches or degrees in a general modeling environment, the system speed can be severely reduced. Rebuild Surface is also very effective in such circumstances.

1. Understanding Surface and Parameter Range

In general, chord length and uniform surfaces each have different parameters.
These parameters determine how the curvature will be distributed, how the surface will be defined in the texture mapping and how the surfaces will be attached when using Attach Surface or Stitch. To review how texture is different for chord length and uniform surface, refer back to the section on using the Loft option.
In this section, we will look at how these values affect Attach and Stitch.

Chord Length

For chord length surfaces, the parameter is determined by the curve or surface length.
In other words, if the parameter value of the edit point, the starting point of the curve, is 0, then the parameter will differ, comparatively, based on the edit point and curve or surface length. This takes on an actual decimal number.

Figure 4-55 Chord Length Surface   Figure 4-56 Attribute Editor

Uniform Surface

The parameters of the uniform surface take on the same values as the edit point.

For example, when drawing a curve, if the first edit point is 0, the second edit point is 1, the third edit point is 3 and so on, then the parameter value assumes the same format.

In other words, the parameters of a uniform surface coincide with the span of the surface or curve.

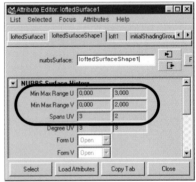

Figure 4-57 Chord Length Surface   Figure 4-58 Attribute Editor

2. The Difference in the Two Types When Using the Attach Option

Let's use the Attach option to see how the two types affect the surface. Let's suppose that we have a chord length surface and a uniform surface, each with the same number of spans. In the figure below, yellow depicts the chord length surface and blue depicts the uniform surface. You will probably guess that when these two surfaces are attached, they will do so without affecting the current isoparms of the surfaces.

However, when these two surfaces are attached, a new isoparm is added, as shown in Figure 4-60.

Figure 4-59 2 Types of Surfaces

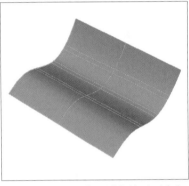
Figure 4-60 Applying Attach Surface

This happens because each of the 2 surfaces has a different parameter range.

When attaching two surfaces, Maya looks for the parameter range so as to decide, which areas of the surfaces will be attached.

If these values are the same, then the 2 surfaces will be attached with the same span and isoparm. However, if they are different, as in the figure above, Maya adds an additional isoparm in order to maintain this value. As a result, you will end up with an unwanted isoparm, which will complicate your work.

This is something that you do not want to happen in patch modeling.

Therefore, we must use Rebuild Surface in order to rebuild the chord length surface as a uniform surface.

3. Rebuild Surface Options

Selecting [Edit NURBS > Rebuild Surface ◘] will open the Rebuild Surface Options window shown below.

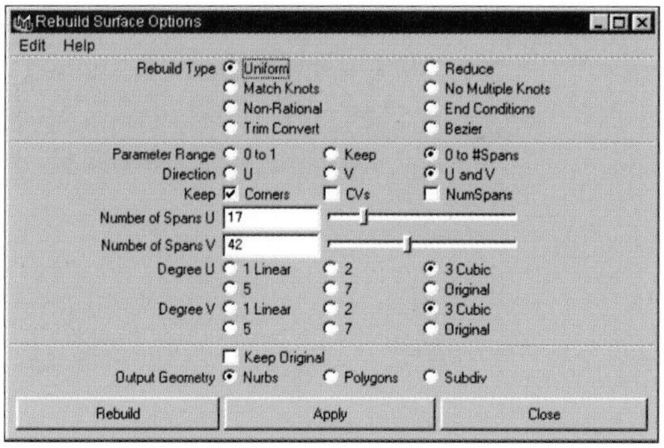

Figure 4-61 Rebuild Surface Options Window

As you can see from the figure, this window offers us many options. We will only look here at the options necessary for patch modeling.

Uniform

All actual patch modeling will be done using Uniform.

The reason for this is, as we mentioned above, in order to match the Span and Parameter Range of the surface for attachment. By selecting Uniform, we can modify the Parameter Range and Number of Spans U, V. For patch modeling, set the option to Uniform, set the Parameter Range to 0 to Span, set Number of Spans U, V to the desired values, and then click the Rebuild button.

Match Knot

This option rebuilds surfaces in accordance with the Degree, Knot, and Span values of another surface. For example, say that you want to rebuild a uniform surface and then want to apply these same values to another surface. Simply select all of the surfaces to rebuild, select the rebuilt uniform surface, and then apply this option. A new surface will be rebuilt using the same values of the rebuilt uniform surface.

Parameter Range

This allows us to establish the parameter range.

● 0 to 1
This option is used to establish the parameter range from 0 to 1. After applying this option, open the Attribute Editor to verify that the Parameter Range has indeed been set from 0 to 1.

● Keep
This option allows us to maintain the Parameter value. In other words, although the Span and Knot values will be rebuilt, the Parameter Range is kept the same as that for the original surface.

● 0 to #Spans
This is the most frequently used option in patch modeling. It matches the Parameter value with the Span value, allowing us to accurately line up the isoparms during patch modeling. In other words, if a surface has 5 spans, then the Parameter Range is also set from 0 to 5.

● Direction
This option rebuilds in the U-and/or V-direction.

● Number of Spans U, V
During Uniform Rebuild, this option allows us to establish the span value of the surface to rebuild. In other words, if these options are set to 4, then the surface will be rebuilt with 4 spans in either direction.

Using a simple example, we will look at how rebuilding is done for patch modeling. Figure 4-62 shows us the surface, which will be rebuilt. Figure 4-63 shows us the Attribute Editor, which illustrates how many Spans the surface has and how the Parameter Range is applied.

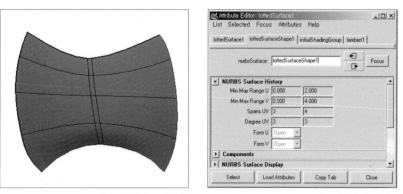

Figure 4-62 Surface to Rebuild   Figure 4-63 Attribute Editor

Select the surface and then select [Modeling > Edit NURBS > Rebuild Surface] to open the Rebuild Surface Options window. Reset the values by selecting [Edit > Reset Settings], and enter the following values:

Rebuild Type: Uniform
Parameter Range: 0 to # Spans
Number of Spans U: 4
Number of Spans V: 5

Click on the Rebuild button at the bottom.
As shown in Figure 4-64, a surface will be rebuilt with 4 spans in the U-direction and 5 spans in the V-direction. Looking at the Attribute Editor, as shown in Figure 4-65, we can see that the Parameter Range is in accordance with the Span values.

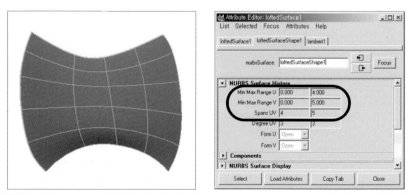

Figure 4-64 Surface to Rebuild   Figure 4-65 Attribute Editor

1-4. STITCH EDGE TOOL

The Stitch Edge Tool, which will be explained here, and the Global Stitch Tool, which will be explained in the following section, are essential and very important tools for Multi-Patch modeling. In Multi-Patch modeling, we need to attach several surface fragments together and add a tangent line to the seams so that it looks like one, smooth surface.

In the past, this was a very tedious and complex step. However, the Stitch Tool makes this step very quick and easy.

In this section, we will look at how this tool is used and the options used with it.

First, select [Modeling > Edit NURBS > Stitch > Stitch Edge Tool ▢] to open the Tool Settings window shown in Figure 4-66.

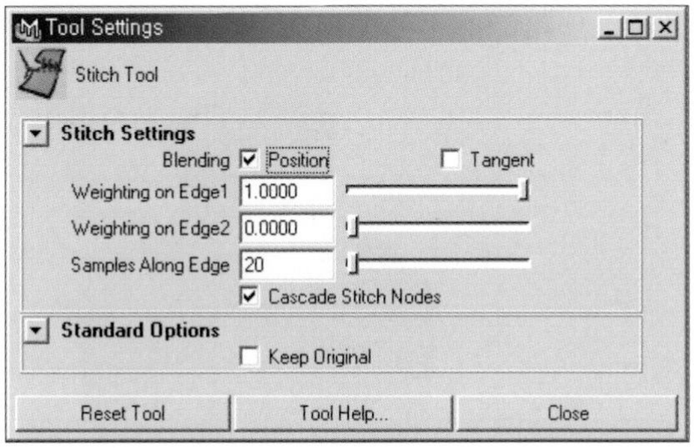

Figure 4-66 Tool Settings Window

1. Blending

Selecting Position will add positional continuity between the stitched surfaces.

Selecting Tangent will add a tangent (i.e., contact continuity, between the stitched surfaces).

2. Weighting Factor on Edge

Before the edges are stitched, the 2 selected isoparms will be standardized in Weighting Mode. The 2 surfaces will meet as they change along the continuing tangent. Now we can select along which isoparm this will occur.

The default is for the isoparm selected first to have a Weight of 1.0 and the second isoparm to have a Weight of 0. As follows, a tangent will be made for the surface selected first and the CV of the second surface will move. If the Weight values are both set to 0, then a tangent continuity will be made as the CV of both surfaces move.

3. Cascade Stitch Node

When the Cascade Stitch Node option is turned on, it will ignore any previous Stitch operations that were conducted. If this option is turned off, then the Stitch Node that was used previously will be reused. The default setting for this option is On.

4. Keep Original

When turned on, this option creates a new, stitched geometry.

Let's look at how to use this option through a simple example.
Figure 4-67 shows an example model that was made by revolving a NURBS curve. Let's look at how each option is used to stitch these 2 surfaces.

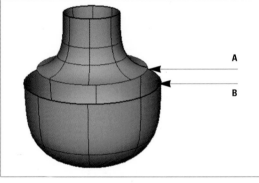

Figure 4-67 Example Modeling

First select [Modeling > Edit NURBS > Stitch > Stitch Edge Tool] to select the isoparm of A and then the isoparm of B.

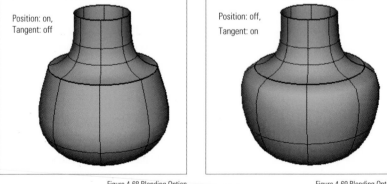

Figure 4-68 Blending Option   Figure 4-69 Blending Option

Turning the History on allows us to modify these values at any time.

Select the surface, and then select and modify the desired property from the Channel Box INPUTS. We can also change the properties by selecting ⊠ from the Minibar and using the Manipulator.

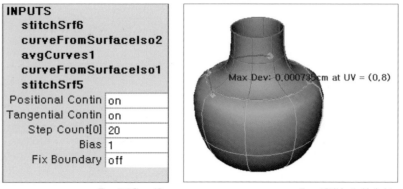

Figure 4-70 Channel Box   Figure 4-71 Using the Manipulator

After applying the Stitch Edge Tool, click and drag on the areas indicated in Figure 4-72 using the mouse to adjust the range of the stitch.

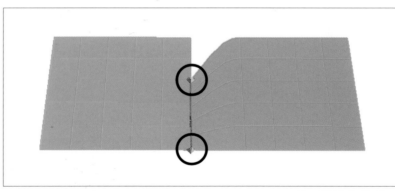

Figure 4-72 Adjusting Stitch Range

1-5. GLOBAL STITCH TOOL

Whereas the Stitch Edge Tool is used to stitch together 2 surfaces, the Global Stitch Tool can be applied to several surfaces at a time. This tool can save a lot of time in the once complex patch modeling phase.

Let's first look at how to use each option.

Select [Modeling > Edit NURBS > Stitch > Global Stitch Tool ▢] to open the Global Stitch Options window as shown in Figure 4-73.

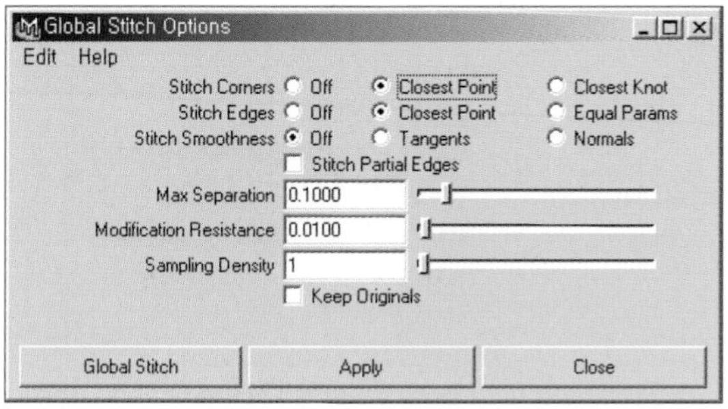

Figure 4-73 Global Stitch Options Window

1. Stitch Corner

This option specifies where the corners of a surface edge will be stitched.

If the point is within the range of the Max Separation, then the Stitch will be applied without regard to which option is selected. The stitch is applied at the point between 2 corners or the point between the corner and the top of the surface edge.

Selecting Closest Point will stitch the corner to the point of the closest edge.

Selecting Closest Knot will stitch the corner to the knot of the closest edge.

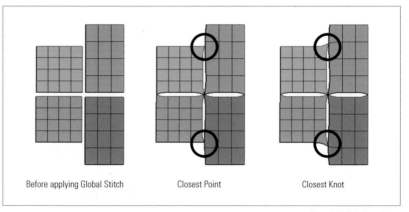

Before applying Global Stitch   Closest Point   Closest Knot

Figure 4-74 Selecting a Corner

2. Stitch Edge

The Stitch Edge option determines the stitch placement of an adjacent edge. If the length of the edge is within the Max Separation range, then the stitch will be applied without regard to which option is selected.

Closest Point ignores the Parameter value between the edges and stitches it to the closes point. It is possible to have a mismatching number of patches for inaccurate stitching. Selecting Equal Params will stitch the edge to the point on top of the surface edge with the same parameters while ignoring the number of Spans. In order to obtain the best result using this stitching method, there must be the same number of UVs, Spans, and Knots between each surface edge.

Turning this option off will deactivate it.

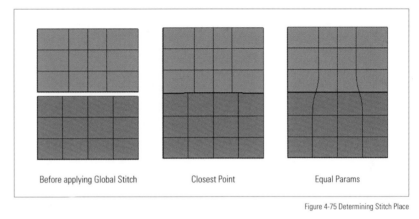

| Before applying Global Stitch | Closest Point | Equal Params |

Figure 4-75 Determining Stitch Place

3. Stitch Smoothness

Selecting Tangents, the isoparms will bend in order for the intersections of the stitch edges to cross at right angles.

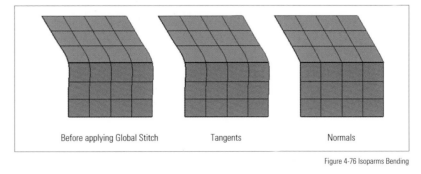

| Before applying Global Stitch | Tangents | Normals |

Figure 4-76 Isoparms Bending

This results in the greatest continuity between surfaces. Selecting Normal will not cause the isoparms to cross at right angles, but a smooth stitching will occur on the surface. Turning off this option deactivates it causing the surfaces to attach in an abnormal fashion.

4. Stitch Partial Edges

Turning this option on will cause all of the areas between the edges within the Max Separation length to be stitched. Turning this option off will only apply the Stitch to the edges between surfaces if they are within the Max Separation length. If the edges are not within this range and this option is turned off, then only the points within this range will be stitched. Because this option takes a lot of time, I recommend that it not be turned on unless absolutely necessary.

5. Max Separation

Max Separation refers to the maximum length between surface edges or corners that can be stitched. If you will not be applying the stitch, then this value can be raised. However, if the surface is abnormally stitched and twists, then simply lower this value.

6. Modification Resistance

This option determines how much the surface CV will maintain its position when the surfaces are stitched. Although raising this value will prevent the surface from rippling and wrinkling, a value that is unnecessarily high will prevent satisfactory stitching of the surface.

7. Sampling Density

This option determines the amount of sampling that will take place on top of the edge as the stitch is in progress. As the Sampling Density is increased, the stitch will occur properly, but it will take longer to calculate the stitch time. In the beginning, set this value to 1, and then if the stitch does not occur properly, try raising this value slowly. In most cases, you will not need to exceed a value of 5.

We have now concluded our look at the basic menus for NURBS modeling. Although some other menus may come in handy to fit your individual needs, this review of the NURBS modeling menus has been fairly comprehensive. We will now begin NURBS modeling.

2. ONE PATCH MODELING

The simplest and easiest to control method of NURBS character modeling is the One Patch Modeling method.

It is much easier to work with than the Multi-Patch modeling method we will look at later, and because the face is made up of one surface, it is also easier to animate.

However, it does have its share of disadvantages. One Patch modeling cannot produce accurate and precise models. Many unnecessary isoparms must be added to create detail, which can interfere with handling the data and the model.

In this example, we will first create a simple character using One Patch modeling and then consider what methods are available to overcome the problems we face.

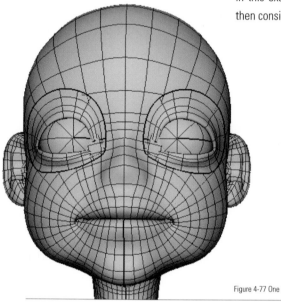

Figure 4-77 One Patch Modeling

2-1. FACE MODELING

step 1 First, draw 3 curves that will serve as the base of the model. As shown in Figure 4-78, Curves 1 and 3 are used to make the profiles of the face in Side View and Curve 2 is used to add dimension in Front View.

This curve is the one that flows from the mouth, down the cheek to the neck. This curve does not need to be perfect in the beginning because we will need to make modifications here and there in order to make the surface.

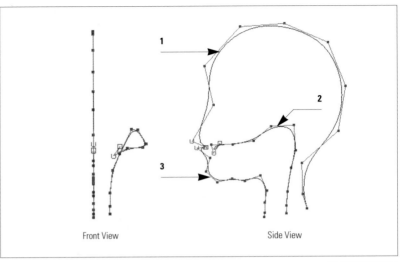

Front View   Side View

Figure 4-78 Draw Curve

When drawing the curve in the beginning, just make sure that it looks like the curve in the figure above. Also, after drawing the curve, we must apply Rebuild Curve in order to make the Span values of the curve the same.

The figure above shows the result after applying Rebuild Curve.

To rebuild the curve, first, select all 3 curves and then select [Modeling > Edit Curves > Rebuild Curves ▢] to open the Options window. As shown in Figure 4-79, set the Rebuild Type to Uniform, the Parameter Range to 0 to # Span, and the Number of Spans to 9 before clicking the Rebuild button at the bottom of the Options window.

Figure 4-79 Options Window

step 2 After selecting Curves 1, 2, and 3, in that order, as shown in Figure 4-78, select [Modeling > Surface > Loft]. This will create the Loft Surface shown in Figure 4-80. Select and delete the 3 curves. Select the surface and make a mirror copy in Instance, making sure that the model is symmetrical. Trim the shape by adjusting the CVs as shown in Figure 4-81.

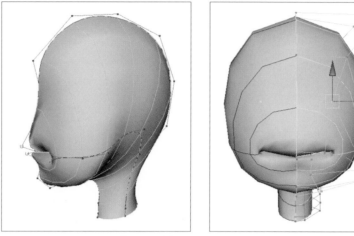

Figure 4-80 Loft Surface   Figure 4-81 Duplicate Instance

step 3 Select the surface, click the RMB and then select Isoparm from the Marking Menu. After selecting the isoparm indicated in the figure below, select [Modeling > Edit Surfaces > Insert Isoparm] to add a new isoparm (see Figure 4-82). After adding the isoparm, adjust the CVs as shown to trim the shape.

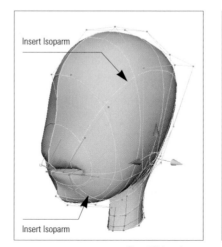

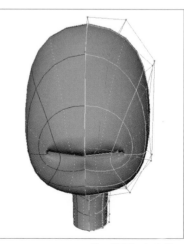

Figure 4-82 Insert Isoparm   Figure 4-83 Trimming the Shape

After roughly trimming the shape, select the isoparm, as shown in Figure 4-83, and select [Modeling > Edit Surfaces > Insert Isoparm] to add a new isoparm. After adding the isoparm, add some more detail.

In the same way, continue to add isoparms and adjust the CVs to add detail.

Figure 4-84 shows a roughly detailed shape. Isoparms are only added when the current CVs are not enough to add more detail. Adding too many isoparms in the beginning will only complicate your work.

Figure 4-85 shows the completed model.

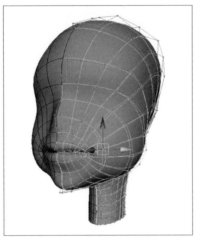
Figure 4-84 Trimming the Shape

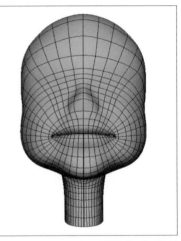
Figure 4-85 The Completed Model

We have now completed trimming the overall shape.

We now have to model the eyes and the ears. The only problem is that in adding the eyes and the ears we need to add many isoparms to sufficiently model their shapes. Also, if there is a great difference in the details, especially for characters with large eyes, this method becomes difficult to use.

As we can see in Figure 4-77, this character has large eyes. In such cases, it is actually quite impossible to make the eyes by adding isoparms.

Problems with One Patch Modeling

Let's look at the following example. This character's eyes are not very big and his nose does not have a great amount of detail.

It is possible to model this type of character using One Patch modeling.

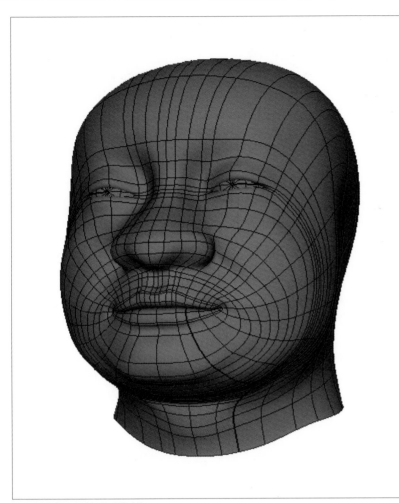

One of the biggest advantages of One Patch modeling is that we can quickly conduct Blend Shape Modeling for animation.

Multi-Patch modeling, which we will look at later, requires much more time and effort.

Now let's look at what methods we have available for effectively solving these problems. The most effective method is to model the eyes and the ears separately and then attach them later.

Figure 4-86 An Example of One Patch Modeling

2-2. MODELING THE EYES

In order to make the eyes for the character, first, make a NURBS sphere, as shown in Figure 4-87, and adjust its size and position.

Use the CV Curve Tool to make the shape of the eye as shown.

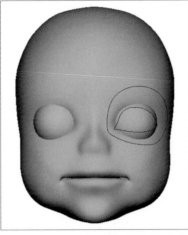

Figure 4-87 Modeling the Eye

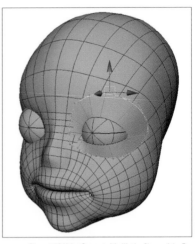

Figure 4-88 Using Curves to Modify the Shape of the Eye

Select the curve and then use [Modeling > Surface > Loft] to make the Loft Surface. Because the History is active, modifying the shape of the curve, as shown in Figure 4-88, will automatically modify the shape of the surface.

As shown in Figure 4-87, apply Rebuild Curve to the curve as necessary so that it takes on an adequate Span value. Add detail to the eye by adding isoparms as needed, as shown in Figure 4-89. After roughly shaping the eye, adjust the CVs, as shown in Figure 4-90, so that the eye is attached as closely and as naturally to the face as possible.

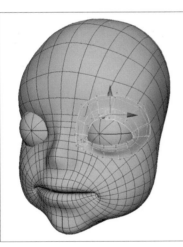

Figure 4-89 Detailing the Eye

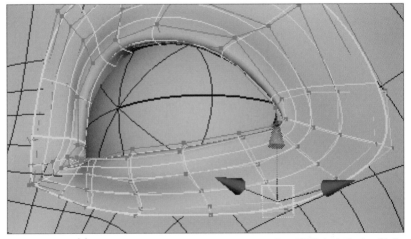

Figure 4-90 Aligning the Curvature of the Eye

2-3 MODELING THE EARS

Use NURBS Sphere to model the ears. Make a NURBS sphere and adjust its size and location as shown in Figure 4-91.

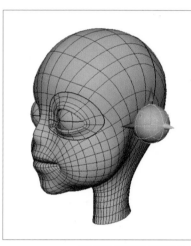

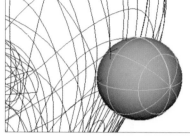

Figure 4-92 Selecting the Isoparm in the Area to Detach

After selecting the isoparm, as shown in Figure 4-92, select [Modeling > Edit NURBS > Detach Surface] to delete the inner surface.

Figure 4-91 Making the NURBS Sphere

Adjust the CV to make the rough shape shown in Figure 4-93. Then, add isoparms, as shown in Figure 4-94, to add detail to the ear.

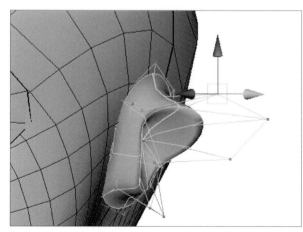

Figure 4-93 Making the Shape

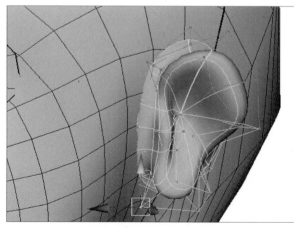

Figure 4-94 Adding Detail

Continue in this way until the ear is complete (see Figure 4-95).

We must also make sure that the ear attaches smoothly and naturally to the face, as we did for the eye.

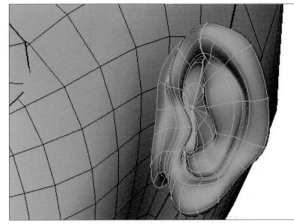

Figure 4-95 The Completed Ear

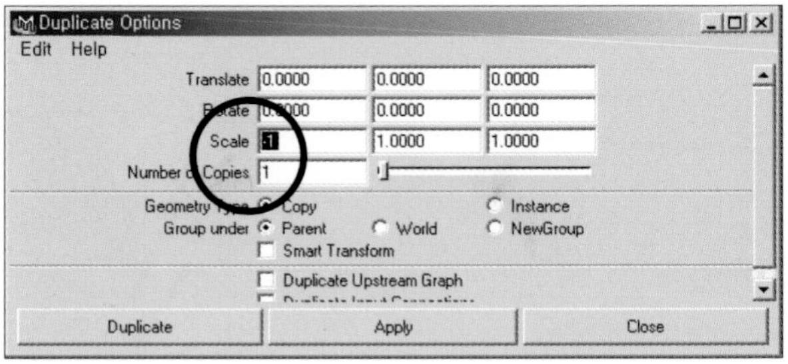

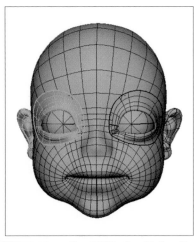

Figure 4-96 Duplicate Options Window

After making the ear and eye, select them both and then select [Edit > Group] to group them together. Select [Edit > Duplicate ▢] to open the Duplicate Options window. After selecting [Edit > Reset Setting] in this window to reset the values, enter **-1** for the Scale X Field, and then press the Duplicate button.

This will create a mirror copy of the eye and ear, as shown in Figure 4-97.

Figure 4-97 Mirror Copy of the Ear and Eye

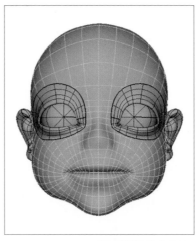

Figure 4-98 Selecting the Isoparm

Complete the modeling by selecting the surface isoparms on either side of the face, as shown in Figure 4-98. Select [Modeling > Edit NURBS > Attach Surface ☐] to open the Options window. Then, as shown in Figure 4-99, set the Attach Method to Blend, Keep Originals to Off, and then press the Attach button.

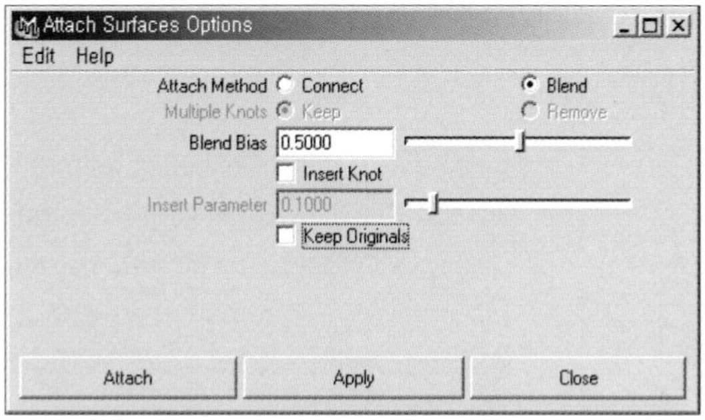

Figure 4-99 Attach Options Window

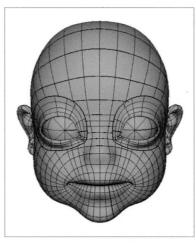

Figure 4-100 The Completed Model

After attaching, select [Modeling > Edit NURBS > Open/Close Surface] to close the surface. If the surface does not close properly, cancel this step, open the Open/Close Options window and change the Surface Direction. The figure on the left shows the final completed model.

2-4. MATCHING SURFACE CURVATURE IN MAPPING

Figure 4-101 Making the Directional Light

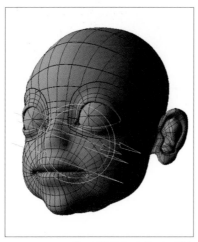

Although the model is complete, it has one big problem: The curvature between the eyes, ears and head are broken up.

To test this, select [Create > Light > Directional] to make a directional light and adjust the direction of the light as in Figure 4-101. Press the **7** key on the keyboard to convert to Light Mode when doing this.

Select [Windows > Rendering Editors > Render Global] to open the Render Globals window. As shown in Figure 4-102, set the Resolution to 640X486, the Anti-aliasing Quality to Production Quality, and then render the image.

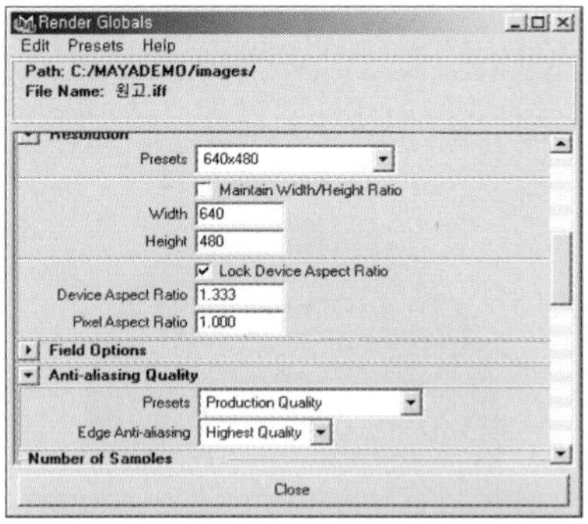

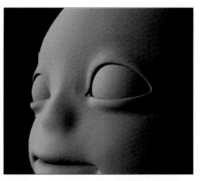

Figure 4-102 Render Global

Figure 4-103 Rendering the Image

Let's examine Figure 4-103. We can see that the curvature where the eye meets the face is broken up. It will be virtually impossible to obtain a good result in this state.

Let's use Map to fix this problem. Select [Windows > Rendering Editors > HyperShade]. (See Figure 4-104.) After making a Blinn Material and a Ramp Texture in Hypershade, link the ramp to the color and assign it to the eye.

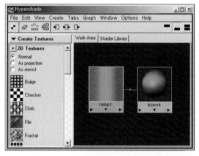

Figure 4-104 Hypershade

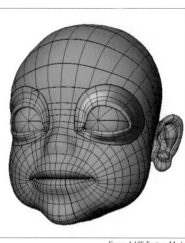

Figure 4-105 Texture Mode

Press the **6** key on the keyboard to verify the direction of the texture in Texture Mode. If, as in Figure 4-105, the direction of the ramp has not been established, open the Attribute Editor of the Ramp Texture and change the Type to U- or V-Ramp.

Adjust the ramp color and range to look like Figure 4-106.

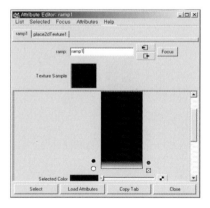

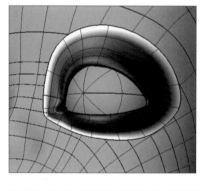

Figure 4-106 Adjusting the Color Range of the Ramp Texture

Break the connection between the ramp and the Blinn Shader color in Hypershade.

Reconnect the ramp to the Blinn Shader Transparency. Assign this Blinn Shade to the other eye. Make another Blinn Shader and assign it to the NURBS sphere made above the face and the eyeball. Render the image.

The rendered result is shown in Figure 4-107.

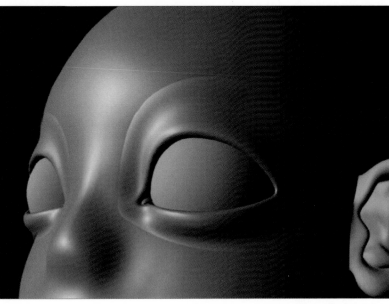

Figure 4-107 Rendering the Image

A basic Blinn Shader has a specular. This is why, even though the corners of the eyes are transparent, a specular is made and it takes on a shine. This is also why the edges are more distinct.

This problem is fixed in the following way.

Make a Reverse Utility in the Hypershader, and double-click on it to open the Attribute Editor.

Use the MMB to drag the ramp texture, which was made, over the Input to link them as shown in Figure 4-108.

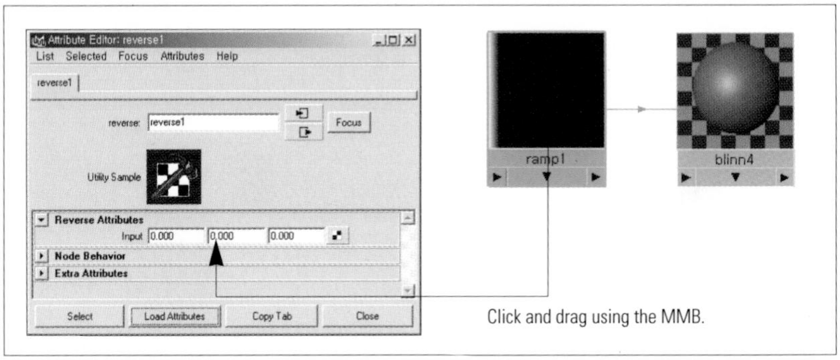

Click and drag using the MMB.

Figure 4-108 Linking the Reverse Utility to the Ramp Texture

Link the Reverse Utility to the Blinn Shader Specular

This will endow the Blinn Shader Specular with a Ramp Map. Because the Reverse Utility was used, a white specular will be made on the black portion of the ramp, but a specular will not be made on the white portion.

Because the default specular of the Blinn Shader used on the face is gray, we need to change this specular color to white.

Render the image once again.

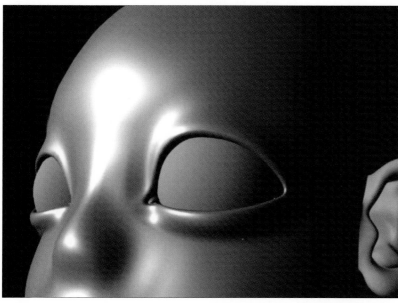

Observing the rendered image in Figure 4-109, we can see that the eyes and the ears are now smoothly connected to the face.

If the shadow of the light was used, a shadow will appear on the eyes in the form of a line at the edges.
To prevent this line from forming, first, select the eye, then open the Attribute Editor, as shown in Figure 4-110, and turn off Cast Shadow under Render State.

Figure 4-109 Rendering the Image

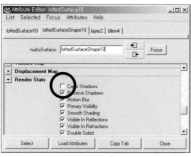

Figure 4-110 Attribute Editor

The same thing is done for the ear.

So far, we have looked at how to align surface curvatures using mapping. However, using this type of method on lifelike characters is not advised.
This is because no matter how accurately you have done this, the movement of the area where the eyes meet the face will be portrayed differently when creating expression.
However, when creating rather simple characters, this method is more effective than any other.

3. MULTI-PATCH MODELING

3-1. FACE MODELING

We have already covered One Patch modeling in the previous section. Many people, I am sure, are already familiar with the One Patch as a general form of modeling.

One Patch modeling is very effective as a basic modeling tool. In reality, if such a basic form of modeling did not exist, it would take an incredible amount of time and be very difficult to use simple patches to split a surface. I have used a variety of different methods for patch modeling in my career, and I have experienced how difficult it is to draw a random 3D curve in space and use that curve to make a surface.

Recently, I have even asked myself why it's necessary to even use patches in modeling. However, if you are going to use patches, it is very effective if you use One Patch or Subdivision Surfaces as your basic form.

First of all, it is a good idea to practice patch modeling using a very simple model.

In this example, we will use the model that we created using One Patch modeling and learn what methods there are for splitting and attaching surfaces.

Load the data that you made in the previous section, or open CD-ROM/CHARACTER/scenes/childHEAD.mb.

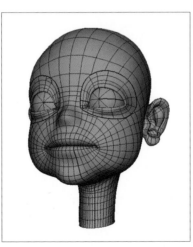

Figure 4-111 One Patch Model

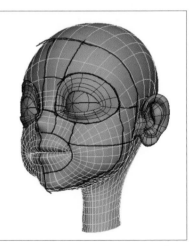

Figure 4-112 Plans for Splitting the Surface

 First, we need to plan how we are going to split the surface. This step involves deciding which patch will be divided by splitting a surface.

Because all characters have their own unique movements, we must devise this plan to fit the movements of our particular character.

Figure 4-112 shows a sketch on top of the model depicting how the surfaces will be divided.

It is a good idea to make a sketch before beginning to model or, if you are using a One Patch model, as we are doing here, to draw a sketch on top of the model to set up your plan.

step 2 In order to split the surface, we need to do the following. First, make a duplicate of the face surface and then press Ctrl+H to hide the duplicated surface. Select the surface, click the RMB, and then select Isoparm from the Marking Menu so that we can select the isoparms as shown. Divide the selected surfaces using [Modeling > Edit NURBS > Detach Surface]. Then, select the isoparms from left to right in the figure shown below to detach the surfaces.

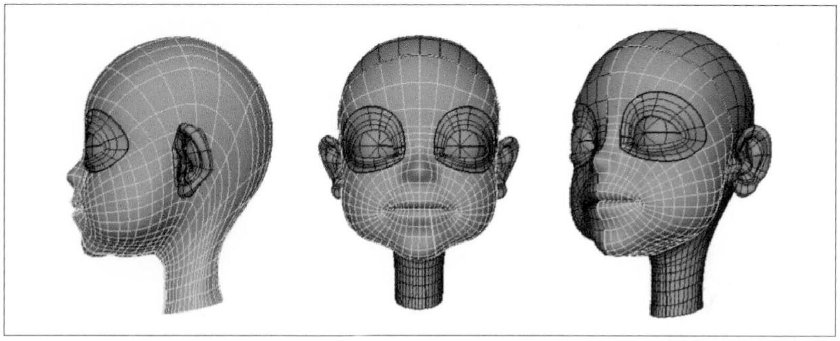

Figure 4-113 Detaching the Selected Isoparms

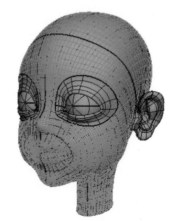

Figure 4-114 Using Make Live

step 3 Press Ctrl+Shift+H to display the duplicate surfa ce, which was hidden in the previous step. Select ⟨c⟩ from the Status Line. The selected surface will change, as shown in Figure 4-114. Now, all we have do is draw a curve directly on this surface to make a Curve on Surface.

Make Live allows us to draw a curve directly on this surface. By drawing the 3D curve, which is somewhat difficult to work with, directly on the surface, we can make our work much easier.

We duplicated a surface at random earlier is so that we can observe its shape in Shading Mode when the Wireframe is made after applying Make Live.

step 4 Now, according to our plan, we will draw the Curve on Surface. Figure 4-115 illustrates the areas that will be split and the curve that we drew. These are the areas that will make up the actual surface. Select the isoparms on the outer edges of the surface we detached at the beginning, and select [Modeling > Edit Curves > Duplicate Surface Curves] to make the curve and draw the remaining divided surfaces on the inside. Exit from Make Live Mode by pressing ⟨ 🗘 ⟩ again. We have divided the eyes and the mouth for convenience, but, in actuality, we could just use the model we made earlier instead of dividing them.

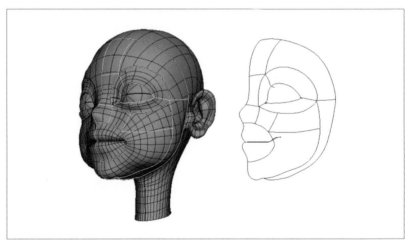

Figure 4-115 3D Curve Made Using Curve on Surface

There are certain things we need to be careful of when using Make Live to make a curve or when selecting isoparms and using Duplicate Surface Curves.

First of all, when using Make Live to make a curve, the curve is drawn directly on the surface (Curve on Surface) and, therefore, has a direct effect on the surface. When we adjust the surface, the curve will also be adjusted. To prevent this from happening, use [Modeling > Edit Curves > Duplicate Surface Curves] to duplicate the Curve on Surface as a separate, 3D curve. Furthermore, if the Curve on Surface is affected by the History, the duplicated curve will also be affected. Therefore, we must delete the history of the duplicated curve by selecting [Edit > Delete by Type > History].

Reviewing the steps once again, we first select the Curve on Surface, apply [Edit Curve > Duplicate Surface Curves] to duplicate the curve on surface, and then select [Edit > Delete by Type > History] to delete the history.

We must also delete the history for curves that are duplicated by selecting the isoparms. As a final step, the curve on the surface must be deleted in its entirety.

The difficult step lies in distinguishing between the independent curve and the curve on surface because the curves overlap. The overlap makes it difficult to distinguish and select the curves. In such cases, we use the Component Mask. First of all, turn off the Component Mask by clicking ⊘ to prevent the surface from being selected, and then click the RMB on the curve icon, as shown below, to select the desired menu. In Figure 4-116, Curve On Surface will not be selected, and in Figure 4-117, NURBS Curve will not be selected.

Figure 4-116 Curves On Surface: OFF   Figure 4-117 NURBS Curve: OFF

step 5 We will now make the surface that will be placed inside each divided region. How proficient you are at this will determine how fast this step is completed. This method is just the one that I happen to use frequently. First, let's observe Figure 4-118. This figure illustrates an example of a curve that was drawn to make the nose and cheek. The curve is drawn using the method described in Step 4. These curves show the position of the isoparms in the surface that will be made. Therefore, we must take this into consideration when first drawing the curve. We must decide how many isoparms the respective surface will have, and we must maintain adequate spacing between the curves because they reflect the spacing between the isoparms.

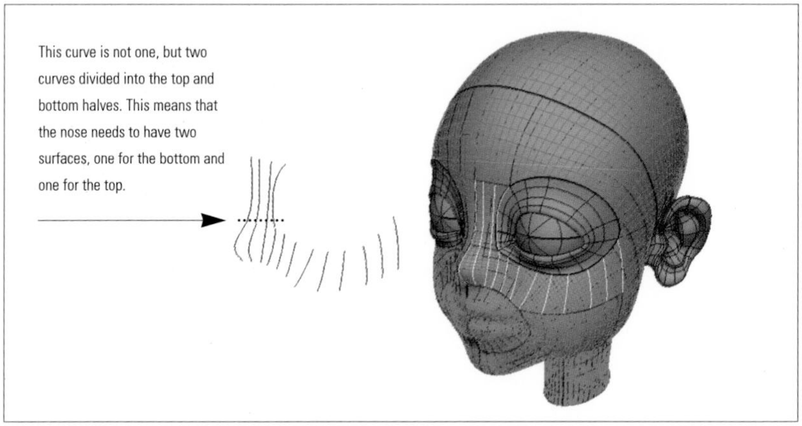

This curve is not one, but two curves divided into the top and bottom halves. This means that the nose needs to have two surfaces, one for the bottom and one for the top.

Figure 4-118 Drawing a New Curve On Surface in the Divided Region

Select the curve and use Loft to make the surface. The figure below illustrates the lofting process.

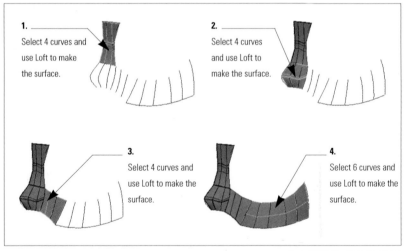

1.
Select 4 curves and use Loft to make the surface.

2.
Select 4 curves and use Loft to make the surface.

3.
Select 4 curves and use Loft to make the surface.

4.
Select 6 curves and use Loft to make the surface.

Figure 4-119 Lofting Each of the Curves

In this way, draw a Curve On Surface for the remaining areas, convert it into a NURBS curve, and then use Loft to make the surface. It is okay to ignore the general isoparm arrangement. We can ignore the isoparm arrangement now because they will be modified again through Rebuild Surface.

When lofting the curve, you may find it necessary to use Rebuild Curve. Review the section "1. Understanding the Basic Menu," and decide which method will be most effective.

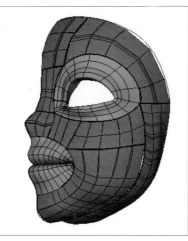

Figure 4-120 The Lofted Surface

step 6 We now have to arrange the surfaces we made using Rebuild. To stitch the surfaces in the end, the Span and Parameter Range between the surfaces must be in accord. One thing we need to be mindful of in this process is the link between the U and V surfaces. While some surfaces have 3 spans in both the U- and V-directions, some have 3 spans in the U-direction and 5 spans in the V-direction.

Let's take a look at the Rebuild process. First of all, delete all of the curves that we made and delete the history of each surface by selecting [Edit > Delete by Type > History]. Select the surface to rebuild and open the Attribute Editor.

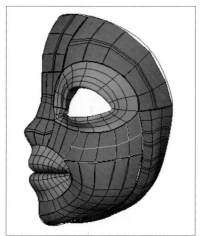

Figure 4-121 Selecting the Surface to Rebuild

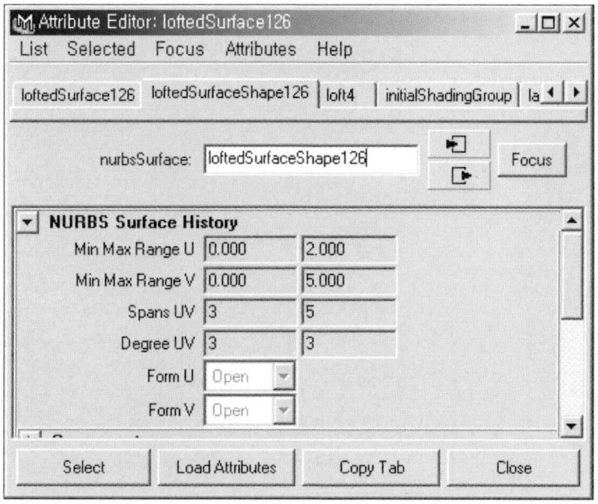

Figure 4-122 Attribute Editor

The values for the Min Max Range U and V and the Span U and V used in Figures 4-121 and 4-122 can be different, depending on the situation.

The surface selected in Figure 4-121 has 3 and 5 span values in the U- and V-directions, respectively, as shown in the Attribute Editor in Figure 4-122. We can also see that this Span value is different from the Min, Max Range value.

In order to maintain the 3 and 5 span values in the U- and V-directions and to have the Min, Max Range value coincide with this, we need to use Rebuild Surface.

Select [Modeling > Edit NURBS > Rebuild Surface ▢] while the surface is selected to open the Options window. In the window, set the Rebuild Type to Uniform, the Parameter Range to 0 to # Spans, and the Number of Spans U and V to 3 and 5, respectively, as shown in Figure 4-123. Keep the Degree U and V at 3 Cubic, turn off Keep Original, and set the Output, Geometry to Nurbs before clicking the Rebuild button.

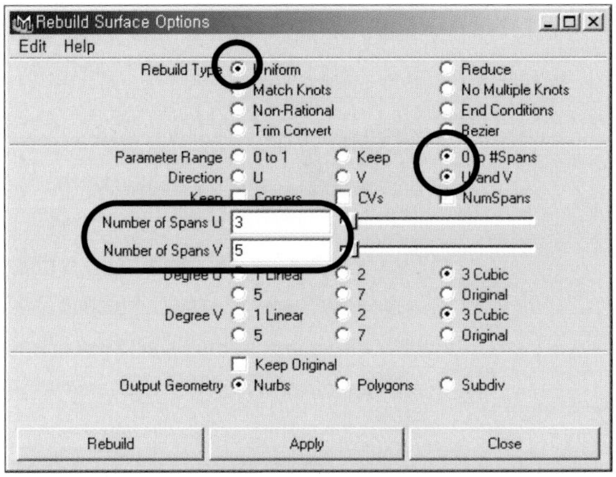

Figure 4-123 Rebuild Surface Options Window

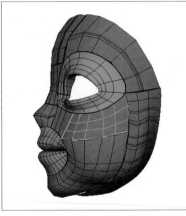

Figure 4-124 Rebuilt Surface

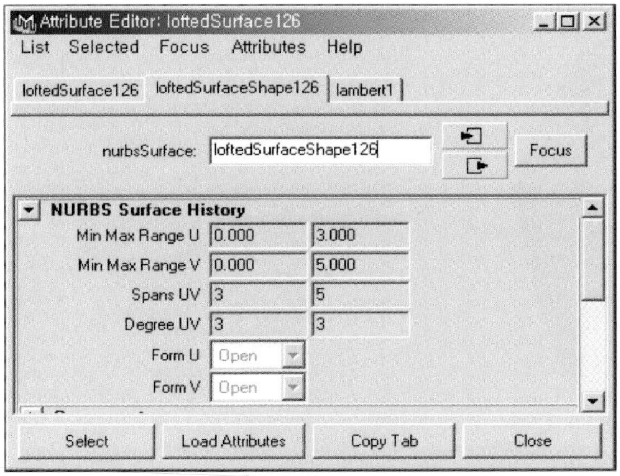

Figure 4-125 Attribute Editor

NURBS MODELING

As shown in Figure 4-124, the selected surface will be rebuilt according to the specifications made in the Options window. We can verify this by opening the Attribute Editor, shown in Figure 4-125.

Now we have to rebuild all the surfaces, excluding the eye and mouth, in the same way. As mentioned before, when rebuilding the surfaces, make sure to match the Span and Parameter Range values of the U- and V-directions with that of the adjacent surface. Figure 4-126 shows how the selected surface is connected to its adjacent surface and how it is rebuilt.

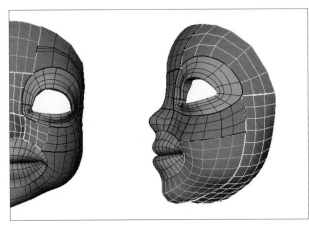

Figure 4-126 Rebuilt Surface

step 7 Let's look at the eye and the mouth. In this case, we will use the data from the existing model.

However, this can create a problem in terms of the modeling method used for this model in the beginning. Generally, these models were made by drawing the curve using the CV Curve Tool and then using Insert Isoparm to add isoparms. As follows, when we open the Attribute Editor for these surfaces, we can see, as in Figure 4-127, that the Min Max Range U and V values are different. If we rebuild the surface in this state, the arrangement of the isoparms will appear very different, as we can see in Figure 4-128.

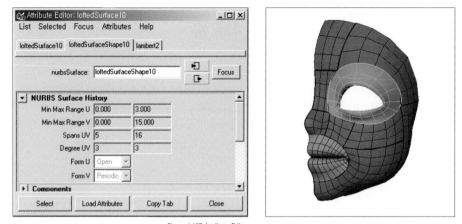

Figure 4-127 Attribute Editor

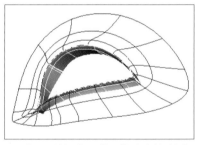

Figure 4-128 Rebuilding the Eye

In order to prevent this from happening and to maintain the isoparm arrangement in the eye, we must alternate between using Detach and Attach. First of all, detach the eye into 3 surfaces, as shown in Figure 4-129. The surfaces have been colored using a Shader for easy distinction. Make sure to detach the surface in accord with the split side of the adjacent surface.

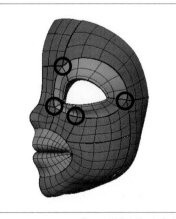

Figure 4-130 Detailing and Detaching the Inside of the Eye

Figure 4-129 Detaching the Surface

Detach each of the surfaces on the inside of the eye as shown in Figure 4-130.

We will now rebuild each of these surfaces by matching them to the Span value of the adjacent surfaces, as we have done up until now. When rebuilding the surfaces in this way, we can see, as in Figure 4-131, that the initial arrangement of the isoparms is maintained.

Attach only the surfaces on the inside of
the eye as shown in Figure 4-130. To
attach, open the Options window, set the
Attach Method to Blend, turn off the Keep
Originals option, and set everything else to
the default setting. (See Figure 4-131.)

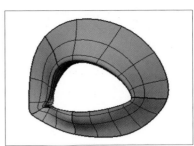

Figure 4-131 Rebuilt Surface

Do the same thing for the mouth. First, detach each of the surfaces where they connect
and then rebuild them so that they have an adequate Span value.

Figure 4-132 illustrates the surface divisions of the mouth, and Figure 4-133 illustrates
how each of these surfaces were rebuilt.

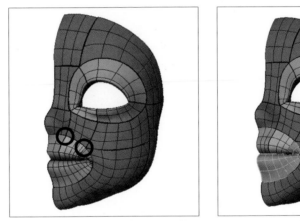

Figure 4-132 Detaching the Mouth   Figure 4-133 Rebuilding the Surface

step 8   Now, we will use Stitch to stitch these surfaces together. To effectively
stitch these surfaces together, we need to alternate between using the
Stitch Edge Tool and the Global Stitch Tool. First, use the Stitch Edge Tool to stitch each
of the surfaces together and then, finish up with the Global Stitch Tool.

However, these 2 tools are not enough to smoothly link the surfaces together. We need
to adjust the CVs at certain points while we stitch. First, select [Modeling > Edit NURBS >
Stitch > Stitch Edge Tool], then select the isoparms on the one of the two surfaces that
will be stitched, and then stitch the isoparms as shown in Figure 4-134.

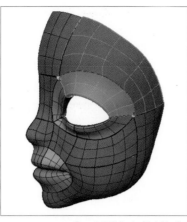

Figure 4-134 Using the Stitch Edge Tool

We use the Stitch Edge Tool with its default settings. When the default settings are used, the isoparm selected first will be stitched to the isoparm selected second. Therefore, select the isoparm on the side that is relatively well arranged. Use this method to stitch all the surfaces together. Although we usually use the Global Stitch Tool, we do an initial stitch in this way for a more effective result. Figure 4-135 illustrates the stitch process.

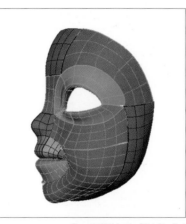

Figure 4-135 Using the Stitch Edge Tool

Figure 4-136 illustrates the stitch process for surfaces with different spans. When the surfaces to stitch have different spans, first select the edge on the surface with the greater number of spans before selecting the surface edge with the lesser number of spans, and then stitch the edges together as shown in Figure 4-136. When the stitch is done this way, because the surface with fewer spans had 3 spans, it will only be stitched to 3 of the spans on the surface with more spans.

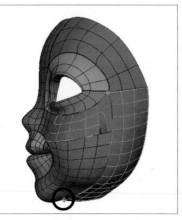

Figure 4-136 Applying the Stitch Edge Tool

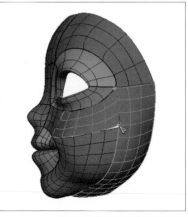

Figure 4-137 Adjusting the Stitching Domain

In order to adjust the stitching domain, click the MMB on the point indicated in Figure 4-136, press the V key on the keyboard to apply the Point Snap, and then position the points in Figure 4-137 as shown.

Use the same method to stitch the surfaces on the bottom. Once all the surfaces have been stitched using the Stitch Edge Tool, we will have to fix the areas that are twisted. Fix the surfaces by modifying the CVs as shown in Figure 4-138.

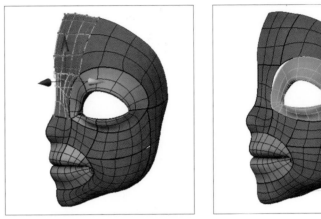

Figure 4-138 Modifying the Surfaces by Adjusting the CV   Figure 4-139 Attach Surface

After modifying the CVs, we need to attach the loose surfaces of the eye and mouth before using the Global Stitch Tool. This is done because during the final animation step, control is easier if the surfaces are attached. Figure 4-139 shows the final attachment of the loose surfaces. For the eye, close the surface using Open/Close Surface after attaching each surface.

Now, select the entire surface, and then select [Modeing > Edit NURBS > Stitch > Global Stitch ◨] to open the Options window. Make the configurations in the Option window as shown in Figure 4-140. Refer to "1. Understanding the Basic Menu" for more information on each of the options.

Stitch all the selected surfaces, as shown in Figure 4-140. It is also possible for some of the CVs to be twisted in this case. After observing each of the CV arrangements in Component Mode, manually smooth the twists and then apply Global Stitch again. Repeating this step twice will give you a more perfect model. When you adjust the CVs, deleting the history ([Edit > Delete by Type > History]) will increase your work speed.

After completing this step, select all the surfaces and then group together the selected surfaces using [Edit > Group]. Then, apply [Edit > Duplicate] to duplicate the group and enter **-1** for the Scale X field in the Channel Box to make the mirror copy.

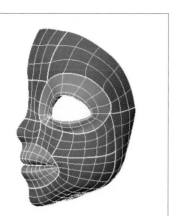

Figure 4-141 Global Stitch

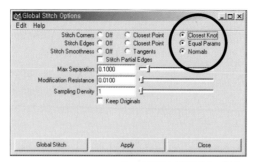

Figure 4-140 Global Stitch Options Window

Finally, select all the surfaces and apply Global Stitch.

Figure 4-142 Grouping All the Surfaces

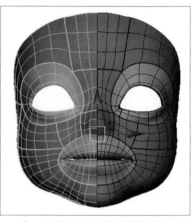

Figure 4-143 Completing the Other Half Using Mirror Copy

Now, display all of the hidden surfaces.
All of the surfaces in Figure 4-144, excluding the head and ear, were created using Multi-Patch.
The surfaces of the ear and the other portions of the head can be split and divided using Multi-Patch as well.

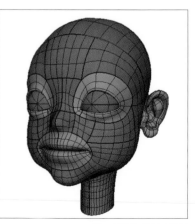

Figure 4-144 The Finished Model

Figure 4-145 shows the final division of all the portions of the head using Multi-Patch. Refer to this diagram as you use Multi-Patch to model the rest of the head. Because I have remained faithful to the basic menus in my explanations, you should have no trouble completing the rest of the head on your own. The face data, made using Patch, is saved as CD-ROM/CHARACTER/scenes/ChildPATCH.mb.

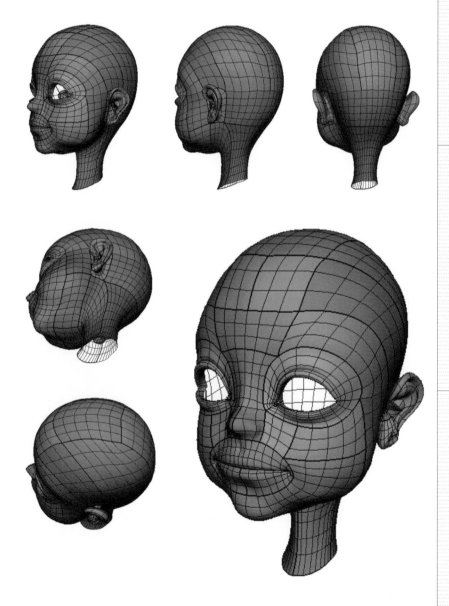

Figure 4-145 The Patch Structure of the Head

3-2. BODY MODELING

The body is comparatively simpler to create than the head or any other part. This section will look at 2 examples of body modeling.

The first example will look at modeling clothes for the face we made in the previous section, and the second example will be the body of a very muscular man. Through these examples, you will come to understand how Multi-Patch modeling is used for modeling clothes and muscles.

First, we will look at how to model clothes for the face we made. Since you should already be well versed in Multi-Patch modeling by now, I will forego explaining the options and concentrate, instead, on effective surface slicing.

1. Modeling Shirts

Let's first look at how to model a shirt for the character. The completed shirt can be seen in Figure 4-146. We will use a simple NURBS Primitive Object for the general shape and then cut the shape of the shirt out of it.

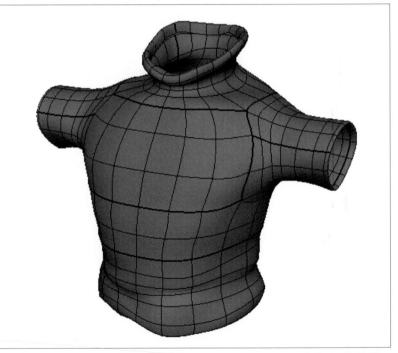

Figure 4-146 The Complete Modeled Shape

step 1 First, select [Create > NURBS Primitive > Cylinder] to make a NURBS Cylinder. Adjust the Span value and the Scale for the Cylinder in the Channel Box, as shown here.

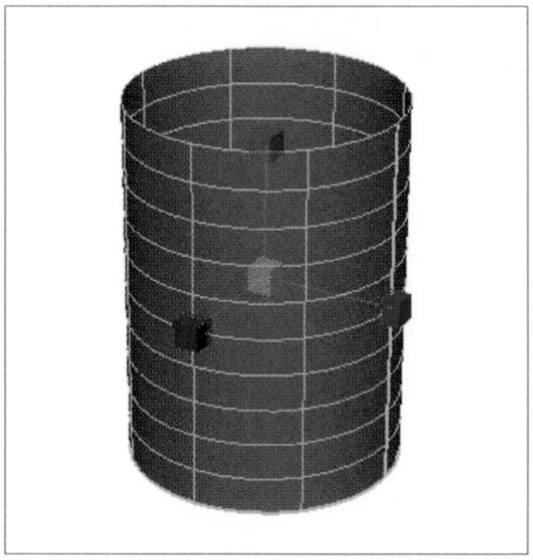

Figure 4-147 Adjusting the Span Value and Scale

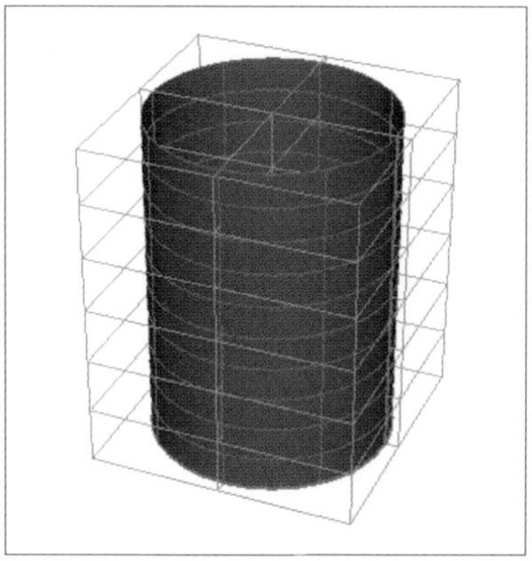

Figure 4-148 Adding a Lattice

Select the NURBS Cylinder and select [Animation > Deform > Lattice] to make a lattice. In the Channel Box, set the S, T, and U Division values of the lattice to 3, 7 and 3, respectively.

step 2 Adjust the points of the lattice to shape the cylinder. Worry about maintaining a big lump rather than about trying to create a detailed shape. After making the lump, select the NURBS surface and select [Edit > Delete by Type > History] to delete the lattice.

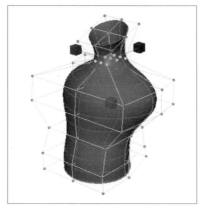

Figure 4-149 Adjusting the Lattice Point

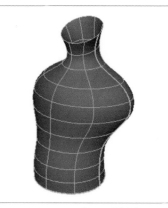

Figure 4-150 Deleting the Lattice

step 3 Add detail by adjusting the CVs of the NURBS surface. Add isoparms as needed to add further details, such as wrinkles in the clothes.

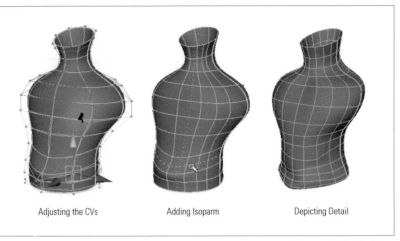

Adjusting the CVs   Adding Isoparm   Depicting Detail

Figure 4-151 The Modeling Process

step 4 Make a NURBS Cylinder and adjust its position and shape to make the sleeves of the shirt. After adjusting the Span value in the Channel Box, adjust the CVs to make the shape.

Once the sleeve has been shaped, use Mirror Copy to make the other sleeve.

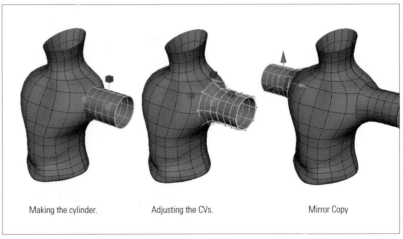

Making the cylinder.   Adjusting the CVs.   Mirror Copy

Figure 4-152 The Modeling Process

step 5 Now, in order to use Multi-Patch modeling, use Detach Surface to adequately detach the surfaces. As shown in Figure 4-153, select the surface isoparms in the front and back of the shirt and select [Modeling > Edit NURBS > Detach Surface] to detach.

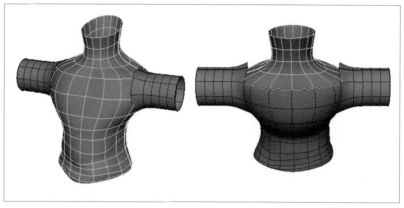

Figure 4-153 Selecting the Isoparms

Figure 4-154 color-codes the detached surfaces so you can easily discern them. Pay close attention to how the surfaces were detached.

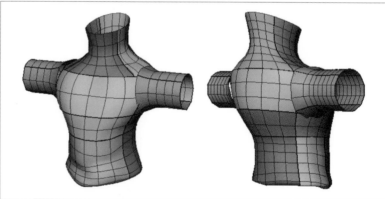

Figure 4-154 Detach

step 6 In order to stitch these surfaces together, we need to rebuild the surfaces using Rebuild Surface. Because the rebuilding process is the same as for the face, I will not explain the options here.

As we can see in the following illustration, the surface has been rebuilt so that each surface can have the same Span value and can be linked in the direction of the diagram.

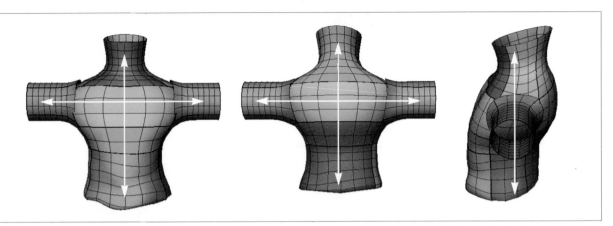

Figure 4-155 The Direction in Which the Surfaces Must Have the Same Span Value

After rebuilding the surfaces, delete the surfaces where the sleeves will be placed.

step 7 Select [Modeling > Edit NURBS > Stitch Edge Tool] to stitch together only the area where the sleeves meet the shirt. First, select the isoparms of the shirt and then the isoparms of the shirt to stitch.

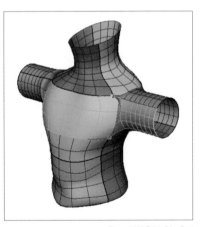

Figure 4-156 Stitch Edge Tool

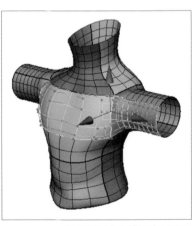

Figure 4-157 Adjusting CVs in Certain Areas

After stitching both sleeves, select all the surfaces and select [Edit > Delete by Type > History] to delete the history. Adjust the CVs in the areas where the stitching does not appear natural.

step 8 Before we can proceed, we must add some detail to the neckline of the shirt.

Adding detail to the neckline now, with the surfaces detached, would be very difficult to do. Therefore, we need to attach all the surfaces, add detail, and then detach the surfaces, returning them to their original state.

First, as shown in Figure 4-158, use Attach and Open/Close Surface to link the surfaces in the neck and then adjust the CVs to add detail.

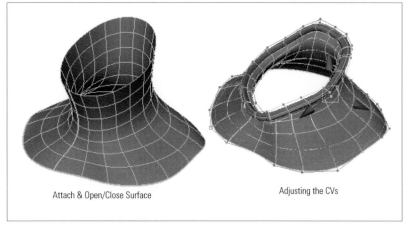

Attach & Open/Close Surface

Adjusting the CVs

Figure 4-158 Depicting Detail in the Neckline of the Shirt

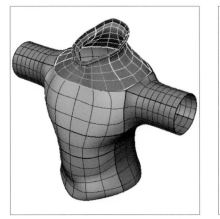

Figure 4-159 Detach Surface

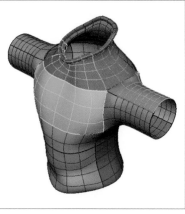

Figure 4-160 Stitch Edge Tool

As shown in Figure 4-159, detach the surfaces again. You may find that you need to use Rebuild Surface again. Use the Stitch Edge Tool to stitch the detached surfaces to the surfaces of the shirt and sleeves.

After all the surfaces have been stitched, delete the history.

step 9 At this point, select all the surfaces and apply [Modeling > Edit Surfaces > Stitch > Global Stitch]. The Global Stitch options should be configured the same as they were for the face. Although there may be differences depending on the modeling method used, generally the Global Stitch is executed as shown in Figure 4-162.

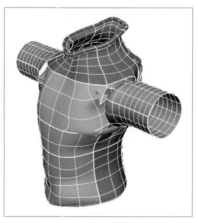

Figure 4-161 Incorrect Global Stitch

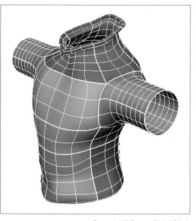

Figure 4-162 Correct Global Stitch

If the Global Stitch is incorrectly applied, as in Figure 4-161, open the Global Stitch Options window, turn off Stitch Partial Edge and then apply the Global Stitch again. If the edges do not attach neatly after applying the Global Stitch, raise the Max Separation value in the Channel Box, as shown in Figure 4-163.

Complete the shirt by adding detail to the sleeves and other parts of the shirt.

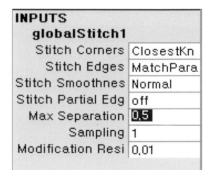

INPUTS	
globalStitch1	
Stitch Corners	ClosestKn
Stitch Edges	MatchPara
Stitch Smoothnes	Normal
Stitch Partial Edg	off
Max Separation	**0.5**
Sampling	1
Modification Resi	0.01

Figure 4-163 Channel Box

2. Modeling Pants

A basic method was used here to make the pants. Instead of using patch-style modeling by dividing many surfaces, it is more effective to model the pants by hiding awkward regions.

step 1 It is best to model the pants using NURBS Primitive.
Select [Create > NURBS Primitives > Cylinder] to make a NURBS cylinder and adjust the size as shown in Figure 4-164. Then, in the Channel Box, set the Span value to around 7.

Figure 4-164 NURBS Cylinder

step 2 Select the cylinder and select [Animation > Deform > Create Lattice] to make a lattice. In the Channel Box, set the S, T, and U Division values to 3, 5, and 3, respectively. Adjust the lattice point to make an overall, large shape.

Figure 4-165 Create Lattice

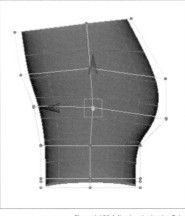

Figure 4-166 Adjusting the Lattice Point

After creating a general lump, select the cylinder and select [Edit > Delete by Type > History] to delete the lattice.

step 3 Adjust some of the CVs to modify the shape. Adjust the CVs until you get the shape shown in Figure 4-167. This shape will create a natural folding of the surfaces during the animation. After the general shape is made, select the center isoparm on the inside of the pants, as shown in Figure 4-168, and select [Modeling > Edit NURBS > Detach Surface] to detach.

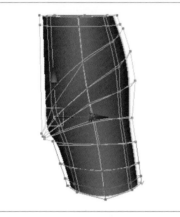

Figure 4-167 Trimming the Shape

Figure 4-168 Selecting the Isoparm to Detach

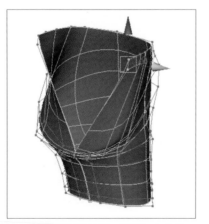

Figure 4-169 Trimming the Shape

Figure 4-170 Adding Isoparms

step 4
As shown in Figure 4-169, move the CVs to trim the waist and the overall shape. Add isoparms as necessary (see Figure 4-170) to add detail.

Continue to model the pants by moving the CVs to trim the shape and by adding isoparms to add greater detail.

Figure 4-171 shows the completed model. Make a mirror copy to make the other side of the pants and create the folds in the pant legs by adding another cylinder and trimming the shape. It is a good idea to make the wrinkles on the pant legs different on each side for a more natural look.

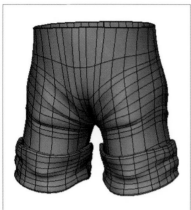
Figure 4-171 The Completed Model of the Pants

3. Muscle Man

In addition to the character we are making, we will look at how to create the body shape of a muscular man.

The file for this example is saved as MuscleBASIC.mb in the supplementary CD-ROM.

Open CD-ROM/CHARACTER/scenes/MuscleBASIC.mb.

This model was made using the Polygon Modeling Source from ViewPoint. Basically, this model was made by using a NURBS cylinder to adjust the CVs. As we can tell by looking at the model, the body was constructed from 3 cylinders (to make the body, arms and legs) and then, Mirror Copy was applied to make the other side.

If you want to work quickly and easily in Multi-Patch modeling, you must make a quick and easy basic shape. As we mentioned before, this will also result in the most accurate shape. This basic shape can be made using NURBS or by using subdivision surfaces and then converting to Polygon. Figure 4-172 shows the arrangement of the isoparms to create the overall flow of muscles in the body. Modeling by following the flow of the muscles will result in a much more natural animation later.

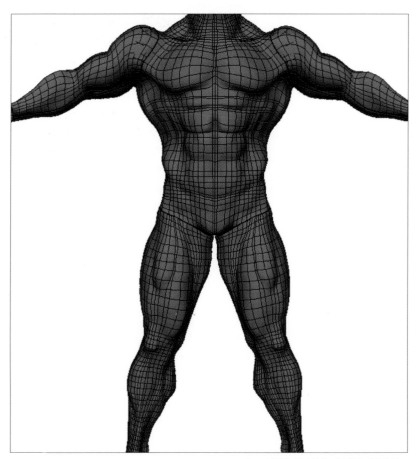

Figure 4-172 The Model before it is Divided into Patches

Up until now, we have looked at how to divide surfaces and use Rebuild and Stitch to complete the face and clothes of a simple character.

In this example, instead of detailed explanations, we will observe how the surfaces have been divided for animation. We will also observe what effect incorrect surface divisions will have on animation. The model in this example is not very detailed. If we were to patch model each of the muscles and its movements, the patch structure would be greater and more complex than it is here. If that were the case, we cannot even begin to fathom the time that we would need to devote to setting up the animation. The example here is for the purposes of a simple animation and the setup is far from perfect.

Keep in mind that the example here is for an animation that will provide minimum movement while maintaining the shape.

Although the trend these days is to use Subdivision Surface rather than Multi-Patch modeling, there are times when Multi-Patch is more useful. It is a good idea to have an understanding of a variety of different modeling methods so that you can apply the most effective one to your project.

Inappropriate Patch Structure

While finishing this model and beginning the setup for the animation, I encountered a serious problem. The animation setup became very difficult due to the surface splitting and an abnormal alteration occurred in the skin.

Let's look at Figure 4-173. The region indicated in the figure is the area where the arm meets the body. This is a very bad structure. This area is where a lot of arm movements take place. In this case, the tangents of each connection do not fit properly leading to unexpected results and an abnormal alteration.

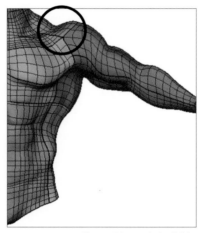

Figure 4-173 Incorrect Surface Splitting

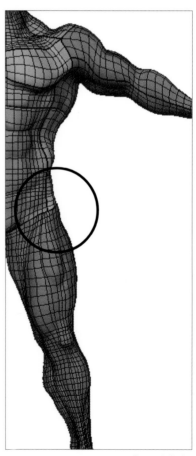

As much as possible, we must refrain from splitting surfaces in areas where there is a lot of movement. Even if you decide to divide the surfaces, having 5 isoparms, as in Figure 4-173, makes it difficult to maintain the tangent.

Figure 4-174 The Leg

The same holds true for the leg. Figure 4-174 shows an example of the leg. In the current state, the leg is the area with the most movement. When using Rigid Bind for character setup, we insert a lattice into the body or other such area for indirect binding. Although it will not be that pronounced here, it is still very difficult to maintain the tangent in areas where there is a lot of movement.

We must fully understand these circumstances and keep them in mind so that the animation setup will proceed easily and the animation itself will appear more natural. Therefore, refrain from dividing surfaces in joints, where there is a lot of movement, and instead, divide surfaces in areas with little or no movement.

Modified Patch Structure

Figure 4-175 shows the modified patch structure. As we can tell by looking at the figure, the arm was made to cross over into the chest region, where there is little movement, and the legs were linked to the waist.

In this type of modeling, a portion of the arm is included in the lattice to easily control the body. Therefore, even if the arm moves a lot, the shoulders will move naturally along without bursting at the seams.

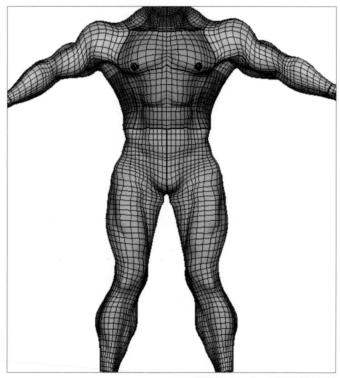

Figure 4-175 Modified Model

Figure 4-176 shows the actual binding.

Observe closely the change that takes place in the area where the arm meets the shoulder. Because some of the arm CVs are included in the lattice, the tangent is maintained for natural movement.

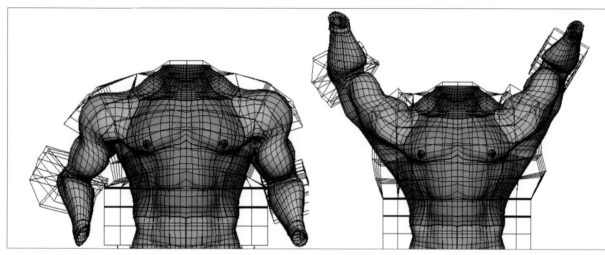

Figure 4-176 Binding Multi-Patch Model

To help you better understand, try practicing this with the models offered in the supplementary CD-ROM.

The divided patch model is saved as CD-ROM/CHARACTER/scenes/musclePATCH.mb. Refer to this for more detail.

4. Modeling Hands

Next, we will look at how to model hands. Hands can be most effectively modeled using Polygon or Subdivision Surface modeling.

Using Multi-Patch modeling requires a lot of time and effort not only for the actual modeling, but also for controlling the hands. Because we have already explained Subdivision Surface modeling, we will look at the process for Patch Modeling here.

First, make a NURBS cylinder by selecting [Create > NURBS Primitives > Cylinder]. Then, after raising the Section and Span values in the Channel Box, adjust the Scale as shown in Figure 4-177.

Select the surface and apply [Animation > Deform > Create Lattice] to make a lattice and set the S, T, and U Division values in the Channel Box to 3, 5, and 5, respectively. Then, adjust the lattice points as shown in Figure 4-178 to make a large, general shape.

Figure 4-177 NURBS Cylinder   Figure 4-178 Making the Shape Using the Lattice

step 2 To make the finger, make another NURBS cylinder, as shown in Figure 4-179, raise the Section and Span values in the Channel Box, and then adjust the size and position. As shown in Figure 4-180, adjust the CVs to detail the finger.

There is no need to add too much detail here. It is enough to create the overall contours of the finger.

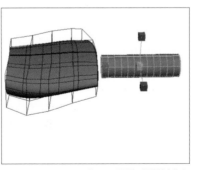
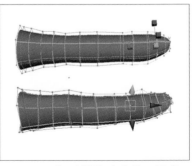

Figure 4-179 Using NURBS Cylinder   Figure 4-180 Trimming the Shape of the Finger

In the same way, make the thumb as shown in Figure 4-181.

After selecting the back of the hand, select [Edit > Delete by Type > History] to delete the lattice and then trim the shape of the back of the hand until it looks like it does in Figure 4-182. Add isoparms as needed.

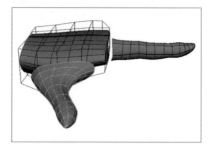

Figure 4-181 Making the Thumb

Figure 4-182 Trimming the Shape of the Back of the Hand

step 3 Now it's time to add more detail. First, let's take a look at the finger. Add isoparms as needed to detail the finger, as shown in Figure 4-183. It is a good idea to use Rebuild Surface now and then to rebuild the entire finger while adding the isoparms. This will minimize changes to the shape during the rebuild later. Detail the back of the hand in the same way as shown in Figure 4-184.

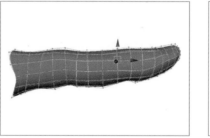

Figure 4-183 Detailing the Finger

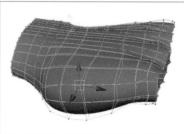

Figure 4-184 Detailing the Back of the Hand

In this step, we must add a lot of overall detail. The detailing process has to be almost completed in this step to minimize the amount of work that we have to do when the surfaces are split using Multi-Patch. It is somewhat difficult to add detail after splitting the surfaces using Multi-Patch.

Let's look at the details in the finger. We need to make the fingernail bed to make the finger look natural.

Figure 4-185 shows an example of how to model the fingernail bed. Aligning it with the length of the fingernail will make a neater model.

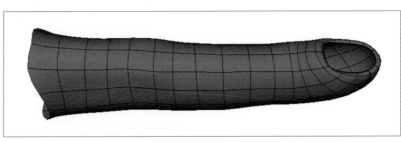

Figure 4-185 Modeling the Finger

In order to model the finger as shown in Figure 4-185, we must detach the finger, as shown in Figure 4-186, and then make a NURBS curve to make the shape shown here.

Detach Surface   Making a NURBS curve.

Figure 4-186 Modeling the Finger

Select the isoparms in the detached region of the NURBS curve of Figure 4-186, select [Edit Curves > Duplicate Surface Curves] to copy it, and then select [Edit > Delete by Type > History] to delete the history. This is the fastest way to make the shape shown here. After making the shape of the curve, select these curves one at a time and use [Modeling > Surfaces > Loft] to loft the curve, as shown in Figure 4-187. Erase the curve and then attach the 2 surfaces.

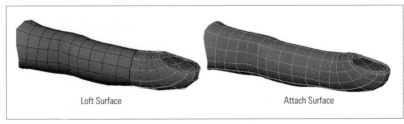

Loft Surface   Attach Surface

Figure 4-187 Modeling the Finger

Finally, adjust the CVs and then make the shape.

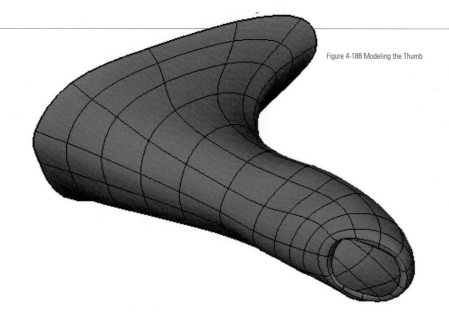

Figure 4-188 Modeling the Thumb

Make the thumb in the same way, and then trim the shape as shown in Figure 4-188. After the fingers have been made, copy them and adjust their sizes before placing them in their proper positions as shown in Figure 4-189. To change the pivot point of the model, press the Insert key and move the pivot point to a more convenient location.

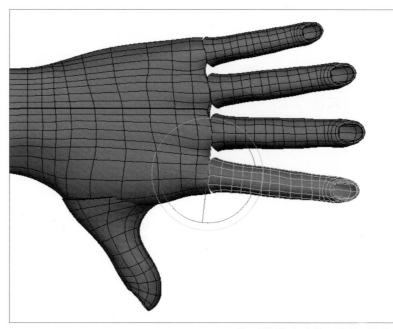

Figure 4-189 Adjusting the Size and Position of the Fingers

step 4 We will now detach the surfaces of the hand using Multi-Patch.

First of all, in order to make the area where the thumb will be placed, select the isoparm, as shown in Figure 4-190, and select [Modeling > Edit NURBS > Detach Surface].

Divide the finger into 1/4ths and detach the surface. Figure 4-191 shows how the surface was detached.

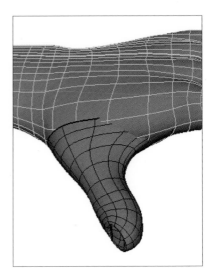

Figure 4-190 Selecting the Isoparm in the Area to Detach

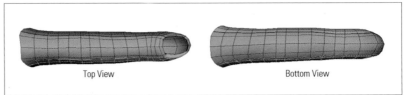

Top View   Bottom View

Figure 4-191 Detaching the Surface of the Finger

Figure 4-192 Detach Surface

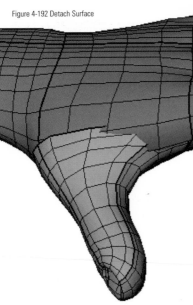

Detach the other fingers and the thumb in the same way.

Figure 4-192 shows how all the fingers were detached. Refer to this illustration while detaching the fingers.

The back of the hand must also be detached in the direction that the fingers were detached. Figure 4-193 shows how the back of the hand was detached.

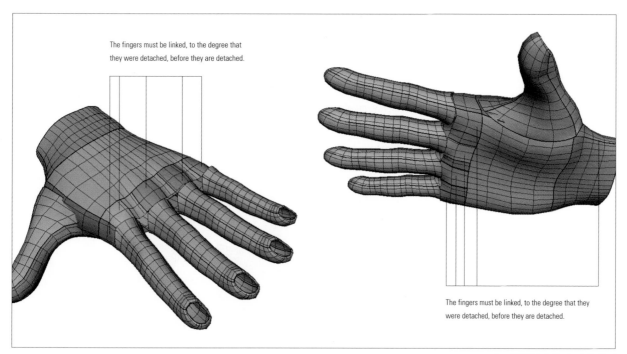

The fingers must be linked, to the degree that they were detached, before they are detached.

The fingers must be linked, to the degree that they were detached, before they are detached.

Figure 4-193 Detach Structure for the Hand

The important thing is that the remaining areas of the hand that have not been detached must be detached in order to fit the arrangement of the fingers and the isoparms.

step 5 Now, we will use the Stitch Edge Tool to stitch together isoparms of surfaces that are especially far apart. Stitch all of the fingers, excluding the thumb, to the back of the hand, and stitch the isoparm of the back of the hand to the isoparm of the thumb. Use the Stitch Edge Tool to stitch together all of the surfaces so that no isoparms are separate from one another. (See Figure 4-194.)

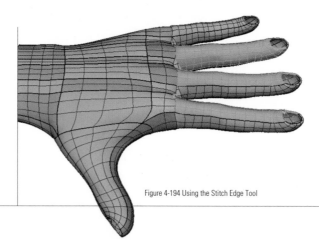

Figure 4-194 Using the Stitch Edge Tool

After deleting the histories of all the surfaces, select all of the surfaces and select [Modeling > Edit NURBS > Global Stitch] to Global Stitch them.

After stitching, delete the histories once again. To fill the spaces between the fingers, select the isoparms of each surface as shown in Figure 4-195. Because we have applied Global Stitch, the starting and ending points of all surface CVs should be linked. After selecting all of the isoparms on each surface, select [Modeling > Surfaces > Boundary] to make the boundary surface on the isoparms, as shown in Figure 4-195.

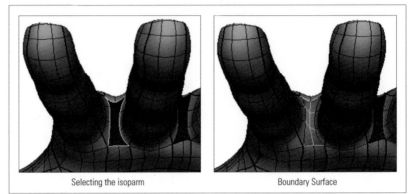

Selecting the isoparm   Boundary Surface

Figure 4-195 Filling in the Surfaces in between the Fingers

Make the remaining surfaces using the same methods.

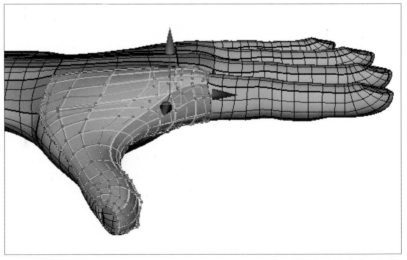

Figure 4-196 Trimming the Surface using CVs

Sometimes, some of the CVs will be tangled or the isoparm arrangement will deviate somewhat from a particular region. In such cases, adjust some of the CVs and arrange the surface as shown in Figure 4-196.

Finally, select the entire surface and apply Global Stitch. Make the fingernails simply by using the Boundary Surface Tool, as explained above, to make and modify their shape. Figure 4-197 shows the completed model of the hand.

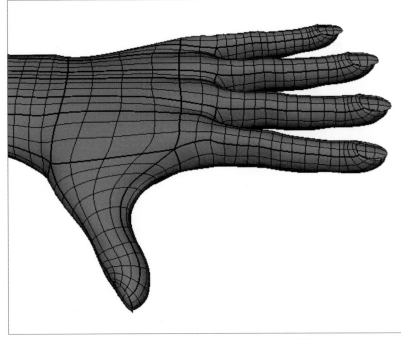

Figure 4-197 The Completed Model of the Hand

We have now looked at Multi-Patch modeling. I have explained how the primary components were modeled. I recommend that you refer to the completed model to observe how the other elements were made. The completed model is saved as CD-ROM/CHARACTER/scenes/ChildModel.mb.

Facial Expression

In character animation, facial animation is the most important and also the most amusing part. Realistic and natural expression of emotion, I believe, is one of the most important, if not the most important, parts of facial animation.

In order to relay your intent to the viewer, you must be able to keyframe the subtle changes that occur in facial expressions. In order to do this, you need to have a complete understanding of facial structure, and you need a facial setup that will move this facial structure.

In this chapter, we will see which muscular structures of the face need to be moved to create various facial expressions. We will also look at what factors are needed for effective movement.

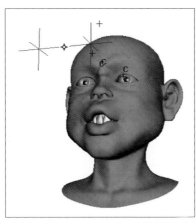

Figure 5-1 Facial Animation

In general, expressions for Blend Shape are largely comprised of (for example, when the character is speaking) five basic vowel sounds and the expressions that are derived from those sounds. The five basic vowel sounds are **"a, e, i, o, u."** Subtle differences in their pronunciations can be added as necessary. These pronunciations can then be mixed to create other sounds using the Blend Shape Editor.

First, we will look at the sequence of steps that we need to follow to create these expressions, and then we will see how each expression is made.

1. USING SKELETON

Facial animation should be completed after performing the procedures in Chapter 7.
Facial animation is important in this section, which is why it is being explained here. This material is also related to the material in "2-4. Setup for Facial Expressions," on page 409.

We will use the subdivision surface modeling data for this section. Subdivision Surface modeling is a quick way to create an accurate shape. We will use the data from the subdivision character modeling.

For this example, open CD-ROM/ CHARACTER/scenes/manFACE.mb or use your own model. The first thing we need to do is to create the basic setting using the skeleton.

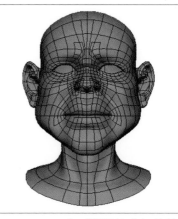

Figure 5-2 Subdivision Surface Modeling

step 1 Make the joints in side view as shown in Figure 5-3.

The important thing here is that the joints in the chin must be configured according to the movements of the chin. Abnormal enunciation will result if the joint is not situated in the center of the movement, as shown here. In order to create precise enunciation, observe where the mandibula is revolving and place the mandibula joint in that spot.

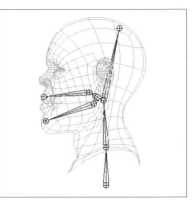

Figure 5-3 Draw Skeleton

step 2 Now, bind the skeleton and the subdivision surface. For the binding, we will use Smooth Binding. If you have worked with subdivision surfaces before, you should have noticed the conspicuous drop in the system speed when binding the subdivision surface. The system speed drops dramatically because, not only is the size of the subdivision surface data large, it requires a lot of time for calculation when binding, unlike NURBS. In such cases, we need to take full advantage of Smooth Binding in binding the subdivision surface by using a quick and easy setup method. First, convert the subdivision surface model into a polygon. To do so, select the model and then select [Modify > Convert > Subdiv to Polygons ▢] to open the Options window. Then, as shown in Figure 5-4, set the Tessellation Method to Vertices, the Level to 0, and the Original Object to Show before clicking the Convert button. As shown in Figure 5-5, a polygon will be made along the vertex of subdivision surface Level 0.

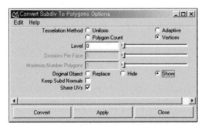

Figure 5-4 Options Windows

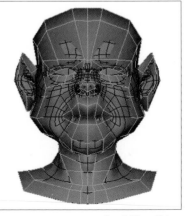

Figure 5-5 Convert Polygon

Select the polygon and the subdivision surface model, and select [Edit > Delete by Type > History] to delete the history.

step 3 Select both the subdivision surface and the polygon model and, while holding down the Shift key, select the skeleton.
Select [Animation > Skin > Bind Skin > Smooth Bind] to smooth bind both the subdivision surface and the polygon model. Hide the subdivision surface and rotate the joint, which was made to manipulate the lower jaw, as shown in Figure 5-6.
The movement will appear abnormal because we have not yet configured the Weight value for the joint cluster.

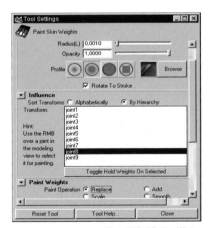

Figure 5-6 Rotating the Joint

step 4 To modify the Weight value, select the model and select [Animation > Skin > Edit Smooth Skin > Paint Skin Weight Tool ▢] to open the Tool Setting window, as shown in Figure 5-7. Select the joint of the lower jaw from Influence Section.

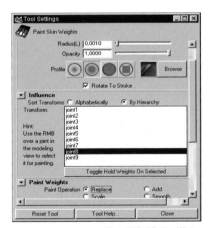

Figure 5-7 Tool Settings Window

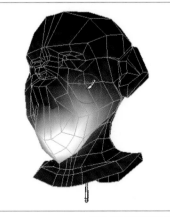

Figure 5-8 Painting Skin Weight

As needed, select the Brush Size and Paint Operation from the Tool Settings window to paint. It is very difficult to paint areas that are folded or rolled over. It is easier to use the Component Editor for these areas. In order to use the Component Editor, first, select the vertex for which the Weight value will be adjusted (see Figure 5-9), select [Windows > General Editors > Component Editor] to open the Component Editor, and then enter the Weight value shown in the figure's Field line.

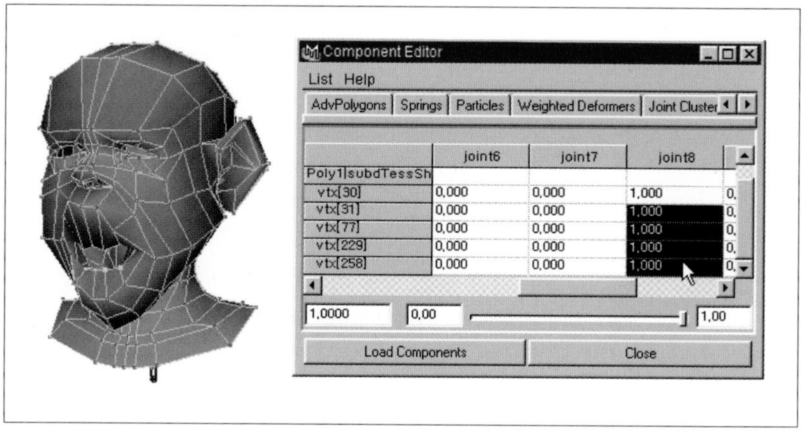

Figure 5-9 Modifying the Weight Value Using the Component Editor

There is no need to configure a Weight value for the entire face. It is enough just to add detail to one-half of the face. The important thing in setting a Weight value is that a great number of vertices must move to create a natural expression. In reality, the action of opening the mouth uses all of the muscles of the face. In order to create the full effect of opening the mouth, the configuration must, as shown in Figure 5-10, be made to affect the sides of the nose, the muscles of the cheek, and the bottoms of the eyes and ears. It is a good idea to look at your own open-mouthed reflection in a mirror to see which muscles are used and affected. Also, in animation, it is a good idea to exaggerate the muscle movements so that almost all of the muscles of the face are affected.

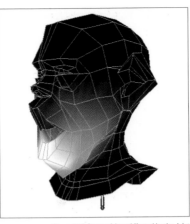

Figure 5-10 Scope of Area Affected by the Joint

In Smooth Bind, unlike Rigid Bind, the vertices are affected by all of the joints. Because it is simply the Weight value that determines how the joint affects the vertex, we need to rotate each joint and see how the shape changes. When adjusting the Weight value, Maya, in order to maintain the average value of 1, automatically raises the values of other joints. Therefore, rotate each joint and configure the Weight value after observing how it affects the skin.

step 5 Because the polygon model is rough, it is difficult to observe specific expression changes. However, the polygon model is still an effective method because it allows us to quickly and easily use the Artisan Tool.

Now, we will look at how to make a Mirror Copy of the Weight value of this polygon model and copy it onto the subdivision surface.

First, select the skeleton and then select [Animation > Skin > Go to Bind Skin] to return the skeleton to the binding pose. Select the polygon model and select [Animation > Skin > Edit Smooth Skin > Mirror Skin Weights ☐] to open the Mirror Skin Weights Options window. Because this model is facing front and because we have modified the Weight value for the left-hand side, (i.e., the + X-direction), configure the options as shown in Figure 5-11 and then press the Mirror button.

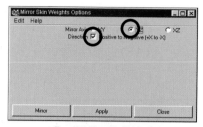

Figure 5-11 Mirror Skin Weights Options Window

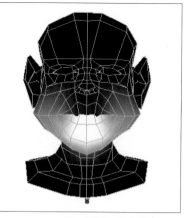

Figure 5-12 Mirror Copied Weight Value

After using the Paint Skin Weight Tool, we can see in Figure 5-12 that the Weight value has been mirror copied.

Now, display the subdivision surface model, which was hidden earlier.

Select the polygon model, select the subdivision surface model while holding down the Shift key, and select [Animation > Skin > Edit Smooth Skin > Copy Skin Weights].

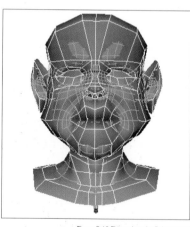

Figure 5-13 First select the Polygon and then select the Subdivision Surface.

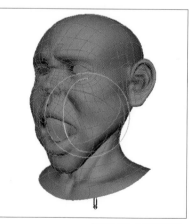

Figure 5-14 Copied Weight Value

Moving the joints, as shown in Figure 5-14, we can see that the Weight value has been copied. Because we configured the Weight value in the polygon, some detailed modifications must be made on the subdivision surface, as well, through the Component Editor.

Select the vertices in areas that do not look natural, as shown in Figure 5-15, an[d]
the Weight value in the Component Editor until the skin looks natural. Becaus[e]
few vertices need to be modified, this should not take too much time or effort.

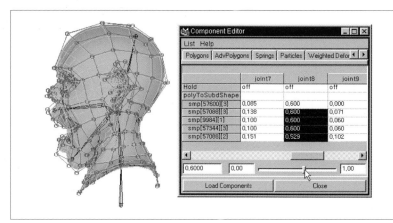

Figure 5-15 Modifying the Weight Value through the Component Editor

2. MODELING BLEND SHAPE

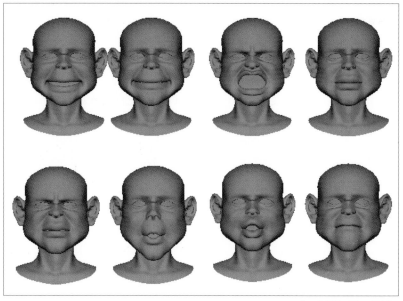

Figure 5-16 Blend Shape Modeling

We have so far completed the basic operations needed to open the mouth. We will now learn how to model basic expressions and pronunciations.

In general, we make anywhere from several to several dozen Blend Shape models to express many different expressions and pronunciations.

For long animations, we need to make Blend Shapes to cover almost all kinds of expressions and pronunciations. Therefore, you can save a lot of time and effort by planning beforehand what expressions and pronunciations you will be using in your animation.

Although there are many different methods for blend shape modeling, the most effective is to use the basic blend shape model and an adequate number of clusters. In general, there are times when all expressions and pronunciations are made using Blend Shape, but this is very inefficient. There is a limit to how many expressions can be mixed in Blend Shape. In addition, a lot of time and effort is needed to blend these expressions naturally and to model them.

However, clusters work naturally with Blend Shape. An adequate number of clusters is sometimes more effective than excessive blend shape modeling.

We will first look at blend shape modeling. Blend Shape using clusters will be explained in "2. Expression Clusters," which starts on page 417.

2-1. UNDERSTANDING THE MUSCULAR STRUCTURE OF THE FACE

Before we begin, let's take a look at the muscular structure of the face. The muscular structure of the face is shown in Figure 5-17.

This anatomy of the face is a 3D recreation of the chart found in *Artistic Anatomy* (Won Kim, Jibmoondang, 1988).

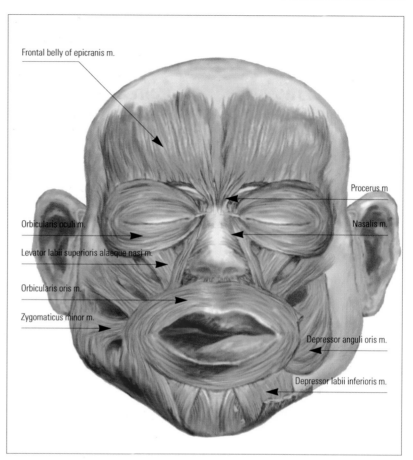

Frontal belly of epicranis m.

Procerus m

Orbicularis oculi m.

Nasalis m.

Levator labii superioris alaeque nasi m.

Orbicularis oris m.

Zygomaticus minor m.

Depressor anguli oris m.

Depressor labii inferioris m.

Figure 5-17 Muscular Structure of the Face

As shown in Figure 5-17, a pair of each of the muscles on each side of the face affects our expressions. In facial animation, instead of just modeling what we can see on the surface, we must understand how the underlying muscles are organized and how they work together to create various expressions. Another thing to remember is that our facial expressions are not determined by the facial muscles but by the wrinkles in the skin. Therefore, it is important to observe how the muscles pull on the skin to create these wrinkles.

Figure 5-18 shows the expression muscles of the face.

Observe how the movements of each of the muscles affect the expressions.

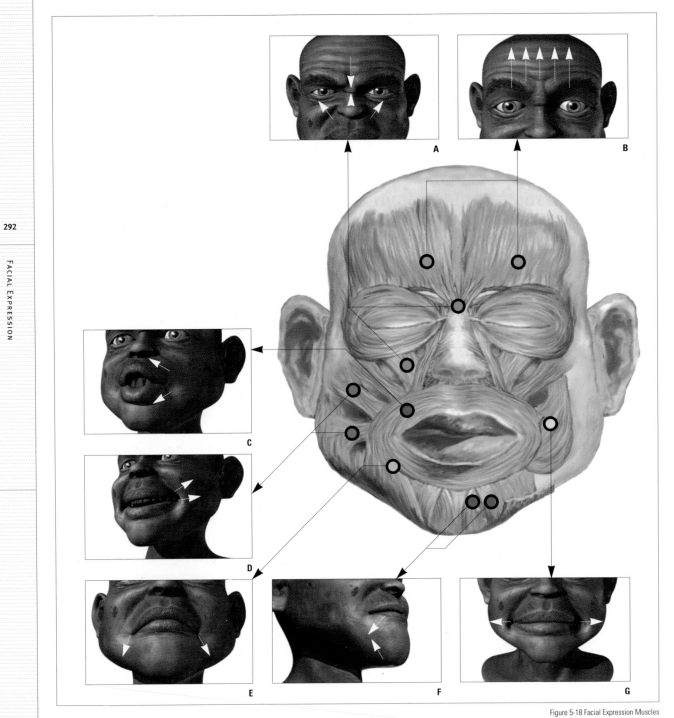

Figure 5-18 Facial Expression Muscles

A. Shows the movement of the procerus and the levator labii superioris alaeque nasi muscles. In terms of the procerus, it is much longer in animals than in humans; therefore, we can clearly observe this muscle at work in an angry animal. In the figure, we can see the procerus at work creating the wrinkles in the forehead of an angry person. The levator labii superioris alaeque nasi muscles are at work when laughing or frowning and are very important in depicting the cheeks and mouth.

B. The frontal belly of epicranius muscles raises the eyebrows to widen the eyes when the person is surprised or tense. In these cases, the wrinkles on the forehead cross at right angles to the muscles. You must remember that the wrinkles always cross at right angles to the muscle.

C. The orbicularis oris muscles determine the shape of the mouth. In making the sound shown here, the lips come together rounded and protrude due to the teeth.

D. Shows the actions of the zygomaticus major and minor muscles. These 2 muscles are responsible for a laughing face. The zygomaticus minor muscle is seen only in humans. As the zygomaticus major is at work, large indentations occur along the sides of the mouth.

E. The depressor anguli oris muscles pull down the corners of the mouth in a frown.

F. These are the depressor labii inferioris and mentalis muscles. The former group of muscles makes the chin firm, and the latter makes the lips firm to make the negative expression shown here.

G. The buccinator muscles raise or lower the rigidity of the mouth.

We have observed how the facial muscles can affect the different expressions. Although there are many more facial expressions than can be mentioned here, you should have no trouble setting up the face knowing these basic muscles. I inserted the diagram on the left in Figure 5-18 because many modelers and animators overlook this part. It is very difficult to create an effective model or a natural animation without accurate knowledge of the muscles. This is also why I used a designed character, instead of an average model, in my explanations. Although most of the features have been exaggerated, the facial animation must be based on the actual human muscular structure in order to create a realistic animation. In terms of body modeling, understanding the human musculoskeletal system of humans will enhance your model. I emphasize such basics because the basics must always serve as your foundation before you can deform your shape. Animation is not the re-creation of living things; it is the exaggeration of living things to create more vivid forms.

We will now look at each blend shape model.

Before modeling, form different pronunciations and expressions in the mirror and, referring to the earlier diagrams, closely observe which muscles move and in what direction and how the skin wrinkles in relation those muscles.

If you're patient and spend the time necessary to study the expressions, you will have no problem attaining the model you need for facial animation.

2-2. THE IMPORTANCE OF MODELING TEETH

Another important thing we need to do before we begin blend shape modeling is make the shape of the teeth. We need to do so because the obribularis oris muscles, which are the muscles that move the most during pronunciation, are affected by the teeth. The teeth will determine how these muscles move.

If blend shape is done without modeling the teeth, later, during the animation, the model will fold into the teeth or the orbicularis oris muscles will not move properly. This, as a result, will lead to a very unnatural and awkward animation.

Therefore, the shape of the teeth must be modeled before blend shape is begun.

This character (see Figure 5-19) includes a model of the teeth.

Either use this character, which is saved as CD-ROM/CHARACTER/scenes/Teeth.mb, or try modeling the teeth yourself. This file was made using Subdivision Surface, based on the Viewpoint model, and then converted over to Polygon.

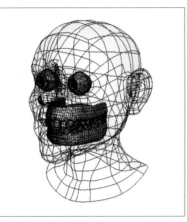

Figure 5-19 Teeth Modeling

● The Sound "ah"

The "ah" sound can be made, simply, by rotating the joint of the lower jaw.

Let's look at which facial muscles are affected by this rotation. The muscles that are affected the most will be the orbicularis oris muscles. Although the masseter muscles also affect the workings of the jaw, the movements of these muscles do not show through the skin.

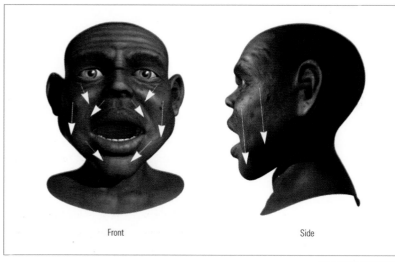

Front   Side

Figure 5-20 The Sound "ah"

The levator labii superioris alaeque nasi and the zygomaticus minor muscles, with the influence of the orbicularis oris muscles, must affect the movement of all the facial muscles. Even if there is little or no actual movement of the muscles during a certain expression, movement must be added to the orbicularis oculi muscles in the cheek to add rich movement to the character during animation. This is very effective in preventing the character from looking like a mannequin, just opening and closing its mouth, when speaking.

As we can see in Figure 5-20, the skin swells in the direction of the arrows shown. If you do not see such rich and abundant movements, modify the Weight values of the vertices and slightly move all the vertices of the face.

● The Sound "e"

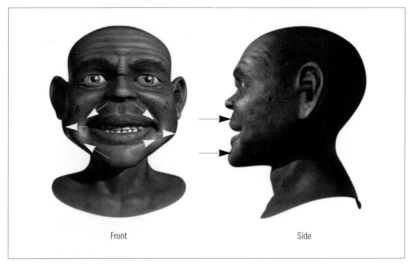

Front   Side

Figure 5-21 The Sound "e"

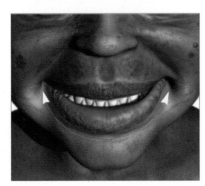

Figure 5-22 The Shape of the Lips

The "e" sound is made without the widening of the chin. The lips become wider while the chin remains still. We model this as if the zygomaticus minor muscles on either side are pulling on the orbicularis oris muscles.

We can see, in Figure 5-21, that because of the teeth, the lips cannot fold over inside the mouth, causing the lips to thin. We must model this as if the corners of the mouth are being pulled out to the sides, and the lips, as shown in Figure 5-22, must remain rounded due to the effect of the teeth.

● The Sound "WOO"

The orbicularis oris muscles cause the lips to become pursed and rounded. The back teeth cause the lips to protrude, and there is no movement of the chin.

The protrusion of the orbicularis oris muscles affects the levator labii superioris alaeque nasi muscles, which link the orbicularis oris and the orbicularis oculi, causing the orbicularis oris muscles to be pushed forward.

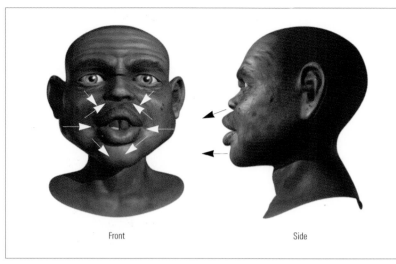

Figure 5-23 The Sound "woo"

The buccinator and zygomaticus minor muscles, which affect the smile, are also affected by the orbicularis oris to bring about a change in either cheek.

● The Sound "eh"

The shape of the lips for the "eh" sound is basically the same as that for the "e" sound.

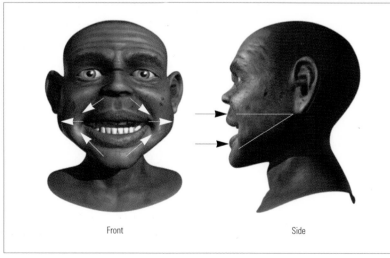

Front   Side

Figure 5-24 The Sound "eh"

The only slight difference is that the philtrum of the upper lip moves down slightly, but this is not very important.

We can make the "eh" sound from the "e" sound by simply moving the lower jaw. Therefore, if we Blend Shape Model the "e" sound and set up the joint so that it can be controlled later on, we can easily resolve the "eh" sound.

● The Sound "oh"

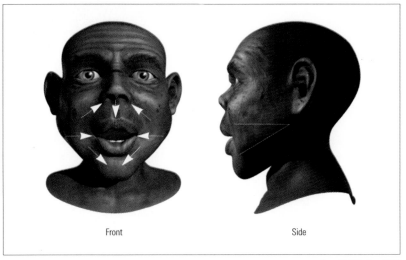

Front   Side

Figure 5-25 The Sound "oh"

Just like the "woo" sound, the orbicularis oris muscles round the lips and the lower jaw moves to open the mouth. The buccinator muscles in the cheeks also adhere to the teeth.

● Other Expressions

In general, even a character that does not speak should have facial expression. If the character were to just sit there without any expression on its face, the animation would be pretty boring. Just as in regular motion, there needs to be some subtle expression changes in facial animation.

In making the blend shape for these other expressions, link them to clusters, as far as it is possible, and plan for them to make other new expressions.

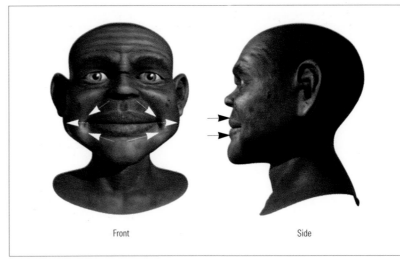

Front   Side

Figure 5-26 Modeling Other Expressions

Let's look at Figure 5-26. This expression is a very practical and useful one. This expression, made by the effect of the buccinator muscles on the orbicularis oris muscles, pulls out the corners of the mouth and thins the lips.

This expression is enough to portray someone licking their lips or listening attentively to someone. If needed, we can strengthen the expression by adjusting the Slider Bar in the Blend Shape Editor.

In addition, one cluster was made to control the corners of the mouth, which can then be manipulated to portray many other expressions. We will save the detailed explanation of clusters for later and, right now, just concentrate on what kinds of expressions can be made using clusters and the skeleton setup.

Raising the cluster slightly will create a slight smile.

Pulling down the cluster slightly will create a frown, due to the effect of the depressor anguli oris muscles.

Raising the cluster and rotating the joint of the chin will create a hearty laugh.

Figure 5-27 Expressions Created by Altering Clusters

Figure 5-27 illustrates several examples. These are just simple examples that result from one another, and many other diverse expressions can be made.

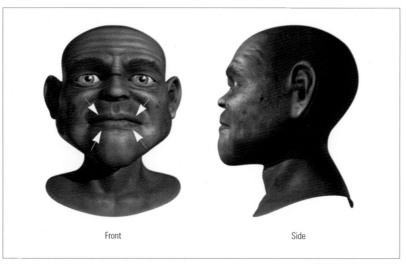

Front

Side

Figure 5-28 Modeling Other Expressions

Another important expression is illustrated in Figure 5-28. The orbicularis oris muscles tense up to tighten the lips. The depressor labii inferioris muscles also tighten. This expression can be used for "anticipation" in facial animation. Anticipation is a method that is used in animation to draw the viewer's gaze to an intended spot, and it is an action that is conducted by the character before assuming a certain stance.

For example, when the character stretches out his arms, bends his back, and raises his legs, we know that he is getting ready to run. Figure 5-28 shows why these expressions are similar to anticipation. Let's suppose that the character is making a rather harsh sound. If the harsh sound is part of a dialogue and it is emitted without any warning, the audience may not understand what is said. If we are simply absorbed in that one harsh sound, the result is rather awkward.

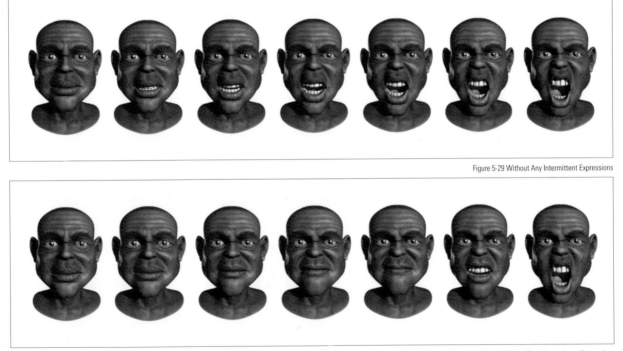

Figure 5-29 Without Any Intermittent Expressions

Figure 5-30 The Addition of Some Intermittent Expressions

Figures 5-29 and 5-30 show this sound emitted without and with some intermittent expressions, respectively. Perhaps the difference is not clearly visible through an illustration, but the difference is dramatic in an actual animation.

This can be a very subtle difference. However, these subtle differences are what determine the quality of the finished product.

Just how detailed the character's feelings are portrayed depends on understanding such differences and appropriately utilizing facial animation. Although animation flips through the screen in no time at all, such subtle differences will determine the quality of your animation.

Many more expressions can be modeled than have been explained here. In the long run, however, it is best if they are made using clusters. Although I recommend modeling expressions that are difficult or impossible to make using clusters, I actively promote the use of clusters when they can be used. Using clusters allows you to effectively create a variety of different expressions.

Of course, the ability to determine which expressions should be modeled and which should be made using clusters comes from much experience. Basically, however, expressions that require the division of many levels in subdivision surfaces and those that transition severely, such as "ah, e, woo, eh, and oh," should be modeled and all others that come from a slight change in the mouth or expression should be made using clusters.

Figure 5-31 shows how the remaining expressions were modeled.

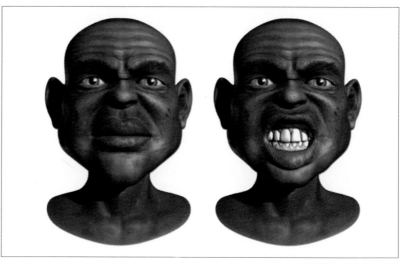

Figure 5-31 The Remaining Expressions

We have covered the basics for facial animation. The important thing is to always remember the theory.

You must understand how the muscles of the face move for different expressions and pronunciations. If you ignore this and just model what you can see on the surface, you will have a very empty and shallow animation.

I recommend that you refer to the example file, which is included in the supplementary CD-ROM, to see which blend shapes were made and to see if clusters were used. The complete data is saved as CD-ROM/CHARACTER/scenes/ManSETUPFinal.mb.

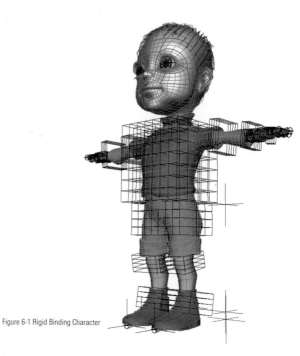

Figure 6-1 Rigid Binding Character

6

Binding Character

1. RIGID BIND

Maya has 2 types of character binding options.

The first, which we will look at here, is Rigid Bind, and the other, which we will cover later, is Smooth Bind. Both types have their share of advantages and disadvantages. You must understand the differences between these 2 types of binding and know which one to use for your particular character and working conditions. In this chapter, we will apply Rigid Bind to a character modeled using Multi Surface. I will use the modeling source offered in the supplementary CD-ROM to explain the binding process.

Open the CD-ROM/CHARACTER/scenes/ChildModel.mb file.

1-1. DRAW SKELETON

We start the binding process by, first, making the skeleton. Making the skeleton is, in general, the same as the character setup process.

 step 1 We will first make the spine in Side View.
Select [Animation > Skeleton > Joint Tool] and make the skeleton as shown in Figure 6-2.
Make the skeleton by looking at the figure below and understanding what changes are brought upon the model by the skeleton. Although it may differ in some cases, usually 3 joints are enough to make the spine and 2 joints are enough to control the neck.

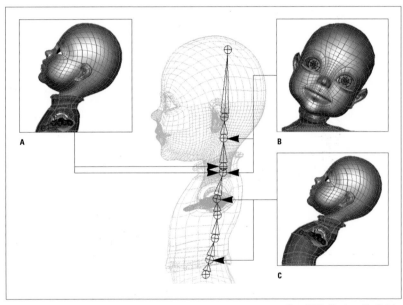

Figure 6-2 The Structure of the Skeleton

A Shows the structure of the neck. As I mentioned before, we use 2 joints to control the neck. However, this character uses a total of 3 joints. We give this character 3 joints because he will be wearing a turtleneck and we want to set up the skeleton so that the neck moves independently, to some degree, inside the shirt. Although this point is not that important, it is helpful in making more precise and detailed movements.

B When a human moves their head from side to side or turns their head, the movements in the top and bottom of an actual cervical vertebra are different from a character's. Therefore, these 2 joints must be moved adequately to portray the movement of the head, and the skeletal structure must be made at the position of the cervical vertebra.

C Use approximately 3 joints to portray the movement of the spine. Although 3 joints are enough, 4 joints may be used if you want a more natural movement.

 step 2 The next step is to make the arms of the skeleton. Figure 6-3 shows the skeletal structure of the arm.

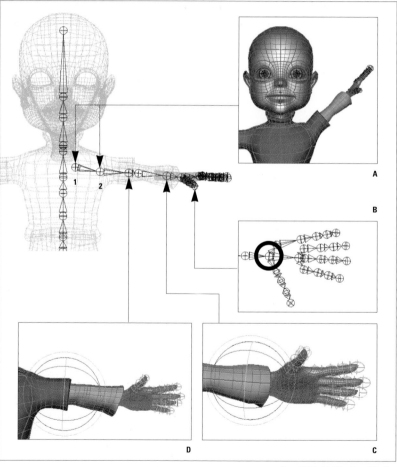

Figure 6-3 Skeletal Structure of the Arm

A These joints are used to control the shoulder. Joint 1 is the joint that controls the movement of some of the muscles in the chest when the shoulder moves, and Joint 2 represents the movement of the shoulder.

B Shows the structure of the hand. We must make all of the joints for each of the fingers. The area indicated here is the wrist joint.

C This controls the twist of the wrist. This is a joint that is not seen in humans, but, because there is a difference in how the skin changes when bending and twisting the wrist, we need to add this joint to portray these actions.

D This, also, is not a joint seen in humans. This joint is added here to affect the twisting of the entire arm. If we do not add this joint and use IK Handles instead to twist the arm, the shoulders will twist severely. Detailed explanations on the setup will be covered later in this chapter.

step 3 Next is the skeletal structure for the leg. Please refer to Figure 6-4.

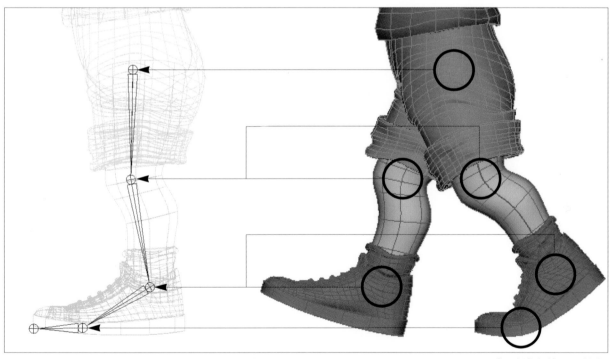

Figure 6-4 Skeletal Structure of the Leg

The basic skeletal structure of the leg is shown in Figure 6-4. As we can see in the figure, each joint controls a joint of the leg as it moves. Carefully observe the modeled character to see where the joints are placed.

 step 4 Joints in the face have no significant meaning. The joints shown in Figure 6-5 are placed to control the teeth.

The pronunciations and expressions of this character have been made using Blend Shape, and joints do not affect them. In actuality, it is very difficult to control facial expressions using joints in Multi-Patch. We will learn how to control facial expressions using joints when we learn about Subdivision Surface Binding later in this chapter.

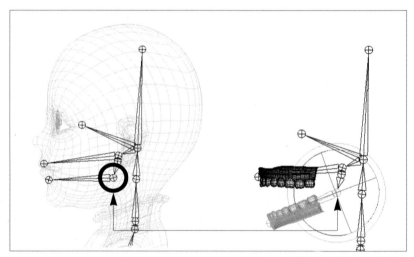

Figure 6-5 Make the Joints to Control the Teeth

step 5 If you made the skeleton by following along with the steps here, your skeletal structure should like the following (Figure 6-6). Generally, we make half of the skeleton, as shown here, and then use Mirror Copy to make the other side. Because the arms and legs are not connected to the body at this point, we must connect them before moving further.

In order to connect the arms, first select Joint A, shown in the figure, and then, while holding down the Shift key, select Joint B. Then, either select [Edit > Parents] or press the P key on the keyboard.

In the same way, apply Parents to join Joint C to Joint D.

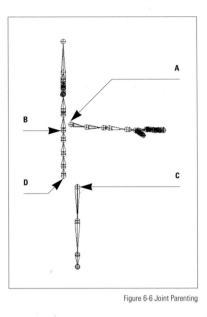

Figure 6-6 Joint Parenting

step 6 After connecting the leg and arm, it is time to make a mirror copy of the other arm and leg.

However, there is one more thing we need to do before we can make the mirror copy. That is, we need to align local axes to each of the joints of the skeleton.

If the default options were used to make the very first joint, then its local axis will be aligned automatically to the next joint. However, if the joints were rotated or moved at random or another method was used to modify them, the local axes will not automatically follow along with such movements. For example, let's suppose that we made the skeleton shown in Figure 6-7 using defaults. Selecting the skeleton and then pressing the F8 key to convert to Component Mode and then pressing [?] to display the local axes will give us the result seen in Figure 6-8.

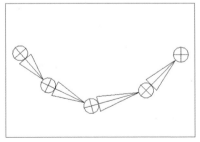

Figure 6-7 Draw Skeleton

Figure 6-8 Display Local Axes

Looking at the alignment of the local axes in Figure 6-8, we can see that the X-axis automatically aligns to the next joint.

The last joint, because there are no more joints, aligns to the absolute axis of the window.

Suppose we moved the Move frame or the Pivot of these joints to align them to the character, as shown in Figure 6-9. In such cases, as shown in Figure 6-10, the local axes do not change with the joints and, instead, maintains their original bearings.

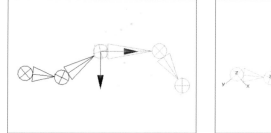 

Figure 6-9 Move Joint   Figure 6-10 Display Local Axes

If this is the case, it is very difficult to keyframe the joint rotation using the Rotate Manipulator. This is especially the case for fingers or areas that have been keyframed using Forward Kinematics. Because we must align the joints to the character, this is something that happens quite frequently.

In such cases, you must readjust the direction of the local axes.

Select the joint for which the direction of the local axes will be readjusted, press the F8 key to convert to Component Mode, click ? and then select the Local Axes.

Use the Rotate Tool so that the X-axis faces the next joint, as shown in Figure 6-11. Adjust the Y- and Z-axes as needed.

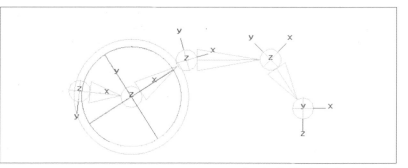

Figure 6-11 Modifying the Direction of the Local Axes

Align the local axes of the arm and leg in this way before making a mirror copy. Figure 6-12 shows the arrangement of the local axes.

Figure 6-12 Alignment of the Local Axes

After aligning the local axes, it is now time to make a mirror copy of the arm and leg.

First of all, select the arm joint. Select Joint A (see Figure 6-6) and then select [Animation > Skeleton > Mirror Joint ▢] to open the Options window (see Figure 6-13).

Figure 6-13 Options Window

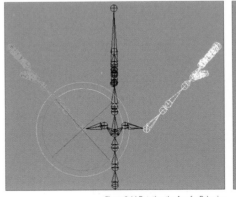

Figure 6-14 Rotating the Arm for Behavior

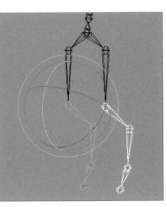

Figure 6-15 Rotating the Leg for Orientation

Because the Mirror Across was made by facing the character in Front View, select YZ.
When the Mirror Function is set to Behavior, the direction of the joint, which will be made, faces the direction opposite the original joint. This option rotates the arms, for example, in different directions allowing us to control the movements of both arms at the same time (see Figure 6-14).
Selecting Orientation causes the joint to follow the direction of the original joint. As follows, this option allows us to rotate the character's legs in the same direction, as shown in Figure 6-15.

This option is not very important when keyframing in Inverse Kinematics using IK Handles. It can, however, be used as needed in Forward Kinematics.

Set the Mirror Function to Behavior and then click the Mirror button.
Mirror the legs in the same way.
Figure 6-16 shows the completed skeletal structure.

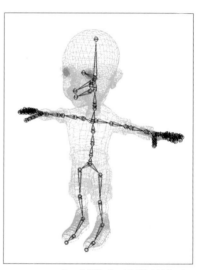

Figure 6-16 The Completed Skeletal Structure

1-2. BIND SKIN

After the skeleton is made, we need to start binding. We will be using Rigid Binding in this chapter. In general, indirect binding is most often used when binding. This allows us to make one Lattice Deformer and control the character using a small amount of lattice points rather than using the many CVs or vertices.
In such indirect binding, we usually create 2 lattices, one that encompasses the upper body and one that encompasses the waist and the bottom.

step 1 First, we will make the lattice for the upper body. Figure 6-17 illustrates the CVs of the upper body that are included in the lattice.

A portion of the pants must also be included in the lattice at this time. Also, because this area was made using Multi-Patch, the CVs of the detached surfaces must be selected so that they are included in the lattice. If this is not done, it will cause the curvature of the connecting surface to easily crack. As shown in the figure, a sufficient number of CVs in the arms and neck must be selected so that the surfaces of the arms, where it meets the shoulders, and the surfaces of the lower part of the neck are included in the lattice.

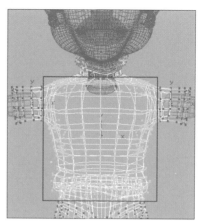

Figure 6-17 CVs Included in the Lattice

After selecting the CV, select [Animation > Deform > Create Lattice ▢] to open the Options window. In the Options window, set the S, T, and U values to 8, 8, and 5, respectively, and then click the Create button.

As shown in Figure 6-18, this will create a Lattice Deformer that surrounds the body.

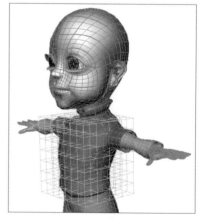

Figure 6-18 Making the Lattice

step 2 Now, let's look at the lower part of the body. There is one thing we need to do before we can select the CVs in the lower body.

Control becomes difficult if there is an empty space in between the upper and lower lattices and if a CV is included in both lattices. Therefore, we must make sure that we select a CV that is not included in the upper lattice. To do so, we must first select the CVs that are included in the upper lattice.

First of all, select the shirt and the pants and then press the F8 key to switch to Component Mode.

Select [Windows > Relationship Editors > Deformer Sets...]. This will open the Relationship Editor. On the left-hand side of this window, under Deformer Sets, we can see the name (ffd1Set01) of the lattice that we made. Click on the lattice name to select it and then select [Edit > Select Set Members] as shown in Figure 6-19.

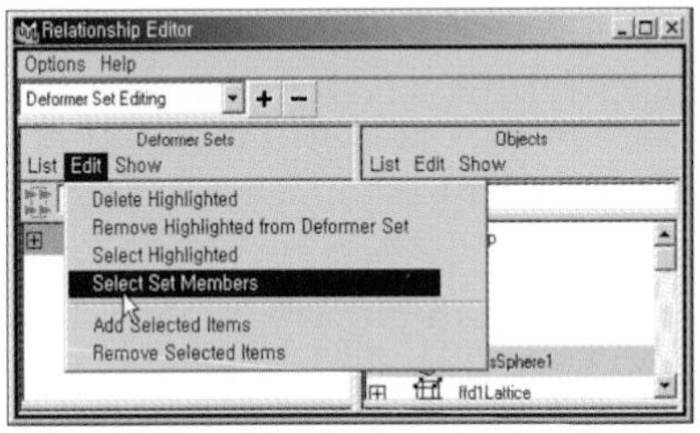

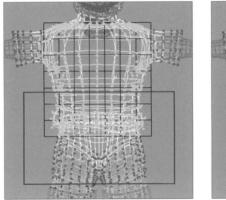

Figure 6-19 Relationship Editor

As a result, all the CVs that are included in the lattice will be selected, as shown in Figure 6-20. Holding down the Shift key and dragging down the lattice to the red line shown in the figure will select the CVs as shown in Figure 6-21. The remaining upper portions will become deselected.

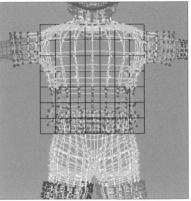

Figure 6-20 Selecting the CVs

Figure 6-21 Selecting the CVs

After selecting the CV, select [Animation > Deform > Create Lattice ⬚] to open the Options window. In the Options window, set the S, T, and U values to 8, 5, and 3, respectively, and then click the Create button. A lattice will be made as shown in Figure 6-22.

Figure 6-22 Create Lattice

We will now look at how to use a lattice for the hands. A flexor will be used on the joints of each finger later, but this is rather difficult to do for the thumb.

The thumb must move as shown in Figure 6-23. This movement will affect many surfaces; therefore, the CVs in this area must be bundled into a lattice.

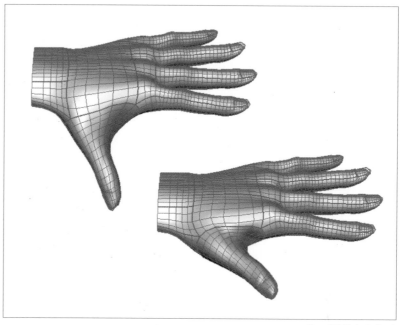

Figure 6-23 Moving the Thumb

Because the hand was made using Multi-Patch, we must set up the hand so that there is little bursting of the surfaces. Figure 6-24 shows how the CVs were selected to insert a lattice.

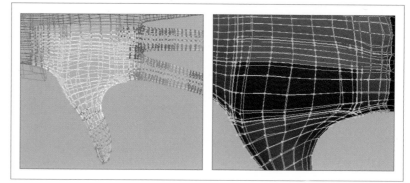

Figure 6-24 Selecting the CVs

One thing we need to remember is that the CVs of the first and second hulls, which affect the curvature in the connecting region of each surface, must be joined together.

To help in understanding, each of the surfaces were colored in Shading Mode to show how the CVs in each surface were selected.

If there is anything that you do not understand, refer to the CD-ROM/CHARACTER/scenes/childSETUP.mb file.

Select [Animation > Deform > Create Lattice] and change the S, T, and U values to 6, 5 and 3, respectively, in the Channel Box.

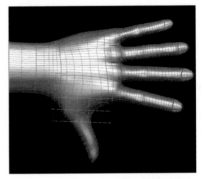

Figure 6-25 Create Lattice

Make a lattice for the other hand, as well (see Figure 6-25). This completes the basic binding steps. We need to now bind the character to the skeleton we made.

step 3　As shown in Figure 6-26, select all the CVs, excluding the CVs of the eye and those included in the lattice, in Component Mode. Refer back to Step 2 to review how lattice CVs are excluded. By turning off the Deformer under Show in the Panel menu, the lattice will be hidden, making it easier to select the CVs. We, generally, do not bind the eyes, and instead, will be parented to the joint later.

With the CV selected, select [Windows > Hypergraph] to open the Hypergraph. Select the Lattice Node, which was made, and then select the skeleton.

step 4　What we select in the window is the CV, and what we select in the Hypergraph is the object. In this way, we can use the Hypergraph or the Outliner to select the component and the object simultaneously. Select [Animation > Skin > Bind Skin > Rigid Bind]. This will bind the selected lattices and all the CVs to the skeleton.

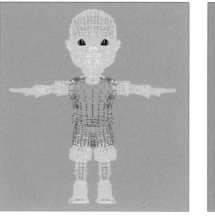

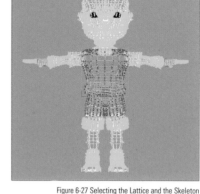

Figure 6-26 Selecting the CVs   Figure 6-27 Selecting the Lattice and the Skeleton

1-3. USING THE EDIT MEMBERSHIP TOOL AND ADJUSTING THE CV AND POINT WEIGHTS

When binding in Maya, the points, due to the option configurations, are bound to the adjacent joint. However, because the points are bound based on average values, we must arrange them manually for more precision. We must also modify the CV Weight values for each joint at the same time. We do this so that Maya knows which CV to bind to which joint.

We use the Edit Membership Tool and Artisan's Paint Set Membership Tool to selectively define the CVs, which affect the joints. Their Weight values are adjusted using the Component Editor and Artisan's Paint Cluster Weight Tool. We will now use these tools to define the joints so that they affect the modeled character to create proper movement.

First, in order to control the body, which has been indirectly bound using lattices, adjust the lattice point using the Edit Membership Tool and the Component Editor. Let's first rotate the shoulder joint and observe the changes. Although there may be some differences between characters, the shoulders do not yet move naturally because the CVs have not yet been arranged. Using [Animation > Deform > Edit Membership Tool], click on the joint indicated in Figure 6-28. As shown here, the lattice points included in the selected joint will become activated.

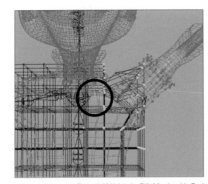

Figure 6-28 Using the Edit Membership Tool

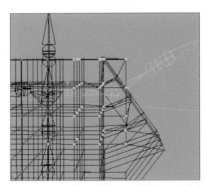

Figure 6-29 Using the Edit Membership Tool

Press the Shift key and select the CVs you wish to add to the selected joint. Refer to Figure 6-29 and make sure that the selected joint is included in the lattice point. If you wish to exclude the selected joint from the lattice point, select the point while holding down the Ctrl key.

Set [Show > Nurbs] to Off in the Panel menu to make it easier to select the lattice point.

After selecting the joints in the rotating shoulder, use the same method to make the selections shown in Figure 6-30 so that appropriate lattice points are added. Observe the change in the shoulder by displaying the NURBS surface and make sure that the sleeve of the shirt is also included in the selected joint, as shown in Figure 6-31.

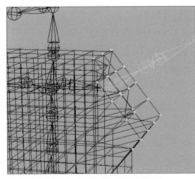

Figure 6-30 Using the Edit Membership Tool

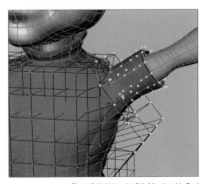

Figure 6-31 Using the Edit Membership Tool

It is a good idea to adjust the Weight values while you work. Select the lattice point and modify the Weight values for the movement of the arm. As shown in Figure 6-32, select the lattice point for which the Weight value will be adjusted, then select [Window > General Editors > Component Editor], and then modify the Weight value in the Component Editor.

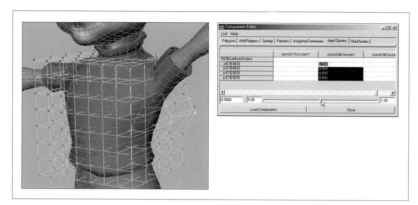

Figure 6-32 Adjusting the Weight Value

The Component Editor has 3 tabs used to adjust the Weight value. As shown in Figure 6-32, Weighted Deformers is the used to adjust the Weight value of a cluster and Joint Clusters is the tab used to adjust the Weight value during a rigid bind. Because Rigid Bind was applied to this character, we use the Joint Clusters Tab to adjust the Weight value for this character. Finally, Skin Clusters is the tab used to adjust the Weight value during a smooth bind.

Also, we can click and drag to select all the Weight fields for a selected point and type in the Weight values using the keyboard or use the Slider Bar at the bottom to adjust the values.

Use the Edit Membership Tool so that the joint moves in a natural fashion.

Figure 6-33 illustrates the rotation of the joint after the Weight values have been modified. Refer to the figure below as you adjust your Weight values.

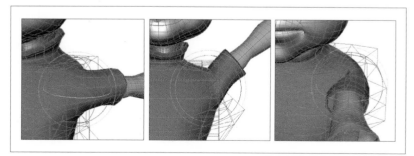

Figure 6-33 The Change in the Surface Due the Movement of the Joint

Now let's modify the joint made for twisting the arm. When this character twists his arm, the sleeve of the shirt should not move. Therefore, the sleeve of the shirt has been included in the joint of the shoulder. To twist the arm, select [Animation > Deform > Edit Membership Tool] and then, after clicking on the joint indicated in Figure 6-34, select the CV of the sleeve.

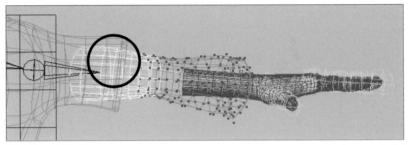

Figure 6-34 Using the Edit Membership Tool

Rotate this joint to see if it twists as shown in Figure 6-35.

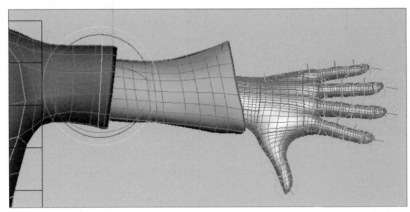

Figure 6-35 Twisting the Arm

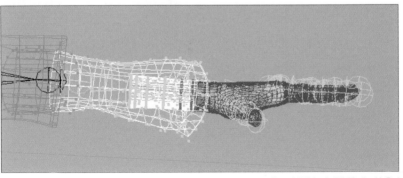

Figure 6-36 Using the Edit Membership Tool

The elbow will be made using a flexor, so a precise setting is not necessary. Have it assume appropriate CVs as shown in Figure 6-36. There is no need to adjust the Weight value.

By observing the inclusion of the CVs in the selected joint, as shown in Figure 6-36, we can see that all the CVs of the sleeve are included in the selected joint. This is because the setting is such that the hand should move separately.
The CVs must be included in the sleeve joint, as shown here, so that the wrist joint does not affect the sleeve.

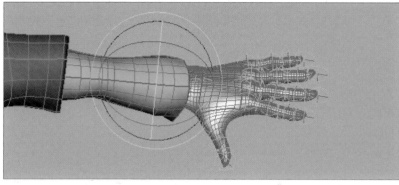

Figure 6-37 Twisting of the Wrist

Next is the wrist movement. In general, flexors allow us to easily control the wrist joint. However, the setting for the twisting of the wrist, as shown in Figure 6-37, must be done separately. There is no need to adjust the Weight values for the CVs on the inside of the wrist, which are not readily visible.

Although flexors have been used for almost all the joints of the fingers, we still need to modify the areas of the thumb that used a lattice.
We do this by rotating each of the joints until the most natural movement is obtained.
In actuality, it is very difficult to achieve perfect movement of the fingers using Multi-Patch modeling. Therefore, in most cases, it is more effective to use Polygon or Subdivision Surface.
Refer to the illustration in Figure 6-38 as you adjust the lattice points of the thumb.

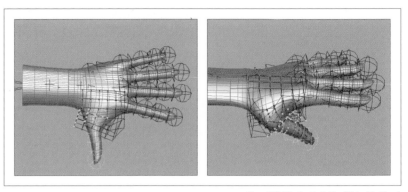

Figure 6-38 Adjusting the Lattice Points of the Thumb

Finally, we need to adjust the lattices used in the pelvic region. We must pay careful attention to the movement of the legs as the legs are spread.

Figure 6-39 shows an example of a modification using the Edit Membership Tool and the Component Editor.

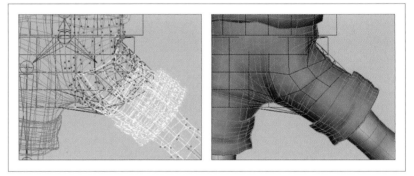

Figure 6-39 After Modifying the Lattice Points

In order to achieve the somewhat natural movement seen in Figure 6-39, we need to use the Component Editor to appropriately adjust the Weight values. Also, when making the very first lattice, the lattice division in the center of the character must not be divided so that the movement of one leg affects a portion of the CVs in the pants of the other leg to create a natural movement.

Continue moving the legs, as shown in Figure 6-40, and keep adjusting the Weight values until the optimal result is obtained.

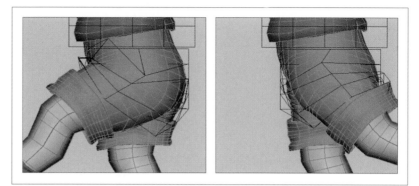

Figure 6-40 Adjusting the Lattice Weight Values of the Leg

Instead of using the Edit Membership Tool, we can use Artisan's Paint Set Membership Tool to more directly assign the CVs to each joint. First, select the surface, and then select [Animation > Deform > Paint Set Membership Tool ▣]. After selecting the desired joint name in Set Membership, as shown in Figure 6-41, paint and select the CV.

Tool Settings Window

Figure 6-41 Using the Paint Set Membership Tool

This tool displays in color the selected CVs of each joint on the surface, allowing us to easily assign the CVs to each joint. It is very effective to use the Paint Set Membership Tool and the Edit Membership Tool interchangeably.

Finally, we will look at how to use the Edit Membership Tool to reassign the CVs and how to modify the Weight value to manipulate the character. Repeat the same process to create the settings for the other side.

1-4. USING FLEXORS

After modifying the basic Weight values, we will use flexors to create more natural movement at each of the joints.

First of all, select the elbow joint, as shown in Figure 6-42, to control the elbow.

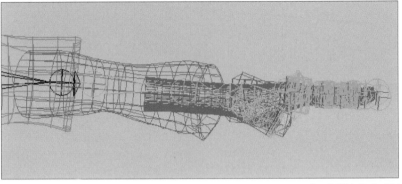

Figure 6-42 Selecting the Joint

Select [Animation > Skin > Edit Rigid Skin > Create Flexor]. The Create Flexor window will appear, as shown in Figure 6-43. Select At Selected Joint (s) from Joint, and use the default settings for the remaining fields.

Click on the Create button at the bottom of the window.

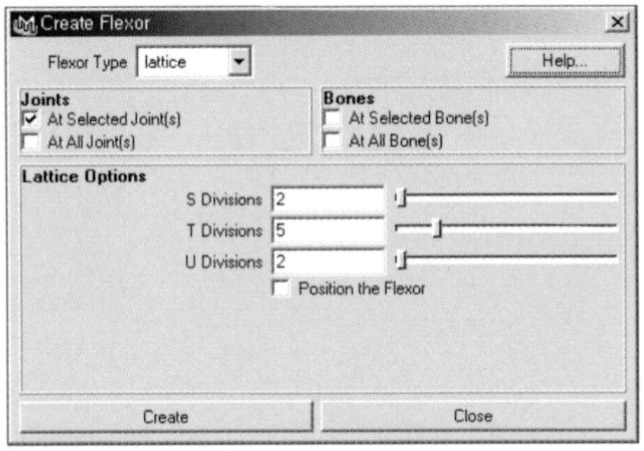

Figure 6-43 Create Flexor Window

The size of the flexor we made might not be appropriate for the character. If that is the case, select the flexor and then select [Windows > Hypergraph]. In Hypergraph (see Figure 6-44), press the F key on the keyboard to display the selected node in the screen, and then select Group Node from the top. Adjust the size of the flexor using the Scale Tool, as shown in Figure 6-45.

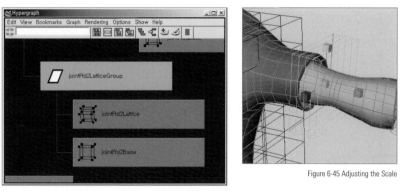

Figure 6-44 Hypergraph

Figure 6-45 Adjusting the Scale

Rotating the elbow joint at random, select the Lattice Flexor and then define the flexor properties in the Channel Box, as shown in Figure 6-46.

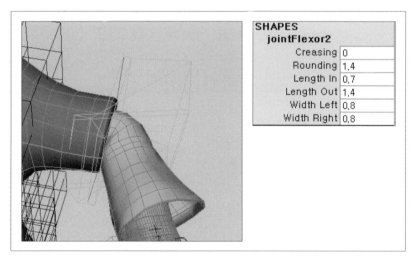

SHAPES	
jointFlexor2	
Creasing	0
Rounding	1.4
Length In	0.7
Length Out	1.4
Width Left	0.8
Width Right	0.8

Figure 6-46 Defining the Flexor Properties

Using the same method, add a flexor to each of the joints of the fingers and the wrist and then define the properties in the Channel Box.

Figure 6-47 shows the movement of the fingers after adding a flexor to all the joints of the fingers and wrist. Refer to CD-ROM/CHARACTER/scenes/childSETUP.mb file if you wish to observe this section more closely.

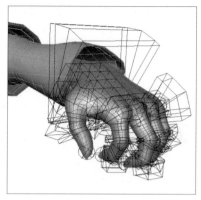

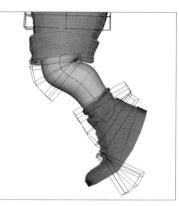

Figure 6-47 Finger Movements after Application of Flexors

Figure 6-48 Flexors Used in the Legs

Figure 6-48 shows the use of flexors in the joint of the leg.

Three flexors were used in each joint of the knee, ankle, and toes. Appropriately define the properties in the Channel Box.

Using Copy Flexor

Up until now, we have looked at how to control one side of the character using lattice flexors. We must add lattice flexors to the joints on the other side of the body, as well.

If the properties of the each of the flexors have been defined in the Channel Box, all we need to do, simply, is to copy the flexors to the other side.

In order to copy the flexors, first, select the flexor to copy and then select the desired joint while holding down the Shift key (see Figure 6-49).

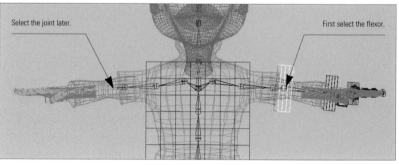

Select the joint later.

First select the flexor.

Figure 6-49 Selecting the Joint and the Flexor

Select [Animation > Skin > Edit Rigid Skin > Copy Flexor].
If the selected flexor is copied onto the joint, as shown in Figure 6-50, and the properties for that flexor have been defined in the Channel Box, the properties will be copied, as well.

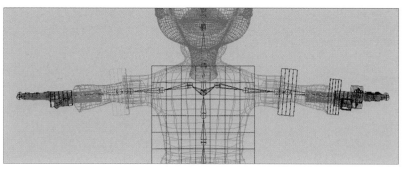

Figure 6-50 Executing Copy Flexor

If portions of the flexor have been scaled, this adjusted flexor may not copy properly. In such instances, we must adjust the size of the copied flexor again.

Using the same method, copy all the flexors to the other side to complete the character.
Figure 6-51 shows the final illustration after all the flexors have been applied to each of the joints. After you finish, save this scene under an appropriate name to prepare for the next example. We will use this character to explain the Character Setup process later.

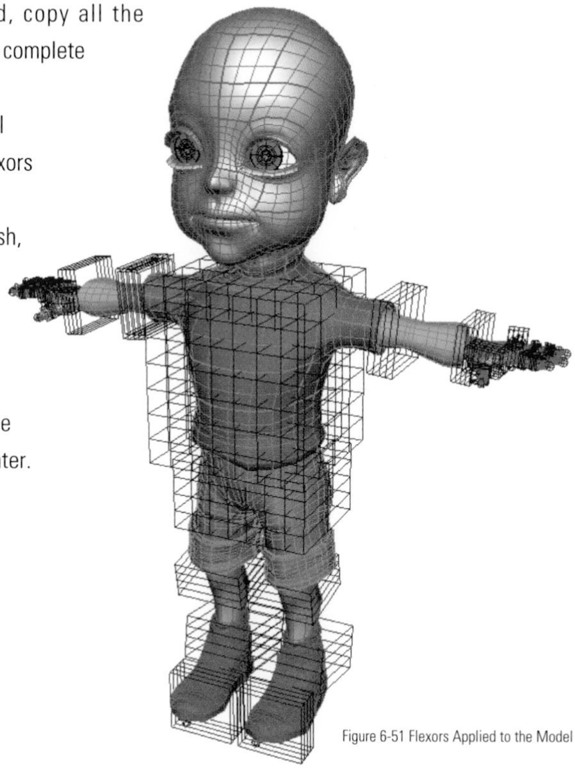

Figure 6-51 Flexors Applied to the Model

2. SMOOTH BIND

In this section, we will look at smooth binding. Although smooth binding does not use flexors, like rigid binding, it offers us an environment in which to easily and precisely manipulate the characters.

Although each method has its share of advantages and disadvantages, as a person who uses mostly Subdivision Surface and Polygon modeling, I prefer smooth binding to rigid binding. This will be explained further in the back. However, in contrast to rigid binding, once the Weight values for one side of the character have been made, the values for the other side can simply be mirror copied. Also, Weight values can be exported to use in the setup of a similar character.

We will first cover the basic options for smooth binding and then move on to an example of character binding using subdivision surfaces.

2-1. SMOOTH BIND OPTIONS

Select the surface and the skeleton and then [Animation > Skin > Smooth Bind] to open the Smooth Bind Options window shown in Figure 6-52.

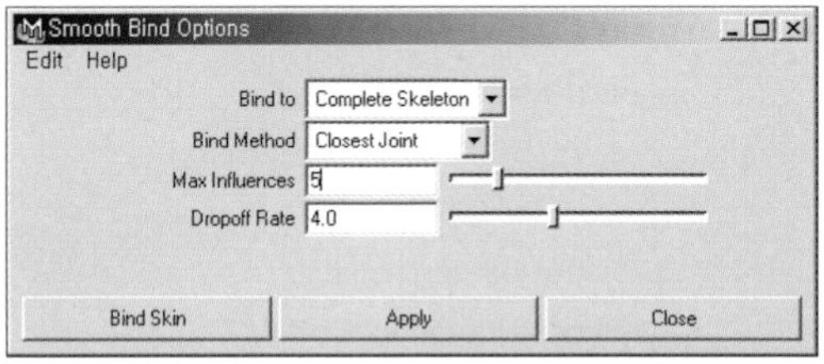

Figure 6-52 Smooth Bind Options Window

● Bind To

Complete Skeleton will bind the entire skeleton, whereas Selected Joint will bind only the selected joint. If you only want to bind portions of the character, select the desired joint and then select Selected Joint in this window.

● Bind Method

Close Joint, the default setting, binds the skeleton based on its class structure.
In other words, it is affected by the adjacent skin point. For example, we can alleviate, to

some degree, the binding of the skin point of the left thigh on the right joint.

Closest Distance ignores this skeleton structure and binds the joints, first, to the nearest point.

● Max Influences

This allows us to specify the number of joints that will affect each skin point. The default setting is 5, which is an appropriate value for almost all characters. We can also specify the range of joint movement using the Dropoff Rate.

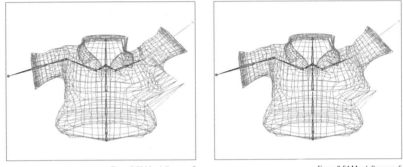

Figure 6-53 Max Influences: 2   Figure 6-54 Max Influences: 5

Comparing figures 6-53 and 6-54, we can see that the greater the value of the Max Influences, the smoother the change.

● Dropoff Rate

This determines how the skin points will be affected by each joint.

In other words, the affect of the joint accompanies the distance and determines how much the ratio will be diminished. The greater this value, the greater the rate of diminishment. The smaller the value, the more abruptly the rate is decreased. When Smooth Bind is used, a Dropoff Rate is applied to all selected joints and the slider bar is used to adjust this value anywhere from 0.1 to 10. The default value is 4, which is an appropriate value for almost all characters.

Figure 6-55 and 6-56 compare two images with a Max Influences value of 5 and a varying Dropoff Rate.

Figure 6-55 Dropoff Rate: 2   Figure 6-56 Dropoff Rate: 7

2-2. EDIT SMOOTH SKIN

1. Add Influences

When Smooth Bind is used, NURBS or Polygon Geometry is used to affect the bound skin. This allows us to control the change in the shape of the skin, much as we do joints or clusters. Let's use the example file to see how this is used.

Open the file, CD-ROM/CHARACTER/scenes/polyhand.mb.

You will see the image of a hand created using Smooth Bind (see Figure 6-57). First, make a NURBS sphere, as shown in Figure 6-58, and then adjust its size and position.

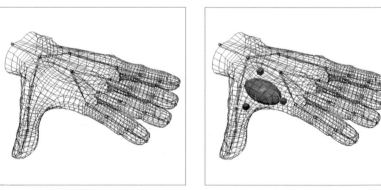

Figure 6-57 Smooth Bind Model   Figure 6-58 Making a NURBS Sphere

After first selecting the hand and then the NURBS sphere, select [Animation > Skin > Edit Smooth Skin > Add Influence].

Rotating the thumb, as shown in Figure 6-59, we can see that the vertices around the NURBS sphere is affected by the sphere, but not by the selected joint.

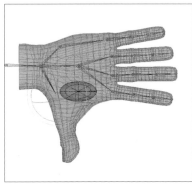

Figure 6-59 Rotate Joint

We can also use Influence Object to obtain a more precise setting.

Select [Animation > Skin > Edit Smooth Skin > Add Influence ▢] to open the Options window, as shown in Figure 6-60.

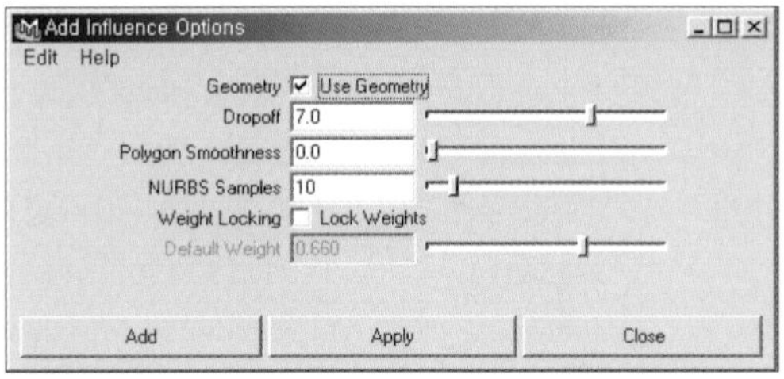

Figure 6-60 Add Influence Options Window

● **Geometry**

When this option is turned on, we can also influence the Transform (Translation, Rotation, Scale) of the Influence Object. In other words, when this option is turned on, moving the Influence Object, as shown in Figure 6-61, will also affect the skin point.

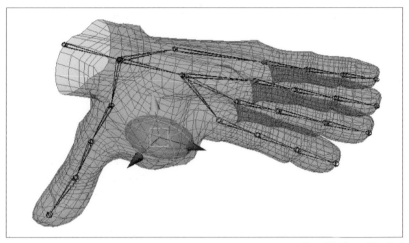

Figure 6-61 Influence Object Move

● Dropoff

This determines how much the influence will diminish. A lower value will bring about a steady diminish, whereas a high value will bring about an abrupt diminish.

● Polygon Smoothness and NURBS Samples

These 2 options determine how the skin points will be influenced when using Polygon and NURBS.

Polygon Smoothness determines how much the skin point will follow the polygon influence object. The larger the value, the smoother the change will be. The range of values is from 0.0 to 50, with the default value being 0. NURBS Sample is the number of samples used to calculate the forming of the NURBS Influence Object. The higher this value, the more it is calculated to remain faithful to the NURBS shape. The range of values is from 1-100, with the default value being 10.

● Weight Locking

When this option is turned on, a hold is placed on the object using the Weight value specified at the bottom. This Weight value will remain fixed until the hold is removed.

This option produces satisfactory results from the specified value and is used to prevent the Weight value from being modified when Artisan's Paint Skin Weight Tool is used.

2. Remove Influence

This option is used to remove the Influence Object. Select the smooth bound surface and then the Influence Object. Then, select [Animation > Edit Smooth Skin > Remove Influence] to remove the influence on the skin object.

3. Set Max Influence...

This option is used to change the initial Max Influence setting made in Smooth Bind Options. Select the smooth bound surface, then select [Animation > Edit Smooth Skin > Set Max Influence...], and enter a new value.

4. Paint Skin Weight Tool

Artisan's Paint Skin Weight Tool is used to quickly and easily modify the Weight value of the smooth bound surface. For more detailed modifications in certain areas, alternate the use of this option with the Component Editor.

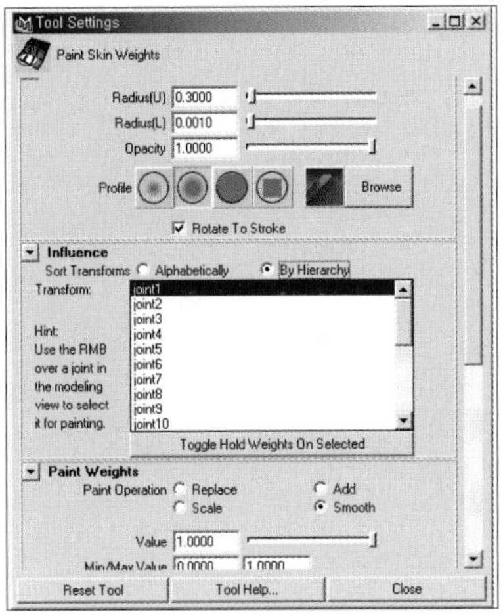

Figure 6-62 Tool Settings Window

As an example, we will use the CD-ROM/CHARACTER/scenes/polyhand.mb file.
Select the polygon object, and then, either click the RMB and select [Paint > Skin Cluster - Skin Cluster1 > Paint Weight] from the Marking Menu or select [Animation > Edit Smooth Skin > Paint Skin Weight ☐].
This will reveal the Tool Settings window, shown in Figure 6-62.
As shown in the figure, select the desired joint name from the Influence Section box in the middle of the window. The range of the skin point, influenced by the selected joint, will appear white.

The area shown in white is influenced by the Weight value 1 of the selected joint. The black areas are influenced by the Weight value 0, indicating that there is no movement in this region.

The middle portions will receive values between 0-1 depending on the concentration.

For practice, try rotating the thumb joint as shown in Figure 6-63.

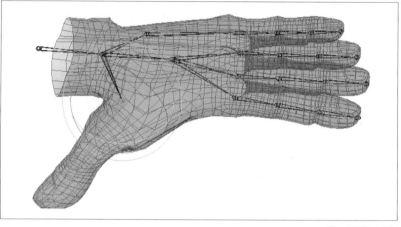

Figure 6-63 Rotate Joint

After verifying the name of the selected joint in the Channel Box and selecting the polygon object, select [Animation > Edit Smooth Skin > Paint Skin Weight ▢] to open the Tool Settings window. In Artisan's Tool Settings window, select the joint name. The joint name here is "Joint21," meaning that joint number 21 has been selected.

The area influenced by the selected joint is shown in Figure 6-64.

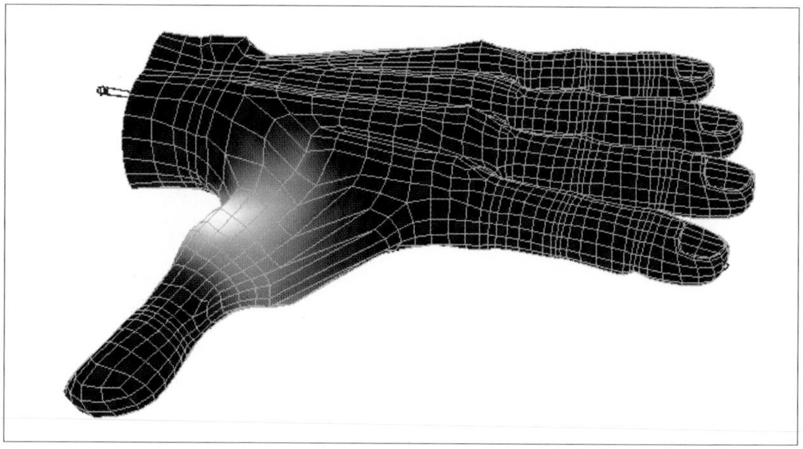

Figure 6-64 Paint Skin Weight Tool

In the Tool Settings window, select Smooth from within the Paint Operation menu in the Paint Weight section and paint the edges as shown in Figure 6-65. This will soften the Weight values of the skin point in this area.

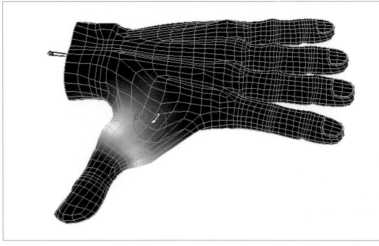

Figure 6-65 Painting Value

If necessary, modify the Weight values of the nearby joints so that an appropriate value is assigned to the skin point.

Select Joint3 from Influence in the Tool Settings window. Enter a value around **0.7** for the Paint Weight value and set the Paint Operation to Replace.

As shown in Figure 6-66, paint the region of the thumb so that Joint3 influences the skin point.

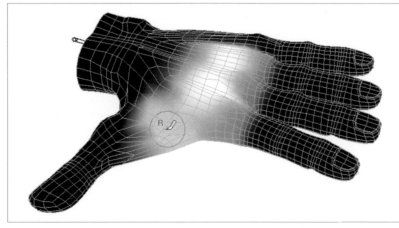

Figure 6-66 Paint Operation: Replace

Set the Paint Operation to Smooth in the Tool Settings window, convert the painted main surface to Smooth Mode, and continue to paint until a smooth surface is achieved (see Figure 6-67).

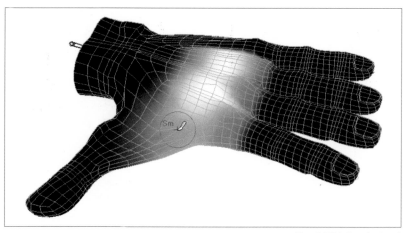

Figure 6-67 Paint Operation: Smooth

In this way, adjust the Weight value such that the rotating joint helps smooth the skin joint. If you are satisfied with your results, click on the Toggle Hold Weight On Selected button in the Tool Settings window, as shown in Figure 6-68, to hold the skin point Weight value of the selected joint.

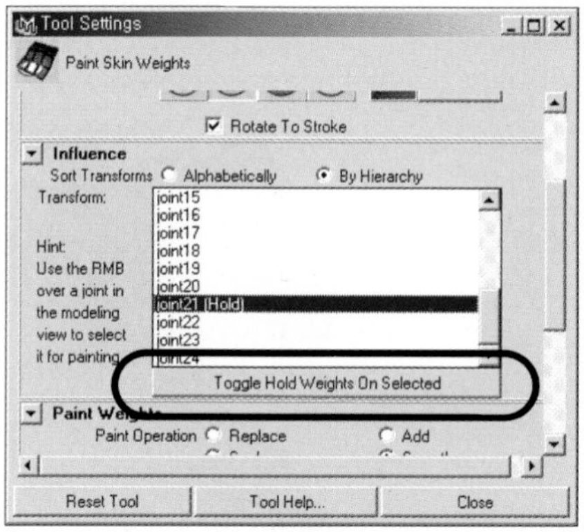

Figure 6-68 Tool Settings Window

This prevents this Weight value from being changed when the Weight values of other joints are modified.

5. Export Skin Weight Tool

This menu is very useful. It is very effective when it comes to creating a setup of several, similar characters. If careful consideration was given to the entire process from modeling to skinning, after first setting up the basic shape and UV-axis, you can model the object by altering this basic shape.

This is an even more useful menu for subdivision surfaces and when converting to Polygon.

This menu saves the set skin point Weight values on the map so that it may be used again on another character, which is loaded onto the map. Therefore, when making similar characters, you should pay special attention to the initial character setup. Afterwards, this Weight value can be exported and used on different characters.

The following conditions must be met before this menu can be used:
The names for the skeleton's hierarchy structure and the joint must be the same. In other words, if the name for the joint hierarchy of the skeleton with the Weight value that will be exported is different from the name of the joint hierarchy of the skeleton that has the surface with the Weight value that will be imported, then we will not be able to use this menu properly.

The surfaces with the Weight values to export and import must have the same UV-axis.
In general, because the Weight values are made into a black and white image file, the UV-axis, which will serve as the foundation, must be set up first.

Therefore, first make the initial, basic model and then set up the UV-axis. Then, this basic model can be modified to create many different characters.

We use this menu as follows. For example, let's suppose that we have set up the Weight values for the polygon hand shown in Figure 6-69. In order to export this Weight value, first select the polygon hand and then select [Animation > Edit Smooth Skin > Export Skin Weight Tool ▢].

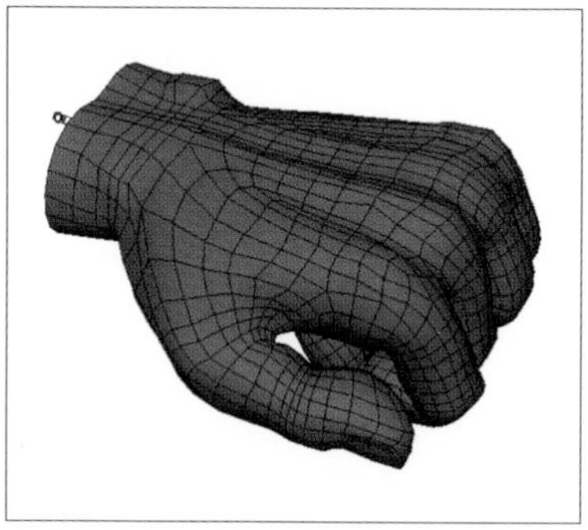

Figure 6-69 A Model with Adjusted Weight Values

This will open the Export Skin Weight Map Options window, as shown in Figure 6-70.

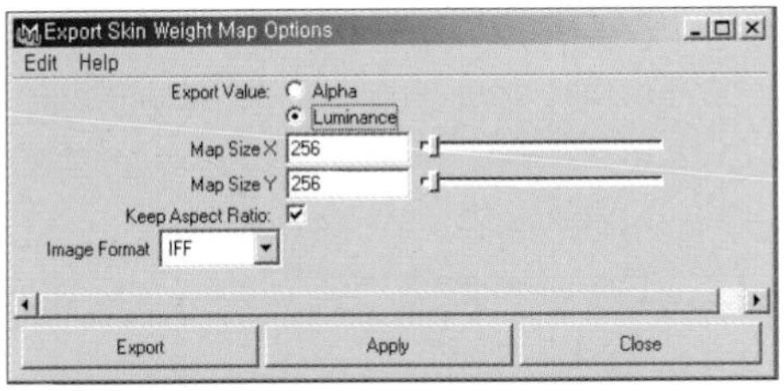

Figure 6-70 Options Window

The Options window is made up of the following menus:

- **Export Value**

  Alpha This is the Alpha Channel value. In other words, an opacity value is used to export.

  Luminance This is the Luminance value. In other words, a brightness (luminance) value is used to export.

- **Map Size X, Y**

  This determines the resolution of the map to export. For a more precise value, use values greater than 512.

- **Keep Aspect Ratio**

  When this option is turned on, it matches the length and breadth of the map to export.

- **Image Format**

  This determines the format of the map to export.

In my case, I usually set the Export Value to Luminance and the Image Format to JPEG.
After setting the Export Value to Luminance, the Map Size X,Y to 512 and the Format to JPEG, click the Export button.
A Save dialogue box will open as shown in Figure 6-71.
After selecting the desired directory, type an appropriate file name.
For example, type **maptest**, and then click the Write button.

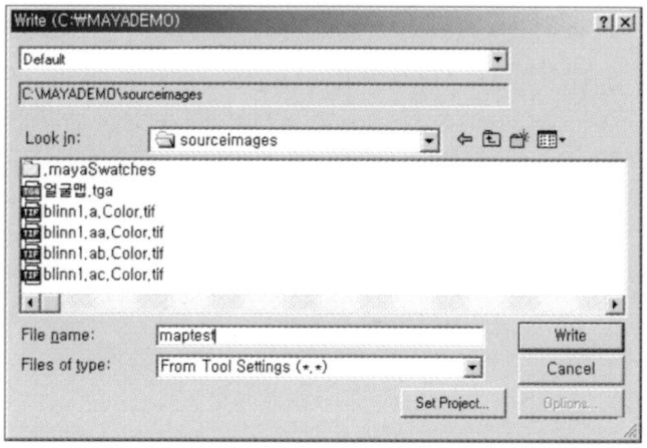

After clicking the Write button, Maya will ask if you wish to proceed (see Figure 6-72). Click the Yes button.

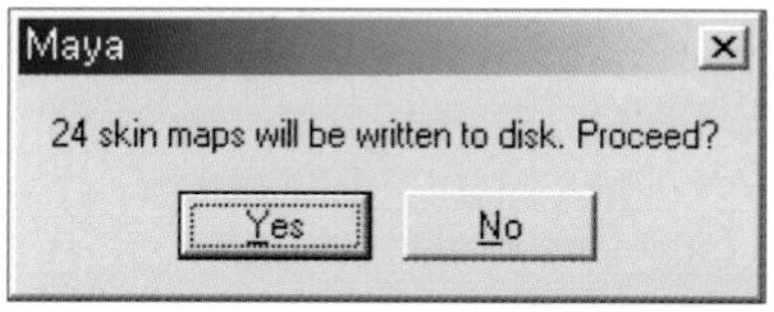

Figure 6-71 Save Map

A directory is made with the given name, and the Weight values of each of the joints are saved on a map in that directory.

Figure 6-72 Save Map

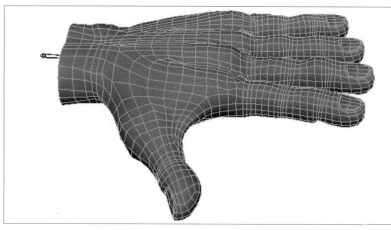

6. Import Skin Weight Tool

Load the exported Weight value from the previous section.

The figure in 6-73 is the image of the hand that has undergone changes from the previous steps. Therefore, the names for the UV-axis, the skeleton's hierarchy structure, and the joint should be the same as above.

Figure 6-73 The Altered Model

Select the model and then select [Animation > Skin > Edit Smooth Skin > Import Skin Weight Maps].

An Import dialogue box will appear as in Figure 6-74.

We named the file "maptest" when we exported. Maya automatically creates a folder named "maptest" and saves the weight map inside it. Maya also creates a filname.weightMap file inside the directory with the maptest folder in order to conduct Batch Import. Because we exported maptest, select the maptest.weightMap file and click the Import button.

In other words, when maptest, (inside folder A) is exported, a maptest folder along with the maptest.weightMap file is created inside folder A.

Maya then applies this new Weight value to the model (see Figure 6-75).

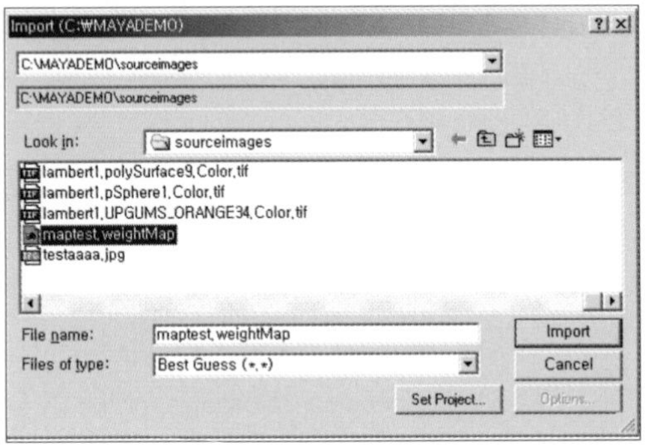

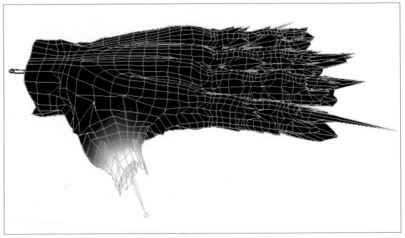

Figure 6-74 Import Dialogue Box

Figure 6-75 Import Skin Weight

The maptest.weightMap file and the maptest folder are created inside CD-ROM/CHARACTER/sourceimages. Open the polyhand.mb file and test it.

7. Mirror Skin Weight

In contrast to Rigid Bind, in Smooth Bind, we can create Weight values for one half of a symmetrical character and mirror copy them to the other side.

For example, as shown in Figure 6-76, after setting up the Weight values for one hand, select both hands, select [Animation > Skin > Edit Smooth Skin > Mirror Skin Weight], configure the options, and then click the Mirror button. (See Figure 6-77.)

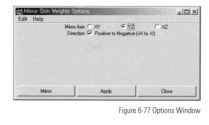

Figure 6-77 Options Window

Figure 6-76 Modifying the Weight Values of One Hand in Order to Mirror Copy

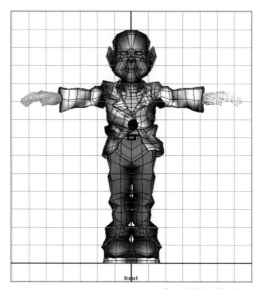

Figure 6-78 Mirror Skin Weight

We use the Options window to determine how and along which axis the object will be copied. In other words, Figure 6-78 shows us a front view of the model. If we want to copy the Weight values of the left hand to the right, in the Options window, the Mirror Axis should be set to YZ and the Direction to Positive to Negative (+X to -X). If the right hand were being copied to the left, the Direction option must be turned off.

This option is based upon the absolute axis of the window. Therefore, the character, as shown in Figure 6-78, will be arranged symmetrically around the centerline of the window.

Also, as shown above, the surfaces do not need to be separated from each other. For example, in terms of the jacket above, after setting the Weight values for half of the jacket, the other side can be mirror copied.

8. Copy Skin Weight

This feature copies the skin point Weight value of A onto B.

This feature comes in handy when making many similar characters. After setting the Weight values for one, they can be simply copied onto the others. However, you must make sure that the skeletal structures for each of the characters is the same and that the poses are also similar. If not, the Copy function will not work properly.

First, select the object for which the Weight value has been configured and then select the object to copy before selecting [Animation > Skin > Edit Smooth Skin > Copy Skin Weight].

I fully utilize this feature when binding in subdivision surfaces.

This will be covered in greater detail when we cover the binding process later in this chapter.

9. Reset Weight to Default

This initializes the Weight value to the initial binding state.

10. Prune Small Weight

This option deletes all Weight values below the value specified in the Options window and sets them all to 0. For example, by rotating a random joint on the smooth bound hand in Figure 6-79, we can easily see that this movement has an undesirable effect on some skin points.

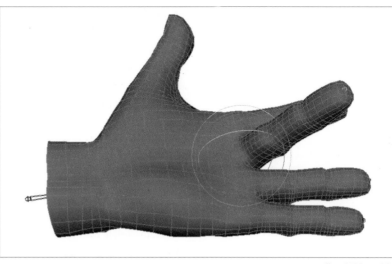

Figure 6-79 Rotate Joint

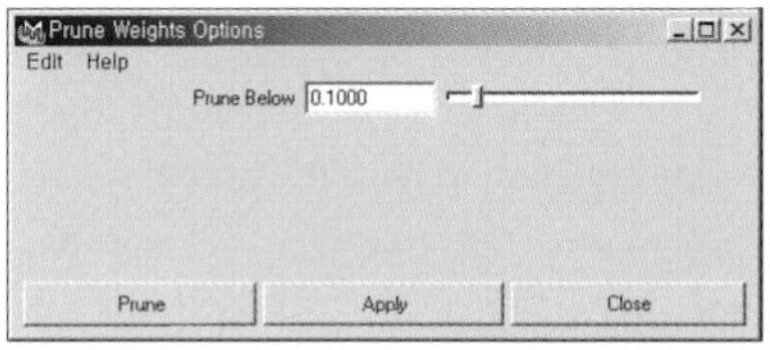

Figure 6-80 Options Window

In such instances, select [Animation > Skin > Edit Smooth Skin > Prune Small Weight ☐] to open the Options window. Enter an appropriate value (the Weight value of the skin point that is influenced) as shown in Figure 6-80, and then press the Prune button so that all values below this specified value will be set to 0.

11. Remove Unused Influences

When using Smooth Bind, at times, we will need to use many Influence Objects. Also, when using the Paint Skin Weight Tool to adjust Weight values, the values may take on a value of 0 depending on the Influence Objects. When the Weight value is set to 0, the Influence Object will not work.

In such cases, select the bound surface and apply this command to automatically delete these Influence Objects.

12. Normalization

The greatest difference between Smooth Bind and Rigid Bind is that in Smooth Bind, we can create a setup that causes one skin point to be influenced by all of the joints. This is possible because the skin point distributes the same Weight value to each of the joints. Maya automatically sets the sum of all Weight values to 1. Suppose that one skin point is affected by two joints, A and B. If the Weight value of A is set to 0.8, Maya, in order to maintain a sum of 1 for the Weight values, will automatically sets the Weight value of B to 0.2. This is called "Normalization."

There will be times when you want to have this number be greater than 1. The following options are used in such cases.

● Disable Weight Normalization

Selecting the bound surface and this menu allows us to use a value greater than 1. In other words, if the Weight value is 1 and the Paint Skin Weight Tool was used to paint at 0.5, then the Weight value will be 1.5.

● Enable Weight Normalization

Selecting the bound surface and this menu will bring the value back to 1.

The effects of this menu are not immediately visible. When using the Paint Skin Weight Tool, Maya automatically sets the value to 1 using the adjusted Weight value.

● Normalize Weight

If the bound surface has a value greater than 1 and you want to immediately change this value back to 1, select the bound surface and then select this menu.

These menus can be applied to the entire surface or to selected skin points.

3. SMOOTH BIND EXAMPLE

We have just finished taking a look at the basic menus for Smooth Bind.

We will now look at how to use Smooth Bind in character binding.

The character we will use in this example is the one that was modeled using subdivision surfaces earlier in the book. Because the subdivision surfaces have not yet been optimized, the example has more data than a Polygon or NURBS and binding this type of model directly is more difficult.

However, because we do not have to divide the character into multi-patches, as in NURBS, and because we do not have to control many vertices, as in Polygon, the end result will appear smoother and more natural.

As follows, directly binding a subdivision surface will create a highly polished result.

As I explain how to smooth bind subdivision surfaces, I will focus my attention on explaining the overall Smooth Bind environment. Please I make a mental note of how Smooth Bind is different from Rigid Bind as you follow along with the example.

In order to more effectively follow along with this example, open the CD-ROM/CHARACTER/scenes/ManBeforeBind.mb file. This file will help you to understand the flow of the entire process, and you will more effectively be able to bind your individual characters. If you do not use this file, you could encounter some difficulties in following along.

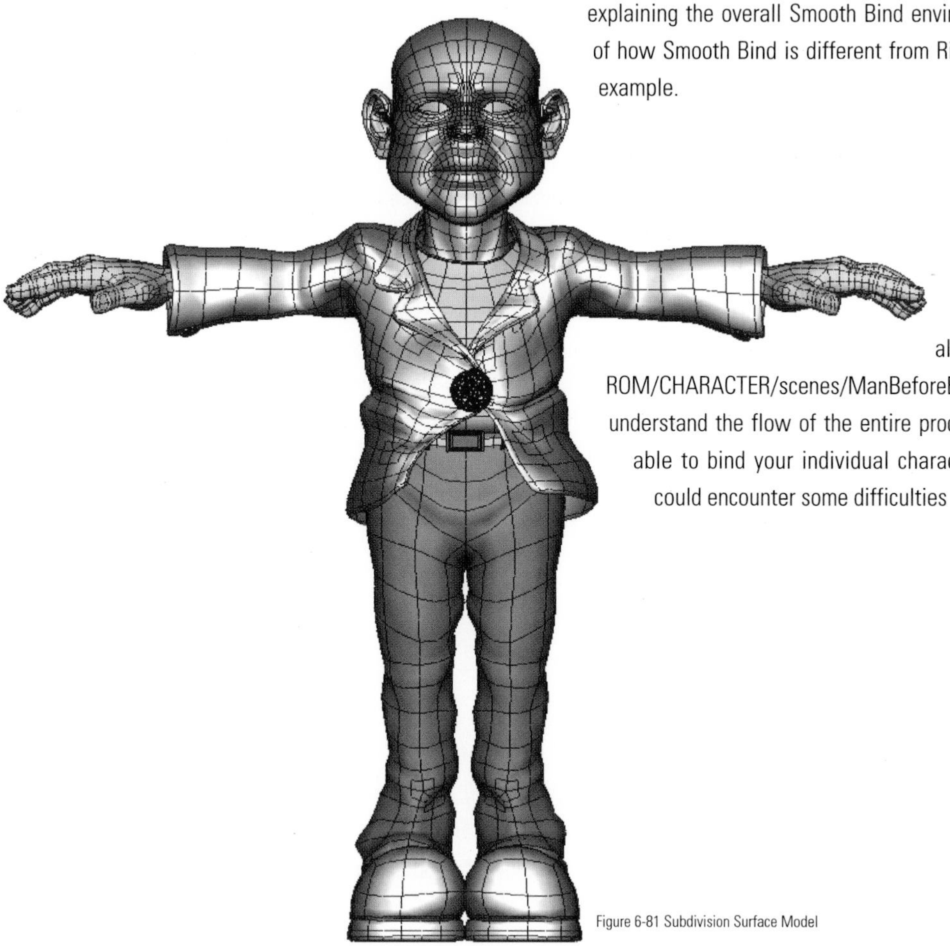

Figure 6-81 Subdivision Surface Model

Before Beginning

Before binding, make sure that all geometry transformations (Translate, Rotate, Scale) are set to default. If they are not, select all geometries and select [Modify > Freeze Transformation] to initialize their settings.

Also make sure that each model does not have any unnecessary histories. For example, if the model has an unnecessary UV-axis or history, select them all and delete them by selecting [Edit > Delete by Type > History]. Make sure that the Blend Shape of the face and any other miscellaneous deformers necessary for animation are not erased. Inspecting the data before binding prevents unnecessary errors from occurring while working.

3-1. PREPARATIONS FOR BIND

When animating characters, we usually assign layers by distinguishing it as a Low Polygon Model for the model that will be used in the actual rendering and animation keyframing.

The keyframing is set to Low Polygon, which has a comparatively fast display speed, and the rendering is done in the original model. This way, a lot of time and effort is saved.

This is especially the case for subdivision surfaces. It is very difficult to directly control a bound subdivision surface.

Therefore, the Low Polygon Model is created first. This Low Polygon Model also plays an important role when directly binding the subdivision surface.

step 1 First, select the face model made in Subdivision Surface. Then select [Modify > Convert > Subdiv to Polygon ◘] to open the Options window (see Figure 6-82).

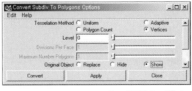

Figure 6-82 Options Window

In the Options window, set the Tessellation Method to Vertices and the Level to 0. Check the Show option next to Original Object, and then click the Convert button at the bottom.

As shown in Figure 6-83, the subdivision surface is converted to a polygon. Selecting the polygon, select [Edit > Delete by Type > History] to delete the polygon's history.

This history pertains to the conversion and is not needed for the animation. Therefore, it is deleted because it can increase the size of the data and reduce system speed.

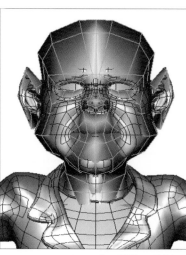

Figure 6-83 Convert to Polygon

step 2 In the same way, convert all subdivision surfaces to polygons. After converting, make sure to delete all the histories.

Figure 6-84 shows the converted polygon model.

Figure 6-84 Convert to Polygon

step 3 Click on the button in the Layer Editor, at the bottom of the Channel Box, to create two layers. Double-click on the layer name to open the Layer Editor, and change the name from Subdiv to Poly, as shown in Figure 6-85.

Figure 6-85 Layer Editor

step 4 Selecting all the polygon objects (excluding the model of the teeth), click the RMB on top of the Poly Name in the Layer Editor, as shown in Figure 6-85, and select Add Selected Objects from the Marking Menu. This puts the polygon object inside the Poly layer.

Next, select all subdivision surface models, and then click the RMB on top of the Subdiv Name in the Layer Editor, as shown in Figure 6-85, and select Add Selected Objects from the Marking Menu. The selected subdivision surface will be placed inside the Subdiv layer.

We have now completed the necessary preparations for binding.

3-2. DRAW SKELETON

The saved modeling data includes the skeleton. The basic skeletal structure is the same as Rigid Bind, which we learned about in the previous chapter. The only difference is that an extra joint has been added in the area indicated in Figure 6-86.

This joint is added to prevent the pelvis from twisting severely later when the leg is twisted. Because we learned how to make this skeleton in the previous chapter and because the structure is the same, I will not discuss the skeleton any further at this point. If you are still unsure about the skeleton, refer to "1-1. Draw Skeleton," under "1. Rigid Bind."

One thing that is different from Rigid Bind is that the joints, rather than Blend Shape, will be used to control the skeleton. Therefore, it is very important that the joints be placed very carefully. Figure 6-87 illustrates the positions of the joints.

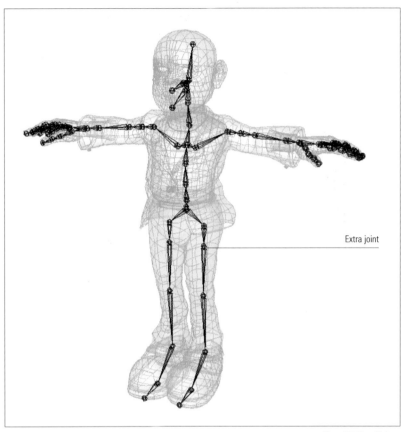

Extra joint

Figure 6-86 Draw Skeleton

Joint A becomes the central axis around which the lower jawbone rotates when the mouth is opened. Therefore, the placement of this joint will determine how the chin is moved and should be placed so that it closely resembles an actual chin.

Joint B will control the movement of the head. This joint correlates to the position of the cervical vertebrae.

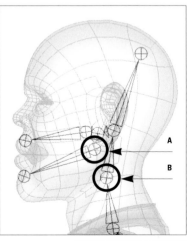

Figure 6-87 Joint Structure of the Head

3-3. BINDING SKIN

Once the skeleton has been made, select all the polygons, subdivisions, and NURBS surfaces, excluding those of the eyes and teeth. The eyes and teeth are not selected because they will be parented to the joint, instead of bound.

Select [Animation > Skin > Bind Skin > Smooth Bind ▢] to open the Options window. In the Options window, select [Edit > Reset Setting] to reset the options and then click on the Bind Skin button at the bottom. (See Figure 6-88.)

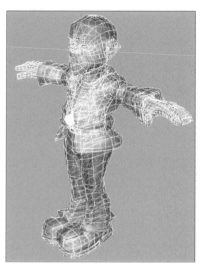

Figure 6-88 Selecting Surfaces and the Skeleton for Binding

This will smooth bind the low polygon, the subdivision surface, and the NURBS surface, which has been used here and there.

3-4. EDITING SKIN WEIGHT

We will now learn how to set the Weight values for bound models. As mentioned earlier, directly binding the subdivision surface and then modifying the Weight value, due to problems with system speed, is harder to do than with NURBS or Polygon.

Also, although we are now able to use Artisan tools when modifying subdivision surface Weight values (starting with version 4), the system speed drops drastically and we cannot work as precisely as we can with NURBS or Polygon.

Therefore, we will actively use the converted polygon.

In smooth binding, as for rigid binding and particularly for subdivision surfaces, a lot of time and effort is needed to obtain an accurate and precise character setup.

step 1 First, hide the NURBS surface and turn off the Subdiv in the layer to hide the subdivision surface. Only the skeleton and the polygon will be displayed, as shown in Figure 6-89.

Figure 6-89 Display Polygon & Skeleton

step 2 Let's first modify the Weight value for the shirt. Select the shirt and the skeleton and then press Alt+H to hide all unselected objects. Rotate the arm as shown in Figure 6-90.

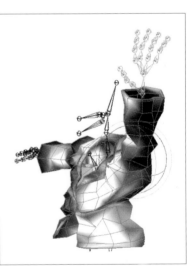

Figure 6-90 Rotate Joint

Verify the name of the selected joint in the Channel Box. If you have bound the example file, it will probably be named "joint22."

step 3 Select the shirt and select [Animation > Skin > Edit Smooth Skin > Prune Small Weight ☐].

In the Options window, set the Prune Below value to 0.1 and then press the Prune button at the bottom (see Figure 6-91).

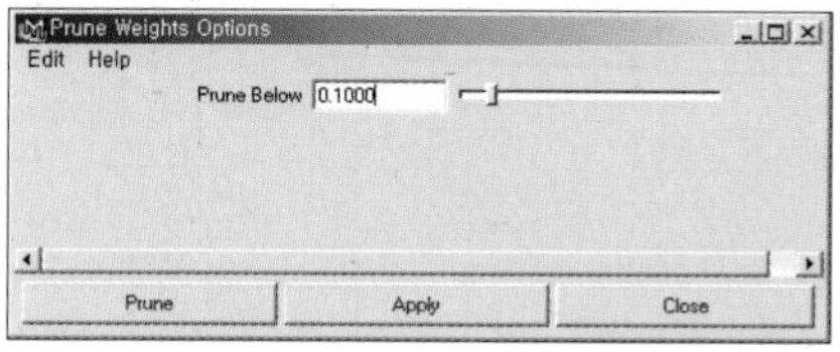

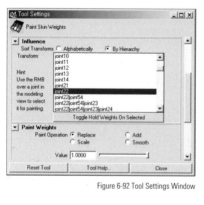

Figure 6-91 Options Window

All skin points of the shirt with a Weight value less than 0.1 will be set to 0. This prevents each joint from being affected, no matter how subtle, by the skin points.

step 4 Select the shirt, and select [Animation > Skin > Edit Smooth Skin > Paint Skin Weight Tool ☐].

Select the joint of the rotated arm from under Influence Settings in the Tool Settings window. Then, set the Paint Operation to Replace, the Value to 1 and then paint so that appropriate sections get a Weight value of 1 (see Figure 6-93).

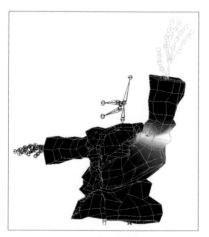

Figure 6-92 Tool Settings Window

Figure 6-93 Painting Weight Value

It world be better do this job while alternating between the use of the Replace and Smooth Paint Operations. Rotate the joint from time to time to make sure that the movement appears natural.

Set the value for the shirt collar to less than 0.1 so that it is slightly influenced by the moving arm.

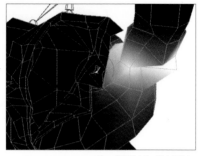

Figure 6-94 Painting Weight Value

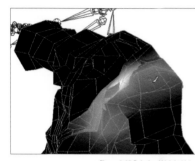

Figure 6-95 Painting Weight Value

Figure 6-95 shows the lowering of the arm. To make this appear natural, set the Paint Operation to Smooth before painting. Select joint21 from the Tool Settings window of the Paint Skin Weight Tool when working so that the joint affects the skin point of the shoulder. This creates a more natural movement.

Joint21 is used to portray the slight movements of the shoulder in response to the arm movements. Therefore, the Weight value must be modified by alternating between the use of the Replace and Smooth Paint Operations (see Figure 6-96). Also, as we did in Figure 6-97, rotate the joint from time to time to make sure that the movement appears natural.

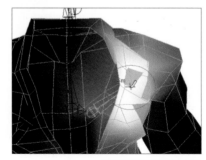

Figure 6-96 Painting Weight Value

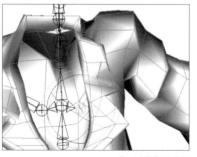

Figure 6-97 Rotate Joint

Next, let's look at the elbow. When the hand moves, the supervising joint must not affect the sleeve. Therefore, as shown in Figure 6-98, set the Weight value to 1 so that the sleeve is entirely affected by the elbow joint.

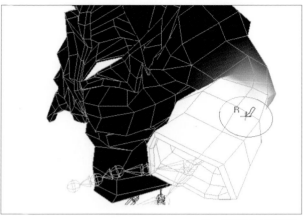

Figure 6-98 Painting Weight Value

Select the skeleton and then select [Animation > Skin > Go to Bind Pose] to change the skeleton to Bind Pose. Then, modify the Weight value of the spine by rotating the joint, as shown in Figure 6-99, before painting. Figure 6-99 illustrates the modification of Joint 4.

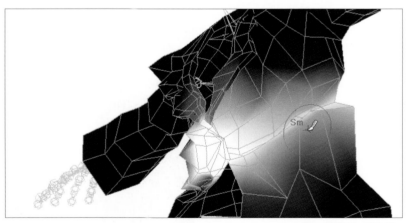

Figure 6-99 Painting Weight Value

In this way, paint all the skin point Weight values of each joint.

After the weights have been set for one side, Bind Pose the skeleton and then, selecting the shirt, select [Animation > Skin > Edit Smooth Skin > Mirror Skin Weight ☐].

Configure the options as shown in Figure 6-100 and press the Mirror button.

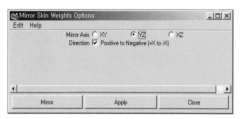

Figure 6-100 Mirror Skin Weights Options Window

Verify the mirror result by rotating the joint as shown in Figure 6-101.

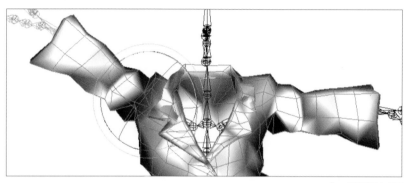

Figure 6-101 Rotate Joint

The Weight values will not be mirrored accurately through this step because the shirt itself is not symmetrical.

Because the Weight values are not mirrored properly, we must use the Paint Skin Weight Tool to modify Weight values on parts of the other side.

step 5 Because we are currently using a low polygon model, we cannot know for sure how the subdivision surface is changing. The subdivision surface has a smooth surface, and we have no way of knowing if the Weight values adjusted in Polygon have been applied correctly to the subdivision surface.

Let's now learn how to modify Weight values in areas of the subdivision surface after copying the Weight values, configured in polygon, to the subdivision surface.

Display the shirt made in subdivision surface. First select the Weight values, which have been set in Polygon, and then select the subdivision surface while holding down the Shift key.

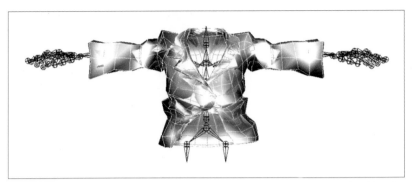

Figure 6-102 Selecting the Polygon and Subdivision Surface

Select [Animation > Skin > Edit Smooth Skin > Copy Skin Weight].

The polygon skin weight values will be copied directly onto the subdivision surface.

By modifying the Weight values in areas of the subdivision surface, we can create more precise detail. Rotate the joint to observe the subdivision surface. Select vertices, which have an inappropriate Weight value, and select [Windows > General Editors > Component Editor] (see Figure 6-103).

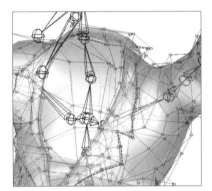

Figure 6-103 Selecting the Vertex

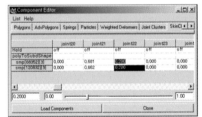

Figure 6-104 Component Editor

In the Component Editor (see Figure 6-104), magnify the Skin Cluster Tab on the farthest right-hand side. Slide the slider bar until the respective joint Weight value is displayed and then type in an appropriate Weight value.

Because we are only adjusting the Weight values for certain parts of the subdivision surface, this step does not take a lot of time. Also, because we can modify the vertices one at a time, we can obtain a very precise setup.

In this way, rotate each joint to verify the movements of the surface in response to the character's movements as you adjust the Weight values.

 step 6   Let's now adjust the Weight values of the hand.

First, in order to portray the movements of the wrist, rotate it as shown in Figure 6-105. Of the two wrist joints, select and rotate the one closer to the elbow. This is Joint24 of the left hand.

Use the Paint Skin Weight Tool to set the Weight values as shown in Figure 6-105. This setup creates a more natural twist of the wrist.

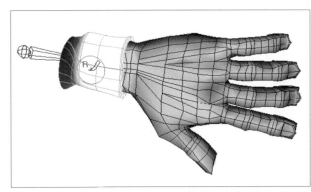

Figure 6-105 Painting the Weight Value of the Wrist

The next step is to paint the Weight value of the hand. To create a more natural movement, we need to adjust the Weight values while rotating the joints of the hand in various positions. (See Figure 6-106.)

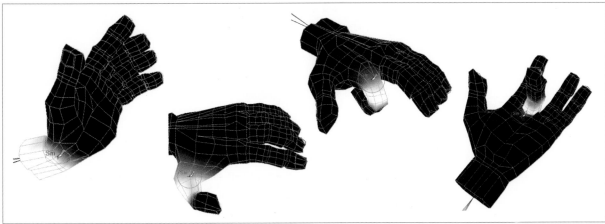

Figure 6-106 Painting Weight Value

Use the Paint Skin Weight Tool to adjust the Weight value as best as you can.

Afterward, copy the polygon Weight value to the subdivision surface. Display the subdivision surface hand. After first selecting the polygon hand and then selecting the subdivision surface hand, select [Animation > Skin > Edit Smooth Skin > Copy Skin Weight]. (See Figure 6-107.)

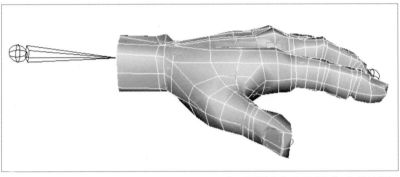

Figure 6-107 Selecting the Model to Copy the Weight Value

If necessary, use the Component Editor to adjust the Weight values of some of the vertices, just as we did for the shirt.

Figure 6-108 illustrates a test of the hand movements.

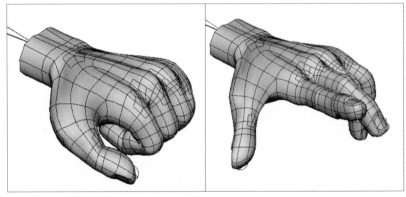

Figure 6-108 Testing the Hand

To mirror copy the hand Weight values, first select both hands, as shown in Figure 6-109, and then select [Animation > Skin > Edit Smooth Skin > Mirror Skin Weight]. The option settings are the same as for the shirt. Mirror copy the hands and the NURBS sleeve at the wrist.

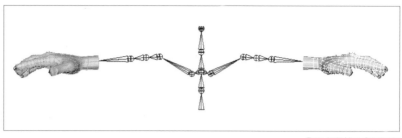

Figure 6-109 Mirror Skin Weight

step 7 In order to adjust the Weight values of the leg, rotate the joints of the legs to spread them, as shown in Figure 6-110.

The legs move as they do in the figure because the joints of both legs affect different skin points.

Figure 6-110 Rotate Joint

As shown in Figure 6-111, select the skin points of the left leg that are not affected by the rotating joint. Select [Windows > General Editors > Component Editor] to open the Component Editor. After expanding the Skin Cluster Tab, set the Weight value of the current joint to 1. This is Joint15 in this example.

Set the Weight value of the vertex on the other leg to 1 also. You should be setting the Weight value of Joint16 of the other leg to 1.

Figure 6-111 Selecting the Vertex

Component Editor

List Help

	joint14	joint15	joint16	joint16	jo
Hold	off	off	off	off	off
subdTessShape9					
vtx[8]	0.000	1.000	0.000	0.000	0.000
vtx[9]	0.000	1.000	0.000	0.000	0.000
vtx[36]	0.000	1.000	0.000	0.000	0.000
vtx[52]	0.000	1.000	0.000	0.000	0.000
vtx[60]	0.000	1.000	0.000	0.000	0.000
vtx[76]	0.000	1.000	0.000	0.000	0.000
vtx[100]	0.000	1.000	0.000	0.000	0.000
vtx[108]	0.000	1.000	0.000	0.000	0.000
vtx[173]	0.000	1.000	0.000	0.000	0.000
vtx[174]	0.000	1.000	0.000	0.000	0.000

| 1.0000 | 0.00 | | 1.00 |

| Load Components | Close |

Figure 6-112 Component Editor

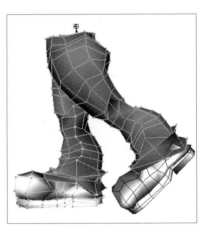

Use the Paint Skin Weight Tool to set the Weight values and rotate the leg joints, as shown in Figure 6-114, to adjust the movements of the legs. We set the Weight values on this shape so that the model will move naturally. Some of the skin points of the shoes have been set to the Weight value of the upper leg joint leading to this abnormal movement.

Figure 6-113 Adjusting the Weight Values

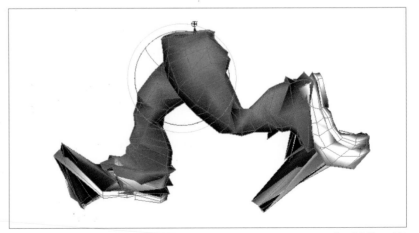

Figure 6-114 Rotate Joint

Let's first adjust the Weight values for the left shoe. In the Channel Box, select the names of the joints on the left that are used by the shoe to view the image.

Select the left shoe and then select [Animation > Skin > Edit Smooth Skin > Paint Skin Weight Tool ☐].

As shown in Figure 6-115, paint to adjust the Weight value of the shoe.

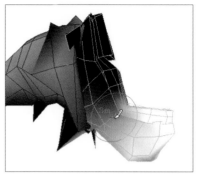

Figure 6-115 Painting Weight Value

Adjust the Weight values for the pants in the same way. There will be some vertices for which the Weight values cannot be adjusted by painting. The vertex in the area indicated in Figure 6-116 sticks out much more than other areas. It is much more effective to use the Component Editor, rather than the Paint Skin Weight Tool, to adjust the Weight values in such areas.

Figure 6-116 Painting Weight Value

After adjusting the Weight values, mirror copy the Weight values of the pants and the shoe to the other side. Select the skeleton and then select [Animation > Skin > Go to Bind Pose] to return the skeleton to a Bind Pose.

First, select the pants and then select [Animation > Skin > Edit Smooth Skin > Mirror Skin Weight]. Select both shoes and apply Mirror Copy in the same way.

Now, display the subdivision surface models for the pants and shoes in order to copy the Weight values onto the subdivision surface.

Select, first, the polygon model of the pants and then select the subdivision surface while holding down the Shift key. Apply [Animation > Skin > Edit Smooth Skin > Copy Skin Weight Tool].

Copy the Weight values of both shoes in the same way. After copying all the Weight values, rotate the joints to make sure that the subdivision surface moves properly.

If some areas do not move naturally, edit them using the Component Editor.

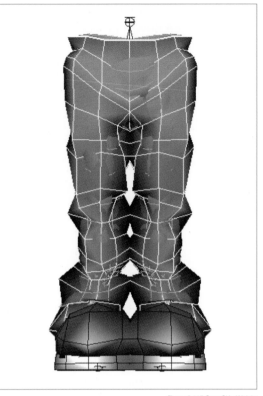

Figure 6-117 Copy Skin Weight

step 8 Let's now modify the Weight values for the face. We must pay particular attention to the face to get an accurate setup.

Generally, the opening of the mouth is made using joints. Therefore, the set up for the facial muscles, coinciding with the movements of the jaw, must be set up precisely so that Blend Shape can be used simultaneously or so that a natural expression can be made when using clusters.

Although when using the Paint Skin Weight Tool, we usually create the set up for one side and simply mirror copy it to the other side, in this case, we will be using another tip for the Paint Skin Weight Tool. First, in the Tool Settings window, check the box next to Reflection X under the Stroke section.

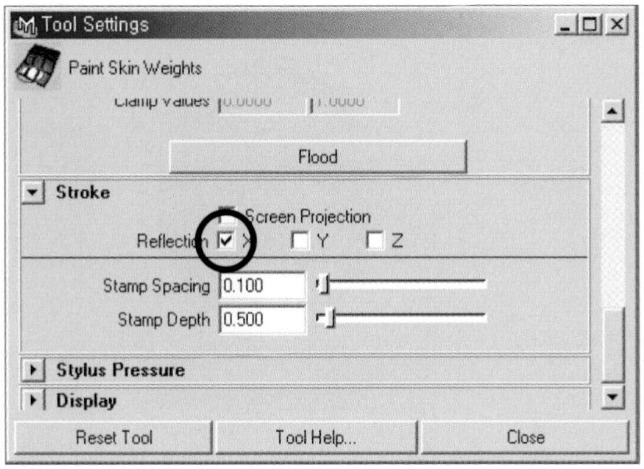

Figure 6-118 Tool Settings Window

This option allows us to paint symmetrically across the X-axis.

The Screen Projection option at the bottom allows us to paint symmetrically about, not the X-axis, but the entire screen, and, therefore, should be turned off. This option is not used all the time, but by learning it now, it may become handy in the future.

As shown in Figure 6-119, rotate the joint that controls the lower jaw and paint the Weight values so that the mouth opens.

One thing to note here is that the setup must be made to affect all the skin points of the face. In reality, the cheeks, the edges of the nose, and the bottoms of the eyes must be made to move slightly to create natural expressions during the animation.

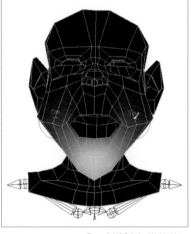

Figure 6-119 Painting Weight Value

Because the Weight values of the face must be configured precisely, we must first copy the Weight value onto the subdivision surface and then more precisely adjust the vertex Weight values in the subdivision surface through the Component Editor. The shape of the mouth, in particular, is especially important. Therefore, adjust the vertex Weight values of the mouth in the Component Editor as shown in Figure 6-120.

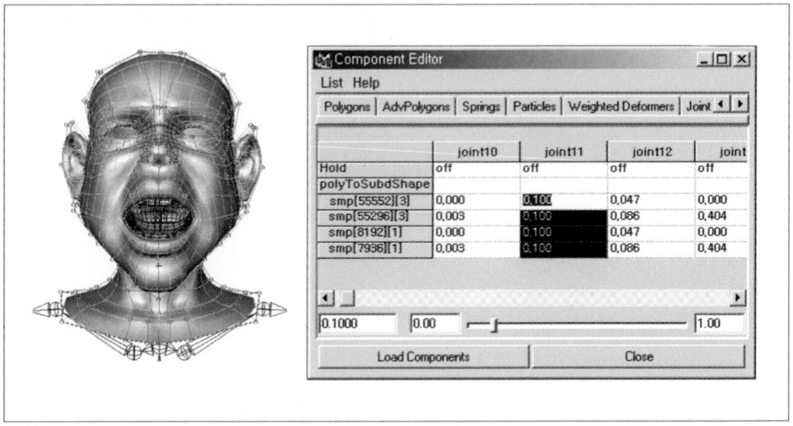

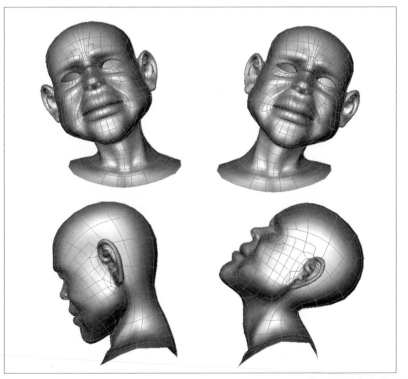

Figure 6-120 Modifying Weight Values in the Component Editor

Figure 6-121 shows an example of how the Weight values were configured to portray the movements of the head. In this way, modify the Weight values in the Component Editor so that the shape changes as the joints are rotated.

Figure 6-121 Moving the Head

Continue to rotate the joints and adjust the Weight values in the Component Editor until the shape of the mouth appears natural.

step 9 This character has objects, such as buttons and belts, on his clothes. These objects must move along with the model. Therefore, after observing how the nearby Weight values are configured, adjust the Weight values of these objects in the same way.

Let's look at Figure 6-122. In the beginning, only the Weight value for the shirt was adjusted, which is why, when the joints of the spine are rotated, the button distorts abnormally.

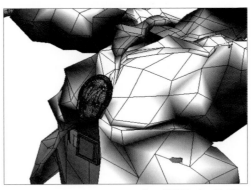

Figure 6-122 Distortion of the Button

Because this button serves to fix the clothes in place, it must have its own movement and not be affected by the movements of the clothes. Therefore, the Weight values for this button must all be the same.

First, if you would like for the button to fall perfectly into step with the movements of the clothes, only one joint must influence the Weight value of several of the vertices around the button.

Rotate the joint as shown in Figure 6-123. The joint seen here is the joint nearest the button, and this is the joint that should influence the button.

In this example, this joint is joint3.

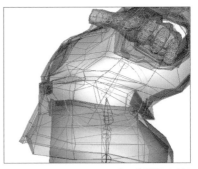

Figure 6-123 Rotate Joint

As shown in Figure 6-124, select several of the vertices around the button.

Select [Windows > General Editors > Component Editor...] to open the Component Editor and, after expanding the Skin Cluster Tab, set the Weight value of joint3 to 1, as shown in Figure 6-125.

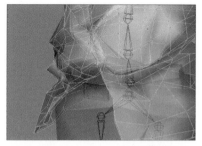

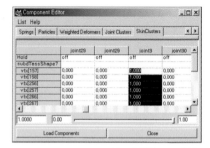

Figure 6-124 Select Vertex | Figure 6-125 Component Editor

Display the button and select all the vertices of the button. (See Figure 6-126.)

In the same way, set the Weight value of joint3 to 1 in the Component Editor. Now, when we rotate the joint, the button should move with the joint, as shown in Figure 6-127.

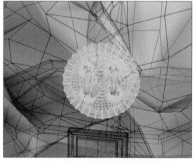

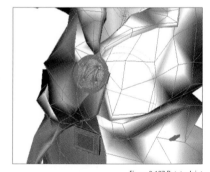

Figure 6-126 Select Vertex | Figure 6-127 Rotate Joint

Copy the adjusted polygon Weight value onto the subdivision surface so that the subdivision surface takes on the Weight value of the polygon.

Set up the remaining buttons on the sleeves in the same way.

To adjust the movement of the belt, select some of the CVs of the NURBS torso, all the CVs and vertices of the belt, and some of the vertices of the pants, as shown in Figure 6-128. We must create the setup so that only some of the joints affect these skin points. Therefore, in order to facilitate the re-selection of the current skin points, select [Create > Set > Quick Select Set...].

As shown in Figure 6-129, type **BeltPoint** and click OK.

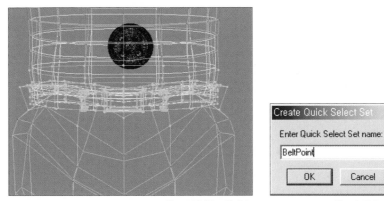

Figure 6-128 Select Skin Point

Create Quick Select Set

Enter Quick Select Set name:

BeltPoint

OK   Cancel

Figure 6-129 Create Set

Select [Windows > General Editors > Component Editor] and then set the Weight value of joint1 to 1 so that the selected skin points receive the full effect of the root joint.

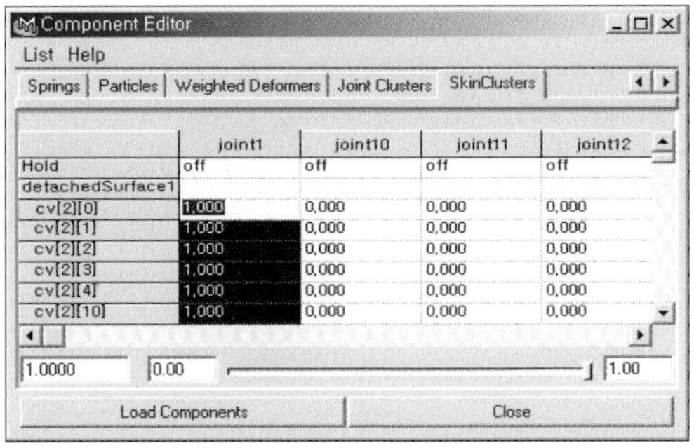

Figure 6-130 Component Editor

Rotate joint2 as shown in Figure 6-131. Select [Edit > Quick Selection Set > BeltPoint], and then adjust the Weight value of joint2 in the Component Editor so that the rotating joint2 affects the selected skin point. A value of approximately 0.35 was used here.

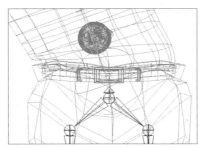

Figure 6-131 Rotate Joint

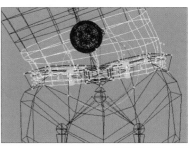

Figure 6-132 Weight Value: 0.35

As shown in Figure 6-133, after rotating joint3, select the BeltPoint set and adjust the Weight value through the Component Editor. Set the Weight value to 0.05 so that the influence is slight.

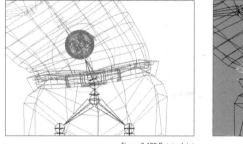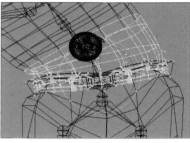

Figure 6-133 Rotate Joint   Figure 6-134 Weight Value: 0.05

Using the same procedure, adjust the Weight values appropriately by rotating each of the joints.

After all the Weight values are modified, copy the polygon Weight value of the pants to the subdivision surface pants.

In this chapter, we learned how to bind a character using smooth bind and how to effectively setup the Weight values.

The more you practice, the more skilled you will become at binding and character setup. Therefore, I recommend that you practice with a lot of binding styles until you find the one that is right for you.

It is also possible to use a lattice deformer, as we saw for Rigid Bind earlier, in Smooth Bind for indirect binding.

Try tying up some of the vertices of the subdivision surface into a lattice and testing the indirect bind in order to see for yourself which method is more effective.

The important thing is to create the best result you can in the shortest amount of time. How and what steps you use to get there do not matter.

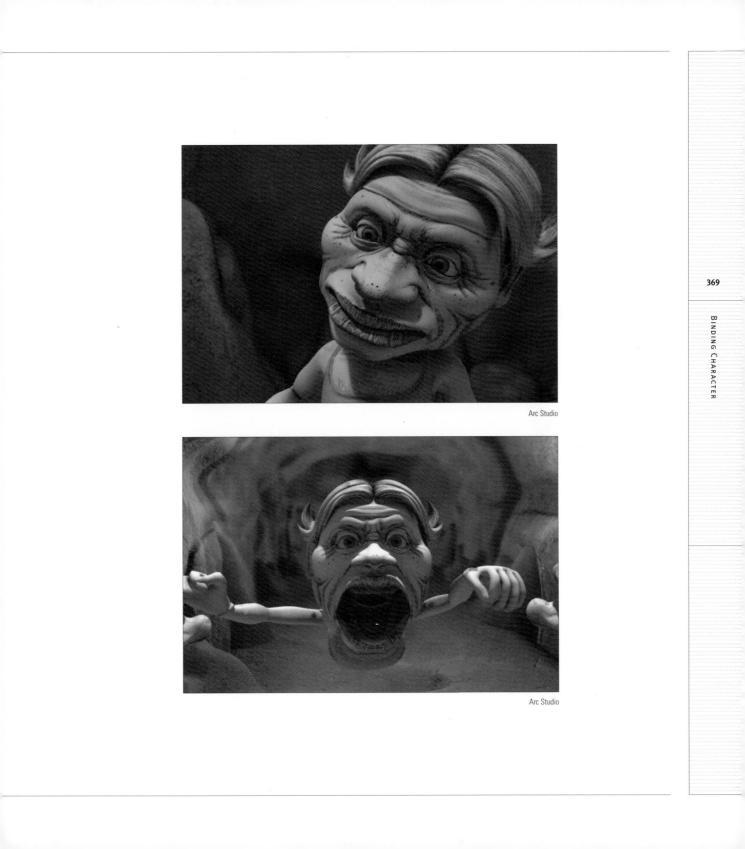

Arc Studio

Arc Studio

7

Character Setup

In order to create the desired movements, users must set up the character environment when animating. This series of steps is referred to as Character Setup, and it will be different depending on the preferences of each user. This chapter will seek to explain general character setup.

By adapting the steps explained here, users will be able to handle a wide variety of movements. Users familiar with Maya should have no trouble understanding the concepts explained here.

1. FORWARD KINEMATICS AND INVERSE KINEMATICS

In 3D Animation, there are two types of keyframing. One is Forward Kinematics and the other is Inverse Kinematics. This is completely dependent on user preference. Users may use the type of keyframing that is more convenient for them.

In general, partial movements of arms and hands use Forward Kinematics and leg movements use Inverse Kinematics.

Now we will use a bound character to observe the differences between the two keyframing types.

1-1. FORWARD KINEMATICS

The organization of the skeleton is hierarchical. In other words, joints are the parents of the upper joints so that when these upper joints are moved or rotated, the lower joints follow.

Forward Kinematics does not require a special setup.

The following Figure 7-1 is the character that was bound using the Rigid Bind in the previous chapter.

We will use this character as an example.

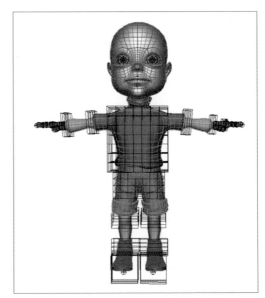

Figure 7-1 Rigid Bind Character

Human characters, like this character, usually use Forward Kinematics for the arm movements. Selection Handles are used so that each arm joint can be easily selected. In order to bring out the Selection Handles, the joints are selected as shown in Figure 7-2.

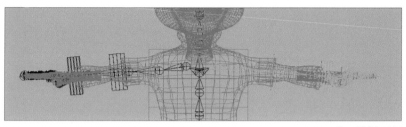

Figure 7-2 Select Joint

Select [Display > Component Display > Selection Handle] to display the selection handles. Because the handles appear in the center of the currently selected joint, they are hard to distinguish with the naked eye. After pressing the F8 key to convert to Component Mode and clicking on Component Mask, select the selection handle and move to an appropriate position, as shown in Figure 7-3.

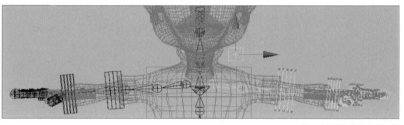

Figure 7-3 Move Selection Handle

After displaying all the other selection handles on the arm joints, position them as shown in Figure 7-4.

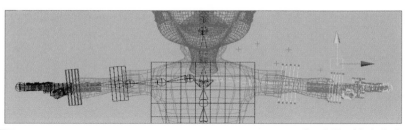

Figure 7-4 Move Selection Handle

Display the selection handles on the other arm, and position them so that they are easy to select.

After displaying the selection handles as such, select the joints that will be keyframed, add a motion, and then give it a key.

This method is more complicated than Inverse Kinematics. This is because in order to give each joint an appropriate motion, all of the joints must be modified and the key value must also be modified using the Graph Editor. All in all, there is a lot of work involved in this method.

However, this method does have its share of advantages. In contrast to Inverse Kinematics, this method can create more precise hand motions. If there are several elements to control, a more precise movement will result.

Actually, experienced animators strongly prefer Forward Kinematics over Inverse Kinematics. I will explain why later when we compare these two methods, after we first take a look at Inverse Kinematics.

1-2. INVERSE KINEMATICS

In Forward Kinematics, the lower joints moved in response to the movements of the upper joints. However in Inverse Kinematics, the opposite is true. In other words, this time, the upper joints will move in response to the movements of the lower joints.

Maya offers the IK Handle made especially for Inverse Kinematics, and users can use these handles to control the movements of the joints.

Inverse Kinematics is most often used to create leg movements.

Because the legs are fixed on the ground and the body moves independently of the legs, this type of movement is difficult to do using Forward Kinematics. Therefore, it is more effective to add IK Handles to the legs and use Inverse Kinematics.

We will use the character from above to go over the process for leg setup.

Figure 7-5 shows an example of a leg with IK Handles.

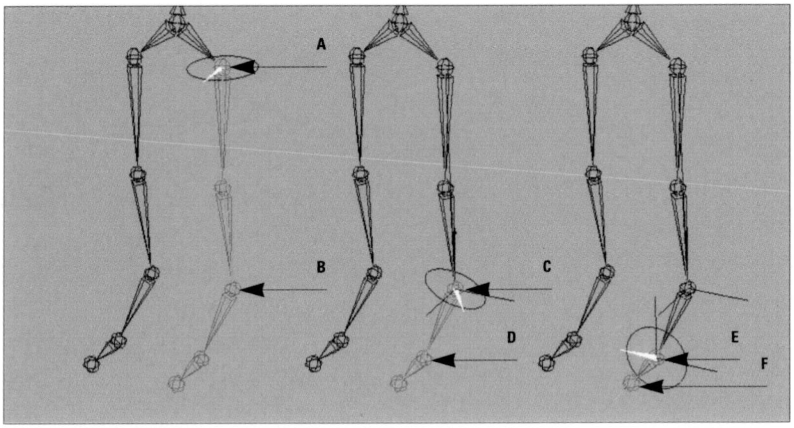

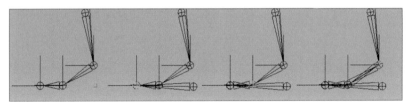

Figure 7-5 Using IK Handles

Select [Animation > Skeleton > IK Handle]. We will work with the IK Handle options set to Default. As shown in Figure 7-5, select Joint A and Joint B consecutively. The name was changed to L1 for convenience in the Channel Box. Next, insert IK Handles into Joint C and D and into Joints E and F. Name them L2 and L3, respectively.

Now make a new support joint and parent it to the support joints with the IK Handles. First of all, make a support joint in Side View as shown in Figure 7-6.

Figure 7-6 Making Support Joints

If the joints were made in the order shown in the figure, press the Enter key to finish this step. Select [Edit > Duplicate] to duplicate the joints and position them as shown in Figure 7-7.

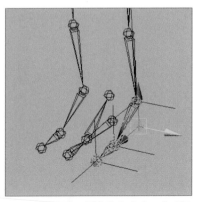

Figure 7-7 Positioning the Supporting Joints

Select [Windows > Hypergraph] to open the Hypergraph Window.

As shown in Figure 7-8, click the MMB for the IK Handle in the Hypergraph, and drag it on top of the joint. This is the process of parenting the IK Handle to the joint.

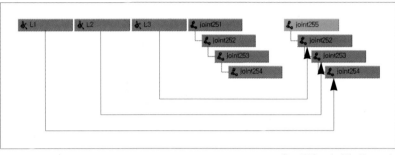

Figure 7-8 Parenting Using Hypergraphs

In other words, we are parenting the IK Handle to the support the joint in the IK Handle. Use the same process to create the IK Handle and the support joint on the opposite leg, and parent the IK Handle to the joint. By moving the created support joint, we can see, as shown in Figure 7-9, the joint moving as a result of Inverse Kinematics. By moving the root joint, as in Figure 7-10, we can see that the leg is fixed on the ground.

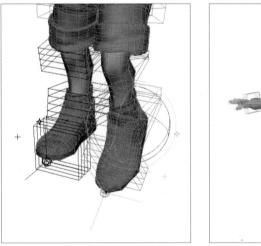

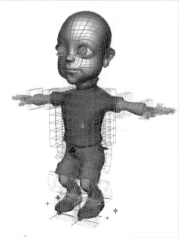

Figure 7-9 Moving the Supporting Joint   Figure 7-10 Moving the Root Joint

For more about detailed character setup, please refer to "2. Advanced Character Setup," later in this chapter.

1-3. SWITCHING FORWARD AND INVERSE KINEMATICS

Users can, as needed, switch between FK (Forward Kinematics) and IK (Inverse Kinematics). This allows users to selectively choose the appropriate keyframing for special motions when creating character animation. For example, this technique is useful when creating arm movements.

As seen in Figure 7-11, the arm moves to form an arc. This type of animation can be very difficult to create using IK. In FK, all we would need to do is keyframe a selected shoulder joint; however, in IK, the IK Handles are used to draw the arc and then keyframing is done. Therefore, keyframing with IK is very complex

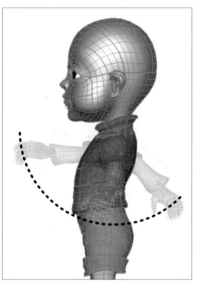

Figure 7-11 Arm Movements

In contrast, let's suppose that we are trying to keyframe the motion of a character climbing up a ladder. In order to affix the character's hands to the ladder, we need to use IK.

As follows, there are going to be situations when users need to switch between IK and FK as needed. In order to facilitate this, Maya offers convenient options that allow users to switch between the two modes.

The options for IK and FK include Set IK/FK Key, Enable IK Solver, and Connect to IK/FK, and they are located within [Animation > Animate > IK/FK Keys].

Through the use of these three options, users can switch from IK keyframing to FK keyframing and vice versa.

We will look at how these options are used through a simple example.

First of all, as shown in Figure 7-12, draw a simple skeleton and add IK Handles. For convenience, the joint names have been changed as shown.

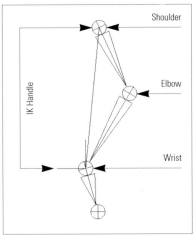

Figure 7-12 Drawn Skeleton

1. Switching to IK from FK

In order to conduct FK keyframing, we first need to stop the operation of the IK Handle Solver. After selecting the IK Handle, select [Animation > Animate > IK/FK Keys > Enable IK Solver] and then set it to Off.

In order to set the currently selected IK Handle Solver to On or Off, select [Display > Head Up Display > Animation Detail]. As shown in Figure 7-14, the relevant text is displayed at the bottom of the window. As in the figure, make sure that the currently selected IK Solver Enable is set to Off.

IK/FK Keys   ✕
Set IK/FK Key
Enable IK Solver
Connect to IK/FK
Move IK to FK

Figure 7-13 Enable IK Solver: Off

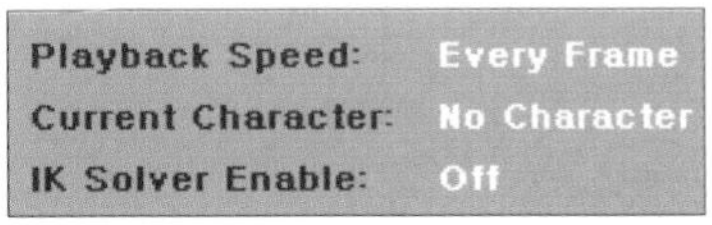

Playback Speed: Every Frame
Current Character: No Character
IK Solver Enable: Off

Figure 7-14 Animation Detail

First, move the frame to Frame 1 and then, as in Figure 7-12, select the shoulder joint and then rotate the joint, as shown in Figure 7-15.

Rotate the elbow joint also, as shown in the figure.

Select either the shoulder or elbow joint, and click [Animation > Animate > IK/FK Keys > Set IK/FK Key].

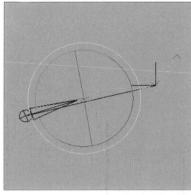

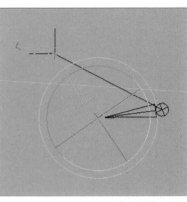

Figure 7-15 Rotate Joint   Figure 7-16 Rotate Joint

Move the frame to Frame 10. After rotating the elbow and shoulder joints as shown in Figure 7-16, click on the [Animation > Animate > IK/FK Keys > Set IK/FK Key] button.

Play the animation. From Frames 1-10, the rotation value of the joints is animated. Now let's use the IK Handles to conduct IK keyframing.

Move to Frame 20 and select the IK Handle. Select [Animation > Animate > IK/FK Keys > Enable IK Solver] and set it to On. Verify that the IK Solver Enable is set to On in the Animation Detail at the bottom of the window.

After moving the IK Handle as shown in Figure 7-17, click [Animation > Animate > IK/FK Keys > Set IK/FK Key].

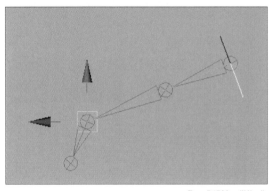

Figure 7-17 Move IK Handle

Play the animation to verify the result. FK animation should take place between Frames 1 and 10, and IK animation between Frames 20 and 30.

2. Switching to FK from IK

After moving to Frame 1, select [Edit > Delete All by Type > Channel] and remove all the keys. Select the IK Handle and verify that [Animation > Animate > IK/FK Keys > Enable IK Solver] is checked. If it is set to Off, click on it to set to On. Move the IK Handle to the position shown in Figure 7-18, and click [Animation > Animate > IK/FK Keys > Set IK/FK Key]. Move to Frame 10. After moving the IK Handle as shown in Figure 7-19, click [Animation > Animate > IK/FK Keys > Set IK/FK Key]. Move to Frame 20 and, after positioning the IK Handle as shown in Figure 7-20, click [Animation > Animate > IK/FK Keys > Set IK/FK Key].

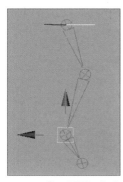

Figure 7-18 Move Handle

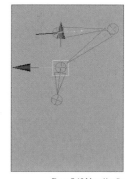

Figure 7-19 Move Handle

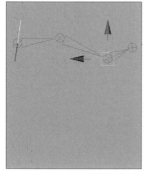

Figure 7-20 Move Handle

Playing the animation, we can see the IK Handle animation in effect from Frames 1 to 30. Move to Frame 30.

Select the IK Handle and click [Animation > Animate > IK/FK Keys > Enable IK Solver] to set it to Off.
After rotating the shoulder and elbow joints as shown in Figure 7-21, click [Animation > Animate > IK/FK Keys > Set IK/FK Key].

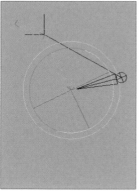

Figure 7-21 Rotate Joint

Play the animation to verify the results. IK animation occurs from Frames 1 to 20, and FK animation occurs from Frames 20 to 30.

3. Connecting to IK / FK

When doing character setup, at times, users will use a random object to constrain the use of the IK Handle for convenience. At times like this, users do not have to separately select the IK Handle through a menu, but simply select the IK Handle-constrained object to set the IK/FK key.

For example, look at the instance below. In order to point-constrain the IK Handle, make the polygon cube as shown in Figure 7-22 and set it to an appropriate size and position.

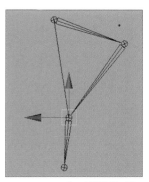

Figure 7-22 Making Cubes

In order to point-constrain the IK Handle of the cube, first select the cube, then select the IK Handle, and then select [Constraint > Point].

With both the cube and the IK Handle selected, click [Animation > Animate > IK/FK Keys > Connect to IK/FK]. When the cube is selected, we can see that the IK Solver Enable is set to On or Off at the bottom of the window.

Now, users do not have to select the IK Handle to set the IK/FK key, but simply do so by selecting the cube. Users will be better able to understand this by going through the examples given above again, this time by selecting the cube.

4. Move IK to FK

When IK is moved to FK, the position of the IK handle will not follow the joint controlled by FK. The position of the IK handle will be fixed at the point where it converts to FK, which can make things confusing for the animator and make it difficult to convert back to IK at the point controlled by FK.

In such instances, we use Move IK to FK. Simply by selecting the IK handle and then selecting this menu, we can move the IK handle to the joint.

5. Using IK Blend to Move IK to FK

The latest version of Maya allows us to move easily from IK to FK and vice versa. This menu, which is introduced for the first time in version 5.0, is called IK Blend.

Make the joint and the IK handle shown in Figure 7-23. After you've made the joint and the IK handle, look in the Channel Box and you'll find the IK Blend option at the bottom (Figure 7-24).

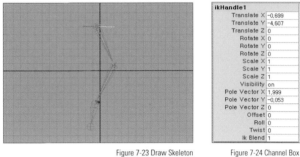

Figure 7-23 Draw Skeleton   Figure 7-24 Channel Box

Insert frame 1 and, after positioning the IK handle as shown in Figure 7-25, keyframe it. Insert frame 10 and, after positioning the IK handle as shown in Figure 7-26, keyframe it, too.

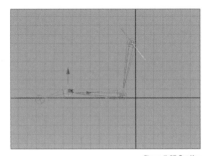

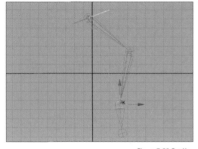

Figure 7-25 Set Key   Figure 7-26 Set Key

Right-click the mouse on IK Blend in the Channel Box and select Key Selected. Insert frame 20, set the IK Blend value to 0 in the Channel Box, and then keyframe it.

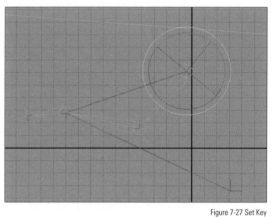

Figure 7-27 Set Key

Now, after controlling the joint using FK (Figure 7-27), keyframe it and play the animation. You will see that, from frames 1 to 10, the animation is controlled using IK; from frames 10 to 20, we move from IK to FK.

As we saw in this example, by keyframing the IK Blend value of the IK handle in the Channel Box, we can easily move from IK to FK and from FK to IK.

2. ADVANCED CHARACTER SETUP

Up to this point, we have looked only at basic character setup. From now on, we will look at a more effective setup procedure for controlling character movements.

Users will have their own individual styling methods, but by using setup as a foundation, they will be able to control almost all character motions.

In reality, the human body is made up of 206 bones. The joints connecting each of these bones and the spine and vertebra are able to move. Portraying this wealth of movement is very complex and calls for accurate and precise operations.

The skeleton generated by most software programs, excluding skin transformation systems based on muscular structure, affect the skin, creating small differences compared to human structure.

Now we will look at the character setup process using the skinning data from the smooth binding created earlier.

For the example, open the CHARACTER\scenes\ManBind.mb file in the accompanying CD-ROM.

If you are not too familiar with setups, you should first follow along with the example and then practice on your own.

2-1. USING EXTRA JOINTS

The example file is already bound with the skeleton, and the smooth bind and the weight value has already been added.

Through this setup process, which will endow the character with motion, users will be able to more quickly and easily control characters.

First we need to use the support joints to more easily and accurately control movement.

1. Leg Control

Let's look at leg control. Basic leg control is executed in the same manner as the leg setup found in "1-2. Inverse Kinematics" (see page 373).

However, more details will be added to make the setup more elaborate.

step 1 Let's look at the method for leg control through the creation of an extra support joint. As shown in Figure 7-28, copy the leg joint and move it into position.

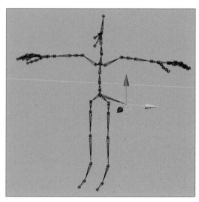

Figure 7-28 Copying to an Appropriate Location

step 2 Now we will do the actual setup that will allow us to control the leg using the support joint made in Step 1.

We are using a more complex method, rather than a simpler one, in order to keep the leg from twisting. Refer to Figure 7-32.

These joints will be connected using the Connection Editor. Select [Windows > General Editors > Connection Editor] and open the Connection Editor.

After selecting Joint A, as shown in Figure 7-29, press Reload Left in the Connection Editor. Select Joint G, and press Reload Right in the Connection Editor.

As shown in Figure 7-30, link the Rotate Y and Z from Outputs to the Rotate Y and Z of Inputs.

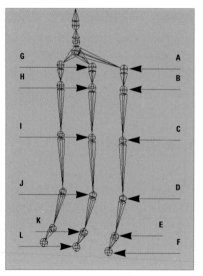

Figure 7-29 Joint Name

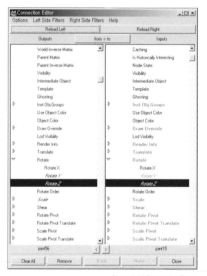

Figure 7-30 Connection Editor

By doing this, we will be able to control the movement of the leg, as shown in Figure 7-31.

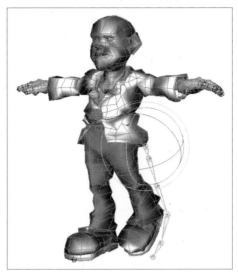

Figure 7-31 Moving the Joints Linked Using the Connection Editor

Now we can see each of the joints connected using the Connection Editor and their corresponding movements.

Referring to the image, link to the attributes in the Connection Editor and verify the movements.

Put Joint A in Outputs and
Joint H in Input.
Link the Outputs of Rotate X and
the Inputs of Rotate X.
As shown in the figure on the right, this method is used to
control the leg twists.

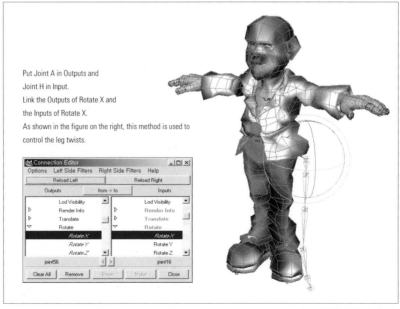

Figure 7-32 Controlling Leg Twists

Put Joint C in Outputs and Joint I in Inputs.

Link the Outputs of Rotate Z and the Inputs of Rotate Z.

As shown in the figure on the right, this method is used to control the movements of the knee joints.

Figure 7-33 Controlling the Knee Joints

Put Joint D in Outputs and Joint J in Inputs.

Link the Rotate Outputs.

As shown in the figure on the right, this method is used to control the movements of the ankles.

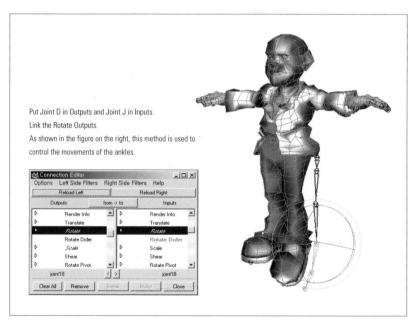

Figure 7-34 Controlling the Movements of the Ankles

Link the rotation of the remaining Joints E and K and Joints F and L. Join them as shown above. Joint B must be removed using [Animation > Skeleton > Remove Joint].

We remove this joint because it is not necessary. If we do not remove this joint, it will cause all of the rotate channels in the Channel Box to lock, which will prevent rotation. This prevents the IK Handles used in the leg from affecting the joints.

step 3 Add an IK Handle to the leg, as shown in Figure 7-35. This IK Handle must be made using IK Rpsolver. Then, move the joint back to its original position, as shown in Figure 7-36. By moving the joint while pressing the V key, we can move the joint to the exact position.

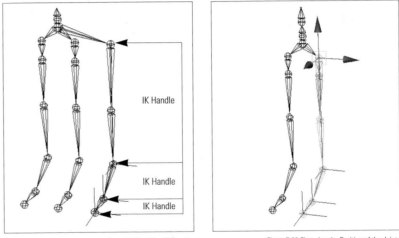

Figure 7-35 Adding IK Handles   Figure 7-36 Changing the Position of the Joints

Now we will make the support joint that will be used to control the leg. All we need to do is parent this joint to the IK Handle. This is the same procedure outlined in "1-2. Inverse Kinematics." The only difference is the use of the Connection Editor in the beginning.

One thing to keep in mind when making the support joint is that it must be aligned precisely with the heel of the shoe, as shown in Figure 7-37. This makes it easier to control the rotation of the ankle when the leg touches the ground.

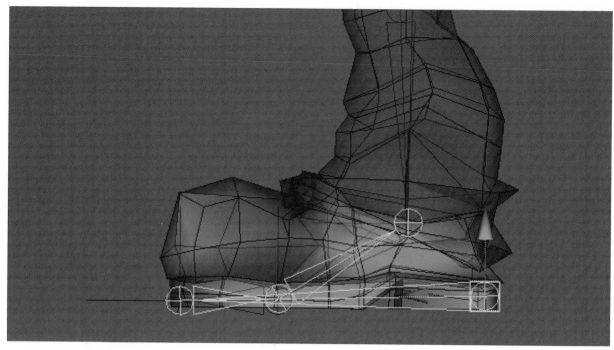

Figure 7-37 Changing the Position of the Joints

The next image, Figure 7-38, shows the parenting of each IK Handle to its respective joint. Make sure that your character moves as shown in the figure.

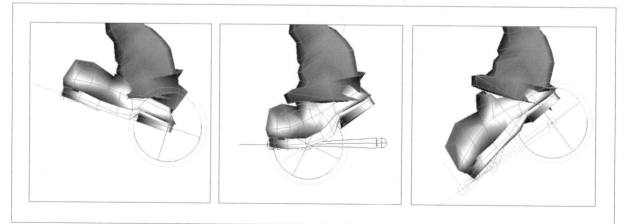

Figure 7-38 Movements of the leg Through the Supporting Joints

Apply the same procedure to the opposite leg. Go through the procedure making sure to pay attention to how to each joint is linked using the Connection Editor.

2. Arm Control

The arms are set in the same way as the legs. The arm, however, is slightly more complex than the leg. This is because the entire arm or just the wrists can be twisted, and setup must portray these details.

 step 1 Duplicate the arm joint as we did for the leg, and move it to an appropriate position, as shown in Figure 7-39.

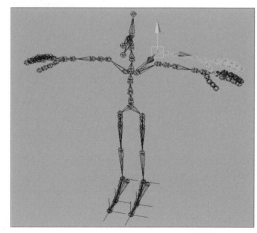

Figure 7-39 Duplicate Joint

Leave only the shape of the duplicated joint as shown in the figure below, and delete everything else. Remove all of the fingers and the center arm joint by selecting [Animation > Skeleton > Remove Joint].

Figure 7-40 Remove Joint

step 2 Select [Windows > General Editors > Connection Editor...] and open the Connection Editor.

As shown in Figure 7-41, select the Joint A and click Reload Left in the Connection Editor. As shown in the same figure, select the Joint E and click Reload Right in the Connection Editor.

As shown in Figure 7-42, link the Rotate Y and Z from Outputs to the Rotate Y and Z of Inputs.

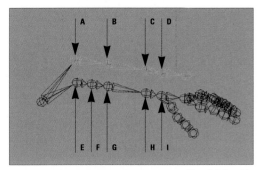

Figure 7-41 Extra Joint

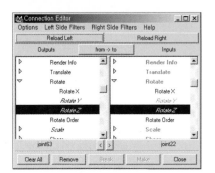

Figure 7-42 Connection Editor

This allows us to control movements, as shown in Figure 7-43.

Figure 7-43 Controlling Arm Movements

The next figure shows the connection state of each joint connected using the Connection Editor and the corresponding movements. Referring to the image, link to the attributes in the Connection Editor and verify the movements.

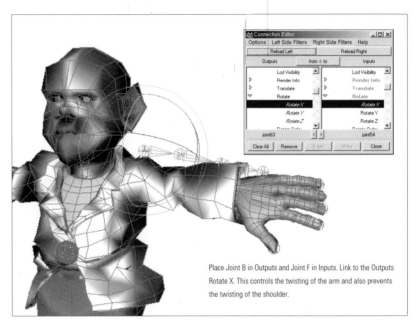

Place Joint B in Outputs and Joint F in Inputs. Link to the Outputs Rotate X. This controls the twisting of the arm and also prevents the twisting of the shoulder.

Figure 7-44 Controlling the Twisting of the Arm

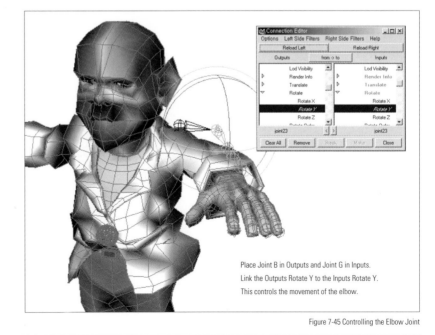

Place Joint B in Outputs and Joint G in Inputs. Link the Outputs Rotate Y to the Inputs Rotate Y. This controls the movement of the elbow.

Figure 7-45 Controlling the Elbow Joint

As shown in Figure 7-45, sometimes it is convenient to constrain the joints using [Animation > Constraint > Orient]. We will leave the explanation at that for now, but using the Orient constraint is sometimes a good idea for accurate joint movement.

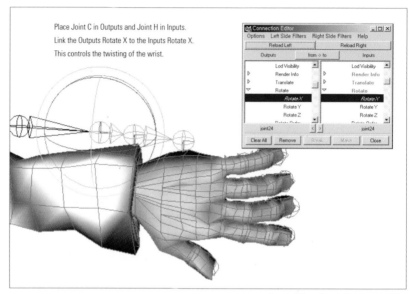

Place Joint C in Outputs and Joint H in Inputs.
Link the Outputs Rotate X to the Inputs Rotate X.
This controls the twisting of the wrist.

Figure 7-46 Controlling the Twisting of the Wrist

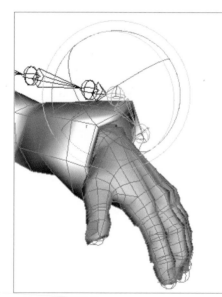
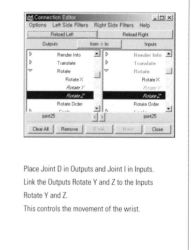

Place Joint D in Outputs and Joint I in Inputs.
Link the Outputs Rotate Y and Z to the Inputs Rotate Y and Z.
This controls the movement of the wrist.

Figure 7-47 Controlling the Movement of the Wrist

We have been looking at the process for arm control using support joints.

This is completely user preference. Support joints can be used to control joint movement using Inverse Kinematics, or this process can be avoided altogether using Forward Kinematics.

Experienced animators strongly prefer to use Forward Kinematics over Inverse Kinematics for arm movements.

The arm has a wider range of movements than the leg. Arms can lift objects, and sometimes, for one reason or another, arms need to be fixed against a wall or some other object. When the arm needs to be fixed against an object, Inverse Kinematics is used.

For example, when simulating lifting weights or climbing a ladder, it is easier to create the arm movements using Inverse Kinematics.

The following example is for a setup that takes into account several situations.

This is just a suggestion, but users should realize that this type of setup is possible and then adapt it to fit their own needs.

● Using Handles for Simple IK

This is for simultaneously using FK and IK as described in "1-3. Switching Forward and Inverse Kinematics," (see page 376).

This setting allows users to insert IK handles for IK or switch between FK and IK as needed.

step 1 First, display the Selection Handles for the support joints, and move it into an appropriate position as shown in Figure 7-48. Selection Handles facilitate the selection of FK-movable joints.

As shown in Figure 7-48, use the IK Rpsolver to make the IK Handle.

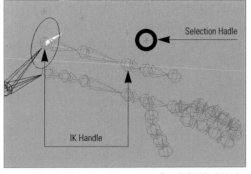

Figure 7-48 Adding IK Handles

step 2 Move the support joint to the original joint position as shown in Figure 7-49. By moving the joint while pressing the V key, we can move the joint to the exact position.

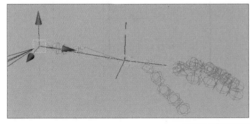

Figure 7-49 Move Joint

Select [Create > Locator] to make the Locator and move it into an appropriate position, as shown in Figure 7-50.

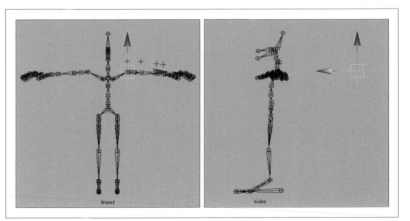

Figure 7-50 Making and Arranging Rocators

step 3 This Locator constrains the IK Handle Pole Vector. Not only does this control arm twists, it also prevents arm distortions during manipulation of the IK Handle.

Details on this setup are introduced in "2-3. Using Constraint and Custer" (see page 402). First, select the Locator and then select the IK Handle while holding down the Shift key. Select [Animation > Constraint > Pole Vector]. The IK Handle Pole Vector becomes constrained by the Locator as shown in Figure 7-51.

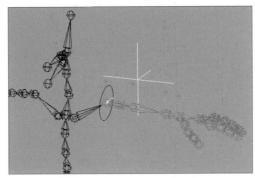

Figure 7-51 Constraining the Pole Vector

Now we can switch between FK and IK to keyframe as explained in "1-3. Switching Forward and Inverse Kinematics" (see page 376).

● **Setup to Fix the Hand in a Particular Spot**

We need a slightly different setup to fix the hand in a particular spot.

First, let's examine Figure 7-52.

step 1 As shown in the following figure, add the IK Handle to the respective joint. Select Joint A and lock the Rotate Y, Z Channel in the Channel Box.

In a previous step, we had already linked, using the Connection Editor, the Rotate Y and Z axes of the Joint C to follow the Rotate Y and Z axes of Joint B.

For a simple setup, select Joint C. After selecting the connected Rotate Y and Z channel in the Channel Box, click the RMB and then select Break Connection in the Marking Menu to break the connection.

Now, first select Joint B, then Joint C, and then select [Animation > Constraint > Orient].

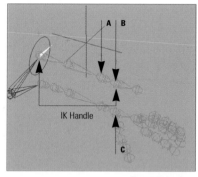

Figure 7-52 Arm Setup

step 2 Select [Create > Polygon Primitives > Cube] to make a polygon cube. Arrange the polygon cube and adjust the scale as shown in Figure 7-53. In order to precisely center the joint in the figure on the polygon cube, move it while pressing the V key on the keyboard.

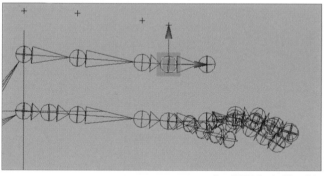

Figure 7-53 Making the Polygon Cube

Press the F8 key to adjust the polygon vertex in Component Mode so that it appears as in Figure 7-54. This is to alter the shape of the polygon without changing the pivot.

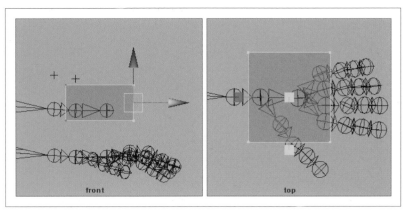

Figure 7-54 Editing the Vertex to Make the Shape

step 3 As shown in Figure 7-55, select the polygon cube and then select [Animation > Constraint > Orient].

Select the polygon cube first and then after selecting the added IK Handle, select [Animation > Constraint > Point].

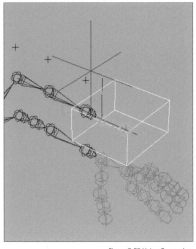

Figure 7-55 Using Constraints

step 4 After selecting the Locator and the IK Handle, select [Animation > Constraint > Pole Vector] to constrain the IK Handle Pole Vector to the Locator. Now move the support joint to the position of the original joint.

Again, we move the joint while pressing the V key, so that we can move the joint to the exact position, as shown in Figure 7-56.

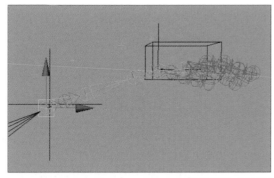

Figure 7-56 Move Extra Joint

Now, use the Rotate and Move tools on the cube to transform it into the one seen in Figure 7-57. Then, after selecting the root joint of the skeleton, move it from side to side along the X-axis.

The arm will appear to move as if the hand is fixed to the wall, as shown in Figure 7-58.

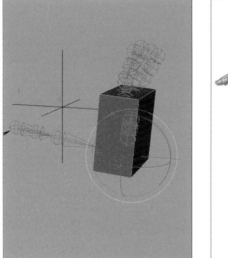

Figure 7-57 Rotate Poly Cube

Figure 7-58 Move Root Joint

This type of setting can be very useful at times.

Apply the same setting to the opposite arm. Because the joint of the opposite arm was basically created using Mirror Copy, the joint can rotate at times when it is Orient-constrained. When this happens, rotate the cube to the original position.

This is further explained on page 427 in the "2. Fixing the Hands Using Constraint" example.

2-2. USING IK SPLINE HANDLE

In general, the IK Spline Handle is usually used to control spine movements in human characters. In this section, we will look at how to make IK Spline Handles and how to control them.

step 1 After selecting [Animation > Skeleton > IK Spline Handle Tool], add an IK Spline Handle to the joint indicated in Figure 7-59. In order to have the handle appear on top, click the lower joint first and then click on the upper joint. Make the IK Spline Handle using the default value.

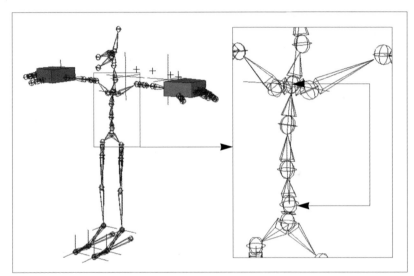

Figure 7-59 Adding IK Spline Handles

step 2 In [Panel Menu > Show], select only NURBS Curve and Deformer and set everything else to Off, as shown in Figure 7-60.
In Figure 7-61, we can see the NURBS Curve made based on the IK Spline Handle.
Observing it in Component Mode (F8), we can see a total of 4 CVs. A curve made from a default 4 CVs is shown.

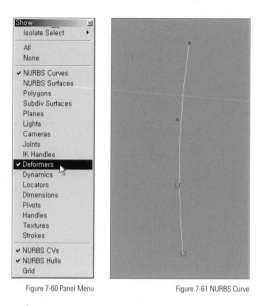

Figure 7-60 Panel Menu

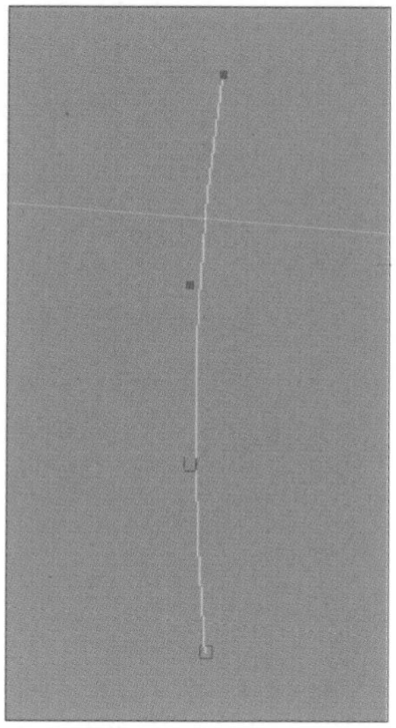

Figure 7-61 NURBS Curve

step 3 Now, selecting only the uppermost CV in the Curve CV in Figure 7-61, select [Animation > Deform > Create Cluster ▢] to open the Options window. After selecting Mode Relative, as in Figure 7-62, click on the Create button below. Immediately thereafter, select [Display > Component Display > Selection Handle] to display the Cluster Selection Handle. In order to view the handle, select Handles in [Panel Menu > Show] of Figure 7-60 and set it to On. The cluster and handle will be displayed as in Figure 7-63.

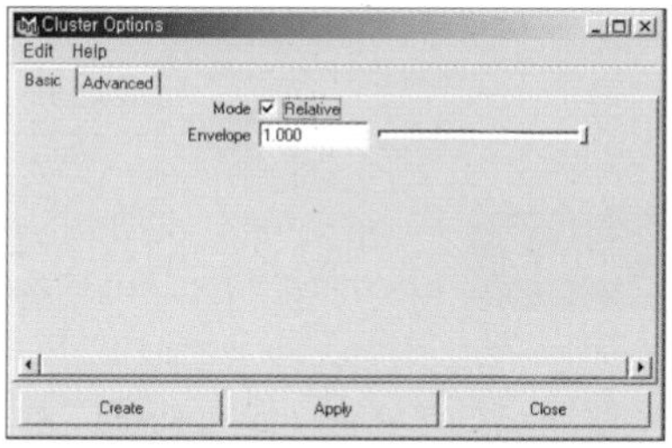

Figure 7-62 Options Window

Figure 7-63 Create Cluster

Using the same method, make clusters for the two remaining CVs, excluding the Start CV at the very bottom, as shown in Figure 7-64.

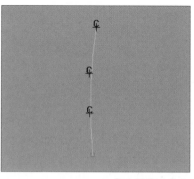

Figure 7-64 Create Cluster

Now we can control the spine movements using the cluster and IK Spline Handle we just made.

As in Figure 7-65, select the cluster and move it to observe the movements of the character. Also, as shown in Figure 7-66, after selecting the IK Spline Handle, adjust the Twist value in the Channel Box to observe the degree of twisting.

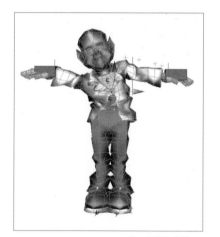

Figure 7-65 Movie Cluster

Figure 7-66 Twist IK Spline Handle

After selecting all the clusters so that they follow the movements of the character, select joint1 of the skeleton's root joint and select [Edit > Parent] to parent the cluster to the joint.

Select the Root Joint and move it so we can see that the cluster follows the movements of the root joint.

2-3. USING CONSTRAINT AND CUSTER

We will now learn how to use Constraint and Cluster for elaborate sectional setting. We will learn how to use basic Constraint using the method outlined below and learn how to use it to create movement through the example in the back.

We will also learn how to use Cluster to elaborately set up the character and the importance of using cluster in facial animation.

First, we will look at how to constrain the IK Handle Pole Vector using the Constraint menu.

1. Constraining the Pole Vector

In the previous process, we learned how to make IK Handles using IK Rpsolver for arm and leg control. Among the IK Handles, the IK Rpsolver, in contrast to the IK Spsolver, has the attribute of a Pole Vector, as seen in Figure 7-67. By constraining this, users will be able to more effectively control joint movements and abnormal leg movements when doing Inverse Kinematics Keyframing.

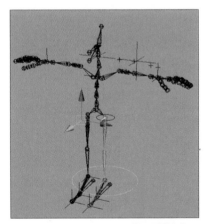

Figure 7-67 Pole Vector

As a short example, select the root of the support joint for leg control and move it at random. This causes an irregular flip of the knee of the Pole Vector Character.

Controlling the constrained Pole Vector can solve this problem. In order to control the Pole Vector, select [Create > Locator] and after making a Locator, arrange it as shown in Figure 7-68. Adjust the scale if necessary.

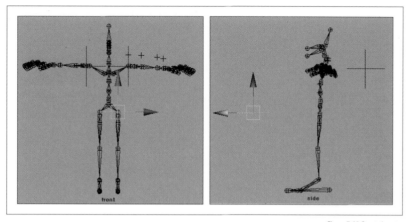

Figure 7-68 Create Locator

Select the Locator, and then select the IK Handle used in the leg. Select [Animation > Constraint > Pole Vector].

As shown in Figure 7-69, the selected IK Handle becomes constrained to the Locator.

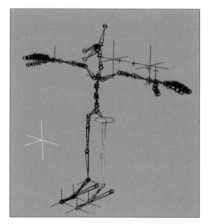

Figure 7-69 Constraining Pole Vectors

Select the Locator and move it from side to side. To observe the movement more closely, after selecting the root of the support joint, rotate a fixed portion of the joint along the Y-axis. We can see that the character's knee is not affected at all by the movements of the character. In order to fix this problem, slightly move the locater. We can now observe the knee responding to the movements.

Figure 7-70 Move Locator

Apply this method of constraining the Pole Vector using the Locator on the remaining feet and arms.

2. Controlling Body Changes

Most 3D graphics software is made up of a system where skin changes are controlled by the skeleton. Although this allows us to quickly and easily control the character, it makes it difficult to create perfect skin changes. Recently, there has been much talk about animation rooted in muscular structure, and I expect muscle-based animation to become active very soon.

This system will cause the muscles to contract and expand according the movements of the skeleton and then cause the skin to change as a result. If this type of animation becomes a reality, character movements will become smoother and more lifelike.

The character used in this example was made using Smooth Binding. Unlike Rigid Bind, Smooth Binding cannot use Flexor, and Influence Object must be used to control partial changes. Influence Object gives us sectional control, such as folding the joints and muscular movement. However, I tend to prefer Cluster over Influence Object. Cluster gives me more detailed control over the epidermis. However, using it does require more time and effort. This is not necessary if an elaborate setup is not used. Some detailing is possible through the mere adjustment of Weight values.

Using a hand as an example, we will look at how to use Clusters here.

step 1 First of all, as shown in Figure 7-71, rotate the finger joints. Do this using Subdivision Surface.

Observing the figure, we can see that the joint at which the finger bends is rounded. This is not all that elaborate. This area protrudes somewhat due to the bone. If this is the desired effect, users will find Cluster to be very effective.

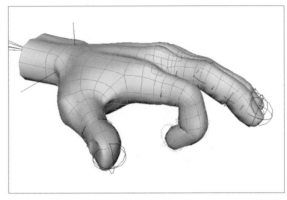

Figure 7-71 Rotate Joint

Move the joint back to its original position. In Component Mode, select the vertex of the Subdivision Surface, as shown in Figure 7-72.

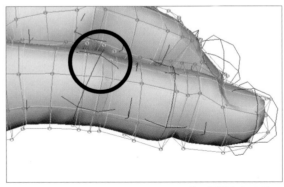

Figure 7-72 Selecting the Vertex

step 2 Select [Animation > Deform > Create Cluster ☐] to open the Options window and verify that Mode Relative has been checked. If it is set to Off, click on it to set it to On.

Click on the Create Cluster button at the bottom to create a cluster that ties together the selected Vertices.

For easier selection, select [Display > Component Display > Selection Handle] and display the Selection Handle of the Cluster.

Select the cluster that has been made and after selecting the joint that is located where the cluster is, press the P key on the keyboard to parent the cluster to the joint, as shown in Figure 7-73.

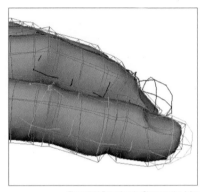

Figure 7-73 Parenting the Cluster to the Joint

The important thing here is to rearrange the Deformation Order.

If the joint is rotated as it is now and the cluster moved, the cluster will move abnormally.

This is because the Deformation Order for the Skin Cluster, used to change the surface, and the cluster made later have not been appointed properly.

In order to control the cluster in the desired way, the cluster made later must come before the skin cluster made through binding.

In order to change this order, select Subdivision Surface and click the RMB to select [Inputs > Complete List] from the Marking menu. The List of History Operation window will open, as shown in Figure 7-74.

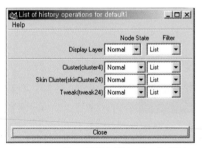

Figure 7-74 List of History Operation Window

As shown in the figure, we can see that the cluster made later comes before the skin cluster.

In order to change this order, click the MMB above the cluster name, and after dragging it behind the Skin Cluster name, release the mouse.

As a result, the cluster comes after the skin cluster.

This creates the proper Deformation Order.

step 3 Select [Animation > Animate > Set Driven key > Set ▣] to open the Set Driven Key window.

After selecting the finger joint parented to the cluster, click on the Load Driver button at the bottom of the Set Driven Key window.

After selecting the cluster, click on the Load Driver button at the bottom of the Set Driven Key window.

Select Rotate Z of the Driver and the Translate X, Y, Z of Driven. The Rotate Z of the joint in Driver is the rotational axis for bending the finger. Creating this axis is different for every skeleton and the axis should be rotated directly before selecting.

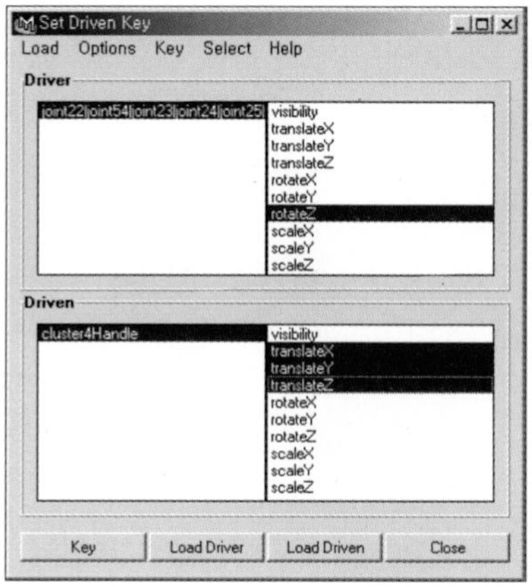

Figure 7-75 Set Driven Key Window

After selecting it, click on the Key button at the bottom of the Set Driven Key window in the current state (without rotating the joint).

As shown in Figure 7-76, randomly rotate the joint along the Z-axis. Select the cluster and then move it so that it protrudes somewhat as shown in Figure 7-77. In the present condition, click on the Key button at the bottom of the Set Driven Key window.

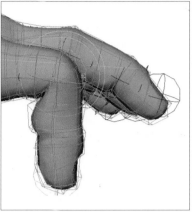

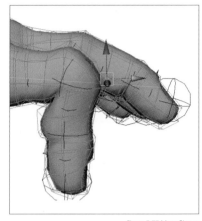

Figure 7-76 Rotate Joint   Figure 7-77 Move Cluster

For a more natural change, adjust the Vertex Weight value for the cluster.

Select the vertex as shown in Figure 7-78, and adjust the Weight value in the Component Editor.

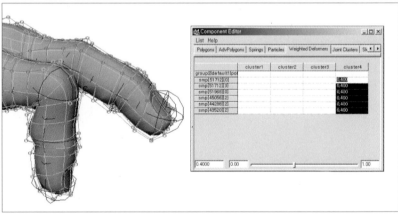

Figure 7-78 Adjusting the Weight Value in the Component Editor

Now let's observe how the skin changes as a result of the joint rotation.

Because it is linked to the Set Driven Key, as the joint rotates, the cluster will move to create a natural shape.

Use this method to apply changes with clusters (i.e., due to skin or clothes) as needed.

Anywhere from a few to a few dozen clusters can be used depending on the degree of detailing in the model. In order to note how specifically the clusters have been added observe the completed data. It is saved as CD-ROM\CHARACTER\scenes\Man SETUPFinal.mb.

2-4. SETUP FOR FACIAL EXPRESSIONS

We already discussed creating Blend Shape for character expressions in Chapter 5.
Cluster, as well as Blend Shape, is used for facial expressions. Users can use Cluster to effectively create more diverse expressions.
Refer to Chapter 5, "Facial Expression," to see how Blend Shape was used to create the facial expressions for this character.

First, let's observe the structure of the character's face. If you have been following along using the ManBind.mb file, found in the supplementary CD-ROM, the structure of the character's face should be like the one seen in Figure 7-79. The face is made up of eyes and teeth and is parented to the joint that controls the entire face.
These elements are generally not bound together. This is because the eyes and teeth should be set up to have their own individual movements to create more elaborate movements.

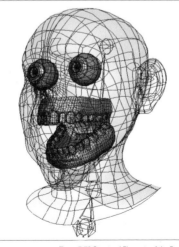

Figure 7-79 Structural Elements of the Face

Let's see how the lower teeth have been parented. All teeth are parented to the gums, and the gum pivots are located on the parented joint. This is so that the teeth will move along with the basic movements of the joint or move independently.

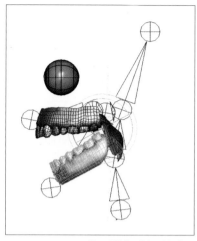

Figure 7-80 Pivot Points of the Gums

Because this character has previous Blend Shape data, we can select [Windows > Animation Editor > Blend Shape] to open the Blend Shape Editor to observe the previously made Blend Shape before we bind it. See Figure 7-81.

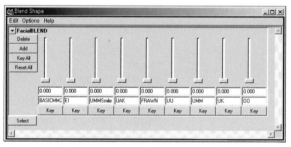

Figure 7-81 Blend Shape Editor

We will run a test to see what expressions and sounds have been made. This is based on the content explained in Chapter 5, "Facial Expression."

The movements were set up to move along with the previously made joints. In other words, a simple opening and closing of the mouth has been created to form the sound "ah."

Other sounds were made using Blend Shape. We will look at how Cluster can be used to create more diverse expressions and sounds.

But first, we will look at eye control.

1. Eye Control

 step 1 Select [Create > Locator] to make two locators and arrange them as shown in Figure 7-82.

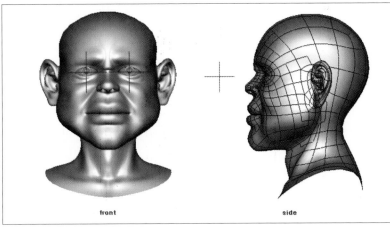

Figure 7-82 Create Locator

Select both Locators and select [Edit > Group] to group them. Change the name of the Group Node to EyeControl in the Channel Box. Again, select [Modify > Center Pivot]. After positioning a pivot between the two locators, select [Display > Component Display > Selection Handle] to display the handles for easy selection.

step 2 The locators made for each eye will be constrained using Aim. In order to observe which axis will be constrained, select the eye and after pressing Ctrl+A key to open Attribute Editor, select Display Local Axis, as shown in Figure 7-83. The local axis will appear on the eyes, as shown in Figure 7-84.

Figure 7-83 Attribute Editor

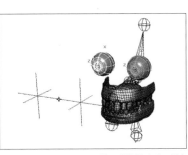

Figure 7-84 Display Local Axis

Let's observe how the local axis has been shaped for each eye. Basic example files have the X-axis on top and the Y-axis opposite the Locator.

First, select the Locator and then the eye. Then select [Animation > Constraint > Aim 🔲] to open the Options window.

As shown in Figure 7-85, enter a **-1** for Y in the Aim Vector. This is because the local axis of the eye is facing the opposite direction due to the Locator.

Set the X-axis of the Up Vector to **1**. This is because the X-axis is facing up.

Click on the Add/Remove button at the bottom.

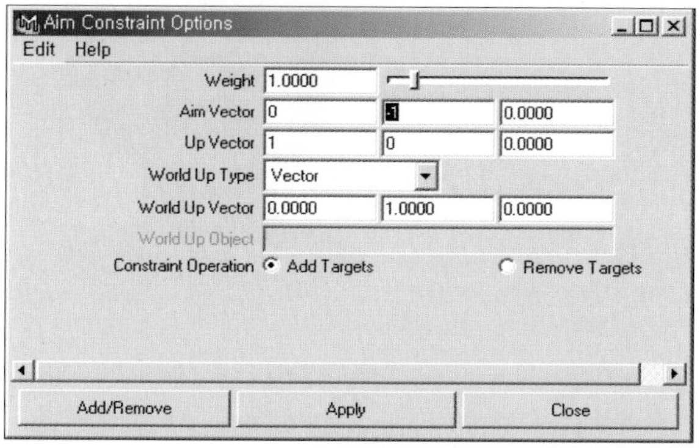

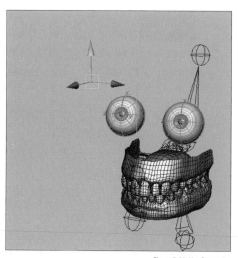

Figure 7-85 Options Window

Constrain the other eye in the same manner.

Now, when we move the EyeControl as shown in Figure 7-86, the eyes will both be facing the Locators on either side.

Figure 7-86 Aim Constraint

There is one thing that we need to keep when mind when creating more natural eye movements.

That is the reaction of the eyelids in response to the eye movements. In a real human eye, the eyelids react to the upward or downward movement of the eyes.

To create this type of movement easily, we use Cluster.

step 3 To make the cluster, select the upper vertex around the eye, as shown in Figure 7-87. Select [Animation > Deform > Create Cluster ▣], select Relative in the Options window, and then click the Create button. Display the Selection Handles of the cluster to make selection easier. Select the cluster and press the Insert key in Rotate Mode, and position the pivot at the center of the eye as shown in Figure 7-88.

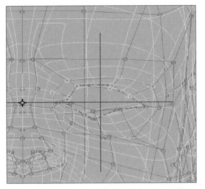

Figure 7-87 Selecting the Vertex

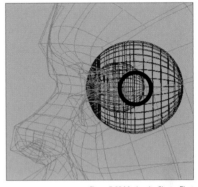

Figure 7-88 Moving the Cluster Pivot

After moving the pivot, press the Insert key again and quit Move Pivot Mode.

Parent this cluster to the parented eye joint.

In order to change the Deformation Order, select the face and click the RMB to select [Inputs > Complete List] from the Marking Menu. Then, in the List of History Operation window shown in Figure 7-89, drag the cluster below the skin cluster using the MMB.

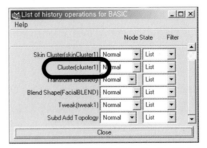

Figure 7-89 List of History Operations Window

step 4 After selecting the cluster, rotate as shown in Figure 7-90 to close the eyes. The transformation will appear severe because the cluster weight value has not yet been established.

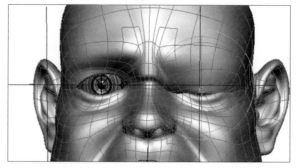

Figure 7-90 Rotate Cluster

This is taken care of by making detailed adjustments in the Component Editor. In the case of the Subdivision Surface, which does not have many vertices, all we need to do is adjust the weight values for a few vertices.

Select [Windows > General Editors > Component Editor...] to open the Component Editor and adjust the weight values so that the eyes form naturally, as shown in Figure 7-91.

Figure 7-91 Adjusting the Weight Values Using the Component Editor

The Cluster Weight value is adjusted in the Weighted Deformers Tab of the Component Editor.

Select a few vertices at the bottom, as shown in Figure 7-92, to make the cluster. After changing the Pivot and Deformation Order as for the cluster above, parent it to the joint. Then, in the same way, edit the weight value in the Component Editor.

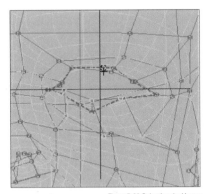

Figure 7-92 Selecting the Vertex

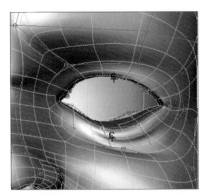

Figure 7-93 Creating the Cluster and Editing the Weight Value

In the same way, make the cluster for the other eye, remembering to edit the Pivot and Deformation Order of the cluster.

step 5 In order to make the eyes open and close, we must verify along which axis the Rotate value of the cluster will rotate. It will rotate along the X-axis. Now, set the Rotate value of all the clusters to 0, and select all four clusters used in both eyes.

Select [Animation > Animate > Set Driven Key > Set ▢] to open the Set Driven Key window. After selecting the EyeControl, the Group Node of the Locator that has been constrained using the aim of the eye, click on the Load Driver in the Set Driven Key window.

As shown in Figure 7-94, select the Translate X of the EyeControl and all ClusterHandles and then select Rotate X. Click on the Key button at the bottom of the Set Driven Key window.

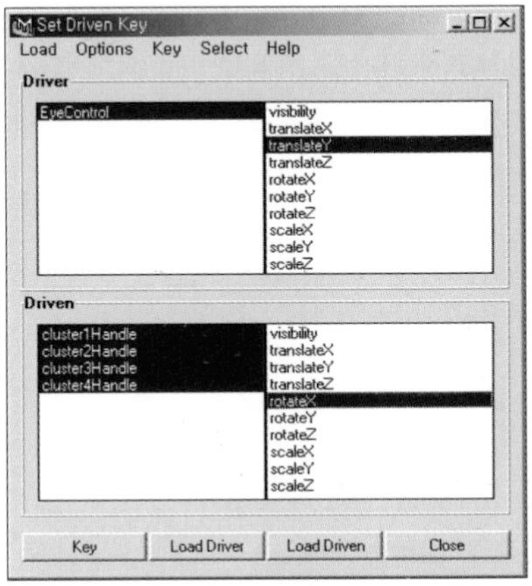

Figure 7-94 Set Driven Key Window

After moving the EyeControl four spaces along the Y-axis, rotate the upper clusters 12 spaces towards the X-axis, as shown in Figure 7-95. Click on the Key button in the Set Driven Key window. After moving the EyeControl four spaces along the Y-axis, rotate the upper clusters 20 spaces towards the X-axis and the lower clusters about seven spaces towards the X-axis, as shown in Figure 7-96. Click on the Key button in the Set Driven Key window.

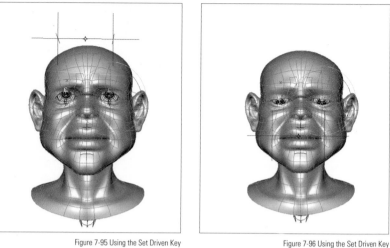

Figure 7-95 Using the Set Driven Key

Figure 7-96 Using the Set Driven Key

step 6 Now select the EyeControl and move it up and down.
The eyelids should now move along with the eye, creating more natural movement.

Now we will use clusters to close the eyes.
Select EyeControl and then select [Modify > Add Attribute...]. This will open the Add Attribute window.

As shown in Figure 7-97, enter EyeClose for Attribute Name, Float for the Data Type, 10 for both the Minimum and Maximum, and 0 for the Default Value, and then click OK. Looking at the Channel box, we can see that the EyeClose has been made into a channel.

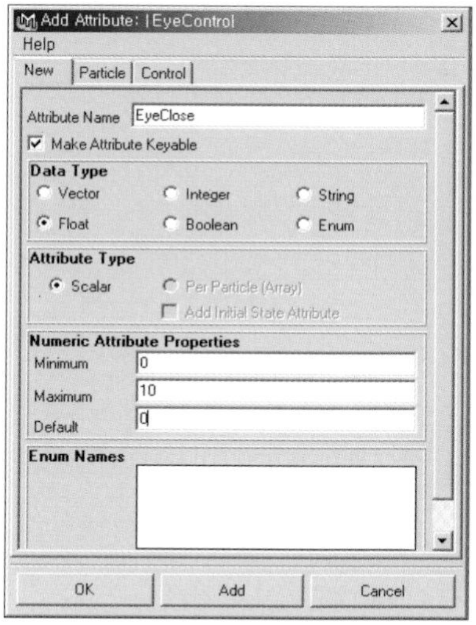

Figure 7-97 Add Attribute Window

step 7 Select the two clusters used in the upper eye and then select [Animation > Animate > Set Driven Key > Set] to open the Set Driven Key window.

After selecting EyeControl, click on the Load Driver button in the Set Driven Key window.

As shown in Figure 7-98, after selecting the EyeClose of the EyeControl and the two ClusterHandles, select rotateX and then click on the Key button at the bottom.

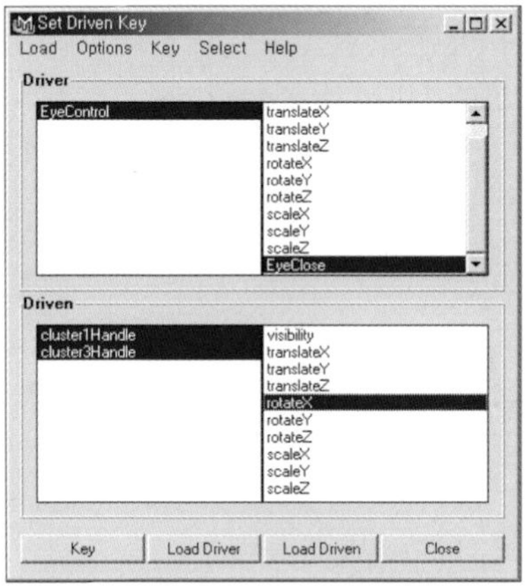

Figure 7-98 Set Driven Key Window

After setting the EyeClose value of the EyeControl to 10 and rotating both cluster handles approximately 35 spaces along the X-axis, click on the Key button at the bottom of the Set Driven Key window.

Select EyeControl and then change the value of the EyeClose in the Channel box. We can see that the eyes close as the value increases.

2. Expression Clusters

Let's create clusters for controlling expressions. This is much more effective when used in conjunction with Blend Shape.

Depending on the details of the expression, we can use up to several dozen clusters.

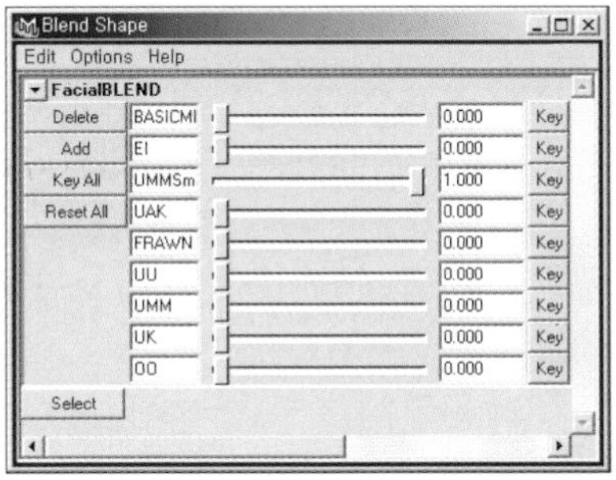

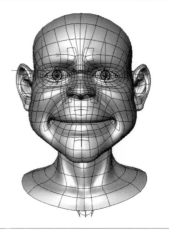

Figure 7-99 Blend Shape Editor

Figure 7-100 Making the Expressions

Select [Windows > Animation Editors > Blend Shape] to open the Blend Shape window. Then set the value of the UMMSmile to 1, as shown in Figure 7-99, to obtain the expression seen in Figure 7-100.

For this expression, we will make the clusters that will allow us to control the corners of the mouth to create a character that is smiling or frowning.

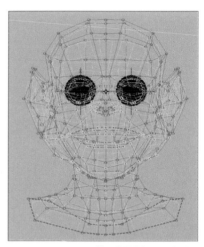

In order to make the cluster, select many vertices from the many areas on the mouth as shown in Figure 7-101. In order to create a variety of movements, we need to select the vertices from many frames other than the ones used for the actual movement.

Figure 7-101 Selecting the Vertices

Select [Animation > Deform > Create Cluster]. Use the previous Option. Display the Selection Handle and then change the Deformation Order.
Then parent this to the joint to which the other clusters have been parented.

As shown in Figure 7-102, move the cluster that has been made to the Y-axis. The expression should change as shown in the figure. Now we need to use the Component Editor to adjust each of the Weight values to create natural expressions.

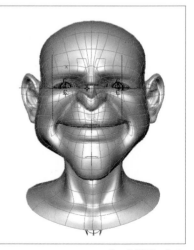

Careful attention to detail and a lot of trial and error are needed here because expressions can change drastically through the slightest changes in Weight values.

Figure 7-102 Move Cluster

The next figure, Figure 7-103, shows examples of different expressions that have been created through the changes in the Weight values of the cluster vertices. In order to create natural expressions as shown here, the Weight values for each of the vertices must be modified very carefully.

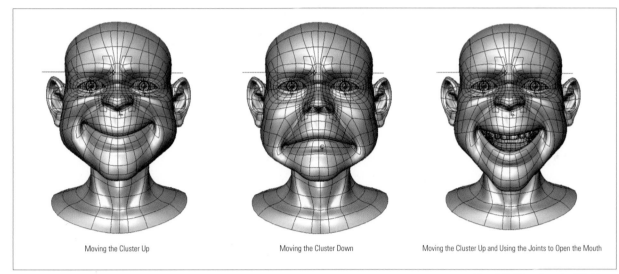

Moving the Cluster Up

Moving the Cluster Down

Moving the Cluster Up and Using the Joints to Open the Mouth

Figure 7-103 Different Expressions Using Clusters

In order to create the furrows between the eyebrows, an abundant number of vertices must be selected, as shown in Figure 7-104. It is important to remember that in order to create natural expressions, we must always select vertices in areas beyond the areas that actually move and then carefully adjust the Weight values.

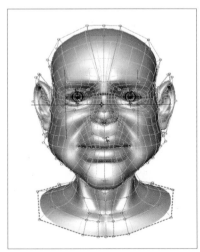

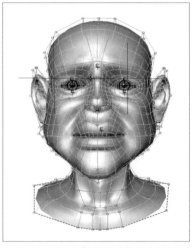

Figure 7-104 Selecting Vertices

Figure 7-105 Adjusting Weight Values

Select [Animation > Deform > Create Cluster] to make the cluster. Using the same technique, parent the cluster to the joint and then change the Deformation Order. Change the Weight value of the cluster to create the expression seen in Figure 7-105.

As shown here, we can use only the necessary clusters to create the expressions we want. We can also use up to several dozen clusters, depending on the details of the expression. Figures 7-106 and 7-107 show the expressions were made using Joint, Blend Shape and Cluster.

The cluster in the picture at the bottom was made to control both eyebrows. Then the expression was made by altering the shape slightly using Blend Shape and then moving the cluster. Clusters were made to control the eye movements that respond to the raising or lowering of the eyebrows.

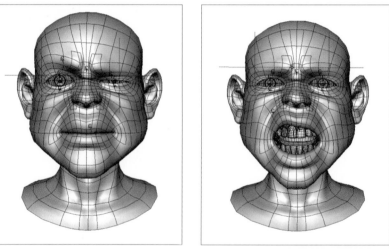

Figure 7-106 Creating Expressions   Figure 7-107 Creating Expressions

This is an example of a cluster that was made on the left side of the face to control lip movements creating a slightly asymmetrical expression. In order to create this asymmetry, which is useful in creating a wide variety of expressions, we can also use clusters in certain areas. This expression was also created using Joint and Blend Shape.

We have, so far, looked at ways to create facial expressions using clusters. Users can create many more clusters to bestow their characters with even more expressions. In order to create and produce various different expressions, users must experiment with many different clusters.

2-5. EXAMPLE CHARACTER CONTROL

We have, thus far, looked at the process of character setup. If you have followed along with the steps outlined here, you should be very familiar with the entire process involved in character modeling and setup.

We will now look at how to use this setup in animation keyframing.

There are methods out there to make characters move, and users are encouraged to use the method that is comfortable for them. No one method that is better than another.

Maya offers an environment that allows diverse character control. It is important that users first understand this environment and then adapt to find their own unique styles. Your individual style is far more important than a set of rules or a certain procedure. The most comfortable method is always best.

Before we begin, let's summarize the setup process that we have looked at so far. First, the use of supporting joints for leg/arm control was covered in "2-1. Using Extra Joint." In "2-2. Using IK Spline Handles," we looked at how to use IK Spline Handles and how to create clusters for spine control.

In "2-3. Using Constraint and Cluster," we looked at how to use clusters for even more detailed, partial modeling and the setup process for using Constraint for IK Handle control and eye control.

Now, we can finally start animating the character and learn how to use this animation to create different situations.

First, we set up the Locator, used to constrain the IK Handle Pole Vector, the Locator used for eye control, and the polygon cubes used in each arm to follow along with the movements of the character.

Figure 7-108 shows us which elements have been parented to which joint.

The Locator and polygon cubes used to control both arms are parented to the first joint that causes the arm to spread out, and the Locator on the leg that controls the Pole Vector is parented to the Root Joint of the Skeleton.

When the polygon cube in the arm, a mirror of the opposite arm, is parented, the Rotate and Scale values can change. To create normal arm movements, the cube is rotated and the scale adjusted.

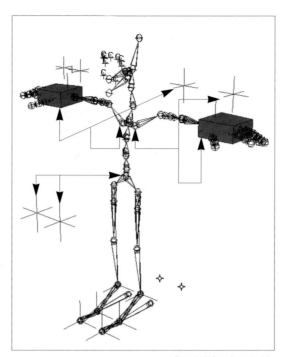

Figure 7-108 Parenting to the Joint

The three clusters used in the spine are also parented to the Root Joint of the skeleton. Also, the Locator Group Nodes used in both eyes are parented to the facial joints. This is done so that the face moves along with the direction of the eyes.

However, when this Locator Group Node is parented directly to the face, the Set Driven Key may not operate normally. In this instance, after selecting the EyeControl of the Locator Group Node, [Edit > Group] is selected or one Group Node is made and parented to the joint.

This parenting follows the same procedure we used to parent the cluster to the joint.

Select the Root Joint of the skeleton and change the name to Pelvis in the Channel Box. Select [Edit > Group] and change the name to Body. As shown in Figure 7-109, this Pivot Node is matched to the Pivot of the Pelvis (Root Joint.)

Press the V key while moving to create an exact match between the two.

After displaying the Selection Handles of the Pelvis and Body, we arrange it as shown in Figure 7-110 for easier selection.

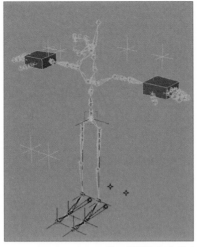

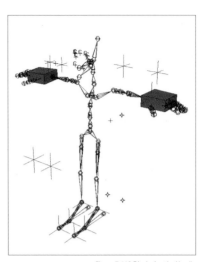

Figure 7-109 Moving the Pivot   Figure 7-110 Displaying the Handle

As shown in Figure 7-110, change the name of the supporting joints used in either leg to L_Foot and R_Foot, respectively.

This concludes the basic setup for the animation. Now we will use examples to explain how to control this character using animation keyframing.

1. Simple Expression for Character Animation

We will look at how to control the character using simple expressions.
Although this is a widely used numerical formula, I believe that many users still do not understand how convenient it really is. This formula is very simple. It's not a problem when the character is merely moving in one direction; however, when the character's movements are random (i.e., the character is constantly changing direction), it becomes more difficult to keyframe the movements of the leg to the movements of the body.
However, if we use an expression that causes the body to respond to the leg movements, control of the character becomes much easier. We will use the character setup that we created earlier to explain.

In the example above, the Root Joint of the skeleton is set to the Pelvis and the joint grouped to create another Body Node. Now, we will configure the setup so that the body is controlled using expression and the pelvis can be keframed independently.

First, select the Body Node.

Select [Windows > Animation Editors > Expression Editor]. Enter the values seen in Figure 7-111 in the Expression Editor. Set the Expression Name to BodyFront.

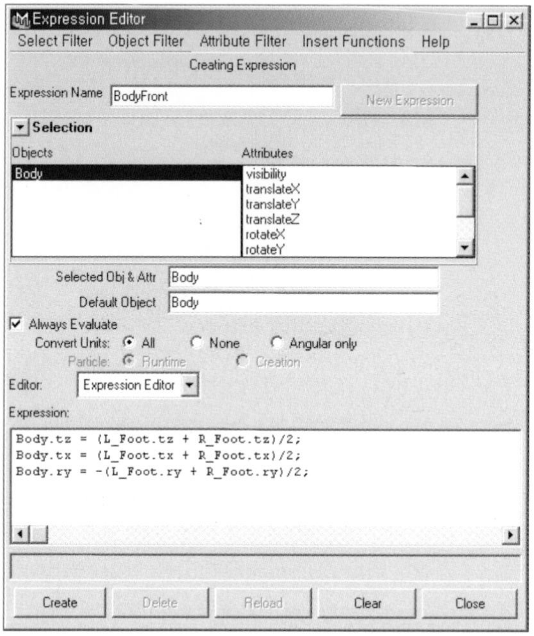

Figure 7-111 Expression Editor

The formulas entered are as follows:

Body.tz = (L_Foot.tz + R_Foot.tz)/2;

Body.tx = (L_Foot.tx + R_Foot.tx)/2;

Body.ry = -(L_Foot.ry + R_Foot.ry)/2;

What this formula means is that the addition of the lengths of both the right and left leg divided by 2 is the Translate Z and X of the body. In other words, the Body Node should always be located between the left and right legs.

The final formula controls the rotation around the Y-axis.

The "-" in this formula represents rotation in opposite directions. When this type of formula is substituted and opposite rotations are required, we insert a "-".

Sometimes, we see the condition illustrated in Figure 7-112. In these instances, we move the expression, using the connected lower body node, the pelvis, as seen in Figure 7-113.

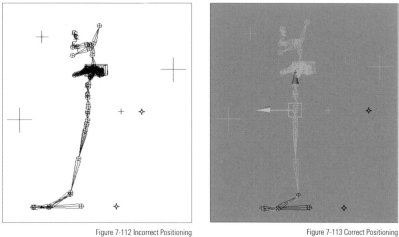

Figure 7-112 Incorrect Positioning

Figure 7-113 Correct Positioning

Now let's move/rotate the R_Foot and L_Foot to observe the motions. We observe that as the leg moves, the body responds in proportion.

In this case, the body is set to move along with the side/forward motions of the leg.

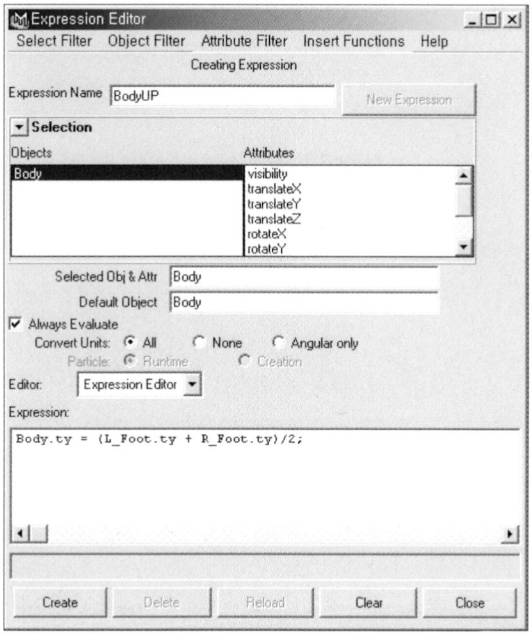

Figure 7-114 Expression Editor

In reality, the body of the human is set to move somewhat in response to the up and down movements of the leg.

In order to reset this, select the Body Node and then select [Windows > Animation Editors > Expression Editor] to open the Expression Editor.
Enter **BodyUP** in the Name Field, and enter the formula seen in Figure 7-114.

Body.ty = (L_Foot.ty + R_Foot.ty)/2;

This formula controls the movement of the body along the Y-axis.
In order to test this, select L_Foot and move it along the Y-axis. We can see that the body moves along with the movement of the leg.
If the position is set too high, select the pelvis and lower the Y-axis slightly.

At times, while using expression to control the movements of the body, users may wish to break off the binding power of the expression.
This problem is particularly seen in Y-axis movements.
For example, in this type of expression constraint, if the character kicks or jumps and the body is set to respond to the Y-axis movements, keyframing becomes very difficult.

Users can use the following method to keyframe the binding force of a character expression to prevent this expression from being applied in certain areas.

step 1 Move the L_Foot and R_Foot to create a simple walking animation, as shown in Figure 7-115.

Figure 7-115 Creating a Walking Animation

step 2 Move to the frame in which we wish to sever the constraint of the Expression. Selecting either the L_Foot or the R_Foot and viewing INPUTS in the Channel Box, we can see the display of the Expression Names, BodyFront, and BodyUP. Click on BodyUP. As shown in Figure 7-116, set the Node State to Normal and click the RMB to select Key Selected in the Marking Menu.

Move one frame from the current frame, and after setting the Node State to Blocking as seen in Figure 7-117, select the Node State and click the RMB to select Key Selected in the Marking Menu.

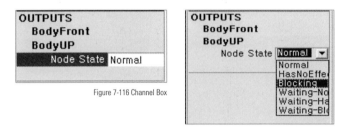

Figure 7-116 Channel Box

Figure 7-117 Channel Box

When the constraint on Translate Y of the Body Node in the current frame is severed, we can keyframe this channel separately.

If we want to establish the constraint again, we first move to the desired frame, block it, give it a key, and then set the Node State to Normal in the next frame.

2. Fixing the Hands Using Constraint

We can use Constraint to fix the hands in the desired spot.

Let's suppose we are keyframing a scene where the character is walking and then pushes a heavy object. While the character is walking, the hands must follow along. When the charcter is pushing the object, the hand must be fixed on the object. In order to keyframe this type of movement, we use constraint.

On page 395, in the section entitled, "Setup to Fix the Hands in a Particular Spot," we explained how to do this kind of setup using constraints. We will go through this example using the character that was set up in the beginning of "2-5. Example Character Control" (page 421). If the setup is not the same as the one shown here, please refer to the two sections above and create the proper setup.

We will use this character to explain in detail how to create movement.

step 1 First, in order to create the motions, use the PolyCube, as shown in Figure 7-118, to create hands that appear to be pushing an object.

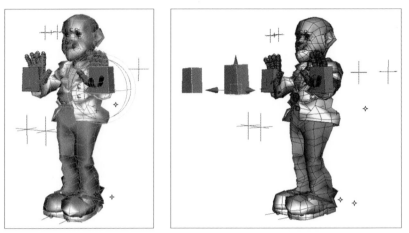

Figure 7-118 Creating Hand Motions   Figure 7-119 Copying Polygon Cubes

After making the hand motions, select the two polygon cubes and then select Edit > Duplicate to copy. (See Figure 7-119.)

This cube, which was parented to the joint in the previous step, is also parented when copied.

Select [Edit > Unparent] to unparent the two duplicated polygons.

 step 2 We will now create the object that the character is pushing. As shown in Figure 7-120, make a simple polygon cube and then move and paste the copied cube.

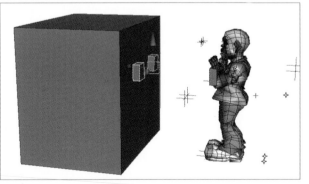

Figure 7-120 Arranging the Polygon Cube

Select the three polygon cubes and then select [Edit > Group] to group the cubes. Select [Modify > Center Pivot] to move the pivot to the center of the Group Node, and then display the Selection Handles to make selection easier.

As shown in Figure 7-121, change the name of the duplicated polygon cube in the Channel Box.

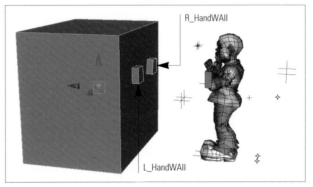

Figure 7-121 Displaying the Handle after Grouping

step 3 The IK Handles and Supporting Joints used in both arms are constrained on each point and orient of the polygon cube in each arm.

Using the same method, constrain these on the point and orient of the duplicated polygon.

The point-constrained IK Handle on the cube of the left hand is point-constrained on L_HandeWall and the orient-constrained joint is orient-constrained.

The position and rotation values for the arm are shown in Figure 7-122.

Figure 7-122 Using Constraints

This shows each IK Handle and supporting joint constrained simultaneously to two objects.

The IK Handles point-constrained to the two polygons are positioned on the center of the two cubes, and the rotation value of the orient-constrained joint follows half the rotation value of the two cubes.

step 4   Select the IK Handle of the left hand and select pointConstraint in the Channel Box to apply the same value of 1 to the two objects as seen in Figure 7-123. In order to have it follow the movements of the arm, set the value of L_Hand Wall W1 to 0.

Now select the supporting joint orient-constrained to the cube. We can see in Figure 7-124 that the same value of 1 has been applied to both cubes. Again, in order to follow the movements of the body, set the value of L_Hand Wall W1 to 0.

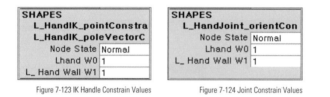

Figure 7-123 IK Handle Constrain Values   Figure 7-124 Joint Constrain Values

Change the constraint values for the opposite arm as well.

step 5   We will now use a simple expression to convert their Weight value. Before making the expression, we need to verify the Attribute Name that will be used for the expression. Because the Attribute Names for each model can be different, users should refer to the following explanation for the proper substitutions.

First, set the name of the IK Handle used in the left hand to L_HandIK and the constrained joint to L_HandJoint. Name the parented cube of the arm **Lhand** and the cube affixed to the wall **L_HandWall**.

Name the IK Handle used in the right hand **R_HandleIK** and the constrained joint **R_HandJoint**. The parented cube of the arm is named "Rhand" and the cube affixed to the wall is named "R_HandWall."

If they have created differently, it is advised that users should keep track of their names and their order.

After selecting the body on the character, select [Modify > Add Attribute] to open the Add Attribute window. Configure the options, as seen in Figure 7-125, and then click OK.

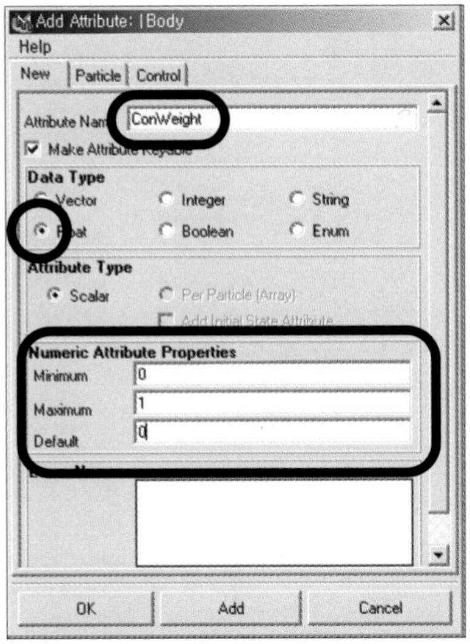

Figure 7-125 Add Attribute Window

With the body selected, select [Windows > Animation Editors > Expression Editor].
Enter the following:

L_HandIK_pointConstraint1.LhandW0 = 1 - Body.ConWeight;
L_HandIK_pointConstraint1.L_HandWallW1 = Body.ConWeight;
L_HandJoint_orientConstraint1.LhandW0 = 1 - Body.ConWeight;
L_HandJoint_orientConstraint1.L_HandWallW1 = Body.ConWeight;
R_HandIK_pointConstraint1.RhandW0 = 1 - Body.ConWeight;
R_HandIK_pointConstraint1.R_HandWallW1 = Body.ConWeight;
R_HandJoint_orientConstraint1.RhandW0 = 1 - Body.ConWeight;
R_HandJoint_orientConstraint1.R_HandWallW1 = Body.ConWeight;

Click on the Create button at the bottom of the Expression Editor. By selecting Body and
changing the value of ConWeight to 1, we can verify the response of the two constrained
cubes of the hands.
Apply the appropriate Attribute Names shown above.

There is no need to follow this formula, but then there is the inconvenience of having to
change each and every constraint value before keyframing. If you wish to keyframe each
hand separately, all you need to do is make two attributes and substitute the appropriate
Attribute for each hand.

step 6 As shown in Figure 7-126, keyframe the simple animation of the character walking toward the object.

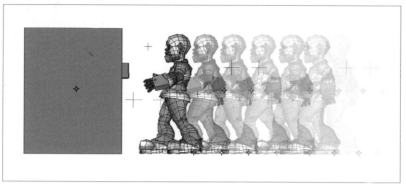

Figure 7-126 Walking Animation

Keyframe the animation of the character standing in front of the object and getting ready to push.

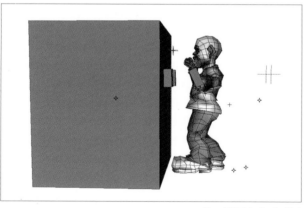

Figure 7-127 Animation Key Work

In the current frame, select the body. After selecting the ConWeight value in the Channel Box, click the RMB and select Key Selected.

After moving the frame appropriately, change the value of the ConWeight to 1. After giving it a key, select the pelvis and create the pushing motion seen in Figure 7-128.

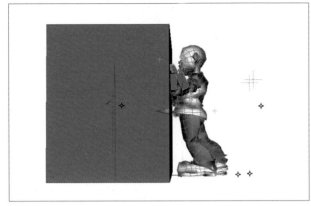

Figure 7-128 Animation Key Work

Now, select the grouped node and move it from side to side. We can see that the arms are fixed to the object.

Move the object and keyframe the character to move along with it.

There is one potentially important problem that can present itself here. That is that the palms of the hands can rotate severely when the constraint values are adjusted.

This can happen because, through various situations, the rotate value of the cube parented to the hands and the rotate value of the cube affixed to the object have been created differently.

This problem is solved by rotating the cube fixed to the object to fit the movement of the cube parented to the hand.

3. Constraining Pivots

There are numerous ways that characters can be set up depending on user preference.

In my case, I prefer the methods that I have described here. Not only do I prefer these methods, these methods are the most popular.

If, as in the example of this setup, the body has been configured to move along with the movements of the leg in the basic expression, one problem can result. Although its not a big problem in itself, this can create a problem in the keyframing process.

The Root Joint of the skeleton of this character has been grouped and another node has been made on top of the root.

This method allows us to control the character in very diverse ways.

This is because the expression can be used and constrained on the uppermost node and the Root Joint can be used to create separate movements.

However, the problem is that, for this character, we used an expression on the body. When the lower node, the pelvis, is used to create another movement, even though the first pivot of the body has been placed on the root joint, when the lower pelvic joint is moved, the body pivot is not fixed to the pelvis.

Figure 7-129 shows us the position of the rotate pivot of the upper body node when the pelvis is moved.

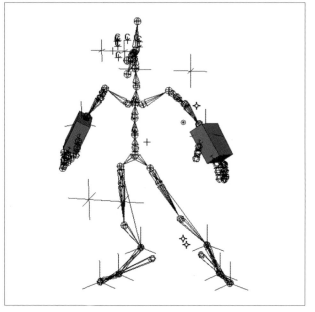

Figure 7-129 Pivot Location

In this case, when we need to coincide the upper pivot node with the lower pivot node, we can constrain the pivot as follows.

Select the upper Body Node and then select [Windows > General Editors > Channel Control...]. This will open the Channel Control window for the body. Select rotatePivotX, Y, Z from Non Keyable, as shown in Figure 7-130, and click the Move button at the bottom.

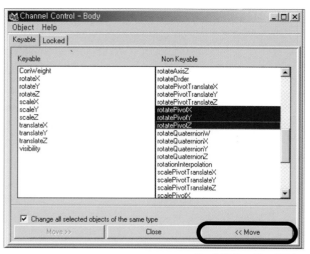

Figure 7-130 Channel Control Window

Looking at the Channel Box, we can see the presence of Rotate Pivot X, Y, Z Channels. Select [Windows > Animation Editors > Expression Editor...] and enter the following formulas.

Body.rotatePivotX = Pelvis.tx;
Body.rotatePivotY = Pelvis.ty;
Body.rotatePivotZ = Pelvis.tz;

Move the Pelvis and verify the result.
The Rotate Pivot of the body should always follow the location of the pelvis.

We have so far looked at the overall details for Character Setup. Although there are many other setup environments depending on certain variables, you should have no problem creating your own animations simply by adapting the procedures outlined here.
As I mentioned earlier, it is more important that you first learn the basics and then adapt them to create your own style.
The complete setup for this example can be found in CD_ROM\CHARACTER\scenes\ManSETUPFinal.mb.

2-6. SURFACE DEFORMATION TIP

In this section, we will move from using one example to set up a character to learning how to elaborately transform a model.

This also is just one of the many methods that can be used with Maya.

Actually, there is a limit to how much we can transform the surface using the skeleton. To overcome these limitations, for Rigid Bind we use Flexor and for Smooth Bind we use Influence Object. For more detailed and elaborate expressions, we use also use clusters, which was described in the previous sections.

We will now look into another method for the more elaborate portrayal of surface transformations. That method is Blend Shape.

Although this will increase our workload, Blend Shape is excellent for portraying detailed muscular movements.

First, open the data for the example found in the supplementary CD–ROM (CD-ROM\ CHARACTER\scenes\ARM.mb.)

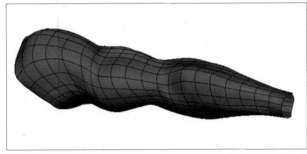

Figure 7-131 NURBS Model

As in Figure 7-131, the model of an arm, created using NURBS modeling, will open. Let's use this model for a simple test. Once you learn how to use it, this method can be effectively utilized and adapted to other parts of the character.

step 1 First, after making the skeleton for the model, add IK Handles, as shown in Figure 7-132.

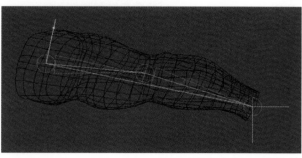

Figure 7-132 Making the Skeleton and IK Handles

step 2 Before binding, we must copy the model of the arm. Select the arm and then select [Edit > Duplicate]. Leave the Duplicate value on the default setting.

After selecting the two models of the arm and the skeleton, execute [Animation > Skin > Bind Skin > Smooth Bind].

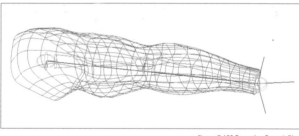

Figure 7-133 Executing Smooth Bind

The two arm models have been smoothly bound to the skeleton. Now we need to hide the copied model of the arm. Select the model and then select [Display > Hide > Hide Selection].

step 3 Now we need to use Artisan to give the smoothly bound arm model a Weight value. As shown in Figure 7-134, use the IK Handle to bend the arm, and then adjust the Weight value to create the most natural model.

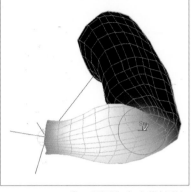

Figure 7-134 Adjusting the Weight Value

Even though we adjusted the Weight value, we will experience many problems with the model. These problems become more severe when models are very muscular like the one used here.

For example, sometimes the muscles will dig in and burrow into each other or the elbows will protrude due to the bone.

Although smaller areas can be fixed using Cluster or Influence Object, it is more effective to just Model the entire shape to create more detail.

First, we need to make a copy of the model with the copy of the Weight value. After selecting the skeleton, select [Animation > Skin > Go To Bind Pose]. Then select [Display > Show > Show Last Hidden] to display the hidden model.

First, select the model with the adjusted Weight value and then select the copied model while holding down the Shift key.

It will be more convenient to use Hypergraph or Outliner.

Select [Animation > Skin > Edit Smooth Skin > Copy Skin Weight]. This will copy the Weight value of the edited surface.

step 4 Hide one of the two models. This is done to prevent one from interfering with the work on the other. As shown in 7-135, use the IK Handle to bend the arm.

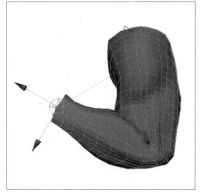

Figure 7-135 Assuming the Shape for Modeling

Looking at the result, as we predicted, the muscles start burrowing into each other. We can also see that the elbow appears too smooth. In order to correct these problems, we need to move the CV of the surface to create the shape.

Let's select the CV of the surface and move it. We have a problem. The CV does not move in the desired direction.

This is because this surface has already been Smooth Bound and the Deformation Order has the Skin Cluster for the Tweak.

In order to verify the Deformation Order, select the arm model made using NURBS Surface and click the RMB to select [Input > Complete List] from the Marking Menu. As we can see in Figure 7-136, there is a Skin Cluster on top of the Tweak.

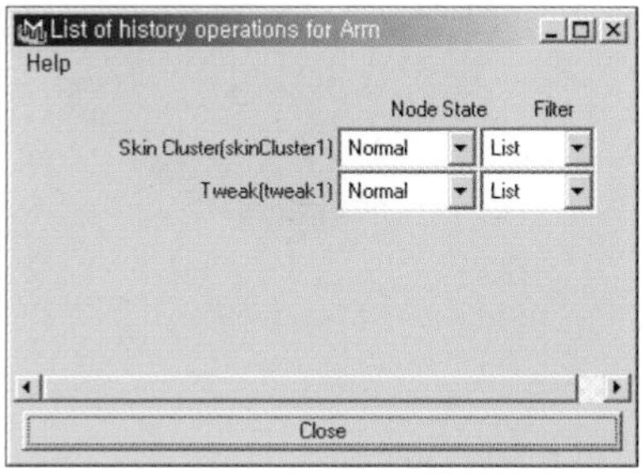

Figure 7-136 Deformation Order

In order to change this order, click the top of SkinCluster (Cluster1) with the MMB and drag on top of the Tweak. This will move the Skin Cluster below the Tweak.

Now we can move the CV to model the shape of the bent arm. For effective modeling, it is a good idea to use Artisan periodically.

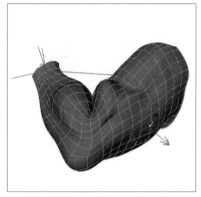

Figure 7-137 Using the Sculpt Surface Tool

When modeling this type of muscle movement, it is important first to observe which portions contract and which portions expand before modeling.
Let's observe Figure 7-138. This illustration is a comparison of the model before and after modification.

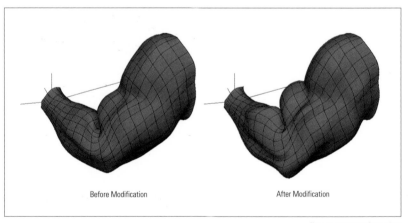

Before Modification

After Modification

Figure 7-138 Model Comparison

Once the Figure has been modeled, it is now time to apply Blend Shape.

step 5 After selecting the skeleton, select [Animation > Skin > Go To Bind Pose]. After selecting the model, select [Edit > Duplicate] to copy the model. After selecting all the channels in the Channel Box, select Unlock Selected to undo the lock and move as shown in Figure 7-139.

Delete the bound model and display again the model that was hidden earlier.

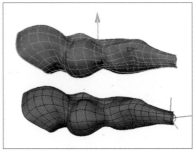

Figure 7-139 Copying the Model

As shown in Figure 7-140, select the surface that was created by remodeling the shape after adjusting the CV first, and then select the original surface. Then select [Animation > Deform > Create Blend Shape ☐] to open the Blend Shape Options window.

After setting the Deformation Order to Front of Chain in the Advanced tab of the Options window as shown in Figure 7-141, press the Create button at the bottom of the window.

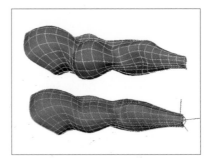

Figure 7-140 Selecting the Surface

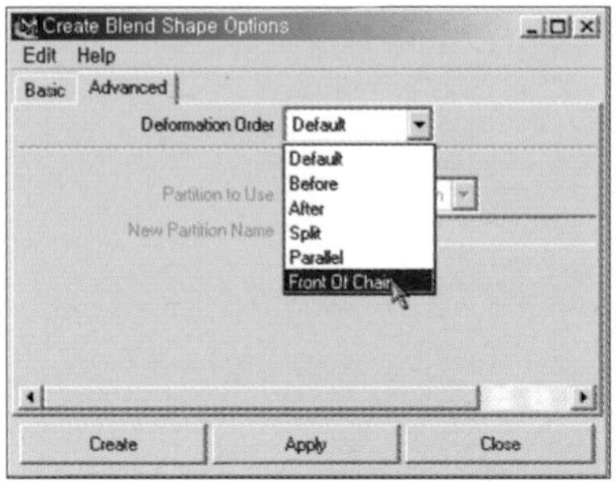

Figure 7-141 Options Windows

Hide the Target Object in which the surface has been transformed.

step 6 Now let's use the Set Driven Key to automate the transformation of this model.

First, select [Animation > Animate > Set Driven Key > Set ▢] and open the Set Driven Key window.

As shown in Figure 7-142, select the joint and then click the Load Driver button at the bottom of the Set Driven Key window.

After selecting the surface, select blendShape1 below INPUTS in the Channel Box, as shown in Figure 7-143, and then click the Load Driver button at the bottom of the Set Driven Key window.

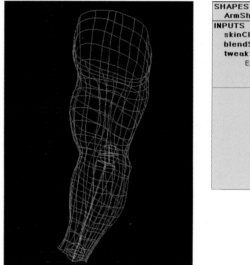

Figure 7-142 Selecting the Joint

Figure 7-143 Channel Box

As shown in Figure 7-144, select the rotateZ of Driver Joint2 and Arm 2 of Driver Joint2 (these names may be different) in the Set Driven Key window. Arm2 is the Target Node that will be blended.

In order to add a key to the current value, press the Key button at the bottom of the window.

Figure 7-144 Set Driven Key Window

After selecting the IK Handle, bend the arm as shown in Figure 7-145. Select [Windows > Animation Editors > Blend Shape] to open the Blend Shape window and set the Weight value to 1, as shown in Figure 7-146.

Click on the Key button at the bottom of the Set Driven Key window.

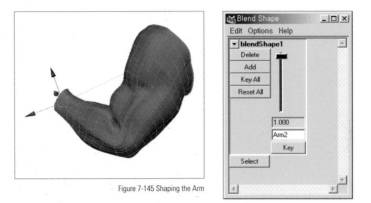

Figure 7-145 Shaping the Arm

Figure 7-146 Blend Shape Window

Now, we can see that the surface transforms naturally when we use the IK Handle to move the arm.

Figure 7-147 The Transformation of the Surface in Response to the Rotation of the Joint

So far, we have used simple examples to illustrate surface transformation using Blend Shape.

Although these were simple examples, they can be adapted to create elaborate surface expressions.

2-7. SETTING UP ANIMAL LEGS

The hind legs of an animal are very different in structure from human legs. For human characters, all we need to do is make one joint for the knee and set up movement in the ankles and toes so that they can move separately. The hind legs of an animal, which are lifted up, require that we bend two joints.

In such instances, we use Inverse Kinematics to control the movement of the joints.

Let's look at an example to see how joint properties are controlled and how to set it up using IK.

First of all, open the example file, leg.mb, that is included on the CD-ROM.

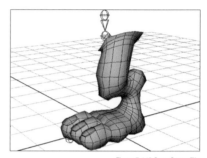

Figure 7-148 Open Scene File

This example file is simply a bound skeleton made for the purposes of our example.

Let's make IK handles and observe the movement of the leg; select [Animation > Skeleton > IK Handle Tool] and select the points shown in Figure 7-149 (in the order indicated).

Move the IK handle along the Y-axis, then take a closer look at Figure 7-150.

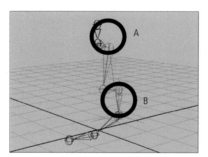

Figure 7-149 Making the IK Handle

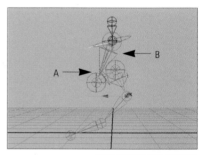

Figure 7-150 Moving the IK Handle

This is what happens when two or more joints are connected to the IK handle. In other words, the IK handle causes joint A to rotate, but joint B does not rotate.

In the real world, in a structure such as this, one joint needs to move and the remaining joint must rotate in turn to make the movement appear natural. In Figure 7-150, the legs overlap (like in Figure 7-151), making natural movement impossible.

Instead, to make movement appear natural, the joints must be set up as shown in Figure 7-152.

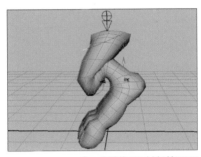

Figure 7-151 Unnatural Joint Movement

Figure 7-152 Proper Joint Movement

In FK, we can use the joint's rotation to adjust the movement. In IK, however, the movements should appear automatically. Let's look at some solutions. First, move the IK handle along the Y-axis so that we get the shape seen in Figure 7-153.

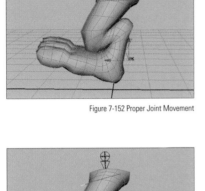

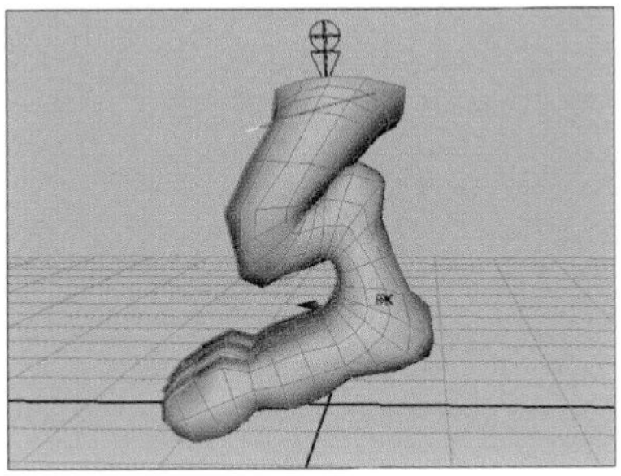

Figure 7-153 Moving the IK Handle

When we use IK handles, we can use some of the joint's properties to control the joint movement. Delete the IK handle we made, select the joint, and then execute Go to Bind Pose.

Select the joint as shown Figure 7-154, then open the Attribute Editor.

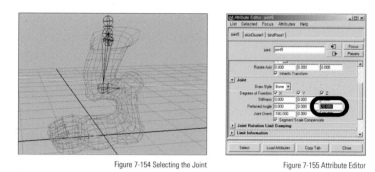

Figure 7-154 Selecting the Joint   Figure 7-155 Attribute Editor

Look at Figure 7-155. As shown here, set the Z-value of the joint's Preferred Angle to 20. As shown in Figure 7-156, select the joint, open the Attribute Editor (Figure 7-157) and set the Z-value of the Preferred Angle to 15.

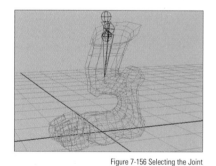

Figure 7-156 Selecting the Joint   Figure 7-157 Attribute Editor

Make another IK handle and move it along the Y-axis. You should see that the two joints now move naturally, one after the other.

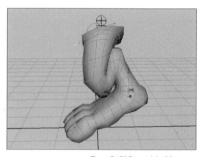

Figure 7-158 Proper Joint Movement

As we saw in this example, we can use Inverse Kinematics and set up Preferred Angle values to give each joint priority so that they move one right after the other. This method is used when we need to control the movement of 2 or more joints, as in the case of animal legs.

3. AN OUTLINE OF 3D CHARACTER ANIMATION

Up until now, we have looked at various Maya modeling methods and their respective setup methods. Now, I will attempt to bring all that knowledge together to make it easier for you to understand. Since we've already looked at the various options relating to modeling and setup procedures, I'll refrain from going into their explanations here. Refer to earlier chapters if you need to refresh your memory.

3-1. CHARACTER MODELING

The most important aspect of modeling is movement. All modeling stems from the question, "How am I going to make this character move?" In other words, the best techniques for modeling, from an animation standpoint, are those by which character setup is both quick and easy. Ultimately, the goal of an animator is to make the character move with the least amount of effort.

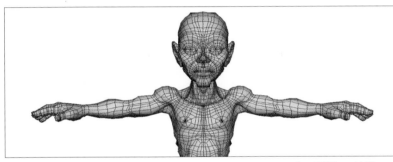

Figure 7-159 Proper Joint Movement

To do that, we need to consider the character's features. Before we begin modeling, we need to consider whether we want our character to look as realistic as possible, or cartoon-like. The range of motion we want our character to have in the realm of facial animation is also a factor, along with the kinds of expressions that will best portray the character's personality.

Let's look at two examples to see the methods involved in character modeling.

1. Which Method of Modeling Should You Choose?

Before you can begin modeling, you're going to need a lot practice sketching the character. Sketching is probably the best and easiest way to gain a better understanding of the character's personality and features. After you've finished designing the character, the time comes to ask yourself, "Which method of modeling should I choose?"

The method of modeling will be different depending on the nature of the project. Depending on whether you used NURBS Patch, Polygon, or Subdivision Surface (the latest trend) will affect the kind of modeling you do. Let's take a look at some of the advantages and disadvantages of each.

● NURBS Modeling

The most optimized method of modeling in Maya right now is NURBS. Data compatibility, file size, and all of Maya features have been optimized for NURBS. NURBS also uses UV coordinates, which makes it appropriate for product and character modeling (thanks to its curve functions).

However, NURBS has one big drawback: all the surfaces are not attached. What this means is that you are going to have to invest a lot of time and effort into animating shapes for character animation.

Despite this drawback, there are many production companies that prefer this method of modeling, and the reason has to do with rendering.

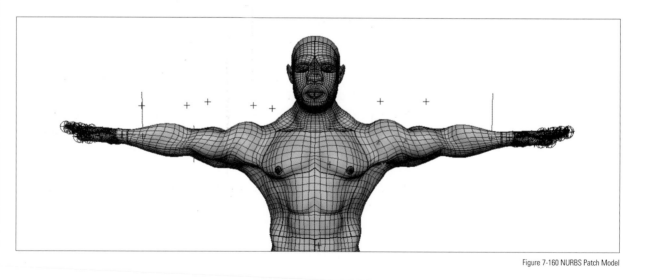

Figure 7-160 NURBS Patch Model

Simply comparing the results from one of Maya's renderers to RenderMan is enough to show a big difference. One of the biggest differences between RenderMan and Maya's renderers is tessellation. Maya's renderers, when rendering NURBS surfaces, convert the calculation units to generate the finished product using polygon faces.

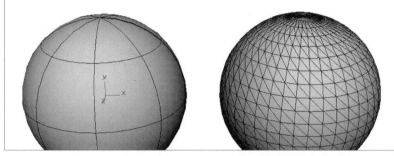

Figure 7-161 NURBS Surface Tessellation

Figure 7-161 shows a demonstration of how tessellation occurs in Maya NURBS surfaces. The shape on the right, which is divided into little rectangles, is the product of surface rendering the object on the left.

As you can see in the figure above, Maya converts NURBS into polygon faces to produce the final image. Curve functions are used in NURBS and, when this is surface rendered, separate surface tessellation does not take place. If the attributes of the curves have been defined, the object will be rendered as a perfect curve, no matter how many span values there are. This is not the case with Pixar's RenderMan.

Taking this into consideration, we can assume that–when we use polygons–we're going to need an enormous number of faces for the movie's output resolution. Since, in Polygon, the number of faces has a direct effect on rendering, Polygon is going to have a longer rendering time than NURBS.

As a result, since Polygon has a negative impact on rendering, NURBS is the method of choice. However, NURBS has its limitations. It can be implemented quickly, easily, and effectively for very simple characters, but for realistic multi-patches, it becomes tricky and time consuming.

The following figures show you how NURBS is used in modeling. Even when using NURBS, it's important to choose the most effective method of modeling.

● Radiating NURBS Modeling

Radiating NURBS models are good for modeling characters with small eyes; they allow for very easy control. This method also allows you to preserve smooth curves (an advantage of NURBS), and, when binding using joints, you can use the Artisan tool to quickly set up Weight values.

(One thing you need to keep in mind is that the Isoparms you add when making the eyes must flow down the cheek and into the neck. The reason is that this area uses a lot more Isoparms than other areas and, if we don't set them up properly, we can create unnecessary wrinkles.)

Radiating NURBS models aren't always ideal, though.

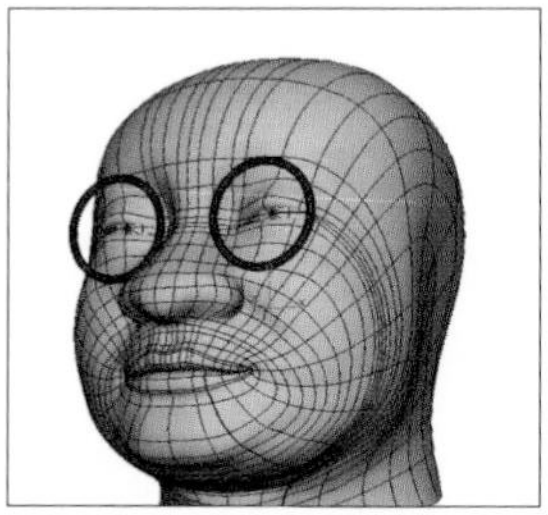

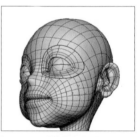

Figure 7-162 Radiating NURBS Model

This character has very large eyes. For this kind of character, it is difficult to make the one-patch structure we made for the character in Figure 7-157. It would require a great many Isoparms to make the eyes for this model.

In this case, it's best to model the eyes, ears, and other elements separately, then paste them onto the character. One potential problem with this solution is the curvature between surfaces, but we can fix this by mapping the area between surfaces so that the curvatures of the surfaces appear to be attached.

Figure 7-163 NURBS Model that Overcomes the Problems of Radiating NURBS Model

● Multi-Patch Modeling

This is an example of the most elaborate kind of modeling you can do using NURBS. Multi-Patch modeling. To make the face, we use several surfaces to respresent the muscles, then put them together. Although this method allows you to perform very elaborate modeling, controlling this sort of model takes a lot of time and effort because the curvature between the surfaces must be maintained throughout the range of motion.

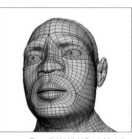

Figure 7-164 Multi-Patch Modeling

Although we can use the Stitch Edge tool or the Global Stitch tool to fit the curves together, curves can break apart very easily in animations. Using Weight values to maintain the curves while making the surfaces move naturally can be very difficult. Compared to other types of modeling, the character setup in this variety calls for a lot of time and effort on the part of the designer.

● Using Multi-Patch Modeling to Make Blend Shapes

In order to make good blend shapes using Multi-Patch modeling, surfaces must be bound together for large movements, and the Deformer—either Cluster or Lattice—should be used for smaller movements. As a final step, CVs should be adjusted to complete the shape and, at times, the Stitch Edge tool or the Global Stitch tool should be used.

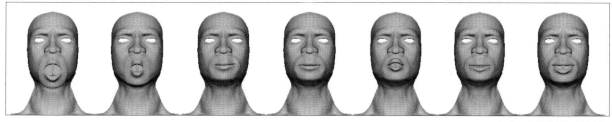

Figure 7-165 Multi-Patch Modeling

We've already covered NURBS modeling in Chapter 4 of this book, so I won't go into more detail here. If you want to refresh your memory, refer back to Chapter 4, "NURBS Modeling."

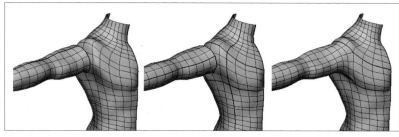

Figure 7-166 Using Multi-Patch to Model the Human Body

● Polygon & Subdivision Surface Modeling

Unlike NURBS, Polygon and Subdivision Surface modeling allow you to attach surfaces. In other words, in NURBS patches are used to produce only rectangles, but in Polygon, we can produce shapes with an infinite number of angles. We can also add on elements and remove unwanted surfaces.

All 3D software supports the Polygon method of modeling. RenderMan also supports Subdivision Surface and this method of modeling is becoming the norm. Since we can easily convert from Polygon to Subdivision Surface, we will talk about them both here.

Maya Subdivision Surface Modeling

In terms of basic usage, Subdivision Surface modeling is the same as Polygon modeling, with the biggest difference being the use of levels. We have already gone over this in great detail in Chapter 3, "Subdivision Surface Character Modeling," so I will briefly summarize it here.

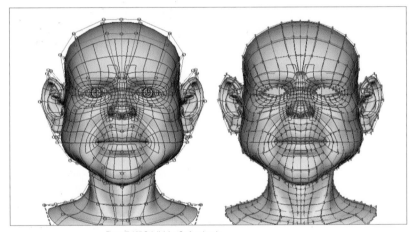

Figure 7-167 Subdivision Surface Levels

As you can see in the figure above, we can divide up the model into more levels depending on how detailed the model is. Levels can also be easily converted to surfaces. In other words, we can divide the model up into many levels to portray the details (the actual binding point on this model is the point at Level 0). What that means is that, since a very small number of vertices are bound to the joint, it is easier to adjust the Weight values, and transformations in the surfaces are also smoother.

Polygon Modeling

If Subdivision Surfaces are too heavy and inconvenient to use, you can use Polygon modeling instead. The modeling method is the same, but in Polygon modeling, the model is not divided up into levels and all modeling takes place at Level 0.

Figure 7-168 is an example of Polygon modeling. The final output of this model is in the form of polygons. What this means is that the model will be rendered using polygons, and you'll need more surface divisions in order to get a softer final image.

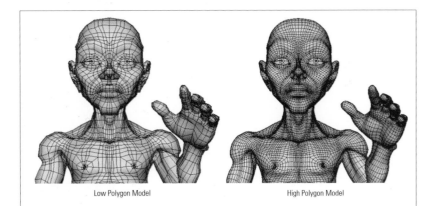

Low Polygon Model   High Polygon Model

Figure 7-168 Polygon Modeling

2. Which Method?

Now that we've looked at the methods involved in each type of character modeling, we're equipped to consider which methods are suitable for specific situations. In this section, we'll look at which modeling method is best for modeling a given character.

Since we've already covered Subdivision Surface modeling in the book, and since both methods use surfaces in the same way, the majority of my explanations here will be based on Polygon modeling. It's time to explore how surfaces flow in the models and movements of the characters.

● Character Modeling

Modeling a static character to look realistic is not very difficult; we just have to make the surfaces look like the final character, and how they are structured doesn't matter. However, adding movement to the model is a different story. If you have a character that looks realistic, its movement must also be realistic.

This is where things get tricky because it can be quite difficult to make your character, human or otherwise, move like the real thing. In human characters, you need to consider the movement of the joints and understand how this movement will affect the overlying muscles. Without this understanding, it will be very difficult to model the movement, and—even if you somehow manage to model the movement—the motion will appear unnatural.

Figure 7-169 Motion Test of a Low Polygon Model

The most important thing in character modeling is to understand the flow of the muscles and to analyze and divide up the surfaces accordingly. This directly affects the character's movement and induces natural transformations in the skin.

Relationship of Muscle to Skin

It is not enough just to understand how the muscles are organized, because what we actually see is not the muscle, but the overlying skin. For that reason, you not only have to understand how the muscles are organized but also how the skin moves in relation to the movement of the muscles. Let's look at the face, for example.

The surface of the face is mostly determined by the structure of the underlying muscles. Therefore, not only should you structure the surfaces according to the flow of the muscles, you should divide the edges of the muscles to make the facial movements look natural.

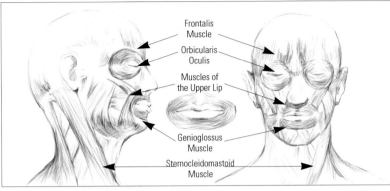

Figure 7-170 Frontal Muscles

In face modeling, the areas we need to worry about the most are the muscles that are diagrammed in the surrounding figures. Since these muscles directly affect the movements in the face, we need to at least understand them–if nothing else. Most users will probably already have a good understanding of these muscles. The sternocleidomastoid muscle, for instance, is very important. How this muscle is organized will largely depend on the movements of the neck, and setting the it up properly is crucial for ensuring realistic motion in the neck.

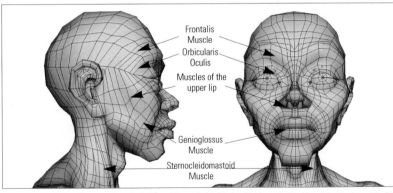

Figure 7-171 A Low-Polygon Model of Surface Division against the Flow of the Muscles and the Skin

How to Model a Face

There are many ways to model a face. The most common method is to draw the profile of the face and extrude it to create the surfaces. Another choice is to use NURBS. With the NURBS method, we make the big block into a simple NURBS surface, convert the surface into polygons, attach them, and then fine-tune the entire model. Still another method is one that starts with cubes. This method is a lot like sculpting, and it's the one I'll use here.

The following illustrations show the steps involved in modeling a face starting with polygon cubes. This method is slightly different from the Subdivision Surface modeling method explained earlier.

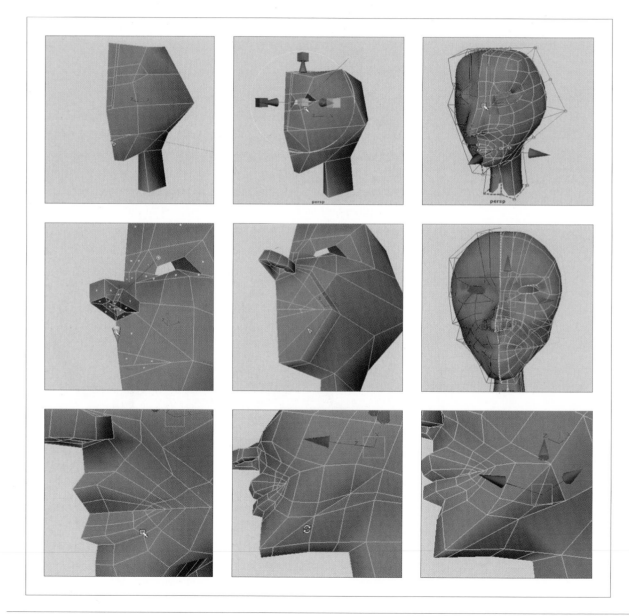

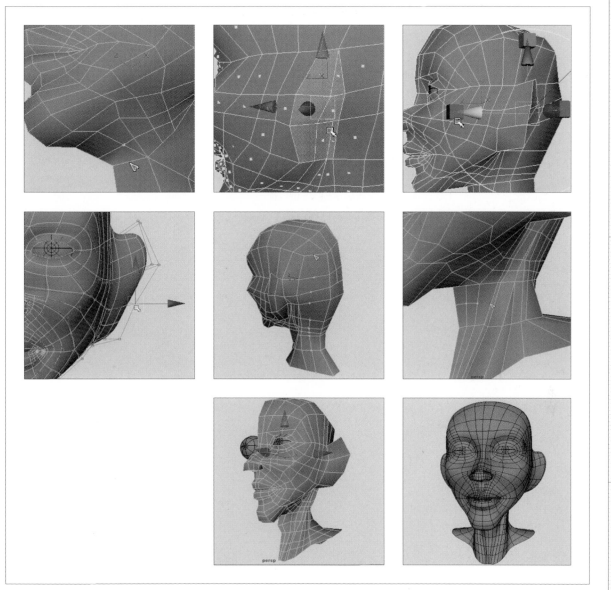

Figure 7-172 Steps Involved in Face Modeling

Muscles, Surfaces, and Movement

Like face modeling, body modeling requires an understanding of muscle flow. You may think this is not as important, as the majority of the character's body will be covered with clothing or some other adornment, but if you want to do character animation, it's a good idea to be familiar with all the bends and twists of the body.

In this section, we will look at how surfaces will be divided depending on the muscles of the body. The important thing is to start with the main muscle mass. In body modeling, how this mass is organized and how the surfaces are divided to fit the flow of the muscles is very important. Understanding this will be a big help when it comes to modeling. Take the last drawing shown here and practice sketching in surface divisions. The flow between the edges is key for sketching in surface divisions, and mastering this is essential to this skill.

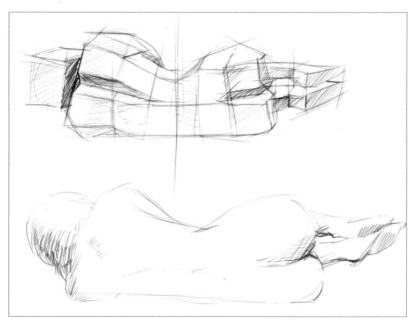

Figure 7-173 Understanding Surfaces

Let's look at the following example. This is a sketch that shows how we plan to divide the surfaces for the model.

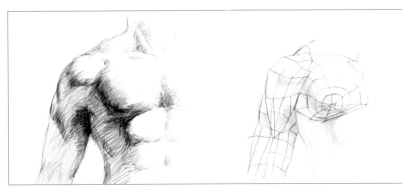

Figure 7-174 Basic Preparations for Surface Division

This is the most important step in terms of work efficiency. It not only allows you to gain perspective to see how the surfaces will be divided (so that you can predict the motion), it will also help save a lot of time once you actually start to model.

Figure 7-175 shows a test model of the sketched portion from the above drawing. Since we have sketched the surface divisions, the subsequent surface divisions and modeling are relatively easy.

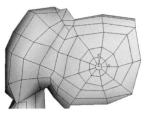

Figure 7-175 An Example of Surface Divisions Based on Our Sketch

The next figure shows an example of body modeling based on an analysis of the body shape as surfaces.

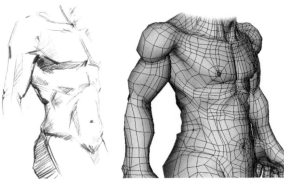

Figure 7-176 An Example of Surface Divisions Based on Our Sketch

Figure 7-176 shows surface divisions of the chest, arm, and abdominal muscles. The surface blocks that we see in the figure are created out of the muscle blocks, and the flow is the direction in which the surface moves as a result of the joint.

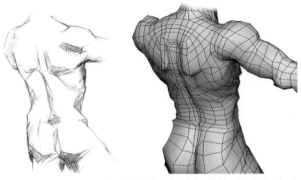

Figure 7-177 An Example of Surface Divisions Based on Our Sketch

Figure 7-177 shows the rear view of the character. The flowing structure for the back is not yet complete. Only the large flows have been linked together, but the details still need to be worked on.

At the end of this chapter, we'll look at an example that covers the binding of this character to a skeleton to see how motion is added.

3-2. CHARACTER SETUP

Up until this point, we've looked at the modeling process itself. Now we will look at how to set up a modeled character. There are many books on the market that deal with character setup. Here, I will use the method that I have found works best for me.

1 Rigid Bind Vs. Smooth Bind

Maya offers two different binding environments. When Maya first came out, its first binding environment, which was used with Alias, was Rigid Bind. After several version upgrades, Smooth Bind, which allows us to perform more elaborate binding, was introduced. Let's take a closer look at the two binding types.

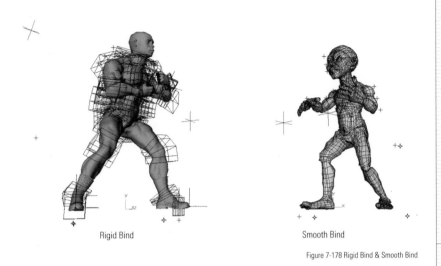

Rigid Bind

Smooth Bind

Figure 7-178 Rigid Bind & Smooth Bind

The biggest difference between Rigid Bind and Smooth Bind lies in how the joints affect the NURBS CV or Polygon Vertex. In Rigid Bind, the CVs and vertices are affected by only one joint, but in Smooth Bind, the user decides how many joints will affect the CVs and vertices.

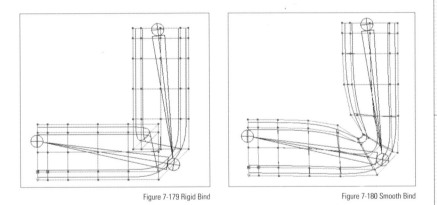

Figure 7-179 Rigid Bind

Figure 7-180 Smooth Bind

Rigid Bind is used in the figure above. Since each CV or vertex can only be moved by one joint, this effect can occur. In order to make the movement more natural, we need to adjust the Weight values for the CVs affected by that joint.

Smooth Bind is used in figure 7-180. The CVs in the joint area are controlled by a total of 3 joints, so–in order to make the movement more natural–we need to adjust the Weight values for the CVs of each joint.

There are advantages and disadvantages to both types of binding. One advantage of the Rigid Bind is the use of Flexors. Flexors make moving joints and the muscles around the bone easier to manipulate. This also saves you a lot of time because you can look at the movement of the joints and arrange the movement of the skin accordingly.

A disadvantage to Rigid Bind is that CVs and vertices are controlled by only one joint. This means that it is very difficult to set things up so that the skin moves naturally and realistically. Also, even though you have a symmetrical model, you need to work on each side separately.

In Smooth Bind, on the other hand, users can determine how many joints will be used to control the CVs and vertices. Also, in symmetrical models, you only need to work on one side and simply copy it over to the other side. Smooth Bind is better for setting up the character to move like real people move.

However, because Smooth Bind does not use Flexors, it is a little inconvenient to adjust Weight values for the joints. Most users believe Smooth Bind to be comparatively easier to use and prefer it over Rigid Bind. This is true to some extent, but don't be fooled! Smooth Bind is definitely not easier than Rigid Bind. In reality, using Smooth Bind for more elaborate setups can take more work and effort than using Rigid Bind.

2 Rigid Bind or Smooth Bind?

Whether you decide to use Rigid Bind or Smooth Bind really depends on personal preference. In my case, because I have been using Alias for a long time and since Rigid Bind was the only type of bind that was offered when Maya first came out, I found myself sticking to Rigid Bind even after Smooth Bind was introduced. When I used Multi-Patch modeling to make hands, for example, I would use a lot of smooth binding and then find it quite tricky to adjust the Weight values. With Rigid Bind, it was simply a matter of using Flexors to control each finger joint. But with Smooth Bind, I had to maintain the curvature of each patch while setting up the Weight values–a process I found to be quite difficult.

As more and more people are starting to use Subdivision Surface modeling, Smooth Bind has emerged as the preferred bind method. In Subdivision Surface modeling, all surfaces are attached and you don't run into the problem of having the curves break up on you–not to mention Smooth Bind creates smoother skin transformations and saves time when working on mirror-image models. And the biggest advantage to Smooth Bind is that you can set it up to be as elaborate as you want.

Ultimately, it's difficult to say which is the 'better' bind method. I would recommend that you test both methods thoroughly and use the method that is more comfortable for you, or the one that is better suited to the project at hand.

3 Smooth Binding

In this section, we will look at how to set up a model for Smooth Bind. The method that I am about to explain may seem unfamiliar and I am not saying that this is the only method that you can use. There is no one 'right' method, other than the one that makes your work easier and faster. This method is simply the one that I have found works best for me.

Which Binding Pose is Better?

Binding Pose is the name that we give to the shape our model takes upon first binding it to the skeleton. The binding pose is very important because the skin must move naturally with the movements of each joint and the movement must proceed in the way we want it to. Figure 7-181 shows us a very basic binding pose.

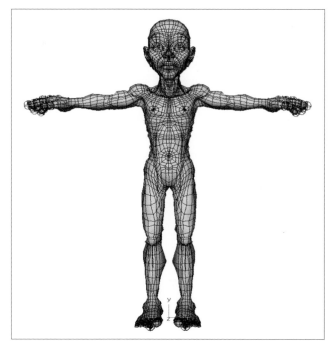

Figure 7-181 Binding Pose

I say that this is a basic binding pose because the arms can be raised up and down and the legs can be moved from side to side and front to back. That's it. This is the binding pose that is used most often because it is adequate for displaying all movement.

Let's stop for a minute and think about which pose would be most effective and efficient for a given scenario. How many scenes in your movie require the character to raise its hands over its head? How many scenes require your character to stretch out its arms as shown in the figure above? Simply by asking a few questions, we have come to the conclusion that a pose such as this is hardly the best one for most situations.

So what poses can we make? Although your character is going to have its arms lowered for much of the time in most animations, quite frequently a character is going to have to raise its arms and spread them out at some point—as shown here. However, the majority of your scenes will probably be ones in which your character's arms are bent. If that's the case, let's see how the bind pose in Figure 7-182 measures up.

Looking at this bind pose, you will notice that the arms are lowered and slightly bent and that the legs are slightly bent, as well.

Figure 7-182 Binding Pose

The binding pose is important because this pose will be the one that directly affects character movement. Let's consider the elbows in the original binding pose figure, for example. If we bind the model with the character's arms stretched out and then bend them again, no matter how great you set up the Weight values, the folds inside the elbow present a problem. You will end up with a surface that sinks into the elbow or a bending action that looks unnatural.

However, if you use the pose here—one with slightly bent arms—the bending action will appear much more natural than the binding of one with completely outstretched arms.

How Are Joints Positioned?

Along with the binding pose, the position of the joints is important. The position of the joints will play an important role in surface transformations.

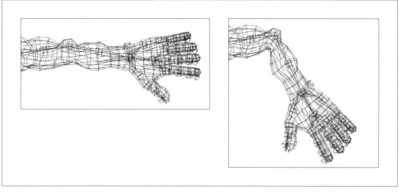

Figure 7-183 How the Skin Moves with Respect to the Placement of the Joint

Let's look at Figures 7-183 and 7-184. Both figures show how the skin moves in relation to the placement of the joints. In Figure 7-183, the joints are placed in the back and in Figure 7-184, the joints are placed in the front. Actually, movements in these joint areas present a problem. The joints should be placed more towards the front, like in Figure 7-184, so that the folds inside the elbow look natural when the arm is bent.

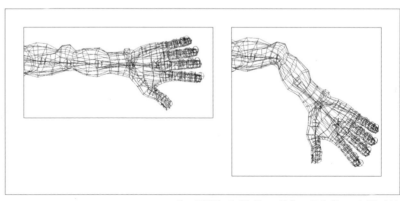

Figure 7-184 How the Skin Moves with Respect to the Placement of the Joints

This method is also a good one for the legs. If we position the joints so that they are positioned like the bones in human bodies (Figure 7-184), movement in the pelvic region will appear more natural.

What's a Good Max Influence Value?

The Max Influence value is the one that determines how many joints will control the CVs and vertices. This value can be changed in the Smooth Bind Options window.

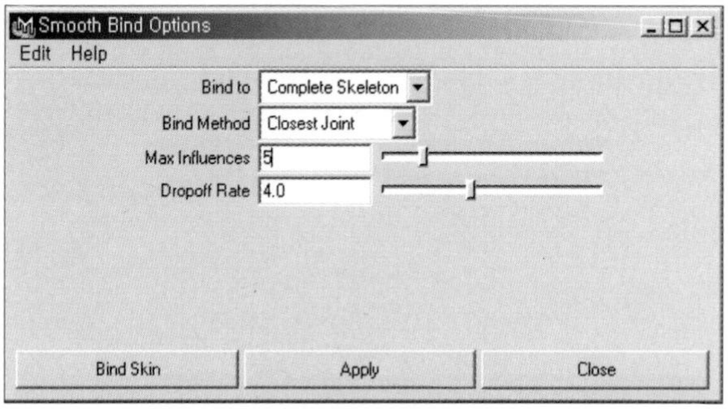

Figure 7-185 Smooth Bind Options Window

I recommend using the default value because, in general, 5 or so joints can control the points in the pelvis, shoulders, and neck regions. Depending on your character, you may have some points that are controlled by more than 5 points, but the higher this number, the trickier it becomes to control your character.

If you want a simpler setup, you can change this value to 4. Even after binding, you can change this value by selecting [Skin > Edit Smooth Skin > Set Max Influences...].

4 Using Clusters

After binding, Weight values are insufficient to set up the flex and release movement of the muscles. Binding only ties points on the model to the joints. Then, by entering an adequate ratio, the joints will rotate accordingly. Movement in the skin caused by the flexing and releasing of muscles is not really related to motion at all–this movement is produced using Influence Objects or Clusters.

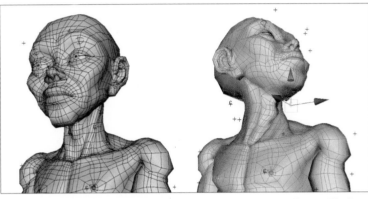

Figure 7-186 Controlling Neck Movements Using Clusters

Figure 7-186 shows how movement in the neck region is controlled using Clusters. When the neck is turned from side to side, the sternocleidomastoid muscles will flex and release accordingly. This is a movement that cannot be portrayed using the Weight value of joint vertices alone. As we can see in the figure, we need to make Clusters on each side so that the neck can move automatically from side to side.

Depending on how detailed the movements of the character are, you can have over a dozen Clusters in your model. The more Clusters you have, the more detailed and elaborate these movements will be.

5 The FInal Method: Blend Shape

There are certain regions that still won't look right no matter how much you adjust the Weight value, or how many Clusters or Influence Objects you have. These areas include the area where the deltoid muscle and the pectoralis major meet when the arms are raised or lowered, the muscles in the pelvis when the legs are raised, and the area where the jaw meets the neck when the mouth is opened. It is difficult to use Clusters in these regions and, when we set up the pose, these are the areas where the surfaces will look strange. The solution calls for the use of Blend Shape.

Let's look at Figure 7-187. This figure shows the area where the jaw meets the neck. The figure on the left shows how we simply used joints to make the movement in this area, and the figure on the right shows how we fixed it using Blend Shape.

Blend Shape is a good method to use to create perfect transformations, as shown here. This method is explained in greater detail in section 2-6 of this chapter, "Surface Deformation Tip."

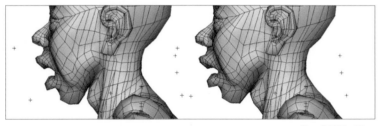

Figure 7-187 Blend Shape

Use this sequence of steps to model using Blend Shape:

1. First, use Weight values and/or Clusters and Influence Objects to set up a model with natural transformations.
2. Move each joint. Observe the regions where the joints move unnaturally to get an idea of how many blend shapes you need.
3. Copying the model made using Blend Shape, clear the History and unlock all channels in the Channel Box.
4. Bind the copied model to the skeleton and then copy the Weight values on the original object.
5. Modify the Deformation Order of the copied object. Move the Twick Node so that it is placed on top of the SkinCluster.

6. Move the joints to set up their positions and then proceed to model the character.
7. After modeling, change the skeleton back into a bind pose, select the model, and clear the history.
8. Make both models into Blend Shapes and automate them as needed by linking joints and Set Driven Keys. When making Blend Shapes, 'Front of Chain' must be selected in the options window. .

This concludes our brief look at Maya's modeling and setup techniques. The most important thing is that you find the method that works best for you.

Nonlinear Animation

What is Nonlinear Animation?

Maya uses Trax Editor to divide all animation sequences into classes to make nonlinear editing possible. This can be used to clip, copy, and paste all 3D animation keyframes or to blend different clips to smoothly link 2 motions. In addition, this allows us to easily adjust the timing of the animations or to easily modify the repetitive actions of a serial animation. Clips can also be exported to other scenes and reused. A variety of motions can be saved as clips and loaded as needed to make a new motion.

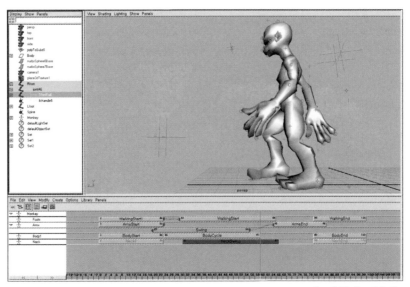

Figure 8-1 Nonlinear Animation

1. UNDERSTANDING CHARACTER

Maya Character refers to a collection of attributes that can be animated simultaneously. This allows us to combine attributes in one Character Node to easily keyframe all attributes. Users will be able to animate a variety of different attributes simply by selecting one character. For example, let's suppose that, in order to animate both hands of the character, we used the IK handle to control the movements of both arms and that, in order to move the fingers, we used a random locator to make a controller and added an attribute to move each of the fingers using Set Driven Keys. We need to select the IK handle, and keyframe in order to animate both arms, select the locater and keyframe the movements of the fingers, and then keyframe the other arm. In this way, we must repeatedly select the object that has the attribute we wish to keyframe, and then configure a key for it. However, if we are to make all of these attributes into one Character Node, we can simply select the Character Node to display all of the attributes in the Channel Box for keyframing. Also, in terms of applying a Set Key, we can apply a Set Key to the selected Character Node to apply a key to all the attributes within. This is a very intuitive way to animate the desired attributes, and it gives us access to a wide variety of different attributes.

However, the ultimate objective is to use the Trax Editor because, as a result, we clip the animation of these Character Nodes.

First of all, let's take a look at the Character menu. The Character menu can be found under [Animation > Character]. Open the file, CD-ROM/CHARACTER/scenes/Alien.mb, for the purposes of this example.

1-1. CREATE CHARACTER SET

This menu is used to create a character set. Figure 8-2 is the example file included in the supplementary CD-ROM.

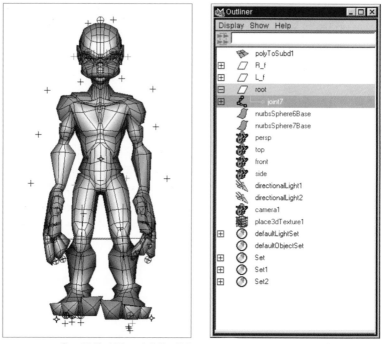

Figure 8-2 Alien.Mb (Image by Ko Yong-Chul)   Figure 8-3 Outliner

In order to make a character, select [Windows > Outliner] to open the Outliner, and select joint7 from under Root, as shown in Figure 8-3. Select [Animation > Character > Create Character Set] to open the Options window. As shown in Figure 8-4, type **Body** for the Name field, and then click on the Create Character Set button at the bottom of the window.

Looking at the Channel Box, we can see that the Translate and Rotate colors for the selected joint7 have changed (see Figure 8-5) and that channels have been made for the INPUTS Body.

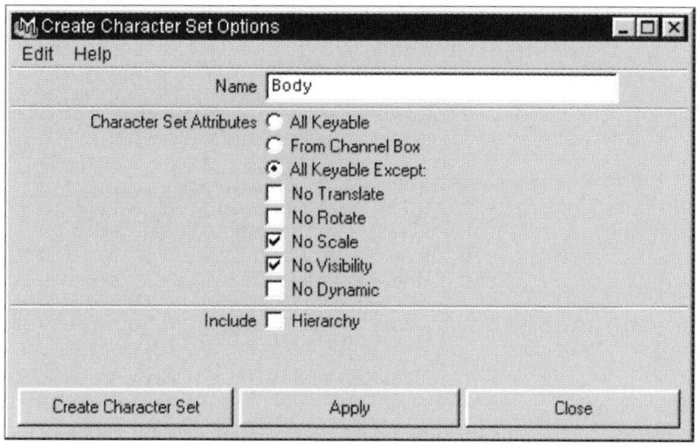

Figure 8-4 Options Window 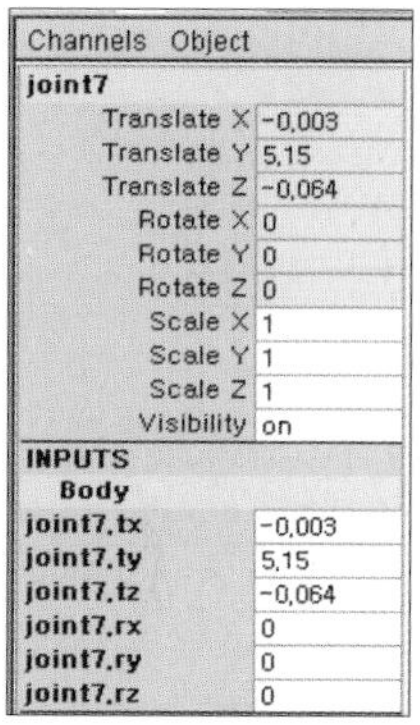   Figure 8-5 Channel Box

A body character node is created in the Outliner, and we can now select this body character node to keyframe the channels within this body. Let's take a quick look at the Options window in Figure 8-4. Character Set Attributes define the channels included in the character. Checking the All Keyable option will include all of the channels in the Channel Box in the character. Selecting From Channel Box will include only those channels selected in the Channel Box in the character. Selecting the default setting, All Keyable Except, allows us to exclude unnecessary channels from the activated channels at the bottom. Selecting the Hierarchy option next to Include will make the character out of all defined channels under the selected node.

1-2. CREATE SUBCHARACTER SET

This option is used to make a subcharacter set. In other words, if the Character Node was made using the Create Character Set menu above, this menu is used to make another, detailed character set. If the skeleton itself is divided into different levels, this hierarchical structure comes in handy when animating such a skeleton. Therefore, it is very convenient to create the character set to have such a hierarchical structure. In other words, when we make the Root Character Node we called "Body" earlier, it will be convenient to create a Character Node to control and govern the movement of both arms, legs, and the neck. For the purposes of the example, select the R_f1 and L_f1 nodes from the Outliner. Select [Animation > Character > Create SubCharacter Set]. In the Options window (see Figure 8-6), type in **Foot** for the Name field and, after configuring the options as shown, click on the Create SubCharacter Set button at the bottom.

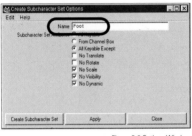

Figure 8-6 Options Window

As a result, a Foot Character Set is created under the Body Character Set. We can verify this by expanding the Body Character Node in the Outliner (see Figure 8-7) to see the Foot Node below the Body Node. We can also see the Foot Node beneath the Body Character by looking at the Character Set beneath the Playback button (see Figure 8-8).

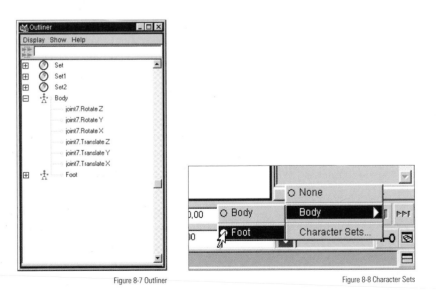

Figure 8-7 Outliner

Figure 8-8 Character Sets

All other options are the same as for the Create Character Set menu, with the exception that the Create SubCharacter Set menu does not have the Include Hierarchy option.

1-3. ATTRIBUTE EDITOR

This menu displays the Attribute Editor of the selected Character Node.

After selecting the Body Character from the Character Set from the Outliner or from below the Playback button, select [Animation > Character > Attribute Editor...] to open the Attribute Editor for the Character Node (see Figure 8-9).

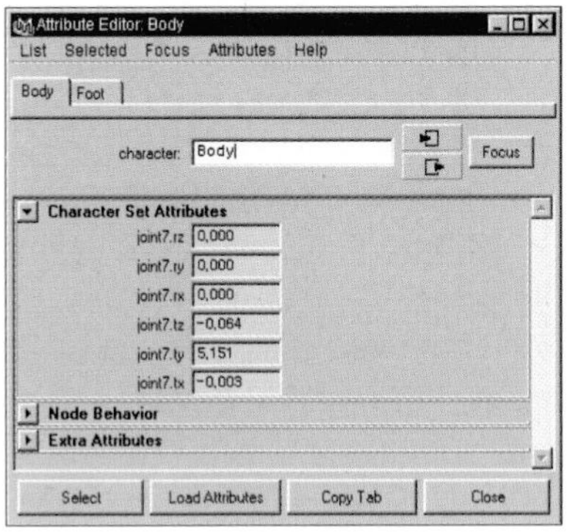

Figure 8-9 Attribute Editor

1-4. ADD TO CHARACTER SET

This menu is used to add channels from different objects to portions of the character set. For example, let's say that we want to add a Rotate Channel to control the joints of the spine in the Body Character Set we created earlier. First, we need to select the Character Set to which the channels will be added. Because the channels will be added to the body, select Body from the Character Set below the Playback button. Select joint8~11, the joints making up the spine, from the Outliner as shown in Figure 8-10. The joints can be selected simultaneously by using the Shift or Ctrl keys. Select all of the Rotate Channels from the Channel Box, as shown in Figure 8-11.

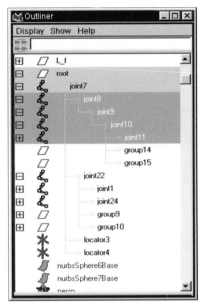

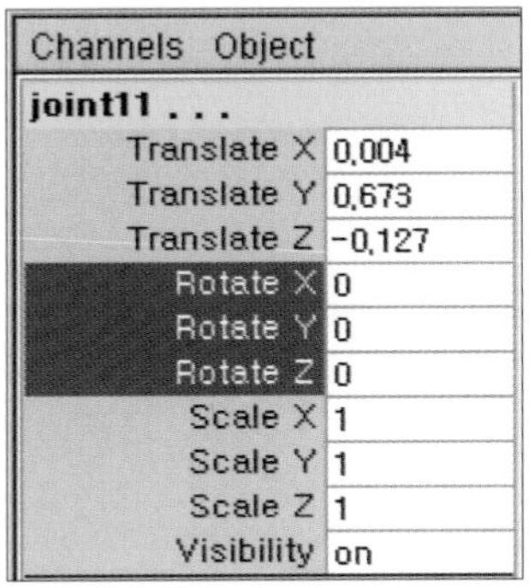

Figure 8-11 Select Channel

Figure 8-10 Outliner

Select [Animation > Character > Add to Character Set].

The result is that all of the Rotate Channels of the selected joints are included in the Body Character Set.

After selecting Body from INPUT in the Channel Box or selecting the Body Character from the Outliner, verify this by selecting [Animation > Character > Attribute Editor].

1-5. REMOVE FROM CHARACTER SET

This menu, in contrast to the Add to Character Set menu, removes particular channels from the character set. For example, let's suppose we want to remove the Rotate Channel of joint11, which we added in the previous section, from the Body Character Set. Select all the Rotate Channels of joint11 from the Channel Box (see Figure 8-12), and then select [Animation > Character > Remove from Character Set].

As a result, the Rotate Channel of joint11 will be removed from the Body Character Set.

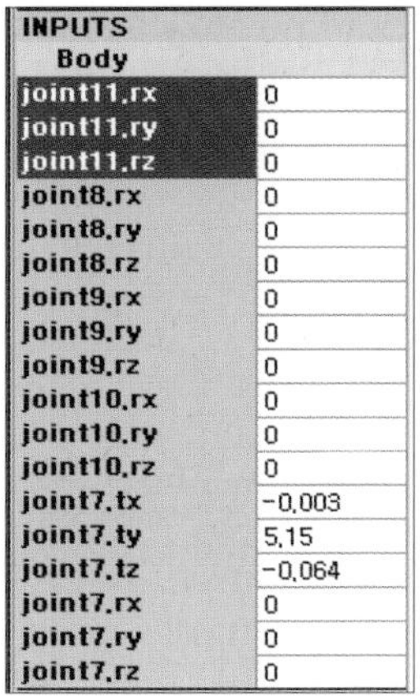
INPUTS
Body
joint11.rx 0
joint11.ry 0
joint11.rz 0
joint8.rx 0
joint8.ry 0
joint8.rz 0
joint9.rx 0
joint9.ry 0
joint9.rz 0
joint10.rx 0
joint10.ry 0
joint10.rz 0
joint7.tx -0.003
joint7.ty 5.15
joint7.tz -0.064
joint7.rx 0
joint7.ry 0
joint7.rz 0

Figure 8-12 Channel Box

1-6. MERGE CHARACTER SET

This menu combines different character sets into one. For example, in order to combine the Foot and Body character sets we made, select the Body and Foot Character Nodes from the Outliner, as shown in Figure 8-13. Then, select [Animation > Character > Merge Character Set] to combine the two sets.

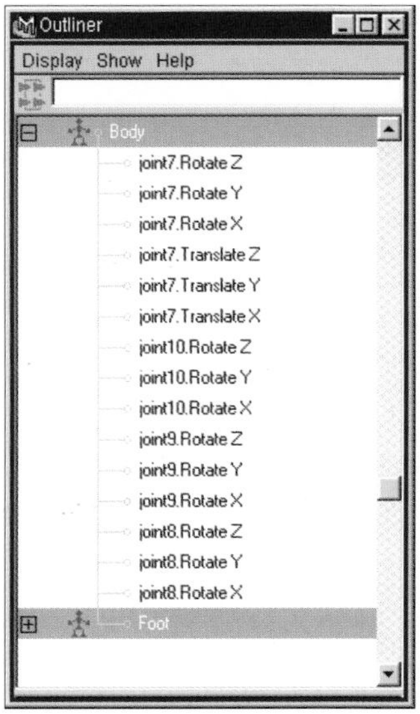
Outliner
Display Show Help
Body
joint7.Rotate Z
joint7.Rotate Y
joint7.Rotate X
joint7.Translate Z
joint7.Translate Y
joint7.Translate X
joint10.Rotate Z
joint10.Rotate Y
joint10.Rotate X
joint9.Rotate Z
joint9.Rotate Y
joint9.Rotate X
joint8.Rotate Z
joint8.Rotate Y
joint8.Rotate X
Foot

Figure 8-13 Outliner

1-7. SELECT CHARACTER SET

We can use the [Animation > Character > Select Character Set] menu to select the desired character node. The desired character node can also be selected from the Outliner or from the character set below the Playback button.

1-8. SELECT CHARACTER SET MEMBERS

Through this menu, we can select all objects included in the character node. For example, let's suppose we want to select all of the joints contained within the Body Character Set. First, select the Body Character Node and then select [Animation > Character > Select Character Set Members] to select all the joints within the Body Character Set.

1-9. SET CURRENT CHARACTER SET

We can use the [Animation > Character > Select Character Set] menu to select the desired character node. No character sets will be selected if None is selected. When the character set is selected, the Character Editing Relationship Editor will appear as in Figure 8-14.

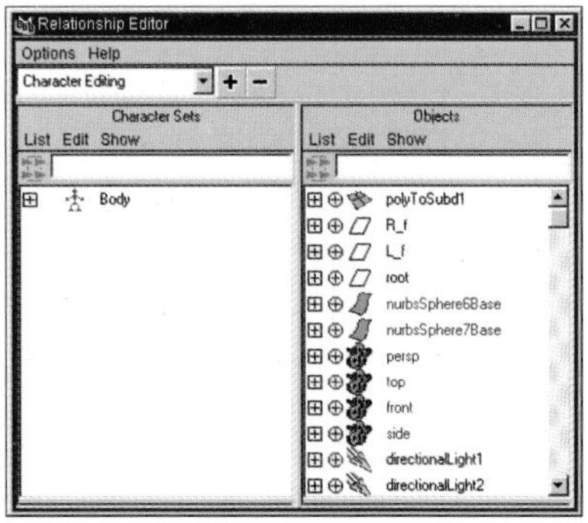

Figure 8-14 Relationship Editor

Through this Relationship Editor, we can edit various properties of the character set.

This completes the overview of the Character menu. Although these commands are useful in intuitively keyframing the channel values of each object, they are the preparatory steps for using the Trax Editor, which we will learn about next, to make each character into a clip and to edit the animation.

2. TRAX EDITOR

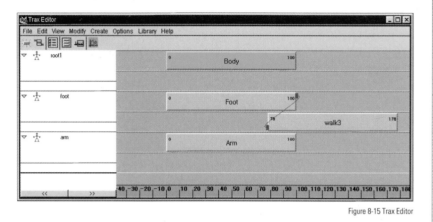

Figure 8-15 Trax Editor

We will now learn about the Trax Editor, which is used to edit nonlinear animation. In terms of animation editing, we previously used Graph Editors or Dope Sheets to modify the overall motion or to control precise and detailed motions. However, it was very difficult to effectively organize previous animation data and to playback keyframes as needed. Such factors (i.e., the effective organization of animation data and the playback of keyframes) are key timesaving elements in actual, large-scale projects.

Maya uses the Trax Editor to make existing animations into clips that can be edited, exported, and imported as needed. We will first take a look at the basic menus and directions for using the Trax Editor and then take a look at nonlinear editing through an example.

2-1. MAKING THE CLIP

We have covered how to make character sets in the previous section. We need this character set in order to make a clip using the Trax Editor.

Clips are made and organized based on these character sets. Although it is not necessary to make a separate character set in recent versions of Maya, if you want to divide and organize the character into areas with special motion, the character set is required. We will cover this point later in this chapter. For now, we will look at how to make a simple clip.

For the purposes of this example, we first need to make a NURBS Sphere. As shown in Figure 8-16, keyframe the bounded ball.

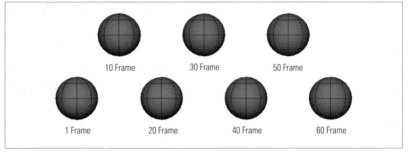

Figure 8-16 Making the Bounding Ball

Make the motion of this sphere into a clip by selecting [Create > Clip] from the Trax Editor. This will open the Create Clip Options window, as shown in Figure 8-17. In the Name field, type **Bounding** and then click on the Create Clip button at the bottom of the window.

Figure 8-17 Create Clip Options Window

A new character is made in the Trax Editor, and a clip for the character is also made. Let's take a quick look at the Create Clip options.

● Name

This option is used to name the clip. The name entered here will be applied to the clip.

● Keys

Selecting Leaves Keys in Timeline will create the clip leaving behind the character keys in the time slider. This is a good option to use if you are not going to be using the clip right away. Also, when the keys are left behind in the time slider, they can be used to make another clip. When this option is turned on, the Put Clip in Trax Editor and Visor option is deactivated. This prevents the animation from being repeated.

● Clip

This option determines where the clip will be arranged.
Put Clip in Visor Only will place the clip only in the Visor and not in the Trax Editor.
Put Clip in Trax Editor and Visor is the default setting and places the clip in both the Visor and the Trax Editor.

● Time Range

This option is used to select the frame range for the clip.
Use Selected will make the clip based on the range selected in the Time Slider, and Use Time Slider Range will make the clip depending on the Playback Start and Playback End range of the time slider.
Use Animation Curve Range is the default setting and makes the clip depending on the entire range of the character's animation curve.
Specify Start and End allows us to randomly assign the starting and ending points of the range.

● Subcharacters

When this option is turned on, if the character has subcharacters, clips are automatically made for the subcharacters as well.

● Time Warp

When this option is turned on, a separate Time Warp animation curve is made.
Select the clip made in the Trax Editor and then select [View > Graph Aim Curves] to open the Graph Editor to edit the animation curve for the clip's channel. Observing Figure 8-18, we can see that the Time Warp Curve is similar to the animation curve for the motion path. By adjusting the clip, as shown in the figure, we can adjust the overall timing.

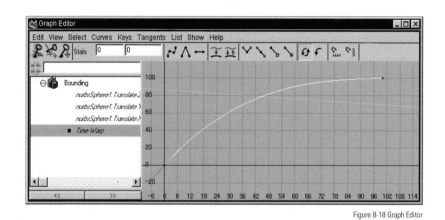

Figure 8-18 Graph Editor

2-2. MANIPULATING THE CLIP

We can edit the various attributes of the clip we made before it is used. This is similar to a 2D video editing program, in which clips are cut and pasted to blend together 2 clips. In this section, we will look at the many ways in which the clip can be manipulated.

1. Editing Clip Attributes

In order to edit clip attributes, select the clip and then select [Modify > Attribute Editor] from the Trax Editor. This will open the Attribute Editor for the selected clip, as shown in Figure 8-19.

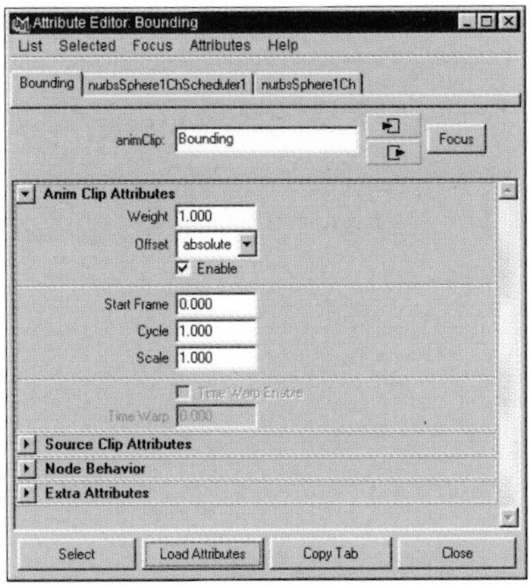

Figure 8-19 Attribute Editor

● Weight

By adjusting this value, we can scale each of the clip's attributes. This affects the entire animation clip from the starting point of the animation. For example, the animation for the clip above, which was made for the bounding ball, is bounded from frames 1-60. In other words, when the ball is bounced, it moves approximately 6 spaces in the Y-direction and -16 spaces in the Z-direction. When this value is set to 0.5, although there is no change in the length of the overall animation, it moves 3 spaces in the Y-direction and -8 spaces in the Z-direction for an approximately 50% scaling in the motion. This affects all attributes excluding the Boolean data (On/Off).

● Offset

This option determines how Maya will interpret the clip values when 2 clips are linked together or when one clip is made to cycle. Absolute uses only the current clip values, without regard to the previous key values.

Relative adds the previous key values to the current clip. For example, in order to successively link the clip made above, select [File > Visor] from the Trax Editor to open the Visor window. Looking at Figure 8-20, we can see that the clip is stored in the Visor Character Clips Tab. Click on this clip using the MMB, and drag it to the track in the Trax Editor. A new clip will be made.

Figure 8-20 Loading the Clip

Open the Attribute Editor for the new clip, set the Offset value to Absolute and then play the animation. The animation will be played according to the values of the first clip and then of the second clip. In this animation, the ball will return to its original position before playing again. However, if the ending point of the first clip animation coincides with the starting point of the second animation, the Offset value must be set to Relative. Set the value to Relative before playing the animation. We can see that the ball will continue to move without returning to its original starting position. This is because Relative causes the key value of the first clip to be added to the value of the current clip.

● Enable

When this option is turned off, the values for the current clip will not be played.

● Start Frame

This determines the starting position of the current clip. We can also define the starting point by selecting the clip in the Trax Editor and then dragging the mouse from side to side.

● Cycle

We use this option to determine the number of times the clip is made to repeat. Since this bounding ball animation is set to run in 60 frames, setting the Cycle value to 2 will cause it to run in 120 frames and setting it to 0.5 will cause the frames to run in half the number of frames (i.e., 30 frames). As shown in Figure 8-21, we can move the mouse to the end of the clip in the Trax Editor. When the cursor changes as such, we can drag the mouse to intuitively adjust the number of cycles. The gradation shown in the figure refers to one cycle.

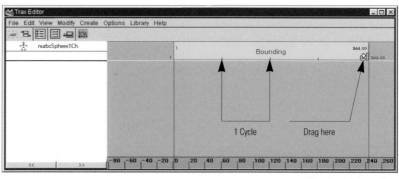

Figure 8-21 Adjusting the Cycle

At this time, we can also adjust the Offset value of the clip to create a repeating animation. Setting the Offset value to Absolute, the ball will return to its original starting position before continuing, and setting the value to Relative will continue the animation without the ball returning to the starting point.

● Scale

This option is used to adjust the time in which the clip plays. Setting this value to 2 will double the length of the animation and slow down the run speed, and setting it to 0.5 will cut the length in half and increase the run speed. We can also intuitively adjust this value in the same way by dragging the mouse on the end of the clip as shown in Figure 8-22. When adjusting the scale, the mouse cursor changes as shown in Figure 8-22.

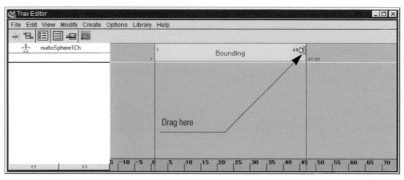

Figure 8-22 Adjusting the Scale

● Source Clip Attribute

This option allows us to edit the attribute for the source clip of the selected clip. The source clip is the clip that was stored in the visor when the clip was first made. Just as it was when we reloaded the source clip of the clip from the visor when we explained Offsets, the source clip is stored in the visor when the clip is made. There is a limit to the attributes we can edit in the source clip. We can edit only the Start Frame and the Duration. Select the clip, and select [Modify > Attribute Editor] from the Trax Editor to open the Attribute Editor. Place the mouse on top of the clip, click the RMB, and then select Select Source Clip from the Marking Menu. By expanding the BoundingSource Tab in the Attribute Editor, as shown in Figure 8-23, we can see that the Source Clip Attribute is activated.

Figure 8-23 Attribute Editor

If we use Animation Pose, instead of Clip, the Pose will be set to On. We will cover poses later in this chapter. We can adjust the length of the animation by adjusting the Start and Duration. Start refers to the starting frame of the clip. In other words, if the Start is set to 30 in an animation that runs from frame 1-60, this does not mean that the animation will change from 30-90, but that the frames 1-30 will be ignored and only frames 30-60 will be played. If the Duration is set to 30, the original bounding ball will only play in frames 1-30. The difference can be seen right away by testing this bounding ball.

2. Cutting, Copying, and Pasting Clips

Clips can be cut or copied in the Trax Editor. We can also copy clips in the Visor. Clips that are cut or copied can be pasted on the same character or, generally, on another character with the same attributes. When the clip is copied and pasted onto the same character, an Instance Clip is created. When copying and pasting clips onto another character, it is best if both characters have the same attributes. If the two characters are different, a Character Map must be exported to edit the characters before the clip can be used. Let's take a closer look at exporting and editing using a Character Map.

1. Cut
To cut a clip, first select the clip to cut and then select [Edit > Cut] from the Trax Editor.

2. Copy
To copy a clip, first select the clip to copy and then select [Edit > Copy] from the Trax Editor.

3. Paste
To paste the clip onto the same character, select the character and then select [Edit > Paste] from the Trax Editor. If the characters are different, select the character to which the clip will be pasted and then select [Edit > Paste] from the Trax Editor to open the Options window. The following options are available in the Option window:

● **Paste Method**

> **By Attribute Name** Selecting this option will look for same attribute values in the character to paste the clip and ignore the object name.
>
> **By Attribute Order** This option will paste the clip according the order of the attributes as seen in the Channel Box.
>
> **By Node Name** This option will paste the clip in characters with the same object name and attributes.
>
> **By Current Map** This option can only be used after the Character Map is exported to edit the character. Exporting character maps is further described on page 500, "2-5. Exporting and Editing Character Maps."
>
> **Start Frame** This option is used to determine where on the time slider the clip will be pasted.
>
> **Current Time** This option pastes the clip in the current frame.
>
> **Timeline Start** This option pastes the clip at the start of the scene.
>
> **Clipboard Start** This option pastes the clip at the start of the original clip.

3. Duplicate Clip

When using Duplicate, instead of Copy, we can create a new Source Clip. This Source Clip refers to the original clip, which is stored in the Visor. For example, when making a clip of a walking character, the original for this clip is stored in the Visor. After modifying portions of this clip, it can be duplicated to create a new Source Clip. When using the Copy command, a new Source Clip is not made, rather an Instance Clip for the Source Clip is made. This is what makes the Copy command different from the Duplicate command. After selecting the clip to duplicate, select [Edit > Duplicate] from the Trax Editor. Then, looking in the Visor, we can see that a new Source Clip is made.

4. Instancing Clips

When a clip is instanced, the same animation curve as the source clip is used. In other words, when the animation curve of the Source Clip is modified, the animation for the instance clip is also modified. We instance clips for the main purpose of reducing the calculation time. Clips that are instanced take lesser time to calculate than clips that are copied, thereby preventing the system speed from falling. For example, when a walking motion is repeated in a certain clip, instead of copying this clip, less calculation time is used if this clip is instanced instead. Using Cycle Attribute to repeat the clip is another way to save calculation time.

In reality, when making a clip with many complex movements, the playback speed for the animation falls drastically. In order to instance the clip, first, select the clip and then select [Edit > Instance] from the Trax Editor.

Clips that are cycled cannot be sliced directly. In order to slice cycled clips, we need to first merge the clip to create a new clip and then slice.

5.Slicing Clips

One clip can be sliced to create several clips.

For example, let's suppose that we are keyframing a fight scene. After making stabbing, kicking and other aerial fight motions, we can slice each of them by movements and store them as Source Clips to be used and linked to other movements as needed. To slice a clip, select the clip to be sliced, select [Edit > Split] from the Trax Editor to open the Options window, and after making the appropriate configurations, click on the Split Clip button at the bottom.

Figure 8-24 Options Window

● Source Clip

This determines how to deal with the Source Clip of the sliced clip. Selecting Delete Original Source will delete the Source Clip before 2 new, sliced clips are made. Selecting Keep Original Source will maintain the original Source Clip even after the 2 new, sliced clips are made.

● Split Time

This determines where the clip will be sliced. Selecting Current Time will slice the clip according to the Current Time in the time slider and selecting Specify Time allows us to enter the frame to slice.

6. Merge Clip

Several clips or even one clip can be merged. Merge combines together clips that have been sliced. Merge can be applied to clips that are arranged consecutively on a track or even to those that overlap. When merging clips, they can be moved easily and it also becomes quite easy to use Scale and Cycle. Also, when editing the original clip, the merged clip is not affected.

In addition, when merging blended clips, the animation curve of the blended region can be modified using the Graph Editor to create a more natural movement. Merge can also be used to slice cycled clips. After selecting the clip to merge, select [Edit > Merge] from the Trax Editor to open the Options window, configure the options, and then click on the Merge Clip button at the bottom of the window.

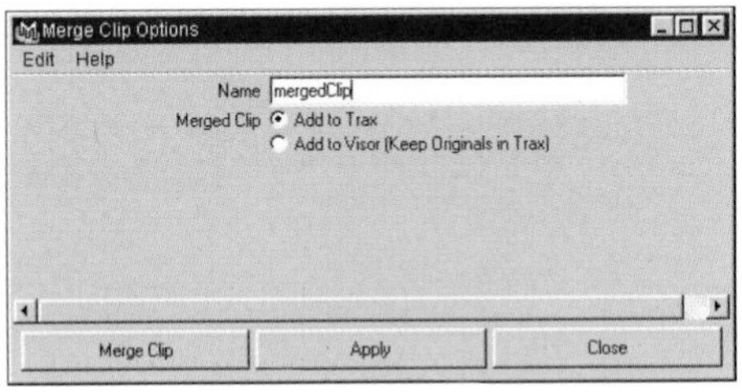

Figure 8-25 Options Window

- **Name** The field where we specify the name of the clip to merge.
- **Merged Clip** Merged Clip When Add to Trax is selected the merged clip replaces the existing clip in the Trax Editor. Selecting Add to Visor (Keep Originals in Trax) will add the merged clip to the Visor, and the original clip in the Trax Editor will not be replaced.

7. Blend Clip

This is the option used to blend together two different animation clips of a character. Blend combines 2 clips naturally together. Blending clips with similar movements will bring good results; however, clips with different movements will not blend together naturally.

For example, blending together a clip of a walking and then a running character will bring fairly good results, but blending together a clip of a character who runs and then falls will appear awkward. A blended clip can be edited at any time, just as long as it has not yet been merged.

It does not matter whether the clips are arranged consecutively on the track or whether they overlap. If 2 clips overlap, the overlapping region will be blended.

step 1   To blend the clips, select the 2 clips, which will be blended.

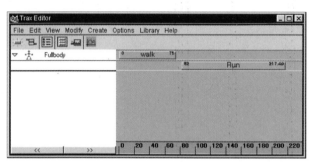

Figure 8-26 Selecting the 2 Clips

The clips to blend must have common character attributes. If they don't, we cannot use Blend.

step 2   Select [Create > Blend] from the Trax Editor to open the Option window.

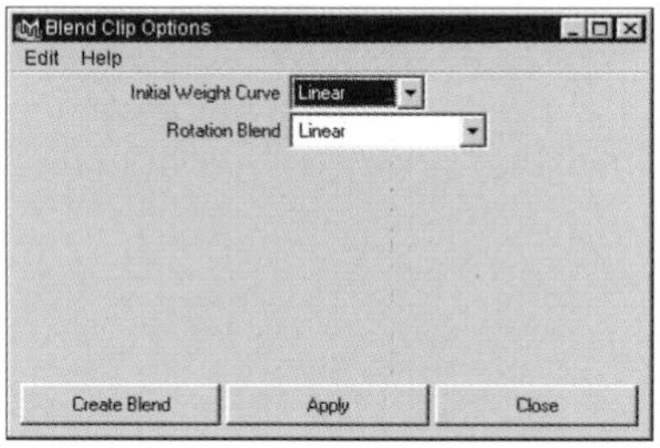

Figure 8-27 Options Window

● **Initial Weight Curve**

This option specifies the method of blending and preserving each clip. Simply put, this defines the shape of the blend curve that will be made in the Graph Editor.

Using the default options in the Options window, click the Create Blend button to blend the 2 clips and then select the blend curve created between the 2 clips in the Trax Editor. Select [View > Graphc Anim Curve] from the Trax Editor menu to open the blend Graph Editor. Because the default setting is Liner, the curve will look like it does in Figure 8-28.

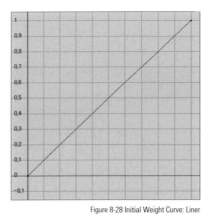

Figure 8-28 Initial Weight Curve: Liner

Let's now take a look at the different curves that can be seen in the Graph Editor.

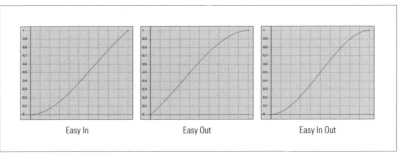

Figure 8-29 Different Curves

● Rotation Blend

This property determines how the rotation value for each attribute within the clip will be assigned. Quaternion Shortest will preserve the clip based on the smallest value between the rotation value of one curve to the rotation value of another curve. Quaternion Longest, in contrast to Quaternion Shortest, will preserve the clip based on the largest rotation value. For example, let's suppose that Rotate Y value of the character in Clip A is 0 and that the same value for Clip B is 90. In this instance, the Y-axis can be rotated in 2 different ways. Rotating from 0 to 90 degrees in the positive direction, we can simply rotate it to 90 degrees. In the negative direction, however, we need to rotate it to 270 degrees. The Quaternion Shortest is then, simply rotated to 90 degrees and the Quaternion Longest is rotated to 270 degrees and matched to the rotation value of Clip B. Liners are not rotated in the 2 different ways mentioned above. This is the method for versions prior to Maya version 4.

step 3 After configuring the options, click on the Create Blend button at the bottom of the Blend Clip Options window. A line is made that links the 2 clips together, and their motions are blended.

8. Editing the Animation Curve of the Clip

Each clip that is made has its own animation curve, which can be freely edited to modify the motions of the clip. Select the clip and then select [View > Graph Anim Curves] from the Trax Editor. As shown in Figure 8-30, the animation curve of the selected clip is displayed in the Graph Editor.

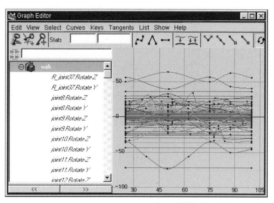

Figure 8-30 The Graph Editor of the Clip

By modifying this animation curve, we can modify the character's motion.

9. Modifying the Original Animation Curve of the Clip

When modifying the animation curve of the clip, it is not as intuitive as the methods described earlier. When the clip is selected, the attributes of the character in the clip are merely displayed in the Graph Editor. In order to intuitively edit the animation, it is much more effective to select the constituents of the character in the scene and then modify them through the Graph Editor.

However, doing this for character motions that have already been made into clips will not be displayed as animation curves in the Graph Editor. Such instances call for the use of the Activate/Deactivate keys. Select the clip and then select [Modify > Activate/ Deactivate Keys] from the Trax Editor.
As shown in Figure 8-31, the color of the selected clip will change, and we can see that the animation key values for the character are displayed in the time slider.

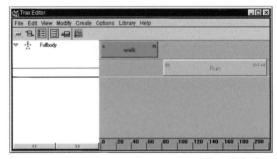

Figure 8-31 Trax Editor

Now, we can select the constituents of the character directly in the scene and intuitively adjust the animation curve through the Graph Editor or adjust the movement directly in the scene. To reactivate the clip, select [Modify > Activate/Deactivate Keys] from the Trax Editor.
In other words, this function temporarily returns the animation curves of each character in the clip back to the state they were in before the clip was made. When the clips are made into a library and used and you want to convert the loaded clip into an animation curve, select the clip, execute Activate/Deactivate Keys, and then delete the respective clip.

10. Enable / Disable Clip

We can use this option to selectively enable or disable the clips. In certain circumstances, this can be a very useful option. For example, when many clips have been made to create a variety of different motions, we can use Enable/Disable Clip to select the clip that we want to use at a certain time.

To temporarily disable a clip, simply select the clip and then select [Modify > Enable/Disable] from the Trax Editor. To enable the clip again, simply select [Modify > Enable/Disable].

11. Adding to/Deleting from Tracks

When loading many clips into one character for editing, the Trax Editor requires many tracks. This is because it is much more effective to arrange each clip onto a track for editing.

We can add or delete tracks as needed. In order to add tracks, select the character to which the track will be added in the Trax Editor, as shown in Figure 8-32, and then select [Modify > Add Track]. Then, a new track will be made, as shown in Figure 8-33. Now all we need to do is to simply click and drag the desired clip from the Visor onto the track to edit.

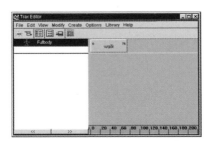

Figure 8-32 Selecting the Character

Figure 8-33 Making the Track and Loading the Clip

12. Motion Wrap

There are times when we need to configure a new key for a character, for which an animation clip has already been made. Such a key will affect the character related to the existing clip animation. This can, at times, be used to effectively alter the movement. Let's suppose we have the following situation. Suppose we want to create a city street scene where many people are walking to and fro. It is much more effective to make these movements into clips rather than to keyframe them all. In addition, instancing these clips is even more effective for data management. In reality, using one clip to apply an instance to the entire character will save an incredible amount of animation data than the character was supposed to have. One disadvantage, however, is that all the characters need to have the same movement making them rather homogenous and non-unique. Modifying some of the character's motions will not only save data, but lead to greater diversity in movement.

For the purposes of this example, open the CD-ROM/CHARACTER/scenes/m_walk.mb file. Select the root character, the monkey, and make it into a clip. A clip is made of the walking character. You may want to modify some of these motions. For example, if you want to raise the height of the character's leg as it walks, do the following:
Select Foots Character from Set the Current Character Set under the time slider.
As we can see in the diagram on the right in Figure 8-34, we move to the frame where the foot is placed on the ground. Select the joint that controls the leg, as shown in the figure, and press Shift+W to create a key for the movement. Again, moving to the frame where the foot is placed on the ground (see Figure 8-35), press Shift+W again to make a key.

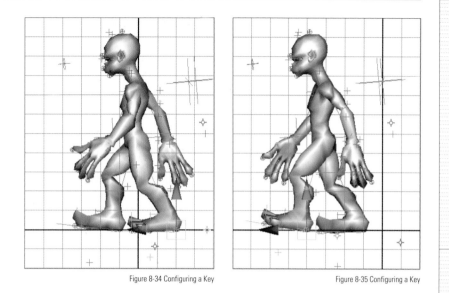

Figure 8-34 Configuring a Key   Figure 8-35 Configuring a Key

As shown in Figure 8-36, raise the frame as high as the leg can be raised in the Y-direction.

As shown in Figure 8-37, move to the Y-axis, raise the foot higher and then press Shift+W to configure the key.

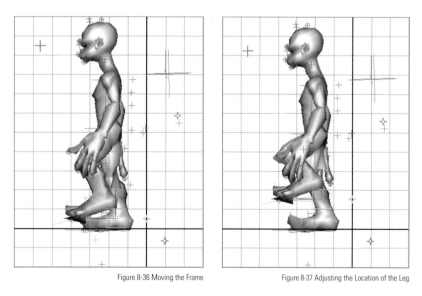

Figure 8-36 Moving the Frame   Figure 8-37 Adjusting the Location of the Leg

Once the keyframing is complete, the keyframing range will appear blue in the time slider of the Trax Editor as shown in Figure 8-38.

Figure 8-38 The Keyframing Range in the Time Line of the Trax Editor

Select the Foots Character in the Trax Editor, and execute Create Clip to create a new clip with a new keyframing range as shown in Figure 8-39.

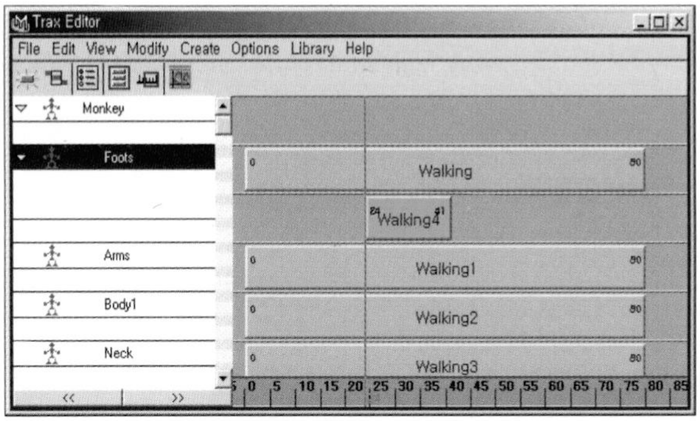

Figure 8-39 Create Clip

We can change the Weight value of this new clip and use it in the same way as the original clip. Double-clicking on the new clip will display its attributes in the Channel Box. Setting the Weight value to 0.5 in the Channel Box will raise the leg to a height between that of the original clip and the newly created clip. We can use this Weight value to easily control how much of an influence this new clip will have. One thing to note here is that cycling a clip for a repetitive walking motion and setting the Offset to Relative can create abnormal results. In such cases, select [Edit > Merge] from the Trax Editor to merge the clip in the beginning and then set the Offset to Absolute.

2-3. USING POSE

When animating the character, we can take a snapshot of the current location anywhere on the time slider. This can be done easily using Pose. In addition, Poses, like clips, can be instanced using the Trax Editor and can also be copied and pasted. The beginning and end of a cycled clip can be posed for easy reference when working.

This pose, also, can be keyframed for animation. In 2D cell animation, the original creator adds key motions at the appropriate times and then animators add the intermediary motions. In such an efficient way, a proficient animator creates the poses and then other animators add the intermediary poses.

To create a pose, move to the frame in which the pose will be made. Select [Create > Pose] from the Trax Editor to open the Create Pose Options window (see Figure 8-40). After typing in the desired name, click on the Create Pose button at the bottom of the window.

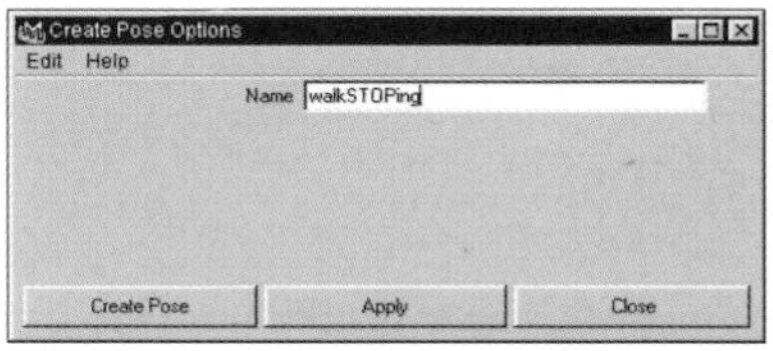

Figure 8-40 Create Pose Options Window

Select [File > Visor] from the Trax Editor to open the Visor. As shown in Figure 8-41, open the Character Poses Tab to verify that the pose we just made has been saved. Drag this pose to the track of the character to use as freely as the clip.

Figure 8-41 Visor

2-4. EXPORTING/IMPORTING CLIPS

The clip we made can be exported at any time and reused in any scene. When a project is made a Clip Director is made automatically. We can organize the clips in this directory to be used at any time. To export a clip, select the clip to export in the Trax Editor and then select [File > Export Clip]. Then, select the Clip Directory, type in the File Name and then click the Export button. Import a clip by selecting [File > Import Clip] from the Trax Editor.

The imported clip is saved in the Unused Clip Tab of the Visor and is used by clicking the MMB on the imported clip and dragging it onto the track of the desired character.

2-5. EXPORTING AND EDITING CHARACTER MAPS

In scenes with several characters, in order to quickly and easily edit the movements of the characters, there are times when you will want to copy the clip of Character A onto Character B. For instance, look at the following Figure 8-42.

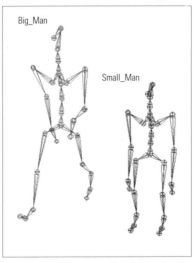

Figure 8-42 Two Characters

This figure shows two characters. Let's suppose that the Big_Man Character has a walking clip and we want to copy this clip onto the Small_Man Character. Figure 8-43 shows the Trax Editor for these 2 characters. If the 2 characters have the same hierarchical structure or if their Attribute Order (the order of the attributes in the Channel Box) is the same, all we need to do is to simply copy and paste the Big_Man Clip using the Paste Option By Attribute Name or By Attribute Order.

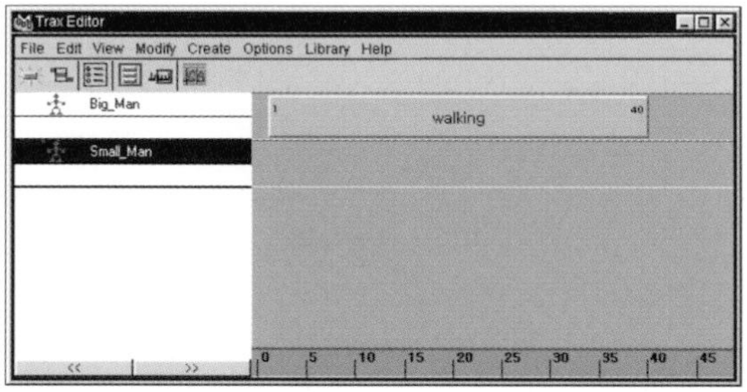

Figure 8-43 Trax Editor

However, if this is not the case, the clip will not paste properly. For instance, the rotation value of the neck could end up affecting the arm and the rotation value of the arm could end up affecting the leg. In such cases, we can export the Character Map to modify the character.

Selecting the Big_Man and Small_Man Characters in the Trax Editor, select [File > Export Character Map] and configure the following options.

● **By Attribute Name**

This option is used to map the attributes of the character to copy onto the attributes of the character to paste. In other words, this option will make the attributes for both characters the same.

● **By Attribute Order**

This option is used to map the attributes of the character to copy onto the attributes of the character to paste according to the order in the Channel Box. In other words, this option will make the attribute order for both characters the same.

● By Node Name

This option is used to map the object name attributes of the character to copy onto the attributes of the character to paste with the same name. In other words, this option is used when the Node names of both characters are the same.

● By Current Map

This option can only be used after the character map is exported and the Mel Script is modified. Let's take a closer look at this option.

After selecting the desired option, click the Export button. Type in the desired name for the project in the mel folder and then click on the Write button. Let's suppose we use the name "walking." The walking.mel will be created inside the Mel folder.

Select [Windows > General Editors > Script Editor...] to open the Script Editor. Under the Script Editor, after selecting [File > Open Script...], open walking.mel. This will open the Script Editor, as shown in Figure 8-44.

Big_Man 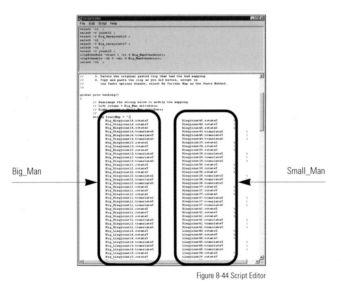 Small_Man

Figure 8-44 Script Editor

As we can see in the figure, the script for the Big_Man Character is recorded in order of Attribute Name and right next to it, and the script for the Small_Man Character is also recorded in order of Attribute Name.

We must modify this script so that the order for the two characters is the same. For example, the Attribute Name for the joint of the neck of the Big_Man must be next to the Attribute Name for the joint of the neck of the Small-Man in order for the key value of the Big_Man's neck to be copied onto the neck of the Small_Man. As follows, each of the joint names must be modified. After editing, select both columns and then select [File > Save Selected] from the Script Editor to overwrite the existing file.

Selecting [File > Source Script] from the Script Editor, select walking.mel. Now we can simply enter **Walking** in the Command Line and execute the script. As shown in Figure 8-45, type **Walking** in the Command Line and press the Enter key.

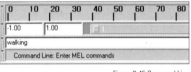

Figure 8-45 Command Line

The walking.mel file is now executed, and we are now ready to copy the clip of the Big_Man Character onto the Small_Man.

After copying the Big_Man clip, select [Edit > Paste] from the Trax Editor to open the Options window. In the Options window, set the Paste Method to By Current Map and then click the Paste Clip button. The Big_Man clip will be copied onto the Small_Man, and the key values for each joint will also be copied properly.

We have just covered the basics for Nonlinear Animation in Maya. We will now use a brief tutorial to see how nonlinear animation is done.

3. BASIC TUTORIAL

We will now use a brief tutorial to go through the process of editing animations.

It is important that you understand the overall workflow, and this tutorial will be based on the options we covered in the first half of this chapter. A good tutorial for the Trax Editor is the source offered at the Alias/Wavefront homepage. Alternating between the tutorial here and the tutorial in this Web site will be of tremendous help to you as you learn about the Trax Editor. The address for this homepage is www.aliaswavefront.com. Go to the How To's under Learn Maya|Studio in Community.

3-1. MAKING AND EDITING CLIPS

The tutorial for this example is offered in the supplementary CD-ROM.
Open the file, CD-ROM/CHARACTER/scenes/m_walk.mb.

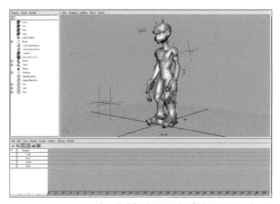

Figure 8-46 Opening m_walk.mb (Animated by Yang Eun-Ja)

This file contains one walking animation cycle and is already made into a character. Below the monkey characters are the subcharacters Foots, Arms, Body1, and Neck. Verify which channel each of these subcharacters has by selecting the channels one by one. To verify which channels they have, select the desired Character Node from [Animation > Character > Select Character Set] and verify the channels in the Channel Box.

1. Making a Walking Cycle

In this scene, after one walking animation cycle, the character comes to a standstill. Using one walk cycle, we will make the character appear as if it is continuing to walk.

step 1
We first need to create a clip for each character.
Although we can select the subcharacter for which the clip will be made and then select [Create > Clip] from the Trax Editor, it is better to use the Root Character to make a clip for all the subcharacters at once. First, select the monkey, the root character, from the Trax Editor. Select [Create > Clip] from the Trax Editor to open the Options window. As shown in Figure 8-47, type **Walking** for the Name, select the other options, and then click on the Create Clip button at the bottom.

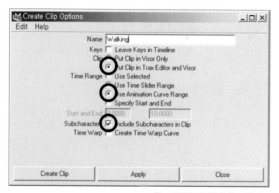

Figure 8-47 Create Clip Options Window

As shown in Figure 8-47, the Include Subcharacter in Clip option must be turned on in order for the clip to be created for the subcharacter.

The clip will be created in the Trax Editor as shown in Figure 8-48.

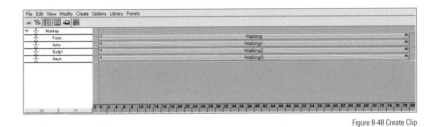

Figure 8-48 Create Clip

The root character monkey does not have a clip. This is because the monkey does not have a character channel.

step 2 Play the animation and observe from which frame to which frame one walking animation cycle occurs. In order for the cycle to move continuously, we must precisely configure the starting and ending points of the cycle. Move to Frame21 in the time slider. As shown in Figure 8-49, select all the clips of the subcharacters.

Figure 8-49 Selecting the Clip

Select [Edit > Split] from the Trax Editor. The clip will divide according to the current frame.

Move to Frame60 in the time slider and then select, once again, all the subcharacter slips on the right-hand side. Then select [Edit > Split] from the Trax Editor. We can see in Figure 8-50 that each clip is divided into 3 portions.

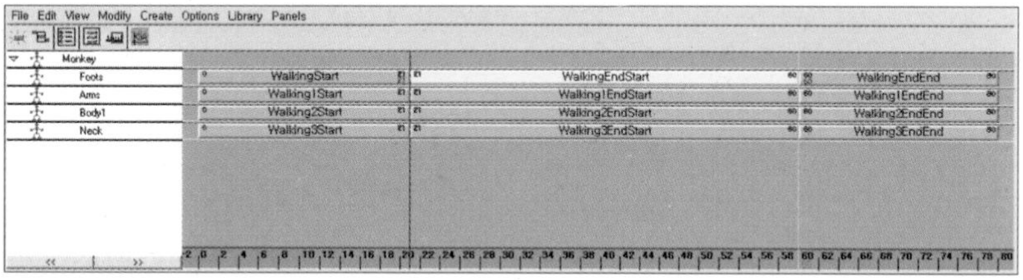

Figure 8-50 Slicing the Clip

New names will be created automatically for the divided clips. We can change these names through the Channel Box, which is accessed by double-clicking on the clip name or through the Attribute Editor, which is accessed by selecting the clip. It is a good idea to change the names of these clips for easy distinction.

step 3 As shown in Figure 8-51, select all the clips on the right and move them to the right. We do this because the clips in the center will be cycled and we want to prevent any clips from overlapping.

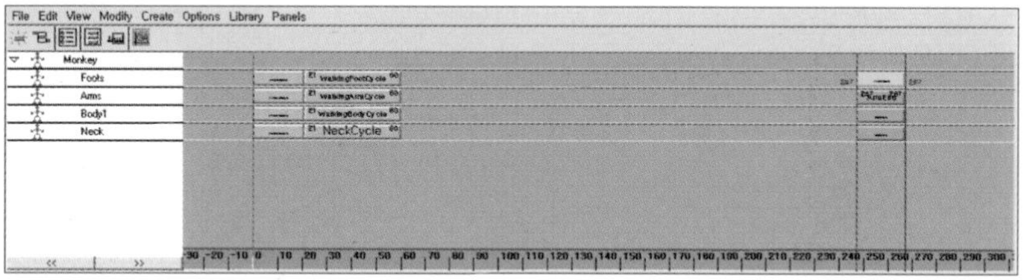

Figure 8-51 Arranging the Clips

Double-click on the center clip of the Foots Character to open the Channel Box and type in **3** for Cycle. Playing the animation, we can see that it repeats 3 times. However, we can also see that, instead of continuously repeating, the character returns to the original starting position before continuing 3 times. We can correct this by modifying the Offset value in the Channel Box. We can see in the Channel Box that the Offset value is set to Absolute, which causes the animation to return to its starting position before continuing. Change the Offset value to Relative and then play the animation again. The character now continues to walk forward as the walking animation is cycled 3 times.

Cycle the clips for the other subcharacters 3 times as shown in Figure 8-52. Set the Offset value back to Absolute.

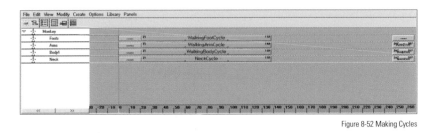

Figure 8-52 Making Cycles

step 4 We encounter a problem here. This is a problem that occurs when the Offset value for the cycled clip is set to Relative. If the cycles are not computed properly before they are keyframed for the animation, there will be a big difference in the animation values for the beginning and end of the cycle. This difference becomes more pronounced when the Offset value is set to Relative, so much so that at the end of the cycle, there will be a big difference in the placement of the object. Let's look at Figure 8-53. If you have followed the example from the beginning, the pose of the character should look like the following. The problem is that the placement of the character pose is very different in Frame60, at the end of the first cycle, and in Frame130, the end of the third cycle.

As we can see in the overlapping poses of the two characters from each frame (see Figure 8-53), we can see that the angles for the feet are not the same. This happens

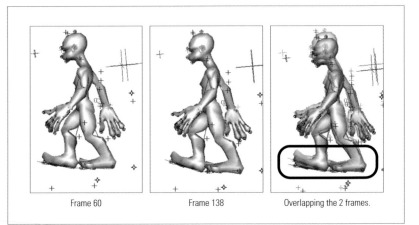

| Frame 60 | Frame 138 | Overlapping the 2 frames. |

Figure 8-53 The Character Pose per Frame

because the starting and ending points of the animation curve do not meet and the Offset value acts to escalate this problem.

Select the cycled center clip of the Foots Character and then select [Modify > Active/Deactive Keys] from the Trax Editor.

This will change the color of the selected clip, and we will be able to modify the animation curve of this clip through the Graph Editor. Select Rfoot from the Outliner and then select [Windows > Animation Editors > Graph Editor].

Select the Rotate Z Channel from the Graph Editor in Figure 8-54. Looking at the animation curve, we can see that the starting and ending points of the curve do not match. To have these points coincide, select the keys on either end as shown and then, as shown in Figure 8-55, enter the value **-6.4** in the Value field and then select Flat from the Tangent menu.

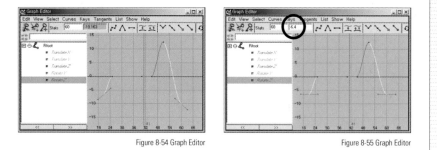

Figure 8-54 Graph Editor   Figure 8-55 Graph Editor

In the same way, select Joint46 from below Rfoot in the Outliner and then use the Graph Editor to match the animation curve of the Rotate Z Channel.

After editing the animation curve, select the clip and then select [Modify > Active/Deactive Keys] from the Trax Editor to restore the clip. Play the animation to view the result. By matching the cycles of all the clips in this way, we will end up with a much more natural motion.

Now, move back the clips that we had moved off to the right as shown in Figure 8-56.

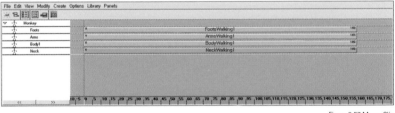

Figure 8-56 Arranging the Clips

Play the animation. Because the Offset value of the rightmost clip of the Foots Character is set the Absolute, the character continues to walk and then goes back to its original position before stopping. Play the animation again after changing the Offset value to Relative. As a result, this clip will link to the cycled clip so that the character merely stops.

step 6

After we have the desired cycle, we now need to merge each of the clips. First, after selecting all of the clips of the Foots Subcharacter, select [Edit > Merge] from the Trax Editor to merge the 3 clips. After merging the other clips in the same way, change the name of the clips in the Channel Box so that they can be easily differentiated.

Figure 8-57 shows the merged clips.

Figure 8-57 Merge Clip

It is a good idea to modify parts of the animation curve of this completed clip using the Graph Editor. This is because parts of the animation curve could have been linked unnaturally during the merging process. To use the animation curve, select the clip of the desired character and then select [View > Graphic Anim Curves...] from the Trax Editor.

2. Modifying Motion Using a New Clip

So far, we have learned how to make a clip and how to cycle them. We will now learn how to use the motion from a cycled clip to make and modify a new clip. Actually, such clips are all exported and managed as data. Therefore, other motions can be created easily by loading these clips and reediting the motions as needed.

We will continue to use the same example we used above.

step 1 In order to modify the walking animation of the clip, select Foots Character from Set the Current Character Set, as shown in Figure 8-58.

Figure 8-58 Selecting the Character

Move to Frame20 in the time slider, and then press the S key to give a key to all the channels in the Foots Character. Move to Frame40 and then press the S key again to make a key for the channels, and then move the Frame60 and repeat this step again.

step 2 Move to Frame30 in the time slider and, in Side View, raise the level of the leg and give it more rotation (see Figure 8-59).

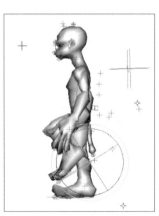

Figure 8-59 Position of the Leg and the Rotation Value   Figure 8-60 Position of the Body and the Rotation

This animation clip is saved as CD-ROM/CHARACTER/Clip/jump.ma. Refer to this file as needed.

Select Body1 from the Set Current Character Set. Select the Body from the Outliner and, as shown in Figure 8-60, modify the position and rotation of the body. In the current frame, press the S key to create a key for the channels. Playing the animation, we can see that channels that have been given a new key will play according to the new key and ignore its original key.

step 3 Select the Foots Character from the Trax Editor. Select [Create > Clip] to open the Options window. As shown in Figure 8-61, name the clip **WalkingUP**, configure the rest of the options, and then click on the Create Clip button at the bottom.

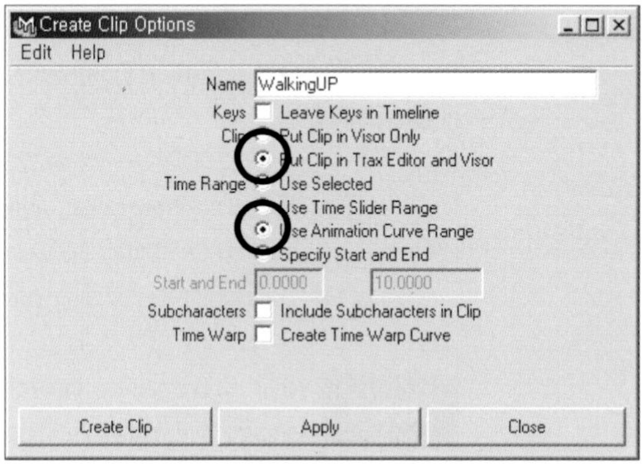

Figure 8-61 Options Window

As shown in Figure 8-62, a new track will be made in the Foots Character and we can see the creation of a new clip.

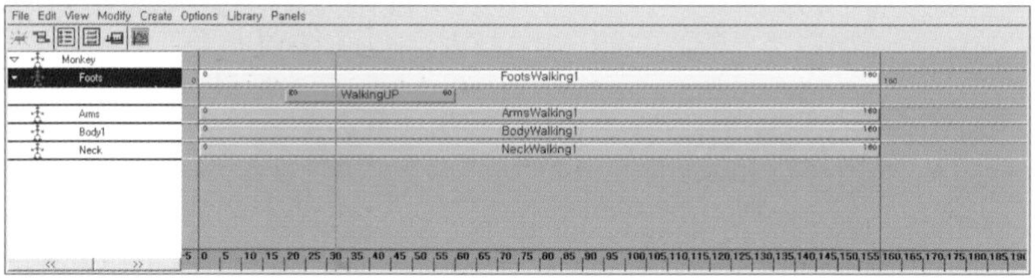

Figure 8-62 Create Clip

As shown here, we can use several clips in the Trax Editor. If the several clips have been piled up as shown here, the key that will directly affect the character is the key value of the bottommost clip. However, we can modify the Weight value of the clip to determine how much the old clip will affect the new clip.

Double-click on the new clip and adjust the Weight value in the Channel Box. The current value is set to 1, which means that the respective clip will influence the character 100%. We will run a test by setting this value to 0.5. The influence of the clip drops to 50%. In this way, we can adjust the Weight value to determine how much the clip will be affected by the animation key value. Make a clip for Body1 and adjust the Weight value in the same way. Create a key value and clip for the remaining characters, and test them in the same way.

For the purposes of the next example, we will delete the new clip.

3. Blending Two Animations

Using the Trax Editor, we can easily blend and link together two, entirely different animations. In this section, we will create a new animation and link it to the previous walking animation. For the purposes of this example, open the file CD-ROM/CHARACTER /scenes/m-walkCycle.mb. This is the file of the walking animation cycle we made earlier. Select [File > Visor] from the Trax Editor. Selecting the Character Clips Tab from the Visor, we can see that it contains the animation clip (see Figure 8-63).

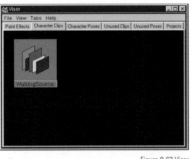

Figure 8-63 Visor

This is the clip we practiced on earlier. We will make a new clip, in addition to this one, and create an animation by linking the 2 clips together.

step 1 Let's keyframe the motion of a jumping character. As shown in Figure 8-64, we will keyframe, in Side View, a character jumping for around 60 frames.

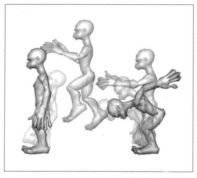

Figure 8-64 Keyframing

Try keyframing this motion yourself for practice.

step 2 After keyframing the motion, we will now convert this animation into a clip. Select the uppermost character, the monkey, in the Trax Editor and then select [Create > Clip] to open the Options window. After naming this character **Jump**, configure the options as shown in Figure 8-65, and then click on the Create Clip button.

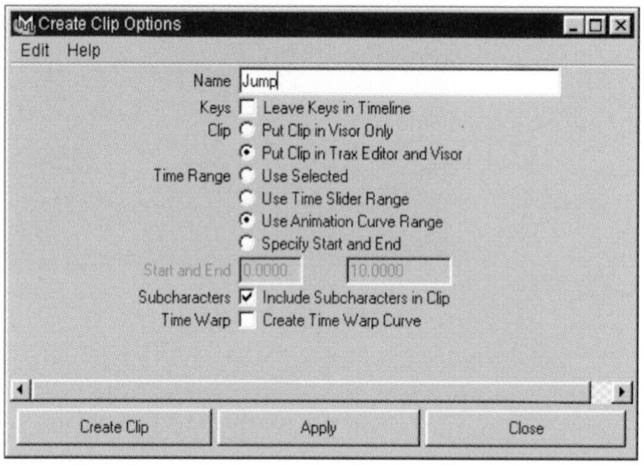

Figure 8-65 Options Window

A new clip is made. Move this clip to the back, as shown in Figure 8-66.

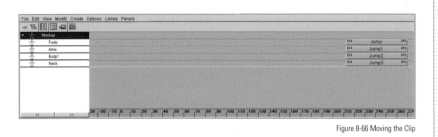

Figure 8-66 Moving the Clip

step 3 Click the MMB on the WalkingSource Clip in the Visor and then, after dragging it onto the track in the Trax Editor, arrange it as shown in Figure 8-67.

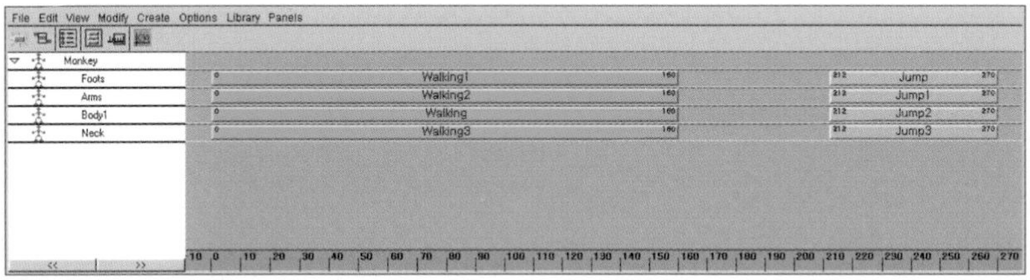

Figure 8-67 Arranging the Clip

step 4 This character will now walk and jump. By playing the animation, we can see that after the walking animation clip, the jumping animation clip will play. Let's now link these 2 clips together.

Select all 4 clips pertaining to the walking animation in the Trax Editor. After moving to Frame80 in the time slider, select [Edit > Split] to split the clips and then, as shown in Figure 8-68, select and delete the clips in the back.

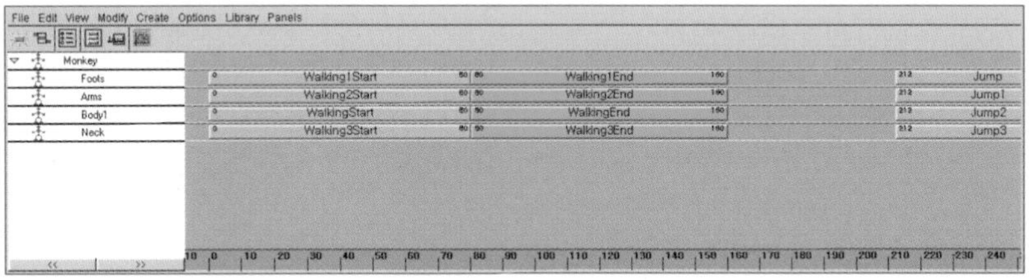

Figure 8-68 Splitting the Clips

Select [Options > Large Track Height] from the Trax Editor, so that we can observe a larger clip, and then, arrange the Jump clip of the Foots Character, as shown in Figure 8-69, so that the start frame is around Frame110.

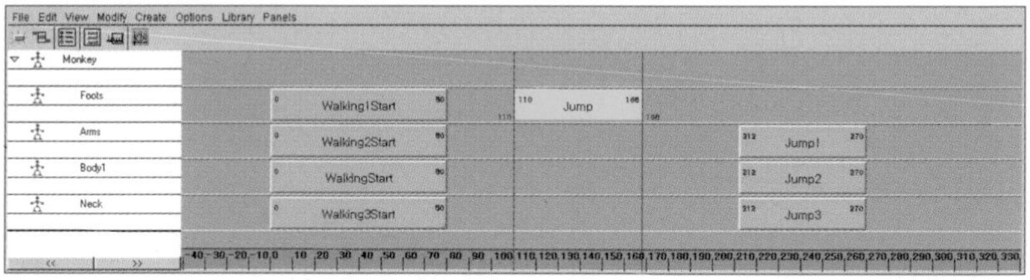

Figure 8-69 Arranging the Clip

We link the 2 clips together using Blend. However, blending the 2 clips together in their current state will create a problem. Let's see what happens. First, select the 2 clips of the Foots Character and select [Create > Blend] in the Trax Editor to blend the 2 clips.

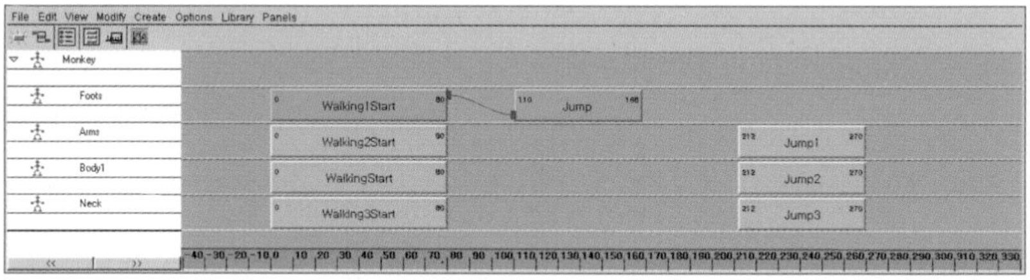

Figure 8-70 Blend Clip

Let's play the animation. The walking clip plays first and then, after a smooth transition, the jumping clip plays. However, we can see that, after walking, the character returns to its original starting position before jumping. Double-click on the Jump clip and set the Offset value to Relative in the Channel Box. This will fix the character's position at the end of the walking clip. However, this, too, creates a problem. The legs should come together before jumping, but that is not the case here. We can fix this problem with Pose. Change the Offset value of the Jump clip back to Absolute and then remove the Blend. We can do this, simply, by selecting the line that connects the 2 clips and by hitting the Delete key.

step 5 Move the start frame of the Jump clip to Frame110. Select the root character, the monkey, from the Trax Editor and then select [Create > Pose]. Set the Name to JumpStart, and then click on the Create Pose button at the bottom. By opening the Visor and the Character Poses Tab, we can see that the JumpStart node has been created. Click the MMB on this node and drag it to the position indicated in Figure 8-71.

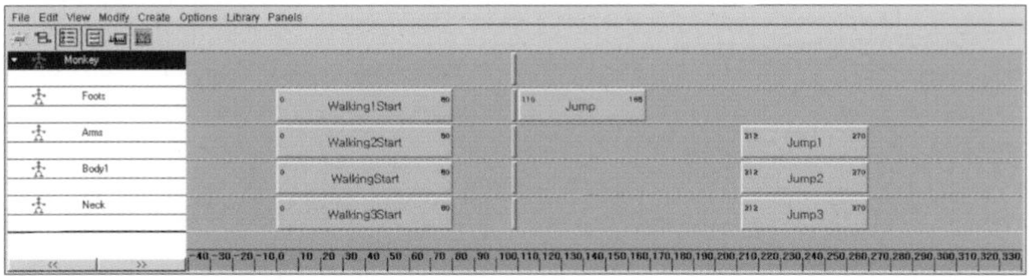

Figure 8-71 Arranging the Pose

Select and delete all the poses in the remaining tracks of the Foots Character Track, excluding the Pose Clip. Select the Walking clip and Pose of the Foots Character, and then select [Create > Blend] from the Trax Editor to open the Options window. Then, configuring the options as shown in Figure 8-72, click on the Create Blend button at the bottom of the window.

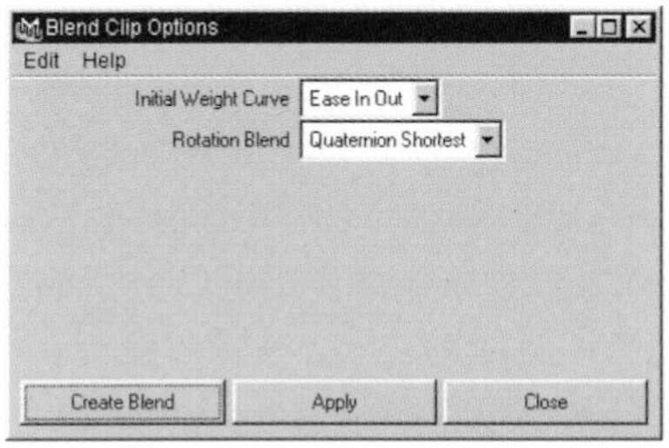

Figure 8-72 Options Window

Because the Offset value of the current pose is set to Absolute, we can see that the character moves in position in order to jump. We now have to match the animation value of the Pose to the animation value of the Walking clip.

step 6 This character has 3 factors that determine its location. These 3 factors are the 2 feet and the body. In other words, how the 2 feet and the body are placed determine the placement of the character in the scene. We can blend the 2 clips together very naturally by matching the location of the 2 feet and body in the clip and the pose. Let's first adjust the placement of the feet. Select the Walking clip of the Foots Character in the Trax Editor and then select [View > Graph Anim Curves] to open the Graph Editor. Select Lfoot, TranslateZ from the Graph Editor, as shown in Figure 8-73. Looking at the key value at the ending point of TranslateZ, we can see the value for the selected key in the Value field. This value corresponds to the Z-direction of the left foot. Copy this value.

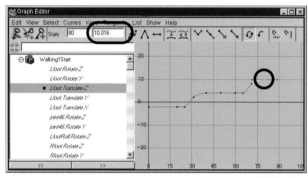

Figure 8-73 Graph Editor

Double-click on the Pose of the Foots Character in the Trax Editor. The key value of the pose will appear in the Graph Editor. However, the curve does not exist. This is because the key for this pose is in only one frame.

Select Lfoot, TranslateZ, as shown in Figure 8-74, and then select the key. In the same way, the current key value will appear in the Value field.

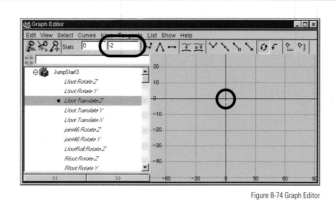

Figure 8-74 Graph Editor

Paste the copied value in the Value field. After moving the frame to where the pose is located, we can see, as in Figure 8-75, that the left leg sticks straight out.

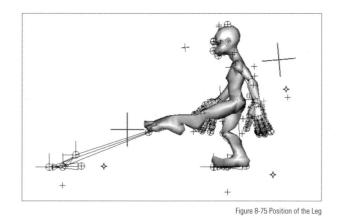

Figure 8-75 Position of the Leg

Now, in order to change the location of the right leg, select Rfoot, TranslateZ and the key in the Graph Editor, as shown in Figure 8-76, and then paste the copied value in the Value field.

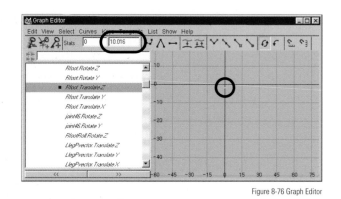

Figure 8-76 Graph Editor

As we can see in Figure 8-77, both legs now stick straight out.

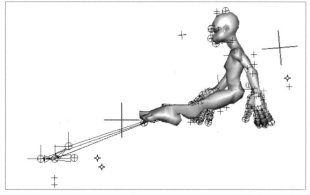

Figure 8-77 Position of the Legs

We also have to change the position of the body. Select Body, TranslateZ from the Graph Editor and change the key value so that the body is positioned as shown in Figure 8-78.

Select the key and then press the W key to select the Move Tool. Hold down the Shift key in this state and drag the mouse up and down. This is, by far, a faster and more intuitive way to change the position.

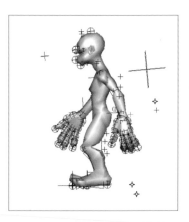

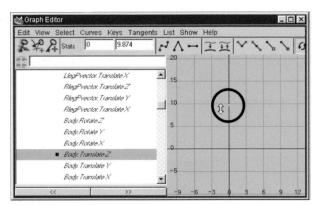

Figure 8-78 Changing the Position of the Body in the Graph Editor

The basic animation steps are now complete. Now, double-click on the Jump clip to change the Offset value to Relative in the Channel Box, and then play the animation. We can see that the character now walks and jumps properly.

Move the Jump clips for the remaining characters, as shown in Figure 8-79, and blend it to the Walking clip. Set the Offset value for the clips to Absolute.

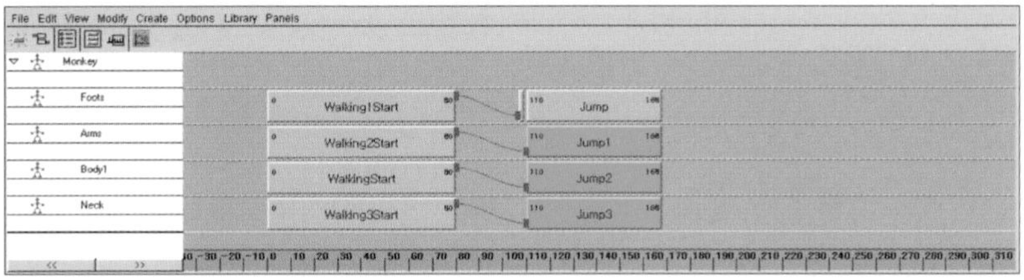

Figure 8-79 Blending the Clips

You will need to modify the details of the animation key values for these clips through the Graph Editor. When using the Graph Editor to modify the animation curve, you can select the clip from the Trax Editor and select [View > Graph Anim Curves...]. However, if you want to be able to select the object directly in the scene, first, merge all the clips together and then select the clip of the character you wish to modify. Selecting [Modify > Active/Deactive Keys] from the Trax Editor will change the color of the selected clip, as shown in Figure 8-80.

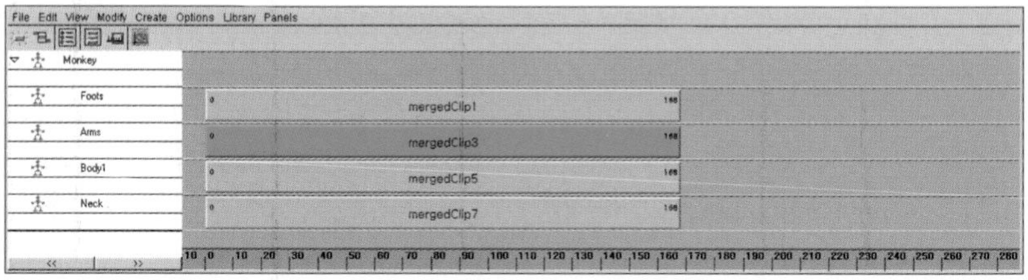

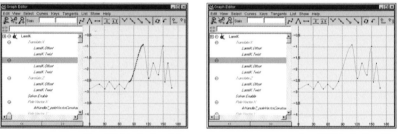

Figure 8-80 Using Active/Deactive Keys

step 7 We can now modify the animation curve for this character's clip using [Windows > Animation Editors > Graph Editor]. Looking at the Graph Editor, we can see that the animation curve does not blend naturally (see Figure 8-81). This must be modified to look like the curve in Figure 8-82.

Figure 8-81 Animation Curve Before   Figure 8-82 Animation Curve After

After modifying the animation curve, select the clip again and select [Modify > Active/Deactive Keys] from the Trax Editor to restore the clip to its original state.

Areas that are not blended correctly should be modified according to the process we saw in "2. Modifying Motion using a New Clip" earlier. For instance, in this example, the movements of the leg need some modification.

3-2. FACIAL ANIMATION USING POSE

We will now learn how to create more effective facial animations using Trax Editor's Pose. For the purposes of this example, open the file, CD-ROM/CHARACTER/scenes/ManSETUPFinal.mb. As shown in Figure 8-83, hide everything except the face and the clusters and joints of the face.

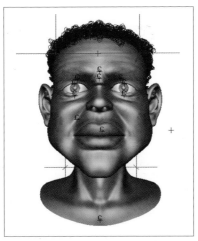

Figure 8-83 Example File

step 1 All the elements that go into making the facial expression should be made into one character.

Select [Animation > Character > Create Character Set] to open the Options window. In the Options window, set the Name to Facial, configure the rest of the options as seen in Figure 8-84, and then click on the Create Character Set button at the bottom of the window. None of the elements should be selected in the window at this time.

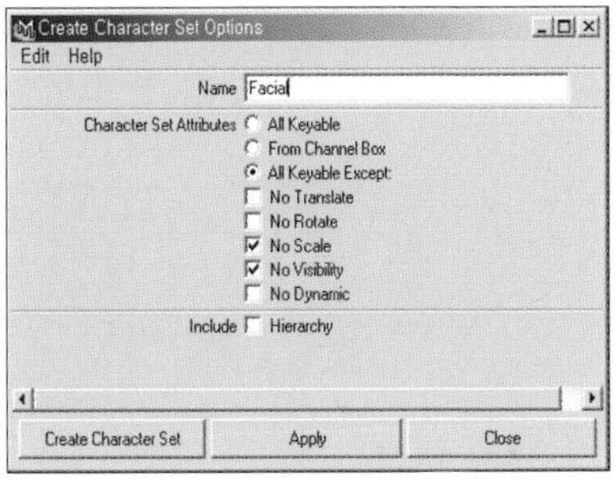

Figure 8-84 Options Window

Select the face and then select FacialBLEND from under INPUTS in the Channel Box, as shown in Figure 8-85. Then, select all the Target Names for the Blend. Select [Animation > Character > Add to Character Set]. All the channels selected in the Channel Box will be included in the Facial Character.

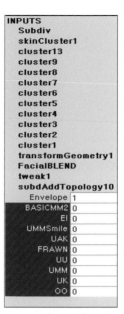

Figure 8-85 Channel Box

Select all the clusters above, excluding the face. Select Translate Channel from the Channel Box and then select [Animation > Character > Add to Character Set]. If the scale needs to be adjusted for some clusters, include the Scale Channel in the Facial Character. In the same way, select the Rotate Channel in the Channel Box to include the joints controlling the lower jaw in the Facial Character.

We are now ready to use Pose. Let's now pose each of the facial expressions.

step 3 I will keep the explanations very brief. If you have an audio source, using the audio source is also a good idea.

Let's pose a few expressions and test them. There are a few things we need to do before we can pose the expressions. Select [Windows > Rendering Editors > Render Global]. Set the Width and Height to 150, as shown in Figure 8-86, and set the Ratio value at the bottom to 1.

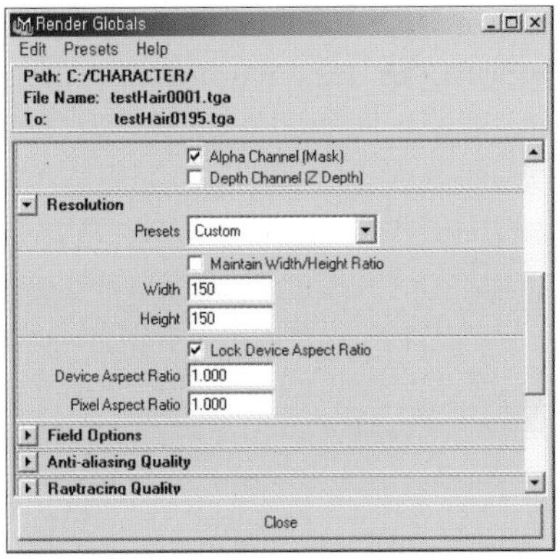

Figure 8-86 Render Global

Create the window layout as shown in Figure 8-87.

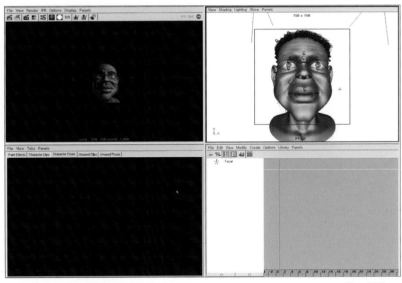

Figure 8-87 Layout

step 4 Select the Facial Character from the Trax Editor, and select [Create > Pose] to open the Options window. Set the Name to Basic, and then click on the Create Pose button at the bottom of the window. Looking at the Character Poses Tab in the Visor, we can see that the Basic Pose has been made. Click on [ ] in the Render View Panel to render the scene.

Select [View > Grab Switch to Hypershade/Visor] in the Render View Panel. Then, as shown in Figure 8-88, select the desired frame in Render View, click the MMB on the frame, and drag it above the pose. As shown here, the pose will change to a rendering image.

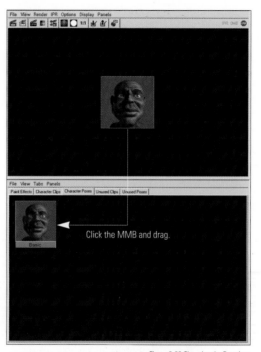

Figure 8-88 Changing the Pose Icon

Change the facial expression using Blend Shape and the clusters and joints, as shown in Figure 8-89.

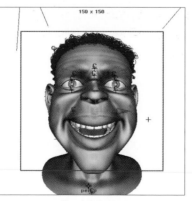

Figure 8-89 Changing the Facial Expression

Select the Facial Character in the Trax Editor and then select [Create > Pose 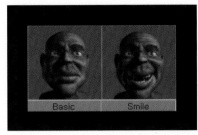]. Set the name to Smile, and then click on the Create Pose button. After rendering the scene, repeat Step 2 to change the pose icon, as shown in Figure 9-90.

Figure 8-90 Changing the Icon

In this way, make the poses for different facial expressions and change the pose icons, as shown in Figure 8-91. By changing the icon, we can easily see which pose corresponds to which facial expression.

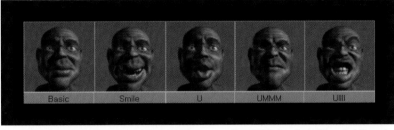

Figure 8-91 The Poses for the Different Facial Expressions

step 5 Now, arrange the poses at random in the Facial Character track. If you have an audio file, the poses must be arranged to fit the given audio. Figure 8-92 illustrates the poses arranged on the track.

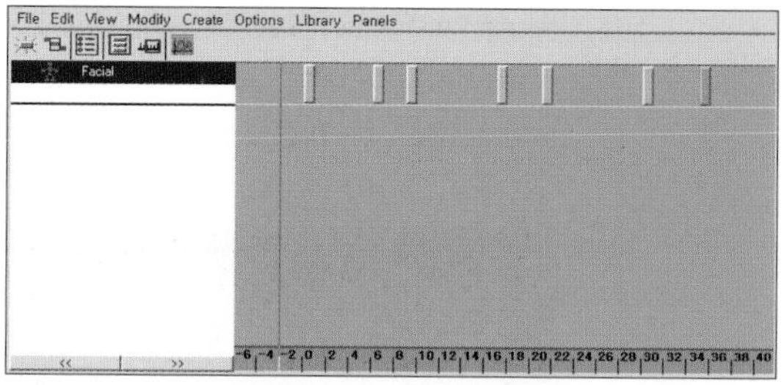

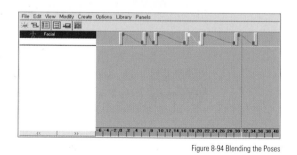

Figure 8-92 Arranging the Poses

All of the poses must be blended together. Select the poses to blend and then select [Create > Blend ▪] in the Trax Editor. Configure the options as shown in Figure 8-93, and then click on the Create Blend button.

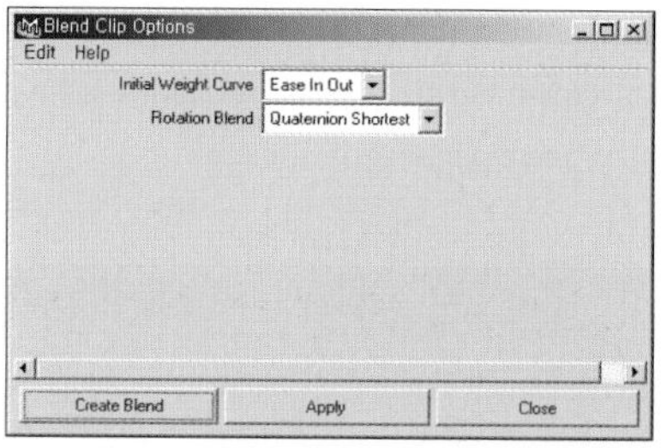

Figure 8-93 Options Window

Blend all the poses as shown in Figure 8-94.

Figure 8-94 Blending the Poses

The animation should be played from time to time to see if the facial expressions are timed right. The timing of the facial expressions are modified simply by moving the poses.

Finally, merge all the poses together and modify the animation curve and save them as clips. This is an efficient way to manage the data.

To merge the poses and convert them into a clip, select all the poses and select [Edit > Merge ▦]. In the Options window, set the name to FacialSource and merge the poses.

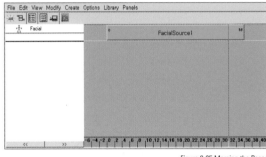

Figure 8-95 Merging the Poses

Modify the animation curve by selecting the clip and then selecting [View > Graph Anim Curves] from the Trax Editor. Because each of the poses were merged after being blended, the animation key values will apply frame by frame, as in Figure 8-96.

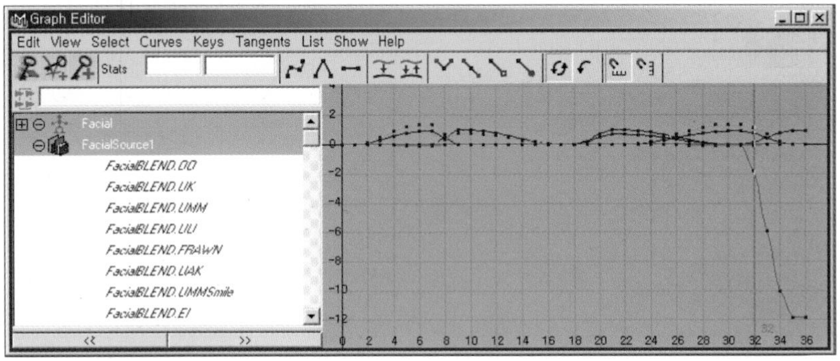

Figure 8-96 Graph Editor

Not only does this make it difficult to modify the curve, it also increases the size of the data. Therefore, we need to simplify this curve. To modify the curve in the Graph Editor, select all the curves and select [Curves > Simplify Curves ▦] to open the Options window.

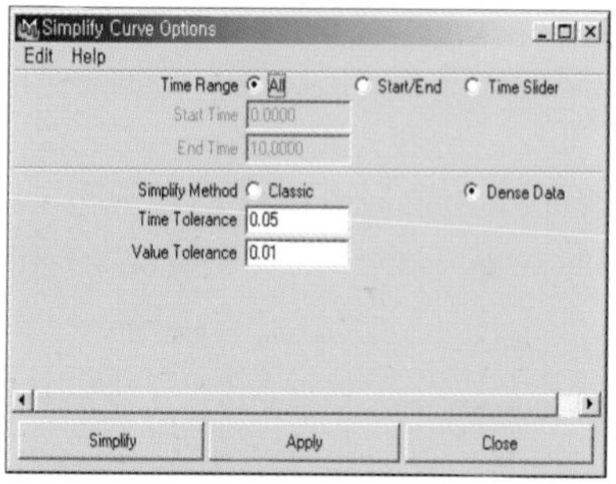

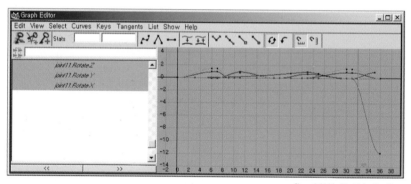

Figure 8-97 Options Window

To simplify the curve, we need to adjust the Time Tolerance and Value Tolerance values in the Options window (see Figure 8-97). Raising these values will simplify the curve, but, at the same time, decrease the accuracy. Therefore, we need to choose an appropriate value to adequately simplify the curve.

After simplifying the curve, we finish up by modifying portions of the curve. Figure 8-98 shows the modified animation curve.

Figure 8-98 Modified Animation Curve

Now we have learned how to use the Trax Editor for nonlinear animation. This feature allows us to edit animations quickly and easily and to store existing animation key values in the library for future use. As with any new feature, the more you use it, the better you will become at using it. Making the most out of the Trax Editor will drastically reduce the time you spend on keyframing animations.

Arc Studio

Arc Studio
(Image by Woo-seung Lee)

Render Utility & Mapping Techniques

In this chapter, we will learn about the Maya mapping environment and the various render utilities. Explanations will be geared toward actual use, rather than a simple explanation of the menus. We will also cover how to use Hypershade and mapping techniques for realistic representations. I will refrain from giving basic explanations.

1. THE MAPPING ENVIRONMENT OF MAYA

Maya offers 2 different texture-editing windows. One, shown in Figure 9-1, is the Multilister and the other, shown in Figure 9-2, is Hypershade. We will be able to use these 2 windows to create and blend many textures.

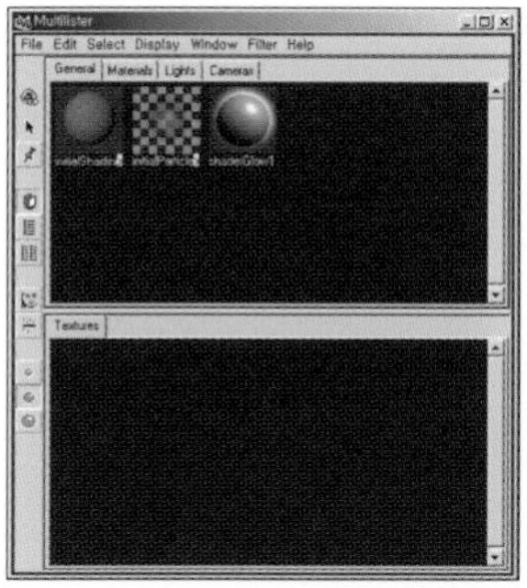

<table>
<tr>
<td>Figure 9-1 Multilister</td>
<td>Figure 9-2 Hypershade</td>
</tr>
</table>

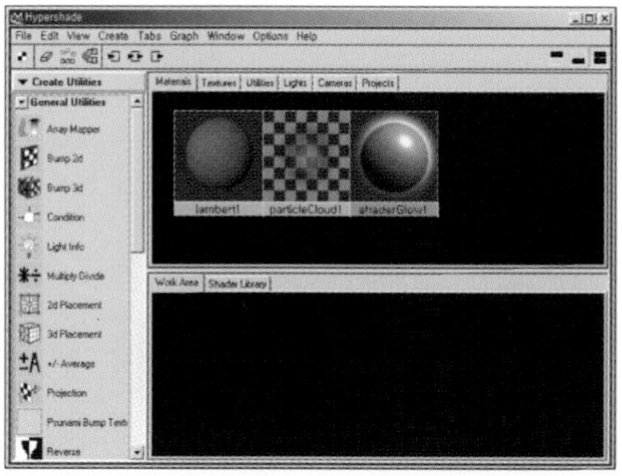

For a more intuitive shading network, I recommend that you use Hypershade rather than the Multilister. Hypershade allows us to create faster, easier, and more intuitive links between the nodes.

1-1. NODE AND SHADING NETWORK

Each node consists of an output, and an input, and they are linked together based on the definition of light and surface representation to create an image.

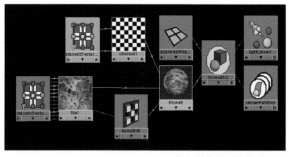

Figure 9-3 Node and Shading Network

A Shading Network refers to how the nodes are linked. By linking these Render Nodes to the network, Maya creates an environment in which various textures can be blended to create the ultimate image.

1-2. USING HYPERSHADE

Hypershade is used to easily create and edit materials, textures, rendering utilities, light, and other special effects. These Render Nodes are linked together to create one shading network. Hypershade is accessed through [Windows > Rendering Editors > Hypershade].

Figure 9-4 shows us the Hypershade window. Let's first take a look at the basic directions for using Hypershade.

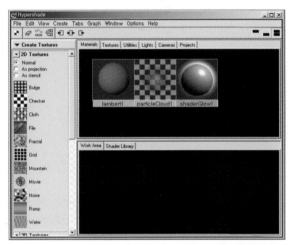

Figure 9-4 Hypershade

1. Hypershade Create Bar

When Hypershade is first opened, the Create Bar is displayed on the left-hand side of the screen. We can create the node we want by clicking on this panel using the MMB and dragging it onto the Hypershade Panel.

This is the same thing as creating a node through the Create Render Node window. To use the Create Render Node window, select [Create > Create New Node] from the Hypershade menu at the top.

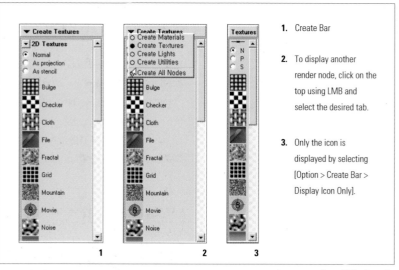

1. Create Bar

2. To display another render node, click on the top using LMB and select the desired tab.

3. Only the icon is displayed by selecting [Option > Create Bar > Display Icon Only].

Figure 9-5 The Create Bar

The Create Bar can be hidden or displayed by clicking on ▪ in the Icon menu.

2. Icon Menu

Hypershade presents frequently used menus in icon format to make our work faster and easier. Let's take a quick look at how to use these icons.

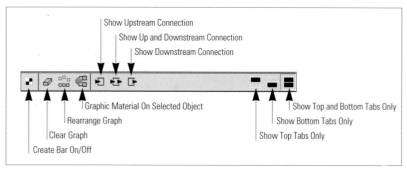

Figure 9-6 Icon Menu

As explained above, this icon is used to turn the Create Bar on or off.

This icon is used to erase a shading network from a work area. The shader is not erased, but merely not displayed in the work area.

This icon is used to realign each render node. Clicking on this icon will realign scattered render nodes in the work area.

Selecting an object in the window and then clicking on this icon will display the shader assigned to the object in the work area. This icon comes in handy when trying to figure out which shader goes with which object in a very complex scene.

These icons show the respective connection states of each node. These icons are used to verify which nodes are connected to the shader.

Selecting this icon will only display the top Select Node Tab of the Hypershader.

Selecting this icon will only display the bottom Works Area Tab of the Hypershader.

The default setting, this icon displays both the top and bottom tabs.

3. Tabs Menu

In general, in order to effectively manage the rendering source and in order to intuitively approach the render node, they should be organized as tabs. Tabs are made using the Tabs menu from the Hypershader menu at the top. We can use the Tabs menu to do the following:

Manage folders where specific images are saved. Let's suppose that we created a folder for a particular image and saved the image source in it. It will be very effective to be able to retrieve this image from the Hypershader. This is because we can convert each image into an icon for faster and easier searching and bring them into the Hypershader. The section below explains how to create tabs out of specific image folders.

Select [Tabs > Create New Tab] from the Hypershade to open the Create New Tab window, as shown in Figure 9-7. Set the New Tab Name to Textures and the Initial Placement to Top so that it is added to the top.

Set the Tab Type to Disk. The Tab Type must be set to Disk so that we can select the image folder from the root directory at the bottom. After finding and entering the desired route from the root directory, click on the Create button at the bottom.

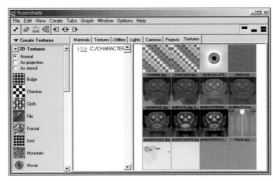

Figure 9-7 Create New Tab Window

As shown in Figure 9-8, a new tab is made in the Hypershader and the image that was specified is displayed as an icon.

Figure 9-8 Create New Tab

As we can see in Figure 9-8, to the left of the tab is the directory and to the right is the file. We can select [Tabs > Current Tab > Show Directories Only] to display only the directory or select Show Files Only to display only the files.

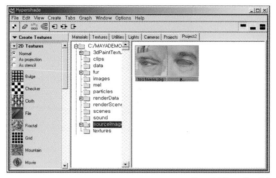

Figure 9-9 Create New Tab

To change the name, select the tab and then select [Tabs > Rename]. Also, we can use Move Tab Left/Right or Up/Down from the Tabs menu to move the tab in the respective directions. To return to the original Hypershade state, select Revert To Default Tab.

In addition, by selecting a project in Maya, we can manage the entire project folder through the Hypershader. When the project folder is selected when specifying the route in the Create New Tab window, the project subfolders will be displayed as seen in Figure 9-9.

4. Shader Library

If the Shader Library was installed when Maya was installed, the Shader Library Tab should be visible in the bottom Hypershader tab. This Shader Library contains a few textures and shaders for quick and easy access.

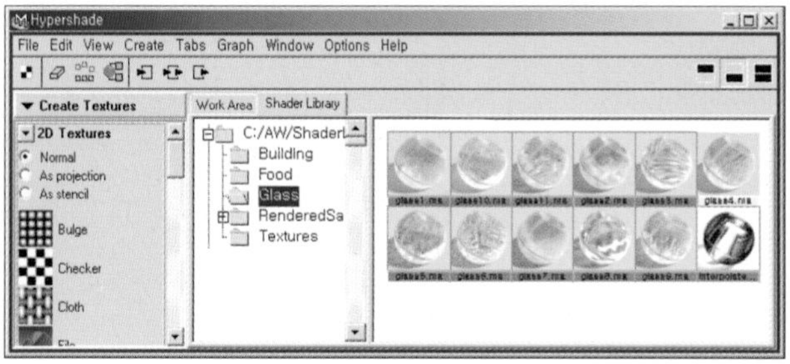

Figure 9-10 Shader Library

All the shaders and textures in the library are showed as rendered images. Click on one of the shaders using the MMB and drag to the Material Tab at the top to load the specific shader into the scene. In order to use a specific texture, select the Texture folder and click on the desired texture using the MMB and drag it to the Texture Tab at the top.

This completes a basic overview on how to use Hypergraph. If you have some experience in using Maya, these menus should be familiar to you. Let's now take a look at shader attributes.

1-3. SHADER ATTRIBUTES

Let's now take a look at a few shader attributes. These attributes are very useful and. very practical; however, they are also frequently misused by many people. Maya offers a total of 9 Surface Materials, 5 Volumetric Materials, and 1 Displacement Material. Each of these materials has their own unique attributes. Figure 9-11 shows the Attribute Editor for the Blinn Shader. Most users stick to using only the attributes that they know. The most frequently used attributes are, without a doubt, Color and Bump, Specular, Transparency, and Reflection. These are the attributes can be used in most shaders, and we will use the Blinn Shader to explain these attributes.

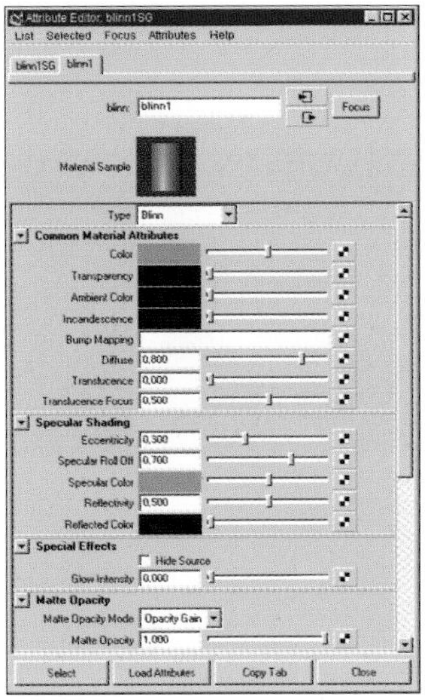

Figure 9-11 Attribute Editor

Actually, we can use these attributes to portray almost all types of materials. However, by understanding how other attributes are used, we can enhance the quality of our portrayal. In this section, we will look at how to use each attribute to create an even more effective material.

First, we will cover the basic concepts of each attribute. As seen in Figure 9-12 above, each attribute has either a color box or a value field in which values can be entered. Color box, like the ones for Color, Transparency, and Ambient Color, means that the attributes use an RGB Channel. This means that the color of the texture will be portrayed as it is by putting in a color texture that has an RGB Channel. However, colors for attributes that have a value field will not be portrayed. Only the value is effective. In other words, most attributes have a value of 0 or 1 (with 0 referring to black and 1 referring to white). Other colors have no meaning for these attributes. In a basic color system, each color has 255 levels. In such a system, gray is also portrayed in a 255-level gradation, but in the shader, this attribute is portrayed from 0-1. Again, 0 refers to total blackness and 1 refers to total whiteness. A value of 0.5 refers to a 50% gray level.

1. Understanding Diffuse

For example, let's look at Diffuse. The default value for Diffuse is 0.8. Figure 9-12 shows the rendered results at different Diffuse values. The lower this value, the darker the Diffuse color. The higher this value, the brighter the Diffuse color.

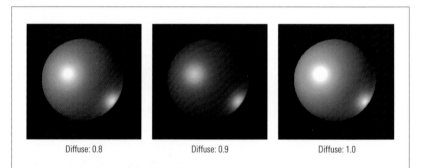

Diffuse: 0.8   Diffuse: 0.9   Diffuse: 1.0

Figure 9-12 Rendered Results at Different Diffuse Values

In other words, by placing a texture in this value, black would make the Diffuse color darker and white would make the Diffuse color brighter. Figure 9-13 shows the result after placing a Checker 2D Texture in the Diffuse value.

Figure 9-13 Using a Checker Texture

Although many people understand this concept, not many people use it in the right way. As an example, let's look at the scene in Figure 9-14. Let's suppose that this scene is for a simple interior and that various directional lights have been placed to light up the room. The rendering of this scene is seen in Figure 9-15. Looking closely at Figure 9-15, we can see that the result is not very realistic. Even though, in an actual room, the collision of light and the reflection of such a collision cover a fixed area, there are still some differences in shading and shadows.

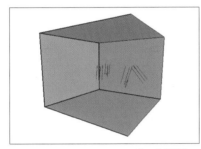

Figure 9-14 3D Scene

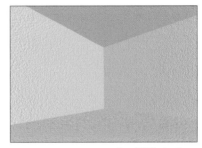

Figure 9-15 Rendered Image

However, it is very difficult to achieve such a result using only directional light. This is because directional light only computes the direction of the light and certain areas are made to receive the same amount of light. Although many people have their own preferences and their own methods for handling such cases, Diffuse is also a very good solution. Figure 9-16 shows the image rendered using a Diffuse Map. We can see that the corners receive comparatively less light for a much more realistic representation of space than seen in Figure 9-15. Figure 9-17 shows the attribute for the Ramp Texture using the Diffuse Map. The Ramp Type is Circular Ramp and the Ramp Color is as shown in the figure.

Namely, a white to gray gradation means that the Diffuse will slowly get brighter and then darker again.

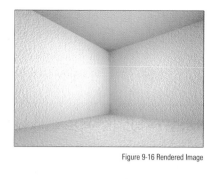

Figure 9-16 Rendered Image

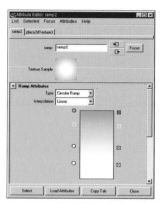

Figure 9-17 Ramp Attribute Editor

Proper use of the Diffuse Map can create highly realistic images.

2. Using Incandescence

In contrast to Diffuse, Incandescence has RGB Channels.

This means that it can be portrayed in color. Incandescence portrays a material that emits its own light. And, because this can be used with color, a variety of different effects can be portrayed. For example, let's suppose we want to portray a hotly burning iron rod. Make a simple polygon cylinder as in Figure 9-18 and render the image. We used Blinn Shader for the material. In order to portray a hotly burning iron rod, only a portion of the cylinder must appear bright. Figure 9-19 shows how this was done by using a Ramp Texture with an Incandescence Map.

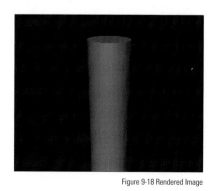

Figure 9-18 Rendered Image

Figure 9-19 Using the Incandescence Map

Figure 9-20 shows the Attribute Editor for the Ramp Texture with the Incandescence Map. As shown in the figure, the black area is where the Incandescence effect does not occur and the original Blinn Shader color (from Figure 9-19) is portrayed. Only the areas that have the RGB shows Incandescence.

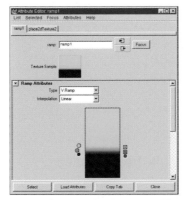

In this way, we can blacken areas to control the amount of Incandescence.

Figure 9-20 Ramp Texture Attribute Editor

3. Using Glow

We can use a Glow Map to further enhance the Incandescence effect. Namely, we will be adding a Glow effect to the bright areas. Figure 9-21 shows the use of the Glow effect in the redhot area of the iron rod.

Figure 9-21 Image Using a Glow Map

We add a texture to the Glow Intensity to add Glow effects to certain areas. Figure 9-22 shows the Ramp Texture Attribute Editor for the Glow Intensity.

In the same way, areas that are black have a
value of 0 and the Glow is not applied. Areas
that are gray will show a glow according to the
intensity of the gray. In other words, since the
value here is approximately 50% gray, a 0.5
glow intensity will be seen.

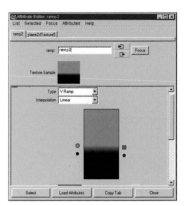

Figure 9-22 Ramp Texture Attribute Editor

4. Using Translucence

This attribute is used to create a material with partial light permeation. It is used in the
following situation. (This effect is available only in Maya versions 4 and later.)

The example file for this example is CD_ROM/CHARACTER/scenes/leaf.mb. Open this
file. This file shows the shadow made by a leaf on a very sunny day. The light in this
example will be shining down on the leaf, but in the actual rendering of the image, the
camera will be placed in opposition to the light. The rendered scene will show the
reflection of the top leaf on the bottom leaf. We simply select [Perspective > Camera]
from the Panels menu and render Camera1 to blacken the bottom portion, as shown in
Figure 9-24.

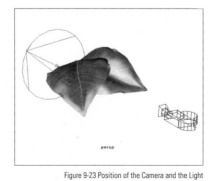

Figure 9-23 Position of the Camera and the Light

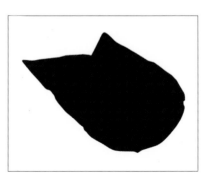

Figure 9-24 Rendered Image

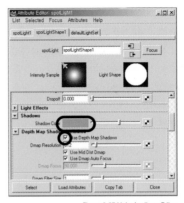

Figure 9-25 Light Attribute Editor

This phenomenon will create a problem for a light-permeating material. Open the Light Attribute Editor and put a check by Use Depth Map Shadow to activate this option. Change the gray to 50% to brighten the color of the shadow made by the light.

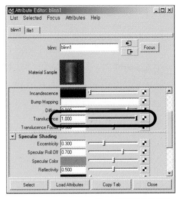

Figure 9-26 Attribute Editor

Open the Hypershade and double-click on the leaf shader to open the Attribute Editor. As show in Figure 9-26, set the Translucence to 1.

Render Camera1. This will create a shadow of the top leaf on the bottom leaf as in Figure 9-27. Translucence is very good for portraying the permeation of light.

Figure 9-27 Rendered Image

This attribute can be applied to the map. For example, the veins of the leaf, which are thicker and do not permeate light, are set to black and the remaining areas are set to white. If the Map Source is used in the Translucence attribute, as in Figure 9-28, the image will render as shown in Figure 9-29. This image is saved as CD_ROM/CHARACTER /sourceimages/leafTranslucenc.jpg. Try testing this attribute on your own.

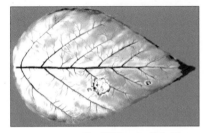

Figure 9-28 Image Used in Translucence

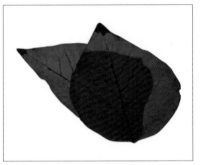

Figure 9-29 Rendered Image

We have covered the basic shader attributes. How and which attributes are used can create a variety of different effects. Therefore, you should test these different attributes on your own to create your own unique mapping style. These attributes alone are enough for the realistic portrayal of materials.

2. SHADING NETWORK USING RENDER UTILITY

Maya usually makes a shader from a node-based network environment. This offers the most optimal environment for intuitively editing materials and specifying objects. Also, through the use of many utilities, it expands the limitations of material representation. These utilities offer a variety of options making it easier to portray materials that were difficult to portray before. There are many utilities and it is, by far, one of the most difficult aspects of Maya. Even I have not fully mastered all of the utilities. The utilities that will be covered here are the ones that are most effective and the ones that are used most often. We can see the nodes for each utility by selecting Create Utility from the Create Bar in Hypershade.

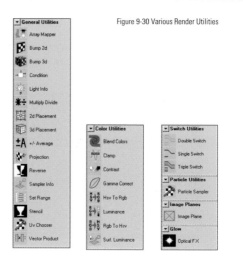

Figure 9-30 Various Render Utilities

Figure 9-30 illustrates the various render utilities. Some utilities are created individually before use, and others are created automatically. Nodes that are created automatically use particles and include the Bump2d and 3d nodes, which are created when an Array Mapper or Bump Map is created, and the 2d and 3d Placement Nodes, which are created when the texture is loaded.

Utilities that are used frequently will be explained in the following sections.

2-1. BUMP2D 🔲 AND BUMP3D 🔲

In general, these nodes are those that are created automatically when a bump texture is used in the shader attributes. However, there is one instance when these nodes are necessary and that is when a bump is placed on top of another bump. For example, let's look at the following case.

Let's suppose that we created a random texture to portray the stitches in a piece of clothing. Using this node to use another bump to portray the thread pattern on the clothes will bring good results. In this instance, we are creating another bump map on top of the bump we already created. Let's test this using the following example.

step 1 In Hypershade, create one Lambert Material from Create Material, one Water and Cloth Texture from Create Texture, and 2 Bump2ds from Create Utility and arrange them in the work area as shown in Figure 9-31.

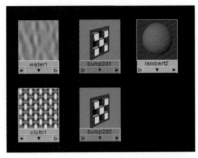

Figure 9-31 Hypershade

We need to do the following in order to link the nodes.

First, click the MMB on the Water Node and drag it above the Bump Node, as shown in Figure 9-32. Because of the default setting, the nodes will be linked automatically. Next, click the MMB on the Bump Node and drag it above the Lambert and link it to the Bump. Then, click the MMB on the Cloth Node and drag it above the Bump Node.

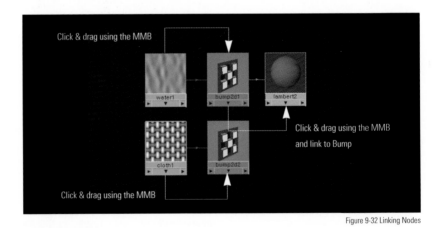

Figure 9-32 Linking Nodes

step 2 Double-click on the Water Texture to open the Attribute Editor and enter 2 for both the Repeat U and V values in the plce2dTexture tab, as shown in Figure 9-33.

Open the Attribute Editor for the Bump Node, which is linked to the Water Node, and set the Bump Depth value to 2.5, as shown in Figure 9-34.

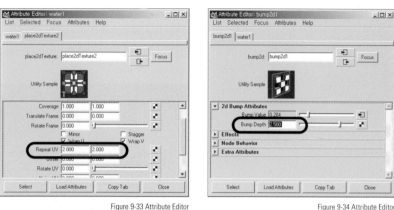

Figure 9-33 Attribute Editor   Figure 9-34 Attribute Editor

Now, make a NURBS sphere and assign the Lambert Node to it. After adequately arranging the light, render the scene. The rendered image is shown in Figure 9-35.

Figure 9-35 Rendered Image

step 3 Now, link the Cloth Texture to the Bump on top of this bump. First of all, we need to see to which Lambert attribute the Water Bump Node is attached. In order to verify how the Bump Node is attached to the Lambert, place the mouse over the line connecting the 2 nodes, as shown in Figure 9-36.

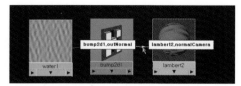

Figure 9-36 Link Status of the Nodes

As we can see in the figure, the outNormal of the Bump Node is linked to the normalCamera of the Lambert Node. Now, click the MMB on the Bump Node of the Cloth Texture and drag it above the Bump Node of the Water Node.

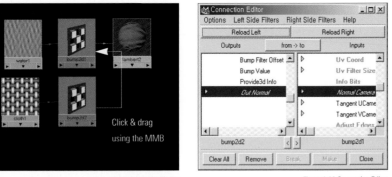

Figure 9-37 Linking the Nodes   Figure 9-38 Connection Editor

Because there is basically no attribute to link to, the Connection Editor will open, as shown in Figure 9-38. Link OutNormal and NormalCamera in the Connection Editor.

Open the Attribute Editor of the Cloth Node and, as shown in Figure 9-39, set the Repeat U and V values to 60 in the place2dTexture tab. Open the Attribute Editor of the Bump Node and, as shown in Figure 9-40, set the Bump Depth value to 0.05.

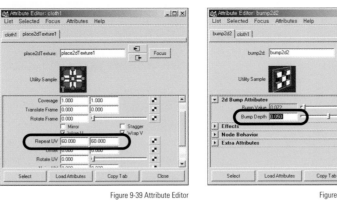

Figure 9-39 Attribute Editor   Figure 9-40 Attribute Editor

Render the final scene. As shown in Figure 9-41, we can see that the Cloth Texture is bumped on top of the Bump Map with the Water Node.

Figure 9-41 Rendered Image

In this way, we can link the Bump Nodes and use them as we please. There is no limit to how many bump nodes can be used. This kind of effect is actually very difficult to create using a map source, but it can be easily accomplished by simply linking nodes together. The Bump3d is used in the same way. The only thing to remember is that the outNormal needs to be linked to the normalCamera of each bump node.

2-2. SAMPLER INFO

This is probably the most frequently used utility. This utility can be used to create a variety of different shaders. The most frequently used attributes of this utility are Facing Ratio and Flip Normal. Let's see what kinds of shaders can be made using these 2 attributes.

1. Facing Ratio

This attribute creates the changing value, between 0 and 1, created by the angle between the Normal of the surface and the direction of the camera.
Let's look at Figure 9-42. This figure shows the yield of the Normal value of the surface according to the direction of the camera when this node is used.

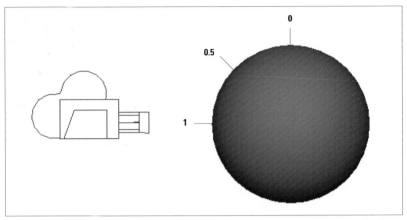

Figure 9-42 Yield of the Facing Ratio According to the Angle of the Camera

As we can see in the figure, when the camera faces the Normal of the surface, the value is 1, and when the camera is perpendicular to the Normal, the value is 0.

The Normal can have any value between 0 and 1.

Let's run a simple test of this theory. Arrange the camera as shown, and render the scene in Camera View. After making one Blinn Shader and one Sampler Info Node in Hypershade, click the MMB on the Sampler Info Node while holding down the Shift key, and drag it on top of the Blinn Shader as shown in Figure 9-43. As shown in Figure 9-44, the Connection Editor will open. Placing the node while holding down the Shift key will also the Connection Editor right away. In the Connection Editor, link the Facing Ratio to the Transparency R, G, B.

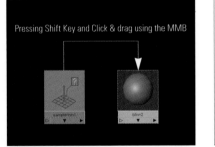

Figure 9-43 Hypershade

Figure 9-44 Connection Editor

Render the scene. The scene will render as shown in Figure 9-45. A check texture was placed in the background so that the scene can be easily observed.

Figure 9-45 Rendered Image

As we can see in the figure, areas in which the direction of the camera is the same as the Normal of the surface appear transparent, whereas areas in which the direction of the camera and the Normal of the surface are perpendicular (the outer regions) are opaque. This theory is based on the fact that when the Transparency value is 0 or black, it appears opaque and when the value is 1 or white, it appears transparent. Therefore, the transparency of the surface is determined by the value in the Sampler Info. The important thing here is to have a complete understanding of these numerical concepts. In Hypershade, almost all values are between 0 and 1. Therefore, observe the characteristics of the material when the attributes are at 0 and 1 and understand how these attributes can be controlled using various utilities.

As a simple example, let's look at the Diffuse attribute. The Diffuse range is from 0 to 1 and the default is 0.8. Figure 9-46 shows the renderings of the images at different Diffuse values. When the Diffuse is 0, the image will be black, and when it is 1, the image brightens considerably. Here, 0 refers to black and 1 refers to white.

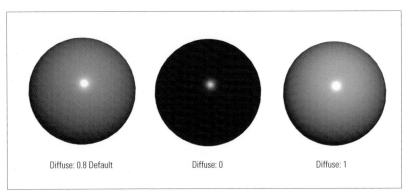

Diffuse: 0.8 Default   Diffuse: 0   Diffuse: 1

Figure 9-46 Rendered Image

Now, let's disconnect the Sampler Info, which was linked to Transparency in the shader above. All we have to do is to simply select the connecting line in the Hypershade and press the Delete key on the keyboard. Link the Sampler Info to the Diffuse of the Blinn Shader. Rendering the image, it should like the image in Figure 9-47. As seen in the figure, areas where the camera and the Normal coincide will appear brighter, and areas where they are perpendicular to each other will appear darker.

Figure 9-47 Rendered Image

2. Flip Normal

This attribute, much like Condition Utility, is used in making double-sided materials. Let's now look at how to use the Condition utility.

2-3. CONDITION

This utility offers options in which shaders are created using conditions. It is linked to Flip Normal of the Sampler Info Node to create a surface with different textures on both sides. Namely, it is used to display different textures in the normal and anti-normal direction of the surface. Let's look at a simple example.

step 1 Make a NURBS sphere as shown in Figure 9-48, and use Detach to cut out and delete the upper portion.

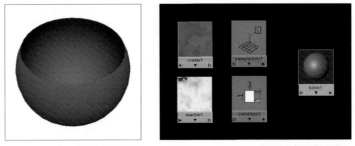

Figure 9-48 Making a Sphere   Figure 9-49 Create Render Node

In Hypershade, make one Blinn Shader in the Create Material Bar, one crater and marble in the Create Texture Bar, and one Sampler Info and Condition Node in the Create Utility Bar and arrange them as shown in Figure 9-49.

step 2 First, click the MMB on the Sampler Info Node while holding down the Shift key and drag it on top of the Condition Node. When the Connection Editor opens (see Figure 9-50), link Flip Normal and First Term.

Figure 9-50 Connection Editor

step 3 After dragging the Crater Texture on top of the Condition Node, link the Out Color to Color 1 in the Connection Editor as shown in Figure 9-51. Drag the Marble Texture on top of the Condition Node and link the Out Color to Color 2 in the Connection Editor, as shown in Figure 9-52.

Figure 9-51 Connection Editor   Figure 9-52 Connection Editor

step 4 Click the MMB on the Condition Node and drag it on top of the Blinn Shader, and link the Out Color to Color in the Connection Editor, as shown in Figure 9-53. After assigning the Blinn Shader to the NURBS sphere, render the scene. As shown in Figure 9-54, an image with different textures on the inside and outside will be rendered.

Figure 9-53 Connection Editor

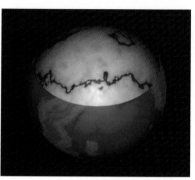

Figure 9-54 Rendered Image

Flip the textures on the outside and the inside by double-clicking on the Condition Node to open the Attribute Editor. As shown in Figure 9-56, select Not Equal from under Operation. Rendering the image, we can see that the outside and inside textures have been flipped (see Figure 9-56).

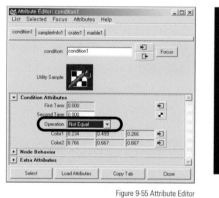

Figure 9-55 Attribute Editor

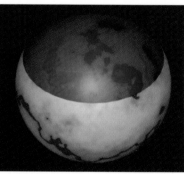

Figure 9-56 Rendered Image

We can also change entire materials, not just textures. In order to change the material, we do the following.

step 5 As shown in Figure 9-57, make a shader with the same structure in Hypershade. Link the Env Chrome of the 3D Texture to the Reflected Color of the Blinn Shader, open the Blinn Shader Attribute Editor and set the Reflectivity value to 1. Link the Checker Texture to the Lambert color. We will leave the Sampler Info and the Connection Node as they are. One thing to note here is that when changing materials, we must use Layer Shader. Select the Layer Shader from the Create Material Bar and arrange it as shown.

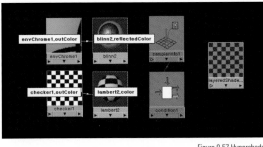

Figure 9-57 Hypershade

step 6 Click the MMB on the Blinn Shader and drag it on top of the Connection Node. In the Connection Editor, link the Out Color to Color 1. Click the MMB on the Lambert Shader and drag it on top of the Condition Node. In the Connection Editor, link the Out Color to Color 2.

step 7 Double-click the Layer Shader to open the Attribute Editor. In Hypershade, click the MMB on the Condition Node and drag it onto Color in the Layer Shader Attribute Editor.

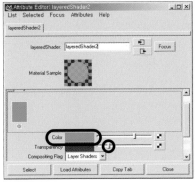

Figure 9-58 Attribute Editor

As a default, we can see in the Layer Shader Attribute Editor that some Transparency is applied. Move the slider bar, seen in Figure 9-58 on the previous page, to the left so that the color is black and the Transparency is not applied.

Assign the Layer Shader to the NURBS sphere and render the scene. We can see in Figure 9-59 that the Blinn and the Lambert have been applied to the inside and outside of the surface, respectively.

Figure 9-59 Rendered Image

2-4. REVERSE ☑

The Reverse utility reverses a given input value. In other words, a value of 0 for black will be switched to a value of 1, or white, with this utility. This utility can be used in many ways. In this example, we will use a sphere with a reflective texture and apply a transparency.

step 1 First, make a Render Node in Hypershade, as shown in Figure 9-60. Make one Blinn Shader, one Reverse Utility from Utility and one Checker and Env Chrome from Texture, and arrange them as shown. The color of the Blinn Shader should be set to Black.

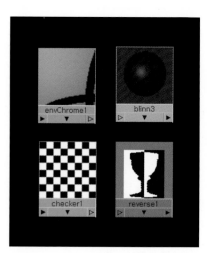

Figure 9-60 Create Render Node

step 2 Click the MMB on the envChrom and drag it on top of the Blinn Shader and then link it to Reflected Color. Click the MMB on the Checker Texture and drag it on top of the Blinn Shader and then link it to Transparency. Make a simple NURBS sphere, assign the Blinn Shader to it and then render the image.

The rendered image should look like the image in Figure 9-61.

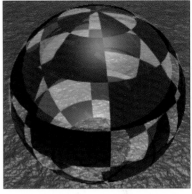

Figure 9-61 Rendered Image

step 3 A completely transparent image is rendered only when the Transparency value is 1 or white. As follows, it considers the white portions of the checker in Figure 9-61 to be white and makes them transparent. In the same way, the black portions of the checker are thought to be black and made opaque. Therefore, as we can see in the figure, despite the Transparency value, the Reflection value creates reflection even in the transparent regions.

Let's suppose we want to remove the reflection only from the transparent regions. The Specular Color of the transparent regions must be black. And the Specular Color of the opaque regions, because we want the Reflection value to be applied and the Specular to show through, must be white. However, because the transparent regions of the Checker Texture applied to the Transparency are white, we must make another checker that is the opposite of this.

This is where the Reverse utility comes in handy.

step 4 Click the MMB on the Checker Texture in the Hypershade and drag it on top of the Reverse Node. The Connection Editor will open automatically. In the Editor, we link the Out Color to Input, as shown in Figure 9-62.

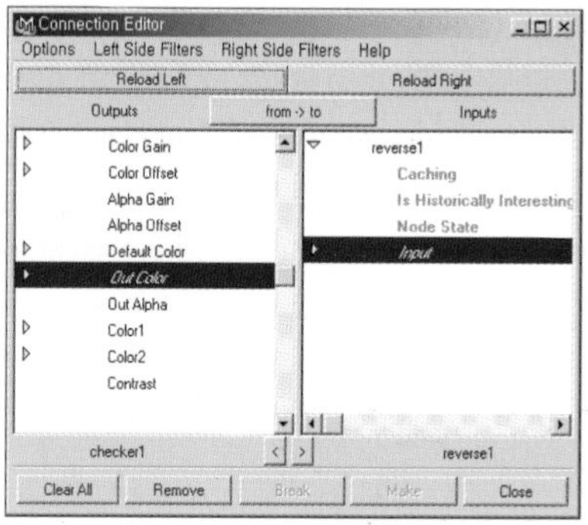

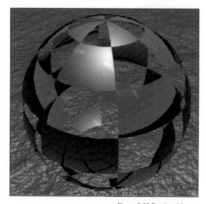

Figure 9-62 Connection Editor

Click the MMB on the Reverse Node, drag it above the Blinn Shader and link it to the Specular Color. Rendering the image, we can see that the reflection and the specular is not applied to the transparent regions making it appear as if there are holes in the sphere (see Figure 9-63).

Figure 9-63 Rendered Image

In this way, the Reverse utility is useful for creating contrary textures and linking them to the shader.

2-5. SET RANGE AND CLAMP

Set Range and Clamp acts to change the attribute values given to a shader. This utility is useful for changing attributes that cannot be changed or are difficult to change by hand. The following figures show the Set Range and Clamp node icons.

Set Range acts to change the given range. In other words, if the given range is 0-10, we can use Set Range to change the range to 0-1.

Figure 9-64 Set Range Node Icon

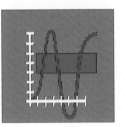

Clamp is a utility that allows us to use a certain range of values within a given range. In other words, we would use this utility if we wanted to use only the range of 0.2-0.4 within the given range of 0-1.

Figure 9-65 Clamp Node Icon

Many people make the mistake of confusing these 2 utilities. There is a big difference in what these 2 utilities do. One acts to reduce a given range, and the other allows us to use a specific range within a given range. Let's look at a simple example. Once you understand the concept, these utilities can be used to easily create a particular shader.

step 1   First of all, make a simple NURBS plane and make and arrange a Directional Light. Make a Blinn Shader and apply the Fractal from 2D Texture to the Bump. Open the Fractal Attribute Editor and, as shown in Figure 9-66, set the Repeat UV value to 0.2 in the 2dTexture tab. Double-click on the Bump Node to open the Attribute Editor, and set the Bump Depth value to 2 as shown in Figure 9-67.

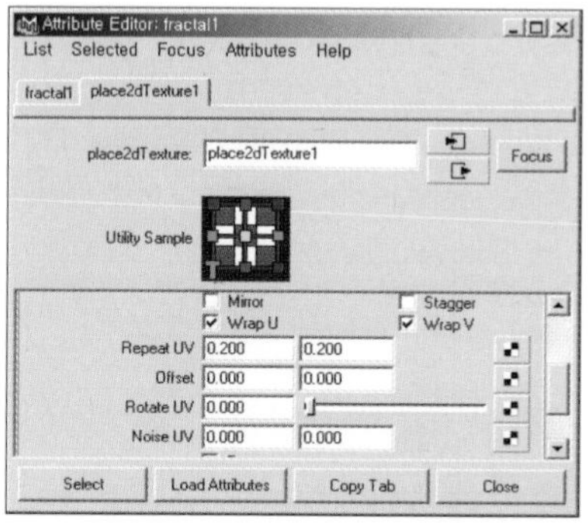

Figure 9-66 Attribute Editor 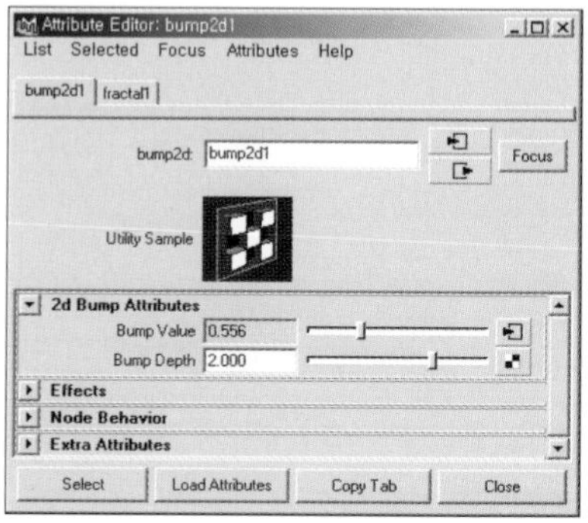   Figure 9-67 Attribute Editor

step 2 Assign the Blinn Shader to the NURBS plane and render the scene. It should like the image in Figure 9-68.

![Rendered Image]

Figure 9-68 Rendered Image

Now, let's see what differences come about by linking the Set Range and Clamp to the Bump. First, select the line connecting the Fractal and the Bump in the Hypershade and press the Delete key on the keyboard to disconnect the 2 nodes. Make a Set Range Node and arrange it as shown in Figure 9-69.

Figure 9-69 Hypergraph

Click the MMB on the Fractal and drag it above the Set Range. In the Connection Editor, link Out Alpha to Value X, as shown in Figure 9-70. Click the MMB on the Set Range and drag it above the Bump. In the Connection Editor, link Out Value X to the Bump value, as shown in Figure 9-71.

RENDER UTILITY & MAPPING TECHNIQUES

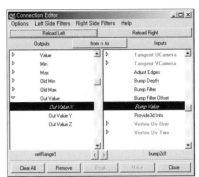

Figure 9-70 Connection Editor

Figure 9-71 Connection Editor

Rendering the image, we can see that there is no change.

First, let's take a look at the attributes we linked above. The Bump receives only one channel. In other words, even though it is a colored texture, when the Bump is calculated, the color is calculated as Luminance because only the luminosity is calculated.

The Out Put value is the value we use when we want to put out attributes from the Texture and Shader and link them to other attributes. In other words, when we want to link it to Color, we select Out Color, as we did in Figure 9-70. However, because it is being linked to Bump here, we use Out Alpha, instead of Out Color. Out Alpha is the value that only calculates the luminosity of the color and then sends it out. Therefore, we must link it to Out Alpha.

The problem lies with the value of the Input attribute of Set Range. This value generally has 3 channels, X, Y, and Z. This is because the range that we can adjust using Set Range includes, not only the one channel Alpha Channel, but the 3 R, G, B channels and the 3D X, Y, Z channels, as well.

However, we will generally use only one channel here. That is why we linked it to Value X. The value selected is entirely up to you. You could easily have linked it to Value Y or Value Z. Just make sure that you select the same channel as the one selected here when you select the Out Value (see Figure 9-71). In other words, because the Input Value is linked to Value X here, we must select Out Value X for the Out Put value of this node. In general, when the Bump is given a texture, the texture is linked to the Bump value. That is why we link Out Value X and the Bump value (see Figure 9-71).

step 3 Let's use the Set Range and see how it affects the Bump.

Double-click the Set Range Node to open the Attribute Editor.

Looking at the Attribute Editor (see Figure 9-72), we can see that the value is calculated by linking the Fractal Out Alpha to Value X. The 3 channels refer to, from left to right, the X, Y and Z channels.

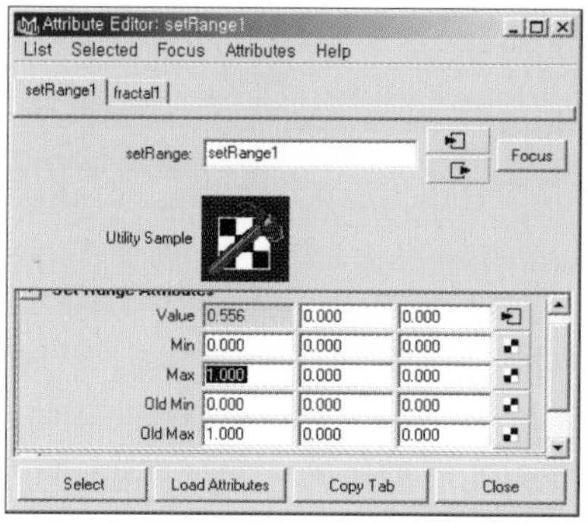

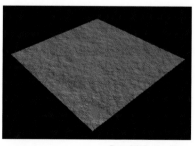

Figure 9-72 Attribute Editor

Opening the initial Attribute Editor, the Min, Max values and the Old Min, Max values should be set to 0. Change the values as shown in Figure 9-72. The Old Min, Max values are used to configure the first fractal range. In other words, this is where we specify the range of the Fractal Out Alpha. The range of one channel in Maya is 0-1. As explained before, 0 refers to black and 1 refers to white.

The Min, Max values are used to determine how the Old Min, Max values will be changed. Enter 0-0.2 here. Again, as explained before, we are reducing the range from 0-1 to 0-0.2. By rendering the image, we can see that the Bump Depth is rendered lightly (see Figure 9-73).

Figure 9-73 Rendered Image

Actually, although we set the Bump Depth to 2 in the beginning, the input value is merely between 0 and 0.2. So what we have done is reduce the Bump Depth value to 0.2 without using the Set Range. Keep testing different Min, Max values. You should be able to see that the amount of the Bump changes with the values.

 step 4 Let's test the Clamp Node this time. Delete the Set Range Node from Hypershade, and make and arrange the Clamp Node as shown in Figure 9-74.

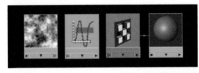

Figure 9-74 Hyphershade

Click the MMB on the Fractal, and drag it above the Clamp Node. In the Connection Editor, link Out Alpha to Input R, as shown in Figure 9-75. Click the MMB on the Clamp Node and drag it above the Bump Node. In the Connection Editor, link Output R to the Bump Value.

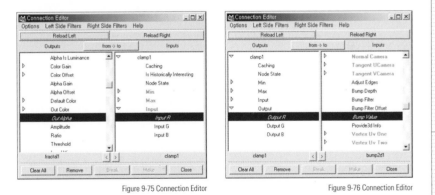

Figure 9-75 Connection Editor   Figure 9-76 Connection Editor

The Clamp Node, like the Set Range, also has 3 channels and is used in the same way.

step 5 Double-click on the Clamp Node to open the Attribute Editor and change the Min, Max value to 0.5-1.0, as shown in Figure 9-77.

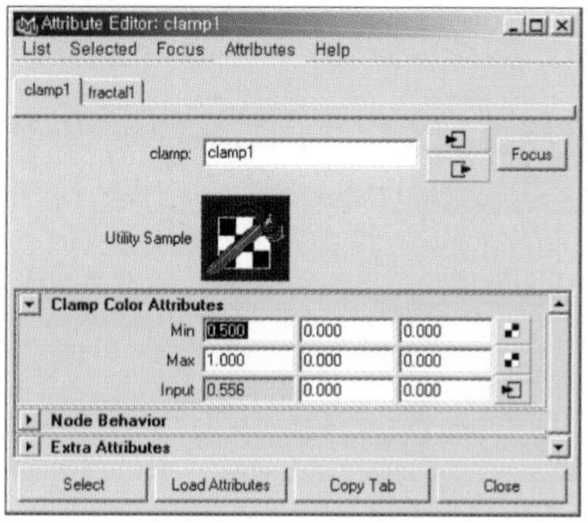

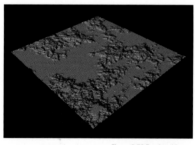

Figure 9-77 Attribute Editor

This means that we only want to use the range of 0.5-1 of the given range 0-1. As follows, rendering the image will give us the result seen in Figure 9-78. In other words, all values below 0.5 are ignored and the Bump is created as shown.

Figure 9-78 Rendered Image

Test the image by changing the Max value. This will change the concavity of the image.

We have finished looking at the differences in these 2 utilities. Summing up what we have learned, the Set Range acts to reduce the entire range so that the Bump is applied but with a weaker depth, much like adjusting the Depth value. Clamp cuts out a section of the range and, although it has no effect on the Bump Depth, the Bump only appears within the specified Min, Max value. The Bump was used here to simplify the explanation of these 2 utilities, but, in actuality, these utilities are not commonly used on the Bump.

On a lighter note, if we use the Clamp like the Bump and use the Min, Max value to keyframe, we get the following result.

For example, let's suppose that there is a very rough piece of wood and a carpenter is sanding the wood to create a smooth surface. A Bump is given using the rough texture of the wood, and the keyframing of the sanding process is done by gradually raising the Min value of the Clamp. This allows us to easily create a scene in which a rough texture becomes gradually smoother.

2-6. STENCIL UTILITY ▼

There are many ways to blend textures in Maya. We can mix several textures together using Layer Texture or we can blend shades using Layer Shader. No matter which other program you use, you will mix textures with Maya. If a mask is not available, we can use a particular color as a mask. The utility for this kind of work is the Stencil utility. Let's see how the Stencil utility is used through a simple example.

First, create a Blinn Shader, a Stencil utility and a File Texture in Hypershade and arrange them as shown in Figure 9-79. This file is saved as CD-ROM/CHARACTER/sourceimages/mayalogo.jpg.

Figure 9-79 Create Render Node

After clicking on the File Texture using the MMB and dragging it on top of the Stencil, link the Out Color and the image in the Connection Editor. Click the MMB on the Stencil, drag it above the Blinn Shader, and then link it to Color in the Connection Editor. Make a NURBS cube, assign a Blinn to the top, and then render the scene. The result, seen in Figure 9-80, is the simple rendering of the File Texture on the Blinn Color.

Figure 9-80 Rendered Image

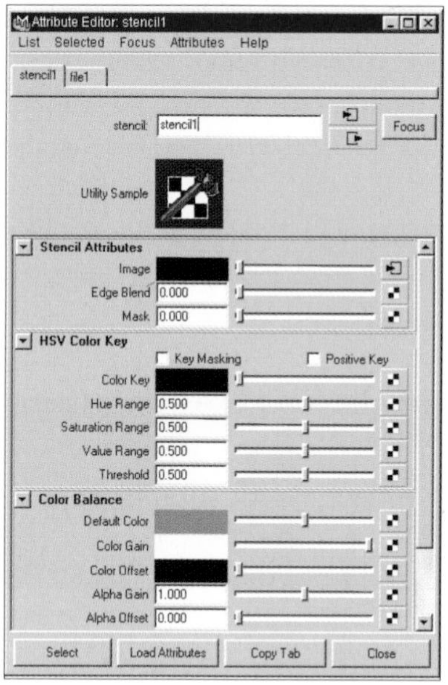

Figure 9-81 Attribute Editor

Double-click on the Stencil utility in the Hypershade to open the Attribute Editor. Make the configurations shown in Figure 9-81.

1. Image

We have already linked the File Texture to the image. In this way, we can place the desired texture in the image to decide the texture of the shader. Instead of using the Connection Editor, we can simply link the File Texture here by clicking the MMB on the File Texture in the Hypershade and dragging it into place.

2. Edge Blend

We can create a softer texture by blending the edges of the textures. This will be easier to understand by comparing the figure below.

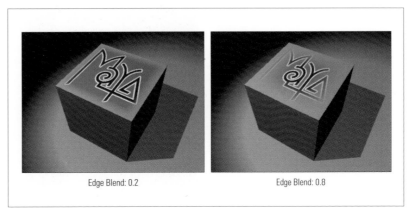

Edge Blend: 0.2   Edge Blend: 0.8

Figure 9-82 Using Edge Blend

3. Mask

We specify here the texture we want to use as a mask. We will be using the image in Figure 9-83 as the mask.

Figure 9-83 The Image to Be Used as the Mask

We usually use black-and-white images as a mask. As it was for the Transparency Map, the white areas will be cut out and only the black areas will remain as the image.

Open the Create Render Node window by clicking on ⬛ next to the slider bar. Select the file, and open CD-ROM/CHARACTER/Sourceimages/mayalogomask.jpg. By rendering the image, we should see the image in Figure 9-84.

Figure 9-84 Rendered Image

The background color, red, disappears due to the mask and the image is rendered in gray. The image is rendered in gray because this is the default color of the Stencil utility.
As shown in Figure 9-85, in the Stencil Utility Attribute Editor, change the default color to blue under Color Balance.

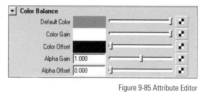

Figure 9-85 Attribute Editor

Rendering the image again, we can see that the image now renders in blue (see Figure 9-86). If we place a texture here now, the 2 textures will be blended using the mask. Figure 9-87 is the image rendered after placing the 3D texture, Crater, in the image.

For simple structures, like the one above, a mask is not necessary.

Figure 9-86 Rendered Image

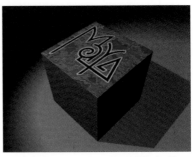

Figure 9-87 Rendered Image

4. HSV Color Key

Using the HSV Color Key allows us to easily use the specified color as the mask.

If you have been following along with the example above, erase the mask image linked to the Stencil utility in the Hypershade. In order to use the red area as the mask, put a check by Key Masking in the HSV Color Key. To select the desired color, click on the color box next to the Color Key to open the Color Chooser window (see Figure 9-88). Click on the Eyedropper Tool and click on the background of the File Texture Node displayed in the Hypershade (see Figure 9-89).

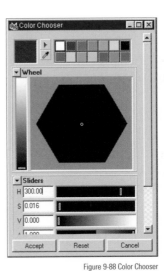

Figure 9-88 Color Chooser

Figure 9-89 Texture Node

Rendering the image will show the same image rendered in Figure 9-88. This utility is useful when using a simple color as a mask.

Hue, Saturation, and Value Range correspond to the ranges for color, saturation, and luminosity, respectively. For example, let's use the Ramp Texture, instead of the File Texture, for the Stencil utility image. Set the Ramp Type to Four Corner Ramp and render the image. The rendered image should look like the image in Figure 9-90.

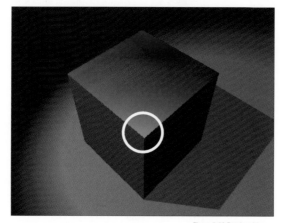

Figure 9-90 Rendered Image

Turn the Key Masking on and, select the green area indicated in Figure 9-90, using the Color Key to render the image seen in Figure 9-91.

Figure 9-91 Rendered Image

This is an example of how the green color disappears due to the mask. We use the Hue, Saturation, and Value Ranges to adjust this green range. The Hue Range is the color range. In other words, this range is used to determine how precisely the selected color will be masked. A lower value means that only colors close to the selected color will be masked.

In the same way, the lower the Saturation, for the color saturation, the lower the range. Value determines the luminosity range for the color. Again, a lower value refers to a narrower range. Adjust the values and see for yourself how the rendered image changes.

2-7. 2D ▦, 3D ▦ PLACEMENT

This is the utility that is created automatically when a 2D texture is made in Normal Mode or when a 3D texture is made. These Placement utilities, generally, determine how the 2D texture will be arranged in the UV-axis of the surface, and where and how big of a rotation value the 3D texture will have in space. Although these are utilities that are created automatically, they are especially useful in the following circumstances. Let's suppose that we have several surfaces and that each of the surfaces has a different texture (see Figure 9-92).

Figure 9-92 Surfaces with Different Textures

Figure 9-93 Hypershade

The Hypershade will look like that in Figure 9-93.

At times, you might want to make uniform the Placement attributes of all 3 textures. However, if the 3 textures each have different Placements, you will have to modify them one at a time. This is, without a doubt, both a very intricate and tedious thing to do.

However, we can link one Placement to each of the Texture Nodes to change the Placement attributes of all 3 textures at once. This is quite simple to do. Leaving behind the Checker Placement, delete the remaining two by selecting them and hitting the Delete key. Holding down the Ctrl key, click the MMB on the Placement Node and drag it above the Cloth Node and above the Bulge Node to link them together. The structure is shown in Figure 9-94. Now, we can control the Placement attributes of all textures using this Placement Node.

Verify the result by double-clicking the Placement Node to open the Attribute Editor. Test the results by changing the Repeat U, V and other attributes.

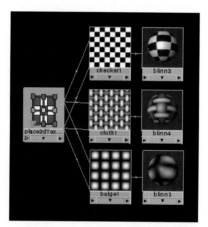

3D Placement is used in the same way.

Figure 9-94 Hypershade

2-8. CONTRAST

This utility is used to adjust the contrast of a Color Map. The contrast can be adjusted by adjusting each of the RGB channels. For example, make a File Texture, Contrast Utility and Blinn Shader in the Hypershade, as shown in Figure 9-95.

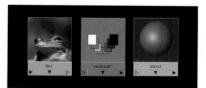

Figure 9-95 Attribute Editor

Clicking the MMB on the File Texture, drag it on top of the Contrast Node, and then link the Out Color of the File Texture to the Value of the Contrast in the Connection Editor. Clicking the MMB on the Contrast, drag it above the Blinn Shader and link it to the Color of the Blinn Shader. Double-click on the Contrast Node to open the Attribute Editor (see Figure 9-96). The Values refer to, from left to right, the RGB values of the given texture and the Contrast below that refers to the contrast of each channel. The Contrast will not be applied if this value is 1.

Figure 9-96 Attribute Editor

Figure 9-97 shows the images rendered at different Contrast values.

Contrast: 1, 1, 1   Contrast: 2, 2, 2   Contrast: 5, 5, 5

Figure 9-97 Images Rendered at Different Contrast Values

By adjusting the Contrast vale of the Texture file, we can obtain clearer results.

2-9. BLEND COLORS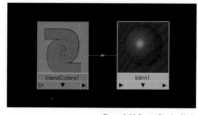

This utility is used to blend 2 colors together. This utility can also be used to blend textures together. First of all, make a Blinn Shader and Blend Color Node, as shown in Figure 9-98, and link the Blend Color to the Blinn Color.

Figure 9-98 Create Render Node

Double-click on the Blend Color Node to open the Attribute Editor. As shown in Figure 9-100, Color 1 is red and Color 2 is blue. Set the Blender value to 0.5. As follows, Color 1 and Color 2 will blend together in a 5:5 ratio to give a violet Out Color.
The lower the Blender value, the closer the Out Color will be to Color 2 and the higher the value, the closer it will be to Color 1.

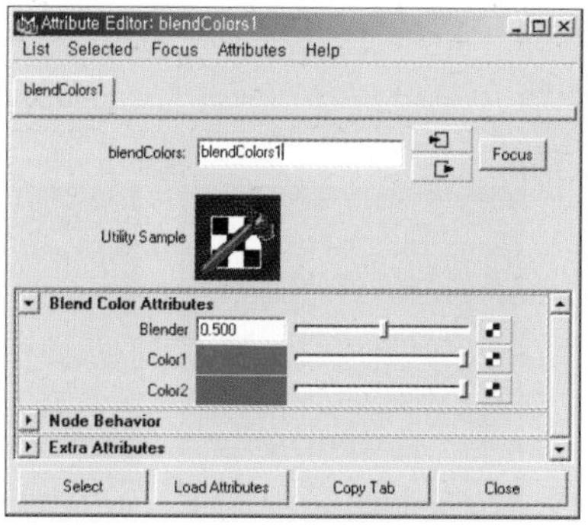

Figure 9-99 Attribute Editor

Let's run a simple test by linking this to the Sampler Info we learned about earlier.
As shown in Figure 9-100, make a Sampler Info Node in the Hypershade and link the Facing Ratio of the Sampler Info to the Blender attribute of the Blend in the Connection Editor.

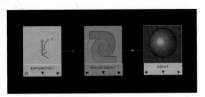

Figure 9-100 Linking the Sample Info to the Blend Color

Make a NURBS sphere and assign it to the Blinn Shader. Then, render the scene (see Figure 9-101). As we learned earlier, when the camera faces the Normal of the surface, the Normal value is 1, and when they are perpendicular, the Normal value is 0. Therefore, as we move from the front of the sphere to the outside, the color changes from Color 1 to Color 2.

Figure 9-101 Rendered Image

We can change the texture to have a dissolving effect by keyframing the Blender attribute. Place the Checker Texture in Color 1 and the Fractal Texture in Color 2 and move the time slider to Frame1. Then, set the Blender to 0 and keyframe it. After moving the time slider to Frame30, set the Blender to 1 and keyframe it. To make a keyframe, click the RMB on the Blender Text and select Set Key. After rendering in IPR, move the frame.

We can see that the texture dissolves from Fractal to Checker.

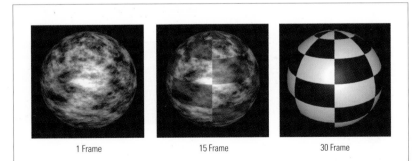

| 1 Frame | 15 Frame | 30 Frame |

Figure 9-102 Dissolving the Texture

2-10. SURFACE LUMINANCE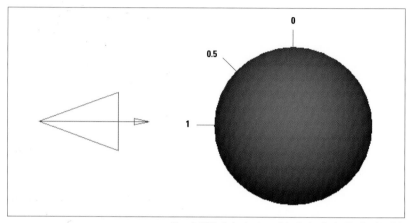

This utility is similar to Sampler Info, but whereas Sampler Info depicted the relationship between the camera and the Normal of the surface, Surface Luminance deals with the relationship between the light and the Normal of the surface. Let's look at Figure 9-103. As shown in the figure, when the light faces the Normal, the value is 1 and when the Light is perpendicular to the Normal, the value is 0.

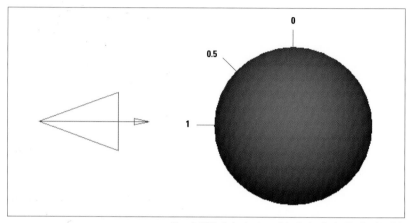

Figure 9-103 The Surface Luminance Value Depicted by the Direction of the Light

At times, this utility can be very useful. We can make a certain area of the surface that is illuminated by the light brighter than any other area.

Let's look at a simple example using Surface Luminance together with Blend Color. First, make a Surface Luminance, aBlender, and a Blinn Shader in Hypershade, as shown in Figure 9-104, and then link the Out Value of the Surface Luminance to the Blender of Blend Color and link the Blend Color to the Blinn Color.

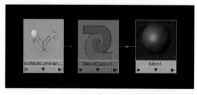

Figure 9-104 Create Render Node

Now, make a NURBS sphere and a Directional Light. Assign the Blinn Shader to the NURBS sphere and render the image. As shown in Figure 9-105, the area of the surface illuminated by the light will be displayed in red, Color 1. Test the image by changing the Directional Light. You should continue to see the color red.

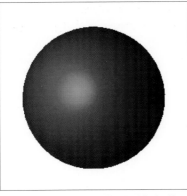

Figure 9-105 Rendered Image

We can use the Surface Luminance utility to make a fun shader. We can have the illuminated surface portrayed using color. Make a Surface Luminance, Ramp Texture, and Surface Shader in Hyphershade as shown in Figure 9-106. Link the Out Value of the Surface Luminance to the V Coord of the Ramp. Link the Out Color of the Ramp to the Out Color of the Surface Shader.

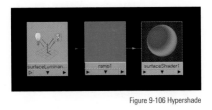

Figure 9-106 Hypershade

Assign the shader to the model and render the image after creating and arranging an appropriate Point Light. The rendered image should like the image in Figure 9-107.

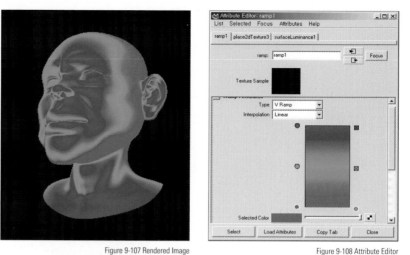

Figure 9-107 Rendered Image

Figure 9-108 Attribute Editor

Open the Ramp Attribute Editor (see Figure 9-108). Because the Type is set to V Ramp, we link the Out Value of the Surface Luminance to the V Coord. This means is that, within the Ramp range of 0-1, areas where the light faces the Normal of the surface will be illuminated using Color 1 and areas where the light is perpendicular to the Normal will be illuminated using Color 2. Figure 9-109 shows a test rendering after changing the ramp color. It is also a good idea to change the direction of the light and see how the color changes as a result.

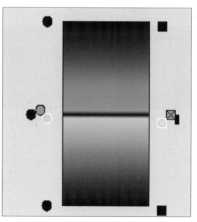

Figure 9-109 Changing the Ramp Color

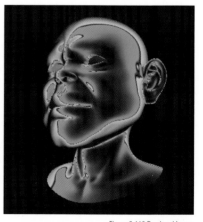

Figure 9-110 Rendered Image

2-11. GAMMA CORRECT

Gamma refers to the light and the relationship between the luminance that is seen on the monitor in response to a video input signal. The objective for all video output devices is to produce a realistic and faithful image. However, not all display devices can create an output for these tones, preventing them from re-creating a faithful image. We can correct this, however, by adjusting the Gamma value as needed. Most graphic programs include an option that allows users to adjust the Gamma value.

The Gamma Correct utility uses this theory and adjusts the Gamma value of each RGB channel to restore the image. It is quite simple to use. In Hypershade, make a random File Texture, Gamma Correct Utility, and Blinn Shader, as shown in Figure 9-111.

Figure 9-111 Hypershade

Link the Out Color of the File Texture to the Gamma Value, and link the Gamma to the Blinn Color. Render the image after making and assigning a NURBS plane.

Figure 9-112 Rendered Image

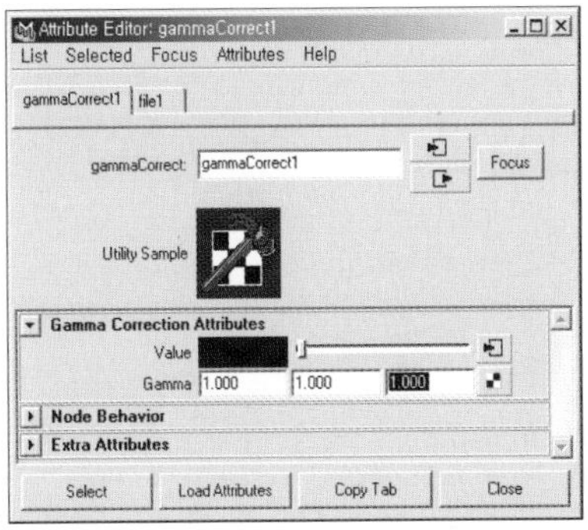

Figure 9-113 Attribute Editor

Adjust the Gamma value by double-clicking on the Gamma Correct Node to open the Attribute Editor. Looking at the Attribute Editor in Figure 9-113, we can see that the Gamma Value of the RGB Channel is currently set to 1. This has no effect on the image whatsoever. Only the lowering or raising of this value will affect the image. Change this value and render the image to see how this value affects the result.

Gamma: 0.5, 0.5, 0.5   Gamma: 2.0, 2.0, 2.0   Gamma: 5.0, 1.0, 1.0

Figure 9-114 Images Rendered at Differing Gamma Values

2-12. LUMINANCE

This utility takes the 3 RGB color channels and makes them into a luminance channel.
In other words, the color is converted to gray. First, make a random File Texture, Luminance Node, and Blinn Shader in Hypershade, as shown in Figure 9-115. Link the Out Color of the File Texture to the Luminance Value, and link the Out Value of the Luminance to the Blinn Shader Color. Because the Out Value of the Luminance has only one channel, we must link the RGB colors separately in the Connection Editor, as shown in Figure 9-116.

Figure 9-115 Hypershade

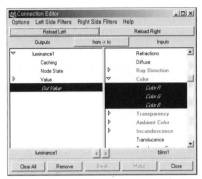

Figure 9-116 Connection Editor

After making a NURBS plane and assigning it to the shader, render the image. As we can see in Figure 9-117, the image is rendered in gray.

Figure 9-117 Rendered Image

In addition to converting the image color to gray, this utility is also used to make visible the Texture Out Alpha value. The attributes of the shader, connected to the Out Alpha of the Texture, include one-channel attributes, such as Bump, Diffuse, or Glow Intensity. In other words, the shader attributes do not have a color box, but a value field in which we can enter the desired value. In general, when textures are linked to such attributes, the Out Value of the texture is linked to the respective attribute and is, therefore, not used frequently. However, it becomes very useful when it is made visible for the purposes of using a precise value. For example, let's suppose we want to link the Color Texture to the Bump. This utility is a good way to link to the Bump.

2-13. HSV TO RGB 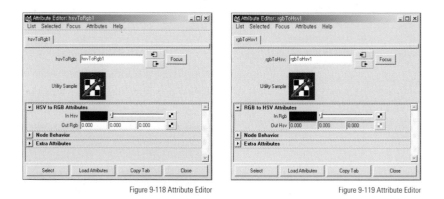, RGB TO HSV

These 2 utilities are used to change the HSV color mode to RGB and the RGB color mode to HSV, respectively. Let's look at the HSV To RGB Attribute Editor in Figure 9-118. Link the texture for which we want to change the color mode to In Hsv and link the Out Rgb to the shader color. Figure 9-119 shows the Attribute Editor for the RGB To HSV. Link the texture for which we want to change the color mode to In Rgb and link the Out Hsv to the shader color.

Figure 9-118 Attribute Editor

Figure 9-119 Attribute Editor

2-14. OTHER GENERAL UTILITIES

There are a few other general utilities in addition to the ones we have covered here. I find it difficult to offer specific examples for these utilities because I have not had much experience with these other utilities. However, I give a brief manual-type description here so that you can have some understanding of what these utilities do. I suggest that you visit the various sites that offer shader samples to help you understand these utilities.

1. Multiply Divide

This utility performs the operations of multiplication and division on the Input values. The Multiply Divide utility has 2 Input attributes, each of which has 3 channels each for color and position.

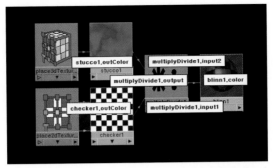

Figure 9-120 Shading Network

Figure 9-120 shows the Shading Network using Multiply Divide. By double-clicking on the Multiply Divide Node to open the Attribute Editor, we can see 4 operations. No Operation, as the name states, does not perform any operations. In this case, it only computes what is linked to Input 1. Multiply multiplies Input 1 and Input 2 and Divide divides Input 1 and Input 2. Power gives us the square of Input 1 and Input 2.

2. Plus Minus Average ±A

The Plus Minus Average utility, as the name suggests, gives the sum, difference, and average of the values. The Attribute Editor for this utility can be seen in Figure 9-121.

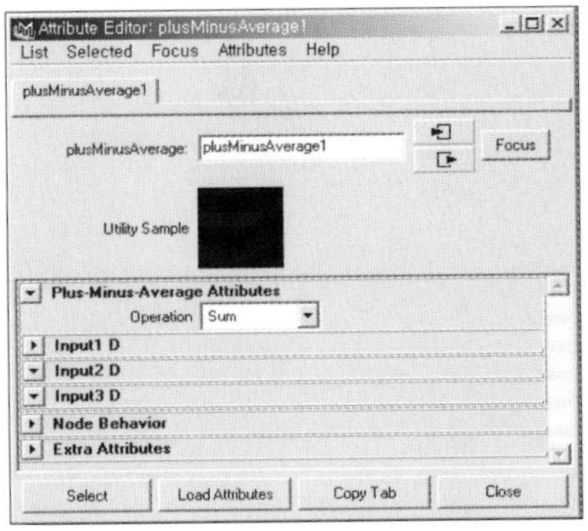

Figure 9-121 Attribute Editor

Looking at the operations, No Operation does not perform any operations and Sum adds up the values. Subtract gives us a difference of the values and Average takes the average of the values.

Let's take a brief look at how these utilities are used. Input1D accepts only one attribute. For example, we can only link to one (either R, G, or B) channel in Color. Input2D can accept 2 attributes. For example, this channel is used when we want to link to 2 values, such as the UV-axis. Input3D can accept 3 attributes. Here, we can link to all three RGB channels or Translate X,Y,Z. We can use a simple expression to restrict the movement of the object. As shown in Figure 9-122, make 3 NURBS spheres and move the X-axis in evenly spaced intervals in Front View.

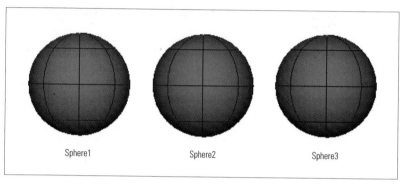

Figure 9-122 Making NURBS Spheres

Make a Plus Minus Average Node in Hypershade. Then, open the Outliner and click the MMB on each sphere and drag them into the Hypershade.

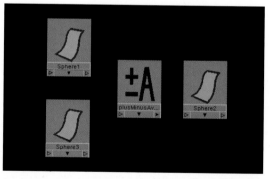

Figure 9-123 Hypershade

Click the MMB on the Sphere1 Node and drag it above the Plus Minus Average Node. Then, link Translate X and Input1D in the Connection Editor. Click the MMB on the Sphere3 Node and drag it above the Plus Minus Average Node. In the Connection Editor, we want to link Translate X of Sphere3 to Input1D, but we can see that these attributes are already connected.

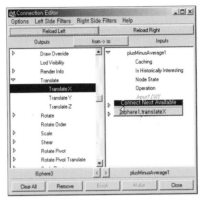

Also, because Translate X is one channel, we must link it to Input1D. At this time, a new Input1D attribute must be made. As shown in Figure 9-124, select Translate X of Sphere3. Then, click the RMB on top of Input1D and select Connect Next Available from the menu.

Figure 9-124 Connection Editor

A new Input1D is made and it is linked to the selected channel. Now, click the MMB on the Plus Minus Average Node and drag it above the Sphere2 Node. In the Connection Editor, link Output1D to Translate X.

Set the Operation to Average and move either Sphere1 or Sphere3 to the X-axis. We can see that Sphere2 is always positioned in the middle of 2 spheres. Let's try setting the Operation to Sum or Subtract. We can see how the expressions limit the movement of the object.

In addition to these utilities, we have Vector Product, Array Mapper, UV Chooser, and Light Info. You will probably need some mathematical knowledge to estimate the output of the Vector Product utility. For me, with limited mathematical knowledge, I find some parts of this utility to be difficult to understand. Array Mapper applies and automatically creates an Age Map on the particle. UV Chooser is a utility that automatically creates when several UV sets are made. Light Info is used to determine the position and direction of the light and the distance between the light and the Shading Point. Using the Intensity Curve of the Spot Light, we can observe the role of this node. Intensity Curve will be covered in further detail later.

2-15. SWITCH

With the Switch utility, we can easily create shaders with several textures of the same material. This utility is useful when used with Multi-Patch to model the face. Although the face uses one material, this utility allows us to easily apply different textures to each patch. There are 3 different types of Switch utilities, Double Switch, Single Switch, and Triple Switch. These different types of switches are related to the shader channels. In other words, for shader attributes that offer a color box and 3 RGB channels, such as Color, Transparency or Ambient, we would use Triple Switch. For attributes that offer only one channel, such as Bump or Diffuse, we would use Single Switch. Double Switch doe not have shader attributes. This switch is used in Placement to control the UV-axis of the texture. In other words, for 2D Placement, for example, Repeat UV or Translate UV would be good examples. To me, Double Switch is not that useful. Of course, it may come in handy in certain occasions; however, the same results can be achieved using the 2D Placement utility. Because these switches are all used in the same way, the only difference being the number of channels that are used, I will explain this utility using Triple Switch.

1. Triple Switch

In Figure 9-125, we have a surface made up of 4 patches. All use the Blinn Material with only a different texture used in each patch. Make a Triple Switch Node in Hypershade, and double-click it to open the Attribute Editor.

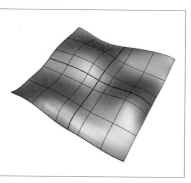

Figure 9-125 4 NURBS Surfaces

Select [Window > Outliner] to open the Outliner. Click the MMB on the NURBS surface name in the Outliner, as shown in Figure 9-126, and drag it to InShape in the Triple Switch Attribute Editor.

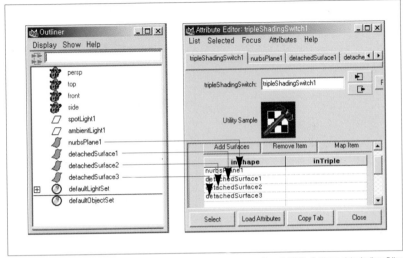

Figure 9-126 The Outliner and the Attribute Editor

As shown in Figure 9-126, click and drag all 4 surfaces to the Attribute Editor. As shown in Figure 9-127, make the textures that will correspond to the 4 surfaces. In order to link these textures to the desired surface, click the MMB on the Checker and then drag it to InTriple in the Attribute Editor.

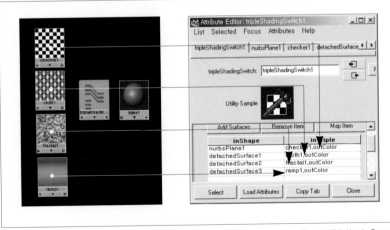

Figure 9-127 Linking the Textures

Now, after linking the Triple Switch Node to the Blinn Color in the Hypershade, assign this Blinn to the 4 NURBS surfaces. Although the surfaces are made up of one material, each of the surfaces will have a different texture (see Figure 9-128) as a result.

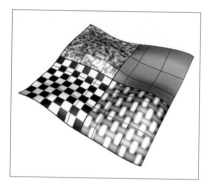

Figure 9-128 An Example of Using Triple Switch

3. FACE MAPPING

Figure 9-129 Face Mapping Example

There are a variety of different colors in the human face. In general, when Map Source is used, the image is usually portrayed using only one color. However, this is not right. If you look carefully at the human face, you can see that it contains shades of red, blue, and green. Therefore, all of these colors must be used to create a rich and realistic source image.

In 3D, in most cases, an actual photograph is used as the map source. This is the quickest way to create a realistic expression. However, I don't recommend this method. Simply scanning a photograph for use is not enough. You must run a series of tests in order to arrive at a source that will fully portray the textures of the skin.

In this section, we will look at a face that has already been created and see how the source was made. I prefer to paint and create the source directly, rather than to scan an image of a face.

Of course, this is simply my preference, and there is no rule that states that one method is better than another. You should select the method that is easiest and works best for you.

In the next section, we will see how the sources, created using Deep Paint 3D, are used.

3-1. COLOR MAP

Figure 9-130 shows the Color Map Source and the image rendered using only the Color Map. I usually use Blinn Shader to portray the skin. I prefer to use Blinn Shader because it is quite easy to adjust the Specular.

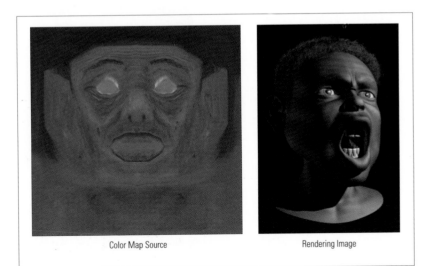

Color Map Source   Rendering Image

Figure 9-130 The Map Source and the Rendered Image

This Color Map is saved as CD-ROM/CHARACTER/sourceimages/MANFACEColor.jpg. Try opening this file in Photoshop, and observe every corner of this file. The completed image is obtained by adding random touches of green and blue to the brown color. Also, brighter areas and areas that are wrinkled and receive less light were made into a map. Since the Color Map will be the base for which the texture of the character's skin will be portrayed, it should be made very carefully.

3-2. BUMP MAP

The presence of a Bump Map makes a huge difference in the texture of the character. The human skin is made up of tiny, miniscule wrinkles. The same is true for the face. Although these tiny wrinkles can be made using Noise, the wrinkles made using the Color Map need to be portrayed using Bump Map. The Bump Map is illustrated in Figure 9-131.

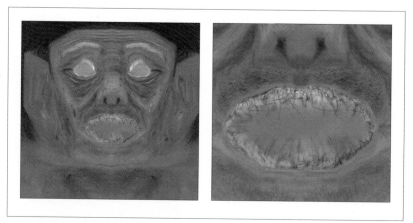

Figure 9-131 Bump Map Source

This file is also saved in the supplementary CD-ROM under CD-ROM/CHARACTER/sourceimages/MANFACEBUMP.jpg. Let's take a closer look at the mouth of the character shown in Figure 9-131. Of all the areas of the skin, the lips are the area with the most wrinkles. We can see in the figure that many lines were drawn to portray the wrinkles of the lips.

The Color Map was converted to gray in Photoshop because it serves as the foundation upon which the Bump Map Source is made. This image was completed by adjusting the brightness and contrast of the color and then by adding detail using Deep Paint 3D.

Figure 9-132 shows the image rendered after applying the Bump.

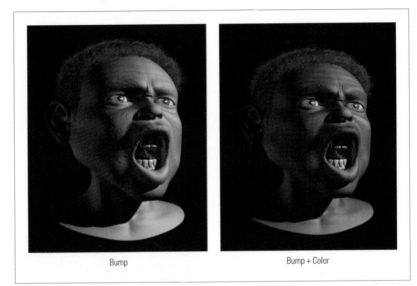

Bump

Bump + Color

Figure 9-132 Rendered Image

3-3. SPECULAR MAP

Many users fail to notice the importance of the Specular Map. The human skin is made up of so many colors because of the abundance of color reflected as light hits the face. Some areas give off a reddish hue, while other areas give off a bluish hue. Depending on the light, a variety of different colors are reflected off the skin. However, despite this fact, many people do not use Specular or use it with black or white only. This is a big mistake. A different Specular Map must be made for the different colors of the human complexion.

Figure 9-133 illustrates an image made using a black-and-white Specular Map.

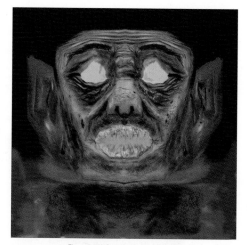

Figure 9-133 Specular Image Made Using Black and White

Figure 9-134 shows the image above rendered using a Specular Map.

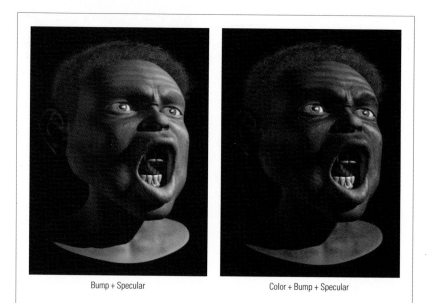

Bump + Specular   Color + Bump + Specular

Figure 9-134 Rendered Image

Perhaps the difference is not so clear by looking at the figures in this book, but the image rendered using a black-and-white Specular looks clouded and turbid. In such cases, it becomes very difficult to accurately portray the colors of the skin.

Let's look at Figure 9-135. This is an image rendered using a color Specular Map.

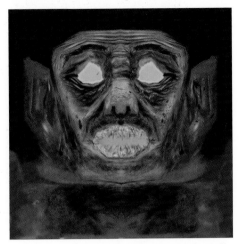

Figure 9-135 Image Rendered Using a Color Specular Map

Looking at the figure, we can see that a variety of different colors have been used in the cheeks, the bridge of the nose, and the lips. We can see shades of pink, yellow, brown, green and blue. A strong pink color is used on the inside and outside of the lips. Strong lines and a dry color are used to portray the parched lips. I would make this Specular Map using Bump. In general, brighter areas protrude in the Bump Map and, therefore, will appear to protrude in the Specular Map.

Taking advantage of this characteristic, a strong contrast will be applied to the Bump Map Source and then color will be applied. Figure 9-136 shows the image rendered using Specular and color. If the results are difficult to distinguish, refer to the data in the CD-ROM. The black-and-white Specular Map is saved as MANFACESP.jpg, and the color Specular Map is saved as MANFACESP2.jpg.

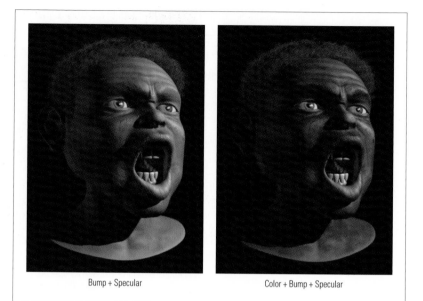

Bump + Specular   Color + Bump + Specular

Figure 9-136 Rendered Image

This completes the study of the basic features necessary for face mapping. For more detailed representation, we can also use Diffuse, Ambient, and Incandescence. Because human complexions are unique and diverse, you should test and practice with many different options until you find a method that works for you.

4. MAPPING TECHNIQUE

In this section, we will look at the entire process from scanning a picture to modeling and then, finally, mapping. Only Maya and Photoshop will be used for this example. No other 3D painting software will be used. Try to understand the overall workflow, from the initial planning to modeling to mapping.

In this example, we will map and model a combat boot using NURBS modeling. This is the work of Oh-deuk Kwon, who teaches Mapping at the Ma-p-ya Academy.

step 1 First of all, scan a picture of the combat boot. All we did was place an actual boot on top of the scanner and scanned it into the computer. After making a NURBS plane of the scanned image in Front, Side, and Top views, map the scanned image in the NURBS plane as shown in Figure 9-138. This kind of modeling technique is very accurate, as you can see the proportions of the model to the actual boot.

Figure 9-137 Scanned Image

Figure 9-138 Mapping in the NURBS Plane

In addition to this method, we can also place the scanned image in the image plane in the Camera Attribute Editor of each view, as shown in Figure 9-139.

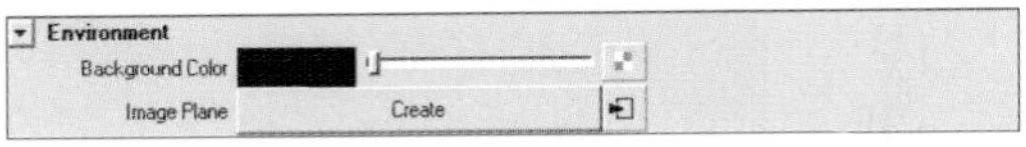

Environment		
Background Color		
Image Plane	Create	

Figure 9-139 Camera Attribute Editor

When using the image plane, the specified image will be placed in the scene, as shown in Figure 9-140. The image plane is affected largely by the system's graphic card. Therefore, some graphic cards may largely reduce system speed. If, after loading the image plane, the system speed drops sharply, it will be better to use the plane mapping method described above.

Figure 9-140 Import Image Plane

step 2 Now, after placing the 3 NURBS planes far away from the work area, make a layer and then include it in this layer as a reference before beginning to work. This NURBS plane only serves as a substitute for the image plane and should be referenced so as not to interfere with work during modeling.

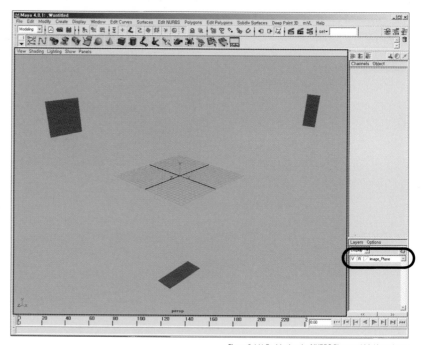

Figure 9-141 Positioning the NURBS Plane and Making a Layer

Before we begin to model, we should closely observe the boot. In order to model it as one NURBS model, we need to effectively slice the surface.

Figure 9-142 Structural Elements of the Model

Let's look at Figure 9-142. We can largely divide the boot into the ankle portion (red), the heel (yellow), and the foot (white).

Let's model the red area first.

step 3 Select [Create > NURBS Primitives > Cylinder] to make a NURBS cylinder, and adjust the basic size and lean as shown in Figure 9-143. Detach the surface as shown in Figure 9-144.

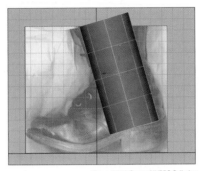

Figure 9-143 Create NURBS Cylinder

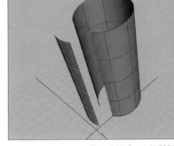

Figure 9-144 Detach NURBS Cylinder

Now, we need to create a large lump by adjusting the CVs. An example of this is shown in Figure 9-145.

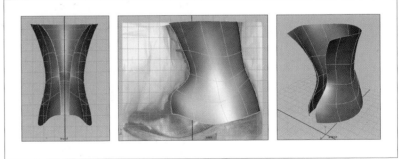

Figure 9-145 The Modeling Process

After modeling the basic lump, we need to add detail. One thing to be careful of here is that, as shown in Figure 9-146, the direction of the isoparm must follow the direction of the wrinkles in the boot as the boot is moved. If this fact is ignored, our task becomes very difficult during the animation. In general, the direction of the surface is made to follow the flow of the isoparm.

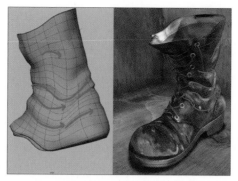

Figure 9-146 The Flow of the Isoparm

Figure 9-148 illustrates the modeling process. We trim the overall shape rather than a specific detail of the boot to easily and accurately portray the boot.

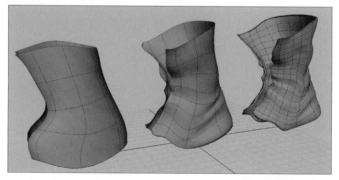

Figure 9-147 Modeling Process

Figure 9-148 illustrates the modeling process of the remaining elements. In general, we use the NURBS cylinder, trim the shape as minimally as we can using CVs, and add isoparms as needed.

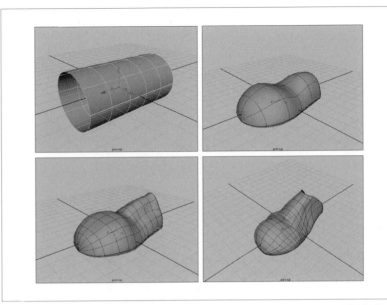

Figure 9-148 Modeling Process

Model all the elements of the boot in this way. We must portray the small wrinkles and the contours of the boot in order to create an effective and realistic portrayal of the boot. Figure 9-149 shows the completed model. Because we need to consider the animation process as we model, think about how the boot will move and add isoparms as needed.

Figure 9-149 Completed Model

There are a few things we need to keep in mind as we model. In order to apply the desired image to the desired position, the spacing between the isoparms must be uniform. If the spacing is not uniform, the map will not be applied evenly as seen in Figure 9-150.

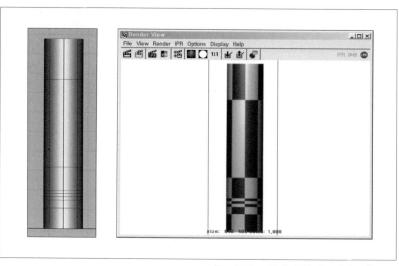

Figure 9-150 Image Rendered Using Unevenly Spaced Isoparms

There are 2 ways to prevent this from happening. One way is to use Rebuild Surface during the modeling process. By checking the CVs in the Rebuild Surface Options window, the spacing between the isoparms will be equalized. It is better to do this during the modeling process rather than at the end. Doing this at the end may change the shape drastically.

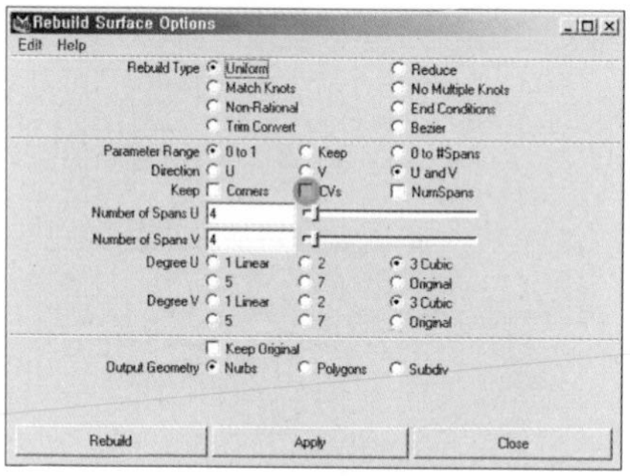

Figure 9-151 Rebuild Surface Options Window

The second method is to open the Surface Attribute Editor and put a check by [Texture Map > Fix Texture Wrap], as shown in Figure 9-152.

Figure 9-153 Attribute Editor

By activating the Fix Texture Wrap and then rendering the image, we can see that the texture is evenly applied to the model.

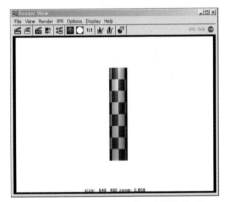

Figure 9-153 Rendered Image

Using these 2 methods together can correct, to some degree, a severely distorted map.

step 4 In this example, an actual boot was taken apart, scanned, the texture modified and used as a map source. Scanned images need to be restored in Photoshop, and a few retouching steps need to be done to correct the image.

Figure 9-154 Scanned Image

In order to spread out the image as shown in Figure 9-154, the areas that are cut need to be fixed in Photoshop. Fill up empty spaces by copying and pasting a rather large and clean area of the scanned image.

Use the Eraser Tool to erase the borders of the pasted image so that it does not stand out from the original image. Select the Eraser Tool and reduce the Hardness value of the Brush options (see Figure 9-155) before using the Eraser Tool.

Figure 9-155 Brush Options

At the same time, we need to remove the light that is reflected on the boot. The areas indicated in Figure 9-156 were illuminated and highlighted during the scanning process, and these areas must be removed.

Figure 9-156 Reflected Areas

Such reflected areas interfere with the adjusting of the Shader Specular later, making it difficult to create a realistic image. We need to do the following in order to remove the reflection.

In Photoshop, make an empty layer as shown in Figure 9-157. After selecting this layer, set the Blend Mode to Multiply and the Opacity to 35 (see Figure 9-158).

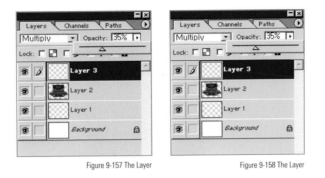

Figure 9-157 The Layer   Figure 9-158 The Layer

Now, after setting the Foreground Color to black, paint over the reflections in the boot using the Air Brush. We will be painting in black in the layer; however, because the Blend Mode is set to Multiply, the 2 layers will overlap only in the bright regions of the boot. The modified image is shown in Figure 9-159. We can see that most of the reflection has been removed from the boot.

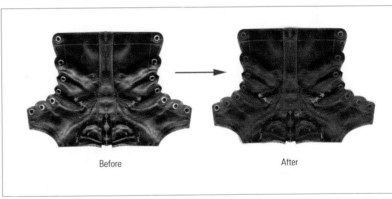

Before   After

Figure 9-159 Modifying the Reflections in the Boot

The holes for the shoestrings in the boot can also be removed using the Stamp Tool. The scanned image is now ready to be used as a map source.

step 5 We will now apply this map to the modeling data. Let's look at how to map the ankle of the boot. Set the File Texture to Projection in Side View, and set the Projection Type to Planer. Figure 9-160 shows the placement of the Projection Manipulator, and Figure 9-161 shows the organization of the Shader in Hypershade.

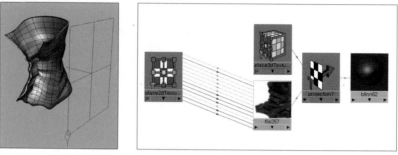

Figure 9-160 Projection

Figure 9-161 Hypershade

step 6 Press the 7 key so that the texture will be displayed in the view. Make the texture clearer by selecting the surface and pressing Ctrl+A to open the Attribute Editor. In the Attribute Editor, select Highest from under Texture Quality in the Hardware section (see Figure 9-162).

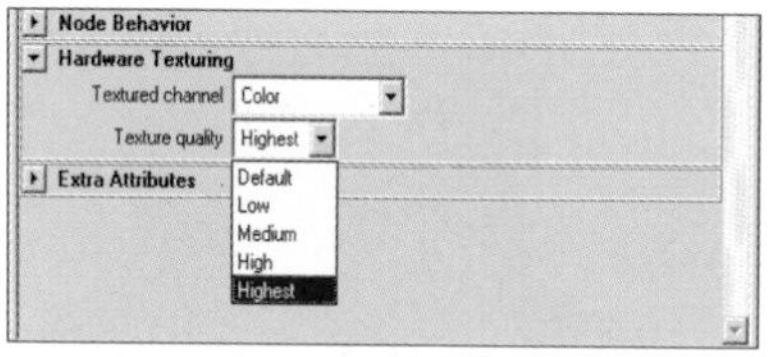

Figure 9-162 Attribute Editor

This should create a cleaner display of the texture, as seen in Figure 9-163.

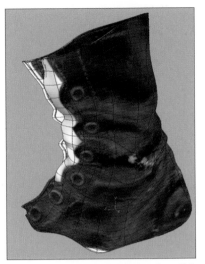

Figure 9-163 Hardware Texture Mode

Figure 9-164 Adjusting the Place3Dtexture

Now, as shown in Figure 9-164, adjust the Place3Dtexture in Side View so that the texture is placed correctly.

After adjusting the Place3Dtexture as accurately as you can (a complete match will be impossible, but try to place it as accurately as you can), select Shader and Surface from the Hypershade. Select [Edit > Convert to File Texture] to open the Convert to File Texture Options window. Configure the options as shown in Figure 9-165.

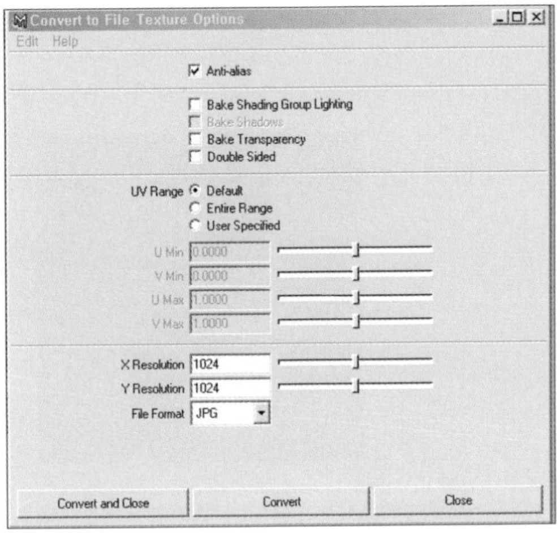

Figure 9-165 Options Window

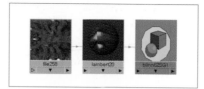
Figure 9-166 The New File and Shader

After applying the Convert to File Texture and observing the Hypershade, we can see the files shown in Figure 9-166. Convert to File Texture. Make and link the images to the file texture. This image is then loaded back into Photoshop for more editing.

step 7 By looking at the image in Photoshop, we can see that the map seems to be pushed to one side.

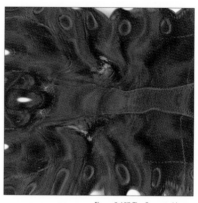
Figure 9-167 The Converted Image

Because the image was converted using Projection, the map is pushed off to one side as it tries to match itself to the surface UV. We need to clean up this image. This step takes a lot of time. Let's compare the original and the converted images. We can see these 2 images in Figure 9-168.

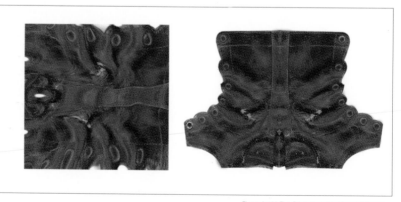
Figure 9-168 The Original and the Converted Images

Now let's compare the 2 images. In contrast to the original image, we can see that parts of the converted image are pushed to one side and severely distorted. We can modify this by copying the similar area from the original image and pasting it onto the severely distorted area of the converted image.

Figure 9-169 shows the similar regions in both the original and converted images. Let's now copy this area onto the converted image.

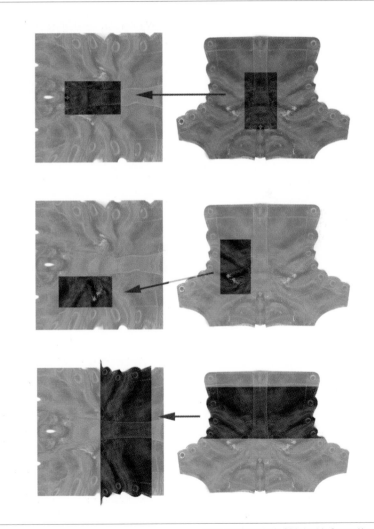

Figure 9-169 Comparing the Original and the Converted Images

Figure 9-170 shows how the similar region in the original image was copied and pasted onto the converted image. After pasting the image, use the Eraser Tool to erase the edges so that the pasted image blends into its surroundings.

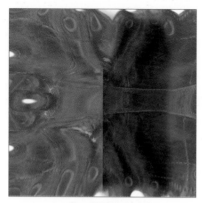

Figure 9-170 Restoring the Converted Image

In order to restore sections that are different, we copy a reasonably acceptable region from the original image and paste it onto the converted image. In such instances, each surface must be mapped and the map source must be modified using Photoshop.

step 8 Looking at Figure 9-171, we can see that some areas in the boot are severely worn. This is a good way to portray the faded textures of the boot.

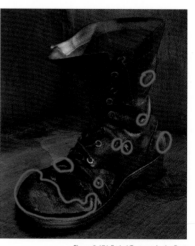

Figure 9-171 Faded Textures in the Boot

In order to create these textures, first, we need to open the texture in Photoshop. Then, as shown in Figure 9-172, we make a layer and, after selecting a portion of the frame, color it in as shown.

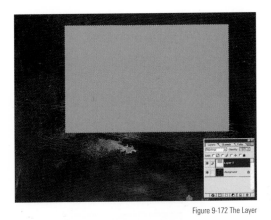

Figure 9-172 The Layer

Set the Blend Mode of the layer to Multiply (see Figure 9-173). We can see that, as a result, the colored top layer is blended into the bright areas of the lower layer (see Figure 9-174).

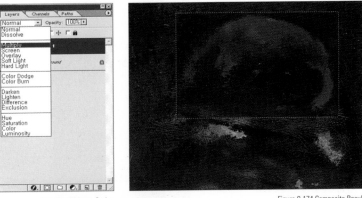

Figure 9-173 Layer Option

Figure 9-174 Composite Result

Figure 9-175 Completed Image

Use the Eraser Tool on the edges of the selected region so that it blends in with its surroundings. The completed image is shown in Figure 9-175.

We have now completed the map sources, which will be used in the boot.
Figure 9-176 shows the final Color Map sources of each constituent.

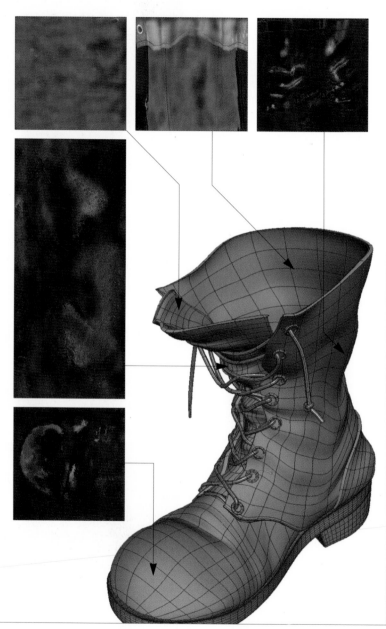

Figure 9-176 Color Sources to Be Used in Each Constituent of the Boot.

step 9 Let's now make the Specular Map. The Specular Map will brighten the areas that are illuminated by light.

The 3D Paint Tool is a good tool to use to find these illuminated areas. First of all, disconnect the Color and the File Texture, so that we can use the 3D Paint Tool to link to the color. First, select the surface to be painted and then select [Rendering > Texturing > 3D Paint Tool] to open the Options window. Click on the Assign Texture button and adjust the resolution of the texture, as shown in Figure 9-177.

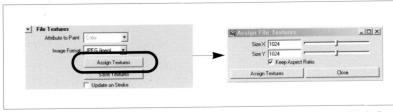

Figure 9-177 Assign Texture

Select the color red, and color in the areas on the boot that will be illuminated and for which a Specular will be made.

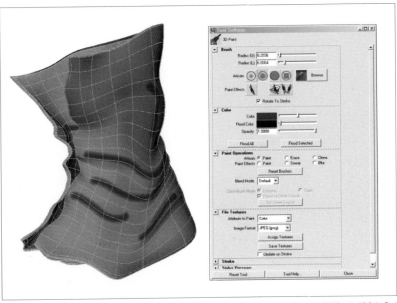

Figure 9-178 Using the 3D Paint Tool

Load both the Color Map and the image created using the 3D Paint Tool into Photoshop. Paste the 3D Paint Tool image onto the Color Map. A new layer will be made and the image will be pasted into the layer. Set the Opacity of the 3D Paint Tool image to 50. As we can see in Figure 9-179, we can see the original image on the bottom.

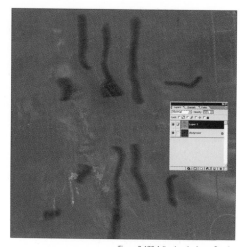

Figure 9-179 Adjusting the Layer Opacity

Select the layer of the Color Map at the bottom, and use the Dodge Tool to paint the red areas.

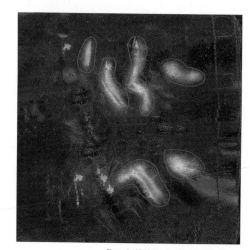

Figure 9-180 Making the Specular Map Source

We can see that areas that were painted using the Dodge Tool appear brighter than the other areas (see Figure 9-181). These are the areas that will be illuminated by light.

In the same way, make a Specular Map for the Color Map for each constituent of the boot. The Bump Map can be rendered simply by using the Specular Map Source, or we can simply convert the Color Map to gray and adjust the Brightness and Contrast before using it. Figure 9-181 shows the completed image.

Figure 9-181 Completed Image

We have covered how to use Maya and Photoshop to scan and map textures. Mapping requires a lot of time and effort. A satisfactory result can only be obtained after careful observation of the actual object and through much practice.

5. FACE MAPPING USING TEXTURE REFERENCE OBJECTS

In this section, we will look at how to make a Multi-Patch Modeling map source without using 3D painting software. Maya offers several methods for mapping textures, and you should practice with each one to find the method that works best for you.

For this example, open the file CD-ROM/CHARACTER/scenes /ChildModel.mb. This file contains a model that was made using Multi-Patch. As shown in Figure 9-182, hide all the surfaces, excluding the face.

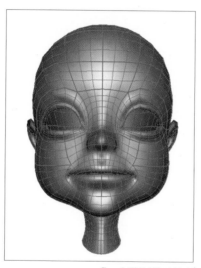

Figure 9-182 Multi-Patch Model

step 1 First of all, convert this NURBS model into a polygon in order to create a texture axis. Select all of the surfaces of the face, and then select [Modify > Convert > NURBS to Polygons] to open the options window and configure the options as shown in Figure 9-183.

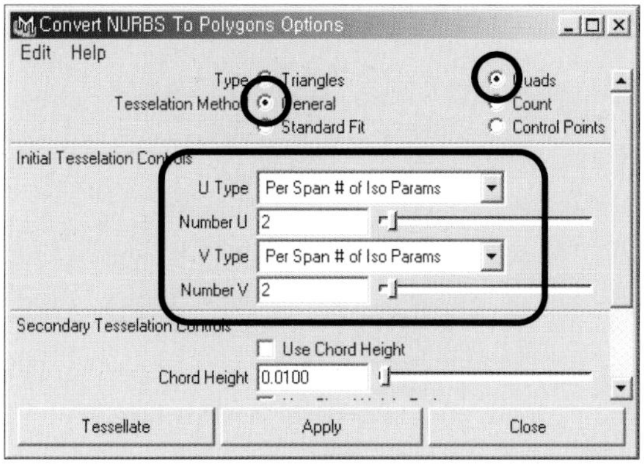

Figure 9-183 Options Window

Click on the Tessellate button at the bottom of the Options window. Select [Edit > Delete by Type > History] to delete the history and, as shown in Figure 9-184, hide the NURBS leaving behind only the polygon.

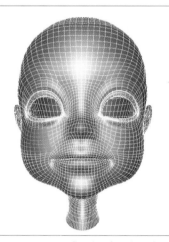

Figure 9-184 Converting the Polygon

step 2 Select the entire polygon, and then select [Modeling > Polygons > Combine]. Because the NURBS patch was converted into a polygon, each of the polygons will be displayed as fragments. Therefore, we must tie these fragments together using Combine. After applying the Combine, select the polygon and then select [Modeling > Edit Polygons > Textures > Cylindrical Mapping]. If [Modeling > Polygons > Tool Options > Convert Selection] is not turned on, we must select the polygon face and do Cylindrical Mapping. In the Channel Box, set the Projection Center to 0.001 and set the Projection Horizontal to 360, as shown in Figure 9-185. The Texture Manipulator will appear as shown.

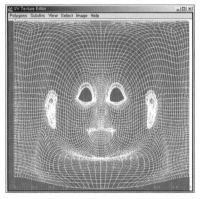

polySurfaceShape1	
INPUTS	
polyCylProj1	
Projection Center	0,001
Projection Center	3,337
Projection Center	0,786
Image Center X	0,5
Image Center Y	0,5
Rotate X	0
Rotate Y	0
Rotate Z	0
Projection Horiz	360
Projection Height	4,711
Image Scale U	1
Image Scale V	1
Rotation Angle	0

Figure 9-185 Cylindrical Mapping

For more information on polygon mapping, refer to Chapter 2, "Polygons, Subdivision Surface Mapping."

Now, select the polygon and select [Windows > UV Texture Editor] to open the Texture Editor. We can see that the UV-axis is made in Figure 9-186.

Figure 9-186 UV Snapshot

step 3   Select [Polygons > UV Snapshot] in the UV Texture Editor. Enter the route and the file name, and configure the resolution and the color as shown in Figure 9-187. Set the Image Format to TGA and then click the OK button.

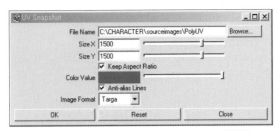

Figure 9-187 UV Snapshot

 step 4 Run Photoshop. Open the UV specified in Step 3 in Photoshop. As seen in Figure 9-188, the UV-axis of the polygon will be connected to the image.

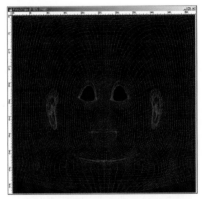

Figure 9-188 Opening the UV Snapshot in Photoshop

This image will have an alpha channel because the Image Format was set to TGA in Step 3. As follows, we can isolate only the UV wire. From the Photoshop menu, select [Select > Load Selection] and select Alpha1 from Channel. After copying the image by pressing Ctrl+C, select [File > New] to open a new window and press Ctrl+V to paste the copied image. A structure will be made as shown in Figure 9-189. At this time, make an empty layer below the UV image.

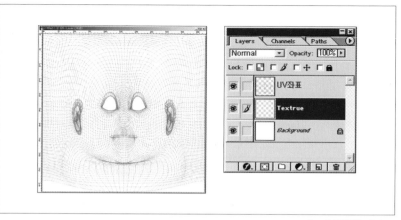

Figure 9-189 Making the Layer

By doing this, we have created a UV-axis for the NURBS surface. We now need to create the texture according to this UV-axis. We can paint the texture directly in Photoshop or distort a photograph to fit the UV-axis. Details on distorting a photograph can be found on page 702 under the section "Mapping Using a Picture Source."

In this way, create the texture seen in Figure 9-190.

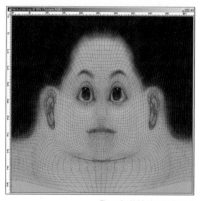

Figure 9-190 Making the Texture

After converting this texture to grayscale in Photoshop, make a Bump Map and add color to portions of the Bump Map to make a Specular Map.

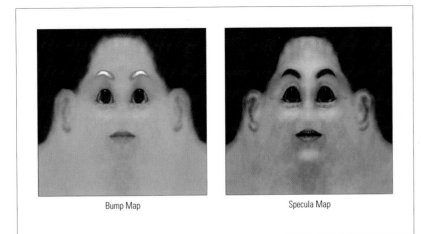

Bump Map

Specula Map

Figure 9-191 The Bump and the Specular Map Source

Figure 9-191 shows the Bump and Specular Maps.

We will now Multi-Patch model these sources in Maya.

step 5 As shown in Figure 9-192, open the NURBS face in Maya and delete the polygon we created earlier.

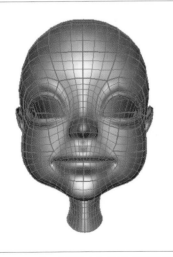

Figure 9-192 Displaying Only the NURBS Surface

As shown in Figure 9-193, make 3 File Textures, one 3D Placement, 3 Projection Nodes and one Blinn Material in the Hypershade.

Load the texture we made into each of the 3 File Textures. For this example, you may refer to the files CD-ROM/CHARACTER/ sourceimages/face_color.jpg, face_bump.jpg, and face_sp.jpg. Link each of the file textures to each Projection. We do this by linking the Out Color of the file textures to the Projection image. Link, also, the Blinn Material Color, Bump and Specular to the Projection. Link the Projection linked to the Color Texture to Color, the Projection linked to the Bump Texture to Bump, and the Projection linked to the Specular to Specular. The connection network is shown in Figure 9-194.

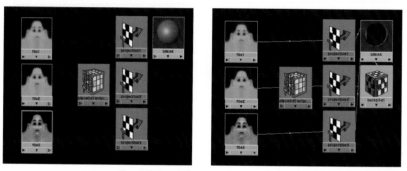

Figure 9-193 Hypershade

Figure 9-194 Hypershade

Click the MMB on the place3dTexture Node and drag it above the Projection Node. Then, in the Connection Editor, link the World Inverse Matrix (0) and the Placement Matrix as shown in Figure 9-195. This links the 3D texture to the default attribute of the place3dTexture.

Link the remaining 2 projections in the same way.

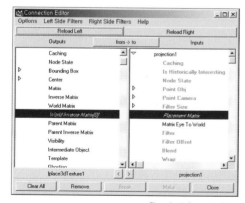

Figure 9-195 Connection Editor

Open the Projection Node Attribute Editor (see Figure 9-196) and set the Proj Type to Cylindrical and the U Angle to 360. Configure the attributes for the other Projections in the same way.

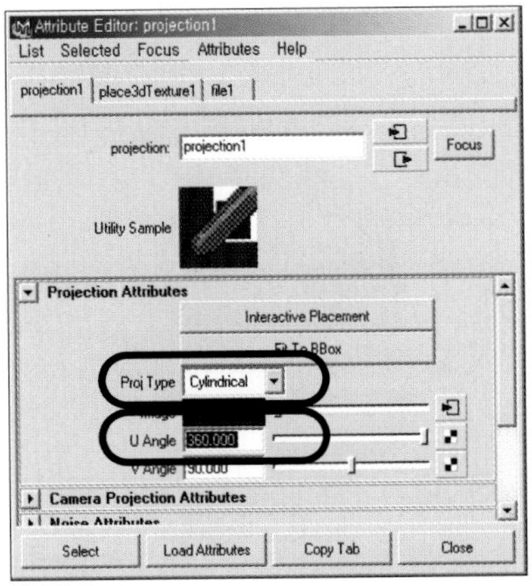

Figure 9-196 Attribute Editor

We need to set the Projection Type here to Cylindrical and the U Angle to 360 because, in general, the UV-axis that we obtained from converting to polygon uses Cylindrical Mapping.

step 6 Arrange a Directional Light and render the Perspective View in IPR. Double-click on the place3dTexture Node in Hypershade to open the Attribute Editor, and click on the Fit To BBox button, as shown in Figure 9-197.

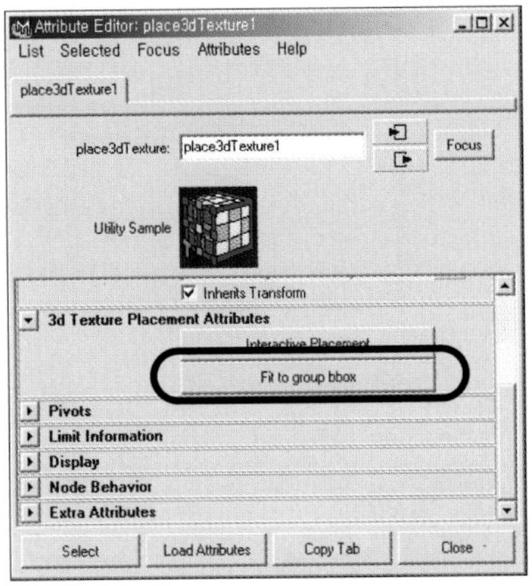

Figure 9-197 Attribute Editor

This will display the 3d Texture Placement Manipulator. Adjust the Manipulator as shown in Figure 9-198. In general, because we rendered the image in IPR, the adjusted values will be rendered right away. Adjust the Manipulator so that the image is rendered as shown in Figure 9-199.

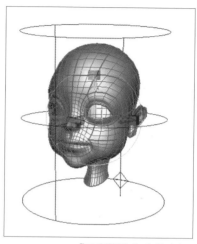

Figure 9-198 Adjusting the Manipulator

Figure 9-199 Rendered Image

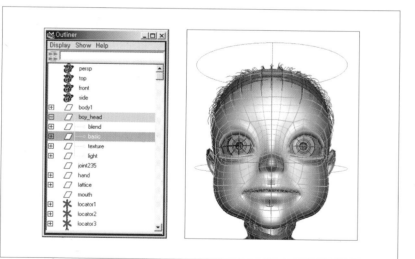

Figure 9-200 Selecting the Face

step 7 Because the 3 projection nodes are linked together, we need to manipulate only one of the them to adjust the Color, Bump, and Specular. This data is

saved in the supplementary CD-ROM. Open the file, CD-ROM/CHARACTER/
scenes/ChildSetup.mb. Open the Outliner and select basic from beneath boy_head, as
shown in Figure 9-200.

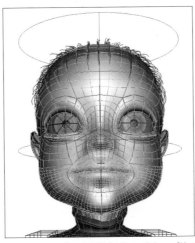

Select [Rendering > Texturing > Create
Texture Reference Object]. A reference
object will be made, as shown in Figure 9-
201.

Figure 9-201 Create Texture Reference Object

Now, the texture axis will follow the direction of the surface without the need to convert
the texture. Figure 9-202 shows a test rendering of different facial expressions. In this
way, the 3D texture is made to follow the changes in the surface.

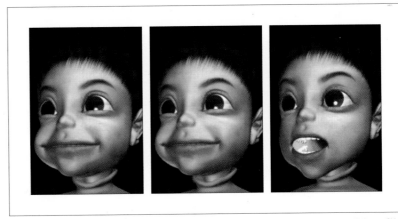

Figure 9-202 Create Texture Reference Object

Collection of Insects

Spurred on by my love of insects, I organized this collection
of my work that dates back to when I first began using Maya.
Unfortunately, these insects will become rare, both in Korea and overseas, in the next 5 years.

images by Kwon Young-jin

Allomyrina dichotoma Linnaeus. 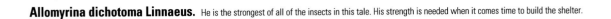 He is the strongest of all of the insects in this tale. His strength is needed when it comes time to build the shelter.

The Adams Stag-Horned Beetle With his scissor-like hands, he begins to form the outer surface of the shelter.

Fly. Although this is not an insect that will become extinct in the next 5 years, it was included in the story because of its adaptability to the human race.

Attelabidae. Apoderus erythrogaster Vollenhoven sucks up the dirt and sand that is created during the construction of the shelter, much like a vacuum cleaner.

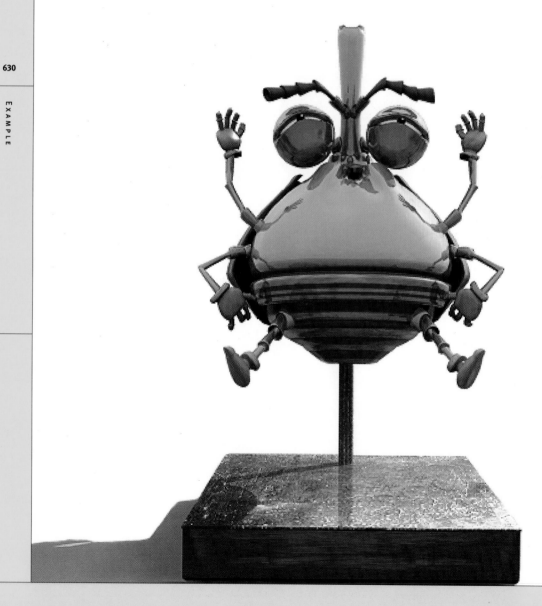

Larva. He is looked after by all the other bugs in the shelter.

Long-Horned Beetle. He is the oldest and wisest of all the insects. He finds a method of escape and acts as leader.

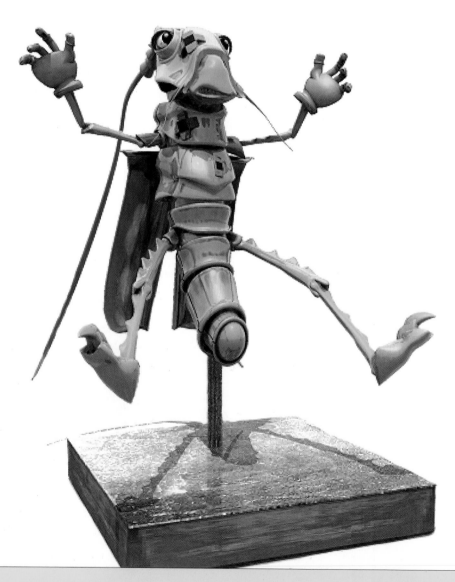

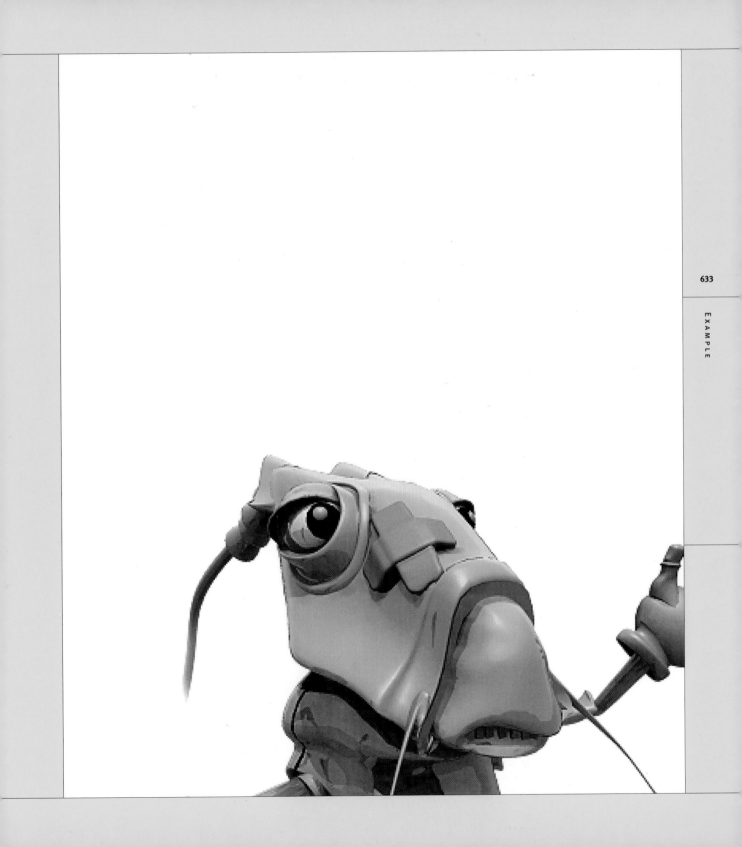

Bamboo worm. He always carries around a ruler and tells the other bugs the height and width of the shelter.

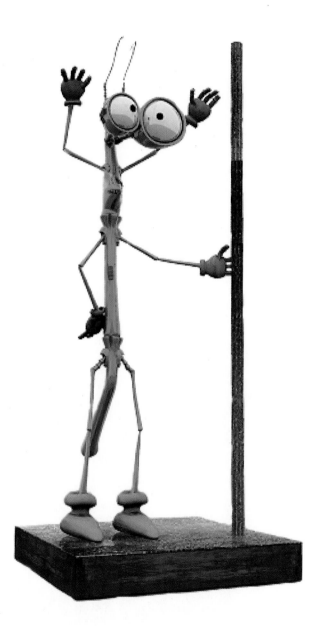

Gryllotalpa orientalis Burmeister. His large shovel-like mouth acts like a fork crane when he builds the shelter.

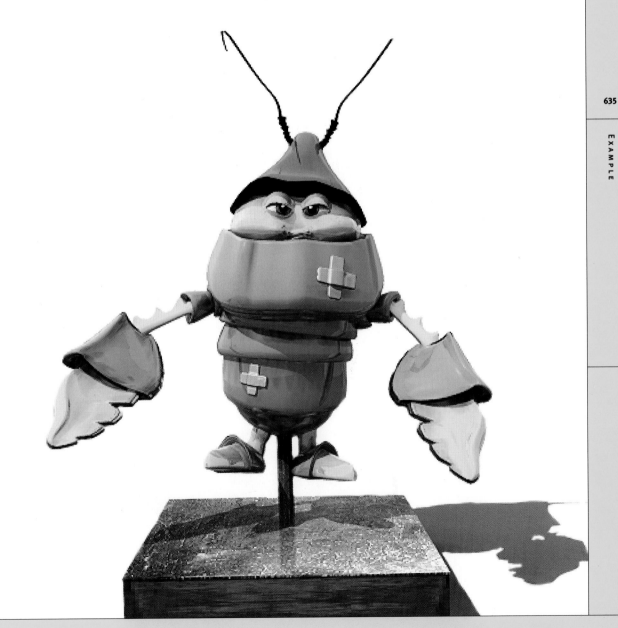

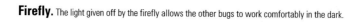

Firefly. The light given off by the firefly allows the other bugs to work comfortably in the dark.

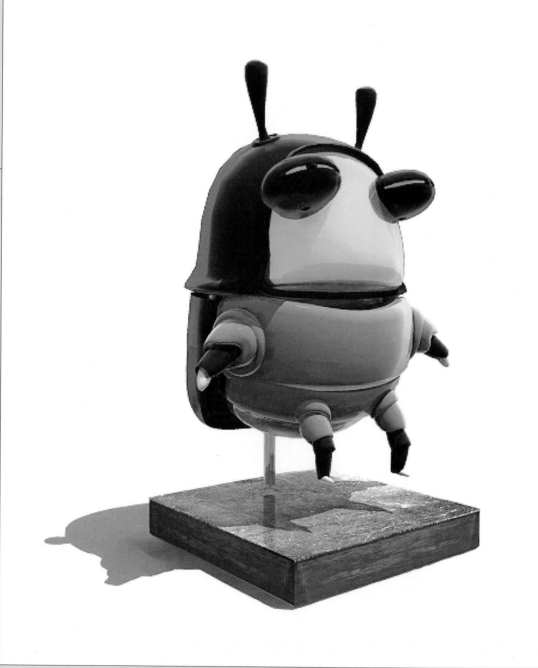

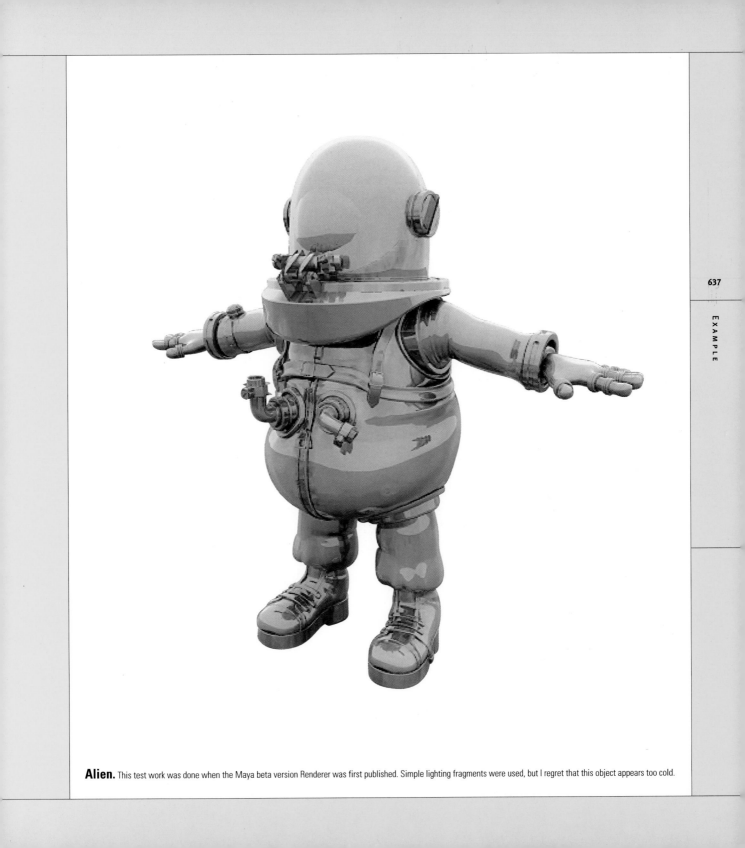

Alien. This test work was done when the Maya beta version Renderer was first published. Simple lighting fragments were used, but I regret that this object appears too cold.

PART_2

MAYA AND BEYOND

10 Essential Features in Maya

With the release of version 5.0, Maya's list of features is more extraordinary than ever. In this chapter, we'll review the most useful and applicable features of Maya, with an eye toward improving your overall productivity.

Note that the following chapter is presented in an instructional format; for a more fundamental, manual-like description of Maya's features, consult the documentation that came with your software.

1. BASIC FEATURES

1-1. ENHANCEMENTS TO ALIGN AND SNAP OBJECTS

The Align and Snap Together Tools have been added to the [Modify > Snap Align Objects] menu. These tools are used in a variety of different ways to align and organize objects.

1. Align Tool

The Manipulator is used to quickly and easily align a selected object to another object in 3D space. While working, there are times when you may need to align objects to the center or other standard line of another object. This tool comes in very handy in such cases. By looking at the following example, we can see how effectively and quickly this tool can be used to align objects. Let's suppose that we are using Polygon Cubes to pile up blocks. First, make the Polygon Cube as shown in Figure 10-1.

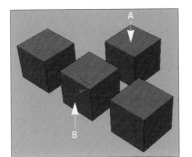

Figure 10-1 Making the Polygon Cube

Figure 10-2 Using the Align Tool

After selecting [Modify > Snap Align Objects > Align Tool], select Object A, indicated in Figure 10-1, and then, holding down the Shift key, select Object B. The Align Manipulator will be displayed as shown in Figure 10-2. In terms of the order in which the objects are selected, we first select the object that will be moved. By holding down the Shift key, we can select many objects at the same time. All selected objects will be aligned.

Click the MMB on the point indicated in Figure 10-3. This will activate the Manipulator, and we can see beforehand where the objects will be aligned. Releasing the mouse button will align the cube as shown in Figure 10-4.

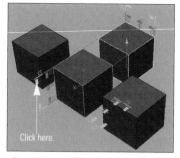

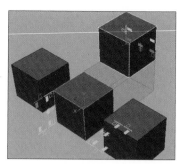

Figure 10-3 Selecting Where the Objects will be Aligned

Figure 10-4 The Aligned Cube

Looking at the shape of the handle of the selected Manipulator, we can see that two small boxes are arranged above and below the Edge. This type of handle indicates that the alignment will take place on the outer part of the edge. Looking at Figure 10-3, we can see that the object has been aligned to the outer edge. The handle selected in Figure 10-4 has already been aligned and, therefore, is inactivated. Only the handle that will be aligned to the inside is activated.

Continue to align the cubes in this way, and pile up the blocks as shown in Figure 10-5.

Figure 10-5 Piling up the Blocks Using Align

2. Snap Together Tool

This tool moves and/or rotates and snaps objects to a specified point on another object. When this tool is selected, an arrow appears showing which point on one object the point of another object will be connected to. This tool is very easy to use. Let's suppose we have 2 objects, as shown in Figure 10-6. First, select [Modify > Snap Align Objects > Snap Together Tool]. After clicking on the objects in the order shown in Figure 10-7, press the Enter key on the keyboard. This will snap the point of the object that was selected first in Figure 10-7 to the point on the object that was selected second.

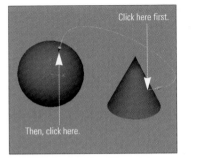

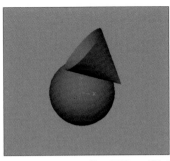

Figure 10-6 Selecting the Snap Point

Figure 10-7 Snapped Object

One thing to note is that the snap will only occur in the direction of the surface Normal. For example, if you wish to snap the object to the inside of the sphere, you must first change the direction of the Normal. As a default, the object that will be snapped is configured to rotate automatically in that direction. If you do not wish to rotate, open the Tool Settings window, as shown in Figure 10-8, and select Move object(s) Only.

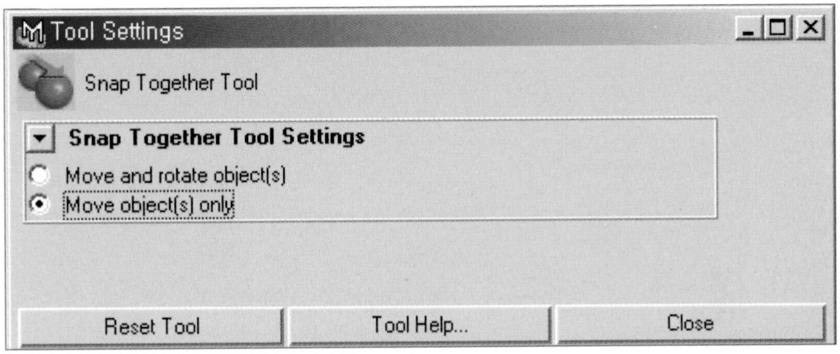

Figure 10-8 Tool Settings Window

1-2. SELECTION ENHANCEMENTS

1. Select Hierarchy

In older versions of Maya, it was rather difficult to select all of the nodes in the Hierarchy. However, this process is now much easier. For example, selecting the desired node from the Outliner and then selecting [Edit > Select Hierarchy], as shown in Figure 10-9, will select all the nodes in the hierarchy below the selected node.

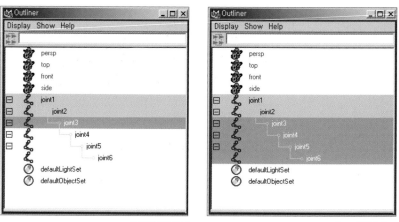

Figure 10-9 Outliner

Figure 10-10 Outliner

2. Changing the Names of Several Objects at Once

While working, you will find that many objects will be arranged on a scene and that various names will be created for those objects. It is very easy to get confused by joint names that are created automatically for characters. In such instances, we are able to change the names of all these objects at once. For example, let's suppose we have the joint names shown in Figure 10-11. Let's change the names to Man.

Figure 10-11 Hypergraph

Select all of the nodes for which you wish to change the name in Hypergraph. As shown in Figure 10-12, click the RMB in the Popup Menu of the Status Line, and select Quick Rename. Type **Man** in the Name Field, and then press the Enter key. Looking at the Hypergraph, we can see that the names of the nodes have changed accordingly.

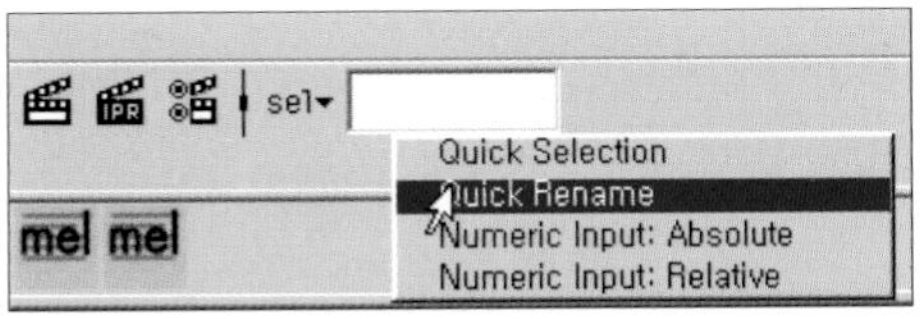

Figure 10-12 Selecting Quick Rename

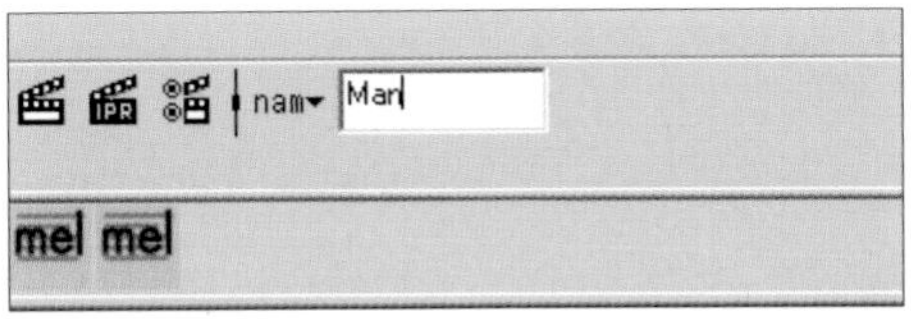

Figure 10-13 Typing in a New Name

3. Annotating Nodes in the Modeling View

Many objects can be arranged in a scene while working. Animating these objects or changing the properties can be made easier if there is some way to discriminate between these objects. Annotating these objects makes it easier to tell them apart. Annotation is very easy to do. First, after selecting the desired object, select [Create > Annotation...] to open the Annotate Node window and type in the desired name.

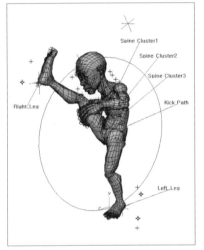

Figure 10-14 Annotation

2. IMPORTANT FEATURES

Let's look at some of the important features that can be found in Maya 5.0.

2-1. BEVEL PLUS

I believe that many users had a lot of problems with Maya's Bevel feature in the past. As someone who has had a lot of experience making TV station logos, I believe that the Bevel feature was one of the areas that needed a lot of improvement. Now, I believe many people will be quite satisfied.

In order to use Bevel Plus, first (if you have a test with a hole as shown in Figure 10-15), select the outer curve first and then select the inner curve. Selecting [Modeling > Surfaces > Bevel Plus] will bevel the curve as shown in Figure 10-16.

Figure 10-15 Selecting the Curve

Figure 10-16 Executing Bevel Plus

Selecting [Modeling > Surfaces > Bevel Plus ▣] will open the Options window as shown in Figure 10-17. This window can be used to define the Bevel options.

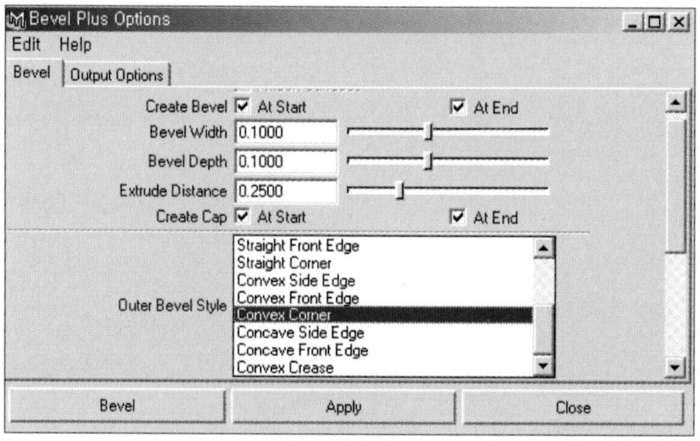

Figure 10-17 Options Window

Figure 10-18 explains the Bevel options.

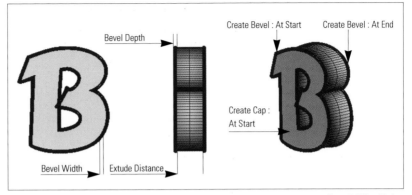

Figure 10-18 Bevel Options

If the Same as Outer Style option is turned off in the Options window of Figure 10-17, we will be able to define the Outer and Inner Bevel Styles separately. In the OutPut Options, select either the NURBS or polygon shape to apply to the result.

2-2. CUT FACES

This menu is very useful for easily dividing up polygons. This menu, which is now included in the program, was offered as a plug-in in older versions. Let's see how easy it is to cut up Polygon Objects. First of all, select the Polygon Object to cut up and then select [Modeling > Edit Polygons > Cut Faces ◻] to open the Options window. As shown in Figure 10-19, put a check next to Extract to turn it on and then set all of the Extract Offset values to 0. Click on the Enter Cut Tool And Close button at the bottom.

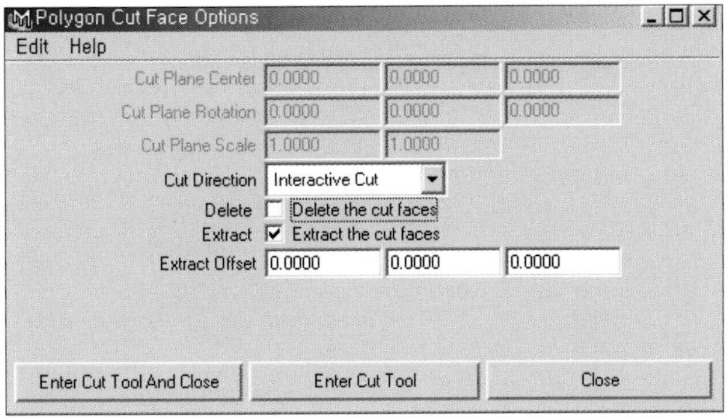

Figure 10-19 Options Window

Click the LMB on the portion that will be cut, and drag it down to establish the cutting direction as shown in Figure 10-20.
After the direction has been established, release the mouse button. Select [Modeling > Edit Polygons > Separate], and move to the cut portion on the top as shown in Figure 10-21.

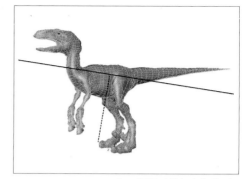

Figure 10-20 Establishing the Cut Direction

In this way, we can use the Cut Faces Tool to easily divide up polygons.

More detailed explanations of each of the Options can be found in your user documentation.

Figure 10-21 Moving the Cut Polygon

2-3. POKE FACES

This feature is used to add detail to the model by adding a vertex to the selected surface to newly divide up the surface. This feature can be used to easily create fun, new shapes and figures. First, make a Polygon Cube and select all the faces, as shown in Figure 10-22. After selecting [Modeling > Edit Polygons > Poke Faces], move it, as shown in Figure 10-23, to make the shape.

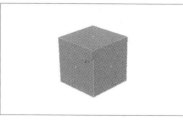

Figure 10-22 Selecting the Faces

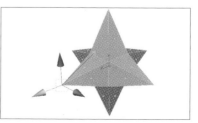

Figure 10-23 Executing Poke Faces and Moving

The following figure shows an example of a shape that was made using this feature.

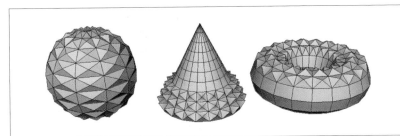

Figure 10-24 An Example of a Shape that was made Using Pole Faces.

2-4. WEDGE FACE

This feature will, when extruding faces, extrude the face in the shape of an arc along the given edge. It is quite simple to use. Select the face to extrude, as shown in Figure 10-25 and then select the edge that will serve as the base while holding down the Shift key. Then, execute [Modeling > Edit Polygons > Wedge Face].

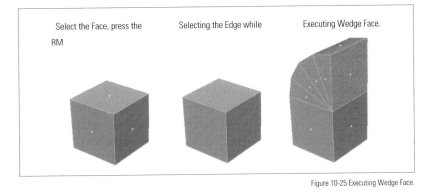

Select the Face, press the RM

Selecting the Edge while

Executing Wedge Face.

Figure 10-25 Executing Wedge Face.

We can control the extruding shape by adjusting the options in the Options window. The following figure shows how the extrude shape changes according to the different options values.

Figure 10-26 Wedge Angle : 120, Wedge Divisions : 10

2-5. SMOOTH PROXY

This tool is used to facilitate Subdivision Surface Modeling. Previously you had to use the In_Out Mesh, but now a menu simplifies the work. Selecting the Low Polygon and executing this tool will make the Low Polygon Model into a Proxy as, shown in Figure 10-27 and Smooth will be applied to the bottom to make the Model. Moving the face as shown in Figure 10-28 will adjust the Smooth Shape below the Proxy Shape.

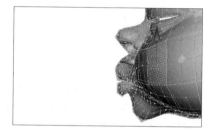

Figure 10-27 Selecting the Face

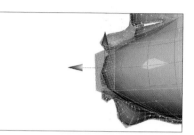

Figure 10-28 Moving the Face to make the Shape

Select the desired polygon, and select [Modeling > Polygons > Smooth Proxy]. For the Smooth values, raise the Divisions values in the Channel Box, as shown in Figure 10-29. This is the same as selecting [Modeling > Polygons > Smooth] in older versions of Maya and then changing the options. Executing Smooth Proxy will automatically create the Proxy Mesh

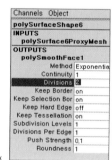

Figure 10-29 Channel Box

Layer and the Smooth Mesh Layer in the Display Layer, and we can easily define the mesh display.

2-6. SUBDIV TO NURBS

This feature allows us to convert Subdivision Surfaces to NURBS. This also means that polygons can be converted to NURBS. The following figure organizes the NURBS surfaces by showing an example of a polygon converted to a Subdivision Surface and then converted back to NURBS.

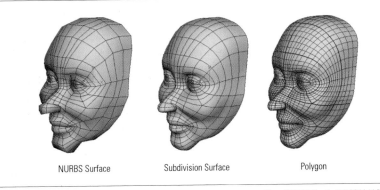

NURBS Surface   Subdivision Surface   Polygon

Figure 10-30 Making the NURBS Multi-Patch.

It is very difficult to work with Multi-Patches using the basic shape. In such cases, it is much more effective to model the basic surface as a polygon or Subdivision Surface and then to convert it to NURBS before modification.

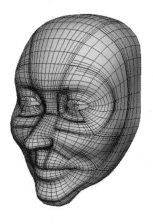

In order to convert to NURBS, all we need to do is select the Subdivision Surface and then select [Modify > Convert > Subdiv to NURBS]. Converting the Subdivision Surface to NURBS will create many isoparms, as shown in Figure 10-31, in order to maintain the curvature of the given Subdivision Surface.

Figure 10-31 The Model converted to NURBS.

We must match the number of spans in the U-and V-directions of such converted models.
This is the same as Multi-Patch Modeling.

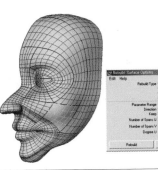

Figure 10-32 Rebuild Surface

Finally, [Modeling > Edit NURBS > Stitch > Global Stitch] is used to match the curvature between surfaces. This makes Multi-Patch Modeling that much easier. Figure 10-33 shows an example of a model completed in this way.

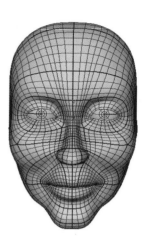

Figure 10-33 Completed Model

There is one thing to keep in mind when Subdivision Surface modeling in order to convert to NURBS. When modeling using Subdivision Surfaces, the flow of the edges must be arranged in the same way that the isoparms are in Multi-Patch. This is because the flow determines how the surface will be divided when Maya converts the Subdivision Surface to NURBS. Let's look at the next figure. Looking at the area indicated in Figure 10-34, we can see that the edges are not continuous and that the polygon has triangular surfaces. If we convert to NURBS under such conditions, it will be divided into many surfaces, as shown in Figure 10-35, and it becomes very difficult to organize these surfaces.

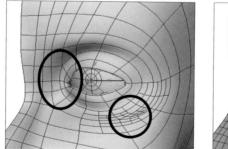

Figure 10-34 Non-Continuous Edges

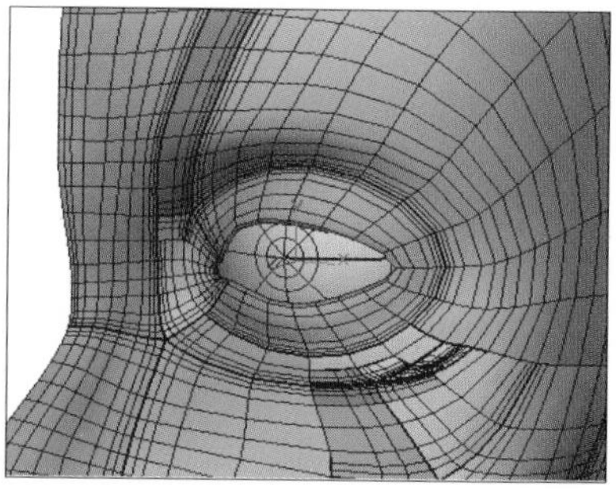

Figure 10-35 Converted Model

Figure 10-36 shows how this problem was solved. The difference is readily available by comparing it to Figure 10-34 above. Converting this model will create fewer surface divisions, as shown in Figure 10-37, which are, consequently, easier to organize.

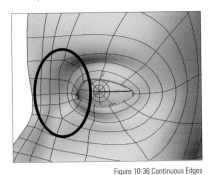

Figure 10-36 Continuous Edges

Figure 10-37 Converted Model

2-7. RAMP SHADER

The Ramp Shader is an excellent feature. The Shader can be used to render simple cartoons. Cartoon shaders that were made previously using Utility and Ramp Texture can now be made simply using this Shader.

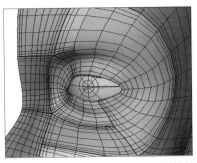

Figure 10-38 Image rendered using Ramp Shader

Figure 10-39 illustrates the Attribute Editor for the Ramp Shader. It is used in the same way as other Ramp attributes and is, therefore, not very difficult to use. I will skip the basic explanations and move onto the attributes needed for the Cartoon Shader.

Figure 10-39 Ramp Shader Attribute Editor

1. Color

This defines the basic color of the Shader. It uses Position and Color to change the color across different positions. The following figure shows the rendered image as it changes with the different Interpolation values. Although no large differences excluding None are readily visible to the naked eye for the options, specific and minute differences exist.

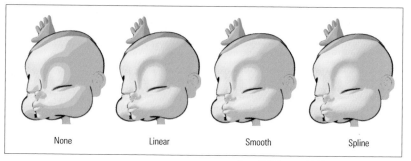

Figure 10-40 Changes with Different Interpolation Values

2. Incandescence

This feature creates a reflection of light and is the same attribute as other Maya Shaders. An important use of this attribute in the Ramp Shader is to create the outline for the shader.

In order to make the Shader Outline, make 2 levels of color, A and B, as shown in Figure 10-41, and then set the Interpolation value to None. Set the V value of Color A to -1 in the Color Chooser window as shown in Figure 10-42.

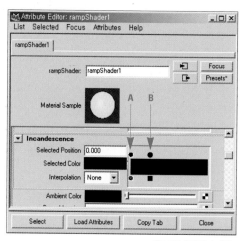

Figure 10-41 Attribute Editor

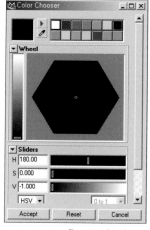

Figure 10-42 Color Chooser

The figure below shows the shape of the Outline. We can control the thickness of the Outline by adjusting the positions of A and B, as shown in Figure 10-41.

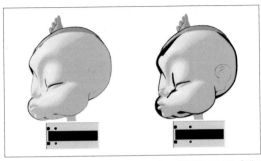

Figure 10-43 Changes in the Outline

2-8. VOLUME LIGHT

Volume Light is a recent addition to the Light feature. This feature is used to illuminate light within the given volume. Within the boundaries of the volume, we can randomly control the direction of the light and the Light Color Decay. One of the biggest advantages of Volume Light is that we can now easily control the scope of the light.

Figure 10-44 Image Rendered using Volume Light (Image by Kwi-Hoon, Jung)

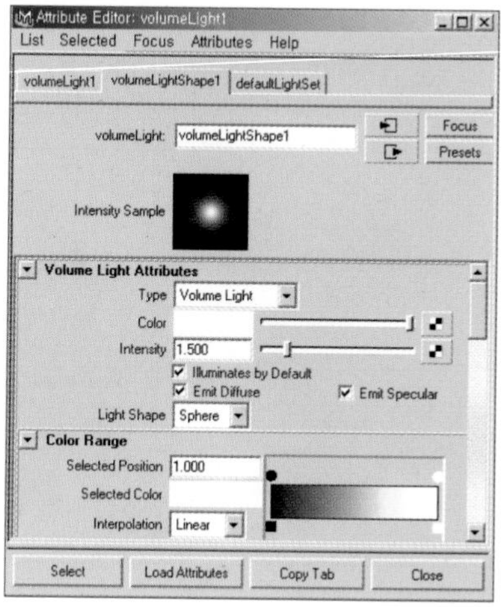

Figure 10-45 Attribute Editor

Figure 10-45 shows the Volume Light Attribute Editor. It is basically the same as general Light attributes with the exception of the Light Shape and Color Range.

Light Shape offers the general Maya Volume Type shape. Volume Light will illuminate the given frame in the form of the specified shape. This means that we can illuminate a given frame in a variety of different shapes. In actuality, Volume Light can be used to achieve the same effect as Spot Light. Figure 10-46 is an example of specifying the illuminated frame using the Transformation Tool and setting the Light Shape of the Volume Light to Cone. Figure 10-47 shows the rendered image.

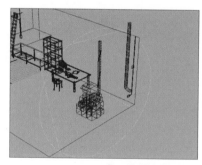

Figure 10-46 Light Shape: Cone

Figure 10-47 Rendered Image

When the Light Shape is set to Cone or Cylinder, the Penumbra Section in the Attribute Editor is activated. The following figure shows an example rendering using the Penumbra attributes.

Figure 10-48 Rendering the Image

Such attributes of Volume Light can, at times, be more useful than Spot Light. In addition to Penumbra, the Shape Scale can be adjusted to make the illuminated area more flexible than if we had used Spot Light.

We can create a variety of different changes to the Light Color by adjusting the Ramp Color of the Color Range. The following figures show how the Light Color changes in response to the Ramp Color.

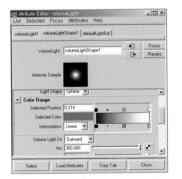

Figure 10-49 Adjusting the Ramp Color

Figure 10-50 Rendered Image

We've just taken a look at some of the more useful features you can exploit in Maya 5.0. Many other improvements have been made since the last edition, however, so please consult your user documentation for a more exhaustive list.

3. FLUID EFFECTS

The many Maya upgrades have brought us new technology in the form of improved tools. One example of this is Fluid Effects, which maximizes your results. Fluid Effects are used to naturally portray the effects to naturally portray the dynamic simulation of clouds, fog, smoke, and explosions.

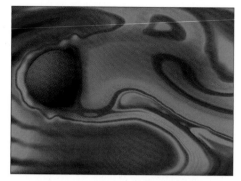

Figure 10-51 Fluid Effect Image

This section will be devoted to understanding the basic concept behind Fluid Effects. First, in order to make dynamic or unmoving Fluid Effects, we need to specify the space where the effects will take place. This space is called a Container. The Fluid Container, in other words, refers to a 2D or 3D space, as shown in Figure 10-52, where fluid is contained.

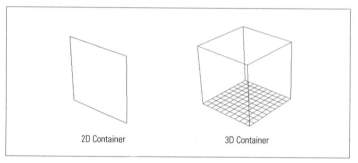

2D Container   3D Container

Figure 10-52 Fluid Container

The numerical values of the fluid properties are entered in the Container to realistically portray the movement and shape of the fluid.

These properties refer to the density and velocity, which determine the characteristics of the fluid, or to the temperature, which acts upon the fluid to create a reaction.
In addition, we can use fuel and temperature to ignite the fuel and to create explosive effects. We can also create provisions for the density color.

We will go over, step by step, the basic steps for creating Fluid Effects. First, we need to make a Fluid Container]. Fluid Containers are made by selecting [Dynamics > Fluid Effects > 2D, 3D Container]. If you wish to make an Emitter along with the Container, select 2D, 3D Container With Emitter. You can add properties to the Container to define the effects of the fluid within the container.

We can create a variety of different effects, including explosions and the flow of fluid. We can change the Fluid properties at any time to create the desired effects.

For more information, refer to your user documentation. We will take a quick look at Fluid Effects using a tutorial here.

3-1. MAKING SIMPLE CLOUD EFFECTS

In this tutorial, we will learn how to make a Container and paint a density within the container to create the desired cloud. We will learn how to use Fluid Textures to create lifelike clouds. To facilitate your understanding of this tutorial, you should first read over the basic concepts in your user documentation.

1. Making a Fluid Container

First, select [Dynamics > Fluid Effects > Create 3D Container] to make a 3D Container. Select the Container and open the Attribute Editor. The first thing we need to do is to set up the Container Properties. In Container Properties, set the Resolution and Size to the values shown in Figure 10-53.

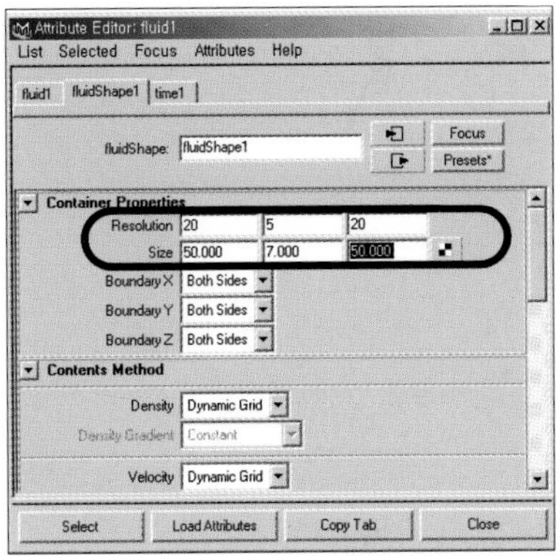

Figure 10-53 Attribute Editor

As the terms suggest, Resolution refers to the resolution of the Container, and Size refers to its size. Resolution and Size are rather closely related. A Voxel (Volume Pixel) is defined for 2D and 3D Containers through a grid.

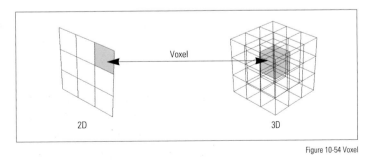

Voxel

2D   3D

Figure 10-54 Voxel

Grids are used to precisely control the values that are given to the Container and to create a Dynamic Simulation using the fluid. In addition, Voxel Resolution is defined by this grid. As follows, the Resolution increases in proportion to the increasing Size in the Container Properties. A greater Resolution will create a better quality image, but also increase the calculation time.

After specifying the Resolution and Size in Container Properties, the Container will take on the shape seen in Figure 10-55.

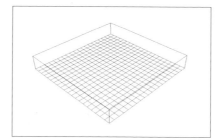

Figure 10-55 3D Container

2. Painting Fluid Density

Particles are added to the Container to create Fluid effects. We can use the Emitter along with Maya's Particle, create even density within the Container, or create particles using the gradient of each axis. In order to add an Emitter to the Container, we simply select the Container and then select [Dynamics > Fluid Effects > Add/Edit Contents > Emitter]. If you wish to make particles without an Emitter, select [Add/Edit Contents > Gradients]. Open the Options window (see Figure 10-56) and adjust the options to create the desired particles. However, in order to obtain the desired Fluid effects, you will need to make your own custom particles. To do so, paint particles with the desired density to define their shape. The tool used here is the Paint Fluid Tool. First, select the Container and then select [Dynamics > Fluid Effects > Add/Edit Contents > Paint Fluid Tool ▣] to open the Tool Settings window.

Figure 10-56 Options Window

The Tool Settings window is shown in Figure 10-57. The basic options are similar to Maya's Artisan options. In Paint Attributes, when Auto Set Initial State is turned on, all attributes in the current frame will be initialized. Paintable Attributes allows us to paint using the desired attributes. The default value is set to Density, and the particle will be made using this value. The Opacity value in the Brush section should be put to good use. This value, to be described later, adjusts the transparency and is useful in controlling the details of the cloud.

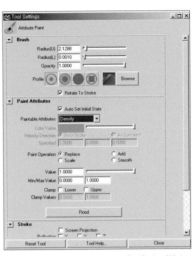

Figure 10-57 Tool Settings Window

Looking at the Container, we can see, in Figure 10-58, that the Manipulator has appeared. Tumbling the scene, we can see that the Manipulator is aligned to each axis as shown here. Select the desired directional arrow in each axis. That direction will turn yellow, meaning that it is activated. Moving to the respective axis, we can see on which grid we can paint.

Figure 10-58 Using the Manipulator to Specify the Frame on Which to Paint.

Clicking on the lock icon in the middle will fix the current frame to prevent the scene from moving and being affected by the actions of the mouse.

In order to paint along the Y-axis, tumble the scene and then paint as shown in Figure 10-59. When painting, it is a good idea to lower the transparency for the bottommost part. When painting the bottom, lower the Opacity value in the Tool Settings window before painting. Then raise the Opacity for the middle portion to add volume to the painting.

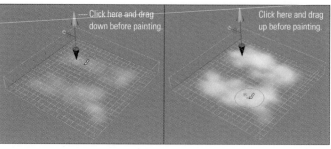

Figure 10-59 Density Painting

Continue painting in this way to control the density to fit the clouds.

3. Rendering Fluid Effects

Let's now render the scene. Rendering the scene right now will create the result seen in Figure 10-60. No attributes have been defined in this current rendering.

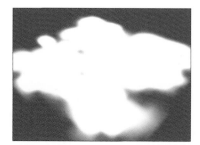

Figure 10-60 Rendering Images

First, in order to add volume to the clouds, let's create a Lighting environment. Select the Container, and then open the Attribute Editor and expand the Lighting section.

As we can see in Figure 10-61, turn on Self Shadow and put a check next to Real Light. We need to put a check next to Real Lights in order to use the light that will be used in the actual scene. Specify the values shown here for Shadow Opacity. This is used to control the degree of darkness in the clouds.

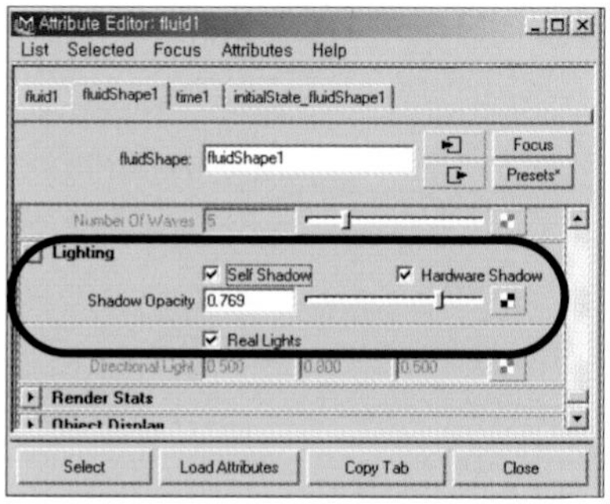

Figure 10-61 Attribute Editor

Rendering the scene again, we can see that the clouds appear more voluminous, as shown in Figure 10-62.

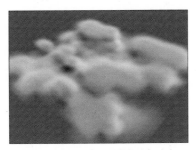

Figure 10-62 Rendering the Image

4. Controlling Transparency

Let's now control the transparency to make the clouds appear softer and more lifelike. There are 2 ways to control transparency. One way is to adjust the entire transparency and the other way is to control the transparency of the density. Adjusting the Transparency in Shading, as shown in Figure 10-63, will adjust the entire transparency (Figure 10-64).

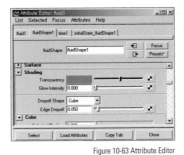

Figure 10-63 Attribute Editor

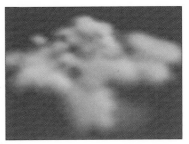

Figure 10-64 Rendered Image

In order to use density to adjust the transparency, adjust the Ramp under Opacity as shown in Figure 10-65. Drag the area indicated in the figure to the right to make transparent the areas of lower density. At this time, the Opacity Input must be set to Density, and Interpolation must be set to None. By rendering the scene, we can see that areas of lower density have become transparent (see Figure 10-66).

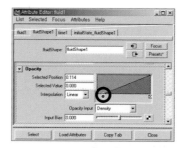

Figure 10-65 Attribute Editor

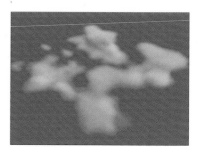

Figure 10-66 Rendering the Images

Continue to adjust these two attributes to create a softer image. In order to observe detailed changes, run a test of different Opacity Ramp values. You can see how the shape of the clouds changes as a result.

5. Adding Texture

After adjusting the transparency, it is now time to make the image appear more realistic by using Texture. Figure 10-67 is an example of an image rendered using Texture. Texture can be used to portray the details of the cloud particles to allow us to easily create more realistic images.

Figure 10-67 Rendering the Images

In order to obtain the results shown above, set the Texture options as shown in Figure 10-68. First, put a check next to Texture Opacity. Select the desired texture from Texture Type. Perlin Noise, which is used most often for this, reduces rendering time while creating effective results.

This is the 3D Noise used in the SolidFractal Texture. We can select Billow to create more realistic effects. However, this will also take up a lot of memory and increase the computation time. Volume Wave creates 3D waves in the space, Wispy creates vague fog effects, and Space Time is 4th dimension Perlin Noise.

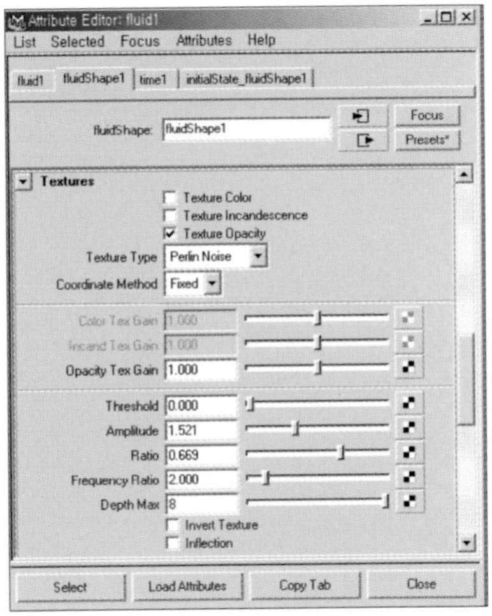

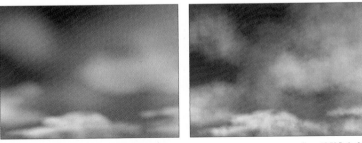

Figure 10-68 Attribute Editor

The following configurations are used for controlling cloud particles. Amplitude is used to adjust the strength of the Noise. In other words, raising this value will cause the lighter regions to protrude and make the darker areas appear deeper. Ratio adjusts the Fractal Noise frequency. Increasing this value will increase the Fractal detail.

Figure 10-69 Ratio: 0.3   Figure 10-70 Ratio: 0.8

Frequency Ratio adjusts the frequency of the Noise to the space. Depth Max is used to determine the computation from Volume Noise Texture. In other words, the greater the number of computations, the more detailed the fractal will be, but this will also increase computation time.

We can animate Textures to create simple flowing cloud movement. Try keyframing Texture Time or adjusting the Texture Scale. This is an easier way to create cloud movement than by defining the Dynamic Simulation of the Container.

We will use a simple example to see how quickly and easily we can create the effect of fluidity (for instance, the fluidity of lava). Through this example, we will familiarize ourselves with configuring Rendering, Collision, and simple Dynamic Simulations to the fluid.

1. The Basics

First, as shown in Figure 10-71, make a simple NURBS Surface.

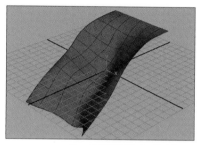

Figure 10-71 NURBS Surface Modeling

Select [Dynamics > Fluid Effects > Create Container] with Emitter to make a container that has an Emitter. After adjusting the size as shown in Figure 10-72, select the Emitter and arrange it on top of the NURBS Surface as shown in Figure 10-73.

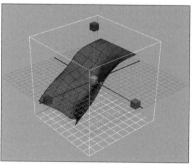

Figure 10-72 Making the Container

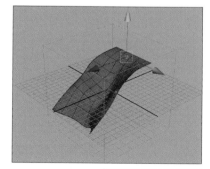

Figure 10-73 Arranging the Emitter

After selecting the Emitter, open the Attribute Editor and select Volume from the Basic Emitter Attributes, as shown in Figure 10-74. Select Sphere from the Volume Emitter Attributes. This shapes the Emitter into a Volume Sphere.

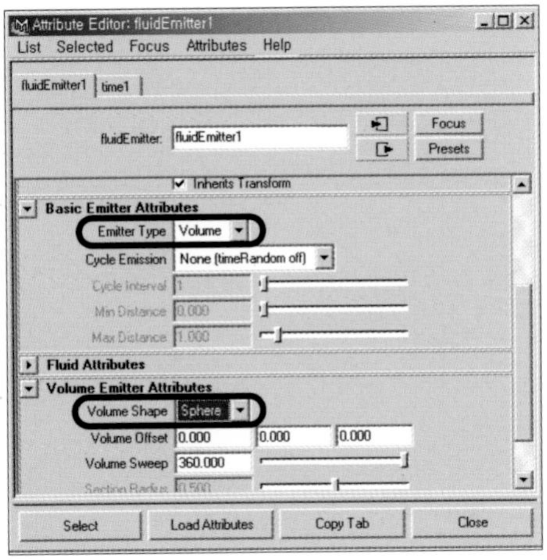

Figure 10-74 Attribute Editor

This completes the basic steps. By playing the animation, we can see that the particles are emitted straight up into the air.

2. Making the Dynamics Simulation

In this current animation, the fluid effects are emitted upward. Because it must be emitted back down due to the force of gravity, we open the container's Attribute Editor, set the Density Scale to 1, and the Buoyancy to -1, as shown in Figure 10-75.

Playing the animation, we can see, as in Figure 10-76, that the particles are emitted downward. In order to facilitate understanding, the Numeric Display in the Display section has been set to Density in the container's Attribute Editor.

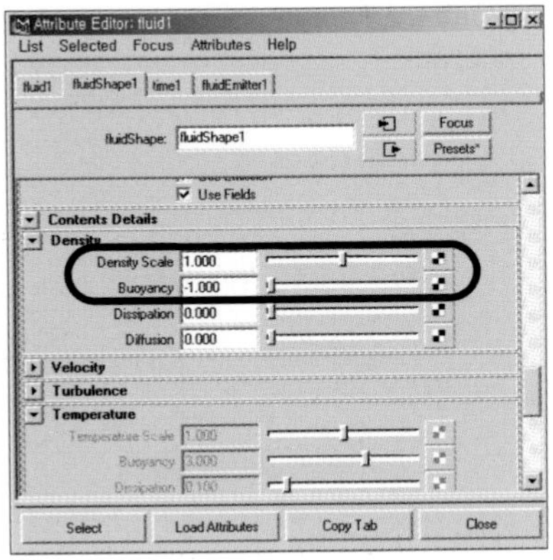

Figure 10-75 Attribute Editor

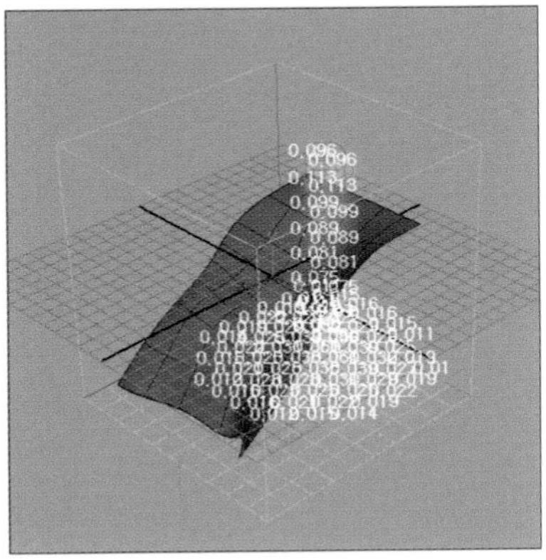

Figure 10-76 Play Animation

We must now configure the emitted particles to recognize the NUBS Surface. First, select the container and then select the NURBS Surface. Select [Dynamics > Fluid Effects > Make Collide]. This is a simple way of having the particles recognize the NURBS Surface. By playing the animation, we can see, as in Figure 10-77, that the particles follow the NURBS Surface downward.

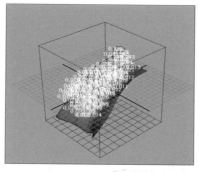

Figure 10-77 Play Animation

3. Rendering

Let's render the simulation to create a lava-like effect. Fluid Effects can be rendered in 2 different ways. One type, Volume Render, is used to create particles, such as smoke and clouds and the other, Surface Render, is used to render particles as surfaces. To create fluid lava-like effects, it is more effective to use Surface Render. In order to set the fluid to Surface Render, open the container's Attribute Editor. Then, as shown in Figure 10-78, select Surface Render and then select Hard Surface. The fluid will be displayed as shown in Figure 10-79.

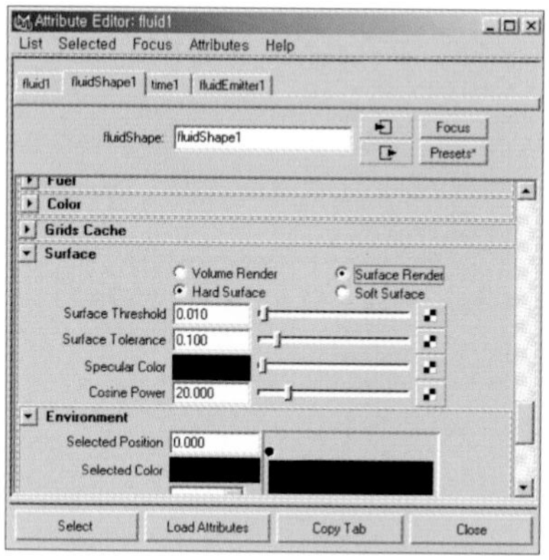

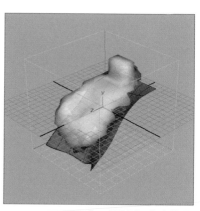

Figure 10-78 Attribute Editor

Figure 10-79 Surface Render Display

By playing the animation, we can see that the fluid flows down the surface. Increase the container resolution to create more accurate Collision and fluid effects.

Open the container's Attribute Editor, and set each of the Resolutions to 20 in the Container Properties.

After rendering the scene, we can see, as in Figure 10-80, that there is more accurate Collision and smoother fluid rendering.

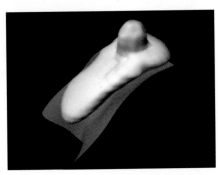

Figure 10-80 Rendering the Image

Let's insert Texture to make the scene more realistic. To portray the hot lava, use Incandescence. First, open the Container Attribute Editor. Figure 10-81 shows the configurations made in the Attribute Editor. First, make sure that there is no Transparency in the Shading and set the Glow Intensity to 0.18 to make the lava look hot. Because we will be using only Incandescence, the color should be set to black. Configure the Ramp Color structure of the Incandescence as shown here. This Ramp Color needs to be adjusted in great detail while verifying the results to create a good image.

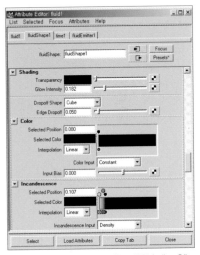

Figure 10-81 Attribute Editor

Rendering the scene in its current state will create the result seen in Figure 10-82. Detailed lava effects are not apparent as we have not yet applied the texture.

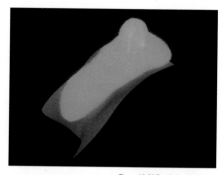

Figure 10-82 Rendering the Image

Figure 10-83 shows the configuration values for Texture, and the image that is rendered as a result is shown in Figure 10-84. Because Texture will only be used in Incandescence, we put a check next to Texture Incandescence. The Incand Text Gain is used to adjust the texture Gain value. The higher the Gain, the greater the Texture contrast. When used in conjunction with Amplitude, lighter regions can be made lighter and darker regions darker. Adjusting the Frequency Ratio and Depth Max of Ratio can control the degree to which Fractal is detailed. These values, too, can be adjusted in great detail and tested to achieve the desired results.

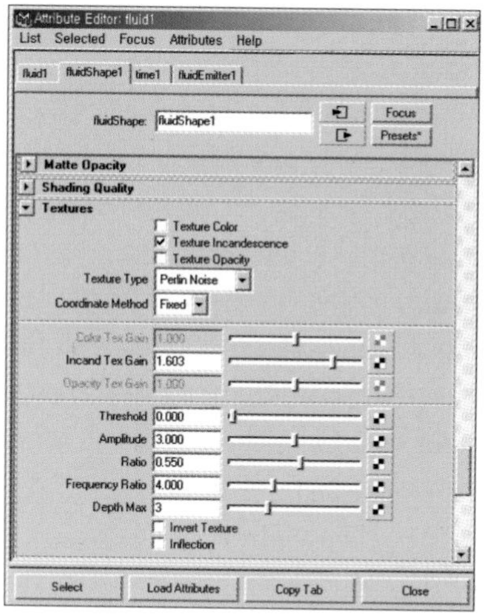

Figure 10-83 Attribute Editor

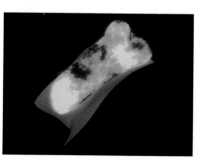

Figure 10-84 Rendering the Image

We have covered how these features are used using a simple example. For more information, refer to your user documentation and example files. You must test with a variety of different values to achieve the desired results.

3-3. CREATE OCEAN EFFECTS

Figure 10-85 The Example Date to be Rendered

In order to use Ocean Effects in older versions of Maya, we needed to use a plug-in such as Arete. Now, we can easily and quickly create Ocean Effects without using plug-ins. Fluid Effect's Ocean Effects are made into one plane to which Ocean Shader has been assigned. This assigned Ocean Shader can be used to create a variety of different effects or they can be turned into animations to create waves. We can also use the movement of the waves to affect the simulation of the boat's movements.   Let's take a look at a simple example to see just how easy these effects can be made.

1. Create Ocean

In order to create Ocean Effects, select [Dynamics > Fluid Effects > Ocean > Create Ocean]. This will create the Ocean Plane seen in Figure 10-86. An Ocean Shader is assigned to this plane, and by adjusting the Shader attributes we can create a variety of different Ocean Effects.

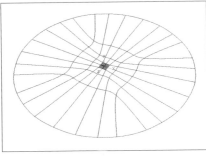

Figure 10-86 Create Ocean

Selecting [Dynamics > Fluid Effects > Ocean > Create Ocean] will open the Options window seen in Figure 10-87.

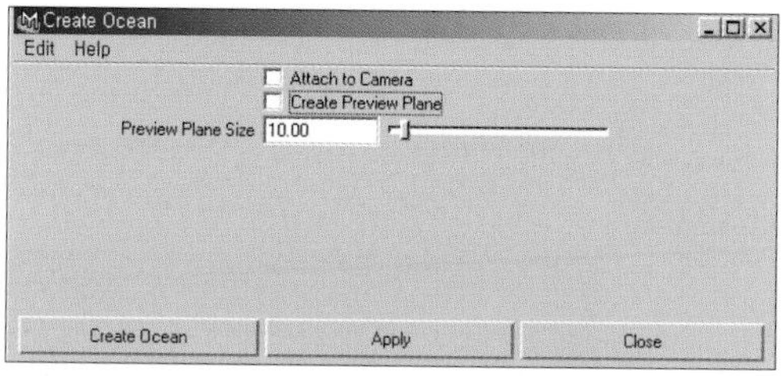

Figure 10-87 Options window

Attach to Camera

This option is used when attaching Ocean to a camera.

Create Preview Plane

Turning this option on will open the Preview Panel, which allows us to intuitively preview the Ocean Effect in Shading mode and easily adjust the height and acceleration of the waves (see Figure 10-88). When this option is turned on, the Preview Plane Size at the bottom is used to adjust the size.

Figure 10-88 Create Preview Plane

2. Adjusting the Ocean Shader Attributes

Simply rendering the Ocean we made will create the default rendering seen in Figure 10-89.

Figure 10-89 Rendering the Image

As we can see in the figure, this renders an image of very tranquil waves. We can use the Ocean Shader's Attribute Editor and adjust these attributes to create a variety of different waves. Let's now try editing the wave attributes. Figure 10-90 shows the Ocean Shader's Attribute Editor. First of all, in order to control the shape of the waves, we need to adjust the Ocean Attribute. Scale adjusts the scale of the overall wave. A lower value will create comparatively thicker ripples. Wind UV can be used to control the direction of the waves. This option, in other words,

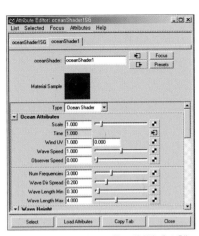

Figure 10-90 Attribute Editor

simulates the effect of the wind on the waves. The speed of the waves is controlled using Wave Speed and, in order to prevent the overlapping of the waves, we use Observer Speed. Num Frequencies is used to control the frequency of the waves and Wave Length Min and Max is used to randomize the height of the waves.

In order to create more random wave effects, we use Wave Height and Wave Turbulence Ramp. These ramps can be used to create more random and more realistic wave heights. An example is shown in the next illustration.

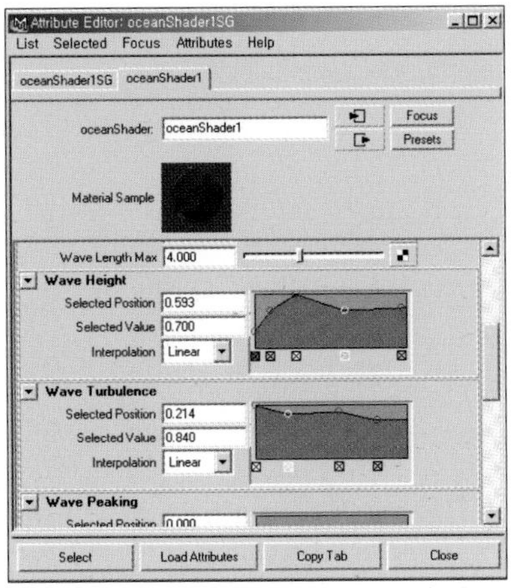

Figure 10-91 Attribute Editor

Figure 10-92 Rendering the Image

Water bubbles appear when large waves surge against each other. This kind of effect is created using Foam Emission from under the Ocean Shader attributes.

Foam Emission determines the density of the foam that is emitted above the Foam Threshold. Foam Offset applies foam evenly over any area and is useful when using Foam Texture.

The following image shows the rendering of Foam. It is applied to the edges of the surging waves making the image more realistic.

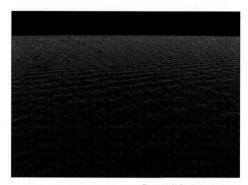

Figure 10-93 Rendering the Image

The color of the waves and foam and the reflective properties are adjusted in Common Material Attributes, as shown in Figure 10-94. For more information on each of these options, refer to your user documentaion.

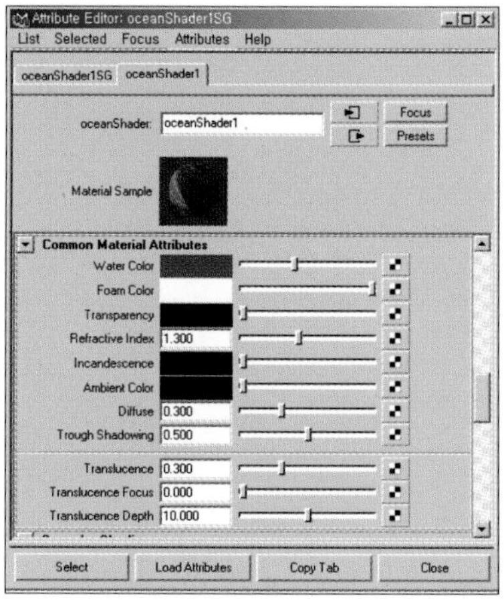

Figure 10-94 Atribute Editor

3. Object Keyframing that Follows the Movement of the Waves

Let's suppose we want to keyframe objects to follow the movement of the waves. For example, we may want to keyframe a boat or ball that is afloat in the water. In such cases, these objects should be made to move along with the waves.

Several different types of such keyframing exist in Ocean Effects. We can make wave surface movements, dynamic movements, or boat movements that follow the waves. As an example, let's create dynamic movements that follow the movement of the waves. This movement can, depending on the speed and height of the waves, make the object rise in the air or sink below the surface of the water. First, let's make a simple Ocean Plane and adjust the movement of the waves. In the figure below, we set the Scale to 0.58. the Num Frequencies to 20, the Wave length Max to 20, and left all the other values at the default in Ocean Attributes.

Figure 10-95 Ceate Ocean

Select [Create > NURBS Primitives > Sphere] to make a NURBS Sphere. First, select the NURBS Sphere and then select the Ocean Plane. Selecting [Dynamics > Fluid Effects > Ocean > Float Selected Object] will create a Locator that moves dynamically along with the waves. The selected NURBS Sphere is then automatically parented to this Locator and follows its movements.

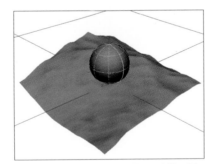

Figure 10-96 Float Object

Using this method, we can very easily keyframe boat and motorboat movements.

4. Ocean Effects

Maya now allows you to create a simple water-ripple effect. This effect is usually used to create ripples in the water as objects glide across the surface. Simulating the movement of a fast-moving motorboat is an excellent example.

To get started, select [Fluid Effects > Ocean > Create Ocean] to make the ocean effect. Then select [Fluid Effects > Ocean > Add Preview Plane] to adjust the size of the effect as shown in Figure 10-97.

Open the Attribute Editor in the Preview Plane and set the resolution to about 30, as shown in Figure 10-98. Select [Fluid Effects > Ocean > Create Ocean > Create Wake]. This will create the Volume Emitter and 3D Container as shown in Figure 10-99. Play the animation; you should see the water ripples shown in Figure 10-100.

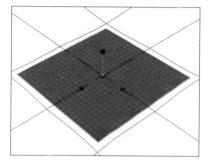

Figure 10-97 Add Preview Plane

Figure 10-98 Attribute Editor

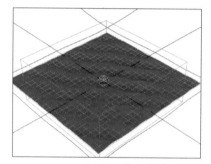

Figure 10-99 Create Wake

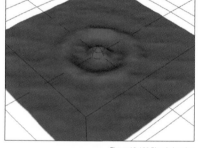

Figure 10-100 Play Animation

Let's now try rendering the effect to see the result. Set the view to where the ripple starts and render it.

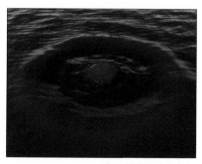

Figure 10-101 Rendering Image

Let's now move the Volume Emitter to vary the water ripple simulation. As shown in Figure 10-102, draw in a random curve in Top view. Now select the Volume Emitter, then the curve. Select [Animation > Animate > Motion path > Attach Motion Path]. If you want, you can open the Attach Motion Path options window and enter the desired value.

Play the animation. As seen in Figure 10-103, we have created a ripple effect that moves along with the Volume Emitter.

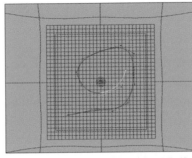

Figure 10-102 Random Curve in Top View

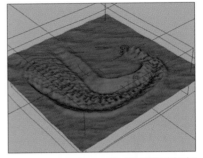

Figure 10-103 Play Animation

When we render the effect, we can see that the Wake effect is created on top of the Ocean effect (Figure 10-104).

Figure 10-104 Rendering the Wake Effect

3-4 CREATE POND EFFECT

The Pond effect is a ripple effect that uses the 3D Fluid Container. Although it's used in the same way as the Ocean Wake effect seen in the previous section, the rendering method follows that of a Fluid Effect.

Select [Fluid Effects > Pond > Create Pond] to create the meshed 3D Container seen in Figure 10-105. Select [Fluid Effects > Pond > Create Wake] and play the animation to see the circular rippling effect seen in Figure 10-106.

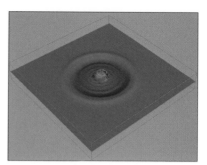

Figure 10-105 Create Pond

Figure 10-106 Create Wake

This tool is used in the same way as the Ocean effect. We can keyframe the Volume Emitter to make a rippling water effect, or we can simulate the movement of an object or boat on the water using Dynamic Locator or Make Boat.

The only difference between the Pond and Ocean effects lies in how the effects are rendered. The Pond effect follows the Fluid Effects rendering method. Consequently, Volume Render and Surface Render give us two different results.

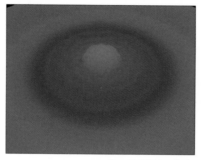

Figure 10-107 Volume Render

Figure 10-108 Surface Render

4. IMPROVED PAINT EFFECT TOOLS

The latest update to Maya allows us to convert paint effects into polygons. This is a vast improvement over the limitations of earlier paint effects, which produced poorer results when it came to model details and shading. By converting the Paint Effect brush into a polygon, we can quickly and easily add more subtle details and more realistic shading.

Let's look at a simple example to see just how much the paint effects have been improved. Press the '8' key on the keyboard to convert to Paint Effect mode. Press the **V** in the menu bar to open the visor.

As shown in Figure 10-109, select the tree folder in the visor and select the birchBlowingLight.mel brush.

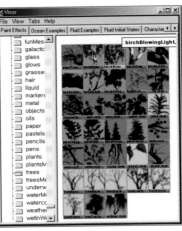

Figure 10-109 Brush Selection

Use the brush to paint the picture of a tree as shown in Figure 10-110. If you would like to render the picture using Paint Effects, select [Panel > Stroke Refresh > Rendered].

Figure 10-110 Drawing the Tree

Now, let's convert the tree into a polygon. Press '8' on the keyboard again to exit from the Paint Effect mode. After selecting the brush stroke we just made, select [Modify > Convert > Paint Effect To Polygon] to open the Options window (Figure 10-111).

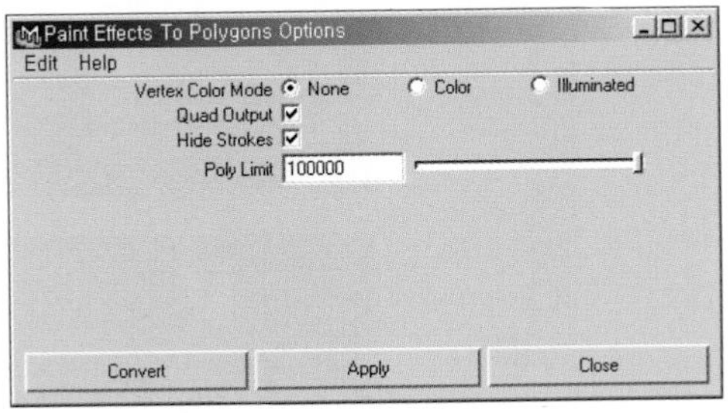

Figure 10-111 Options Window

Select Quad Output so that the polygons remain in rectangular form, then select Hide Strokes to hide the original brush stroke. Poly Limit shows us how many polygons we have; the higher this number, the more elaborate and detailed the converted model.

After making the configurations, click on the Convert button at the bottom. As shown in Figure 10-112, the Paint Effect brush will convert into a polygon

Figure 10-112 Convert To Polygon

Figure 10-113 Rendering Image

As the brush is converted into a polygon, a shader will be made based on the shading properties of the original brush. We can adjust the shader to render the image we want. You can see the shader by selecting [Windows > Rendering Editors > HyperShade].

Figure 10-114 shows us the HyperShade window that contains the shader that was made. If we adjust the shader properties to account for light and other conditions, we can obtain a more realistic and detailed image.

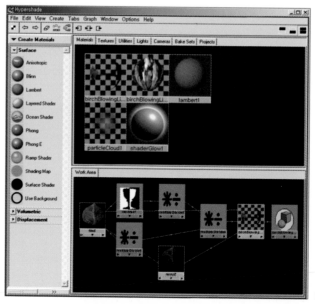

Figure 10-114 HyperShade

4-1 USING THE PAINT EFFECT ATTRIBUTES TO SIMULATE TREE MOVEMENTS

Select the converted tree model and open the Attribute Editor. In the Attribute Editor, after expanding the birchBrowinLight1 tab, click on [Tube > Behavior > Turbulence] and select 'Tree Wind' from Turbulence Types.

Play the animation. You should see the simulation of a tree blowing in the wind. Adjust the strength of the wind by adjusting the Turbulence value. The higher this value, the stronger the wind. A high value will make it look as if the tree is caught in the midst of a tornado.

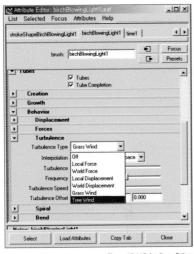

Figure 10-115 Attribute Editor

Polygon-converted paint effects can also be rendered in other Maya rendering types, such as Vector Rendering and Mental Ray. Since we can convert all brush types into polygons, shapes that were difficult to make in the past can be much easier to produce.

This concludes a quick overview of the most useful features in Maya 5.0. Without a doubt, the most important factor is adaptability. The software is only effective as long as you understand and use the features to fit your needs. Simple examples have been used to illustrate some of the features here. This, I hope, will make it easier for you to approach these. For more detailed information on these features, refer to the documentation that came with your software. However, the fastest and best way for you to get a handle on these features is to use them to create your own effects.

Deep Paint 3D

1. TUTORIAL

Now, we will use a tutorial to observe the mapping process using subdivision surfaces in Maya. We have already learned how to edit basic UVs of subdivision surfaces in Chapters 2 and 3. Now, to wrap things up, we will look at how to edit UVs in Maya, paint in Deep Paint 3D, and then move back to Maya for shading.

1-1. EDITING THE UV-AXIS ON THE SUBDIVISION SURFACE

We will first look at how to edit the UV-axis. This method is slightly different from the method we learned earlier. We will use another feature of Maya to edit subdivision surface UVs faster and easier. First, open the example file located in the CD-ROM. The file is saved as CD-ROM/CHARACTER/scenes/FaceMap.mb. The file is shown in Figure 11-1.

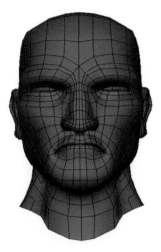

Figure 11-1 Example File (Modeling by Kang Min-Ho)

This modeling file was made into a subdivision surface. We need to map the subdivision surface in order to use the subdivision surface without converting it first into a polygon. We will be using the method learned in Chapters 2 and 3 from time to time.
If you are not familiar with mapping, read Chapters 2 and 3 before continuing.

step 1 Select the model and then select [Edit > Duplicate] to copy the model. Use the default Duplicate options. Select [Display > Hide > Hide Selection] to hide the copied model.

step 2 Select [Modify > Convert > Subdiv To Polygons ▣] to open the Options window. After setting the Tessellation Method to Vertices, the Level to 0, and the Original Object to Replace, as shown in Figure 11-2, click the Convert button at the bottom of the window.

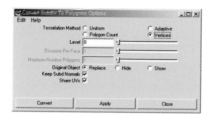

Figure 11-2 Options Window

As shown in Figure 11-3, the subdivision surface will be converted into a polygon at level 0.

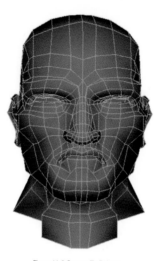

Figure 11-3 Convert To Polygon

step 3 Currently, this model does not have any UVs. Nothing should appear when we select [Windows > UV Texture Editor] to open the Texture Editor.

We must now create UVs for this polygon model. We have already gone over creating and editing UVs in depth. As mentioned earlier, editing UVs requires little effort in 3D painting. The most important thing to remember when editing UVs is that they must be spread out evenly without any overlapping regions. Let's use Cylindrical Mapping as we have learned. First, select all the faces on the model and then select [Modeling > Edit Polygons > Textures > Cylindrical Mapping]. Using the Channel Box, set the Projection Horizontal to 360. As we can see in Figure 11-4, the Cylindrical Mapping is applied and the UV Texture Editor will look as it does in Figure 11-5.

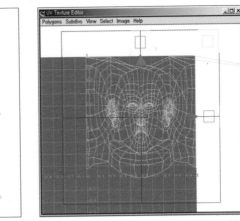

Figure 11-4 Cylindrical Mapping   Figure 11-5 UV Texture Editor

In order to have the UVs spread out as it does in Figure 11-5, the Projection Center must be set to 0.0001 in the Channel Box. Let's look at the UVs in Figure 11-5. We can see that the UVs near the mouth, eyes, and the nose overlap. Overlapping UVs will share textures, and this is not desirable. Therefore, in order to edit these UVs, we must first modify the UVs. If a picture map source was used, we could modify these UVs by referring to the picture. However, if you want to use Deep Paint to create a precise texture, the overlapping UVs must be modified using the various options offered by Maya. One useful option is Relax UV.

step 4   We must do the following in order to use Relax UV. First, as shown in Figure 11-6, select the overlapping UVs in the edges around the eyes. Select [Polygons > Cut UVs] from the UV Texture Editor to cut the UVs, as shown in Figure 11-7.

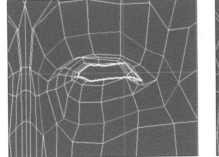

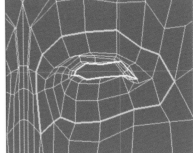

Figure 11-6 Selecting the Edge   Figure 11-7 Applying Cut UVs

Click the RMB and select UV from the Marking Menu. Then, select a few of the UVs from around the eyes, as shown in Figure 11-8. Select [Select > Select Shell Border] from the UV Texture Editor. As shown in Figure 11-9, the UVs in the edge making up the borders of the shell will be selected.

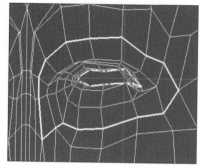

Figure 11-8 Selecting the UVs

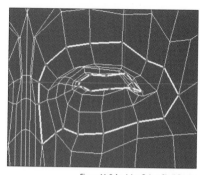

Figure 11-9 Applying Select Shell Border

Remove the outer UVs from the selection and use the Scale Tool to adjust the size of the only the inner UVs, as shown in Figure 11-10. Select [Polygon > Relax UVs] from the UV Texture Editor. This will smoothen out the overlapping UVs around the eyes, as shown in Figure 11-11.

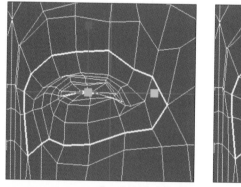

Figure 11-10 Adjusting the Scale

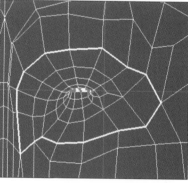

Figure 11-11 Applying Relax UVs

In order to paste severed UVs, select the edges around the eyes in the UV Texture Editor as shown in Figure 11-12. Select [Polygon > Sew UVs] from the UV Texture Editor to paste back together the cut UVs as shown in Figure 11-13.

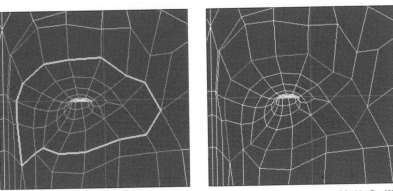

Figure 11-12 Selecting the Edge

Figure 11-13 Applying Sew UVs

By using Relax UVs in certain areas, we are able to manage the UVs more efficiently. If you find this to be too complex, you can simply apply Relax UVs to all the UVs as in Figure 11-14.

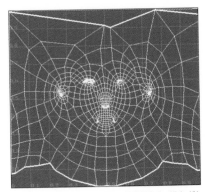

Figure 11-14 Relaxing All the UVs

However, depending on the model, this may or may not be such a good choice. Next, we will look at another method for doing this.

step 5 Select the model, and then select [Edit > Delete by Type > History] to erase the entire history. Select the model, and select [Modeling > Edit Polygons > Sculpt Polygon Tool □] to open the Artisan Tool Settings window. As shown in Figure 11-15, set the Opacity to 1, the Operation to Smooth, the Ref. Vector to Normal, and the Max Displacement to 1 in the Tool Settings window.

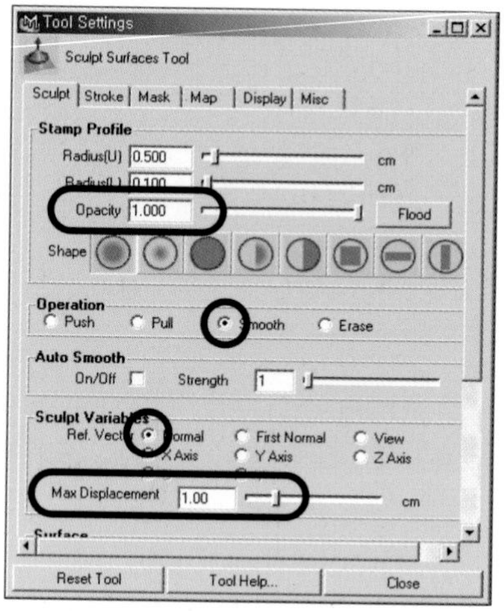

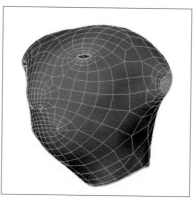

Figure 10-15 Tool Settings Window

Click the Flood button next to the Opacity slider bar in the Tool Settings window (Figure 11-15) until you get the shape seen in Figure 11-16.

Figure 10-16 Applying the Flood

Doing this will prevent the surfaces of the model from overlapping and create a sphere-like shape. Artisan's Smooth feature acts to soften the model in this way. Observe the areas of the ears, nose, and lips to make sure that there are no overlapping regions before continuing.

step 6 Select the model, and then select [Modeling > Edit Polygons > Textures > Spherical Mapping]. Use the default settings for the Spherical Mapping. In the Channel Box, set the Projection Center to 0.0001, the Projection Horizontal to 360, and the Projection Vertical to 180.

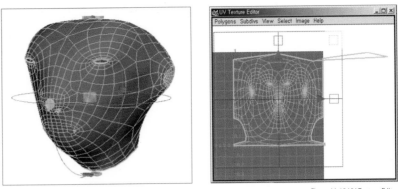

Figure 11-17 Spherical Mapping   Figure 11-18 UV Texture Editor

By opening the UV Texture Editor, we can see that the UVs are spread out, as in Figure 11-18.

This method makes the model into a sphere-like shape so that the model can be mapped once using Spherical Mapping.

Move UVs that have not spread out properly in the UV Texture Editor as shown in Figure 11-19, and then use Sew UVs to organize the UVs in certain areas.

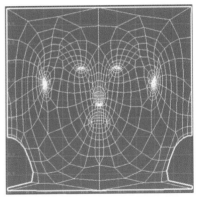

Figure 11-19 Organized UVs

This is a faster and easier method of organizing UVs. We must now apply these UVs to the subdivision surface. This can be done easily using Blend Shape.

 step 7 Select the polygon model and then select [Modify > Convert > Polygons to Subdiv]. The model will be converted to a subdivision surface, as shown in Figure 11-20.

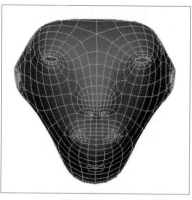

Figure 11-20 Convert To Subdivision Surface

Select [Display > Show > Show All] to display all the models that were hidden in the beginning. Select first the models that have not been altered (see Figure 11-21) and then select the models for which the UVs have been altered. Select [Animation > Deform > Create Blend Shape.] After a short computation time, the Blend Shape will be made. The unaltered model, which was used as the target object, is no longer needed and may be erased.

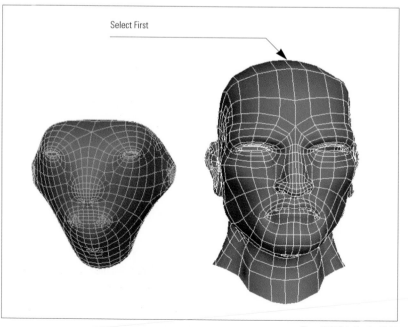

Select First

Figure 11-21 Selecting the Model

step 8 Select [Windows > Animation Editors > Blend Shape] to open the Blend Shape window.

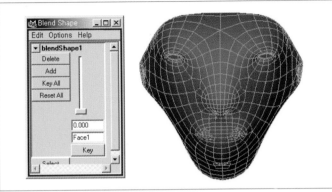

Figure 11-22 Blend Shape Window

We can see in Figure 11-22 that, because we used only one target object, only one slider is made. Now, drag this slider to give a Weight value of 1, and blend the model until it takes on the original shape as shown in Figure 11-23.

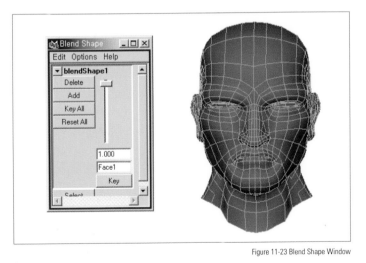

Figure 11-23 Blend Shape Window

After selecting the model, select [Edit > Delete by Type > History] to delete the blend shape and the history of the model. Select [Windows > UV Texture Editor] to open the UV Texture Editor. We can see in Figure 11-24 that the UV-axis we created in Polygon Mode is applied to the subdivision surface.

In such a way, we can use Blend Shape to easily carry over the UV-axis from Polygon Mode to Subdivision Surface Mode. This method can also be used to facilitate working with polygons.

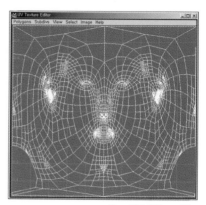

Figure 11-24 UV Texture Editor

1-2. TURNING OVER THE MODEL TO DEEP PAINT

Let's now turn the subdivision surface with the modified UVs over to Deep Paint 3D. Deep Paint 3D does not directly support Maya subdivision surfaces. Therefore, it must first be converted to a polygon before it can be carried over into Deep Paint 3D.

step 1 Select the model and after selecting [Edit > Duplicate] to copy the model, select [Display > Hide > Hide Selection] to hide the copied model. In order to convert the subdivision surface to a polygon, select the model and then select [Modify > Convert > Subdiv To Polygons ▢] to open the Options window. In the Options window, set the Tessellation Method to Vertex and the Level to 1 before clicking on the Convert button, as shown in Figure 11-25.

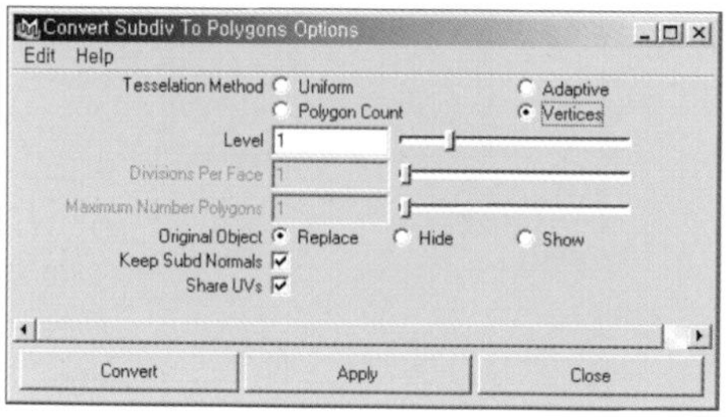

Figure 11-25 Options Window

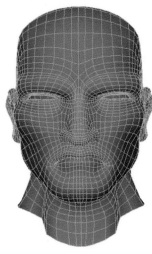

The subdivision surface will be converted over to polygon as shown in Figure 11-26.

Figure 11-26 Convert To Polygon

step 2 If the Deep Paint 3D Plug-In has been installed in Maya, select [Windows > Settings/Preferences > Plug-In Manager] to display DeepPaint3Dmaya 40.mll, as shown in Figure 11-27. Put a check by Loaded and Auto Load.

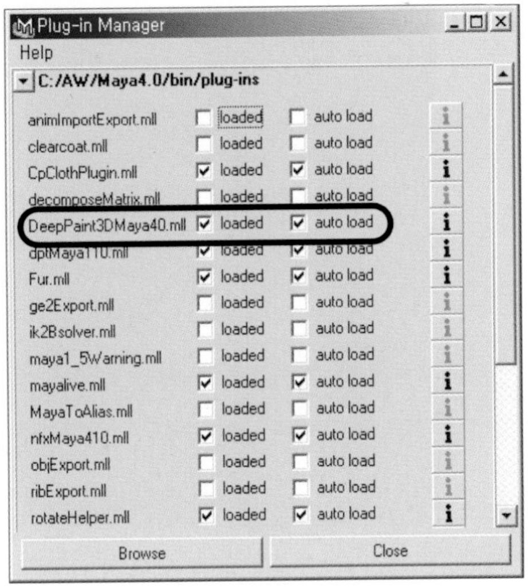

Figure 11-27 Plug-In Manager

The Deep Paint 3D menu will appear in Maya's main menu at the top.

Select [Deep Paint 3D > Launch Deep Paint 3D] to execute Deep Paint 3D.

step 3 Make a Blinn Shader in Hypershade or Multilister and assign it to the polygon object. First of all,

let's look at how the model can be carried over directly into Deep Paint without additional steps. After selecting the polygon model, select [Deep Paint 3D > Paint Selected]. When the Deep Paint 3D window is active, the Material Import window will open in Deep Paint 3D as shown in Figure 11-28.

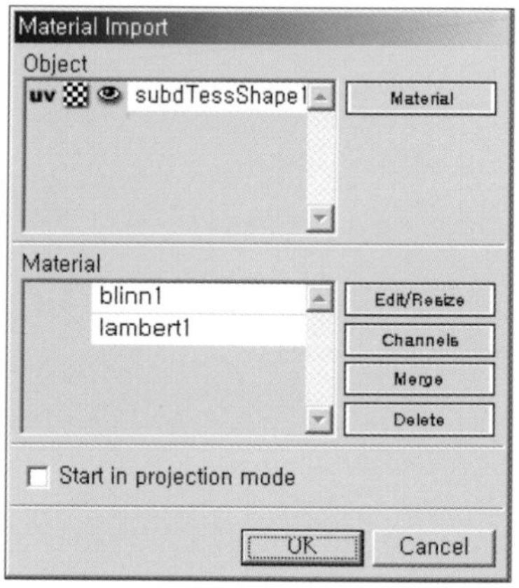

Click the OK button in the current state.

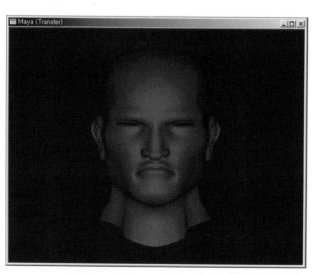

Figure 11-28 Material Import Window

The polygon model will be carried over into Deep Paint 3D as shown in Figure 11-29.

Figure 11-29 Deep Paint 3D Window

However, in this state, we will not be able to paint directly on the model. A warning message (see Figure 11-30) will appear when we try to select a brush and paint on the model.

Figure 11-30 Warning Message

This warning message appears because the modeling does not yet have a source file. If a file had been assigned in Maya before the model was carried over to the Deep Paint, this message would not appear. The next step looks at how to assign a file to the model.

 step 4   As shown in Figure 11-31, click the mouse on the Layer Sub Tab Color in the Element Tab of the Command Panel.

Figure 11-31 Command Panel

The Add New Channel window will open, as seen in Figure 11-32.

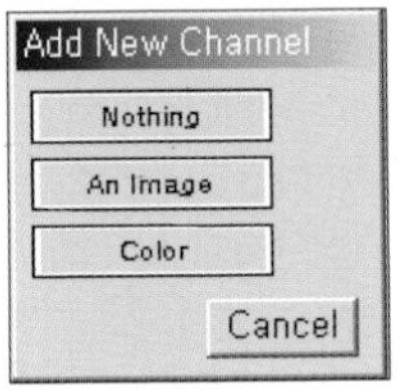

Figure 11-32 Add New Channel Window

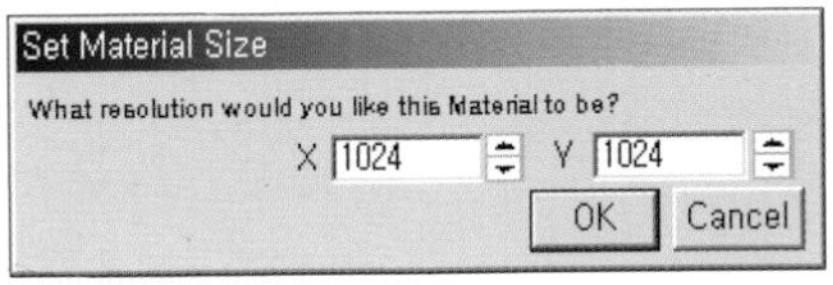

Figure 11-33 Set Material Size

Select Color from the Add New Channel window (see Figure 11-32). This will open the Set Material Size window seen in Figure 11-33. This is where we adjust the resolution of the image. As shown in the figure, set both X and Y to 1024 and then click the OK button. This will create the Select Color window as shown in Figure 11-34. Selecting the desired color in this window and clicking the OK button will apply the selected color and resolution to the model (see Figure 11-35).

Figure 11-34 Selecting the Color

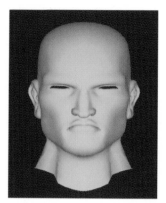

Figure 11-35 A Color Map Made for the Model

We have now created the environment for painting. We can now paint the desired map source shape to create the source. If you wish to use Bump and Shine along with the Color Map, the resolution and colors for each must be assigned separately. The Shine Map can be thought of as the Specular Map in Maya. In my case, instead of making a map of each channel, I prefer to make the Bump and Shine Maps later and then insert them into the Color Map. This can be a much more effective method. In the next section, we will look at a more efficient method for creating the map source.

1-3. MAPPING USING A PICTURE SOURCE

Using a picture to create a map source is a very effective method for those not familiar with painting. Although it may be different for different characters, using a picture is a good way to create a very realistic image. We will now look at how to use pictures to create a mapping source. First, prepare a scanned image.

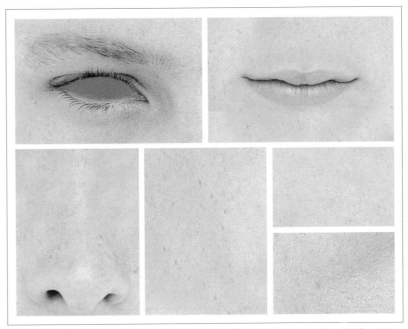

Figure 11-36 Scanned Image

step 1 Let's look at the scanned image. This is an image that has been created by splitting up a scanned image. It is merely a collage of different areas of a scanned image. The Clone Tool has been used to modify areas of the image in Photoshop.

The sources that will be used for the face, as shown in Figure 11-36, consist of the eye, nose, mouth, and the basic skin. This image is saved in the CD-ROM and will be used throughout this process.

step 2 Let's use Photoshop to modify areas of the image. First, after running Photoshop, open the file, CD-ROM/CHARACTER/sourceimages/Eye Picture.jpg. As shown in Figure 11-37, after using Quick Mask in Photoshop to paint the area that will be masked, make it into an Alpha Channel as shown in Figure 11-38.

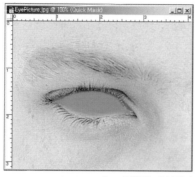

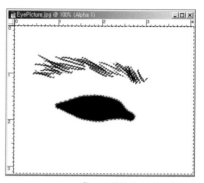

Figure 11-37 Using Quick Mask

Figure 11-38 Making an Alpha Channel

Name the source and save it as a 32-bit TGA file. This file is saved as EyePicture.tga on the CD-ROM.

A picture source is very different from a model. This can be readily seen by looking at the eye and mouth. As follows, we need to match the eye in the picture to the eye in the model.

We will now take a look at how to match and alter the picture image to the model.

step 3 First, after making a NURBS plane, arrange it as shown in Figure 11-39. After making a Lambert Shader in Hypershade, load the TGA file made in Step 2 into Color and assign it to the NURBS plane. Adjust the opacity of the Lamber Shader slightly, and press the 6 key on the keyboard to convert to Hardware Texture Mode. The texture will be displayed as shown in Figure 11-40.

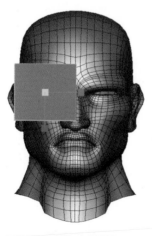

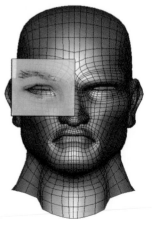

Figure 11-39 Making the NURBS Plane

Figure 11-40 Hardware Texture Mode

The reason we make an Alpha Channel in Photoshop is so that the a slight opacity will be applied to the Hardware Texture Mode (see Figure 11-41). Now, add isoparms to the NURBS plane, as shown in Figure 11-41, and move the CVs so that the eye mapped in the plane becomes similar to the modeled eye. Now, use the EyePicture.jpg, without the Alpha Channel, instead of the EyePicture.tga used in Lambert to remove the opacity in Lambert. The result is that the altered eye image will be displayed clearly as in Figure 11-42.

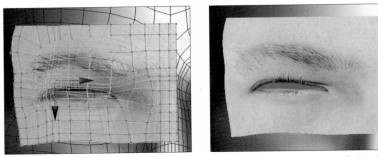

Figure 11-41 Using the CVs to Make the Shape

Figure 11-42 The Altered Image

Maya's Hardware Texture Mode is quite exceptional. The mapped image will retain a resolution quite close to the original image. Let's now capture this entire screen. This can be done by using a basic capture program or by simply pressing the Print Screen key on the keyboard. Load the captured image from the clipboard into Photoshop by selecting [File > New] and then pressing Ctrl+V to paste the image.

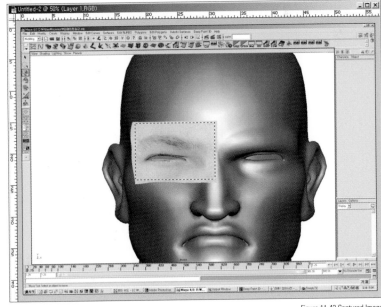

Figure 11-43 Captured Image

This will load the captured image as seen in Figure 11-43. Select the area around the eye as shown and press Ctrl+C to save the image in the clipboard.

step 4 Activate the Deep Paint 3D window. Change back to Project Paint Mode by clicking on ⤓. Turn off the Bump and Shine channels in the Tool Palette. Press Ctrl+V to load the image saved in the clipboard. This will load the copied image onto the model in Photoshop. Adjust the size and position of the image as shown in Figure 11-44. Using the Move Tool will automatically adjust the size and position of the image.

We can also adjust the size and position of the image in the Move Options window, as shown in Figure 11-45.

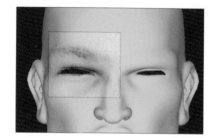

Figure 11-44 Loading the Image

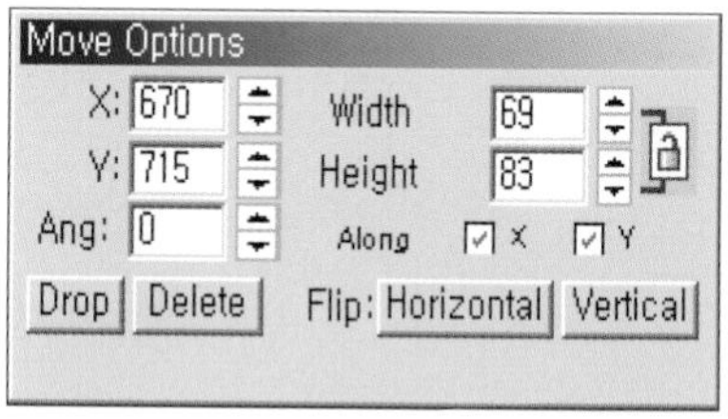

Figure 11-45 Move Options Window

After selecting the position, either press the Enter key or click on the Drop button, as shown in Figure 11-45. Using the Rotate Tool from the Tool Palette to rotate the scene, we can see that the loaded image has been applied to the model (see Figure 11-46).

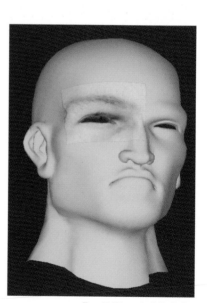

Figure 11-46 Image Applied to the Face

step 5 Now, in order to map in Maya, make a map on the plane (see Figure 11-47) to alter the image. The source file for the mouth is saved as CD-ROM/CHARACTER/sourceimages/MouthPicture.jpg.

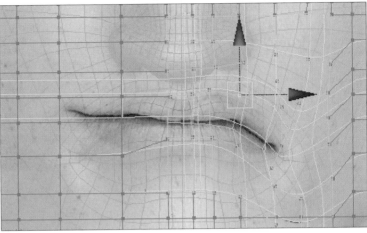

Figure 11-47 Altering the Image

Load the altered texture into Deep Paint 3D by repeating Steps 3 and 4. Figure 11-48 shows the image pasted onto the model. This is the result that you should see. As you can see in the figure, there is no need to work on both sides of the face. Simply work on one side of the face and then we will copy and paste it onto the other side.

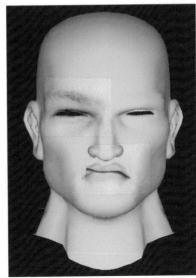

Figure 11-48 Pasted Image

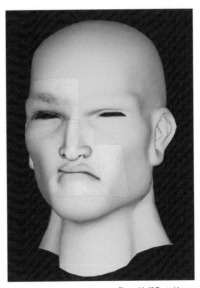

Figure 11-49 Pasted Image

Make the nose in the same way. Figure 11-49 shows the pasted image of the nose. The source file for the nose is saved as CD-ROM/CHARACTER/sourceimages/ NosePicture.jpg.

step 6 We have looked at how to make the eye, nose, and mouth that are different in the picture image and the model. We will now look at how to use Deep Paint 3D s Painting feature to finish the image. The feature used to paint using a picture image is Texture Paint. There are a few things we need to do before we can use Texture Paint. First, load the file, CD-ROM/CHARACTER/sourceimages/Skin2.jpg, into Photoshop. Then, as shown in Figure 11-50, use the Lasso Tool to select the imported image as shown.

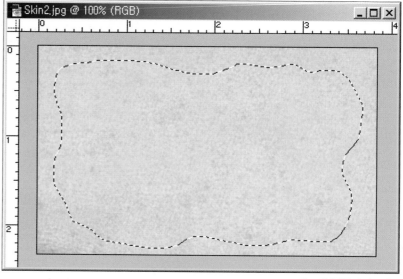

Figure 11-50 Using the Lasso Tool

After specifying an Alpha Channel for the selected frame, apply a Gaussian Blur to the Alpha Channel as shown in Figure 11-51.

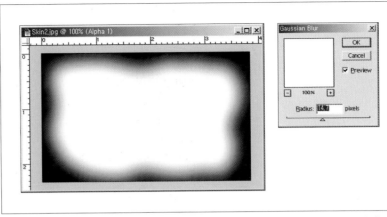

Figure 11-51 Adding a Gaussian Blur to the Alpha Channel

Save this Alpha Channel as a separate image. This image is saved as CD-ROM/ CHARACTER/sourceimages/Skin2Alpha.jpg.

step 7 Activate the Deep Paint 3D window. Click on the arrow icon of the Brush Tab in the Command Panel as indicated in Figure 11-52 and select New from the menu. This will create the Brush & Paint Present Builder window (see Figure 11-53). As shown here, set the Brush Type to Air Brush, the Paint Type to Texture Paint, and then click the OK button.

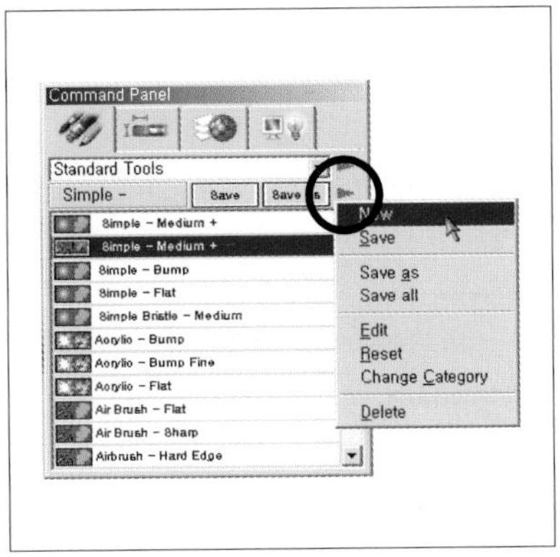

Figure 11-52 Command Panel

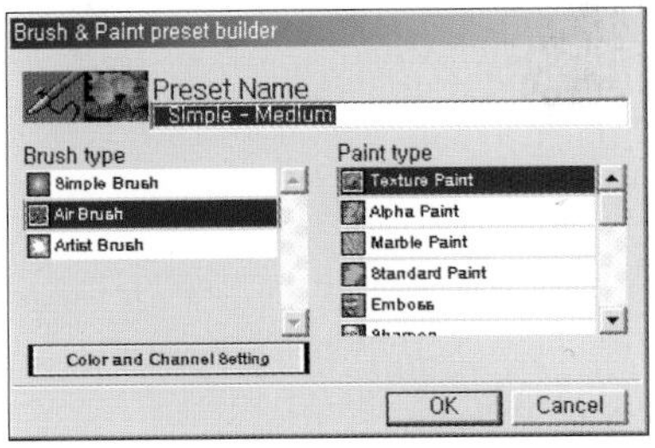

Figure 11-53 Brush & Paint Preset Builder Window

As shown in Figure 11-54, select the Brush & Paint Settings Tab in the Command Panel. Then, place the CD-ROM/CHARACTER/sourceimages/Skin2.jpg in Color of the Texture Channel, and place the Skin2Alpha.jpg file into Alpha.

Figure 11-54 Putting Images in the Channel

DEEP PAINT 3D

Now, select the Brush from the Tool Palette, and paint on top of the model. Adjust the brush size by holding down the Ctrl key and moving the mouse up and down. Hold down the Ctrl key and drag the mouse from left to right to adjust the intensity of the brush. Paint evenly over the entire surface as shown in Figure 11-55. Because we are painting in Project Mode, we must use the Rotate Tool from the Tool Palette to rotate the scene while we paint so that no one area of the map gets bunched up.

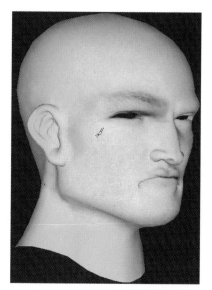

Figure 11-55 Painting Texture

step 8 Let's look at another way to make the texture. Select [File > Open] from Deep Paint 3D, and open the file CD-ROM/CHARACTER/sourceimages/ Skin1.jpg. Opening the image file in a new window will create 2 windows side by side, as shown in Figure 11-56.

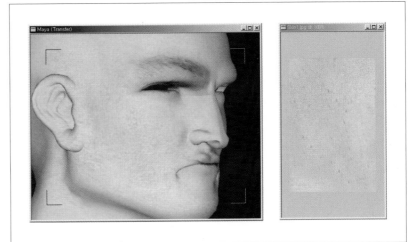

Figure 11-56 Arrangement of the Windows

Select the Clone Tool from the Tool Palette and, while holding down the Alt key, click on the area of the Skin1.jpg file that we wish to replicate. By painting over the model, we can see that the 2D image is painted over the 3D model. Continue painting so that the texture is applied differently to portions of the image.

step 9 When the painting is almost finished, edit the image again in Photoshop. Click on the ⬇ icon in the icon menu to exit from Project Paint Mode. Select [File > Export > Material Photoshop]. This will activate the Photoshop window, and a new window will be opened as shown in Figure 11-57. This picture is composed of 2 layers. The painted texture is placed in the Background layer, and the UV coordinates are placed in the new layer.

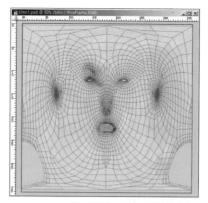

Figure 11-57 Image Imported into Photoshop

It is time to copy the side completed using the UV coordinates and paste it to the other side. In order to do so, edit the image as shown in Figure 11-58. After editing the image, merge the layers so that the image only has 2 layers, as it did when it was first imported into Photoshop. Figure 11-58 shows the edited image. The UV coordinate layer has been hidden.

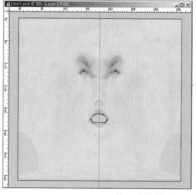

Figure 11-58 Edited Image

Activate the Deep Paint 3D window. Select [File > Import > Photoshop]. This will import the image edited in Photoshop into Deep Paint 3D, as shown in Figure 11-59.

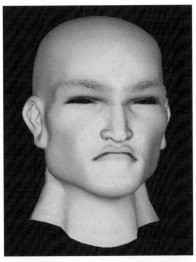

Now, all we need to do is to touch up awkward areas using Texture Paint or the Clone Tool. Figure 11-60 shows the modified image. Touch up the image so that no awkward areas remain.

Figure 11-59 Image Imported from Photoshop

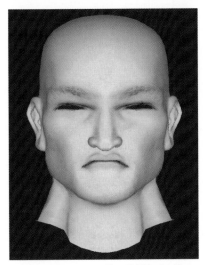

Figure 11-60 Completed Texture

step 10 The final step is to save the completed image. Save the image by selecting [File > Save All Map]. If you are still in Project Paint Mode, you must exit from this mode before applying Save All Map. The Save All Map Options window will appear as in Figure 11-61.

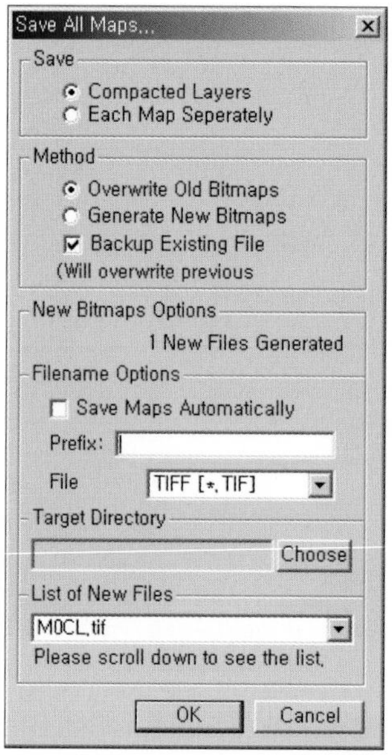

Save All Maps...

Save
- Compacted Layers
- Each Map Seperately

Method
- Overwrite Old Bitmaps
- Generate New Bitmaps
- ☑ Backup Existing File
  (Will overwrite previous

New Bitmaps Options
1 New Files Generated

Filename Options
- ☐ Save Maps Automatically

Prefix: [   ]

File [TIFF [*.TIF] ▼]

Target Directory
[   ] Choose

List of New Files
[M0CL.tif   ▼]
Please scroll down to see the list.

OK   Cancel

Figure 11-61 Options Window

Keep the default settings, and click on the OK button at the bottom of the window. Then, select Directory and File Format and save the image under an appropriate name.

Now, all we have to do is to make an appropriate shader in Maya, load the saved image, and then insert it into the Color Map. Display the subdivision surface and assign the shader to the model. Figure 11-62 shows the completed image.

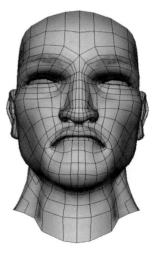

We can create a Specular Map and a Bump Map faster by using the Color Map image in Photoshop.

Figure 11-62 Completed Color Texture

2. MULTI-PATCH MODELING

In this section, we will look at how to turn the multi-patch modeling data over to Deep Paint 3D. In general, we can only use polygons in Deep Paint 3D. However, if the Deep Paint 3D Plug-In has been installed in Maya, the NURBS surface will be converted automatically into a polygon and exported into Deep Paint 3D.

Let's look at how to turn the multi-patch modeling data (see Figure 11-63) over to Deep Paint 3D.

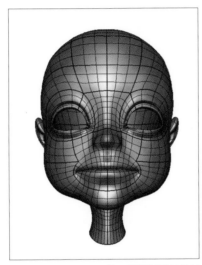

Figure 11-63 Multi-Patch Model

step 1 In contrast to the subdivision surface seen in the last section, many surfaces will have to be turned over into Deep Paint 3D in this section. If there is only one polygon, it is more effective to make the map source in Deep Paint 3D. If, like this multi-patch, there are numerous surfaces, it can be very difficult to assign a map source for each surface in Deep Paint 3D. However, if the Deep Paint 3D Plug-In has been installed in Maya, this becomes rather easy to do. First, make a Blinn Shader in Hypershade or Multilister and select and assign all the surfaces of the face.

Select [Deep Paint 3D > Material Splitter] from Mayas main menu.

This will open the Material Splitter window as shown in Figure 11-64. Select the name of the blinn 1 Shader, which has been assigned to the Multi-Patch, and click on the indicated Select button. Strengthen the color as shown in Figure 11-65, click on the Select button, and then click on the Assign Shading Switch button at the bottom of the window.

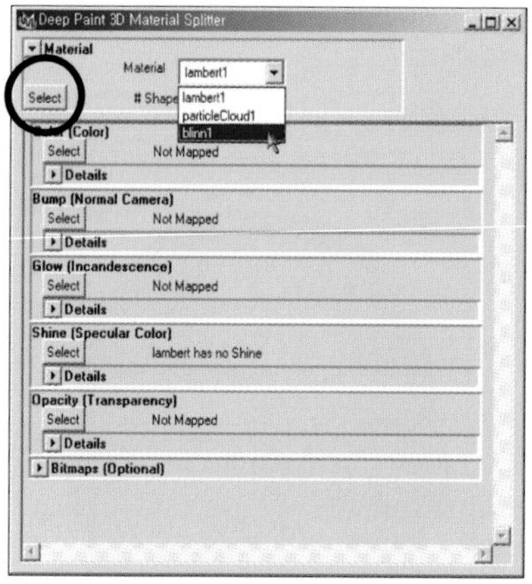

Figure 11-64 Material Splitter Window

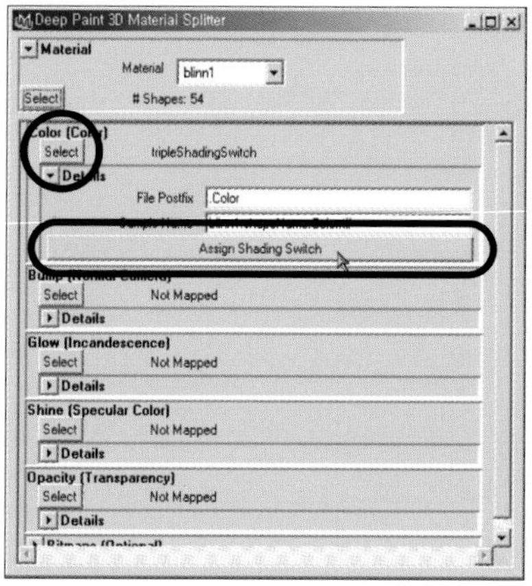

Figure 11-65 Material Splitter Window

Looking at the Multilister window, we can see that a Triple Switch Utility is made automatically and that a file map is made for each surface (see Figure 11-66).

This file will automatically be given the name specified in Sample Name (see Figure 11-66). In other words, looking at the Sample Name, we can see that it reads blinn1.shape-Name.color.tif. If the surface name is A1, the name of the file texture that is applied to the A1 surface will be blinn1.A1.color.tif.

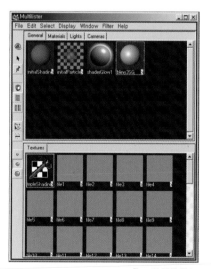

Figure 11-66 Mulilister

If the file is successfully made, the file image will appear gray as shown in Figure 11-66. If the file is made but appears in black, this means that the file was not successfully made and the texture will not be exported from Deep Paint 3D. This can happen for the following reasons:

One reason why this occurs is a missing Temp folder. Select [File > Preference > Directory] in Deep Paint 3D, and we can see, in Figure 11-67, that the Temp folder is missing from the Temp folder route. If there is no folder in C:/temp, the texture has nowhere to be saved temporarily and, therefore, fails to be made. As follows, we must make a C:/temp folder ourselves and specify the route as shown.

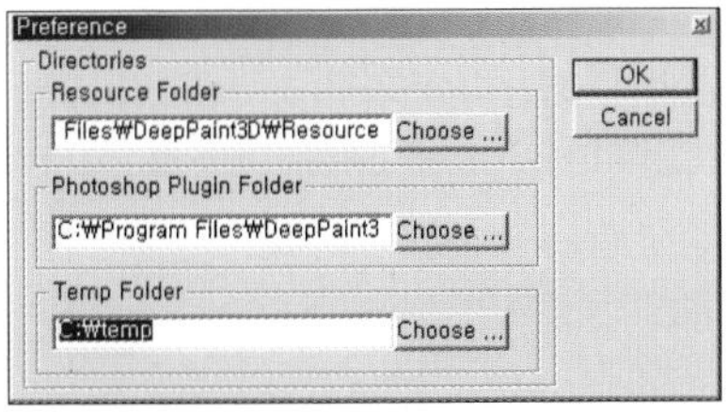

Figure 11-67 Preferences Window

When Deep Paint 3D is first installed, it automatically looks for and specifies the system Temp folder. Therefore, although this step may not have to be done as a separate step, it is a good idea to create a Temp folder that will only be used by Deep Paint.

A second reason why this may occur is that the project is not correctly assigned in Maya. In such cases, we must specify the project by selecting [File > Project > Set] from Mayas main menu.

A third reason for this phenomenon is that the surface name is too long. There is a limit to the number of characters that can be recognized by the window. Files that have names longer than this limit will not be recognized and a file texture will not be made. Actually, when working in Multi-Patch, we apply Attach and Detach many times. Every time this is done in Maya, the respective surface name gets longer. As follows, when the surface name exceeds the limit that can be recognized by the window, a file texture for such a surface will not be made. When you are using Deep Paint 3D, it is a good idea to change the name of the completed patch to something that is short and easily recognizable.

By avoiding these 3 situations, a successful file texture will be made. So far I haven't discovered any other situations that would prevent a texture from being made properly.

step 2 It is a good idea to inspect the Normal of the surface before exporting. This is because, when there are many surfaces, it is very difficult to correct abnormal surface Normals in Deep Paint 3D.

In order to export the surface into Deep Paint 3D, select all the surfaces in the face and select [Deep Paint 3D > Paint Selected] from Maya's main menu. You must make sure to execute Deep Paint 3D prior to this step. The time that it takes for the model to be exported into Deep Paint 3D will depend on the number of surfaces and the system itself. As the surface is exported into Deep Paint 3D, the Material Import window will open (see Figure 11-68). Click on the OK button at the bottom of the window.

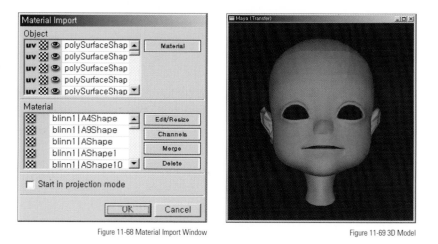

Figure 11-68 Material Import Window   Figure 11-69 3D Model

As shown in Figure 11-69, the NURBS model will be converted into a polygon as it is imported.

step 3 Now, as we described earlier, paint over the object. In general, using Project Paint Mode assures that the texture is applied correctly.

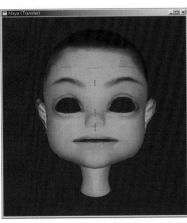

Figure 11-70 Painting over the Model

step 4 If you are not familiar with the painting process, please refer back to the Tutorial.

It is now time to export the texture back into Maya.

Before exporting the texture into Maya, we must exit from Project Paint Mode. To exit from this mode, click on the icon in Texture Weapon.

After selecting [File > Save All Maps] in Deep Paint 3D, leave the options in the default setting and click on the OK button. Activate Maya. Select [Deep Paint 3D > Update All Textures] from Maya's main menu.

Press the 7 key on the keyboard to convert to Hardware Texture Mode. Now we can see that the texture that was created using Deep Paint 3D is imported into Maya.

Figure 11-71 Texture loaded into Maya

In this section, we looked at how to create Texture map sources using Deep Paint 3D. Such 3D painting software programs can make character mapping very quick and easy. It also reduces the time needed to edit UVs because maps are automatically applied to fit the UVs even without having to equalize the UV spacing of the subdivision surface or polygon. If the Deep Paint 3D Plug-In has not been installed in Maya, convert the model to a polygon first, in Maya, and then export it in OBJ format before importing into Deep Paint 3D. Although there is the added hassle of having to save this separately because only the texture is being used, it should not be that much of a problem. When exporting in OBJ format, we can maintain the UV coordinates when exporting into other software programs.

|ma-p-ya| Woo-seung Jeong

|ma-p-ya| Jin-pyo Hong

Remains When did we become so used to saving time and looking for shortcuts? We seem to associate faster with being better.

Remains When I'm down, nothing cheers me up like ramen noodles cooked in an old silver pot, served with a bottle of soju. And accompanied by the perfume of cigarettes from long ago.

Underground Parking Lot 2. Another angle of the underground parking lot seen earlier.

Park A park bench in the fall. Taking a small break to merely gaze at the sky.

Tunnel A re-creation of the harmony created by the intensity of light and darkness.

PART _ 3

In Part 3, we will look at how to use Maya to create a short animation story.
I believe that you will have no trouble understanding the modeling, animation, and rendering environments in Maya. Although there are many things that go into making a video, the focus here will be placed on using Maya features to effectively carry out a planned project.

If you have never created a short-piece animation on your own, by following along with the steps here, you will, however indirectly, come to understand the processes that are involved in creating an animation.

MAKING
AN ANIMATION
WITH MAYA

Modeling

It is not easy to create a story and turn it into a short animation. Although I have assumed responsibility for major television broadcasts and other projects, I realize that creating a story and turning it into an animation piece is not easy. Frog is the title of just one of my pieces. A colleague of mine wanted to make an animation piece using a frog. And this was an idea I gave him. Not having a talent for storytelling, I made this piece using a popular story. I will use this piece and explain how the overall process was done using Maya.

Figure 12-1 Frog (Low-Polygon Modeling)

The major elements that need to be modeled for this piece are 2 characters, a tree and leaves and flowers. This chapter will focus on modeling the frog and the bee. Brief explanations will be given regarding the modeling of the other elements. In general, to model the frog and the star, I used NURBS and Subdivision Surfaces. Let's first take a look at the process of modeling the frog.

 This was done in Maya 3.0. Please note that some menu sections have been modified in later versions.

1. FROG MODELING

The frog was modeled using subdivision surfaces. If we had used NURBS, we would also have had to use Multi-Surface. A lot of time is needed to model and set up a character in Multi-Surface, and the results are not all that effective. Therefore, we will use subdivision surfaces here. After the subdivision surface is made and it is bound directly to the skeleton, the speed of the system drops sharply when using Maya version 3 (I used version 3). Because we are not able to use Artisan tools at all, it becomes very difficult to control the character after setup. Therefore, although it is a little bothersome, it is best to create the subdivision surface modeling and then convert it into a polygon when modeling.

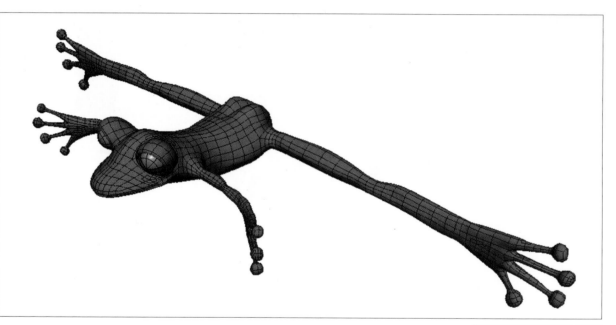

Figure 12-2 Frog (Subdivision Surface Model)

At times, it is more effective to convert the subdivision surface model to a polygon rather than to bind it to the skeleton right after modeling. One of the largest advantages of converting the subdivision surface to a polygon is that character manipulation becomes faster when it is bound to the skeleton. One of the disadvantages is that after the subdivision surface model is converted to a polygon, we can only work in Hierarchy Level 0. This is because after converting Subdivision Surface Level 0 to a polygon and applying Smooth, we get the same result as if we had done subdivision surface modeling.

This will be covered in greater detail later in this chapter.

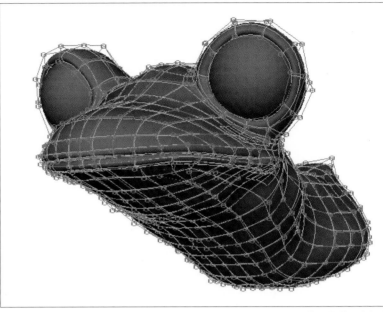

Figure 12-3 Hierarchy Level = 0

1-1. SETTING UP THE MODELING POSE

In order to model a character, the first thing we have to consider is the character's pose. In general, when modeling people, we usually model them standing with their arms stretched out to the sides. This is in preparation for making the skeleton and the binding work that will be done later. The frog character, because it must perform a variety of different actions, is posed with all 4 of its limbs spread out as shown below.

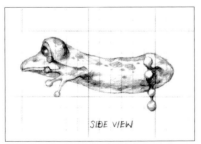

Figure 12-4 Side View

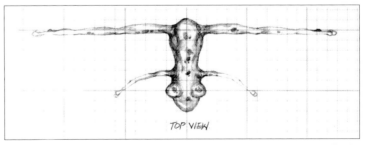

Figure 12-5 Top View

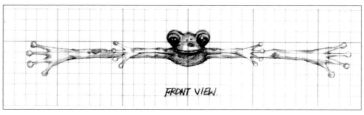

Figure 12-6 Front View

The figures above show sketches of the frog in different views. It is a good idea to create such sketches so that we can accurately observe the shape of the character from all angles. As much as possible, the pose of a character should be such that the character is spread out on the canvas as above. After planting the skeleton, such a pose makes it easy to control the character during modeling and binding.

1-2. MODELING FROG

1. Head Modeling

As mentioned earlier, the frog will be made using subdivision surface modeling and then converted into a polygon. If you are not familiar with subdivision surfaces, you should review the earlier sections on subdivision surfaces. Modeling methods will not be covered here. Instead, we will be adding movement to the character and learn how to divide surfaces for configuring movements.

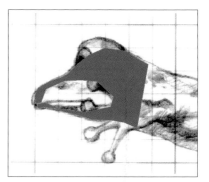

Figure 12-7 Modeling the Frog's Head

First of all, after loading the image plan in Side View, use [Polygons > Create Polygon Tool] to convert the head of the frog into a polygon as shown in the figure above. After the basic shape has been made, use Extrude Edge to make the surfaces. First, extrude the edges as shown in Figure 12-8. Before we convert to subdivision surface, we need to delete unnecessary faces. Therefore, we delete the faces on the side and on the neck. Select the polygon and then select Create Subdivision from the Subdiv Surface menu to convert the polygon in to a subdivision surface, as shown in Figure 12-9.

Figure 12-8 Extrude Edge

Figure 12-9 Create Subdivision Surface

We can now begin modeling using the subdivision surface. One thing to keep in mind here is that, because we will eventually end up using the polygon, we must make sure to work only in Hierarchy Level 0 of the subdivision surface.

Figure 12-10 The Modeling Process of the Head

The figure above illustrates the modeling process for the head. As we can see, we start out by first modeling a big lump, and then we slowly add details for the eyes and other features of the face. We always model by first creating a big lump and then slowly adding the detailed features. Detailed information on modeling can be found in Chapter 1, "Subdivision & Polygon Modeling." Using shortcut keys for the modeling commands, which are used frequently, can save a lot of time. Remember to Mirror Copy the other side using Instance to maintain symmetry. This is a very effective way to make sure symmetry is maintained because Instance creates a copy that conforms to the original object.

Figure 12-11 shows the completed model of the head that was converted into a polygon using the Extract Vertex command. This figure illustrates how the surfaces have been divided to add movement to the head. We must decide how the surfaces will be divided to add movement during the initial modeling step. Dividing correctly is essential to creating natural movement.

It would be a shame to have an awkwardly moving character because we divided the surfaces too much or too little.

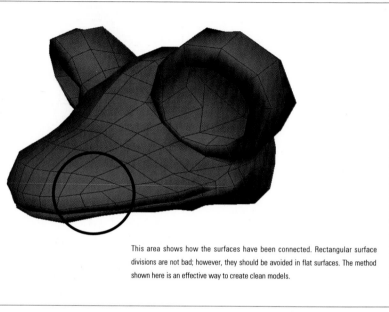

This area shows how the surfaces have been connected. Rectangular surface divisions are not bad; however, they should be avoided in flat surfaces. The method shown here is an effective way to create clean models.

Figure 12-11 Dividing the Surfaces

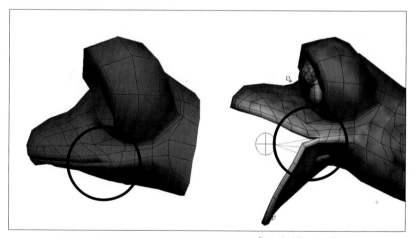

Figure 12-12 Dividing the Surfaces Near the Mouth

Figure 12-12 illustrates how to divide the surfaces near the mouth. The divisions shown are for creating a natural opening of the mouth. Surface divisions for opening the mouth in humans are different and also depend on the expressions of the face. In this way, keep in mind the average of the expressions as you divide the surfaces.

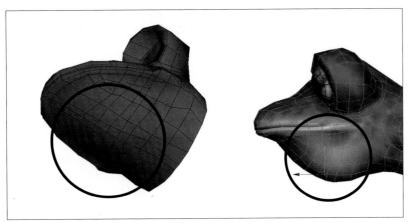

Figure 12-13 Dividing the Surfaces of the Lower Jaw

Figure 12-13 shows how the surfaces were divided, when a cluster was added for deformation, to create a natural transformation in the lower jaw. As we can see, just the right number of surfaces has been divided, not too little and not too much. If there are too few surfaces, the final output during rendering, when the lower jaw is made to transform as shown here, will appear very rough. Although a large number of surfaces are not needed for viewing the image in full shot, it is a good idea to have an adequate number of surfaces in the event that the image is zoomed in on.

Before Deform   After Deform

Figure 12-14 Dividing the Surfaces of the Eyes

Figure 12-14 shows how the surfaces of the eyes were divided to adjust the size of the eyes. We detailed the surfaces, indicated in the figure, to adjust the size of the eyes while maintaining their overall shape. By adjusting the Weight value of the indicated area later, we can maintain the shape of the eyes while naturally changing their size.

2. Body & Legs Modeling

Surface divisions in the body must be uniform. We want to avoid focused surface divisions on any one specific part of the body because it will make the body difficult to control later when we add the skeleton.

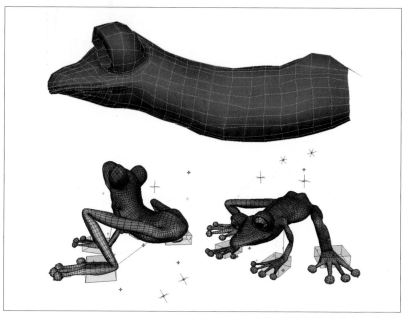

Figure 12-15 Dividing the Surfaces of the Body

As we can see in Figure 12-15, the body of the frog must be made to move naturally from side to side and from front to back. This should be clear to anyone with even a little modeling experience, but in order for such movements to take place naturally, uniform surface divisions must be made.

As we can see in the figures below, we select a few surfaces from the side and apply Extrude Face to make the surfaces of the legs.

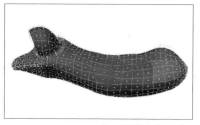

Figure 12-16 Selecting the Face

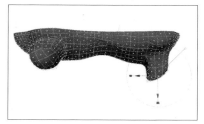

Figure 12-17 Extrude the Face

The figure below shows how the surfaces of the leg model were divided. Making adequate surface divisions are important to creating natural movements.

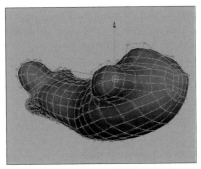

Figure 12-18 Modifying the extruded Surfaces

After extruding the faces, shape the leg as shown in Figure 12-18. Because we need to keep applying Extrude to make the surfaces, shape the leg before applying Extrude to save an extra step later.

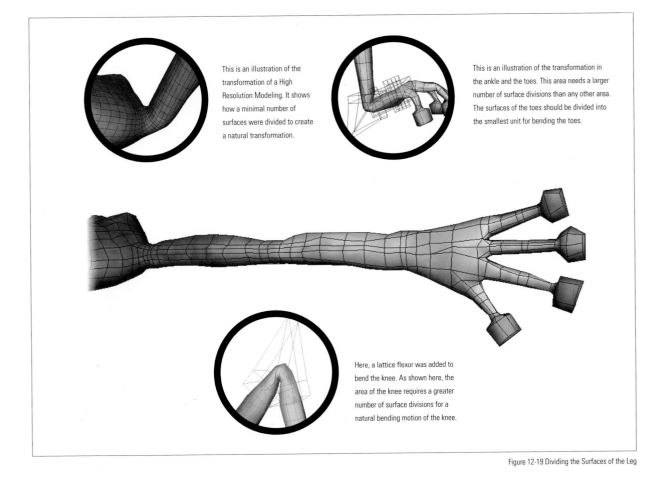

This is an illustration of the transformation of a High Resolution Modeling. It shows how a minimal number of surfaces were divided to create a natural transformation.

This is an illustration of the transformation in the ankle and the toes. This area needs a larger number of surface divisions than any other area. The surfaces of the toes should be divided into the smallest unit for bending the toes.

Here, a lattice flexor was added to bend the knee. As shown here, the area of the knee requires a greater number of surface divisions for a natural bending motion of the knee.

Figure 12-19 Dividing the Surfaces of the Leg

The basic structure of the front legs is the same as the hind legs. In such instances, there is no need to model all 4 legs. All we simply need to do is to copy the hind legs, adjust the size and position, and paste it in front. As shown in the figure below, we first need to delete the surfaces where the front legs will be placed. Before we delete the surfaces, we apply Extract Vertex to the subdivision surface and then convert it into a polygon.

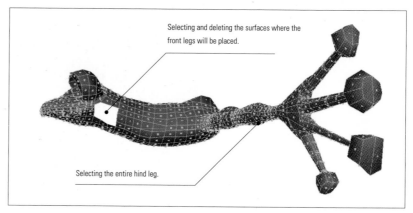

Selecting and deleting the surfaces where the front legs will be placed.

Selecting the entire hind leg.

Figure 12-20 Duplicate Face

Select the faces of the hind legs, and select [Edit Polygons > Duplicate Face] to copy the selected faces. As shown in the figure below, adjust the size and position of the copied leg.

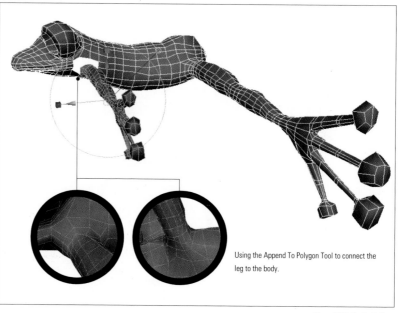

Using the Append To Polygon Tool to connect the leg to the body.

Figure 12-21 Duplicate Face

We need to map the model before we can apply Mirror Copy to complete the modeling. Mapping will be explained later in this chapter.

In order to connect the leg to the body, first, select the body and the leg and then select [Polygons > Combine] to combine the 2 objects. Then, use [Polygons > Append To Polygon Tool] to connect the body and the leg, and then convert back to subdivision surface. Slightly modify the shape of the front leg and then apply Mirror Copy and Attach to complete the model of the frog.

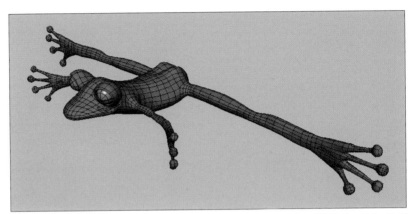

Figure 12-22 The Complete Frog Model

2. BEE MODELING

The bee is modeled in a completely different way. We polygon model the bee using NURBS and subdivision surfaces. Figure 12-23 shows how portions of the bee are modeled.

The head, body, and wings are made using NURBS. Since the structures of these areas are not very complex, we use NURBS, which is relatively easy to control. The radial structure of the head makes NURBS an effective choice.

The arms and legs are modeled using subdivision surfaces and then converted into a polygon. The hands and the feet have individual fingers and toes. This can be quite complex when done using NURBS modeling. The fact that the arms and the legs do not have important motions is another reason why we convert to polygon.

Fur was used to represent the hair on the body. This will be explained in detail later in this chapter.

Figure 12-23 Modeling Structure of the Bee

2-1. HEAD MODELING

The head takes on a radial structure basic to NURBS modeling. The advantage of this is that it is very easy to control. NURBS is optimized in Maya to have far less data than subdivisions and to be faster to work with. However, the story changes when it is divided into many patches. Such patch modeling is very difficult to control in animation. Therefore, if you need the character to be so accurate as to use patches, then you should choose to model using subdivision surfaces. However, for simple characters like this bee, NURBS is more effective.

step 1 Radial modeling begins with 3 curves. The 3 curves consist of the 2 curves that give shape to the face seen from the side and the 1 curve that extends from the cheek down to the neck. Each of these curves must have the same number of CVs. Therefore, after making the curves, Rebuild Curve must be used to give each curve the same number of CVs.

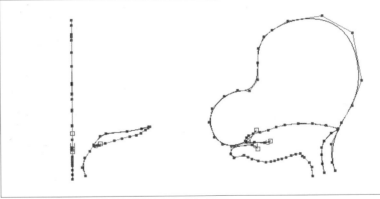

Figure 12-24 Making the 3 Curves

step 2 Now, we need to loft the curves. First, select [Modeling > Surface > Loft Tool] to select the curves in order from top to bottom, and then quit Loft by pressing the Enter key. This will create a lofted surface. This is not enough, however, and we need to add isoparms, as shown in Figure 12-25, and adjust the CVs to make the shape.

The important things here are to first complete the shape as much as you can using a minimum number of isoparms and then add additional isoparms as needed to add detail. If too many isoparms are added in the beginning, it increases the number of CVs that need to be moved, which takes a lot of time.

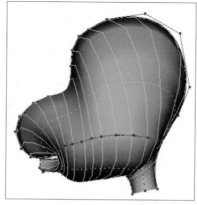

Figure 12-25 Adding Isoparms

step 3 Once the model is complete, we need to make the other half of the face. This is done, generally, by making a copy of the completed model. Select the model and select [Edit > Duplicate] to open the Options window. In the Options window, enter **-1** for Scale X and press the Duplicate button to make a mirror copy of the selected model across the X-axis. This mirror copy of the model is then attached using [Edit NURBS > Attach Surface Tool] and [Edit NURBS > Open/Close Surface].

The same result can be achieved by simply copying the mirror copy of the model and entering **-1** in the Scale X field in the Channel Box.

Selecting [Edit NURBS > Attach Surface Tool], select the isoparms on either surface and press the Enter key to attach the 2 surfaces.

Select the model, and select [Edit NURBS > Open/Close Surface] to close the surface. In the Options window, we must indicate the direction along which the surface should be closed.

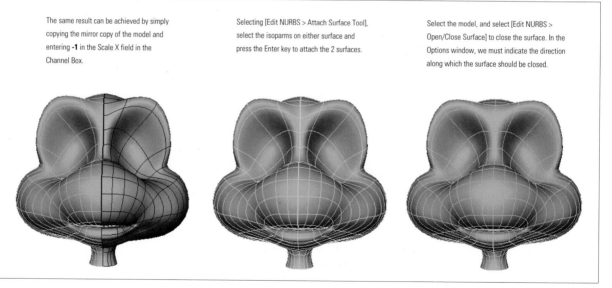

Figure 12-26 Completing the Other Half of the Face

The completed head is saved as BeeHead.mb.

2-2. EYE MODELING

The eye was modeled by referring to the structure of the eyeball. The eye consists of the 2 surfaces of the eyeball and the one surface of the eyelid. Figure 12-27 shows the structure of the eye. The eyelid will be explained separately as it must be modeled keeping the animation in mind. As shown in the figure, the eyeball is composed of a surface made by revolving one NURBS sphere and NURBS curve. Looking at the eyeball curve, we can see that the structure has been kept simple. This type of modeling, when rendered, will diversely reflect light to create a very realistic looking eye.

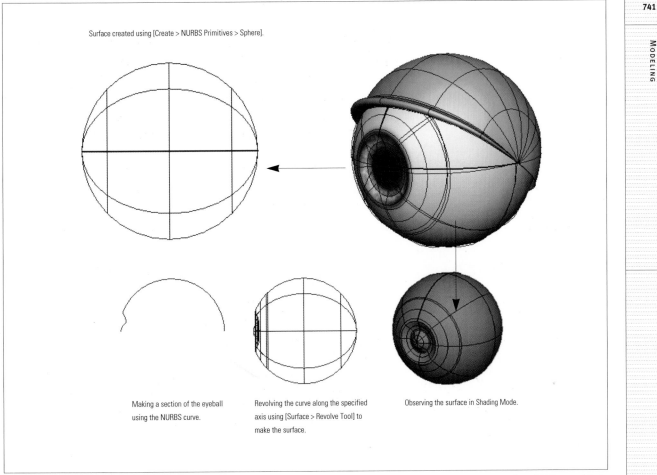

Surface created using [Create > NURBS Primitives > Sphere].

Making a section of the eyeball using the NURBS curve.

Revolving the curve along the specified axis using [Surface > Revolve Tool] to make the surface.

Observing the surface in Shading Mode.

Figure 12-27 Structure of the Eye

1. Modeling the Eyelid

We must keep the animation in mind while we model the eyelid. All models that will be used for animation must be made keeping the animation in mind. The eyelid will control the closing and opening of the eyes during the animation, and in order for that to be done quickly and easily, we need to create the setup during the initial modeling.

step 1 First, select [Create > NURBS Primitives > Sphere] to make a NURBS sphere. Click on makeNurbsSphere1 under INPUT in the Channel Box, and either select ⬚ from the Minibar or press the Y key on the keyboard. A Manipulator will appear in the window.

Press the X key on the keyboard to activate the Grid Snap, and adjust the Manipulator as shown in Figure 12-28.

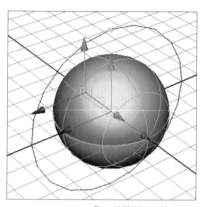

Figure 12-28 Using the Manipulator

step 2 In the Channel Box, set the Start Radius value of makeNurbsSphere1, under INPUT, to 151. Add isoparms using the Insert Isoparm Tool as shown on the left in Figure 12-29. Adding isoparms will add a few rows of CVs to the Component Mode as shown in Figure 12-29 below. We can easily make the curves of the eyelid by adjusting these CVs.

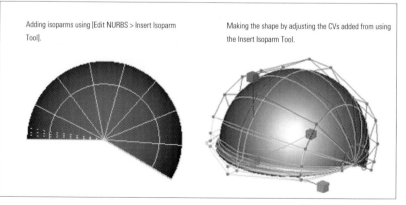

Adding isoparms using [Edit NURBS > Insert Isoparm Tool].

Making the shape by adjusting the CVs added from using the Insert Isoparm Tool.

Figure 12-29 Modeling the Eyelid

step 3 We will now take this shape and create an environment in which the eye can be made to blink. In general, we use Blend Shape to transform the shape. However, when it is used here to open and close the eye, the movement does not appear natural. Therefore, instead of using Blend Shape, we use clusters. Figure 12-30 illustrates the process of making clusters.

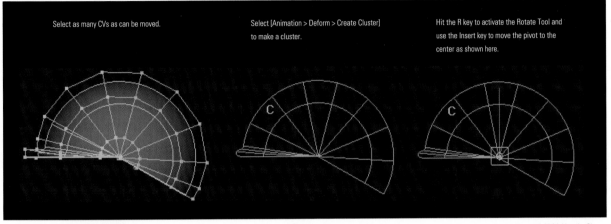

Select as many CVs as can be moved.

Select [Animation > Deform > Create Cluster] to make a cluster.

Hit the R key to activate the Rotate Tool and use the Insert key to move the pivot to the center as shown here.

Figure 12-30 Making the Cluster

step 4 After making the cluster, we now have to modify the Weight values for the CVs of the clusters. The leftmost image in Figure 12-31 shows the Weight values of the CVs in each hull. The figures below show how they change in response to the Weight values as the clusters are rotated. The Weight values for the CVs must be adjusted by observing how naturally the surface transforms due to the rotation of the cluster. In such cases, the Weight values should be modified using the Component Editor, rather than Artisan, in order to create an accurate setup. If you want a more natural-looking surface, add an abundant number of isoparms, raise the Mesh density of the surface, and then plant the cluster. This will create a much more natural movement than we have here.

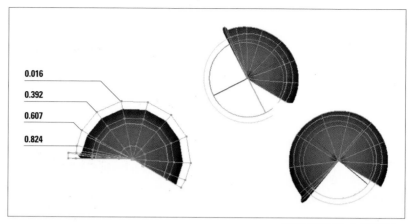

Figure 12-31 Modifying the Weight Values

step 5 To make a new cluster, first, we need to select several CVs as shown in Figure 12-32. Select [Animation > Deform > Create Cluster]. After a new cluster is made, move the pivot of the cluster to the center, as shown in Figure 12-33.

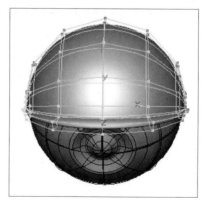

Figure 12-32 Selecting CVs to make the Cluster

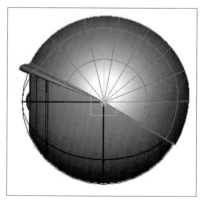

Figure 12-33 Moving the Pivot of the Cluster

step 6 We now need to modify the Weight values. These clusters will be used to portray a squinting expression. All the clusters made during the modeling process were made simply for the blinking of the eye and, as a result, all of the CV Weight values on one side of the hull were the same. However, the CV Weight values for this cluster need to be different. First of all, rotate the cluster, as shown in Figure 12-34, so that we can modify the Weight values by observing the naturalness of the expression that results from rotating the cluster.

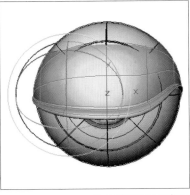

Figure 12-34 Rotating the Cluster

step 7 It is far more effective to adjust these Weight values in the Component Editor than it is to adjust them using Artisan's Paint Cluster Weight Tool. The Weight values must be modified with great precision in order to prevent the eyelid from digging into the eyeball. Open the Component Editor by selecting [Windows > General Editors > Component Editor], and adjust the CV Weight values until a natural shape is made. This adjustment is made simply by using the slider bar at the bottom.

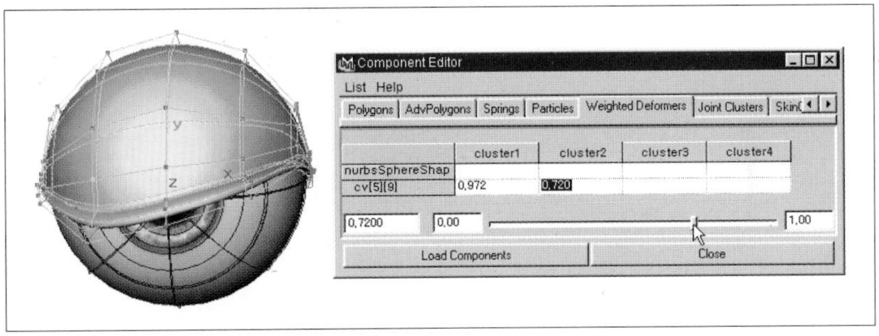

Figure 12-35 Modifying the Weight Values in the Component Editor

Now, with these 2 clusters, we can create a variety of different expressions of the eye.

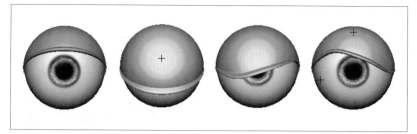

Figure 12-36 Various Expressions of the Eye Using the Clusters

step 8 This character's eyes are slightly oval in shape. The shape of the eye can be adjusted easily using Scale. However, this creates problems later on during the animation when the eye is bound to the Locator. Therefore, in order to prevent these problems, we adjust the shape of the eye using Lattice Deformer. Before using lattice, the 2 clusters and the 3 NURBS surfaces must be parented using the same rules. First of all, 2 clusters are parented to each eyelid.

Then, the eyeball is parented to the NURBS sphere while rotating the eyelid and the curve. Now, select the NURBS sphere and select [Animation > Deform > Create Lattice ☐] to open the Lattice Options window. In the Lattice Options window, reset all settings by selecting [Edit > Reset Settings] and, as shown in Figure 12-37, enter **3**, **5** and **3** for each field next to Divisions, put a check in the box next to Parenting, and then click the Create button at the bottom of the window.

This will create the Lattice Deformer, as seen in Figure 12-38.

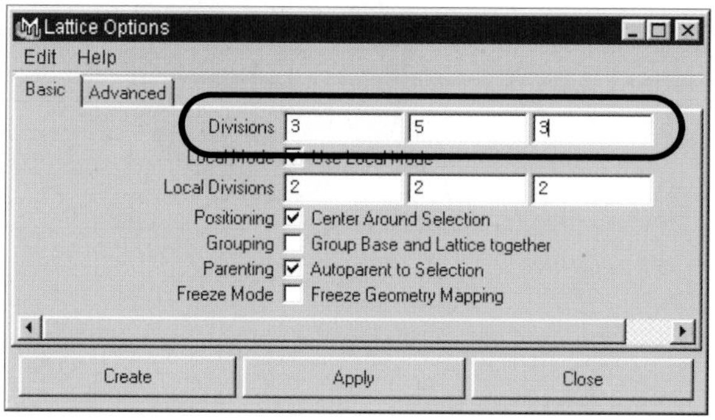

Figure 12-37 Lattice Options Window

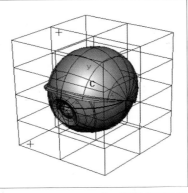

Figure 12-38 Lattice Deformer

2. Using Duplicate to Make the Opposite Eye

step 1 Import the BeeHead.mb file or the CD-ROM/CHARACTER/scenes/
BeeHead.mb file. Select the Lattice Deformer made in the eye, and adjust
the Scale according to the proportions of the face, as shown in Figure 12-39. As shown in
Figure 12-40, select the topmost node, the NURBS sphere, of the eye.

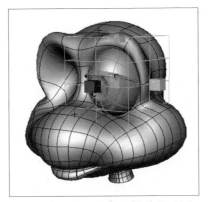

Figure 12-39 Adjusting the Size of the Eye

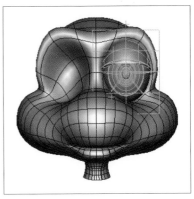

Figure 12-40 Selecting the Topmost Node of the Eye

Select [Edit > Duplicate ☐] to open the Duplicate Options window. As shown in Figure
12-41, put a check next to Duplicate Upstream Graph and then click on the Duplicate
button at the bottom. This option copies all the Deformer attributes of the selected
object.

In other words, the cluster and lattice are all put into the hierarchy structure and linked to the surface and all of their values are duplicated.

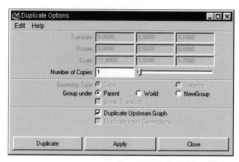

Figure 12-41 Duplicate Options Window

As shown in Figure 12-42, select the position for the other eye and, in the Channel Box, enter a hyphen (-) for the Scale X value to make a mirror. By adjusting the cluster and lattice of the copied eye, we can see how the eye responds accordingly. However, for clusters, we can see that the eye rotates in the other direction. This is the effect of the mirror. Therefore, make sure you take this into account when keyframing.

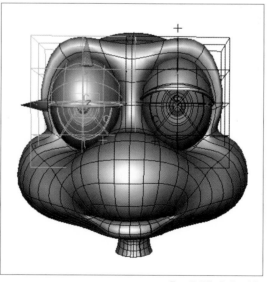

Figure 12-42 The Duplicated Eye

This completes the modeling of the eye. The setup for the animation of this model will be covered later in this chapter.

2-3. BODY MODELING

The body of this character is comparatively simple in structure. First of all, we make the torso by using a NURBS sphere and adjusting the CVs. Because this is a rather simple structure, it will not take much effort on your part to complete the body. As shown in Figure 12-43, the lower body is made by drawing a NURBS curve and using Revolve to rotate it across the Y-axis.

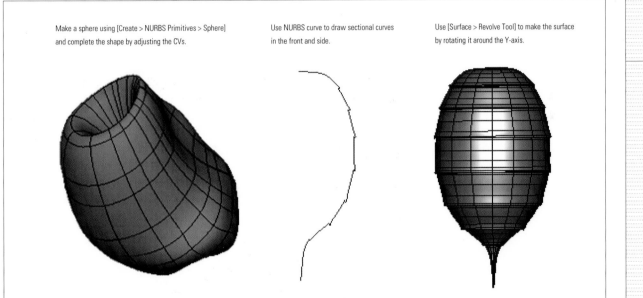

Make a sphere using [Create > NURBS Primitives > Sphere] and complete the shape by adjusting the CVs.

Use NURBS curve to draw sectional curves in the front and side.

Use [Surface > Revolve Tool] to make the surface by rotating it around the Y-axis.

Figure 12-43 Modeling the Body

2-4. MODELING THE ARMS AND LEGS

The arms and legs are made using subdivision surfaces and converted to polygon to facilitate control. Although we can bind the subdivision surface right away, the movements of the arms and legs are not that specific and, therefore, we can convert it to a polygon to make it easier to use. Figure 12-44 shows the modeling of each arm and leg. In this case, the Tessellation Method is set to Vertex and the Level to 0 when converting the subdivision surface to a low polygon model. The figure has been converted into a polygon so that it is easier to observe. Observe how each of the surfaces has been divided.

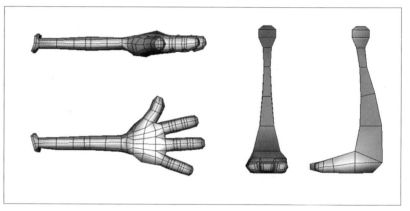

Figure 12-44 Division of the Surfaces in the Arms and Legs

Figure 12-45 shows the final rendering of the completed model. I have not gone into the modeling for the wings and other parts of the bee because they can be made quite simply using NURBS. The hair on the body was made using Fur, which will be covered in greater detail in the rendering section later in the book.

Figure 12-45 The Completed Model of the Bee

13

Character Setting

After modeling the character, we need to move onto endowing the characters with movement. This is referred to as setting the character. Character setting must be done after fully understanding the personality of the character created so that the optimal and most effective movement can be added. In this chapter, we will use the frog and the bee to understand the general setup pattern.

1. FROG SETUP

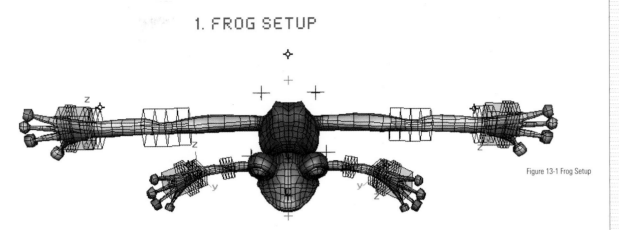

Figure 13-1 Frog Setup

Let's first look at the setup for the frog. The first thing we need to do in character setup for an animation is to fully understand the movements specific and natural to each of the characters. A frog has 4 legs and they move in a very specific way. Figure 13-2 is a snapshot of a leaping frog. As we can see, the 4 legs of the frog are fixed on the ground and the front and hind legs, which are different in size, are used to create this unique motion. When the frog jumps, the hind legs tense up to spring the frog forward and then the frog lands first with its front 2 legs and then its hind legs. Therefore, when creating the character setup for the frog, we must make sure that all 4 legs are free to move from side to side, top to bottom and front to back.

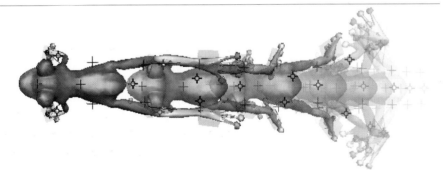

Figure 13-2 Movements of the Frog

The frog was modeled using subdivision surfaces, so we first need to convert it to polygon. We convert the subdivision surface to polygon, because the frog uses an In-Out Mesh in animation and we must be in Polygon Mode to use this mesh. The completed subdivision surface of the frog is saved in the supplementary CD-ROM as CD-ROM/CHARACTER/ scenes/Frogsubdiv.mb. Select the model of the frog and then select [Modify > Convert > Subdiv To Polygons ▣] to open the Options window. In the Convert Subdiv To Polygons Options window, configure each of the options as shown in Figure 13-3.

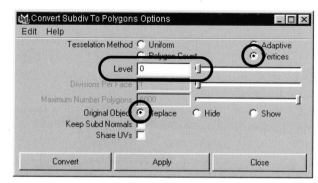

Figure 13-3 Convert Subdiv To Polygons Options Window

Clicking on the Convert button at the bottom of the window will convert the subdivision surface to a low polygon. Change the name of the converted model to LowFrog.

1-1. USING IN-OUT MESH

In this section, we will use the In-Out Mesh to control the High Res Polygon using a Low Res Poygon character during the frog animation. Before subdivision surface modeling became the universal method for modeling, this method was used as an option for controlling models that had been made to some degree using subdivision surfaces. An advantage that this method has over subdivision surfaces is that characters can be controlled efficiently using light data. Let's look how the In-Out Mesh is used.

You do not have to use In-Out Mesh. You can simply keyframe using a low-polygon model and then apply Smooth during the final rendering.

step 1 First of all, in order to use In-Out to link polygon attributes, we need identical model data. In other words, we need to make another copy of this model. This option cannot be used for polygons that have completely different attributes and shapes. First, as shown in Figure 13-4, select the frog model, which has been converted to polygon, and either hit Ctrl+D or select [Edit > Duplicate] to make a copy of the model and move it along the Y-axis as shown.

step 2 Select [Windows > Outliner] to open the Outliner window. Click on the ⊞ + icon next to LowFrog and LowFrog1 to expand the respective menus as shown in Figure 13-5. In the Outliner, after selecting subdTessShape2 from below LowFrog, select [Windows > General Editors > Connection Editor] to open the Connection Editor. Click on Reload Left in the Connection Editor. Now, select subdTessShape2 from below LowFrog1 and click on Reload Right in the Connection Editor.

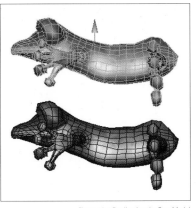

Figure 13-4 Duplicating the Frog Model

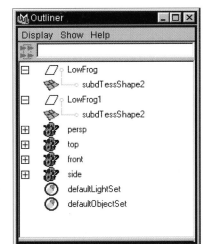

Figure 13-5 Outliner Window

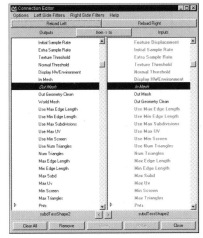

Figure 13-6 Connection Editor

Depending on the system and the size of the data, this step can take anywhere from a few seconds to a few minutes. After all the attributes have been added to the Left and Right columns, link the Out Mesh on the left to the In Mesh on the right. There are many attributes listed in the Connection Editor. Therefore, you must be careful that you connect the proper attributes.

step 3 Now the 2 models have been connected as In-Out. The next thing we need to do is to apply a Smooth value to one of the models to change it to a High Res Polygon. Selecting the duplicated frog, select [Modeling > Polygons > Smooth]. We can see in Figure 13-7 that the mesh density of the model rises to create a smooth model.

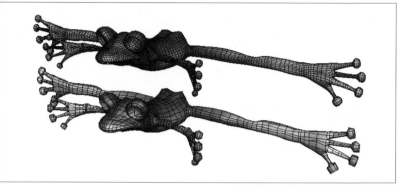

Figure 13-7 Applying a Smooth Value

Since the history is still present, we can select polySmoothFace1 from below INPUTS in the Channel Box and raise the Divisions value to 2 from the menu that appears to make the model even smoother.

step 4 Now, the 2 models, linked as In-Out, are a Low Res Polygon and a High Res Polygon, respectively. Changing the shape of, say, the Low Res Polygon will cause the High Res Polygon to change automatically to match the Low Res Polygon. Make 2 layers, named Low and High, respectively. Then, by conducting the specified animation keyframing in Low and the final rendering in High, we can conduct this step quickly and easily.

1-2. DRAW SKELETON

We begin the actual Character Setup by making a skeleton. This step, also, must be done after deciding how the character will move in the animation. We need to first determine how the spine will move and how the mouth will be controlled to move. If this is not done, then we run into very sticky problems when it comes time to control the character after the setup.

step 1 Let's first make the joints of the spine that crosses through the body. Figure 13-8 shows the structure of the skeleton that connects the spine to the mouth.

Figure 13-8 Skeletal Structure

This is the joint used to control the neck. Although the neck moves only slightly to create the various movements of the character, joints can be added as such to exaggerate the movement.

This is used to control the movement of the spine. How many joints will be added to the spine depends on how naturally you plan to animate it. Using 3 or 4 joints as we did here is enough to cover almost all movements of the spine.

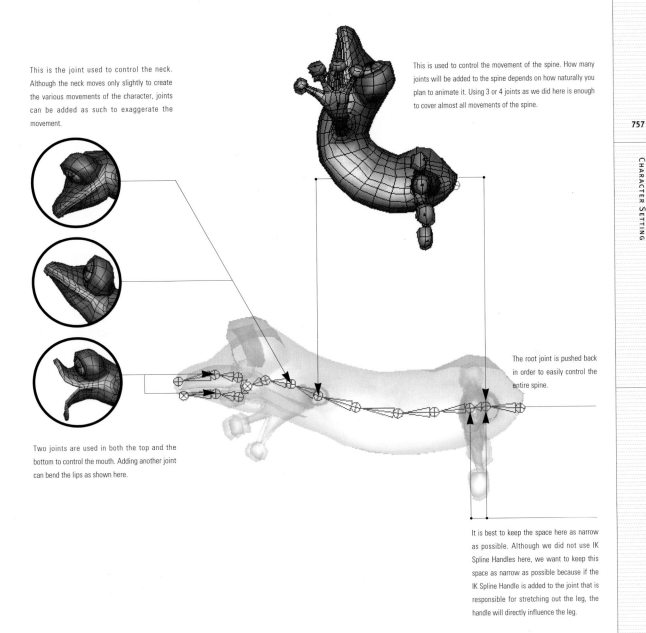

The root joint is pushed back in order to easily control the entire spine.

Two joints are used in both the top and the bottom to control the mouth. Adding another joint can bend the lips as shown here.

It is best to keep the space here as narrow as possible. Although we did not use IK Spline Handles here, we want to keep this space as narrow as possible because if the IK Spline Handle is added to the joint that is responsible for stretching out the leg, the handle will directly influence the leg.

step 2 In this step, we will make the skeleton for the leg. The front and back of the leg should be made using the same structure. The leg skeleton is shown in Figure 13-9.

Figure 13-9 Skeletal Structure of the Leg

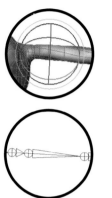
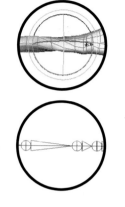
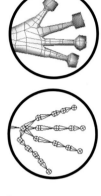
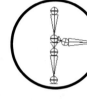

This is the joint where the leg stretches out. The joint indicated here is used to control the movement of the skin as the leg moves.

A joint is added that does not exist in an actual leg. This joint prevents a severe distortion of the body when twisting the leg.

This joint is used for twisting the ankle.

These are the joints of the toes. A joint must be added for each joint of the toe as shown here.

As shown here, this joint is used when bending the ankle. We need to have 2 different joints here because the movement of the skin when the ankle is twisted and when it is bended is different.

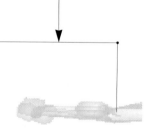

The basic structure of the front legs is the same as that of the hind legs, with the exception of the bending angles. Figure 13-10 shows the skeletal structure of the font leg.

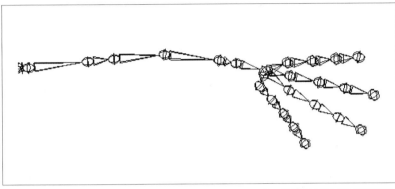

Figure 13-10 Skeletal Structure of the Front Leg

step 3 For the purposes of accompanying control, add additional joints to transform the eyes as shown in Figure 13-11. As we can see in the figure, the purpose of these joints is to increase the size of the eyes. Used to create a cartoon-like effect, these joints are very useful in portraying the movements of the character.

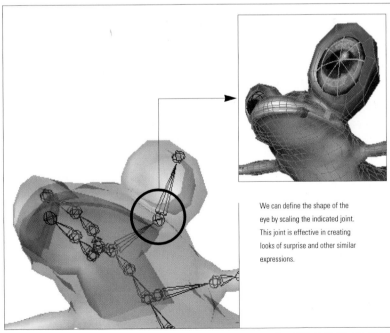

We can define the shape of the eye by scaling the indicated joint. This joint is effective in creating looks of surprise and other similar expressions.

Figure 13-11 Joint Used to Control the Eyes

This completes the basic character setup. Make the other side by simply selecting [Animation > Skeleton > Mirror Joint] to create a mirror copy. Figure 13-12 shows the final skeletal structure.

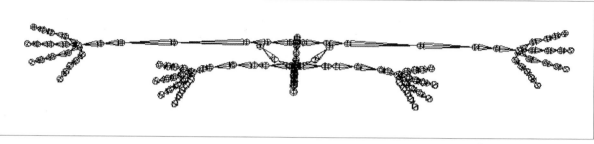

Figure 13-12 The Final Skeletal Structure

1-3. BINDING SKIN

After setting the skeleton, we need to bind the model and the skeleton and manipulate them so that the skin transforms in respond to the movement of the joint. We will see in this section just how the skin transforms in response to joint movement.

This character was bound using Rigid Binding. There are 2 different types of binding in Maya, Rigid Bind and Smooth Bind. Rigid Bind was used for this project. The next step shows how the frog was bound and the vertices edited.

step 1 First of all, in order to bind the model and the skeleton, select the model and, while holding down the Shift key, select the skeleton. Select [Animation > Skin > Bind Skin > Rigid Bind] to bind the model to the skeleton. Maya uses average values to allot the vertices of the model to each joint. Therefore, we will not get the result we desire. We can see in Figure 13-13 that the transformation in the leg surfaces does not look natural.

As you know, binding allots the CVs or vertices of the model to the joints so that the vertices respond to the movement of the joints and animate the skin.

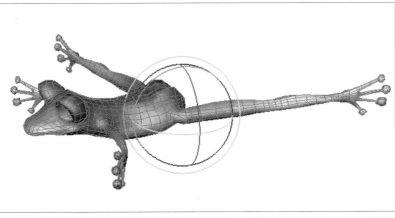

Figure 13-13 Rotating the Joint after Applying Bind Skin

As follows, in order to create transformations in the skin that respond precisely to the movement, each vertex must be allotted to an appropriate joint. However, because Maya uses average values to compute the binding results, the vertices will not be allotted to the appropriate joints. This problem is rectified in the following step.

step 2 We need to use Artisan's Paint Set Membership Tool in order to manually assign each vertex to the appropriate joint. By using this tool, we can simply select the desired joint name from Artisan's Tool Settings window and paint over the model to allot the vertex to the selected joint. To use this tool, first, select the model and then select [Animation > Deform > Paint Set Membership Tool ◘] to open the Tool Settings window, as shown in Figure 13-15. It is a good idea to pose the character in the desired action, as shown in Figure 13-14, so that it is easier to decide which vertices need to be bound by which joints.

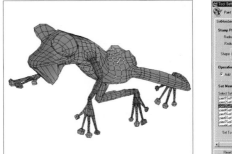

Figure 13-14 Applying the Paint Set Membership Tool

Figure 13-15 Tool Settings Window

Figure 13-14 shows the state of the model after the Paint Set Membership Tool is applied. Different colors will be used to show how the joints have been allotted to each vertex. Each of the colors responds to the binding of each vertex by a different joint. By selecting the desired joint name from the Tool Settings window in Figure 13-15 and painting over the model, we can easily bind the vertex to the desired joint. However, there is a limit to what we can accomplish using this tool. Namely that it is very difficult to control detailed areas using this tool. For instance, the area around the character's mouth is made up of overlapping vertices and it becomes very difficult to use this tool in such areas. In such cases, we would use the Edit Membership Tool to selectively assign the vertex to the joint by clicking the desired vertex on the desired joint.

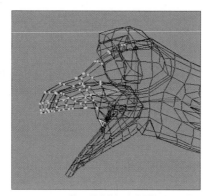

Figure 13-16 Using the Edit Membership Tool

As shown in Figure 13-16, after selecting the desired joint (the joint on top of the mouth) and selecting [Animation > Edit Membership Tool], hold down the Shift key to click the mouse on the vertex we wish to assign to the selected joint. Then, the color of the vertex will change to yellow meaning that it has been bound to the selected joint.

step 3 Next, we need to assign vertex Weight values to each of the joints. Assigning Weight values controls the expansion and constriction of the skin. By entering a movement value for the vertices that responds to the movement of the joints, the vertices assigned to each joint move in uniform proportions to expand and constrict the skin. This can also be done using Artisan tools, making the work proceed quickly and easily. Selecting the bound character, select [Animation > Deform > Paint Cluster Weight Tool ▣] to open the Tool Settings window.

As shown in Figure 13-17, in the Paint Attribute section, clicking on the Name box and then clicking Cluster will list all the clusters for each joint.

By selecting the joint cluster we wish to edit from this list, the respective joint cluster will appear white in the model (see Figure 13-18). Select Smooth from under Paint Operation, and paint the edges to soften the edges.

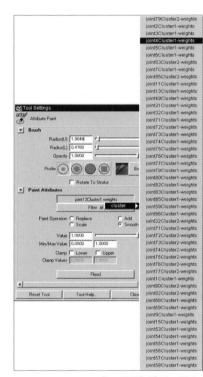

Figure 13-17 Tool Settings Window

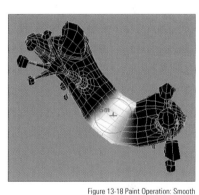

Figure 13-18 Paint Operation: Smooth

In this way, modify the vertex Weight values for each joint cluster. The model will appear in black and white, with the white areas corresponding to a Weight value of 1 and the black areas corresponding to a Weight value of 0. Gray areas, depending on the intensity of the color, correspond to a value between 0 and 1. This tool is also not very good for modifying detailed values. Although this tool is good for obtaining the overall, average value, in order to create detailed movement, we need to select a particular vertex and enter the values by hand. Select the vertex we wish to modify, and select [Windows > General Editors > Component Editor] to display the Component Editor as shown in Figure 13-19. Opening the Joint Cluster Tab, the Weight value for the selected vertex will be displayed and we can type in the desired value here to assign a more precise value.

The following is the Component Editor window.

polySurfaceShape31	joint49Cluster1	joint4Cluster1	joint53Cluster1	joint53Cluster2
vtx[889]		0,490		
vtx[890]		0,490		
vtx[896]		0,446		
vtx[897]		0,149		
vtx[2395]		0,490		
vtx[2401]		0,490		
vtx[2402]		0,490		

Figure 13-19 Component Editor

1-4. WORKING WITH FLEXOR

Flexor is a tool that was designed to control the joints of the character. This tool makes the skin respond smoothly and naturally to the movement of each joint. After editing the Weight values for the character, add flexors to each joint to create a natural transformation of the skin on the surface. Figures 13-20 and 13-21 show the transformation of the skin with and without the use of flexors, respectively. As we can see, the skin changes drastically in response to the presence of flexors.

Figure 13-20 No flexors Used

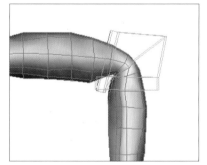

Figure 13-21 Flexors Used to Control the Joints

step 1 Selecting the joint where the flexor will be added, select [Animation > Skin > Edit Rigid Skin > Create Flexor ■]. This will open the Create Flexor window, as shown in Figure 13-22. Setting the Flexor Type to Lattice and selecting At Selected Joint(s), because the flexor needs to be added to the selected joint, we click the Create button at the bottom of the window.

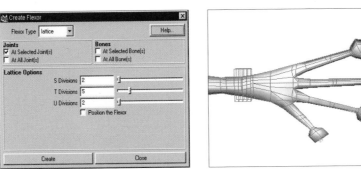

Figure 13-22 Create Flexor Window

Figure 13-23 Flexor Made at the Selected Joint

As shown in Figure 13-23, a flexor will be made at the selected joint. However, we can see that the flexor is quite small. A small flexor means that the area of the skin that it will affect will also be small. Therefore, we need to increase the flexor to an appropriate size. To adjust the scale, first, select the flexor we made and then select [Windows > Hypergraph]. In Hypergraph, pressing the F key will display the flexor nodes for the selected flexor in the middle of the screen. Select the topmost flexor node.

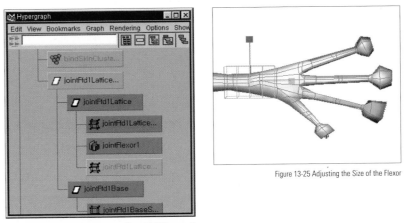

Figure 13-24 Hypergraph

Figure 13-25 Adjusting the Size of the Flexor

As shown in Figure 13-25, adjust the flexor to the desired size.

step 2   We must manipulate this flexor so that it responds differently when the joint is bent and extended. Because the skin responds to the constriction and expansion of the muscles when the joints are moved, we can control this phenomenon using flexors in a certain area to create a natural transformation of the skin.

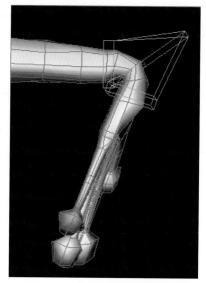

Figure 13-26 Transformation of the Flexor

After selecting the joint and having it bend to some degree, select the flexor and define its attributes in the Channel Box. Figure 13-26 shows how the skin changes in response to changing the flexor attributes in the Channel Box (see Figure 13-27). Try adjusting each of the values to see how it affects the transformation.

SHAPES	
jointFlexor1	
Creasing	-0,4
Rounding	3,6
Length In	1
Length Out	1
Width Left	3,5
Width Right	5,4
INPUTS	
jointFfd1	

Figure 13-27 Channel Box

step 3 Let's now copy this flexor to the opposite joint. Instead of making a flexor for each of the joints, it is more efficient to make the flexor for one side and then copy it to the other side for symmetrical characters. First of all, select the flexor as shown in Figure 13-28 and then, holding down the Shift key, select the joint on the other side.

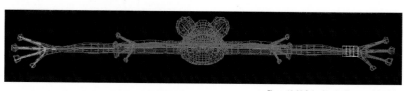

Figure 13-28 Selecting the Flexor and the Joint

Select [Animation > Skin > Edit Rigid Skin > Copy Flexor]. This will copy the flexor onto the selected joint. Because we adjusted the size of the flexor, it is possible that the flexor will be copied in the state it was before the size was adjusted.

If this is the case, we need to adjust the size of the flexor again. We can adjust the size of the flexor using the method described earlier. The copied flexor will retain the attributes of the original flexor, so there is no need to adjust the attributes in the Channel Box again.

Figure 13-29 Copying the Flexor

step 4 Repeat Steps 1-3 to make a flexor for each of the joints. After adjusting the attributes of the flexors using the Channel Box, copy them to the other side. The final model should like the one shown in Figure 13-30.

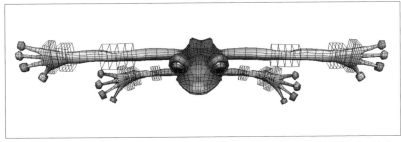

Figure 13-30 The Final Character with All of the Flexors in Place

1-5. USING CLUSTER

Using clusters is an effective way to create individual character deformation in certain areas. When the frog makes its characteristic sound, its lower jaw and belly transforms in an amusing way. The lower jaw bulges out and the belly moves accordingly. Two clusters are used to control these movements. Let's see how these clusters are used.

step 1 We use Artisan's Paint Selection Tool to select the vertices for which a cluster will be made. Select the model, select [Edit > Paint Selection Tool], and select several vertices in the lower jaw, as shown in Figure 13-31. Selecting several vertices and adjusting their Weight values is an effective way to create a more natural and realistic movement.

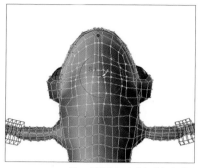

Figure 13-31 Using the Paint Selection Tool

Select [Animation > Deform > Create Cluster ▢] to open the Cluster Options window. After putting a check by Relative in the Cluster Options window (see Figure 13-32), click on the Create button.

Figure 13-32 Cluster Options Window

Relative causes the cluster to follow the movements of the joint when it is parented to the joint later. Instead of configuring this option now, we can open the Attribute Editor of the cluster at any time to configure this option.

step 2 Make a cluster of the stomach region in the same way. As shown in Figure 13-33, use Artisan's Paint Selection Tool to select several vertices in the stomach. Just as we did for the jaw, quite a few vertices should be selected in the belly and clustered and the corresponding Weight values modified.

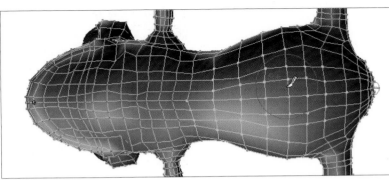

Figure 13-33 Using the Paint Selection Tool

Select the vertex, and make a cluster as we did earlier.

step 3 Now that we have made the 2 clusters, we need to adjust the Weight values for the vertices included in these clusters so that the skin transforms naturally and smoothly when the clusters move. These Weight values can be configured quickly and easily using Artisan's Paint Cluster Weight tool. Figures 13-34 and 13-35 show how the Weight values of the clusters are configured using Artisan.

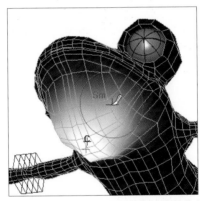

Figure 13-34 Paint Cluster Weight Tool

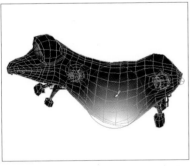

Figure 13-35 Paint Cluster Weight Tool

step 4 These clusters will be listed first in the Deformation Order. This is because these are the first clusters to be made after binding. This Deformation Order will directly influence the transformation of the character.

If (as in this case) the cluster was the last thing to be made, when the cluster is moved, it will either move in the unintended direction or the vertices of the clusters will transform abnormally when the character is moved. Such abnormalities result from an improper Deformation Order. For a proper Deformation Order, the clusters must be made first and then the model should be bound to the skeleton. However, because of the History, this order can be changed at any time. To change the Deformation Order, select the model, click the RMB and select Complete List from under Input in the Marking Menu, as shown in Figure 13-36.

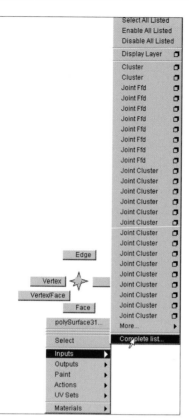

Figure 13-36 Marking Menu

This will open the History List window, as shown in Figure 13-37. We can see that the 2 clusters we made at the end are at the top. These clusters must be moved to the bottom, as shown in Figure 13-38. We move these clusters by simply clicking the MMB and dragging them to the bottom.

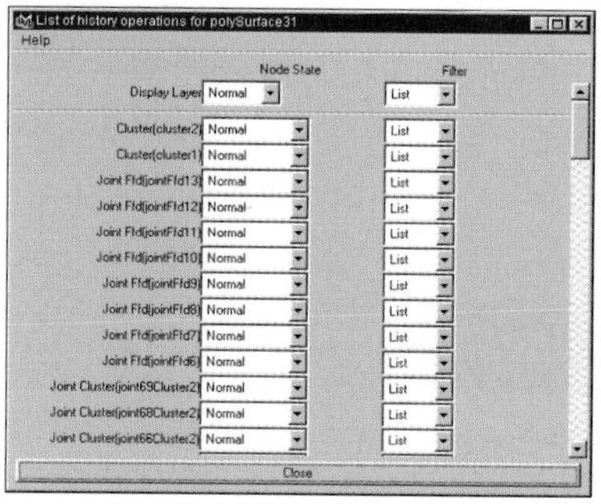

Figure 13-37 History List Window

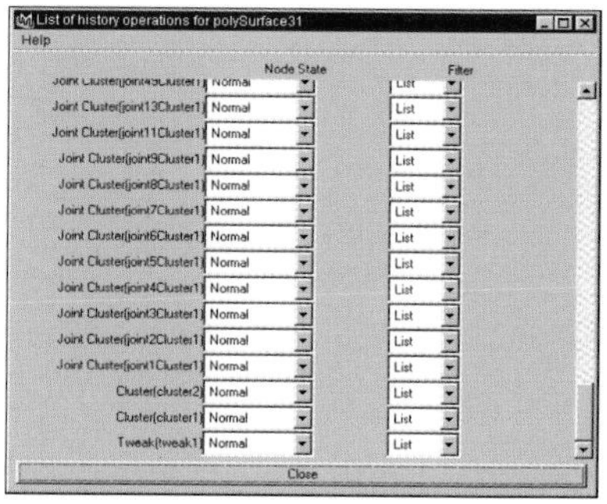

Figure 13-38 History List Window

The Deformation Order has now been modified and, the model should now move properly whether we move the entire character or the clusters individually.

2. SETTING UP THE FROG FOR ANIMATION

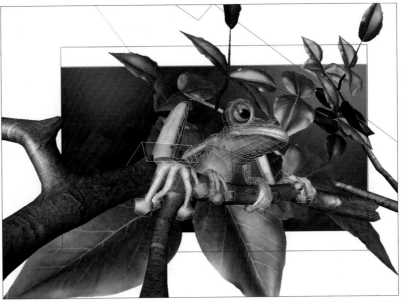

Figure 13-39 Animating Character Shot

Up until now, we have looked at basic character setup. We will now take a look at setting up the character to move. There are many methods available for moving a character. In this project, the movements of the frog will mostly be confined to the tree. Although the body moves, the 4 legs must be fixed on the tree. This type of movement is very hard to control using Forward Kinematics. Therefore, to create effective character motion, we will use Inverse Kinematics. From this point on, the explanations will be geared toward setting up an environment for the motions that will be seen in this animation.

2-1. CONTROLLING THE JOINTS USING AUXILIARY JOINTS

In general, the transformations of the skin that correspond to the movements of the character's joints are very complex and diverse. Because this is not an animation system based on bones and muscle, it is very difficult to perfectly display these movements. Most existing software merely imitates this movement. In this section, we will look at how to create extra joints and use them to move other joints. Most of the explanations here have already been covered in earlier parts of this book.

step 1 First of all, in order to make an auxiliary joint, select the joint of the leg, as shown in Figure 13-40, press Ctrl+D to copy the joint, and move it along the Y-axis.

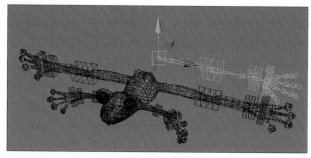

Figure 13-40 Copying the Joint

Because we have already made flexors for the joints, the flexors will also be copied along with the joints. Delete all the flexors. When deleting the flexors, we must make sure that even the topmost flexor nodes in the Hypergraph are deleted. Delete, also, the joints of the toes until only the portion shown in Figure 13-41 remains.

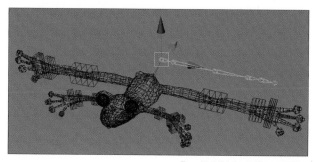

Figure 13-41 Deleting the Flexors and Joints

The local rotating axis will differ depending on how the skeleton is made. In other words, although we are linking the Rotate Y-and Z-axes in this example, it may be different for another skeleton. Therefore, it is necessary to use the Rotate Tool to directly rotate the joints and observe along which axis the rotation will occur in the Channel Box.

 The movements of such duplicated auxiliary joints do not affect the character in any way. We now have to create the environment in which these duplicated joints will control the movements of the original joints. This is done using the Connection Editor. First, select [Windows > General Editors > Connection Editor] to open the Connection Editor.

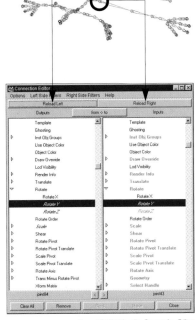

Figure 13-42 Using the Connection Editor

As shown in Figure 13-42, position each of the joints on the left and the right and link the Rotate attributes Rotate Y and Rotate Y to Rotate Z and Rotate Z. Now, rotating the copied joint along Rotate Y and Rotate Z, we can see that the original joint moves as well.

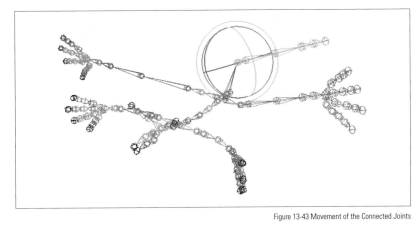

Figure 13-43 Movement of the Connected Joints

Structure the remaining joints as shown in Figure 13-44. Make sure you pay careful attention to which joints are positioned on the left and the right.

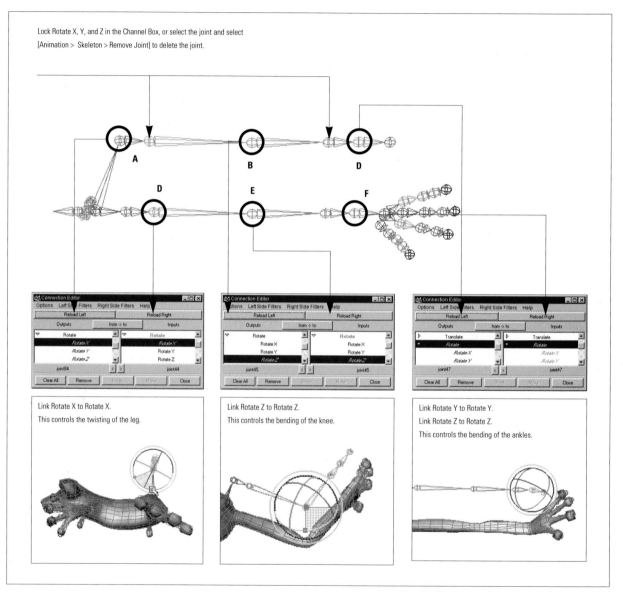

Figure 13-44 The Connection System of the Leg in the Connection Editor

Although the structure in the figure above looks complicated, if you understand the overall connection, it should be easy to understand.

step 3 Make auxiliary joints for the front legs in the same way. Figure 13-45 shows the connection system for the front legs in the Connection Editor.

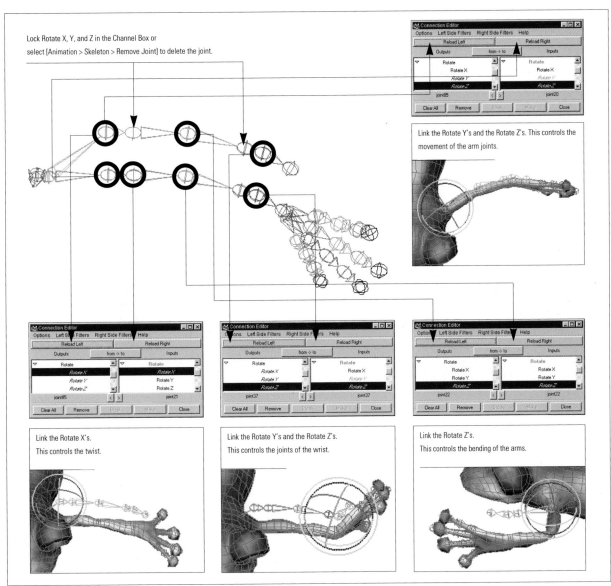

Lock Rotate X, Y, and Z in the Channel Box or
select [Animation > Skeleton > Remove Joint] to delete the joint.

Link the Rotate Y's and the Rotate Z's. This controls the movement of the arm joints.

Link the Rotate X's.
This controls the twist.

Link the Rotate Y's and the Rotate Z's.
This controls the joints of the wrist.

Link the Rotate Z's.
This controls the bending of the arms.

Figure 13-45 The Connection System of the Leg in the Connection Editor

In this section, we looked at how to make auxiliary joints and how to use these joints to control the actual joints. The joints on the other side should be made in the same way.

2-2. USING IK HANDLES

We will now look at using IK handles to set up an Inverse Kinematics environment. The IK handles are planted into the extra auxiliary joints we made in the previous section. Auxiliary joints will also be used in this section for the effective control of the IK handles.

 step 1 A total of 2 IK RPsolvers are used in each of the front and hind legs. Figure 13-46 shows how the IK RPsolvers are linked to each joint.

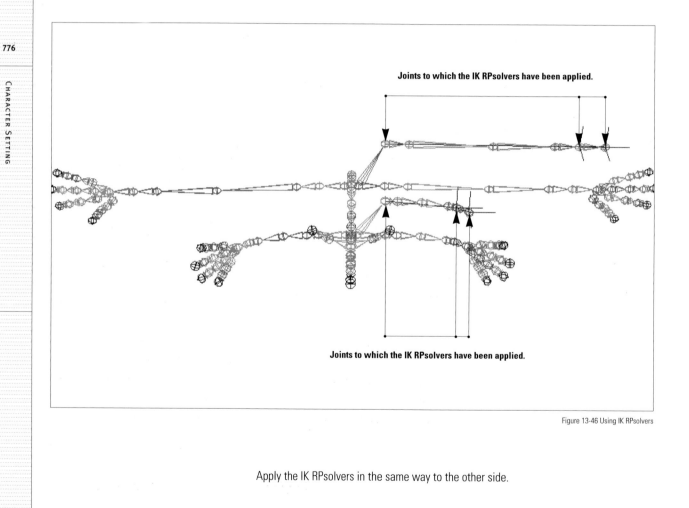

Figure 13-46 Using IK RPsolvers

Apply the IK RPsolvers in the same way to the other side.

step 2 Make the auxiliary joints again. Make the auxiliary joints in Top View so that they are the same size as the respective joints in the bottoms of all 4 feet. Figure 13-47 shows the placement of the auxiliary joints.

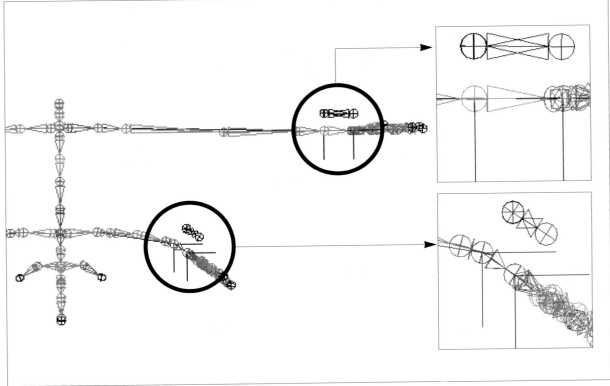

Figure 13-47 The Size and Placement of the Joints

As shown in the figure, we must make the auxiliary joints so that they are the same size as the respective joints in the bottoms of the feet. This is also where the IK handles will be placed. After making the joints, we can move them slightly, as shown in Figure 13-47, so that they can be easily distinguished. This auxiliary joint consists of 3 joints and 2 bones. The auxiliary joint is drawn according to the sequence shown in Figure 13-48.

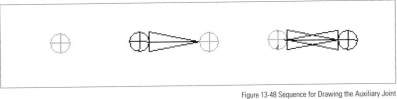

Figure 13-48 Sequence for Drawing the Auxiliary Joint

Joints can be distinguished by adding a prefix to the name. First, select the auxiliary joint root used in the front leg, and select [Modify > Prefix Hierarchy Names...]. In the Prefix Hierarchy Name field, type in R_front_ and then click OK. This will add a prefix to the auxiliary joint of the front leg. In the same way, name the auxiliary joint of the hind leg R_back_.

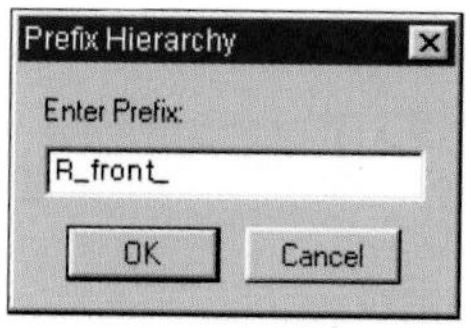

Figure 13-49 Prefix Hierarchy Name

We also change the name of IK handles for distinction. Change the names to match Figure 13-50 by using the Channel Box or the Attribute Editor.

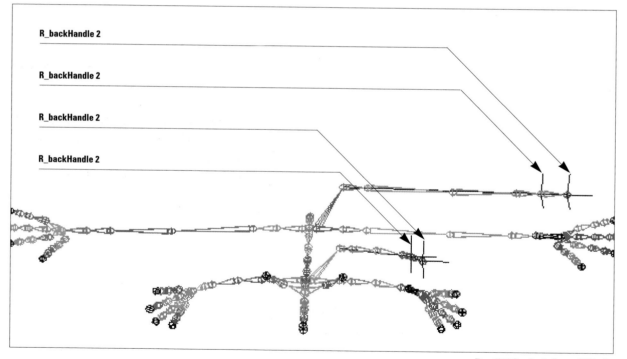

R_backHandle 2

R_backHandle 2

R_backHandle 2

R_backHandle 2

Figure 13-50 Changing the Names of IK Handles

step 3 Move all auxiliary joints to the location of the original joints. In order to accurately align their positions, press the V key on the keyboard to activate the Point Snap. As we can see in Figure 13-51, the auxiliary joints that have been connected through the Connection Editor have been aligned accurately to the original joints to control the bottoms of all 4 feet.

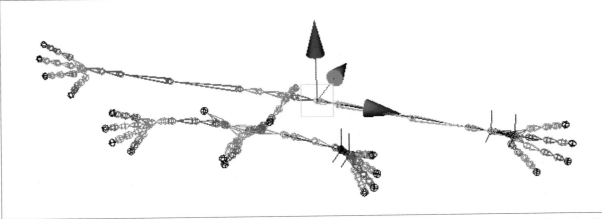

Figure 13-51 Fixing the Placement of the Auxiliary Joints

step 4 We now have to parent the IK handle to the auxiliary joint in order to control the bottoms of the feet. This can be done effectively through the Hypergraph. Select [Windows > Hypergraph] to open the Hypergraph. Parent the IK handles to the joint in the Hypergraph until we get the structure shown in Figure 13-52.

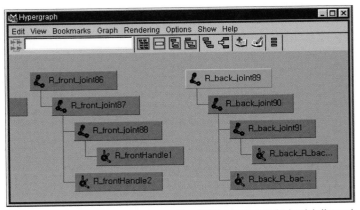

Figure 13-52 Parenting the IK Handles through the Hypergraph

The number of the auxiliary joints can change according to the circumstances. Therefore, all we have to do is to parent the IK handles until we obtain the hierarchy level shown in the figure. All we have to do is click the MMB on the node we wish to parent in the Hypergraph and drag it above the upper node. Select the auxiliary root joint in the hypergraph above, and select [Display > Component Display > Selection Handle] to display the selection handles. This make it easier to select the joints in the window.

The basic configurations are now complete. We now select the auxiliary joints to see if the setup occurred correctly. Move or rotate the auxiliary joints made to control the bottoms of the feet, and make sure that the Inverse Kinematics works correctly.

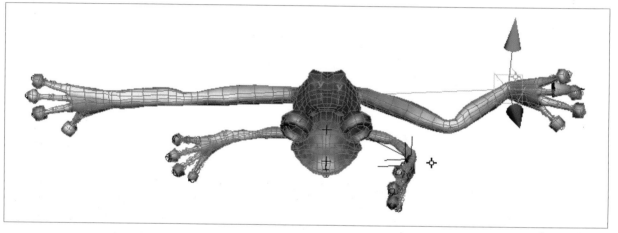

Figure 13-53 Setup Test

Set up the other side in the same way.

2-3. USING CONSTRAINTS

We need to use Constraints to.fine-tune and diversify the movements of the character.
In this example, a Pole Vector, used to control the frog's legs, and a Point, Orient Constraint is used.

step 1 Let's first look at how to use a Pole Vector to control the twisting of the front and hind legs. First of all, use the Locator on the object used to constrain the legs. Apply [Create > Locator] twice to make 2 Locators, arrange them as shown in Figure 13-54 and then change the name of the Locators as shown in the Channel Box.

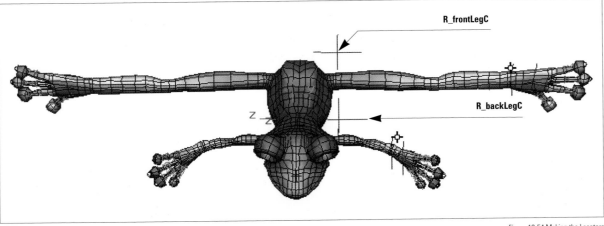

Figure 13-54 Making the Locators

step 2 First, select the R_frontLegC Locator and then select R_frontHandle1 while holding down the Shift key, and then select [Animation > Constraint > Pole Vector]. Next, select the R_backLegC Locator, select R_backHandle1 while holding down the Shift key, and then select [Animation > Constraint > Pole Vector]. Test the result by selecting the Locator and moving it along the Y-axis. We can see that the leg twists, as shown in Figure 13-55.

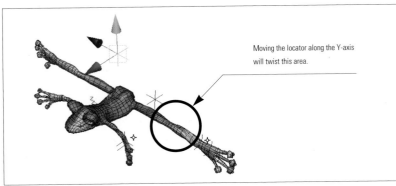

Moving the locator along the Y-axis will twist this area.

Figure 13-55 Testing the Pole Vector Constraint

step 3 Use Polygon Cube to constrain the auxiliary joints in the bottoms of the feet. Why we use the Polygon Cube will be explained during the animation section later in the book. This can be very useful in certain situations. The Polygon Cube allows us to easily determine with the naked eye how much the bottoms of the feet rotate, and it allows us to examine the state of the feet and select them during keyframing. First of all, apply [Create > Polygon Primitives > Cube] twice to make 2 Polygon Cubes and rotate them 90 degrees in the X-axis. If they are not rotated, the bottoms of the feet will flip over 90 degrees. Although this can be modified later, it is more convenient to simply rotate it now. Arrange the 2 cubes as shown in Figure 13-56, and change the names of the cubes in the Channel Box as shown.

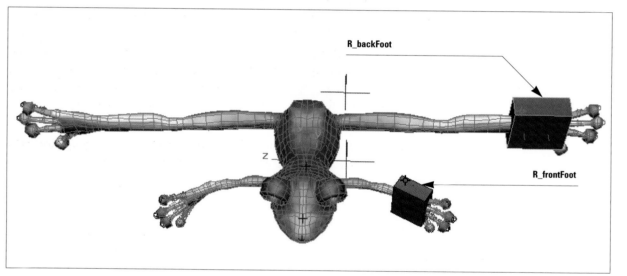

Figure 13-56 Making and Arranging the Polygon Cubes

Before applying the constraint, the pivot of each cube must be aligned to the auxiliary joint root, used to control the bottoms of the feet. In the current state, the pivot is situated in the center of the cube. Therefore, by using Point and Orient Constraint, the auxiliary joint will be centered on the cube and it will also rotate around the pivot. This will create abnormal movements. Therefore, in order to maintain the movements of the auxiliary joints, the pivot of the cube must be aligned to the auxiliary root joint.

Select the cube and use the Move Tool, and then press the Insert key to move the pivot of the cute to the root of the auxiliary joint, as shown in Figure 13-57. Pressing the V key on the keyboard will apply the Point Snap so that alignment will take place accurately.

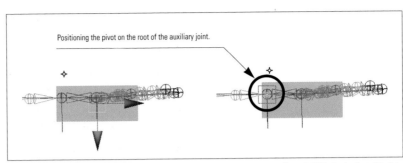

Positioning the pivot on the root of the auxiliary joint.

Figure 13-57 Moving the Pivot of the Cube

step 4 First select R_backFoot Cube and, while holding down the Shift key, select the auxiliary joint of the bottom of the feet, or R_back_joint, which is in the same spot. First, select [Animation > Constraint > Point] and then select [Animation > Constraint > Orient]. Select R_frontFoot Cube and, while holding down the Shift key, select the auxiliary joint of the bottom of the feet, or R_front_joint, which is in the same spot. First, select [Animation > Constraint > Point] and then select [Animation > Constraint > Orient]. The auxiliary joints of the front and hind legs will now be constrained by the Polygon Cube, and we can now control the legs by selecting and moving or rotating the Polygon Cube. The knees are controlled using the Pole Vector constrained Locator. The rest of the legs are set up in the same way.

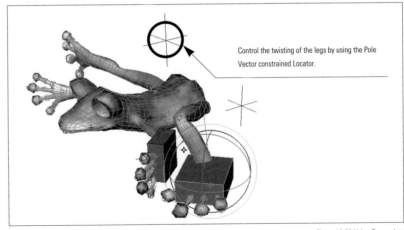

Control the twisting of the legs by using the Pole Vector constrained Locator.

Figure 13-58 Using Constraints

Figure 13-59 shows the completed model. A random shader is made for the 4 cubes used in the legs in HyperShade and the Color and Transparency are adjusted. Also, we can open the Attribute Editor and turn off all options in the Render State so that they do not appear during the final rendering.

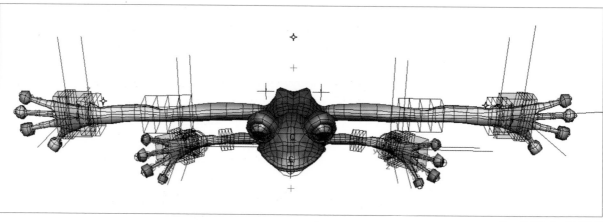

Figure 13-59 The Completed Model

The completed model is saved as CD-ROM/CHARACTER/scenes/FrogSETUP.mb on the CD-ROM. Although the basic structures of the model in the CD-ROM and the model made here are the same, there are slight differences due to changes that have been made in the configuration. However, because the basic shape is the same, you should have no problems using the model supplied on the CD-ROM.

2-4. MAKING THE TONGUE ANIMATION

One characteristic of the frog is that it uses its tongue to catch insects. This section will be devoted to animating the tongue of the frog. The tongue is, basically, made using a NURBS surface and animated using Blend Shape.

step 1 Open the scene file that has been prepared. Open CD-ROM/CHARACTER/scenes/Tongue.mg.

As we can see in the figure below, this file is made up of one NURBS surface and 12 NURBS curves. The NURBS surface was made simply by using Primitive Sphere and a Lattice, or some other deformer, to transform the shape.

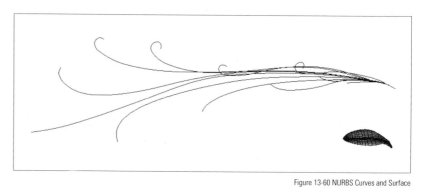

Figure 13-60 NURBS Curves and Surface

The important thing here is the shape of the curves. These curves directly influence the movement of the tongue and their shapes must, therefore, undergo several modification steps.

step 2 Now, these curves are made as a Blend Shape. Select BlendCurves 2-12, in consecutive order, through the Hypergraph or Outliner and then select BlendCurve 1 at the end. Select [Animation > Deform > Create Blend Shape ☐] to open the Create Blend Shape Options window. After configuring the Target Shape options as shown in Figure 13-61, click the Create button at the bottom of the window.

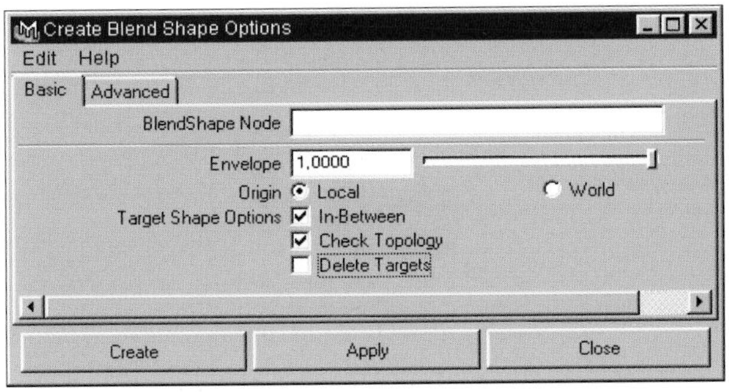

Figure 13-61 Create Blend Shape Options Window

Test the shape by selecting [Windows > Animation Editors > Blend Shape...]. We can see that the NURBS curve transforms accordingly.

step 3 Select [Animation > Deform > Wire Tool]. After first selecting the NURBS surface, press the Enter key on the keyboard. Then, select the NURBS curve and hit the Enter key.

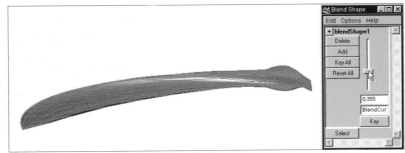

Figure 13-62 Using the Wire Tool

Adjusting the slider bar in the Blend Shape window, we can see that the surface transforms to the movement of the curve. However, we can see in Figure 13-62 that this transformation is not all that smooth.

step 4 Select the NURBS curve and select Wire1 from under INPUTS in the Channel Box. As shown in Figure 13-63, set the Dropoff Distance to 20. Now test it again. We can see that the transformation occurs properly now. The Wire Tool is an effective tool for transforming the surface using the curve.

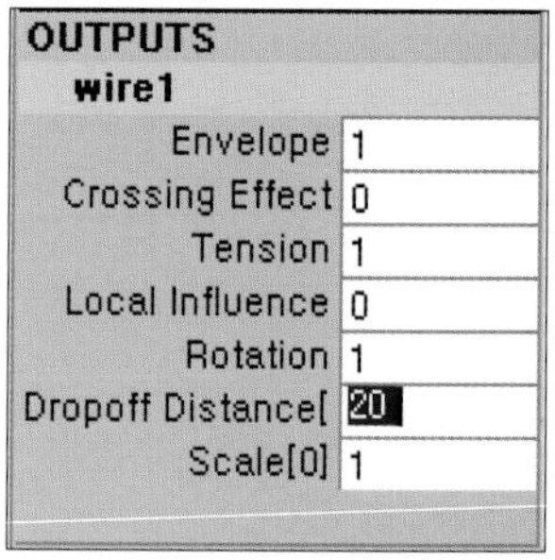

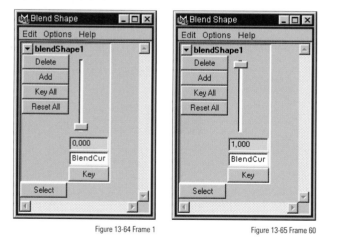

OUTPUTS	
wire1	
Envelope	1
Crossing Effect	0
Tension	1
Local Influence	0
Rotation	1
Dropoff Distance[	20
Scale[0]	1

Figure 13-63 Channel Box

step 5 In order to take a snapshot of the surface, we need to first keyframe the blend shape. After moving the time slider to Frame1, set the Range value to 0 in the Blend Shape window and press the Key button. Move the time slider to Frame60, set the Range value to 1 in the Blend Shape window and press the Key button.

Figure 13-64 Frame 1   Figure 13-65 Frame 60

We can see that the tongue is animated when we play the animation.

step 6 Let's now wrap up this process by copying the animated surface in fixed proportions and making them into a Blend Shape. Select the NURBS surface, and then select [Animation > Animate > Create Animation Snapshot ☐] to open the Options window.

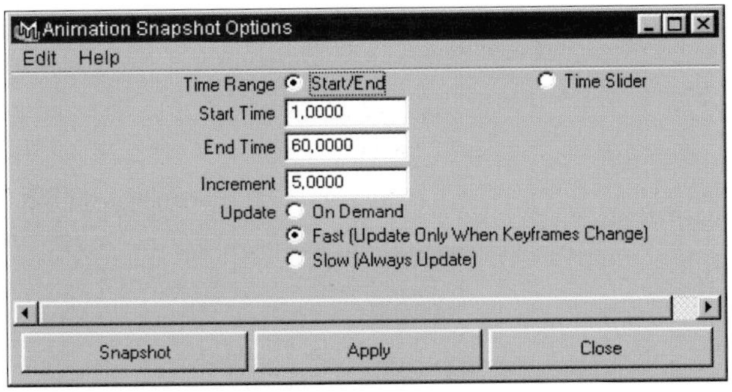

Figure 13-66 Animation Snapshot Window

As shown in Figure 13-66, set the Time Range to Start/End and then set the Start Time to 1, the End Time to 60, and the Increment to 5 before clicking on the Snapshot button. The result is that Frames 1-60 will be copied in 5-frame units to make a total of 12 NURBS surfaces as shown in Figure 13-67.

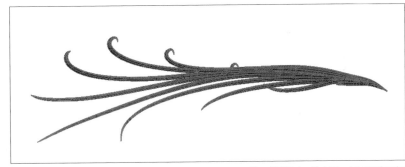

Figure 13-67 Surface Made Using Animation Snapshot

step 7 Delete all of the curves excluding the surface. By opening the Hypergraph, we can see that the NURBS surfaces made using Snapshot are named Transform1-1, Transform1-2, and so on. Select Transform1-2 to Transform1-12 in consecutive order, select Transform1-1, select the original NURBS surface, and select [Animation > Deform > Create Blend Shape]. Apply the same Blend options for the NURBS curve to the Blend Shape.

Dragging the slider bar in the Blend Shape window, we can see that the surface transforms in consecutive order. Save the completed model as TongueANI.mb.

step 8 After the setup of the tongue is complete, put it into the Frog model. Open CD-ROM/CHARACTER/scenes/FrogSETUP.mb. Select [File > Import] to import CD-ROM/CHARACTER/scenes/ TongueANI.mb. Open the frog's mouth and adjust the size and position of the tongue, as shown in Figure 13-68.

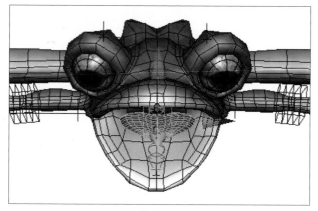

Figure 13-68 Adjusting the Size and Position of the Tongue

Make a joint that will be used to control the tongue separately. Bind the tongue and the new joint (use Smooth Bind here) and apply an appropriate Weight value. As shown in the figure, parent Joint A to Joint B.

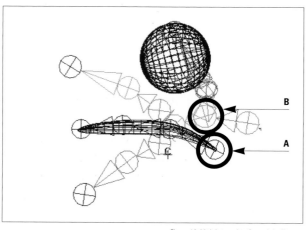

Figure 13-69 Joint used to Control the Tongue

Now, we can use Blend Shape or the joint to control the movements of the tongue.

3. BEE SETUP

Figure 13-70 Animation Snapshot

The setup for the bee is organized in basically the same way as the character setup. The only difference is that this is a two-legged character and we simply need to add wings. The setup of the bee is very simply organized. This is because the bee will not be moving on land but flying around in the air. You can save a lot of time by first thinking ahead to how the bee will be made to move in the storyboard and then setting it up by removing all unnecessary parts. Let's now take a look at the overall process for setting up the animation of the bee. Open the file CD-ROM/CHARACTER/scenes/BeeHead.mb.

It is more effective to create the Blend Shape after making and binding the skeleton. This is because this step will be repeated later. I listed this step first only to aid understanding. In reality, you should do this step after the step in the back.

3-1. MAKING BLEND SHAPE

step 1 The facial expression of the bee does not require a lot of Blend Shapes. Because the bee does not have any speaking parts, all we need to do is simply alter the shape of the mouth. First of all, in order to make the Blend Shape, make a skeleton for the face and rigid bind this by selecting [Animation > Skin > Bind Skin > Rigid Bind].

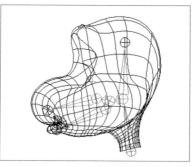

Figure 13-71 Binding Skin: Rigid

step 2 Select the face model and then use [Animation > Deform > Paint Set Membership Tool] or select the joint and then use [Animation > Deform > Paint Set Membership Tool] to allot the CVs of the model to each joint. Then, select the model and then use [Animation > Deform > Paint Cluster Weight Tool] or [Windows > General Editors > Component Editor] to adjust the Weight values of the CV joints.

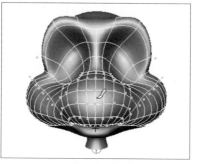

Figure 13-72 Paint Set Membership Tool

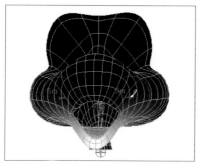

Figure 13-73 Paint Weight Tool

All that's needed here is for the mouth of the character to open naturally. As with all characters, the joints controlling the movements of the lower jaw must have a lot of CVs. This is the only way we can get a natural movement of the face when we rotate the joints to open the mouth after adjusting the Weight values.

step 3 Now, we simply make 2 Blend Shape Targets. If the character had a specific speaking part, we would have to match the Blend Shape Targets to each pronunciation. However, in this case, we only need the two targets.

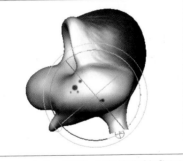

Figure 13-74 Opening the Mouth of the Character

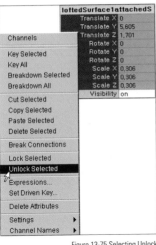

Figure 13-75 Selecting Unlock

First of all, use the Rotate Tool on the joint controlling the lower jaw to open the mouth of the character. In this state, press Ctrl+D to make a copy of the head, select all of the locked channels in the Channel Box, and click the RMB to unlock them (see Figure 13-75). Move the copied model somewhere along the X-axis. In the same way, make 2 copies of the model. The following figure illustrates how the CVs of the duplicated model are adjusted to model the character. A simple opening of the mouth or a laughing mouth will be dealt with using the bound joint or clusters.

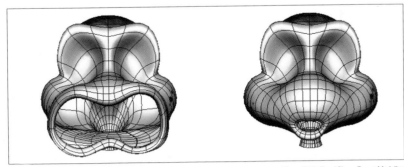

Figure 13-76 Blend Shape Target Modeling

The expressions shown in Figure 13-76 are difficult to create using only joints or clusters. We will model only the expressions, such as these, that are considered difficult to make.

Select and export only the 2 Blend Shape Target Objects. Select [File > Export Selection ▢] to open the Options window, set the File Type to mayaBinary, and then click on Export Selection at the bottom before setting the File Name to BeeBlendTarget.mb.

3-2. DRAW SKELETON

Let's now begin making the skeleton. The skeletal structure is similar to that of a human character and should not be difficult to understand. Figure 13-77 shows the skeletal structure of the body.

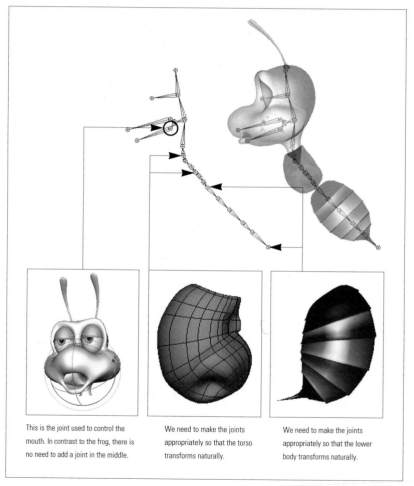

This is the joint used to control the mouth. In contrast to the frog, there is no need to add a joint in the middle.

We need to make the joints appropriately so that the torso transforms naturally.

We need to make the joints appropriately so that the lower body transforms naturally.

Figure 13-77 Skeletal Structure of the Body

Keep in mind that the first joint of the root joint that spreads out from top to bottom must always be as close to the root as possible. Figure 13-78 shows the skeletal structure of the wing. If you want to create the natural movement of the wings as shown here, the joints must be split and each of the joints should be rotated slightly as they are keyframed. However, because the wings move very fast and are not that noticeable, we did not keyframe each individual joint here.

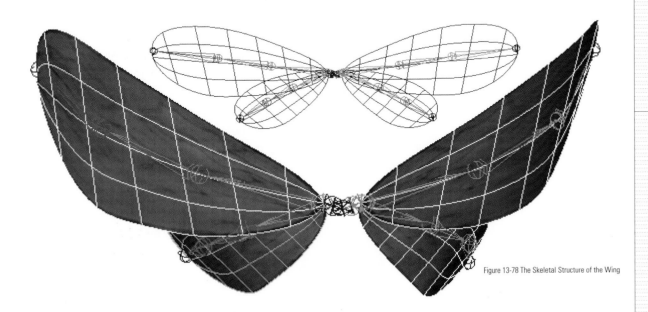

Figure 13-78 The Skeletal Structure of the Wing

Figure 13-79 shows the skeletal structure of the hand and leg. The setup is organized in the same way as a general setup and should not be difficult to understand.

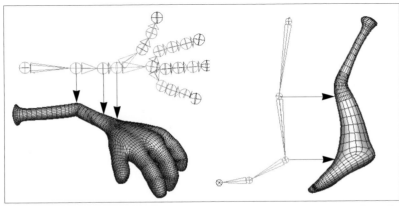

Figure 13-79 The Skeletal Structure of the Hand and Leg

The areas linked by the arrows in Figure 13-79 show how the skin changes due to the joints. The fingers must be made while observing the movement of each joint.
Refer to the completed setup model to see the details of the entire skeleton.

3-3. BINDING SKIN

Binding the bee is quite different than binding the frog. It is more effective to use direct binding using a lattice so that the body moves naturally. This method is very common and a rectified process will be used here rather than a detailed explanation.

step 1 First of all, in order to use a lattice for direct binding, we need to rotate the lower body. This is because the lattice will be made according to the current state of the body if it is not rotated. As shown in Figure 13-80, after rotating and arranging the lower body, make the lattice and then rotate the lattice again to arrange it in the original position.

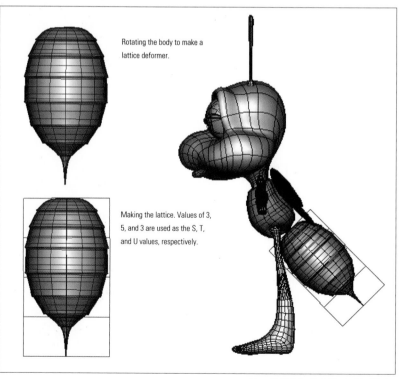

Rotating the body to make a lattice deformer.

Making the lattice. Values of 3, 5, and 3 are used as the S, T, and U values, respectively.

Figure 13-80 Making the Lattice for Direct Binding

step 2 Select all of the surfaces, excluding those of the eye. Because we made a lattice for the lower body in Step 1, we can simply select the lattice rather than the lower body. Select the root joint while holding down the Shift key and select [Animation > Skin > Bind Skin > Rigid Bind]. As shown in Figure 13-81, parent the joint indicated to the lattice surrounding the eye.

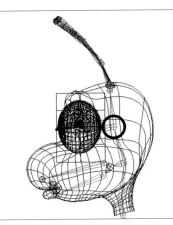

Figure 13-81 The Joint to Which the Eye Will Be Parented

After binding, use the Edit Membership Tool and the Paint Set Membership Tool to readjust the allotment of the CVs to each joint. Modify the joints by rotating the character and aligning it to the actual movement of the character. Figure 13-82 illustrates an example using the Paint Set Membership Tool.

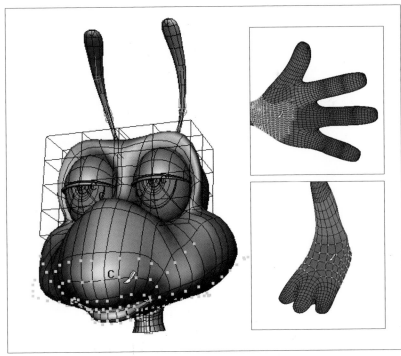

Figure 13-82 An Example of Using the Paint Set Membership Tool

In order to allot the CVs in greater detail in certain regions, we must make adequate use of the Edit Membership Tool. This tool is very effective for working with lattices used in direct binding.

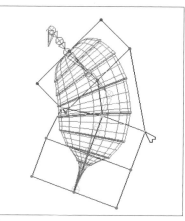

Figure 13-83 Using the Edit Membership Tool

step 3 After using the Edit Membership Tool to edit the CV joints, we now need to modify the Weight values for each of the joint clusters. This step is also done using Artisan's Paint Cluster Weight Tool and the Component Editor. For detailed modifications, we can use the Edit Membership Tool here, as well, to readjust the CVs. This step is illustrated in Figure 13-84.

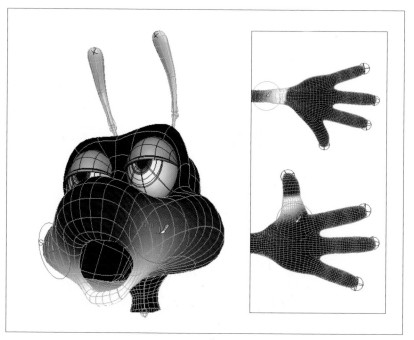

Figure 13-84 An Example of Using the Painting Cluster Weight Tool

Lattice flexors are used in each joint of the hand. However, areas (such as those shown on the left-hand side of Figure 13-85) in which it is difficult to use a lattice are dealt with by adjusting the Weight values. In particular, it is especially difficult to use a lattice flexor and so we use the Paint Cluster Weight Tool. Also, when binding using a lattice, we first select the lattice point, select [Windows > General Editors > Component Editor] to open the Component Editor, and adjust the Weight values one at a time to create a more precise model.

3-4. WORKING WITH FLEXOR

Just as we did for the frog, we usually use flexors in areas that use Rigid Bind to control the movement of the joints. Because we fully covered the use of flexors in the frog setup, we will only go over where to use flexors here. As we can see in Figure 13-85, flexors are used only in the arms and legs. In general, the use of flexors is concentrated in the arms and legs of all characters. In order for the joints to move naturally, the flexor attributes must be defined in the Channel Box.

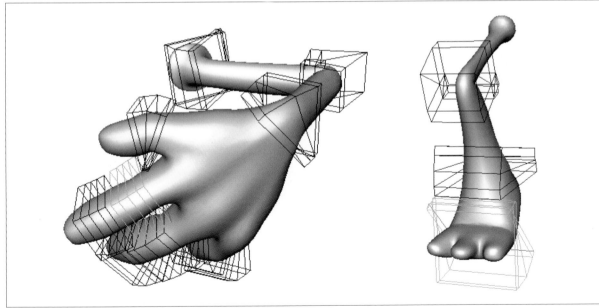

Figure 13-85 Use of Flexors in the Arms and Legs

After setting up one side, copy it using [Animation > Skin > Edit Rigid Skin > Copy Flexor] to make the other side.

Figure 13-86 shows the flexors used in each area of the body.

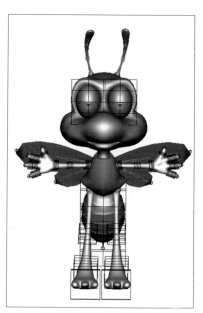

Figure 13-86 Flexors Added to the Model

3-5. CREATE BLEND SHAPE

In order to make the Blend Shape, we need to import the BeeBlendTarget.mb file. As shown in Figure 13-87, select the 2 target objects one at a time and then select the bound face.

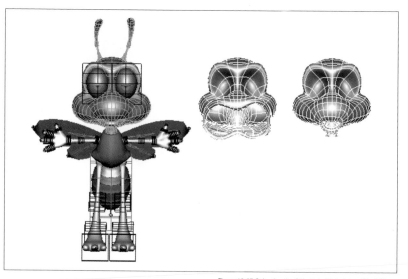

Figure 13-87 Selecting the Objects to Make into a Blend Shape

Select [Animation > Deform > Create Blend Shape ▣] to open the Create Blend Shape Options window. Click on the Advanced Tab in the Options window, as shown in Figure 13-88, select Front of Chain from Deformation Order, and the click on the Create button.

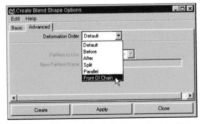

Figure 13-88 Create Blend Shape Options Window

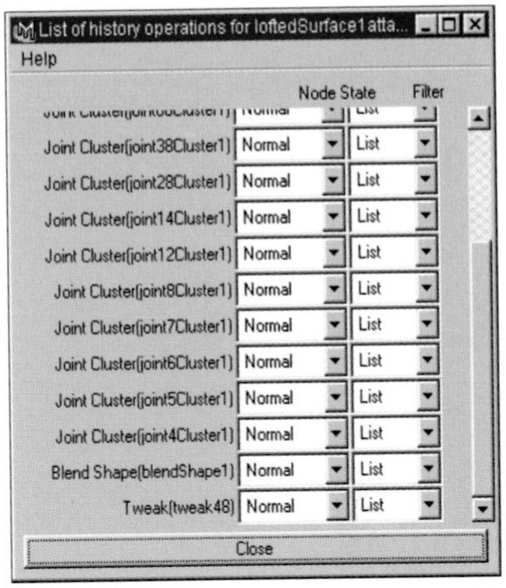

Figure 13-89 Complete List

This option is used to specify the Deformation Order of the Blend Shape and the order is placed in front of the joint cluster. Select the Blend Shape face, click the RMB, and select [Input > Complete List] from the Marking Menu to open the List of History Operation window. In this window, we can see that Blend Shape is listed below the joint cluster (see Figure 13-89).

If the Blend Shape was made using the default values, the Blend Shape will not work properly during the animation.

4. SETTING UP THE BEE FOR ANIMATION

Figure 13-90 Animation Snapshot

We have just completed the basic setup for the bee. In this section, we will look at the animation setup process for controlling the given movements. The majority of the bee's movements consists of floating in the air. Therefore, the animation setup should not be too difficult.

This section will only cover a few, characteristic steps in the animation setup process.

4-1. USING IK HANDLES AND AUXILIARY JOINTS

The frog did not have any auxiliary joints in the hands because, unlike a human character, the movements of the hands are not that significant.

However, the auxiliary joints that were used to control the feet were set up based on the fact that the feet were planted on a surface. In terms of IK handles, IK RPsolvers were used in the hands and legs. An IK Spline Handle, used to control the body, was not used because the animation was made using Scale values, making it was more convenient not to use IK Spline handles.

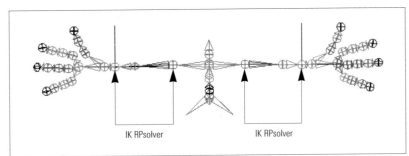

IK RPsolver   IK RPsolver

Figure 13-91 IK RPsolver Used in the Hand

The legs followed the basic character setup. Three IK RPsolvers were made to connect the joints of the leg and were parented to make auxiliary joints that would be used to control the leg, and then these auxiliary joints were parented to the IK RPsolver.

Figure 13-92 shows how the auxiliary joints and IK handles were made and parented.

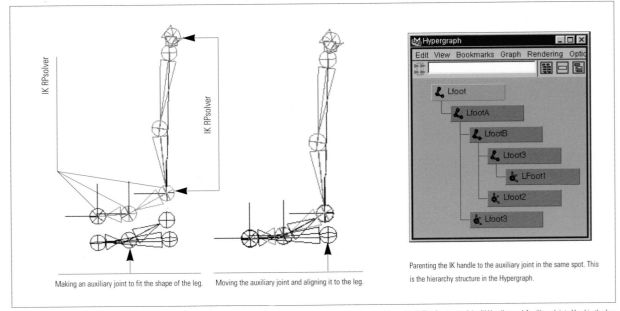

IK RPsolver

IK RPsolver

Making an auxiliary joint to fit the shape of the leg.   Moving the auxiliary joint and aligning it to the leg.

Parenting the IK handle to the auxiliary joint in the same spot. This is the hierarchy structure in the Hypergraph.

Figure 13-92 The Structure of the IK Handles and Auxiliary Joints Used in the Leg

4-2. USING CONSTRAINTS

A comparatively simpler constraint is used in the bee. All we have is the Pole Vector for the IK handles and the Aim Constraint used to control the eyes. Although this may be not

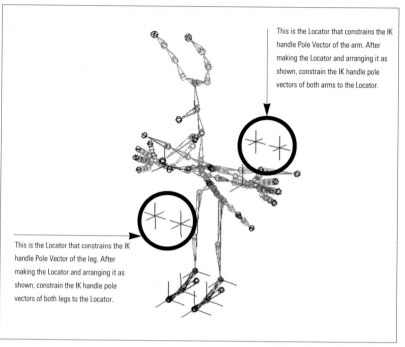

This is the Locator that constrains the IK handle Pole Vector of the arm. After making the Locator and arranging it as shown, constrain the IK handle pole vectors of both arms to the Locator.

This is the Locator that constrains the IK handle Pole Vector of the leg. After making the Locator and arranging it as shown, constrain the IK handle pole vectors of both legs to the Locator.

Figure 13-93 Constraining the IK Handle Pole Vector

be the case for a more complex animation, we do need a large number of constraints for a simpler animation. Figure 13-93 shows the constraining of the IK handle Pole Vectors.

Each of the Locators needs to follow the movements of the character. We do this by parenting the Locator to specific joints. As shown in Figure 13-94, in order to constrain the Pole Vectors of the arms, the 2 Locators need to be parented to the joints of the spread-out arms. In order to constrain the Pole Vectors of the legs, we need to parent the 2 Locators to the root joint of the skeleton. The next step looks at using Aim Constraint on the eyes.

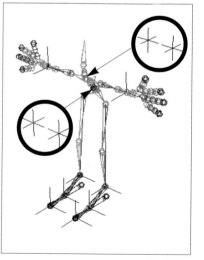

Figure 13-94 Parenting the Locators

step 1 First of all, select [Create > Locator] to make 2 locators. As shown in Figure 13-95, fix the Locators to the gaze of both eyes.

An easier way to do this is to fix the Locator for one eye and then duplicate the Locator and move it along the X-axis to fix it in place for the other eye.

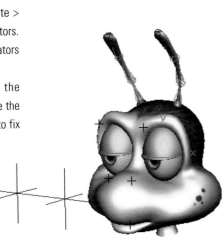

Figure 13-95 Making and Arranging the Locator

step 2 As we saw during modeling, the bee's eyes consist of 3 objects. One is the eyelid that allows the eyes to blink, another is the NURBS sphere (to which Transparency has been applied) that surrounds the eyeball, and the last object is the textured eyeball.

Actually, the object to which the Aim Constraint is applied is the textured eyeball. There is no need to apply Aim Constraint to the other objects.

First of all, select the eyeball and press Ctrl+A to open the Attribute Editor so that we can confirm the local axis of the eyeball. As shown in Figure 13-96, click on the leftmost tab and select Display Local Axis from under Display. This will display the local axis of the eyeball.

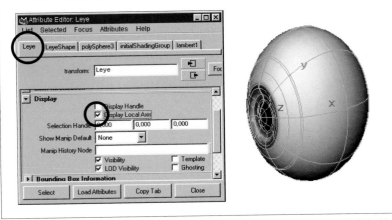

Figure 13-96 Display Local Axis

step 3 First, select the Locator and then, while holding down the Shift key, select the eyeball. Select [Animation > Constraint > Aim ❐] to open the Aim Constraint Options window. In the Options window, as shown in Figure 13-97, set the Z field of the Aim Vector to 1, set the Y field of the Up Vector to 1, and then click the Add/Remove button.

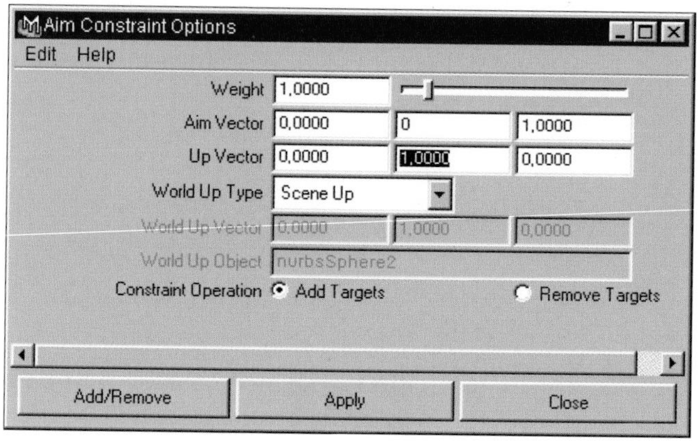

Aim Constraint Options
Edit Help
Weight 1,0000
Aim Vector 0,0000 0 1,0000
Up Vector 0,0000 1,0000 0,0000
World Up Type Scene Up
World Up Vector 0,0000 1,0000 0,0000
World Up Object nurbsSphere2
Constraint Operation Add Targets
Remove Targets
Add/Remove
Apply
Close
Figure 13-97 Aim Constraint Options Window

Constrain the other eyeball in the same way.

step 4 Select both Locators, select [Edit > Group] to group them, and then select [Modify > Center Pivot] to center the pivot on the group node. We can facilitate selection by selecting [Display > Component Display > Selection Handle] to display the handles.

Because this Locator must also follow the movement of the character, we parent it to a joint on the head as shown in Figure 13-98.

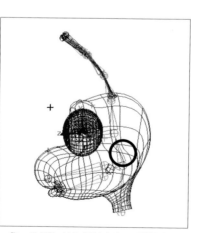

Figure 13-98 The Joint to Which the Locator Will Be Parented

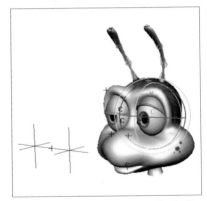

Figure 13-99 Cluster Made So the Eyes Can Close

4-3. USING SET DRIVEN KEY

We will now use Set Driven Key to quickly and easily set up the character's movements. First, we will make the eyelid respond to the gaze of the eyes. We have already covered this in Chapter 7, "Character Setup," and will only explain the process here. We have already made 2 clusters for each of the eyes during modeling. One cluster was set up to blink the eyes, and the other was set up to squint the eyes. We use the eye-blinking cluster to set up the eyelid to respond to the eye movements.

step 1 Select [Animation > Animate > Set Driven Key > Set ▢] to open the Set Driven Key window. As shown in Figure 13-100, select the locator group and place it in Driver, and then select the clusters of each eye and place it in Driven. After selecting Translate Y in Group and selecting both cluster names in Driven, select rotateX. The eyes will rotate as shown. The configuration will be made so that the selected cluster rotates in the X-axis when the Locator moves in the Y-axis. After making the configurations shown here, click on the Key button at the bottom of the Set Driven Key window to make a key.

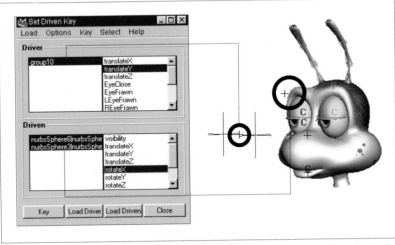

Figure 13-100 Configuring Set Driven Key

step 2 After moving the Locator in the Y-axis as shown in Figure 13-101, rotate the clusters of both eyes as shown. One thing to note here is that the one of the eyes that has been made using Mirror Copy will rotate in the "-" direction because the Scale value of the mirrored eye is -1. Keeping this in mind, let's rotate the eyes in the opposite direction. After making the configurations as shown, click on the Key button at the bottom of the Set Driven Key window to make a key.

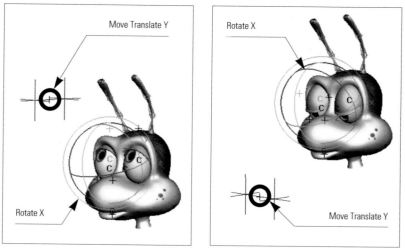

Figure 13-101 Configuring Set Driven Key   Figure 13-102 Configuring Set Driven Key

Next, after moving the locator group in the Y-axis as shown in Figure 13-102 rotate the cluster of both eyes in the X-axis as shown. Click on the Key button at the bottom of the Set Driven Key window to make a key. Now, when we move the locator group, the eyes and the eyelids will move accordingly.

step 3 Other eye movements can be made effectively by making several attributes and linking them to the Set Driven Key. When using the grouped node of the Locator to animate the eyes, it is a good idea to add attributes for this node. After selecting the grouped node of the Locator, select [Modify > Add Attribute] to open the Add Attribute window. As shown in Figure 13-103, set the Attribute Name to EyeClose, the Data Type to Float, the Minimum value to -10, the Maximum value to 10, and the Default to 0 before clicking on the OK button at the bottom of the window. This will create the EyeClose channel in the Channel Box.

Now all we have to do is to change the name of this channel to EyeFrown, LeyeFrown and ReyeFrown, respectively.

Now, link these attributes to the Set Driven key as shown below. The Frown attribute is linked to the eye-squinting cluster as Driven.

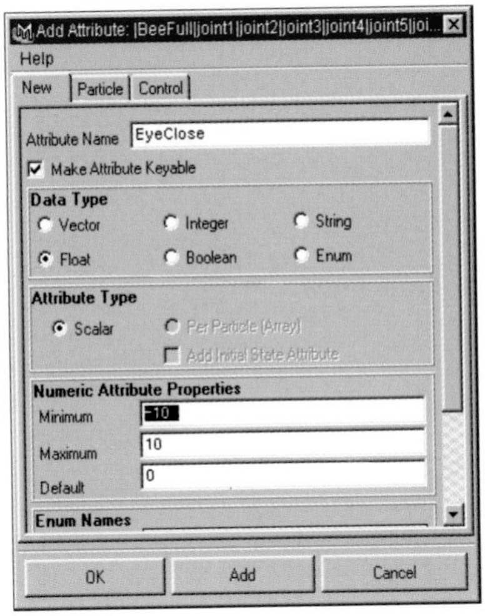

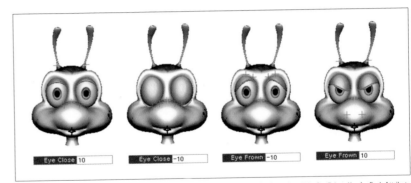

Figure 13-103 Add Attribute Window

Figure 13-104 Configuration of the Set Driven Key for Each Attribute

Configure the Leye Frown and the Reye Frown over the Eye Frown on the left and right eyelids, respectively.

Stretch & Squash

We can use Set Driven Key to easily add a Stretch & Squash effect to the lower body of the bee. Adequate use of such animation elements to transform the shape can bring be used to obtain very effective results. Let's first add attributes. When adding attributes, it is a good idea to make groups of identical attributes. In other words, just as we made a group node for the Locator of the attributes controlling the eye, we make one node for the attributes controlling the body.

Because the majority of this character's movement will be floating in the air, the entire skeleton needs to be grouped. Select the root joint of the skeleton and all the auxiliary joints used in the leg and then select [Edit > Group].

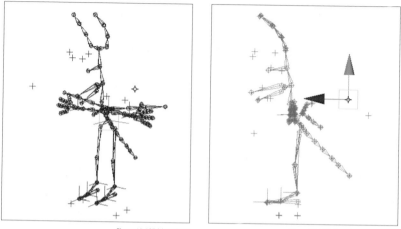

Figure 13-105 Move Pivot

Figure 13-106 Move Selection Handle

Change the name of the group node to BeeFull and align the pivot to the root joint as shown in Figure 13-105. An exact alignment can be made by pressing the V key on the keyboard to apply the Point Snap. Select [Display > Component Display > Selection Handle] to display the selection handle, and move it as shown in Figure 13-106. Now, add an attribute and link it to the Set Driven Key.

step 4 Select BeeFull and then select [Modify > Add Attribute]. In the Add Attribute window, set the Attribute Name to Tail Stretch, the Data Type to Float, the Minimum value to -10, the Maximum value to 10, and the Default to 0 before clicking on the OK button as shown in Figure 13-107. A Tail Stretch channel will be made in the Channel Box.

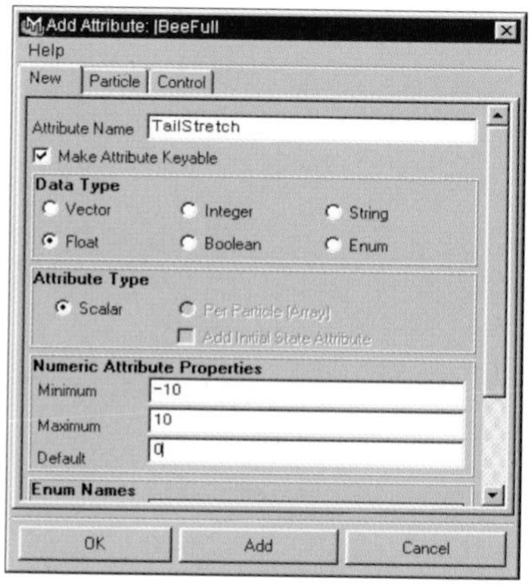

Figure 13-107 Add Attribute Window

step 5 Select [Animation > Animate > Set Driven Key > Set ▣] to open the Set Driven Key window. As shown in Figure 13-108, select the joint and place it in Driven and then select BeeFull and place it in Driver. Select Joints 1-5 in consecutive order.

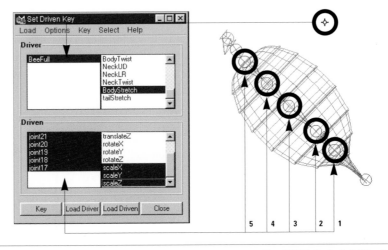

Figure 13-108 Configuring the Set Driven Key

As shown in Figure 13-108, select the Tail Stretch of BeeFull and all the joints in Driven. Select Scale X, Y, and Z from the joint channels before clicking on the Key button at the bottom of the Set Driven Key window to make a key.

step 6 As shown in Figure 13-109, adjust the Tail Stretch and joint Scale values, and then click on the Key button at the bottom of the Set Driven Key window of each to make a key.

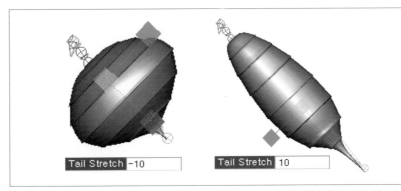

Figure 13-109 Configuring the Set Driven Key

Adjust the Tail Stretch value in the Channel Box and verify that the Stretch & Squash effect is applied correctly to the lower body. We must make sure that the size of the lower body is maintained while it is stretched and squashed.

Character Setup Using Other Set Driven Keys

In order to quickly and easily control complex animations, we use Set Driven Keys to configure areas for which animation keyframing is difficult. One such area that is difficult to animation keyframe is the finger. Each joint must be made to rotate, and because there are many joints in the finger, rotating and keyframing each one is very difficult to do.

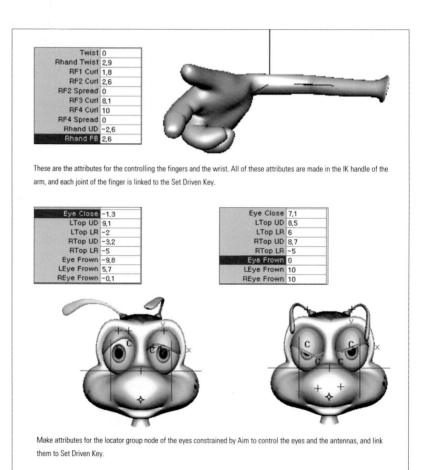

These are the attributes for the controlling the fingers and the wrist. All of these attributes are made in the IK handle of the arm, and each joint of the finger is linked to the Set Driven Key.

Make attributes for the locator group node of the eyes constrained by Aim to control the eyes and the antennas, and link them to Set Driven Key.

Figure 13-110 An Example of Using Set Driven Key

However, if the fingers need to have special movements, the Set Driven Key may not be all that effective. We need to break the connection to the Set Driven Key in order to use a special script. If the connection is not broken, we cannot use any other motion besides the one indicated by the Set Driven Key. In the case of the bee, the fingers do not have a special movement. That is why we use the Set Driven Key to set up the environment beforehand. Our work will proceed much faster if we decide, before using the Set Driven Key, what motion the character will have. Refer to CD-ROM/CHARACTER/scenes/ BeeSETUP.mb for further details. Figure 13-110 shows the movement of the joints manipulated by the Set Driven Key.

4-4. USING LAYERS

The binding data gets very big during animation. Therefore, it is very difficult to use this model for keyframing. The reason it is difficult to keyframe is that the time needed to compute the large amount of data prevents us from seeing a preview of the motion right away. In order to facilitate keyframing in such instances, we use layers. Figure 13-111 shows layers for separate keyframing.

One thing to keep in mind when making layers is that each layer must remain faithful to its respective movement. If not, there will be a big difference in the actual transformation of the model. As follows, the model that will be used as a layer must remain faithful to the shape of the final object. Also, there is no need to bind such layer objects to the skeleton. Binding, in and of itself, acts to increase the amount of data; therefore, it is better to simply parent it to the respective joint.

Figure 13-111 Model for the Layer

14
Animating
a Character Model

Up until now, we have looked at the setup process for character modeling and animation. It is now time to keyframe these setups. However, a detailed explanation of animation is very difficult to do on paper. It is very difficult to explain in words which frames need to be keyed and how the poses should look. Therefore, the majority of the explanations here will deal with setups, which is the fastest and quickest way to obtain the desired motions.

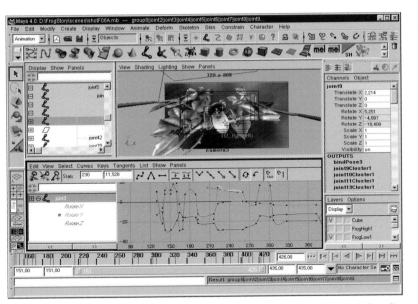

Figure 14-1 Keyframing Screen Shot

1. FROG KEYFRAMING

We have already looked at the basic setup for moving the frog in the previous step. We will now look at the problems that come up during keyframing and how to deal with these problems. This chapter will also offer a brief explanation on the problems that arise while configuring the timing during keyframing. These all have to do with the movements of the characters and, since you may have your own inclinations and preferences, there is no such thing as the exact or proper way. Therefore, I hope that you will carefully read over this chapter and go over the supplied animation, so that it will serve as an opportunity for you to seriously consider timing in keyframing.

1-1. MOVING IN THE TREES

Almost all of the frog's movements are confined to the tree. The ending also consists of the frog moving on a big leaf. The frog and the tree are 2 separate objects. However, the frog's 4 feet need to be fixed on the tree and the tree branches need to respond to the frog's movements. This kind of configuration brings the following thought to mind. Namely, whether the animation should be configured so that the branches are made to respond to the frog's legs or whether the frog's legs should be made to respond to the branches.

As explained before, the 4 legs of the frog have been set up using IK handle Inverse Kinematics. This means that we can fix the frog's legs to a particular spot. Looking at the characteristics of Inverse Kinematics, the latter configuration (i.e., the frog's legs being made to respond to the branches) is the easier choice. This is because we can simply attach the feet to the legs to have the feet respond to the swaying of the branches. However, configuring the branches to respond to the feet can be a very complex and difficult process. When the frog leaps down from the air in the beginning, the legs should follow the movements of the body and when it finally lands on the branch, it should follow the movements of the branch.

1. Point & Orient Constraint

Constraint is used in the configuration of all similar character animations.
By making several constraints and changing the constraint from time to time as needed, we can easily solve these kinds of problems. We have already made a polygon cube and applied Point & Orient to the 4 legs during the initial frog setup process. We need to make polygon cubes for each of the 4 legs and apply a constraint to each. The data for this example is saved as CD-ROM/CHARACTER/scenes/FrogSHOT1.mb. This file may be used if you wish to follow along with this example. By opening this file, we can see, as in Figure 14-2, that there are 4 polygon cubes placed on the branch of the tree.

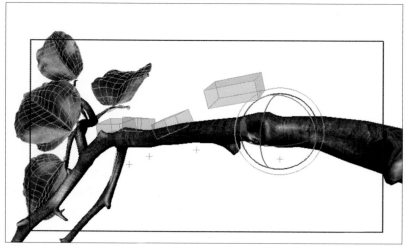

Figure 14-2 Example File

This branch has already been bound to the joint, and each of the polygon cubes has been parented to a nearby joint. The leaves have also been parented to the joints made to manipulate the leaves. Therefore, by rotating each joint, we can see that the parented polygon cubes and leaves respond to the motion. Looking at the example file, we can see that the frog is suspended in the air over the branch. The animation we will be making here is that of the frog landing on the branch and the branch swaying from the weight. The first thing we need to do is apply the Point & Constraint of the polygon cube parented to the branch to the auxiliary joints of the 4 legs.

The polygon cubes on the outsides are used to constrain the auxiliary joints of the hind legs, and the polygon cubes in the middle are used to constrain the auxiliary joints of the front legs.

step 1 Select each of the polygon cubes on the branch and the respective auxiliary joints of the frog's legs, and then select, first, [Animation > Constraint > Point] and then [Animation > Constraint > Orient] to constrain them. This will Point & Orient constrain the 4 auxiliary joints of the legs to their respective polygon cubes, and the legs will be positioned as shown in Figure 14-3.

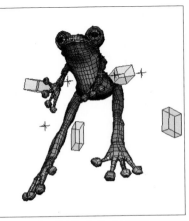

Figure 14-3 After Applying Point & Orient Constraint

Because the auxiliary joint is Point & Orient constrained to 2 objects, the rotation and position of the auxiliary joint will lie somewhere between the 2 objects. If it had been constrained to 3 objects, the rotation and position would lie somewhere between the 3 objects.

step 2 In the current frame, the frog is suspended in air. As follows, the rotation and position of the legs must follow the frog's movements. Therefore, the 4 auxiliary joints of the legs must not be constrained to the 4 polygon cubes. In order to break the constraints, select one of the auxiliary joints. As shown in Figure 14-4, we can look under SHAPES in the Channel Box to see which constraint is applied to which object.

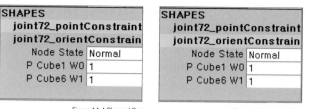

Figure 14-4 Channel Box   Figure 14-5 Channel Box

In other words, the Point Constraint of the currently selected joint is constrained to P Cube 1 and 6 with a constraint value of 1. As follows, because each of the polygon cubes, which constrain the joint, has a constraint value of 1, this means that the joint is located in the middle of these polygon cubes. Even if we select joint72_orientConstraint, below the current joint72_pointConstraint, we will see the same values (see Figure 14-5). As shown in Figure 14-4, select joint72_pointConstraint and set the constraint value of one of the constraining nodes, P Cube6 W1 to 0. In the same way, select joint72_ orientConstraint, as shown in Figure 14-5, and set the P Cube6 W1 value to 0. This will constrain the selected auxiliary joint to the parented polygon cube on the body and break the constraint of the polygon cube on the branch.

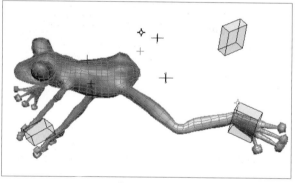

Figure 14-6 Results from Making Changes in the Channel Box

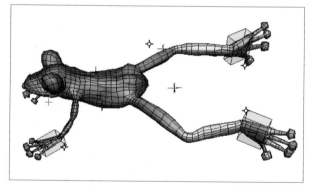

Figure 14-7 Adjusting the Constraint Values of all Auxiliary Joints

In the same way, break the constraints between the remaining auxiliary joints and the polygon cubes of the branches until we get the result seen in Figure 14-7. Because the 4 polygon cubes of the frog have already been grouped in the topmost node in the frog hierarchy, by selecting and moving this node, the polygon cube will follow.

step 3 After moving this to an appropriate frame (approximately Frame13), pose the frog as shown in Figure 14-8.

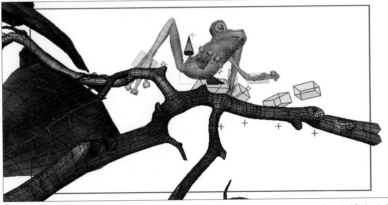

Figure 14-8 Posing the Frog

Select all of names of the polygon cubes constraining the auxiliary joints in the Channel Box (see Figure 14-9), and click the RMB and select Key Selected to make a key. Keyframe the remaining auxiliary joints in the same way. By doing so, we will assign a key to the constraint values of the current frame in its current state.

Figure 14-9 Channel Box

step 4 Now, after moving to Frame 18, keyframe the frog to pose it as shown in Figure 14-10.

Figure 14-10 Posing the Frog

We will now change the constraint value in the Channel Box. In other words, values of 1 will be changed to 0 and values of 0 will be changed to 1 and then given a key. Change the values for the remaining auxiliary joints. By changing the values for one of the legs a few frames later, we can obtain a more natural result.

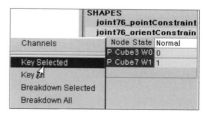

Figure 14-11 Channel Box

By keyframing the joints, the legs are now all fixed on the branch. Rotating each of the joints bound to the branch, we can see that the legs are indeed fixed to the branches as shown in Figure 14-12.

Now, after keyframing the swaying of the branch from the weight of the frog's body landing on it and matching the movements of the frog to it, we can keyframe the exact placement of the legs. We simply reverse the values in the Channel Box to keyframe the ending, when the frog leaps again.

Constraint will be used again in the ending shot, when the frog raises and puts on the glasses.

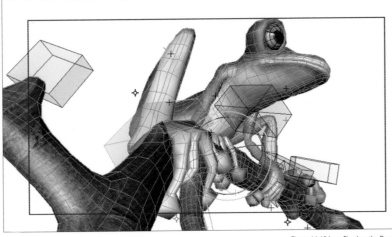
Figure 14-12 Legs Fixed on the Branch

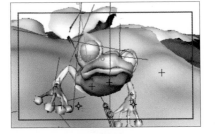

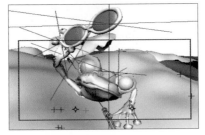

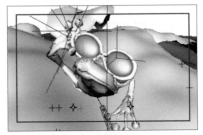

Figure 14-13 Constraint Keyframing

Figure 14-13 shows the frog raising and putting on the glasses. Currently, the frog has 3 Locators and each of the Locators is parented to nearby joints. The 3 locators are the Locator of the hand, the Locator that will be used when the glasses are placed on the face and the hidden Locator beneath. The Locator of the hand is parented to the joint of the palm of the hand, the Locator in the face is parented to the joint in the face (the joint used to control the upper lip), and the remaining Locator is parented to the root joint. The glasses are Point & Orient constrained to all 3 locators. This constraint is keyframed to follow the movements of the hand. When the frog raises the glasses, the glasses are constrained to the Locator parented to the hand. When the glasses are placed on the face, it is constrained to the Locator parented to the face.

In addition, the movement of the glasses is possible by keyframing the Locator constraining the glasses. In this way, one object is constrained to several Locators and these constraints are keyframed to animate diverse motions.

Rendering a Character Animation

In this section we will look at how to create the overall texture, how to shade the project for rendering, and how to configure the environment to render the scene. The map source will be made using mostly Deep Paint 3D and Photoshop. For more information on using Deep Paint 3D, refer to Part 2, "Maya and Beyond."

1. FROG MAPPING

The frog was made using mostly polygons. Although subdivision surface modeling was used, because the final output is in polygon, we use polygon mapping. Because the original plan was to use Deep Paint 3D, one of the most difficult parts of this project was to create the UV coordinates for the polygon.

Figure 15-1 Copyright 2001 (c) Choi Jae-Jin

UV setting must be completed before beginning character binding. We cover UV setting first in this chapter merely for the sake of understanding.

For more information on polygon mapping, refer to Chapter 2, "Polygon, Subdivision Surface Mapping." This chapter will be devoted, not to the use of Deep Paint 3D, but to creating the UV setting and shader.

1-1. UV SETTING

Figure 15-1 shows the UV coordinates for the frog. Although this is a very tedious and complex step, once it is done, we can easily create the texture by simply painting over the object using Deep Paint 3D or any other 3D painting software. We already covered polygon mapping to some degree earlier in this book. Therefore, we will merely look at the steps that were involved in setting up the UV. As mentioned earlier, although it is easier to simply use Layout UV, this is not an effective method for creating precise map sources.

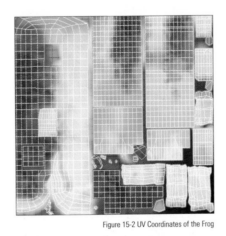

Figure 15-2 UV Coordinates of the Frog

The UVs must be densely packed inside the texture axis as shown to minimize the texture loss. The following steps are needed to setup the UV as shown above.

step 1 First of all, in order to set up the coordinates of the body, select the face of the body as shown in Figure 15-3. Select [Modeling > Edit Polygons > Textures > Cylindrical Mapping] and adjust the Manipulator to obtain the result seen in Figure 15-4.

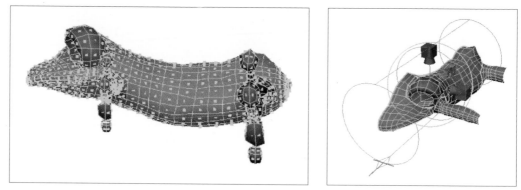

Figure 15-3 Selecting the Face   Figure 15-4 Cylindrical Mapping

Open [Windows > UV Texture Editor] and position the UV-axis by moving the Manipulator as shown in Figure 15-5. If the UV is not moved to the side (see Figure 15-5), deactivating the UV, we can see that the UVs overlap, making it difficult to freely edit the UV.

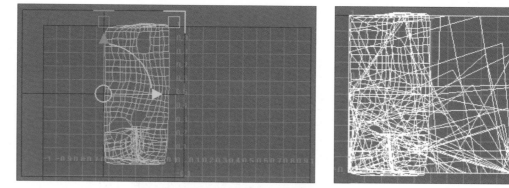

Figure 15-5 Positioning the UV Using the Manipulator   Figure 15-6 Overlapping UV

step 2 Now, select the faces of the legs as shown in Figure 15-7. As we did for the body, select [Modeling > Edit Polygons > Textures > Cylindrical Mapping] and adjust the Manipulator to obtain the result seen in Figure 15-8.

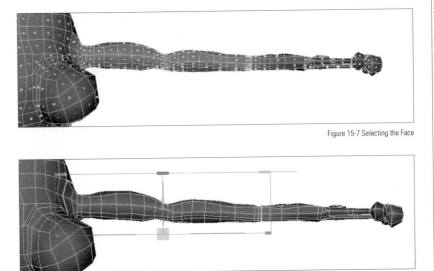

Figure 15-7 Selecting the Face

Figure 15-8 Cylindrical Mapping

Open the UV Texture Editor as we did for the body and after selecting the UV, adjust the size and position (see Figure 15-9) so that the UVs are easily distinguishable. Apply Cylindrical Mapping in the same way to the hind legs.

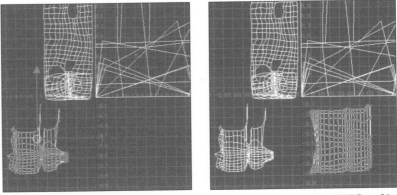

Figure 15-9 UV Texture Editor

Spread out the UVs in this way. Depending on the method used, using polygon mapping will make the work proceed faster and easier. Although we can set up the UV faster and easier without using the method described here, we manually organize the UV made in this way to minimize texture loss and to distribute the texture evenly.

This can be very tedious. To select and align the UV inside the texture map, press the X key on the keyboard to apply the G rid Snap. You must familiarize yourself with almost all of the methods available in the Polygon Texture menu to facilitate this setup process. The most commonly used menus are Cut UVs, Sew UVs, and Move UVs, Other menus include Relax UVs, Normalize UVs and Unitize UVs.

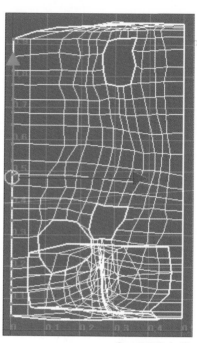

Figure 15-10 Aligning UVs

Figure 15-11 shows the final UV setting. Areas that are not especially important are allotted to a comparatively smaller area of the texture map.

Figure 15-11 Final UV-Axis

1-2. CREATING TEXTURE

Next, we will look at using Deep Paint 3D to make the texture. The map source of the frog was created almost entirely using Painting. Painting is used because it appears smoother than if a picture map was used. A lot of time is needed to paint. The details and folds of the texture require a lot of time and manual work. For more information on using Deep Paint 3D, refer to Part 2, "Maya and Beyond." We have completed the UV setting in Step 2. All we need to do now is to paint over the model. This will automatically create the texture over the UV map to create the color texture seen in Figure 15-12.

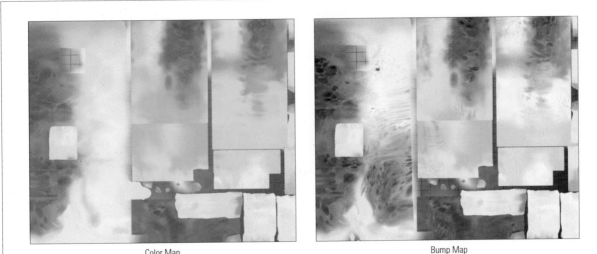

Color Map

Bump Map

Figure 15-12 Map Source Drawn Using Deep Paint 3D

I believe that it is personal preference whether you first make the Bump Map and then the Color Map or vice versa. Here, we will make the Color Map first and then, after converting the source to gray in Photoshop, it will be brought back to Deep Paint 3D to add the details. However, depending on the character and the degree of the bump, it may sometimes be more effective to first create the Bump Map and then base the Color Map on it. Do not be restricted by this. Specular Map is not included in this project.

1-3. SHADING CHARACTER

After making the texture, we then make the shader and assign it to the character. We come across a problem during this process. The problem is illustrated in Figure 15-13. We can see that one side of the Bump Map is made in the "+" direction and that the other side is made in the "-" direction. This phenomenon occurs because only one side of the map was set up and then mirror copied to the other side. When the model is completed using Mirror Copy, open the UV Texture Editor. We see the other side, but in reality, the 2 sides overlap. The 2 sides of the Bump Map are different because although the model is mirror copied, the UV map is not.

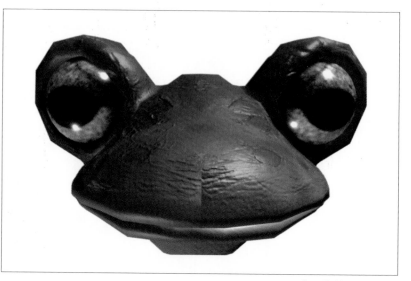

Figure 15-13 Incorrect Bump Map

In order to create a proper map, we need to use [Edit Polygon > Textures > Flip UVs] on the one half of the model to flip the sides and make the map at the same time. However, this is made easier by using one map source and making 2 shaders, one with a Bump value of "+" and the other with a Bump value of "-", and assigning to the faces.

The result is shown in Figure 15-14.

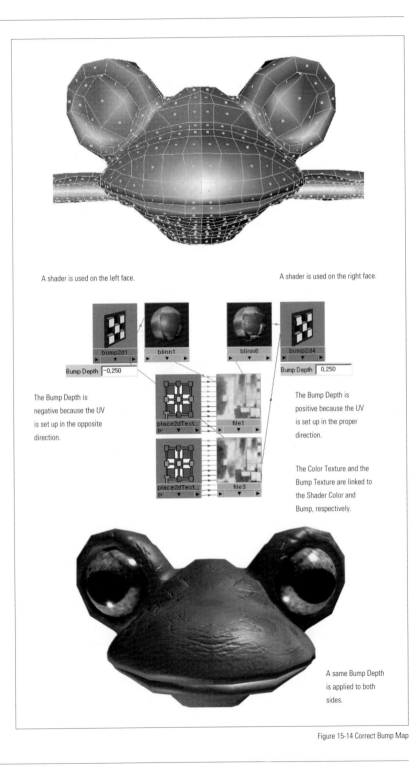

A shader is used on the left face.

A shader is used on the right face.

Bump Depth | -0,250

Bump Depth | 0,250

The Bump Depth is negative because the UV is set up in the opposite direction.

The Bump Depth is positive because the UV is set up in the proper direction.

The Color Texture and the Bump Texture are linked to the Shader Color and Bump, respectively.

A same Bump Depth is applied to both sides.

Figure 15-14 Correct Bump Map

2. BEE MAPPING

The bee is much simpler to map than the frog. The bee was made using mostly Deep
Paint 3D and, therefore, uses only a Color and Bump map.
Figure 15-15 shows the shading of the bee.

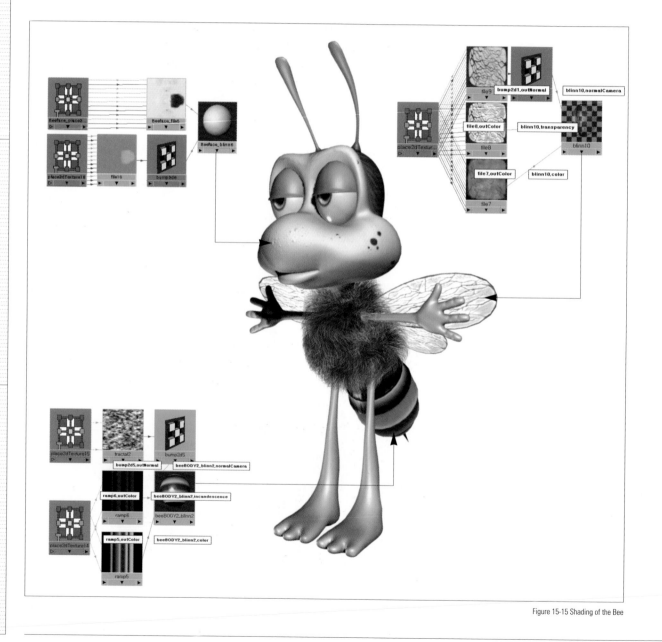

Figure 15-15 Shading of the Bee

2-1. USING FUR

We use Fur to portray the hair on the torso of the bee. For longer hairs, a good result will not be obtained during simulation, but this method is effective for the short hairs of this character.

step 1   To make the fur, first select the torso and then select [Rendering > Fur > Attach Fur Description > New]. The fur will be made as shown in Figure 15-16. After rendering the scene, we can see that the fur still appears rough (see Figure 15-17) because no attributes have yet been defined for it.

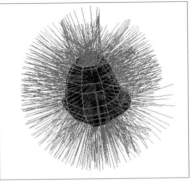

Figure 15-16 Create Fur

Figure 15-17 Rendering Fur

step 2   Let's define the attributes of the fur. Currently, the fur is too thick. To thin out the fur, select [Rendering > Fur > Edit Fur Description > FurDescription1] to open the FurDescription Attribute Editor (see Figure 15-18). Adjust the length of the fur by setting Length to 0.6.

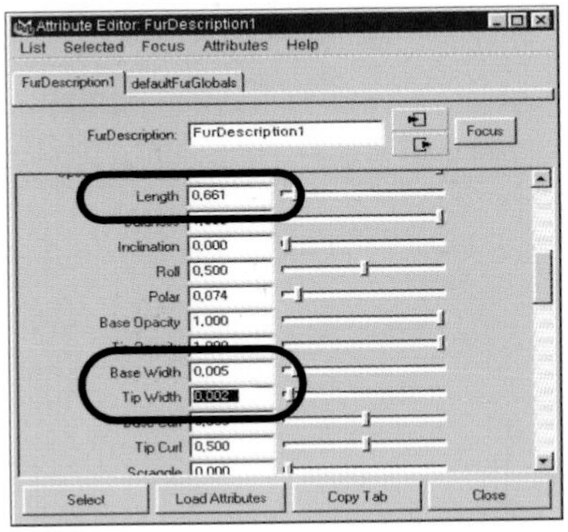

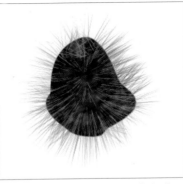

Figure 15-18 Attribute Editor

Figure 15-19 Rendered Image

Adjust the thickness by setting Base Width to 0.005 and the Tip Width to 0.002. These values define the thickness at the base and at the tip of the fur, respectively. Rendering the image, we will see the result shown in Figure 15-19.

We get this kind of result because the density of the fur is still quite low. Let's change the density and color of the fur. In the Attribute Editor, set the Density value to 10,000 and set the Base Color, Tip Color, and Specular Color as shown in Figure 15-20 Density raises the density of the fur and Base Color, Tip Color and Specular Color adjusts the color at the base, the tip and the color of the illuminated areas, respectively. After rendering the image, we will see the result shown in Figure 15-21.

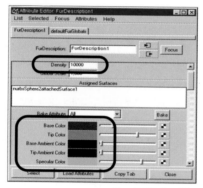

Figure 15-20 Attribute Editor

Figure 15-21 Rendered Image

step 3 The fur right now is too stiff. Let's look at how to soften the fur. First of all, in order to observe the changes in the fur in the window, select the fur and open the Attribute Editor. As shown in Figure 15-22, set the Fur Accuracy to 1. Select [Rendering > Fur > Edit Fur Description > FurDescription1] to open the Attribute Editor, and adjust the indicated options as shown in Figure 15-23. Base Curl and Tip Curl represent the degree of curl at the base and at the tip, respectively, and Scraggle refers to the tangle of the fur. Segment is used to determine how softly the fur will be curled.

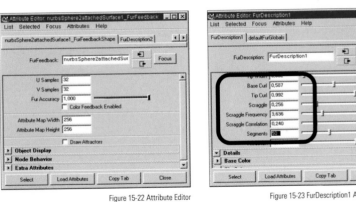

Figure 15-22 Attribute Editor

Figure 15-23 FurDescription1 Attribute Editor

After rendering the image, we will see the result shown in Figure 15-24. Finally, we need to link the Fur and Light. The linked light will act to render the fur in a more realistic way. Not linking the fur and light will create a very unrealistic image (see Figure 15-24). Link the light by selecting the desired light in the scene and selecting [Rendering > Fur > Fur Shadowing Attribute > Add to Selected Light].

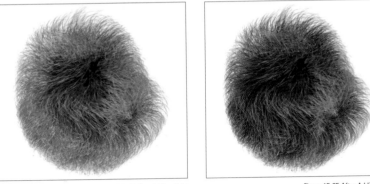

Figure 15-24 Before Adding Light

Figure 15-25 After Adding Light

This concludes the brief look at character mapping. Because the texture requires a lot of time from start to finish, work as slowly and as carefully as you can.

You can make a better tree by using the Convert option, which converts the Paint Effect feature (offered in versions after 5.0) to a Polygon.

3. MAKING THE TREE USING PAINT EFFECTS

Figure 15-26 Paint Effect

3-1. BASIC WORKS

Let's look at how to use Paint Effect to portray the swaying branches. Maya's Paint Effect is a quick and easy way to simulate trees, plants, and other natural elements. However, there is a limit to what we can portray using Paint Effect. Although it adequately portrays things at a distance, detail drops in those objects that are closer.

For this reason, the trunk of the tree is made using modeling, and only the branches and the leaves are portrayed using Paint Effect. Figure 15-27 shows the modeled tree. This tree was modeled using subdivision surfaces and converted to a polygon for the final output.

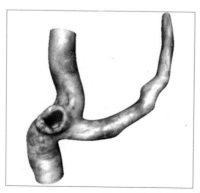

Figure 15-27 Modeling the Tree

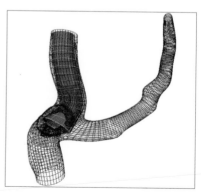

Figure 15-28 Modeling the Tree

However, because Paint Effect can only be used in NURBS, we use NURBS to make the surfaces by fitting it to the shape of the tree, as shown in Figure 15-28.

3-2. PAINTING BRUSH

Select the NURBS surface we made, and then select [Rendering > Paint Effects > Make Paintable] to allow us to paint the NURBS surface. Press the 8 key on the keyboard to convert to Paint Effect Mode. Select [Paint Effect Panel > Paint > Paint Scene ▼]. Click on the Get Brush icon in the Panel menu to open the Visor. Open the Trees folder and select the shrub.mel Brush, as shown in Figure 15-29.

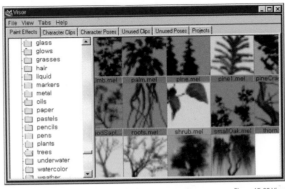

Figure 15-29 Visor

In order to define the attributes for the branches, click on the Edit Template Brush icon ( ) in the Panel menu to open the Paint Effects Brush Settings window. Adjust the overall size by using Global Scale, and randomize the color applied to the leaves by changing the color of Color1.

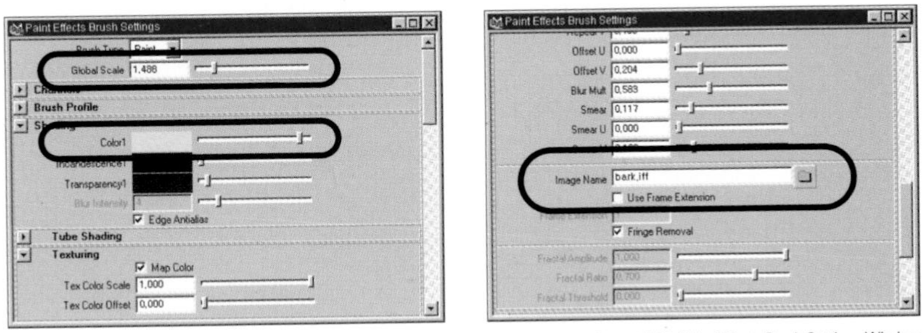

Figure 15-30 Paint Effects Brush Settings Window

Looking at the Texturing section, you should see the Image Name field (see Figure 15-30). The current brush has been applied to the texture of the branches using the Default setting. We can make our own textures, and specify the route here to apply the desired texture to the branches. Make a texture that is the same pattern as the texture used on the modeled tree, and use this field to import it into the image. As needed, expand the Tube section and adjust the Creation Section options. All the Creation options are used to manipulate the shape of the branches, including length, width and a variety of other variables pertaining to the branches. In order to portray the swaying branches, expand the [Behavior > Turbulence] menu, and set the Turbulence Type to Tree Wind.

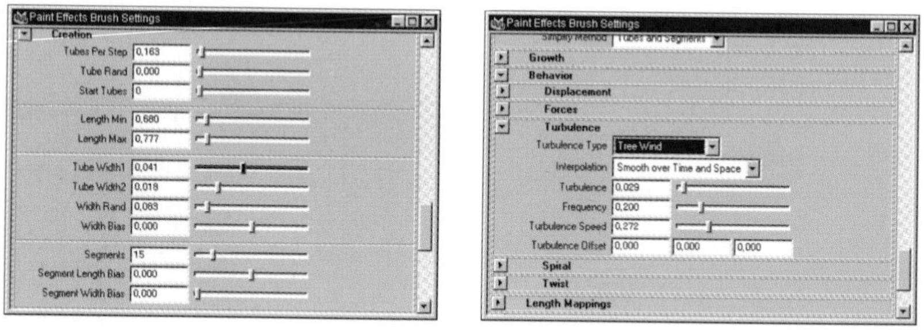

Figure 15-31 Paint Effects Brush Settings Window

Turbulence Type is used to determine how the branches will be affected by the wind. We need to set this type to Tree Wind because the leaves, as well as the branches, should sway. Raising the Turbulence and Turbulence Speed will create a greater wind force to increase the swaying of the branches and the leaves.

After making the basic configurations, paint directly on the NURBS surface to make the branches. Install a light to observe the shape of the painted tree. Selecting [Panel > Stroke Refresh > Rendered] will render the brush as shown in Figure 15-32. However, one thing to remember is that there is some difference in what we see in the view and what is actually rendered.

Figure 15-32 Painting Stroke

Therefore, the scene should be rendered to give us a final confirmation of the scene.

3-3. EDITING BRUSH STROKE

The brush settings can be configured beforehand, as we did above, or at any other time afterward. After painting, open the Hypergraph and you should see that a stroke node has been made (see Figure 15-33). The stroke nodes were grouped here for convenience. Select the node we want to change to view the values in the Channel Box (see Figure 15-34). We can change these values at any time through the Channel Box.

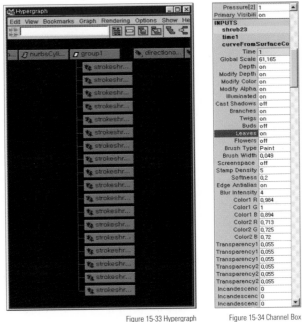

Figure 15-33 Hypergraph   Figure 15-34 Channel Box

Keep changing the values while rendering the scene until the desired result is obtained.

Let's now make the shadows for the branches. Making a shadow for all the branches will make the image look unrealistic. Therefore, an appropriate amount of shadow should be used in certain areas to create a realistic image.

Select the stroke node to which we want to add the shadow in the Hypergraph or the window, and press Ctrl+A to open the Attribute Editor.

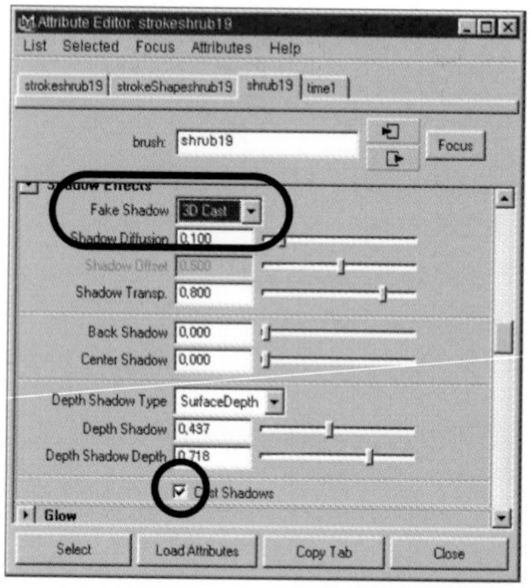

Figure 15-35 Attribute Editor

In order to create a realistic shadow, select 3D Cast from under Fake Shadow. 3D Cast creates the shadow by computing the light in the scene. 2D Offset does not compute the light, but rather offsets the stroke to make it look like a shadow and is not very realistic. Make sure that a check is placed in the box next to Cast Shadow at the bottom of the window. Rendering the scene will create the result seen in Figure 15-36.

Figure 15-36 Rendered Scene

3-4. USING FOG

One of the disadvantages of using Paint Effect is insufficient spacing. Reasons for this can be either that a shadow has not been made for each of the leaves or that there is no difference in placing the concentration of the color nearer or farther away from the camera. Another reason could be that the Paint Effect makes the computation based on particles rather than the object. Fog can be used to effectively deal with such spacing problems.

In actuality, during rest, fine dust particles or the density of air creates depth. This depth can be portrayed using Fog. Compare the 2 figures below. Figure 15-37 shows a scene where Fog was used, and Figure 15-38 shows where Fog was not used. As we can see, the use of Fog emphasizes the depth and spacing of the scene.

Figure 15-37 With the Use of Fog

Figure 15-38 Without the Use of Fog

In order to use Fog, open Render Global and click on the Texture icon next to the Environment Fog field under Render Options (see Figure 15-39).

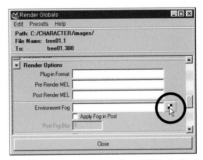

Figure 15-39 Render Global

By opening [Windows > Rendering Editors > Multilister], we can see that the envFogSE Shader has been made. Open the Attribute Editor for this shader, expand the envFogMaterial Tab, and adjust the options. Color is used to adjust the color of the fog, and Color Based Transparency is used to adjust the transparency of the fog depending on the concentration of color. A high Saturation Distance will create a denser fog, and a low Saturation Distance will create a thinner fog. Select Fog Near/Far from Clipping Planes, and adjust the Fog Near and Fog Far Distances to adjust the starting and ending points of the fog.

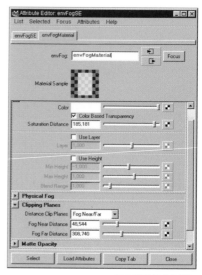

Figure 15-40 Attribute Editor

4. MAPPING THE LEAVES

Let's look at an example of using Paint Effect to model the leaves, in addition to the tree. Figure 15-41 is the texture used as the Color Map for the leaf.

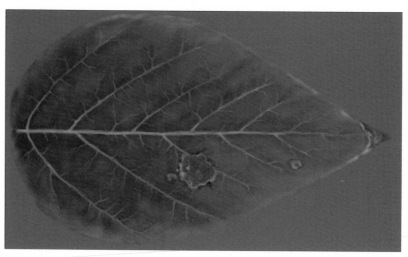

Figure 15-41 Leaf Texture

This texture was made using Photoshop. Details were not portrayed because the leaf will not be that conspicuous in the scene. We simply made a Color Map, converted it into a black and white image, and then used Bump Map. Figure 15-42 shows a test rendering of the leaf. The leaf was modeled using subdivision surfaces. Mapping coordinates were made using Planar Mapping in Polygon Proxy Mode, and the UV Texture Editor was used to align the UV to the shape of the leaf as in figure 15-43. Because we made the leaf using version 3 of Maya, we were able to maintain the coordinates of the mapping from Polygon Proxy Mode in the subdivision surface. Refer to Chapter 2. "Polygons & Subdivision Surface Mapping" for more information on subdivision surface mapping.

Figure 15-42 Test Rendering

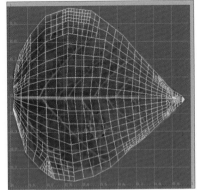

Figure 15-43 UV Texture Editor

Because we simply used a texture to make the leaf, this process is not all that difficult. Next, we will look at how to portray a plant, which has a slightly more complex structure. This is a mapping example of the image that will appear at the end of the animation. The following figure shows each of the mapping sources applied to the shader used in this example.

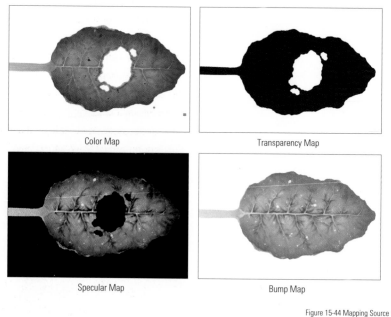

Color Map

Transparency Map

Specular Map

Bump Map

Figure 15-44 Mapping Source

The result rendered using this map source is shown in Figure 15-45.

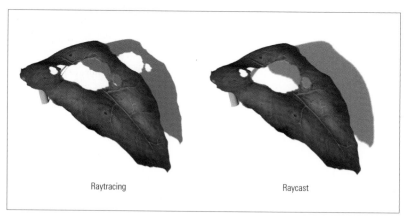

Raytracing

Raycast

Figure 15-45 Rendered Image

As we can tell by looking at Figure 15-45, when using a Transparency Map, we need to use a Raytracing Shadow and render it as Raytracing in order for the shadow to recognize the transparency. If we had used Depth Map Shadow or did not render it as Raytracing, the shadow will not be able to recognize the transparency of the object.

However, simply using the Transparency Map in order for the shadow to recognize the transparency can bring about incorrect results. This problem is especially seen in specular textures, such as Blinn Shader or Phong Shader. Although this problem cannot be observed in great detail in Figure 15-45, we can map the NURBS plane and render the image to see the problem in Figure 15-46. We can see in the figure that a light shadow has been applied to the transparent regions.

Maya renders this type of result because, no matter how transparent the texture, there is still some shadow, however light, that is portrayed.

This problem can be solved using Layer Shader.

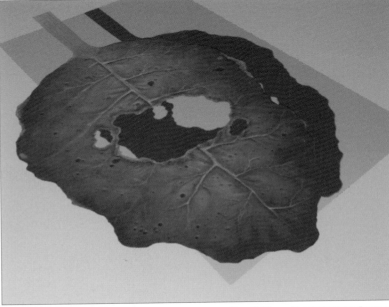

Figure 15-46 Incorrect Representation of the Transparency

Make a Layer Shader and then open the Attribute Editor. Place the shader used in Figure 15-46 in the Layer Shader Attribute, and link the texture used in the Transparency Map to the transparency indicated in Figure 15-47. Set the Compositing Flag to Layer Texture.

Instead of using Layer Shader, you can simply open [Shader - Attribute Editor] and set the Shadow Attenuation (under Raytrace Options) to 0 to achieve the same results.

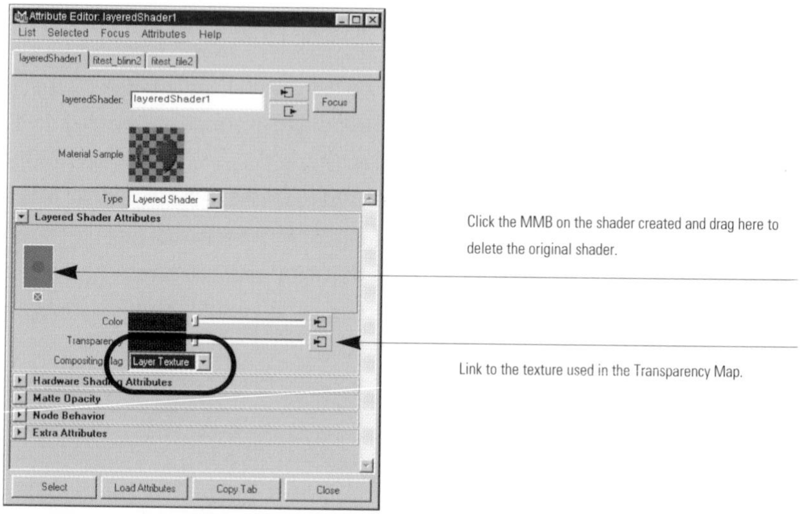

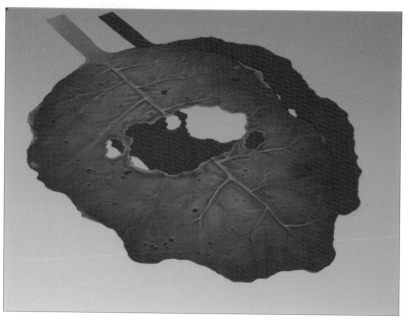

Click the MMB on the shader created and drag here to
delete the original shader.

Link to the texture used in the Transparency Map.

Figure 15-47 Attribute Editor

After assigning the shader and rendering the image, we can see a clean rendering of the
image without the transparency (see Figure 15-48).

Figure 15-48 Rendered Image

5. USING DEPTH OF FIELD

The frog is a small character in the scene. Therefore, in order to create a more realistic mood, a Depth of Field was used in all the scenes. This feature is used to stage the Out Focus effect that is created by adjusting the opening of the iris in an actual camera. We can achieve the desired result by adjusting the focal distance, by opening or closing the iris, and by adjusting the scale of the focus. We will use one of the scenes as an example. Let's look at the example in Figure 15-49. The camera was placed very close to the frog to capture the frog's face. In such instances, the Out Focus effect is applied to all areas of the face, excluding the eyes.

Figure 15-49 Scene used to Describe Depth of Field

The first thing we need to do is to measure the distance between the camera and the subject. After selecting [Create > Measure Tool > Distance Tool], click first on the camera, indicated in Figure 15-50, and then on the frog's eyes. This will compute a numerical value for the distance between the 2 locators.

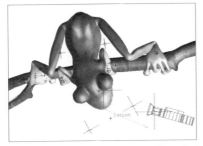

Figure 15-50 Distance Tool

In order to accurately measure the distance, we need to accurately position the locators to fit the positions of the camera and the frog in the 3D space.

It was found that the distance between the 2 locators is approximately 3.016. Now, open the Attribute Editor of the camera that will use Depth of Field. In the Camera Attribute Editor, expand the Depth of Field section and put a check next to the Depth of Field box, as shown in Figure 15-51. Enter the distance between the 2 locators under Focus Distance. F Stop is used to determine whether the iris will be opened or closed. This, as a result, determines how much of an Out Focus effect will be applied. A lower value increases the Out Focus effect. Focus Region Scale allows us to manually configure the focal region. A large value corresponds to a greater focal region.

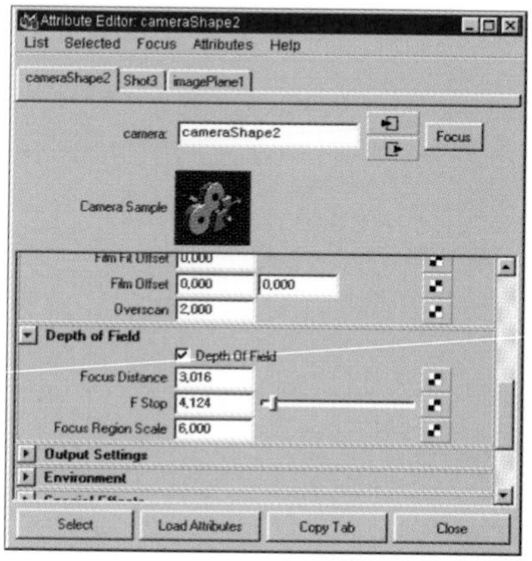

Figure 15-51 Attribute Editor

The result rendered with these options is shown in Figure 15-52.

Figure 15-53 shows a rendering with an F Stop of 15 with all the other options intact. As we can see in the figure, the larger the F Stop value, the smaller the Out Focus effect.

Figure 15-54 shows a rendering with a Focus Region Scale of 2. As we can see, a small value will reduce the focal region.

Up until now, we have looked at how to use Maya to create a short-piece animation. Depending on personal preferences and style, this animation could have been divided into greater parts to create drastically different results. However, since the purpose here was to understand how to use Maya and to understand the steps involved in the overall process, this is where I will leave off.

Figure 15-52 Image Using Depth of Field

Figure 15-53 F Stop: 14 Focus Region Scale: 6

Figure 15-54 F Stop: 4, Focus Region Scale: 2

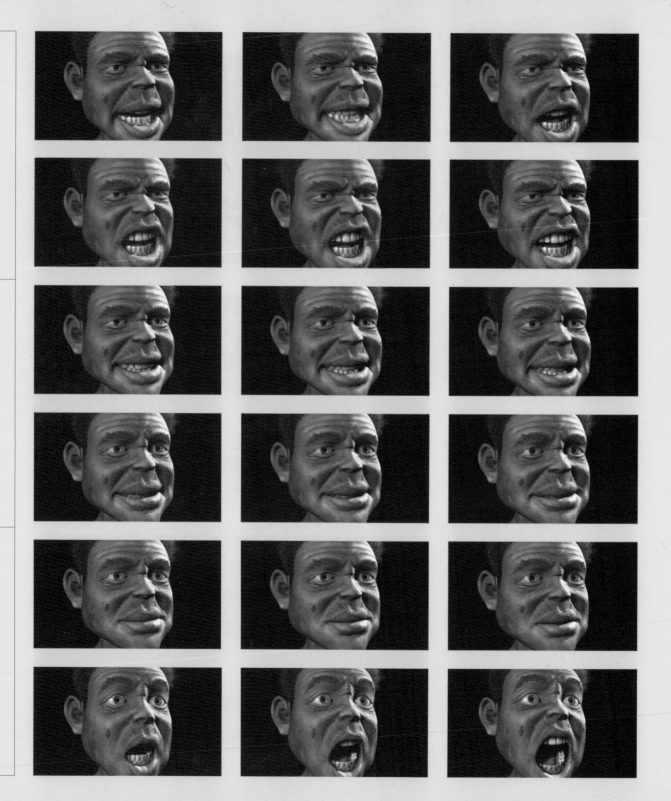

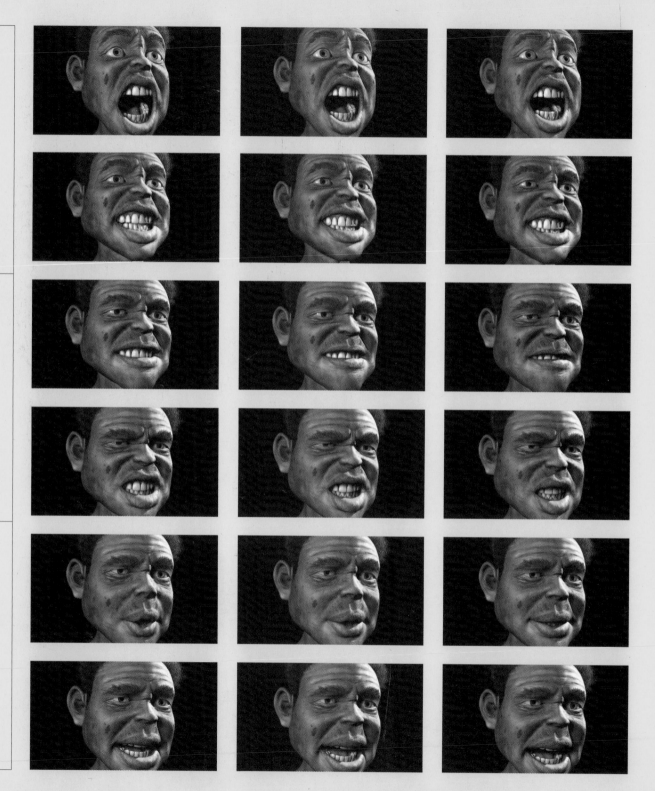

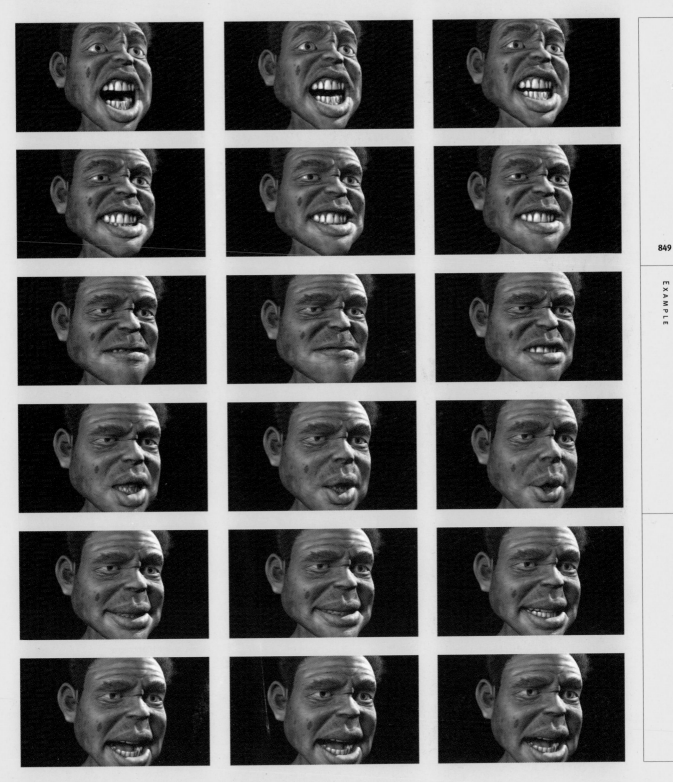